SQL

ALL-IN-ONE

4th Edition

by Allen G. Taylor

with Richard Blum

for

dummies®

A Wiley Brand

SQL All-in-One For Dummies®, 4th Edition

Published by: **John Wiley & Sons, Inc.**, 111 River Street, Hoboken, NJ 07030-5774, www.wiley.com

For general information on our other products and services, please contact our Customer Care Department within the U.S. at 877-762-2974, outside the U.S. at 317-572-3993, or fax 317-572-4002. For technical support, please visit https://hub.wiley.com/community/support/dummies.

Wiley publishes in a variety of print and electronic formats and by print-on-demand. Some material included with standard print versions of this book may not be included in e-books or in print-on-demand. If this book refers to media such as a CD or DVD that is not included in the version you purchased, you may download this material at http://booksupport.wiley.com. For more information about Wiley products, visit www.wiley.com.

Library of Congress Control Number: 2024933440

ISBN 978-1-394-24229-0 (pbk); ISBN 978-1-394-24232-0 (ebk); ISBN 978-1-394-24231-3 (ebk)

SKY10074496_050624

Contents at a Glance

Table of Contents

Introduction

SQL is the internationally recognized standard language for dealing with data in relational databases. Developed by IBM, SQL became an international standard in 1986. The standard was updated in 1989, 1992, 1999, 2003, 2008, 2011, 2016, and 2023. It continues to evolve and gain capability. Database vendors continually update their products to incorporate the new features of the ISO/IEC standard. (For the curious out there, ISO is the International Organization for Standardization, and IEC is the International Electrotechnical Commission.)

SQL isn't a general-purpose language, such as C++ or Java. Instead, it's strictly designed to deal with data in relational databases. With SQL, you can carry out all the following tasks:

>> Create a database, including all tables and relationships.

>> Fill database tables with data.

>> Change the data in database tables.

>> Delete data from database tables.

>> Retrieve specific information from database tables.

>> Grant and revoke access to database tables.

>> Protect database tables from corruption due to access conflicts or user mistakes.

About This Book

This book isn't just about SQL; it's also about how SQL fits into the process of creating and maintaining databases and database applications. In this book, I cover how SQL fits into the larger world of application development and how it handles data coming in from other computers, which may be on the other side of the world or even in interplanetary space.

Here are some of the things you can do with this book:

- >> Create a model of a proposed system and then translate that model into a database.

- >> Find out about the capabilities and limitations of SQL.

- >> Discover how to develop reliable and maintainable database systems.

- >> Create databases.

- >> Speed database queries.

- >> Protect databases from hardware failures, software bugs, and Internet attacks.

- >> Control access to sensitive information.

- >> Write effective database applications.

- >> Deal with data from a variety of nontraditional data sources by using XML.

I've structured this book modularly — that is, it's designed so that you can easily find just the information you need — so you don't have to read whatever doesn't pertain to your task at hand. Here and there throughout the book, I include sidebars containing interesting information that isn't necessarily integral to the discussion at hand; feel free to skip them. You also don't have to read text marked with the Technical Stuff icons, which parses out über-techy tidbits (which may or may not be your cup of tea).

Within this book, you may note that some web addresses break across two lines of text. If you're reading this book in print and want to visit one of these web pages, simply key in the web address exactly as it's noted in the text, pretending as though the line break doesn't exist. If you're reading this as an e-book, you've got it easy — just click the web address to be taken directly to the web page.

Foolish Assumptions

I know that this is a *For Dummies* book, but I don't really expect that you're a dummy. In fact, I assume that you're a very smart person. After all, you decided to read this book, which is a sign of high intelligence indeed. Therefore, I assume that you may want to do a few things, such as re-create some of the examples in the book. You may even want to enter some SQL code and execute it. To do that, you need at the very least an SQL editor and more likely also a database management system (DBMS) of some sort. Many choices are available, both proprietary and open source. I mention several of these products at various places throughout the book but don't recommend any one in particular. Any product that complies with the ISO/IEC international SQL standard should be fine.

Take claims of ISO/IEC compliance with a grain of salt, however. No DBMS available today is 100 percent compliant with the ISO/IEC SQL standard. For that reason, some of the code examples I give in this book may not work in the particular SQL implementation that you're using. The code samples I use in this book are consistent with the international standard rather than with the syntax of any particular implementation unless I specifically state that the code is for a particular implementation.

Icons Used in This Book

For Dummies books are known for those helpful icons that point you in the direction of really great information. This section briefly describes the icons used in this book.

The Tip icon points out helpful information that's likely to make your job easier.

This icon marks a generally interesting and useful fact — something that you may want to remember for later use.

The Warning icon highlights lurking danger. When you see this icon, pay attention, and proceed with caution.

This icon denotes techie stuff nearby. If you're not feeling very techie, you can skip this info.

Beyond the Book

In addition to what you're reading right now, this book comes with a free access-anywhere Cheat Sheet that includes information on SQL system development, normalizing data, and SQL data types and functions. To get this Cheat Sheet, simply go to www.dummies.com and type **SQL All-in-One For Dummies Cheat Sheet** in the Search box.

Where to Go from Here

Book 1 is the place to go if you're just getting started with databases. It explains why databases are useful and describes the different types. It focuses on the relational model and describes SQL's structure and features.

Book 2 goes into detail on how to build a database that's reliable as well as responsive. Unreliable databases are much too easy to create, and this minibook tells you how to avoid the pitfalls that lie in wait for the unwary.

Go directly to Book 3 if your database already exists and you just want to know how to use SQL to pull from it the information you want.

Book 4 is primarily aimed at the database administrator (DBA) rather than the database application developer or user. It discusses how to build a robust database system that resists data corruption and data loss.

Book 5 is for the application developer. In addition to discussing how to write a database application, it gives an example that describes in a step-by-step manner how to build a reliable application.

If you're already an old hand at SQL and just want to know how to handle data in XML or JSON format in your SQL database, or if you'd like to dive into the property graph database world, Book 6 is for you.

Book 7 gives you a wide variety of techniques for improving the performance of your database. This minibook is the place to go if your database is operating — but not as well as you think it should. Most of these techniques are things that the DBA can do, rather than the application developer or the database user. If your database isn't performing the way you think it should, take it up with your DBA. She can do a few things that could help immensely.

Book 8 is a handy reference that helps you quickly find the meaning of a word you've encountered or see why an SQL statement that you entered didn't work as expected. (Maybe you used a reserved word without realizing it.)

1
Getting Started with SQL

Contents at a Glance

Chapter **1**

Understanding Relational Databases

SQL (pronounced *ess cue el*, but you'll hear some people say *see quel*) is the international standard language used in conjunction with relational databases — and it just so happens that relational databases are the dominant form of data storage throughout the world. In order to understand *why* relational databases are the primary repositories for the data of both small and large organizations, you must first understand the various ways in which computer data can be stored and how those storage methods relate to the relational database model. To help you gain that understanding, I spend a good portion of this chapter going back to the earliest days of electronic computers and recapping the history of data storage.

I realize that grand historical overviews aren't everybody's cup of tea, but I'd argue that it's important to see that the different data storage strategies that have been used over the years each have their own strengths and weaknesses. Ultimately, the strengths of the relational model overshadowed its weaknesses and it became the most frequently used method of data storage. Shortly after that, SQL became the most frequently used method of dealing with data stored in a relational database.

Understanding Why Today's Databases Are Better than Early Databases

In the early days of computers, the concept of a database was more theoretical than practical. Vannevar Bush, the 20th-century visionary, conceived of the idea of a database in 1945, even before the first electronic computer was built. However, practical implementations of databases — such as IBM's IMS (Information Management System), which kept track of all the parts on the Apollo moon mission and its commercial followers — did not appear for a number of years after that. For far too long, computer data was still being kept in files rather than migrated to databases.

Irreducible complexity

Any software system that performs a useful function is complex. The more valuable the function, the more complex its implementation. Regardless of how the data is stored, the complexity remains. The only question is where that complexity resides.

Any nontrivial computer application has two major components: the program and the data. Although an application's level of complexity depends on the task to be performed, developers have some control over the location of that complexity. The complexity may reside primarily in the program part of the overall system, or it may reside in the data part. In the sections that follow, I tell you how the location of complexity in databases shifted over the years as technological improvements made that possible.

Managing data with complicated programs

In the earliest applications of computers to solve problems, all of the complexity resided in the program. The data consisted of one data record of fixed length after another, stored sequentially in a file. This is called a *flat file* data structure. The data file contains nothing but data. The program file must include information about where particular records are within the data file (one form of *metadata*, whose sole purpose is to organize the primary data you *really* care about). Thus, for this type of organization, the complexity of managing the data is entirely in the program.

Here's an example of data organized in a flat file structure:

```
Harold Percival 26262 S. Howards Mill Rd.Westminster CA92683
Jerry Appel 32323 S. River Lane Road Santa Ana CA92705
Adrian Hansen 232 Glenwood Court Anaheim CA92640
John Baker 2222 Lafayette Street Garden GroveCA92643
Michael Pens 77730 S. New Era Road Irvine CA92715
Bob Michimoto 25252 S. Kelmsley Drive Stanton CA92610
Linda Smith 444 S.E. Seventh StreetCosta Mesa CA92635
Robert Funnell 2424 Sheri Court Anaheim CA92640
Bill Checkal 9595 Curry Drive Stanton CA92610
Jed Style 3535 Randall Street Santa Ana CA92705
```

This example includes fields for name, address, city, state, and zip code. Each field has a specific length, and data entries must be truncated to fit into that length. If entries don't use all the space allotted to them, storage space is wasted.

The flat file method of storing data has several consequences, some beneficial and some not. First, the beneficial consequences:

>> **Storage requirements are minimized.** Because the data files contain nothing but data, they take up a minimum amount of space on hard disks or other storage media. The code that must be added to any one program that contains the metadata is small compared to the overhead involved with adding a database management system (DBMS) to the data side of the system. (A *database management system* is the program that controls access to — and operations on — a database.)

>> **Operations on the data can be fast.** Because the program interacts directly with the data, with no DBMS in the middle, well-designed applications can run as fast as the hardware permits.

Wow! What could be better? A data organization that minimizes storage requirements and at the same time maximizes speed of operation seems like the best of all possible worlds. But wait a minute . . .

Flat file systems came into use in the 1940s. We have known about them for a long time, and yet today they are almost entirely replaced by database systems. What's up with that? Perhaps it is the not-so-beneficial consequences:

>> **Updating the data's structure can be a huge task.** It is common for an organization's data to be operated on by multiple application programs, with multiple purposes. If the metadata about the structure of data is in the program rather than attached to the data itself, *all* the programs that access

that data must be modified whenever the data structure is changed. Not only does this cause a lot of redundant work (because the same changes must be made in all the programs), but it is an invitation to problems. All the programs must be modified in exactly the same way. If one program is inadvertently forgotten, the program will fail the next time you run it. Even if all the programs *are* modified, any that aren't modified exactly as they should be will fail, or even worse, corrupt the data without giving any indication that something is wrong.

>> **Flat file systems provide no protection of individual data elements.** With flat files, you have read/write access either to the entire file or to none of the file. A flat file system doesn't have a database management system, which allows you to restrict types of access to the data to only authorized users.

>> **Speed can be compromised.** Accessing records in a large flat file can actually be slower than a similar access in a database because flat file systems do not support indexing. Indexing is a major topic that I discuss in Book 2, Chapter 3.

>> **Portability becomes an issue.** If the specifics that handle how you retrieve a particular piece of data from a particular disk drive is coded into each program, what happens when your hardware becomes obsolete and you must migrate to a new system? All your applications will have to be changed to reflect the new way of accessing the data. This task is so onerous that many organizations have chosen to limp by on old, poorly performing systems instead of enduring the pain of transitioning to a system that would meet their needs much more effectively. Organizations with legacy systems consisting of millions of lines of code are pretty much trapped.

In the early days of electronic computers, storage was relatively expensive, so system designers were highly motivated to accomplish their tasks using as little storage space as possible. Also, in those early days, computers were much slower than they are today, so doing things the fastest possible way also had a high priority. Both of these considerations made flat file systems the architecture of choice, despite the problems inherent in updating the structure of a system's data.

The situation today is radically different. The cost of storage has plummeted and continues to drop on an exponential curve. The speed at which computations are performed has increased exponentially also. As a result, minimizing storage requirements and maximizing the speed with which an operation can be performed are no longer the primary driving forces that they once were. Because systems have continually become bigger and more complex, the problem of maintaining them has likewise grown. For all these reasons, flat file systems have lost their attractiveness, and databases have replaced them in practically all application areas.

Managing data with simple programs

The major selling point of database systems is that the metadata resides on the data end of the system rather than in the program. The program doesn't have to know anything about the details of how the data is stored. The program makes *logical* requests for data, and the DBMS translates those logical requests into commands that go out to the physical storage hardware to perform whatever operation has been requested. (In this context, a *logical request* asks for a specific piece of information, but does not specify its location on hard disk in terms of platter, track, sector, and byte.) Here are the advantages of this organization:

>> Because application programs need to know only what data they want to operate on, and not where that data is located, they are unaffected when the physical details of where data is stored changes.

>> Portability across platforms, even when they are highly dissimilar, is easy as long as the DBMS used by the first platform is also available on the second. Generally, you don't need to change the programs at all to accommodate various platforms.

What about the disadvantages? They include the following:

>> Placing a database management system in between the application program and the data slows down operations on that data. This is not nearly the problem that it used to be. Modern advances, such as the use of high speed cache memories have eased this problem considerably.

>> Databases take up more space on disk storage than the same amount of data would take up in a flat file system. This is due to the fact that metadata is stored along with the data. The metadata contains information about how the data is stored so that the application programs don't have to include it.

Which type of organization is better?

I bet you think you already know how I'm going to answer this question. You're probably right, but the answer is not quite so simple. There is no one correct answer that applies to all situations. In the early days of electronic computing, flat file systems were the only viable option. To perform any reasonable computation in a timely and economical manner, you had to use whatever approach was the fastest and required the least amount of storage space. As more and more application software was developed for these systems, the organizations that owned them became locked in tighter and tighter to what they had. To change to a more modern database system requires rewriting all their applications from scratch and reorganizing all their data, a monumental task. As a result, we still have legacy flat file systems that continue to exist because switching to more modern technology isn't feasible, both economically and in terms of the time it would take to make the transition.

Databases, Queries, and Database Applications

What are the chances that a person could actually find a needle in a haystack? Not very good. Finding the proverbial needle is so hard because the haystack is a random pile of hay with individual pieces of hay going in every direction, and the needle is located at some random place among all that hay.

A flat file system is not really very much like a haystack, but it does lack structure — and in order to find a particular record in such a file, you must use tools that lie outside of the file itself. This is like applying a powerful magnet to the haystack to find the needle.

Making data useful

For a collection of data to be useful, you must be able to easily and quickly retrieve the particular data you want, without having to wade through all the rest of the data. One way to make this happen is to store the data in a logical structure. Flat files don't have much structure, but databases do. Historically, the hierarchical database model and the network database model were developed before the relational model. Each one organizes data in a different way, but all three produce a highly structured result. Because of that, starting in the 1970s, any new development projects were most likely done using one of the aforementioned three database models: hierarchical, network, or relational. (I explore each of these database models further in the "Examining Competing Database Models" section, later in this chapter.)

Retrieving the data you want — and only the data you want

Of all the operations that people perform on a collection of data, the retrieval of specific elements out of the collection is the most important. This is because retrievals are performed more often than any other operation. Data entry is done only once. Changes to existing data are made relatively infrequently, and data is deleted only once. Retrievals, on the other hand, are performed frequently, and the same data elements may be retrieved many times. Thus, if you could optimize only one operation performed on a collection of data, that one operation should be data retrieval. As a result, modern database management systems put a great deal of effort into making retrievals fast.

Retrievals are performed by queries. A modern database management system analyzes a query that is presented to it and decides how best to perform it. Generally, there are multiple ways of performing a query, some much faster than others. A good DBMS consistently chooses a near-optimal execution plan. Of course, it helps if the query is formulated in an optimal manner to begin with. (I discuss optimization strategies in depth in Book 7, which covers database tuning.)

THE FIRST DATABASE SYSTEM

The first true database system was developed by IBM in the 1960s in support of NASA's Apollo moon landing program. The number of components in the Saturn V launch vehicle, the Apollo Command and Service Module, and the lunar lander far exceeded anything that had been built up to that time. Every component had to be tested more exhaustively than anything had ever been tested before because each component would have to withstand the rigors of an environment that was more hostile and more unforgiving than any environment that humans had ever attempted to work in. Flat file systems were out of the question. IBM's solution, which IBM later transformed into a commercial database product named IMS (Information Management System), kept track of each individual component, as well as its complete history.

When the ill-fated Apollo 13's main oxygen tank ruptured on the way to the Moon, engineers worked frantically to come up with a plan to save the lives of the three astronauts headed for the Moon. The engineers succeeded and transmitted a plan to the astronauts that worked.

After the crew had returned safely to Earth, querying IMS records about the oxygen tank that failed showed that somewhere between the oxygen tank's manufacture and its installation in Apollo 13, it had been dropped on the floor. Engineers retested it for its ability to withstand the pressure it would have to contain during the mission, and then put it back in stock after it passed the test. But it turns out that in this case, the test did not detect the hidden damage to the tank, and NASA should not have used the oxygen tank on the Apollo 13 mission. The history stored in IMS showed that passing a pressure test is not enough to assure that a dropped tank is undamaged. No dropped tanks were ever used on subsequent Apollo missions.

Examining Competing Database Models

A *database model* is simply a way of organizing data elements within a database. In this section, I give you the details on the three database models that appeared first on the scene:

>> **Hierarchical:** Organizes data into levels, where each level contains a single category of data, and parent/child relationships are established between levels

>> **Network:** Organizes data in a way that avoids much of the redundancy inherent in the hierarchical model

>> **Relational:** Organizes data into a structured collection of two-dimensional tables

After the introductions of the hierarchical, network, and relational models, computer scientists have continued to develop databases models that have been found useful in some categories of applications. I briefly mention some of these later in this chapter, along with their areas of applicability. However, the hierarchical, network, and relational models are the ones that have been primarily used for general business applications.

Looking at the historical background of the competing models

The first functioning database system was developed by IBM and went live at an Apollo contractor's site on August 14, 1968. (Read the whole story in "The first database system" sidebar, here in this chapter.) Known as IMS (Information Management System), it is still (amazingly enough) in use today, over 50 years later, because IBM has continually upgraded it in support of its customers.

TIP

If you are in the market for a database management system, you may want to consider buying it from a vendor that will be around, and that is committed to supporting it for as long as you will want to use it. IBM has shown itself to be such a vendor, and of course, there are others as well.

IMS is an example of a hierarchical database product. About a year after IMS was first run, the network database model was described by an industry committee. About a year after that, Dr. Edgar F. "Ted" Codd, also of IBM, proposed the relational model. Within a short span of years, the three models that were to dominate the database market for decades were spawned.

Quite a few years went by before the object-oriented database model made its appearance, presenting itself as an alternative meant to address some of the deficiencies of the relational model. The *object-oriented database model* accommodates the storage of types of data that don't easily fit into the categories handled by relational databases. Although they have advantages in some applications, object-oriented databases have not captured significant market share. The *object-relational model* is a merger of the relational and object models, and it is designed to capture the strengths of both, while leaving behind their major weaknesses. Now, there is something called the NoSQL model, which stores data as documents instead of tables. The most popular NoSQL model is the MongoDB database system. Because NoSQL stores data as documents, it is designed mostly to work with data that is not rigidly structured. Because it does not use SQL, I will not discuss it in this book.

The hierarchical database model

The *hierarchical database model* organizes data into levels, where each level contains a single category of data, and parent/child relationships are established between levels. Each parent item can have multiple children, but each child item can have one and only one parent. Mathematicians call this a *tree-structured* organization, because the relationships are organized like a tree with a trunk that branches out into limbs that branch out into smaller limbs. Thus all relationships in a hierarchical database are either one-to-one or one-to-many. Many-to-many relationships are not used. (More on these kinds of relationships in a bit.)

A list of all the stuff that goes into building a finished product — a listing known as a *bill of materials,* or BOM — is well suited for a hierarchical database. For example, an entire machine is composed of assemblies, which are each composed of subassemblies, and so on, down to individual components. As an example of such an application, consider the mighty Saturn V Moon rocket that sent American astronauts to the Moon in the late 1960s and early 1970s. Figure 1-1 shows a hierarchical diagram of major components of the Saturn V.

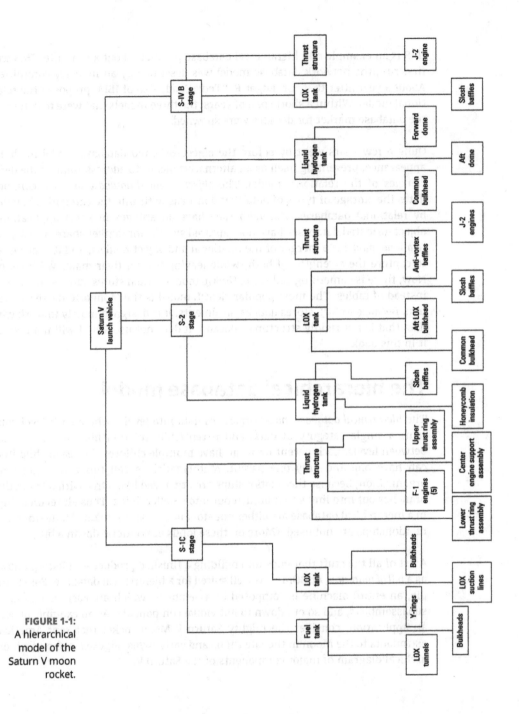

FIGURE 1-1:
A hierarchical
model of the
Saturn V moon
rocket.

Three relationships can occur between objects in a database:

» **One-to-one relationship:** One object of the first type is related to one and only one object of the second type. In Figure 1-1, there are several examples of one-to-one relationships. One is the relationship between the S-2 stage LOX tank and the aft LOX bulkhead. Each LOX tank has one and only one aft LOX bulkhead, and each aft LOX bulkhead belongs to one and only one LOX tank.

» **One-to-many relationship:** One object of the first type is related to multiple objects of the second type. In the Saturn V's S-1C stage, the thrust structure contains five F-1 engines, but each engine belongs to one and only one thrust structure.

» **Many-to-many relationship:** Multiple objects of the first type are related to multiple objects of the second type. This kind of relationship is not handled cleanly by a hierarchical database. Attempts to do so tend to be kludgy. One example might be two-inch hex-head bolts. These bolts are not considered to be uniquely identifiable, and any one such bolt is interchangeable with any other. An assembly might use multiple bolts, and a bolt could be used in any of several different assemblies.

A great strength of the hierarchical model is its high performance. Because relationships between entities are simple and direct, retrievals from a hierarchical database that are set up to take advantage of the way the data is structured can be very fast. However, retrievals that don't take advantage of the way the data is structured are slow and sometimes can't be made at all. It's difficult to change the structure of a hierarchical database to address new requirements. This structural rigidity is the greatest weakness of the hierarchical model. Another problem with the hierarchical model is the fact that, structurally, it requires a lot of redundancy, as my next example makes clear.

First off, time to state the obvious: Not many organizations today are designing rockets capable of launching payloads to the moon. The hierarchical model can also be applied to more common tasks, however, such as tracking sales transactions for a retail business. As an example, I use some sales transaction data from Gentoo Joyce's fictitious online store of penguin collectibles. She accepts PayPal, MasterCard, Visa, and money orders and sells various items featuring depictions of penguins of specific types — gentoo, chinstrap, and adelie.

As shown in Figure 1-2, customers who have made multiple purchases show up in the database multiple times. For example, you can see that Lynne has purchased with PayPal, MasterCard, and Visa. Because this is hierarchical, Lynne's information shows up multiple times, and so does the information for every customer who has bought more than once. Product information shows up multiple times too.

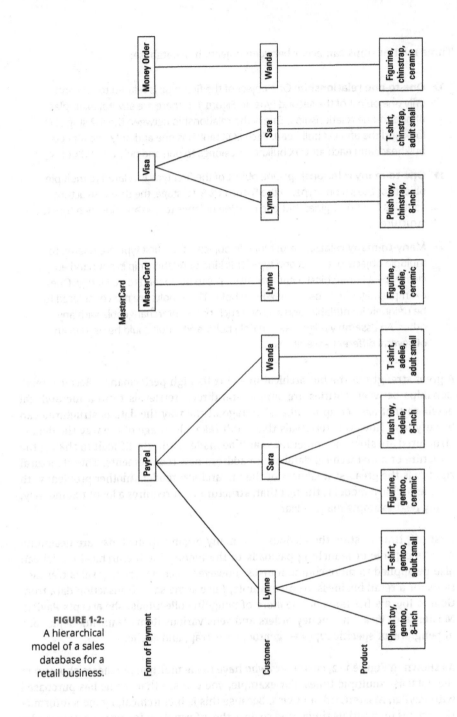

FIGURE 1-2:
A hierarchical
model of a sales
database for a
retail business.

REMEMBER

This organization is actually more complex than what is shown in Figure 1-2. Additional "trees" would hold the details about each customer and each product. This duplicate data is a waste of storage space because one copy of a customer's data is sufficient, and so is one copy of product information.

Perhaps even more damaging than the wasted space that results from redundant data is the possibility of data corruption. Whenever multiple copies of the same data exist in a database, there is the potential for modification anomalies. A *modification anomaly* is an inconsistency in the data after a modification is made. Suppose you want to delete a customer who is no longer buying from you. If multiple copies of that customer's data exist, you must find and delete all of them to maintain data integrity. On a slightly more positive note, suppose you just want to update a customer's address information. If multiple copies of the customer's data exist, you must find and modify all of them in exactly the same way to maintain data integrity. This can be a time-consuming and error-prone operation.

The network database model

The network model — the one that followed close upon the heels of the hierarchical, appearing as it did in 1969 — is almost the exact opposite of the hierarchical model. Wanting to avoid the redundancy of the hierarchical model without sacrificing too much in the way of performance, the designers of the *network model* opted for an architecture that does not duplicate items, but instead increases the number of relationships associated with some items. Figure 1-3 shows this architecture for the same data that was shown in Figure 1-2.

As you can see in Figure 1-3, the network model does not have the tree structure with one-directional flow characteristic of the hierarchical model. Looked at this way, it shows very clearly that, for example, Lynne had bought multiple products, but also that she has paid in multiple ways. There is only one instance of Lynne in this model, compared to multiple instances in the hierarchical model. However, to balance out that advantage, there are seven relationships connected to that one instance of Lynne, whereas in the hierarchical model there are no more than three relationships connected to any one instance of Lynne.

REMEMBER

The network model eliminates redundancy, but at the expense of more complicated relationships. This model can be better than the hierarchical model for some kinds of data storage tasks, but worse for others. Neither one is consistently superior to the other.

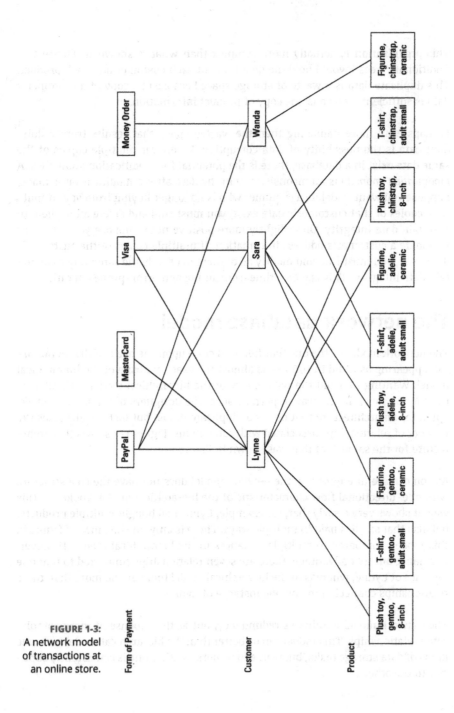

FIGURE 1-3:
A network model of transactions at an online store.

Form of Payment

Customer

Product

The relational database model

In 1970, Edgar Codd of IBM published a paper introducing the *relational database model*. Initially, database experts gave it little consideration. It clearly had an advantage over the hierarchical model in that data redundancy was minimal; it had an advantage over the network model with its relatively simple relationships. However, it had what was perceived to be a fatal flaw. Due to the complexity of the relational database engine that it required, any implementation would be much slower than a comparable implementation of either the hierarchical or the network model. As a result, it was almost ten years before the first implementation of the relational database idea hit the market.

Moore's Law had finally made relational database technology feasible. (In 1965, Gordon Moore, one of the founders of Intel, noticed that the cost of computer memory chips was dropping by half about every two years. He predicted that this trend would continue. After over 50 years, the trend is still going strong, and Moore's prediction has been enshrined as an empirical law.)

IBM delivered a relational DBMS (RDBMS) integrated into the operating system of the System 38 computer server platform in 1978, and Relational Software, Inc., delivered the first version of Oracle — the granddaddy of all standalone relational database management systems — in 1979.

Defining what makes a database relational

The original definition of a relational database specified that it must consist of two-dimensional tables of rows and columns, where the cell at the intersection of a row and column contains an atomic value (where *atomic* means not divisible into subvalues). This definition is commonly stated by saying that a relational database table may not contain any *repeating groups*. The definition also specified that each row in a table be uniquely identifiable. Another way of saying this is that every table in a relational database must have a *primary key*, which uniquely identifies a row in a database table. Figure 1-4 shows the structure of an online store database, built according to the relational model.

The relational model introduced the idea of storing database elements in two-dimensional tables. In the example shown in Figure 1-4, the Customer table contains all the information about each customer; the Product table contains all the information about each product, and the Transaction table contains all the information about the purchase of a product by a customer. The idea of separating closely related things from more distantly related things by dividing things up into tables was one of the main factors distinguishing the relational model from the hierarchical and network models.

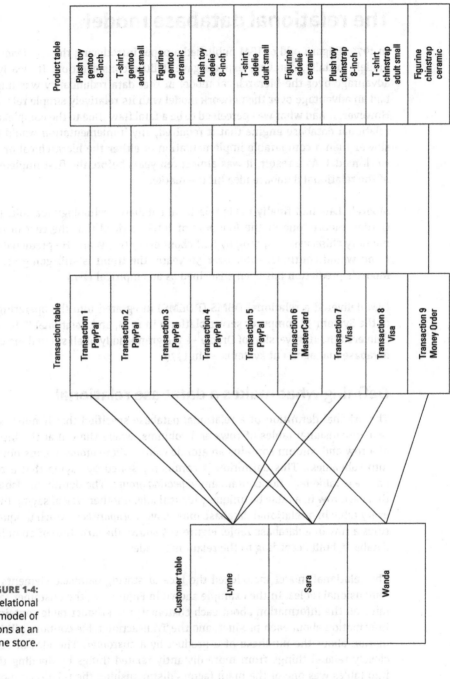

Product table

- Plush toy gentoo 8-inch
- T-shirt gentoo adult small
- Figurine gentoo ceramic
- Plush toy adelie 8-inch
- T-shirt adelie adult small
- Figurine adelie ceramic
- Plush toy chinstrap 8-inch
- T-shirt chinstrap adult small
- Figurine chinstrap ceramic

Transaction table

- Transaction 1 PayPal
- Transaction 2 PayPal
- Transaction 3 PayPal
- Transaction 4 PayPal
- Transaction 5 PayPal
- Transaction 6 MasterCard
- Transaction 7 Visa
- Transaction 8 Visa
- Transaction 9 Money Order

Customer table

- Lynne
- Sara
- Wanda

FIGURE 1-4:
A relational model of transactions at an online store.

Protecting the definition of relational databases with Codd's rules

As the relational model gained in popularity, vendors of database products that were not really relational started to advertise their products as relational database management systems. To fight the dilution of his model, Codd formulated 12 rules that served as criteria for determining whether a database product was in fact relational. Codd's idea was that a database must satisfy all 12 criteria in order to be considered relational.

Codd's rules are so stringent, that even today, there is not a DBMS on the market that completely complies with all of them. However, they have provided a good goal toward which database vendors strive.

Here are Codd's 12 rules:

1. **The information rule:** Data can be represented only one way, as values in column positions within rows of a table.

2. **The guaranteed access rule:** Every value in a database must be accessible by specifying a table name, a column name, and a row. The row is specified by the value of the primary key.

3. **Systematic treatment of null values:** Missing data is distinct from specific values, such as zero or an empty string.

4. **Relational online catalog:** Authorized users must be able to access the database's structure (its *catalog*) using the same query language they use to access the database's data.

5. **The comprehensive data sublanguage rule:** The system must support at least one relational language that can be used both interactively and within application programs, that supports data definition, data manipulation, and data control functions. Today, that one language is SQL.

6. **The view updating rule:** All views that are theoretically updatable must be updatable by the system.

7. **The system must support set-at-a-time insert, update, and delete operations:** This means that the system must be able to perform insertions, updates, and deletions of multiple rows in a single operation.

8. **Physical data independence:** Changes to the way data is stored must not affect the application.

9. **Logical data independence:** Changes to the tables must not affect the application. For example, adding new columns to a table should not "break" an application that accesses the original rows.

10. **Integrity independence:** Integrity constraints must be specified independently from the application programs and stored in the catalog. (I say a lot about integrity in Book 2, Chapter 3.)

11. **Distribution independence:** Distribution of portions of the database to various locations should not change the way applications function.

12. **The nonsubversion rule:** If the system provides a record-at-a-time interface, it should not be possible to use it to subvert the relational security or integrity constraints.

Over and above the original 12 rules, in 1990, Codd added one more rule:

> **Rule Zero:** For any system that is advertised as, or is claimed to be, a relational database management system, that system must be able to manage databases entirely through its relational capabilities, no matter what additional capabilities the system may support.

Rule Zero was in response to vendors of various database products who claimed their product was a relational DBMS, when in fact it did not have full relational capability.

Highlighting the relational database model's inherent flexibility

You might wonder why it is that relational databases have conquered the planet and relegated hierarchical and network databases to niches consisting mainly of legacy customers who have been using them for more than 40 years. It's even more surprising in light of the fact that when the relational model was first introduced, most of the experts in the field considered it to be utterly uncompetitive with either the hierarchical or the network model.

One advantage of the relational model is its flexibility. The architecture of a relational database is such that it is much easier to restructure a relational database than it is to restructure either a hierarchical or network database. This is a tremendous advantage in dynamic business environments where requirements are constantly changing.

The reason database practitioners originally dissed the relational model is because the extra overhead of the relational database engine was sure to make any product based on that model so much slower than either hierarchical or network databases, as to be noncompetitive. As time has passed, Moore's Law has nullified that objection.

The object-oriented database model

Object-oriented database management systems (OODBMS) first appeared in 1980. They were developed primarily to handle nontext, nonnumeric data such as graphical objects. A relational DBMS typically doesn't do a good job with such so-called complex data types. An OODBMS uses the same data model as object-oriented programming languages such as Java, C++, and C#, and it works well with such languages.

Although object-oriented databases outperform relational databases for selected applications, they do not do as well in most mainstream applications, and have not made much of a dent in the hegemony of the relational products. As a result, I will not be saying anything more about OODBMS products.

The object-relational database model

An *object-relational database* is a relational database that allows users to create and use new data types that are not part of the standard set of data types provided by SQL. The ability of the user to add new types, called *user-defined types*, was added to the SQL:1999 specification and is available in current implementations of IBM's DB2, Oracle, and Microsoft SQL Server.

Current relational database management systems are actually object-relational database management systems rather than pure relational database management systems.

The nonrelational NoSQL model

In contrast to the relational model, a nonrelational model has been gaining adherents, particularly in the area of *cloud computing*, where databases are maintained not on the local computer or local area network, but reside somewhere on the Internet. This model, called the NoSQL model, is particularly appropriate for large systems consisting of clusters of servers, accessed over the World Wide Web. CouchDB and MongoDB are examples of DBMS products that follow this model. The NoSQL model is document based, storing all related data in the same document. Because all the related data is stored in the same place, queries for large amounts of data can be quicker than in traditional relational databases. The NoSQL model is not competitive with the SQL-based relational model for traditional reporting applications.

Why the Relational Model Won

Throughout the 1970s and into the 1980s, hierarchical- and network-based technologies were the database technologies of choice for large organizations. Oracle, the first standalone relational database system to reach the market, did not appear until 1979, and initially met with limited success.

For the following reasons, as well as just plain old inertia, relational databases caught on slowly at first:

>> **The earliest implementations of relational database management systems were slow performers.** This was due to the fact that they were required to perform more computations than other database systems to perform the same operation.

>> **Most business managers were reluctant to try something new when they were already familiar with one or the other of the older technologies.**

>> **Data and applications that already existed for an existing database system would be very difficult to convert to work with a relational DBMS.** For most organizations with an existing hierarchical or network database system, it would be too costly to make a conversion.

>> **Employees would have to learn an entirely new way of dealing with data.** This would be very costly, too.

However, things gradually started to change.

Although databases structured according to the hierarchical and network models had excellent performance, they were difficult to maintain. Structural changes to a database took a high level of expertise and a lot of time. In many organizations, backlogs of change requests grew from months to years. Department managers started putting their work on personal computers rather than going to the corporate IT department to ask for a change to a database. IT managers, fearing that their power in the organization was eroding, took the drastic step of considering relational technology.

Meanwhile, Moore's Law was inexorably changing the performance situation. In 1965, Gordon Moore of Intel noted that about every 18 months to 2 years the price of a bit in a semiconductor memory would be cut in half, and he predicted that this exponential trend would continue. A corollary of the law is that for a given cost, the performance of integrated circuit processors would double every 18 to 24 months. Both of these laws have held true for more than 50 years, although the end of the trend is in sight. In addition, the capacities and performance of hard disk storage devices have also improved at an exponential rate, paralleling the improvement in semiconductor chips.

The performance improvements in processors, memories, and hard disks combined to dramatically improve the performance of relational database systems, making them more competitive with hierarchical and network systems. When this improved performance was added to the relational architecture's inherent advantage in structural flexibility, relational database systems started to become much more attractive, even to large organizations with major investments in legacy systems. In many of these companies, although existing applications remained on their current platforms, new applications and the databases that held their data were developed using the new relational technology.

Chapter **2**

Modeling a System

QL is the language that you use to create and operate on relational databases. Before you can do that database creation, however, you must first create a conceptual model of the system to be built. In order to have any hope of developing a database system that delivers the results, performance, and reliability that the users need, you must understand, in a highly detailed way, what those needs are. Your understanding of the users' needs enables you to create a model of what they have in mind.

After perfecting the model through much dialog with the user, you need to translate the model into something that can be implemented with a relational database. This chapter takes you through the steps of taking what might be a vague and fuzzy idea in the minds of the users and transforming it into something that can be converted directly into a robust and high-performance database.

Capturing the Users' Data Model

The whole purpose of a database is to hold useful data and enable one or more people to selectively retrieve and use the data they want. Generally, before a database project is begun, interested parties have some idea of what data they want to store, and what subsets of the data they are likely to want to retrieve. More often than not, people's ideas of what should be included in the database and what they want to get out of it are not terribly precise. Nebulous as they may be, the concepts each interested party may have in mind comes from her own data models. When all those data models from various users are combined, they become one (huge) data model.

To have any hope of building a database system that meets the needs of the users, you must understand this collective data model. In the text that follows, I give you some tips for finding and querying the people who will use the database, prioritizing requested features, and getting support from stakeholders.

Beyond understanding the data model, you must help to clarify it so that it can become the basis for a useful database system. In the "Translating the Users' Data Model to a Formal Entity-Relationship Model" section that follows this one, I tell you how to do that.

Identifying and interviewing stakeholders

The first step in discovering the users' data model is to find out who the users are. Perhaps several people will interact directly with the system. They, of course, are very interested parties. So are their supervisors, and even higher management.

But identifying the database users goes beyond the people who actually sit in front of a PC and run your database application. A number of other people usually have a stake in the development effort. If the database is going to deal with customer or vendor information, the customers and vendors are probably stakeholders, too. The IT department — the folks responsible for keeping systems up and running — is also a major stakeholder. There may be others, such as owners or major stockholders in the company. All of these people are sure to have an image in their mind of what the system ought to be. You need to find these people, interview them, and find out how they envision the system, how they expect it to be maintained, and what they want it to produce.

If the functions to be performed by the new system are already being performed, by either a manual system or an obsolete computerized system, you can ask the users to explain how their current system works. You can then ask them what they like about the current system and what they don't like. What is the motivation for moving to a new system? What desirable features are missing from what they have now? What annoying aspects of the current system are frustrating them? Try to gain as complete an understanding of the current situation as possible.

Reconciling conflicting requirements

Just as the set of stakeholders will be diverse, so will their ideas of what the system should be and do. If such ideas are not reconciled, you are sure to have a disaster on your hands. You run the risk of developing a system that is not satisfactory to anybody.

It is your responsibility as the database developer to develop a consensus. You are the only independent, outside party who does not have a personal stake in what the system is and does. As part of your responsibility, you'll need to separate the stated requirements of the stakeholders into three categories, as follows:

>> **Mandatory:** A feature that is absolutely essential falls into this category. The system would be of limited value without it.

>> **Significant:** A feature that is important and that adds greatly to the value of the system belongs in this category.

>> **Optional:** A feature that would be nice to have, but is not actually needed, falls into this category.

Once you have appropriately categorized the want lists of the stakeholders, you are in a position to determine what is really required, and what is possible within the allotted budget and development time. Now comes the fun part. You must convince all the stakeholders that their cherished features that fall into the third category (optional), must be deleted or changed if they conflict with someone else's first-category or second-category feature. Of course, politics also intrudes here. Some stakeholders have more clout than others. You must be sensitive to this. Sometimes the politically acceptable solution is not exactly the same as the technically optimal solution.

Obtaining stakeholder buy-in

One way or another, you will have to convince all the stakeholders to agree on one set of features that will be included in the system you are planning to build. This is critical. If the system does not adequately meet the needs of all those for whom it is being built, it is not a success. You must get the agreement of everyone that the system you propose meets their needs. Get it in writing. Enumerate everything that will be provided in a formal Statement of Requirements, and then have every stakeholder sign off on it. This will potentially save you from much grief later on.

Translating the Users' Data Model to a Formal Entity-Relationship Model

After you outline a coherent users' data model in a clear, concise, concrete form, the real work begins. Somehow, you must transform that model into a relational model that serves as the basis for a database. In most cases, a users' data model is not in a form that can be directly translated into a relational model. A helpful technique is to first translate it into one of several formal modeling systems that clarify the various entities in the users' model and the relationships between them. Probably the most popular of those formal modeling techniques is the Entity-Relationship (ER) model. Although there are other formal modeling systems, I focus on the ER model because it is the most widespread and thus easily understood by most database professionals.

Graphing tools — Microsoft Visio, for example — make provision for drawing representations of an ER model. I guess I am old fashioned in that I prefer to draw them by hand on paper with a pencil. This gives me a little more flexibility in how I arrange the elements and how I represent them.

SQL is the international standard language for *communicating* with relational databases. Before you can fully appreciate SQL, you must understand the *structure* of well-designed relational databases. In order to design a relational database properly — in hopes that it will be reliable as well as giving the level of performance you need — you must have a good understanding of database structure. This is best achieved through database modeling, and the most widely used model is the Entity-Relationship model.

Entity-Relationship modeling techniques

In 1976, six years after Dr. Codd published the relational model, Dr. Peter Chen published a paper in the reputable journal *ACM Transactions on Database Systems*, introducing the Entity-Relationship (ER) model, which represented a conceptual breakthrough because it provided a means to translate a users' data model into a relational model.

Back in 1976, the relational model was still nothing more than a theoretical construct. It would be three more years before the first standalone relational database product (Oracle) appeared on the market.

REMEMBER

The ER model was an important factor in turning theory into practice because one of the strengths of the ER model is its generality. ER models can represent a wide variety of different systems. For example, an ER model can represent a physical system as big and complex as a fleet of cruise ships, or as small as the collection of livestock maintained by a gentleman farmer on his two acres of land.

Any Entity-Relationship model, big or small, consists of four major components: entities, attributes, identifiers, and relationships. I examine each one of these concepts in turn.

Entities

Dictionaries tell you that an *entity* is something that has a distinct, separate existence. It could be a material entity, such as the Great Pyramid of Giza, or an abstract entity, such as a tetrahedron. Just about any distinct, separate thing that you can think of qualifies as being an entity. When used in a database context, an *entity* is something that the user can identify and that she wants to keep track of.

A group of entities with common characteristics is called an *entity class*. Any one example of an entity class is an *entity instance*. A common example of an entity class for most organizations is the EMPLOYEE entity class. An example of an *instance* of that entity class is a particular employee, such as Duke Kahanamoku.

In the previous paragraph, I spell out EMPLOYEE with all caps. This is a convention that I will follow throughout this book so that you can readily identify entities in the ER model. I follow the same convention when I refer to the tables in the relational model that correspond to the entities in the ER model. Other sources of information on relational databases that you read may use all lowercase for entities, or an initial capital letter followed by lowercase letters. There is no standard. The database management systems that will be processing the SQL that is based on your models do not care about capitalization. Agreeing to a standard is meant to reduce confusion among the people dealing with the models and with the code generated based on those models — the models themselves don't care.

Attributes

Entities are things that users can identify and want to keep track of. However, the users probably don't want to use up valuable storage space keeping track of every conceivable aspect of an entity. Some aspects are of more interest than others. For example, in the EMPLOYEE model, you probably want to keep track of such things as first name, last name, and job title. You probably do not want to keep track of the employee's favorite surfboard manufacturer or favorite musical group.

In database-speak, aspects of an entity are referred to as *attributes*. Figure 2-1 shows an example of an entity class — including the kinds of attributes you'd expect someone to highlight for this particular (EMPLOYEE) entity class. Figure 2-2 shows an example of an instance of the EMPLOYEE entity class. EmpID, FirstName, LastName, and so on are attributes.

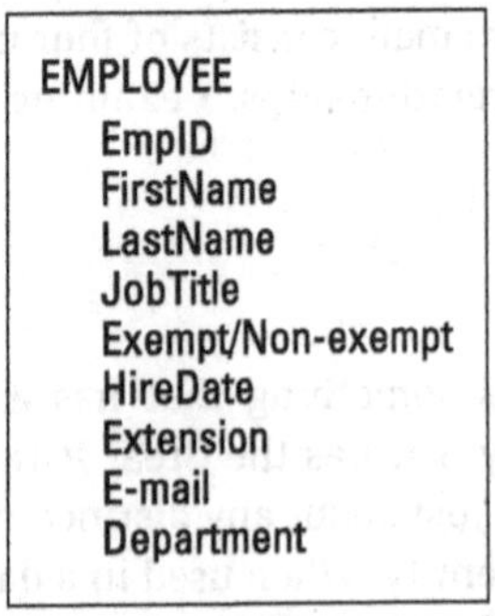

EMPLOYEE
    EmpID
    FirstName
    LastName
    JobTitle
    Exempt/Non-exempt
    HireDate
    Extension
    E-mail
    Department

FIGURE 2-1:
EMPLOYEE, an example of an entity class.

Identifiers

In order to do anything meaningful with data, you must be able to distinguish one piece of data from another. That means each piece of data must have an identifying characteristic that is unique. In the context of a relational database, a "piece of data" is a row in a two-dimensional table. For example, if you were to construct an EMPLOYEE table using the handy EMPLOYEE entity class and attributes spelled out back in Figure 2-1, the row in the table describing Duke Kahanamoku would be the piece of data, and the EmpID attribute would be the identifier for that row. No other employee will have the same EmpID as the one that Duke has.

FIGURE 2-2:
Duke
Kahanamoku,
an example of
an instance of
the EMPLOYEE
entity class.

```
EMPLOYEE
    172850
    Duke
    Kahanamoku
    Cultural ambassador
    E
    01/01/2002
    10
    duck@surfboardsrus.com
    Public Relations
```

In this example, EmpID is not just an identifier — it is a unique identifier. There is one and only one EmpID that corresponds to Duke Kahanamoku. Nonunique identifiers are also possible. For example, a FirstName of Duke does not uniquely identify Duke Kahanamoku. There might be another employee named Duke — Duke Snyder, let's say. Having an attribute such as EmpID is a good way to guarantee that you are getting the specific employee you want when you search the database.

Another way, however, is to use a *composite identifier*, which is a combination of several attributes that together are sufficient to uniquely identify a record. For example, the combination of FirstName and LastName would be sufficient to distinguish Duke Kahanamoku from Duke Snyder, but would not be enough to distinguish him from his father, who, let's say, has the same name and is employed at the same company. In such a case, a composite identifier consisting of FirstName, LastName, and BirthDate would probably suffice.

Relationships

Any nontrivial relational database contains more than one table. When you have more than one table, the question arises as to how the tables relate to each other. A company might have an EMPLOYEE table, a CUSTOMER table, and a PRODUCT table. These become related when an employee sells a product to a customer. Such a sales transaction can be recorded in a TRANSACTION table. Thus the EMPLOYEE, CUSTOMER, and PRODUCT tables are related to each other via the TRANSACTION table. Relationships such as these are key to the way relational databases operate. Relationships can differ in the number of entities that they relate.

DEGREE-TWO RELATIONSHIPS

Degree-two relationships are ones that relate one entity directly to one other entity. EMPLOYEE is related to TRANSACTION by a degree-two relationship, also called a *binary* relationship. CUSTOMER is also related to TRANSACTION by a binary relationship, as is PRODUCT. Figure 2-3 shows a diagram of a degree-two relationship.

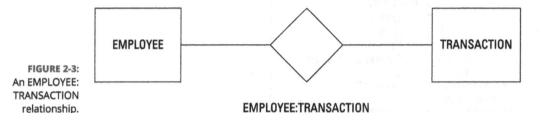

FIGURE 2-3:
An EMPLOYEE:
TRANSACTION
relationship.

EMPLOYEE:TRANSACTION

Degree-two relationships are the simplest possible relationships, and happily, just about any system that you are likely to want to model consists of entities connected by degree-two relationships, although more complex relationships are possible.

There are three kinds of binary (degree-two) relationships:

>> **One-to-one (1:1) relationship:** Relates one instance of one entity class (a group of entities with common characteristics) to one instance of a second entity class.

>> **One-to-many (1:N) relationship:** Relates one instance of one entity class to multiple instances of a second entity class.

>> **Many-to-many (N:M) relationship:** Relates multiple instances of one entity class to multiple instances of a second entity class.

Figure 2-4 is a diagram of a one-to-one relationship between a person and that person's driver's license. A person can have one and only one driver's license, and a driver's license can apply to one and only one person. This database would contain a PERSON table and a LICENSE table (both are entity classes), and the Duke Snyder instance of the PERSON table has a one-to-one relationship with the OR31415927 instance of the LICENSE table.

Figure 2-5 is a diagram of a one-to-many relationship between the PERSON entity class and the traffic violation TICKET entity class. A person can be served with multiple tickets, but a ticket can apply to one and only one person.

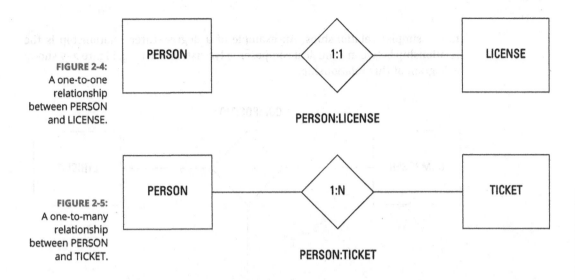

FIGURE 2-4:
A one-to-one relationship between PERSON and LICENSE.

PERSON:LICENSE

FIGURE 2-5:
A one-to-many relationship between PERSON and TICKET.

PERSON:TICKET

When this part of the ER model is translated into database tables, there will be a row in the PERSON table for each person in the database. There could be zero, one, or multiple rows in the TICKET table corresponding to each person in the PERSON table.

Figure 2-6 is a diagram of a many-to-many relationship between the STUDENT entity class and the COURSE entity class, which holds the route a person takes on her drive to work. A person can take one of several routes from home to work, and each one of those routes can be taken by multiple people.

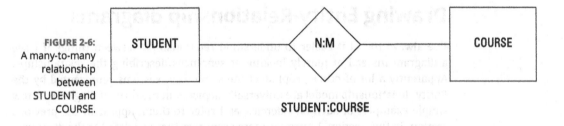

FIGURE 2-6:
A many-to-many relationship between STUDENT and COURSE.

STUDENT:COURSE

Many-to-many relationships can be very confusing and are not well represented by the two-dimensional table architecture of a relational database. Consequently, such relationships are almost always converted to simpler one-to-many relationships before they are used to build a database.

COMPLEX RELATIONSHIPS

Degree-three relationships are possible, but rarely occur in practice. Relationships of degree higher than three probably mean that you need to redesign your system to use simpler relationships. An example of a degree-three relationship is the relationship between a musical composer, a lyricist, and a song. Figure 2-7 shows a diagram of this relationship.

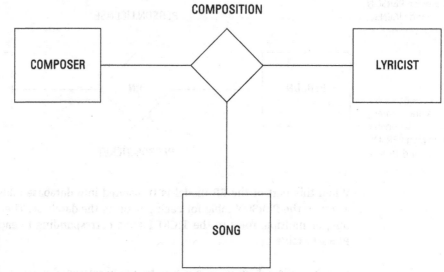

TIP

Although it is possible to build a system with such relationships, it is probably better in most cases to restructure the system in terms of binary relationships.

Drawing Entity-Relationship diagrams

I've always found it easier to understand relationships between things if I see a diagram instead of merely looking at sentences describing the relationships. Apparently a lot of other people feel the same way; systems represented by the Entity-Relationship model are universally depicted in the form of diagrams. A few simple examples of such *ER diagrams*, as I refer to them, appear in the previous section. In this section, I introduce some concepts that add detail to the diagrams.

One of those concepts is *cardinality*. In mathematics, cardinality is the number of elements in a set. In the context of relational databases, a relationship between two tables has two cardinalities of interest: the cardinality — number of elements — associated with the first table and the cardinality — you guessed it, the number of elements — associated with the second table. We look at these cardinalities two primary ways: maximum cardinality and minimum cardinality, which I tell you about in the following sections. (Cardinality only becomes truly important when you are dealing with queries that pull data from multiple tables. I discuss such queries in Book 3, Chapters 3 and 4.)

Maximum cardinality

The *maximum cardinality* of one side of a relationship shows the largest number of entity instances that can be on that side of the relationship.

For example, the ER diagram's representation of maximum cardinality is shown back in Figures 2-4, 2-5, and 2-6. The diamond between the two entities in the relationship holds the two maximum cardinality values. Figure 2-4 shows a one-to-one relationship. In the example, a person is related to that person's driver's license. One driver can have at most one license, and one license can belong at most to one driver. The maximum cardinality on both sides of the relationship is one.

Figure 2-5 illustrates a one-to-many relationship. When relating a person to the tickets he has accumulated, each ticket belongs to one and only one driver, but a driver may have more than one ticket. The number of tickets above one is indeterminate, so it is represented by the variable N.

Figure 2-6 shows a many-to-many relationship. The maximum cardinality on the STUDENT side is represented by the variable N, and the maximum cardinality on the COURSE side is represented by the variable M because although both the number of students and the number of courses are more than one, they are not necessarily the same. You might have 350 different students that take any of 45 courses, for example.

Minimum cardinality

Whereas the maximum cardinality of one side of a relationship shows the largest number of entity instances that can be on that side of the relationship, the *minimum cardinality* shows the least number of entity instances that can be on that side of the relationship. In some cases, the least number of entity instances that can be on one side of a relationship can be zero. In other cases, the minimum cardinality could be one or more.

Refer to the relationship in Figure 2-4 between a person and that person's driver's license. The minimum cardinalities in the relationship depend heavily on subtle details of the users' data model. Take the case where a person has been a licensed driver, but due to excessive citations, his driver's license has been revoked. The person still exists, but the license does not. If the users' data model stipulates that the person is retained in the PERSON table, but the corresponding row is removed from the LICENSE table, the minimum cardinality on the PERSON side is one, and the minimum cardinality on the LICENSE side is zero. Figure 2-8 shows how minimum cardinality is represented in this example.

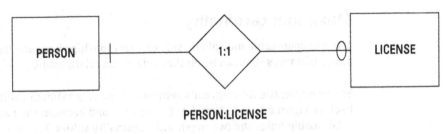

FIGURE 2-8:
ER diagram
showing
minimum
cardinality, where
a person must
exist, but his
corresponding
license need
not exist.

PERSON:LICENSE

The slash mark on the PERSON side of the diagram denotes a minimum cardinality of *mandatory*, meaning at least one instance must exist. The oval on the LICENSE side denotes a minimum cardinality of *optional*, meaning at least one instance need not exist.

For this one-to-one relationship, a given person can correspond to at most one license, but may correspond to none. A given license *must* correspond to one person.

If only life were that simple. . . . Remember that I said that minimum cardinality depends subtly on the users' data model? What if the users' data model were slightly different, based on another possible case? Suppose a person has a very good driving record and a valid driver's license in her home state of Washington. Next, suppose that she accepts a position as a wildlife researcher on a small island that has no roads and no cars. She is no longer a driver, but her license will remain valid until it expires in a few years. This is the reverse case of what is shown in Figure 2-8; a license exists, but the corresponding driver does not (at least as far as the state of Washington is concerned). Figure 2-9 shows this situation.

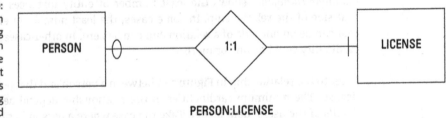

FIGURE 2-9:
ER diagram
showing
minimum
cardinality, where
a license must
exist, but its
corresponding
person need
not exist.

PERSON:LICENSE

REMEMBER

The lesson to take home from this example is that minimum cardinality is often difficult to determine. You'll need to question the users very carefully and explore unusual cases such as those cited previously before deciding how to model minimum cardinality.

If the minimum cardinality of one side of a relationship is mandatory, that means the cardinality of that side is at least one, but might be more. Suppose, for example, you were modeling the relationship between a basketball team in a city league and its players. A person cannot be a basketball player in the league and thus in the database unless she is a member of a basketball team in the league, so the minimum cardinality on the TEAM side is mandatory, and in fact is one. This assumes that the users' data model states that a player cannot be a member of more than one team. Similarly, it is not possible for a basketball team to exist in the database unless it has at least five players. This means that the minimum cardinality on the PLAYER side is also mandatory, but in this case is five. Once again, depending on the users' data model, the rule might be that a team cannot exist in the database unless it has at least five players. The minimum cardinality of the PLAYER side of the relationship is five.

TIP

Primarily, you are interested in whether the minimum cardinality on a side of a relationship is either mandatory or optional and less interested in whether a mandatory minimum cardinality has a value of one or more than one. The difference between mandatory and optional is the difference between whether an entity exists or not. The difference between existence and nonexistence is substantial. In contrast, the difference between one and five is just a matter of degree. Both cases refer to a mandatory minimum cardinality. For most applications, the difference between one mandatory value and another does not matter.

Understanding advanced ER model concepts

In the previous sections of this chapter, I talk about entities, relationships, and cardinality. I point out that subtle differences in the way users model their system can modify the way minimum cardinality is modeled. These concepts are a good start, and are sufficient for many simple systems. However, more complex situations are bound to arise. These call for extensions of various sorts to the ER model. To limber up your brain cells so you can tackle such complexities, take a look at a few of these situations and the extensions to the ER model that have been created to deal with them.

Strong entities and weak entities

All entities are not created equal. Some are stronger than others. An entity that does not depend on any other entity for its existence is considered a *strong entity*. Consider the sample ER model in Figure 2-10. All the entities in this model are strong, and I tell you why in the paragraphs that follow.

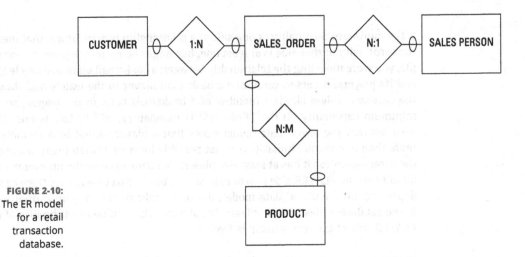

FIGURE 2-10:
The ER model
for a retail
transaction
database.

To get this "depends on" business straight, do a bit of a thought experiment. First, consider maximum cardinality. A customer (whose data lies in the CUSTOMER table) can make multiple purchases, each one recorded on a sales order (the details of which show up in the SALES_ORDER table). A SALESPERSON can make multiple sales, each one recorded on a SALES_ORDER. A SALES_ORDER can include multiple PRODUCTs, and a PRODUCT can appear on multiple SALES_ORDERs.

Minimum cardinality may be modeled a variety of ways, depending on how the users' data model views things. For example, a person might be considered a customer (someone whose data appears in the CUSTOMER table) even before she buys anything because the store received her information in a promotional campaign. An employee might be considered a salesperson as soon as he is hired, even though he hasn't sold anything yet. A sales order might exist before it lists any products, and a product might exist on the shelves before any of them have been sold. According to this model, all the minimum cardinalities are optional. A different users' data model could mandate that some of these relationships be mandatory.

In a model such as the one described, where all the minimum cardinalities are optional, none of the entities depends on any of the other entities for its existence. A customer can exist without any associated sales orders. An employee can exist without any associated sales orders. A product can exist without any associated sales orders. A sales order can exist in the order pad without any associated customer, salesperson, or product. In this arrangement, all these entities are classified as *strong entities*. They all have an independent existence. Strong entities are represented in ER diagrams as rectangles with sharp corners.

Not all entities are strong, however. Consider the case shown in Figure 2-11. In this model, a driver's license cannot exist unless the corresponding driver exists.

The license is *existence-dependent* upon the driver. Any entity that is existence-dependent on another entity is a *weak entity*. In an ER diagram, a weak entity is represented with a box that has rounded corners. The diamond that shows the relationship between a weak entity and its corresponding strong entity also has rounded corners. Figure 2-11 shows this representation.

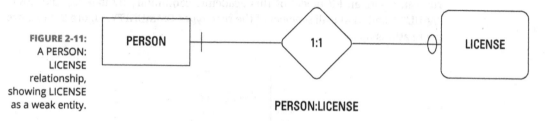

FIGURE 2-11: A PERSON: LICENSE relationship, showing LICENSE as a weak entity.

PERSON:LICENSE

ID-dependent entities

A weak entity cannot exist without a relationship to a strong entity. A special case of a weak entity is one that depends on a strong entity not only for its existence, but also for its identity — this is called an *ID-dependent entity*. One example of an ID-dependent entity is a seat on an airliner flight. Figure 2-12 illustrates the relationship.

FIGURE 2-12: The SEAT is ID-dependent on FLIGHT via the FLIGHT: SEAT relationship.

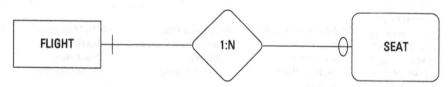

A seat number, for example 23-A, does not completely identify an airline seat. However, seat 23-A on Hawaiian Airlines flight 25 from PDX to HNL, on May 2, 2019, *does* completely identify a particular seat that a person can reserve. Those additional pieces of information are all attributes of the FLIGHT entity — the strong entity without whose existence the weak SEAT entity would basically be just a gleam in someone's eye.

Supertype and subtype entities

In some databases, you may find some entity classes that might actually share attributes with other entity classes, instead of being as dissimilar as customers and products. One example might be an academic community. There are a number of people in such a community: students, faculty members, and nonacademic staff. All those people share some attributes, such as name, home address, home telephone number, and email address. However, there are also attributes that are not shared. A student would also have attributes of grade point average, class standing, and advisor. A faculty member would have attributes of department, academic rank, and phone extension. A staff person would have attributes of job category, job title, and phone extension.

You can create an ER model of this academic community by making STUDENT, FACULTY, and STAFF all *subtypes* of the *supertype* COMMUNITY. Figure 2-13 shows the relationships.

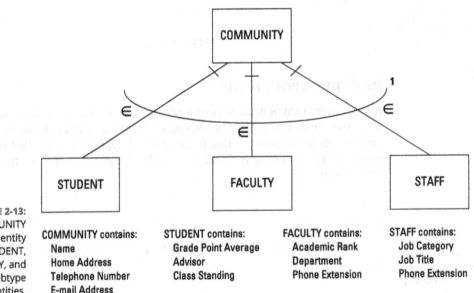

COMMUNITY contains:
  Name
  Home Address
  Telephone Number
  E-mail Address

STUDENT contains:
  Grade Point Average
  Advisor
  Class Standing

FACULTY contains:
  Academic Rank
  Department
  Phone Extension

STAFF contains:
  Job Category
  Job Title
  Phone Extension

FIGURE 2-13: The COMMUNITY supertype entity with STUDENT, FACULTY, and STAFF subtype entities.

Supertype/subtype relationships borrow the concept of *inheritance* from object-oriented programming. The attributes of the *supertype entity* are inherited by the subtype entities. Each *subtype entity* has additional attributes that it does not necessarily share with the other subtype entities. In the example, everyone in the community has a name, a home address, a telephone number, and an email address. However, only students have a grade point average, an advisor, and a class standing. Similarly, only a faculty member can have an academic rank, and only a staff member can have a job title.

Some aspects of Figure 2-13 require a little additional explanation. The ∈ next to each relationship line signifies that the lower entity is a subtype of the higher entity, so STUDENT, FACULTY, and STAFF are subtypes of COMMUNITY. The curved arc with a number 1 at the right end represents the fact that every member of the COMMUNITY must be a member of one of the subtype entities. In other words, you cannot be a member of the community unless you are either a student, or a faculty member, or a staff member. It is possible in some models that an element could be a member of a supertype without being a member of any of the subtypes. However, that is not the case for this example.

The supertype and subtype entities in the ER model correspond to supertables and subtables in a relational database. A supertable can have multiple subtables and a subtable can also have multiple supertables. The relationship between a supertable and a subtable is always one-to-one. The supertable/subtable relationship is created with an SQL CREATE command. I give an example of an ER model that incorporates a supertype/subtype structure later in this chapter.

Incorporating business rules

Business rules are formal statements about how an organization does business. They typically differ from one organization to another. For example, one university may have a rule that a faculty member must hold a PhD degree. Another university could well have no such rule.

Sometimes you may not find important business rules written down anywhere. They may just be things that everyone in the organization understands. It is important to conduct an in-depth interview of everyone involved to fish out any business rules that people failed to mention when the job of creating the database was first described to you.

A simple example of an ER model

In this section, as an example, I apply the principles of ER models to a hypothetical web-based business named Gentoo Joyce that sells apparel items with penguin motifs, such as T-shirts, scarves, and dresses. The business displays its products and takes credit card orders on its website. There is no brick and mortar store. Fulfillment is outsourced to a fulfillment house, which receives and warehouses products from vendors, and then, upon receiving orders from Gentoo Joyce, ships the orders to customers.

The website front end consists of pages that include descriptions and pictures of the products, a shopping cart, and a form for capturing customer and payment information. The website back end holds a database that stores customer, transaction, inventory, and order shipment status information. Figure 2-14 shows an ER diagram of the Gentoo Joyce system. It is an example typical of a boutique business.

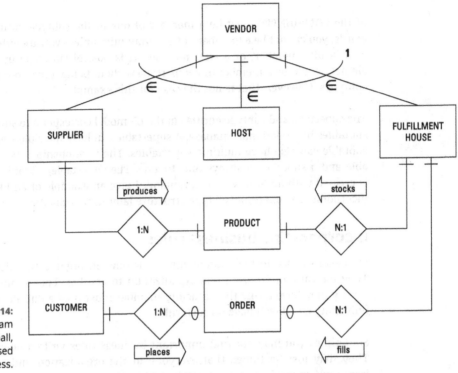

FIGURE 2-14:
An ER diagram
of a small,
web-based
retail business.

Gentoo Joyce buys goods and services from three kinds of vendors: product suppliers, web hosting services, and fulfillment houses. In the model, VENDOR is a supertype of SUPPLIER, HOST, and FULFILLMENT_HOUSE. Some attributes are shared among all the vendors; these are assigned to the VENDOR entity. Other attributes are not shared and are instead attributes of the subtype entities.

REMEMBER

This is only one of several possible models for the Gentoo Joyce business. Another possibility would be to include all providers in a VENDOR entity with more attributes. A third possibility would be to have no VENDOR entity, but separate SUPPLIER and FULFILLMENT_HOUSE entities, and to just consider a host as a supplier.

A many-to-many relationship exists between SUPPLIER and PRODUCT because a supplier may provide more than one product, and a given product may be supplied by more than one supplier. Similarly, any given product will (hopefully) appear on multiple orders, and an order may include multiple products. Such many-to-many relationships can be problematic. I discuss how to handle such problems in Book 2.

The other relationships in the model are one-to-many. A customer can place many orders, but each order comes from one and only one customer. A fulfillment house can stock multiple products, but each product is stocked by one and only one fulfillment house.

A slightly more complex example

The Gentoo Joyce system that I describe in the preceding section is an easy-to-understand example, similar to what you often find in database textbooks. Most real-world systems are much more complex. I don't try to show a genuine, real-world system here, but to move at least one step in that direction, I model the fictitious Clear Creek Medical Clinic (CCMC). As I discuss in Book 2 as well as earlier in this chapter, one of the first things to do when assigned the project of creating a database for a client is to interview everyone who has a stake in the system, including management, users, and anyone else who has a say in how things are run. Listen carefully to these people and discern how they model in their minds the system they envision. Find out what information they need to capture and what they intend to do with it.

CCMC employs doctors, nurses, medical technologists, medical assistants, and office workers. The company provides medical, dental, and vision benefits to employees and their dependents. The doctors, nurses, and medical technologists must all be licensed by a recognized licensing authority. Medical assistants may be certified, but need not be. Neither licensure nor certification is required of office workers.

Typically, a patient will see a doctor, who will examine the patient, and then order one or more tests. A medical assistant or nurse may take samples of the patient's blood, urine, or both, and take the samples to the laboratory. In the lab, a medical technologist performs the tests that the doctor has ordered. The results of the tests are sent to the doctor who ordered them, as well as to perhaps one or more consulting physicians. Based on the test results, the primary doctor, with input from the consulting physicians, makes a diagnosis of the patient's condition and prescribes a treatment. A nurse then administers the prescribed treatment.

Based on the descriptions of the envisioned system, as described by the interested parties (called stakeholders), you can come up with a proposed list of entities. A good first shot at this is to list all the nouns that were used by the people you interviewed. Many of these will turn out to be entities in your model, although you may end up classifying some of those nouns as attributes of entities. For this example, say you generated the following list:

Employee

Office worker

Doctor (physician)

Nurse

Medical technologist

Medical assistant

Benefits

Dependents

Patients

Doctor's license

Nurse's license

Medical technologist's license

Medical assistant's certificate

Examination

Test order

Test

Test result

Consultation

Diagnosis

Prescription

Treatment

In the course of your interviews of the stakeholders, you found that one of the categories of things to track is employees, but there are several different employee classifications. You also found that there are benefits, and those benefits apply to dependents as well as to employees. From this, you conclude that EMPLOYEE is an entity and it is a supertype of the OFFICE_WORKER, DOCTOR, NURSE, MEDTECH, and MEDASSIST entities. A DEPENDENT entity also should fit into the picture somewhere.

Although doctors, nurses, and medical technologists all must have current valid licenses, because a license applies to one and only one professional and each professional has one and only one license, it makes sense for those licenses to be attributes of their respective DOCTOR, NURSE, and MEDTECH entities rather than to be entities in their own right. Consequently, there is no LICENSE entity in the CCMC ER model.

PATIENT clearly should be an entity, as should EXAMINATION, TEST, TESTORDER, and RESULT. CONSULTATION, DIAGNOSIS, PRESCRIPTION, and TREATMENT also deserve to stand on their own as entities.

After you have decided what the entities are, you can start thinking about how they relate to each other. You may be able to model each relationship in one of several ways. This is where the interviews with the stakeholders are critical. The model you arrive at must be consistent with the organization's business rules, both those written down somewhere and those that are understood by everyone, but not usually talked about. Figure 2-15 shows one possible way to model this system.

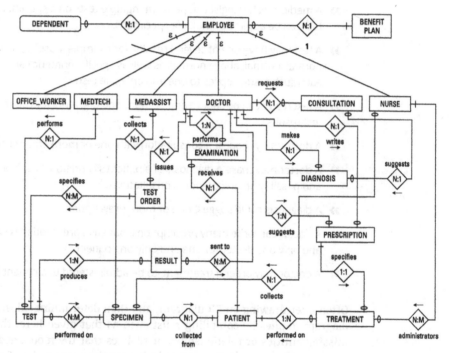

FIGURE 2-15: The ER diagram for Clear Creek Medical Clinic.

From this diagram, you can extract certain facts:

>> An employee can have zero, one, or multiple dependents, but each dependent is associated with one and only one employee. (Business rule: If both members of a married couple work for the clinic, for insurance purposes, the dependents are associated with only one of them.)

>> An employee must be either an office worker, a doctor, a nurse, a medical technologist, or a medical assistant. (Business rule: An office worker cannot,

for example, also be classified as a medical assistant. Only one job classification is permitted.)

>> A doctor can perform many examinations, but each examination is performed by one and only one doctor. (Business rule: If more than one doctor is present at a patient examination, only one of them takes responsibility for the examination.)

>> A doctor can issue many test orders, but each test order can specify one and only one test.

>> A medical assistant or a nurse can collect multiple specimens from a patient, but each specimen is from one and only one patient.

>> A medical technologist can perform multiple tests on a specimen, and each test can be applied to multiple specimens.

>> A test may have one of several results; for example, positive, negative, below normal, normal, above normal, as well as specific numeric values. However, each such result applies to one and only one test.

>> A test result can be sent to one or more doctors. A doctor can receive many test results.

>> A doctor may request a consultation with one or more other doctors.

>> A doctor may make a diagnosis of a patient's condition, based on test results and possibly on one or more consultations.

>> A diagnosis could suggest one or more prescriptions.

>> A doctor can write many prescriptions, but each prescription is written by one and only one doctor for one and only one patient.

>> A doctor may order a treatment, to be administered to a patient by a nurse.

Often after drawing an ER diagram, and then determining all the things that the diagram implies by compiling a list such as that given here, the designer finds missing entities or relationships, or realizes that the model does not accurately represent the way things are actually done in the organization. Creating the model is an iterative process of progressively modifying the diagram until it reflects the desired system as closely as possible. (*Iterative* here meaning doing it over and over again until you get it right — or as right as it will ever be.)

Problems with complex relationships

The Clear Creek Medical Clinic example in the preceding section contains some many-to-many relationships, such as the relationship between TEST and

SPECIMEN. Multiple tests can be run on a single specimen, and multiple specimens, taken from multiple patients, can all be run through the same test.

That all sounds quite reasonable, but in point of fact there's a bit of a problem when it comes to storing the relevant information. If the TEST entity is translated into a table in a relational database, how many columns should be set aside for specimens? Because you don't know how many specimens a test will include, and because the number of specimens could be quite large, it doesn't make sense to allocate space in the TEST table to show that the test was performed on a particular specimen.

Similarly, if the SPECIMEN entity is translated into a table in a relational database, how many columns should you set aside to record the tests that might be performed on it? It doesn't make sense to allocate space in the SPECIMEN table to hold all the tests that might be run on it if no one even knows beforehand how many tests you may end up running. For these reasons, it is common practice to convert a many-to-many relationship into two one-to-many relationships, both connected to a new entity that lies between the original two. You can make that conversion with no loss of accuracy, and the problem of how to store things disappears. In Book 2, I go into detail on how to make this conversion.

Simplifying relationships using normalization

Even after you have eliminated all the many-to-many relationships in an ER model, there can still be problems if you have not conceptualized your entities in the simplest way. The next step in the design process is to examine your model and see if adding, changing, or deleting data can cause inconsistencies or even outright wrong information to be retained in your database. Such problems are called *anomalies*, and if there's even a slight chance that they'll crop up, you'll need to adjust your model to eliminate them. This process of model adjustment is called *normalization*, and I cover it in Book 2.

Translating an ER model into a relational model

After you're satisfied that your ER model is not only correct, but economical and robust, the next step is to translate it into a relational model. The relational model is the basis for all relational database management systems. I go through that translation process in Book 2.

Chapter 3

Getting to Know SQL

I n the early days of relational database management systems (RDBMS), there was no standard language for performing relational operations on data. (If you aren't sure what an RDBMS is, please take a look at the first chapter in this book.) A number of companies came out with relational database management system products, and each had its own associated language. There were some general similarities among the languages because they all performed essentially the same operations on the same kinds of data, structured in the same way. However, differences in syntax and functionality made it impossible for a person using the language of one RDBMS to operate on data that had been stored by another relational database management system. (That's RDBMS, if you missed it the first time.) All the RDBMS vendors tried to gain dominant market share so that their particular proprietary language would prevail. The logic was that once developers learned a language, they would want to stick with it on subsequent projects. This steaming cauldron of ideas set the stage for the emergence of SQL. There was one company (IBM) that had more market power than all the others combined, and it had the additional advantage of being the employer of the inventor of the relational database model.

Where SQL Came From

It is interesting to note that even though Dr. Codd was an IBM employee when he developed the relational database model, IBM's initial support of that model was lukewarm at best. One reason might have been the fact that IBM already had a leading position in the database market with its IMS (Information Management System) hierarchical DBMS. (For the whole hierarchical versus relational divide, check out Book 1, Chapter 1.) In 1978, IBM released System/38, a minicomputer that came with an RDBMS that was not promoted heavily. As a result, in 1979, the world was introduced to a fully realized RDBMS by a small startup company named Relational Software, Inc. headed by Larry Ellison. Relational's product, called Oracle, is still the leading relational database management system on the market today.

Although Oracle had the initial impact on the market, other companies, including IBM, quickly followed suit. In the process of developing its SQL/DS relational database management system product, IBM created a language, code-named SEQUEL, which was an acronym for Structured English Query Language. This moniker was appropriate because SEQUEL statements looked like English-language sentences, but were more structured than most casual speech.

When it came time for IBM to actually release its RDBMS product, along with its associated language, IBM's legal department flagged a possible copyright issue with the name SEQUEL. In response, management elected to drop the vowels and call the language SQL (pronounced *ess cue el)*. The reference to structured English was lost in the process. As a result, many people thought that SQL was an acronym for Structured Query Language. This is not the case. In computer programming, a structured language has some very well-defined characteristics. SQL does not share those characteristics and is thus not a structured language, query or otherwise.

Knowing What SQL Does

SQL is a software tool designed to deal with relational database data. It does far more than just execute queries. Yes, of course you can use it to retrieve the data you want from a database, using a query. However, you can also use SQL to create and destroy databases, as well as modify their structure. In addition, you can add, modify, and delete data with SQL. Even with all that capability, SQL is still considered only a *data sublanguage,* which means that it does not have all the features of general-purpose programming languages such as C, C++, C#, or Java.

SQL is specifically designed for dealing with relational databases, and thus does not include a number of features needed for creating useful application programs. As a result, to create a complete application — one that handles queries as well as provides access to a database — you must write the code in one of the general-purpose languages and embed SQL statements within the program whenever it communicates with the database.

The ISO/IEC SQL Standard

In the early 1980s, IBM started using SQL in its first relational database product, which was incorporated into the System/38 minicomputer. Smaller companies in the DBMS industry, in an effort to be compatible with IBM's offering, modeled their languages after SQL. In this way, SQL became a de facto standard. In 1986, the de facto standard became a standard de jure when the American National Standards Institute (ANSI) issued the SQL-86 standard. The SQL standard has been continually updated since then, with subsequent revisions named SQL-89, SQL-92, SQL:1999, SQL:2003, SQL:2008, SQL:2011, SQL:2016, and most recently, SQL:2023. Along the way, the standard became accepted internationally and became an ISO/IEC standard, where ISO is the International Organization for Standardization, and IEC is the International Electrotechnical Commission. The internationalization of the SQL standard means that database developers all over the world talk to their databases in the same way.

Knowing What SQL Does Not Do

Before I can tell you what SQL doesn't do, I need to give you some background information. In the 1930s, computer scientist and mathematician Alan Turing defined a very simple machine that could perform any computation that could be performed by any computer imaginable, regardless of how big and complex. This simple machine has come to be known as a *universal Turing machine*. Any computer that can be shown to be equivalent to a universal Turing machine is said to be Turing-complete. All modern computers are Turing-complete. Similarly, a computer language capable of expressing any possible computation is said to be Turing-complete. Practically all popular languages, including C, C#, C++, BASIC, FORTRAN, COBOL, Pascal, Java, and many others, are Turing-complete. SQL, however, is not.

Note: Whereas ISO/IEC standard SQL is not Turing-complete, DBMS vendors have added extensions to their versions which *are* Turing complete. Thus the version of SQL that you are working with may or may not be Turing-complete. If it is, you can write a whole program with it, without embedding your SQL code in a program written in another language.

Because standard SQL is not Turing-complete, you cannot write an SQL program to perform a complex series of steps, as you can with a language such as C or Java. On the other hand, languages such as C and Java do not have the data-manipulation facilities that SQL has, so you cannot write a program with them that will efficiently operate on database data. There are several ways to solve this dilemma:

>> Combine the two types of language by embedding SQL statements within a program written in a host language such as C. (I discuss this in Book 5, Chapter 3.)

>> Have the C program make calls to SQL modules to perform data-manipulation functions. (I talk about this in Book 5, Chapter 3 as well.)

>> Create a new language that includes SQL, but also incorporates those structures that would make the language Turing-complete. (This is essentially what Microsoft and Oracle have done with their versions of SQL.)

All three of these solutions are offered by one or another of the DBMS vendors.

Choosing and Using an Available DBMS Implementation

A number of relational database management systems are currently available, and they all include a version of SQL that adheres, more or less, closely to the ISO/IEC international standard for the SQL language. No SQL version available today is completely compliant with the standard, and probably none ever will be. The standard is updated every few years, adding new capability, putting the vendors in the position of always playing catch-up.

In addition, in most cases, the vendors do not *want* to be 100 percent compliant with the standard. They like to include useful features that are not in the standard in order to make their product more attractive to developers. If a developer uses a vendor's nonstandard feature, this has the effect of locking in the developer to that vendor. It makes it difficult for the developer to switch to a different DBMS.

WHAT'S A DATABASE?

There is a lot of confusion about what exactly people are talking about when they mention the word *database*. I have mentioned database management systems (DBMSs), database applications, and databases. Some people lump these things together and call the whole lot databases. Loose usage of this sort just confuses everybody. To keep things clear in your own mind, remember the following distinctions:

- A *database* is a structured collection of integrated records. In other words, it is the data, but organized in a structured way.

- A *database application* is a computer program that operates on a database, which enables users to maintain the database and query it for needed information.

- A *database management system* is the engine that controls access to a database. Database applications must work through a DBMS in order to access the database. Conceptually, the DBMS lies between the database and the database application.

Microsoft Access

Microsoft Access is an entry-level DBMS with which developers can build relatively small and simple databases and database applications. It is designed for use by people with little or no training in database theory. You can build databases and database applications using Access, without ever seeing SQL.

Access does include an implementation of SQL, and you can use it to query your databases — but it is a limited subset of the language, and Microsoft does not encourage its use. Instead, they prefer that you use the graphical database creation and manipulation tools and use the query-by-example (QBE) interface to ask questions of your database. Under the hood and beyond user control, the table-creation tasks that the user specifies using the graphical tools are translated to SQL before being sent to the database engine, which is the part of the DBMS that actually operates on the database.

Microsoft Access runs under any of the Microsoft Windows operating systems, as well as Apple's OS X, but not under Linux or any other non-Microsoft operating system.

To reach the SQL editor in Access, do the following:

1. **Open a database that already has tables and at least one query defined.**

A great place to start is with the Northwind Traders Starter Edition database provided as a free download with Access. The database includes a built-in

Getting to Know SQL

mini-application that uses Access forms to help query and insert data. After you download the database, the application portion automatically starts, showing a form that asks you to create a user account for the application. After you log into the application, you see a database window that looks something like Figure 3-1, with the default Home tab visible. The icon at the left end of the ribbon is the icon for Layout View, one of several available views. In this example, the pane on the left side of the window shows the different tables, forms, reports, queries, and scripts that have been created as part of the Northwind Traders Starter Edition database.

2. **Click the Queries entry in the pane on the left, and then double-click the qryProductOrders query.**

The default view shows the data that's a result of the query, as shown in Figure 3-2.

3. **To see how the query is constructed, click the View icon at the top and then select Design View.**

The Design View for the query is shown in Figure 3-3. At the top is a graphical representation of the tables involved in the query, and below that is a list of the data fields that are retrieved in the query.

4. **Choose SQL View from the View drop-down menu.**

Doing so shows the view displayed in Figure 3-4. It is the SQL code generated in order to display the result of the Team Membership of Paper Authors query.

As you can see, it took a pretty complicated SQL statement to perform that Product Order query.

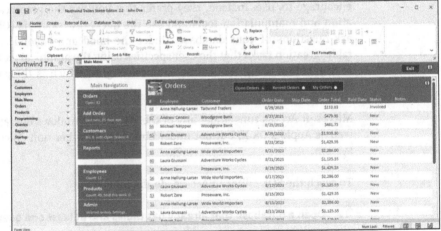

FIGURE 3-1:
A Microsoft Access 365 database window running the Northwind Traders Starter Edition database.

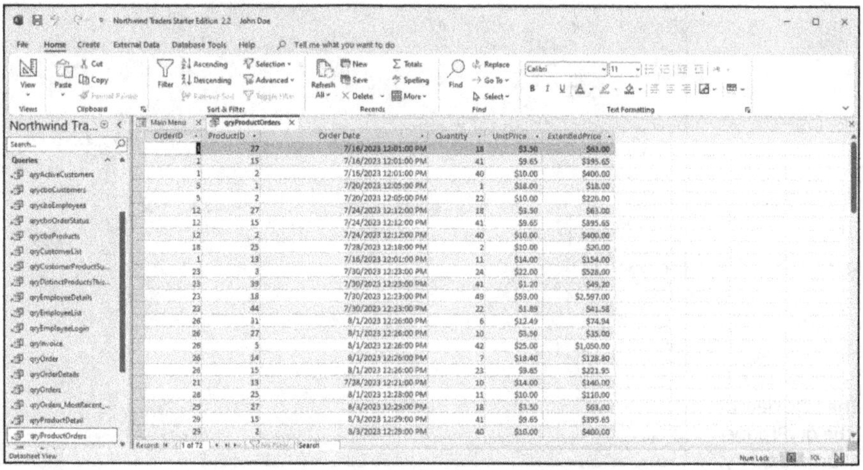

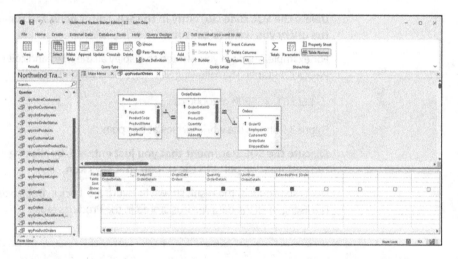

FIGURE 3-2:
Results of the
qryProductOrders
query selected.

FIGURE 3-3:
The Design view
of the qryProduct
Orders query.

This early in the book, and I know many of you do not know any SQL yet. However, suppose you did. (Not an unfounded supposition, by the way, because you certainly will know a lot about SQL by the time you've finished reading this book.) On that future day, when you are a true SQL master, you may want to enter a query directly using SQL, instead of going through the extra stage of using Access' Query by Example facility. Once you get to the SQL Editor, which is where we are right now, you can do just that. Step 8 shows you how.

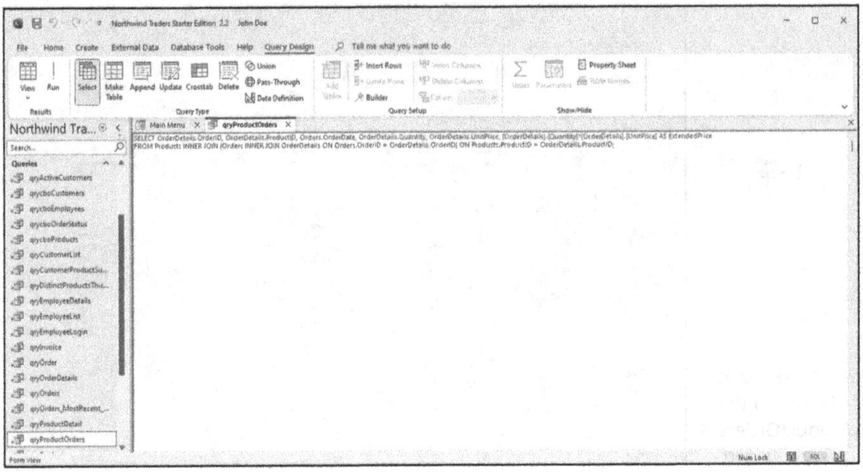

FIGURE 3-4:
The SQL view of the qryProduct Orders query.

5. **Delete the SQL code currently in the SQL Editor pane and replace it with the query you want to execute.**

   For example, suppose you wanted to display all the rows and columns of the PRODUCTS table. The following SQL statement will do the trick:

   ```
   SELECT * FROM PRODUCTS ;
   ```

   Figure 3-5 shows the work surface at this point.

6. **Execute the SQL statement that you just entered, by clicking on the big red exclamation point in the ribbon that says Run.**

   Doing so produces the result shown in Figure 3-6, back in Datasheet View. This is a listing of all the data records stored in the Products table.

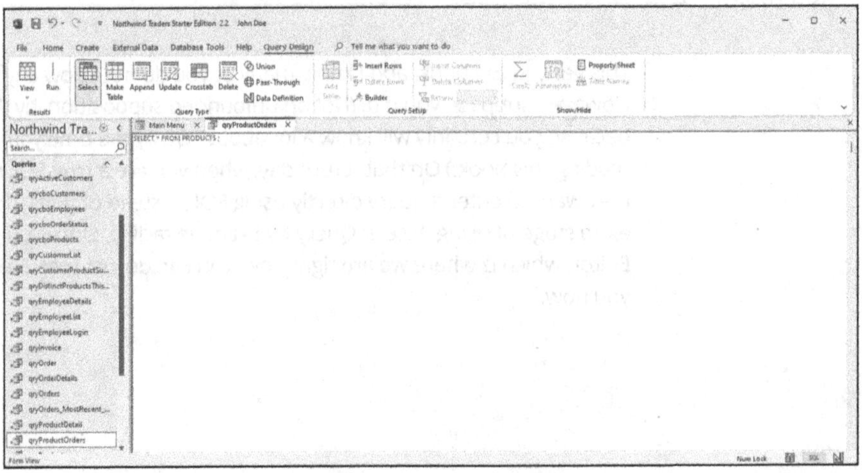

FIGURE 3-5:
Changing the SQL for the query in the qryProduct Orders query to select everything in the PRODUCTS table.

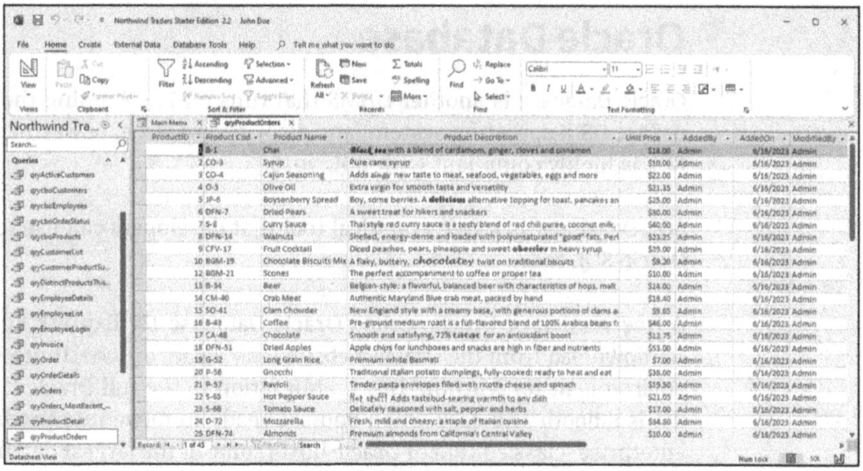

FIGURE 3-6:
The results of the query to display all of the data in the PRODUCTS table.

Don't save your new query as it will replace the standard qryProductOrders query in the Northwind Traders Starter Edition database. Just exit out without saving the changes.

Microsoft SQL Server

Microsoft SQL Server is Microsoft's entry into the enterprise database market. It runs only under one of the various Microsoft Windows operating systems. The latest version is SQL Server 2022. Unlike Microsoft Access, SQL Server requires a high level of expertise in order to use it at all. Users interact with SQL Server using Transact-SQL, also known as T-SQL. It adheres quite closely to the syntax of ISO/IEC standard SQL and provides much of the functionality described in the standard. Additional functionality, not specified in the ISO/IEC standard, provides the developer with usability and performance advantages that Microsoft hopes will make SQL Server more attractive than its competitors. There is a free version of SQL Server 2022, called SQL Server 2022 Express Edition, that you might think of as SQL Server on training wheels. It is fully functional, but the size of database it can operate on is limited.

IBM DB2

DB2 is a flexible product that runs on Windows and Linux PCs, on the low end all the way up to IBM's largest mainframes. As you would expect for a DBMS that runs on big iron, it is a full-featured product. It incorporates key features specified by the SQL standard, as well as numerous nonstandard additions. As with Microsoft's SQL Server, to use DB2 effectively, a developer must have received extensive training and considerable hands-on experience.

Oracle Database

Oracle Database is another DBMS that runs on PCs running the Windows, Linux, or Mac OS X operating system, and also on very large, powerful computers. Oracle SQL is highly compliant with SQL:2016.

SQL Developer is a free graphical tool that developers can use to enter and debug Oracle SQL code.

A free version of Oracle, called Oracle Database 18c Express Edition, is available for download from the Oracle website (www.oracle.com). It provides a convenient environment for learning Oracle. Migration to the full Oracle Database 11g product is smooth and easy when you are ready to move into production mode. The enterprise-class edition of Oracle hosts some of the largest databases in use today. (The same can be said for DB2 and SQL Server.)

Sybase SQL Anywhere

Sybase's SQL Anywhere is a high-capacity, high-performance DBMS compatible with databases originally built with Microsoft SQL Server, IBM DB2, Oracle, and MySQL, as well as a wide variety of popular application-development languages. It features a self-tuning query optimizer and dynamic cache sizing.

REMEMBER

Tuning queries can make a big difference in their execution time. Tuning a query means making adjustments to it to make it run faster. Dynamic cache sizing means changing the size of the cache memory available to a query, based on the resources that the query needs to run as fast as possible. I talk about query tuning in Chapter 2 of Book 3.

MySQL

MySQL is the most widely used open source DBMS. The defining feature of *open source* software is that it is freely available to anyone. After downloading it you can modify it to meet your needs, and even redistribute it, as long as you give attribution to its source.

One amazing feature of MySQL is that it offers multiple ways of storing and managing data, which they call *storage engines.* The most feature-rich of these is the InnoDB storage engine, which provides many of the advanced database features found in commercial databases such as the Microsoft SQL Server. The level of compliance with the ISO/IEC SQL standard differs between storage engines, but the compliance of the MySQL InnoDB storage engine is comparable to that of the proprietary DBMS products mentioned here.

Another popular storage engine is the MyISAM storage engine, which is particularly noted for its speed. Although it lacks many of the advanced features found in the InnoDB storage engine, the MyISAM storage engine is amazingly fast with simple data queries, making it a popular choice for web-based applications. The MySQL server runs under Windows and Linux, but not under IBM's proprietary mainframe operating systems. MySQL is supported by a large and dedicated user community, which you can learn about at www.mysql.com. MySQL was originally developed by a small team of programmers in Finland, and was expanded and enhanced by volunteer programmers from around the world. Today, however, it is owned by Oracle Corporation.

TIP Since the purchase of MySQL by Oracle, the original developers of MySQL have started a new open-source database project named MariaDB. Thanks to the availability of the source code of open-source projects, MariaDB is mostly a clone of MySQL, with just a few feature differences. Most applications written to work with MySQL work fine using MariaDB. You can find more information about MariaDB at https://mariadb.com.

PostgreSQL

PostgreSQL (pronounced *POST gress CUE el*) is another open source DBMS, and it is generally considered to be more robust than MySQL, and more capable of supporting large enterprise-wide applications. It is also supported by an active user community. PostgreSQL runs under Linux, Unix, Windows, and IBM's z/OS mainframe operating system.

Chapter **4**

SQL and the Relational Model

The relational database model, as I mention in Chapter 1 of this minibook, existed as a theoretical model for almost a decade before the first relational database product appeared on the market. Now, it turns out that the first commercial implementation of the relational model — a software program from the company that later became Oracle — did not even use SQL, which had not yet been released by IBM. In those early days, there were a number of competing data sublanguages. Gradually, SQL became a de facto standard, thanks in no small part to IBM's dominant position in the market, and the fact that Oracle started offering it as an alternative to its own language early on.

Although SQL was developed to work with a relational database management system, it's not entirely consistent with the relational model. However, it is close enough, and in many cases, it even offers capabilities not present in the relational model. Some of the most important aspects of SQL are direct analogs of some aspects of the relational model. Others are not. This chapter gives you the lay of the land by offering a brief introduction to the (somewhat complicated) relationship between SQL and the relational database model. I do that by highlighting how certain important terms and concepts may have slightly different meanings in the (practical) SQL world as opposed to the (theoretical) relational database world. (I throw in some general, all-inclusive definitions for good measure.)

Sets, Relations, Multisets, and Tables

The relational model is based on the mathematical discipline known as *set theory*. In set theory, a *set* is defined as a collection of unique objects — duplicates are not allowed. This carries over to the relational model. A *relation* is defined as a collection of unique objects called *tuples* — no duplicates are allowed among tuples.

In SQL, the equivalent of a relation is a table. However, tables are not exactly like relations, in that a table can have duplicate rows. For that reason, tables in a relational database are not modeled on the sets of set theory, but rather on *multisets*, which are similar to sets except they allow duplicate objects.

Although a relation is not exactly the same thing as a table, the terms are often used interchangeably. Because relations were defined by theoreticians, they have a very precise definition. The word *table*, on the other hand, is in general use and is often much more loosely defined. When I use the word *table* in this book, I use it in the more restricted sense, as being an alternative term for *relation*. The attributes and tuples of a relation are strictly equivalent to the columns and rows of a table.

So, what's an SQL relation? Formally, a relation is a two-dimensional table that has the following characteristics:

>> Every cell in the table must contain a single value, if it contains any value at all. Repeating groups and arrays are not allowed as values. (In this context, *groups* and *arrays* are examples of collections of values.)

>> All the entries in any column must be of the same kind. For example, if a column contains an employee name in one row, it must contain employee names in all rows that contain values.

>> Each column has a unique name.

>> The order of the columns doesn't matter.

>> The order of the rows doesn't matter.

>> No two rows may be identical.

If and only if a table meets all these criteria, it is a relation. You might have tables that fail to meet one or more of these criteria. For example, a table might have two identical rows. It is still a table in the loose sense, but it is not a relation.

Functional Dependencies

Functional dependencies are relationships between or among attributes. Consider the example of two attributes of the CUSTOMER relation, Zipcode and State. If you know the customer's zip code, the state can be obtained by a simple lookup because each zip code resides in one and only one state. This means that State is *functionally dependent* on Zipcode or that Zipcode *determines* state. Zipcode is called a *determinant* because it determines the value of another attribute. The reverse is not true. State does not determine Zipcode because states can contain multiple Zipcodes. You denote functional dependencies as follows:

```
Zipcode ⇨ State
```

A group of attributes may act as a determinant. If one attribute depends on the values of multiple other attributes, that group of attributes, collectively, is a determinant of the first attribute.

Consider the relation INVOICE, made up as it is of the following attributes:

- **InvNo:** Invoice number.
- **CustID:** Customer ID.
- **WorR:** Wholesale or retail. I'm assuming that products have both a wholesale and a retail price, which is why I've added the WorR attribute to tell me whether this is a wholesale or a retail transaction.
- **ProdID:** Product ID.
- **Quantity:** Quantity.
- **Price:** You guessed it.
- **Extprice:** Extended price (which I get by multiplying Quantity and Price).

With our definitions out of the way, check out what depends on what by following the handy determinant arrow:

```
(WorR, ProdID) ⇨ Price
(Quantity, Price) ⇨ Extprice,
```

W/R tells you whether you are charging the wholesale price or the retail price. ProdID shows which product you are considering. Thus, the combination of WorR and ProdID determines Price. Similarly, the combination of Quantity and Price determines Extprice. Neither WorR nor ProdID by itself determines Price; they are both needed to determine Price. Both Quantity and Price are needed to determine Extprice.

Keys

A *key* is an attribute (or group of attributes) that uniquely identifies a tuple (a unique collection of attributes) in a relation. One of the characteristics of a relation is that no two rows (tuples) are identical. You can guarantee that no two rows are identical if at least one field (attribute) is guaranteed to have a unique value in every row, or if some combination of fields is guaranteed to be unique for each row.

Table 4-1 shows an example of the PROJECT relation. It lists researchers affiliated with the Gentoo Institute's Penguin Physiology Lab, the project that each participant is working on, and the location at which each participant is conducting his or her research.

TABLE 4-1 **PROJECT Relation**

ResearcherID	Project	Location
Pizarro	Why penguin feet don't freeze	Bahia Paraiso
Whitehead	Why penguins don't get the bends	Port Lockroy
Shelton	How penguin eggs stay warm in pebble nests	Peterman Island
Nansen	How penguin diet varies by season	Peterman Island

In this table, each researcher is assigned to only one project. Is this a rule? Must a researcher be assigned to only one project, or is it possible for a researcher to be assigned to more than one? If a researcher can be assigned to only one project, ResearcherID is a key. It guarantees that every row in the PROJECT table is unique. What if there is no such rule? What if a researcher may work on multiple projects at the same time? Table 4-2 shows this situation.

In this scenario, Dr. Pizarro works on both the cold feet and the warm eggs projects, whereas Professor Shelton works on both the warm eggs and the varied diet projects. Clearly, ResearcherID cannot be used as a key. However, the combination of ResearcherID and Project is unique and is thus a key.

You're probably wondering how you can reliably tell what is a key and what isn't. Looking at the relation in Table 4-1, it looks like ResearcherID is a key because every entry in that column is unique. However, this could be due to the fact that you are looking at a limited sample, and any minute now someone could add a new row that duplicates the value of ResearcherID in one of the existing rows. How can you be sure that won't happen? Easy. Ask the users.

TABLE 4-2

PROJECTS Relation

ResearcherID	Project	Location
Pizarro	Why penguin feet don't freeze	Bahia Paraiso
Pizarro	How penguin eggs stay warm in pebble nests	Peterman Island
Whitehead	Why penguins don't get the bends	Port Lockroy
Shelton	How penguin eggs stay warm in pebble nests	Peterman Island
Shelton	How penguin diet varies by season	Peterman Island
Nansen	How penguin diet varies by season	Peterman Island

The relations you build are models of the mental images that the users have of the system they are dealing with. You want your relational model to correspond as closely as possible to the model that the users have in their minds. If they tell you, for example, that in their organization, researchers never work on more than one project at a time, you can use ResearcherID as a key. On the other hand, if it is even remotely possible that a researcher might be assigned to two projects simultaneously, you have to revert to a composite key made up of both ResearcherID and Project.

REMEMBER

A question that might arise in your mind is, "Is it possible for a relation to exist that has no key?" By the definition of a relation, the answer is no. Every relation *must* have a key. One of the characteristics of a relation is that no two rows may be exactly the same. That means that you are always able to distinguish rows from each other, although you may have to include all the relation's attributes in the key to do it.

Views

Although the most fundamental constituent of a relational database is undoubtedly the table, another important concept is that of the virtual table or *view*. Unlike an ordinary table, a view has no physical existence until it is called upon in a query. There is no place on disk where the rows in the view are stored. The view exists only in the metadata as a definition. The definition describes how to pull data from tables and present it to the user in the form of a view.

From the user's viewpoint (no pun intended), a view looks just like a table. You can do almost everything to a view that you can do to a table. The major exception is that you cannot always update a view the same way that you can update a table. The view may contain columns that are the result of some arithmetic operation on the data in columns from the tables upon which the view is based. You can't update a column that doesn't exist in your permanent storage device. Despite this limitation, views, after they're formulated, can save you considerable work: You don't need to code the same complex query every time you want to pull data from multiple tables. Create the view once, and then use it every time you need it.

Users

Although it may seem a little odd to include them, the users are an important part of any database system. After all, without the users, no data would be written into the system, no data would be manipulated, and no results would be displayed. When you think about it, the users are mighty important. Just as you want your hardware and software to be of the highest quality you can afford, in order to produce the best results, you want the highest-quality people too, for the same reason. To assure that only the people who meet your standards have access to the database system, you should have a robust security system that enables authorized users to do their job and at the same time prevents access to everyone else.

Privileges

A good security system not only keeps out unauthorized users, but also provides authorized users with access privileges tailored to their needs. The night watchman has different database needs from those of the company CEO. One way of handling privileges is to assign every authorized user an authorization ID. When the person logs on with his authorization ID, the privileges associated with that authorization ID become available to him. This could include the ability to read the contents of certain columns of certain tables, the ability to add new rows to certain tables, delete rows, update rows, and so on.

A second way to assign privileges is with roles, which were introduced in SQL:1999. *Roles* are simply a way for you to assign the same privileges to multiple people, and they are particularly valuable in large organizations where a number of people have essentially the same job and thus the same needs for data.

For example, a night watchman might have the same data needs as other security guards. You can grant a suite of privileges to the SECURITY_GUARD role. From then on, you can assign the SECURITY_GUARD role to any new guards, and all the privileges appropriate for that role are automatically assigned to them. When a person leaves or changes jobs, revocation of his role can be just as easy.

Schemas

Relational database applications typically use multiple tables. As a database grows to support multiple applications, it becomes more and more likely that an application developer will try to give one of her tables the same name as a table that already exists in the database. This can cause problems and frustration. To get around this problem, SQL has a hierarchical namespace structure. A developer can define her tables as being members of a *schema*.

With this structure, one developer can have a table named CUSTOMER in her schema, whereas a second developer can also have an entirely different table, also named CUSTOMER, but in a different schema.

THE RELATIONAL DATABASE HIERARCHY

A relational database is organized in a hierarchical structure, where the highest level is the catalog. Generally only the largest, most complex databases have multiple catalogs.

- **Catalogs:** A database catalog comes into play only in large, complex databases that have multiple schemas.

- **Schemas:** A database schema contains metadata. This metadata includes definitions of tables, views, value ranges, indexes, users, and user groups. It can also include stored procedures and triggers.

- **Tables:** A database table is a set of elements organized as a two-dimensional table with horizontal rows and vertical columns. The columns correspond to the attributes in the ER model of an entity. The rows hold the data about individual instances of the entity.

- **Columns:** A column is a component of a database table. Each column in the table corresponds to one of the attributes in the ER model of the entity being actualized by the table.

Catalogs

These days, organizations can be so big that if every developer had a schema for each of her applications, the number of schemas itself could be a problem. Someone might inadvertently give a new schema the same name as an existing schema. To head off this possibility, an additional level was added at the top of the namespace hierarchy. A *catalog* can contain multiple schemas, which in turn can contain multiple tables. The smallest organizations don't have to worry about either catalogs or schemas, but those levels of the namespace hierarchy are there if they're needed. If your organization is big enough to worry about duplicate catalog names, it is big enough to figure out a way to deal with the problem.

Connections, Sessions, and Transactions

A database management system is typically divided into two main parts: a *client* side, which interfaces with the user, and a *server* side, which holds the data and operates on it. To operate on a database, a user must establish a *connection* between her client and the server that holds the data she wants to access. Generally, the first thing you must do — if you want to work on a database at all — is to establish a connection to it. You can do this with a CONNECT statement that specifies your authorization ID and names the server you want to connect to. The exact implementation of this varies from one DBMS to another. (Most people today would use the DBMS's graphical user interface to connect to a server instead of using the SQL CONNECT statement.)

REMEMBER

A *session* is the context in which a single user executes a sequence of SQL statements, using a single connection. A *user* can either be a person entering SQL statements at the client console, or a program running on the client machine.

A *transaction* is a sequence of SQL statements that is atomic with respect to recovery. This means that if a failure occurs while a transaction is in progress, the effects of the transaction are erased so that the database is left in the state it was in before the transaction started. *Atomic* in this context means indivisible. Either the transaction runs to completion, or it aborts in such a way that any changes it made before the abort are undone.

Routines

Routines are procedures, functions, or methods that can be invoked either by an SQL CALL statement, or by the host language program that the SQL code is operating with. *Methods* are a kind of function used in object-oriented programming.

Routines enable SQL code to take advantage of calculations performed by host language code, and enable host language code to take advantage of data operations performed by SQL code.

Because either a host language program or SQL code can invoke a routine, and because the routine being invoked can be written either in SQL or in host language code, routines can cause confusion. A few definitions help to clarify the situation:

» **Externally invoked routine:** A procedure, written in SQL and residing in a module located on the client, which is invoked by the host language program

» **SQL-invoked routine:** Either a procedure or a function, residing in a module located on the server, which could be written in either SQL or the host language, that is invoked by SQL code

» **External routine:** Either a procedure or a function, residing in a module located on the server, which is written in the host language, but is invoked by SQL

» **SQL routine:** Either a procedure or a function, residing in a module located on either the server or the client, which is written in SQL and invoked by SQL

Paths

A *path* in SQL, similar to a path in operating systems, tells the system in what order to search locations to find a routine that has been invoked. For a system with several schemas (perhaps one for testing, one for QA, and one for production), the path tells the executing program where to look first, where to look next, and so on, to find an invoked routine.

Chapter **5**

Knowing the Major Components of SQL

Y ou can view SQL as being divided into three distinct parts, each of which has a different function. With one part, the Data Definition Language (DDL), you can create and revise the structure (the metadata) of a database. With the second part, the Data Manipulation Language (DML), you can operate on the data contained in the database. And with the third part, the Data Control Language (DCL), you can maintain a database's security and reliability.

In this chapter, I look at each of these SQL components in turn.

Creating a Database with the Data Definition Language

The Data Definition Language (DDL) is the part of SQL that you use to create a database and all its structural components, including tables, views, schemas, and other objects. It is also the tool that you use to modify the structure of an existing database or destroy it after you no longer need it.

In the text that follows, I tell you about the structure of a relational database. Then I give you instructions for creating your own SQL database with some simple tables, views that help users access data easily and efficiently, schemas that help keep your tables organized in the database, and domains, which restrict the type of data that users can enter into specified fields.

Creating a database can be complicated, and you may find that you need to adjust a table after you've created it. Or you may find that the database users' needs have changed, and you need to create space for additional data. It's also possible that you'll find that at some point, a specific table is no longer necessary. In this section, I tell you how to modify tables and delete them altogether.

The containment hierarchy

The defining difference between databases and *flat files* — such as those described in Chapter 1 of this minibook — is that databases are structured. As I show you in previous chapters, the structure of relational databases differs from the structure of other database models, such as the hierarchical model and the network model. Be that as it may, there's still a definite hierarchical aspect to the structure of a relational database. Like Russian nesting dolls, one level of structure contains another, which in turn contains yet another, as shown in Figure 5-1.

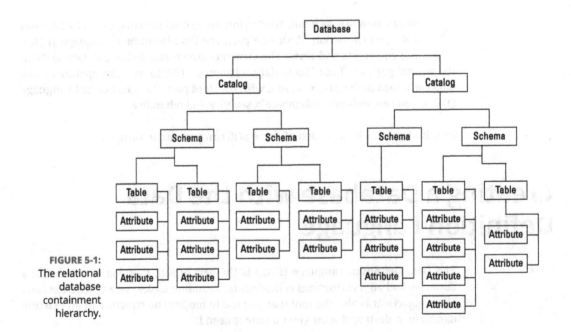

FIGURE 5-1:
The relational database containment hierarchy.

Not all databases use all the available levels, but larger databases tend to use more of them. The top level is the database itself. As you would expect, every part of the database is contained within the database, which is the biggest Russian doll of all. From there, a database can have one or more *catalogs*. Each catalog can have one or more *schemas*. Each schema can include one or more *tables*. Each table may consist of one or more *columns*.

For small to moderately large databases, you need concern yourself only with tables and the columns they contain. Schemas and catalogs come into play only when you have multiple unrelated collections of tables in the same database. The idea here is that you can keep these groups separate by putting them into separate schemas. If there is any danger of confusing unrelated schemas, you can put *them* in separate catalogs.

Creating tables

At its simplest, a database is a collection of two-dimensional tables, each of which has a collection of closely related attributes. The attributes are stored in columns of the tables. You can use SQL's CREATE statement to create a table, with its associated columns. You can't create a table without also creating the columns, and I tell you how to do all that in the next section. Later, using SQL's Data Manipulation Language, you can add data to the table in the form of rows. In the "Operating on Data with the Data Manipulation Language (DML)" section of this chapter, I tell you how to do that.

Specifying columns

The two dimensions of a table are its columns and rows. Each *column* corresponds to a specific attribute of the entity being modeled. Each *row* contains one specific instance of the entity.

As I mention earlier, you can create a table with an SQL CREATE statement. To see how that works, check out the following example. (Like all examples in this book, the code uses ANSI/ISO standard syntax.)

```
CREATE TABLE CUSTOMER (
    CustomerID INTEGER,
    FirstName CHAR (15),
    LastName CHAR (20),
    Street CHAR (30),
    City CHAR (25),
    Region CHAR (25),
    Country CHAR (25),
    Phone CHAR (13) ) ;
```

In the CREATE TABLE statement, you specify the name of each column and the *type* of data you want that column to contain. Spacing between statement elements doesn't matter to the DBMS. It is just to make reading the statement easier to humans. How many elements you put on one line also doesn't matter to the DBMS, but spreading elements out on multiple lines, as I have just done, makes the statement easier to read.

In the preceding example, the CustomerID column contains data of the INTEGER type, and the other columns contain character strings. The maximum lengths of the strings are also specified. (Most implementations accept the abbreviation CHAR in place of CHARACTER.)

Creating other objects

Tables aren't the only things you can create with a CREATE statement. A few other possibilities are views, schemas, and domains.

Views

A *view* is a virtual table that has no physical existence apart from the tables that it draws from. You create a view so that you can concentrate on some subset of a table, or alternatively on pieces of several tables. Some views draw selected columns from one table, and they're called *single-table views*. Others, called *multitable views*, draw selected columns from multiple tables.

Sometimes what is stored in database tables is not exactly in the form that you want users to see. Perhaps a table containing employee data has address information that the social committee chairperson needs, but also contains salary information that should be seen only by authorized personnel in the human resources department. How can you show the social committee chairperson what she needs to see without spilling the beans on what everyone is earning? In another scenario, perhaps the information a person needs is spread across several tables. How do you deliver what is needed in one convenient result set? The answer to both questions is the view.

SINGLE-TABLE VIEW

For an example of single-table view, consider the social committee chairperson's requirement, which I mention in the preceding section. She needs the contact information for all employees, but is not authorized to see anything else. You can create a view based on the EMPLOYEE table that includes only the information she needs.

```
CREATE VIEW EMP_CONTACT AS
    SELECT EMPLOYEE.FirstName,
           EMPLOYEE.LastName,
           EMPLOYEE.Street,
           EMPLOYEE.City,
           EMPLOYEE.State,
           EMPLOYEE.Zip,
           EMPLOYEE.Phone,
           EMPLOYEE.Email
    FROM EMPLOYEE ;
```

This CREATE VIEW statement contains within it an embedded SELECT statement to pull from the EMPLOYEE table only the columns desired. Now all you need to do is grant SELECT rights on the EMP_CONTACT view to the social committee chairperson. (I talk about granting privileges in Book 4, Chapter 3.) The right to look at the records in the EMPLOYEE table continues to be restricted to duly authorized human resources personnel and upper-management types.

Most implementations assume that if only one table is listed in the FROM clause, the columns being selected are in that same table. You can save some typing by eliminating the redundant references to the EMPLOYEE table.

```
CREATE VIEW EMP_CONTACT AS
    SELECT FirstName,
           LastName,
           Street,
           City,
           State,
           Zip,
           Phone,
           Email
    FROM EMPLOYEE ;
```

WARNING

There is a danger in using the abbreviated format, however. A query may use a join operation to pull some information from this view and other information from another view or table. If the other view or table has a field with the same name, the database engine doesn't know which to use. It's always safe to use a fully qualified column name — meaning the column's table name is included — but don't be surprised if you see the abbreviated form in somebody else's code. I discuss joins in Book 3, Chapter 5.

MULTITABLE VIEW

Although there are occasions when you might want to pull a subset of columns from a single table, a much more common scenario would be having to pull together selected information from multiple related tables and present the result in a single report. You can do this with a *multitable view*. (Creating multitable views involves joins, so to be safe you should use fully qualified column names.)

Suppose, for example, that you've been tasked to create an order entry system for a retail business. The key things involved are the products ordered, the customers who order them, the invoices that record the orders, and the individual line items on each invoice. It makes sense to separate invoices and invoice lines because an invoice can have an indeterminate number of invoice lines that vary from one invoice to another. You can model this system with an ER diagram. Figure 5-2 shows one way to model the system. (If the term "ER diagram" doesn't ring a bell, check out Chapter 2 in this minibook.)

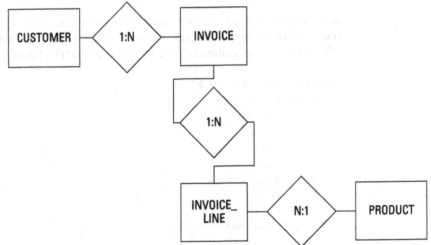

FIGURE 5-2:
The ER diagram
of the database
for an order
entry system.

The entities relate to each other through the columns they have in common. Here are the relationships:

>> The CUSTOMER entity bears a one-to-many relationship to the INVOICE entity. One customer can make multiple purchases, generating multiple invoices. Each invoice, however, applies to one and only one customer.

>> The INVOICE entity bears a one-to-many relationship to the INVOICE_LINE entity. One invoice may contain multiple lines, but each line appears on one and only one invoice.

» The PRODUCT entity bears a one-to-many relationship to the INVOICE_LINE entity. A product may appear on more than one line on an invoice, but each line deals with one and only one product.

The links between entities are the attributes they hold in common. Both the CUSTOMER and the INVOICE entities have a CustomerID column. It is the primary key in the CUSTOMER entity and a foreign key in the INVOICE entity. (I discuss keys in detail in Book 2, Chapter 4, including the difference between a primary key and a foreign key.) The InvoiceNumber attribute connects the INVOICE entity to the INVOICE_LINE entity, and the ProductID attribute connects PRODUCT to INVOICE_LINE.

CREATING VIEWS

The first step in creating a view is to create the tables upon which the view is based.

These tables are based on the entities and attributes in the ER model. I discuss table creation earlier in this chapter, and in detail in Book 2, Chapter 4. For now, I just show how to create the tables in the sample retail database.

```
CREATE TABLE CUSTOMER (
    CustomerID      INTEGER      PRIMARY KEY,
    FirstName       CHAR (15),
    LastName        CHAR (20)    NOT NULL,
    Street          CHAR (25),
    City            CHAR (20),
    State           CHAR (2),
    Zipcode         CHAR (10),
    Phone           CHAR (13) ) ;
```

The first column in the code contains attributes; the second column contains data types, and the third column contains *constraints* — gatekeepers that keep out invalid data. I touch on primary key constraints in Book 2, Chapter 2 and then describe them more fully in Book 2, Chapter 4. For now, all you need to know is that good design practice requires that every table have a primary key. The NOT NULL constraint means that the LastName field must contain a value. I say (much) more about null values (and constraints) in Book 1, Chapter 6.

Here's how you'd create the other tables:

```
CREATE TABLE PRODUCT (
    ProductID      INTEGER      PRIMARY KEY,
    Name           CHAR (25),
```

```
        Description         CHAR (30),
        Category            CHAR (15),
        VendorID            INTEGER,
        VendorName          CHAR (30) ) ;


CREATE TABLE INVOICE (
        InvoiceNumber       INTEGER    PRIMARY KEY,
        CustomerID          INTEGER,
        InvoiceDate         DATE,
        TotalSale           NUMERIC (9,2),
        TotalRemitted       NUMERIC (9,2),
        FormOfPayment       CHAR (10) ) ;


CREATE TABLE INVOICE_LINE (
        LineNumber          Integer    PRIMARY KEY,
        InvoiceNumber       INTEGER,
        ProductID           INTEGER,
        Quantity            INTEGER,
        SalePrice           NUMERIC (9,2) ) ;
```

You can create a view containing data from multiple tables by joining tables in pairs until you get the combination you want.

Suppose you want a display showing the first and last names of all customers along with all the products they have bought. You can do it with views.

```
CREATE VIEW CUST_PROD1 AS
    SELECT FirstName, LastName, InvoiceNumber
    FROM CUSTOMER JOIN INVOICE
    USING (CustomerID) ;

CREATE VIEW CUST_PROD2 AS
    SELECT FirstName, LastName, ProductID
    FROM CUST_PROD1 JOIN INVOICE_LINE
    USING (InvoiceNumber) ;

CREATE VIEW CUST_PROD AS
    SELECT FirstName, LastName, Name
    FROM CUST_PROD2 JOIN PRODUCT
    USING (ProductID) ;
```

The CUST_PROD1 view is created by a join of the CUSTOMER table and the INVOICE table, using CustomerID as the link between the two. It combines the customer's first and last name with the invoice numbers of all the invoices generated for that customer. The CUST_PROD2 view is created by a join of the CUST_PROD1 view and the INVOICE_LINE table, using InvoiceNumber as the link between them. It combines the customer's first and last name from the CUST_PROD1 view with the ProductID from the INVOICE_LINE table. Finally, the CUST_PROD view is created by a join of the CUST_PROD2 view and the PRODUCT table, using ProductID as the link between the two. It combines the customer's first and last name from the CUST_PROD2 view with the Name of the product from the PRODUCT table. This gives the display that we want. Figure 5-3 shows the flow of information from the source tables to the final destination view. I discuss joins in detail in Book 3, Chapter 5.

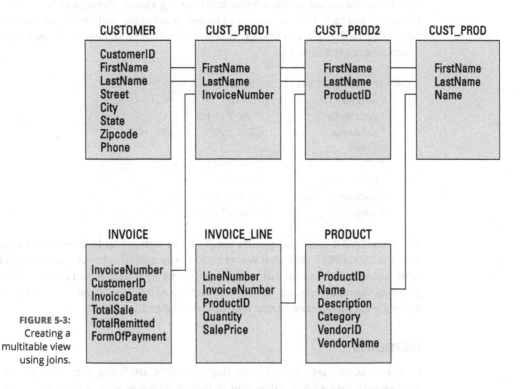

FIGURE 5-3: Creating a multitable view using joins.

There will be a row in the final view for every purchase. Customers who bought multiple items will be represented by multiple lines in CUST_PROD.

Schemas

In the containment hierarchy, the next level up from the one that includes tables and views is the schema level. It makes sense to place tables and views that are related to each other in the same schema. In many cases, a database may have only one schema, the default schema. This is the simplest situation, and when it applies, you don't need to think about schemas at all.

However, more complex cases do occur. In those cases, it is important to keep one set of tables separated from another set. You can do this by creating a named schema for each set. Do this with a CREATE SCHEMA statement. I won't go into the detailed syntax for creating a schema here because it may vary from one platform to another, but you can create a named schema in the following manner:

```
CREATE SCHEMA RETAIL1 ;
```

There are a number of clauses that you can add to the CREATE SCHEMA statement, specifying the owner of the schema and creating tables, views, and other objects. However, you can create a schema as shown previously, and create the tables and other objects that go into it later. If you do create a table later, you must specify which schema it belongs to:

```
CREATE TABLE RETAIL1.CUSTOMER (
     CustomerID          INTEGER          PRIMARY KEY,
     FirstName           CHAR (15),
     LastName            CHAR (20)        NOT NULL,
     Street              CHAR (25),
     City                CHAR (20),
     State               CHAR (2),
     Zipcode             CHAR (10),
     Phone               CHAR (13) ) ;
```

This CUSTOMER table will go into the RETAIL1 schema and will not be confused with the CUSTOMER table that was created in the default schema, even though the table names are the same. For really big systems with a large number of schemas, you may want to separate related schemas into their own catalogs. Most people dealing with moderate systems don't need to go to that extent.

Domains

A *domain* is the set of all values that a table's attributes can take on. Some implementations of SQL allow you to define domains within a CREATE SCHEMA statement. You can also define a domain with a standalone CREATE DOMAIN statement, such as

```
CREATE DOMAIN Color CHAR (15)
     CHECK (VALUE IS "Red" OR "White" OR "Blue") ;
```

In this example, when a table attribute is defined as of type Color, only Red, White, and Blue will be accepted as legal values. This domain constraint on the Color attribute will apply to all tables and views in the schema that have a Color attribute. Domains can save you a lot of typing because you have to specify the domain constraint only once, rather than every time you define a corresponding table attribute.

Modifying tables

After you create a table, complete with a full set of attributes, you may not want it to remain the same for all eternity. Requirements have a way of changing, based on changing conditions. The system you are modeling may change, requiring you to change your database structure to match. SQL's Data Definition Language gives you the tools to change what you have brought into existence with your original CREATE statement. The primary tool is the ALTER statement. Here's an example of a table modification:

```
ALTER TABLE CUSTOMER
    ADD COLUMN Email CHAR (50) ;
```

This has the effect of adding a new column to the CUSTOMER table without affecting any of the existing columns. You can get rid of columns that are no longer needed in a similar way:

```
ALTER TABLE CUSTOMER
    DROP COLUMN Email;
```

I guess we don't want to keep track of customer email addresses after all.

The ALTER TABLE statement also works for adding and dropping constraints. (See Book 1, Chapter 6 for more on working with constraints.)

Removing tables and other objects

It's really easy to get rid of tables, views, and other things that you no longer want. Here's how easy:

```
DROP TABLE CUSTOMER ;
DROP VIEW EMP_CONTACT ;
DROP COLUMN Email ;
```

When you drop a table, it simply disappears, along with all its data.

REMEMBER

Actually, it is not *always* that easy to get rid of something. If two tables are related with a primary key/foreign key link, a referential integrity constraint may prevent you from dropping one of those tables. I discuss referential integrity in Book 2, Chapter 3.

Operating on Data with the Data Manipulation Language (DML)

Just as the DDL is that part of SQL that you can use to create or modify database structural elements such as schemas, tables, and views, the Data Manipulation Language (DML) is the part of SQL that operates on the data that inhabits that structure. There are four things that you want to do with data:

>> Store the data in a structured way that makes it easily retrievable.

>> Change the data that is stored.

>> Selectively retrieve information that responds to a need that you currently have.

>> Remove data from the database that is no longer needed.

SQL statements that are part of the DML enable you to do all these things. Adding, updating, and deleting data are all relatively straightforward operations. Retrieving the exact information you want out of the vast store of data not relevant to your current need can be more complicated. I give you only a quick look at retrieval here and go into more detail in Book 3, Chapter 2. Here, I also tell you how to add, update, and delete data, as well as how to work with views.

Retrieving data from a database

The one operation that you're sure to perform on a database more than any other is the retrieval of needed information. Data is placed into the database only once. It may never be updated, or at most only a few times. However, retrievals will be made constantly. After all, the main purpose of a database is to provide you with information when you want it.

The SQL SELECT statement is the primary tool for extracting whatever information you want. Because the SELECT statement inquires about the contents of a table, it is called a *query*. A SELECT query can return all the data that a table contains, or it can be very discriminating and give you only what you specifically ask for. A SELECT query can also return selected results from multiple tables. I cover that in depth in Book 3, Chapter 3.

In its simplest form, a SELECT statement returns all the data in all the rows and columns in whatever table you specify. Here's an example:

```
SELECT * FROM PRODUCT ;
```

The asterisk (∗) is a wildcard character that means *everything*. In this context, it means return data from all the columns in the PRODUCT table. Because you're not placing any restrictions on which rows to return, all the data in all the rows of the table will be returned in the result set of the query.

I suppose there may be times when you want to see all the data in all the columns and all the rows in a table, but usually you're going to have a more specific question in mind. Perhaps you're not interested in seeing all the information about all the items in the PRODUCT table right now, but are interested in seeing only the quantities in stock of all the guitars. You can restrict the result set that is returned by specifying the columns you want to see and by restricting the rows returned with a WHERE clause.

```
SELECT ProductID, ProductName, InStock
    FROM PRODUCT
    WHERE Category = 'guitar' ;
```

This statement returns the product ID number, product name, and number in stock of all products in the Guitar category, and nothing else. An ad hoc query such as this is a good way to get a quick answer to a question. Of course, there is a lot more to retrieving information than what I have covered briefly here. In Book 3, Chapter 2, I have a lot more to say on the subject.

REMEMBER

I call the query above an *ad hoc query* because it is something you can type in from your keyboard, execute, and get an immediate answer. This is what a user might do if there is an immediate need for the number of guitars in stock right now, but this is not a question asked repeatedly. If it *is* a question that will be asked repeatedly, you should consider putting the preceding SQL code into a procedure that you can incorporate into an application program. That way, you would only have to make a selection from a menu and then click OK, instead of typing in the SQL code every time you want to know what your guitar situation is.

Adding data to a table

Somehow, you have to get data into your database. This data may be records of sales transactions, employee personnel records, instrument readings coming in from interplanetary spacecraft, or just about anything you care to keep track of. The form that the data is in determines how it is entered into the database. Naturally, if the data is on paper, you have to type it into the database. But if it is already in electronic form, you can translate it into a format acceptable to your DBMS and then import it into your system.

Adding data the dull and boring way (typing it in)

If the data to be kept in the database was originally written down on paper, in order to get it into the database, it will have to be transcribed from the paper to computer memory by keying it in with a computer keyboard. This used to be the most frequently used method for entering data into a database because most data was initially captured on paper. People called *data entry clerks* worked from nine to five, typing data into computers. What a drag! It was pretty mind-deadening work. More recently, rather than first writing things down on paper, the person who receives the data enters it directly into the database. This is not nearly so bad because entering the data is only a small part of the total task.

The dullest and most boring way to enter data into a database is to enter one record at a time, using SQL INSERT statements. It works, if you have no alternative way to enter the data, and all other methods of entering data ultimately are translated into SQL INSERT statements anyway. But after entering one or two records into the database this way, you will probably have had enough. Here's an example of such an INSERT operation:

```
INSERT INTO CUSTOMER (CustomerID, FirstName, LastName, Street,
   City, State, Zipcode, Phone)
   VALUES (:vcustid, 'Abe', 'Lincoln', '1600 Pennsylvania
   Avenue NW', 'Washington', 'DC', '20500', '202-555-1414') ;
```

The first value listed, :vcustid, is a variable that is incremented each time a new record is added to the table. This guarantees that there will be no duplication of a value in the CustomerID field, which serves as the table's primary key.

REMEMBER

There are single quotes enclosing the values in the previous INSERT statement because the values are all of the CHAR type, which requires that values be enclosed in single quotes. INTEGER data on the other hand is not enclosed in single quotes. You might say, "Wait a minute! The zip code in the INSERT statement is an integer!" Well, no. It is only an integer if I define it as such when I create the CUSTOMER table. When I created this CUSTOMER table, CustomerID was the only column of the INTEGER type. All the rest are of the CHAR type. I am never going to want to add one zip code to another or subtract one from another, so there is no point in making them integers.

In a more realistic situation, instead of entering an INSERT statement into SQL, the data entry person would enter data values into fields on a form. The values would be captured into variables, which would then be used, out of sight of humans, to populate the VALUES clause of an INSERT statement.

Adding incomplete records

Sometimes you might want to add a record to a table before you have data for all the record's columns. As long as you have the primary key and data for all the columns that have a NOT NULL or UNIQUE constraint, you can enter the record. Because SQL allows null values in other columns, you can enter such a partial record now and fill in the missing information later. Here's an example of how to do it:

```
INSERT INTO CUSTOMER (CustomerID, FirstName, LastName)
    VALUES (:vcustid, 'Abe', 'Lincoln') ;
```

Here you enter a new customer into the CUSTOMER table. All you have is the person's first and last name, but you can create a record in the CUSTOMER table anyway. The CustomerID is automatically generated and contained in the :vcustid variable. The value placed into the FirstName field is Abe and the value placed into the LastName field is Lincoln. The rest of the fields in this record will contain null values until you populate them at a later date.

REMEMBER

A NOT NULL constraint on a column raises a stink if you (or your data entry person) leave that particular column blank. A UNIQUE constraint gets similarly upset if you enter a value into a field that duplicates an already existing value in that same field. For more on constraints, check out Book 1, Chapter 6.

Adding data in the fastest and most efficient way: Bypassing typing altogether

Keying in a succession of SQL INSERT statements is the slowest and most tedious way to enter data into a database table. Entering data into fields on a video form on a computer monitor is not as bad because there is less typing and you probably have other things to do, such as talking to customers, checking in baggage, or consulting patient records.

Fast food outlets make matters even easier by giving you a special data entry panel rather than a keyboard. You can enter a double cheeseburger and a root beer float just by touching a couple of buttons. The correct information is translated to SQL and put into the database and also sent back to the kitchen to tell the culinary staff what to do next.

If a business's data is input via a bar code scanner, the job is even faster and easier for the clerk. All he has to do is slide the merchandise past the scanner and listen for the beep that tells him the purchase has been registered. He doesn't have to know that besides printing the sales receipt, the data from the scan is being translated into SQL and then sent to a database.

Although the clerks at airline ticket counters, fast food restaurants, and supermarkets don't need to know anything about SQL, somebody does. In order to make the clerks' life easier, someone has to write programs that process the data coming in from keyboards, data entry pads, and bar code scanners, and sends it to a database. Those programs are typically written in a general-purpose language such as C, Java, or Visual Basic, and incorporate SQL statements that are then used in the actual "conversation" with the database.

Updating data in a table

The world in the 21st century is a pretty dynamic place. Things are changing constantly, particularly in areas that involve technology. Data that was of value last week may be irrelevant tomorrow. Facts that were inconsequential a year ago may be critically important now. For a database to be useful, it must be capable of rapid change to match the rapidly changing piece of the world that it models.

This means that in addition to the ability to add new records to a database table, you also need to be able to update the records that it already contains. With SQL, you do this with an UPDATE statement. With an UPDATE statement, you can change a single row in a table, a set of rows that share one or more characteristics, or all the rows in the table. Here's the generalized syntax:

```
UPDATE table_name
    SET column_1 = expression_1, column_2 = expression_2,
    ..., column_n = expression_n
    [WHERE predicates] ;
```

The SET clause specifies which columns will get new values and what those new values will be. The optional WHERE clause (square brackets indicate that the WHERE clause is optional) specifies which rows the update applies to. If there is no WHERE clause, the update is applied to all rows in the table.

Now for some examples. Consider the PRODUCT table shown in Table 5-1.

Now suppose that the cost of bike helmets increases to $22. You can make that change in the database with the following UPDATE statement:

```
UPDATE PRODUCT
    SET Cost = 22.00
    WHERE Name = 'Bike helmet' ;
```

TABLE 5-1

PRODUCT Table

ProductID	Name	Category	Cost
1664	Bike helmet	Helmets	20.00
1665	Motorcycle helmet	Helmets	30.00
1666	Bike gloves	Gloves	15.00
1667	Motorcycle gloves	Gloves	19.00
1668	Sport socks	Footwear	10.00

This statement makes a change in all rows where Name is equal to Bike helmet, as shown in Table 5-2.

TABLE 5-2

PRODUCT Table

ProductID	Name	Category	Cost
1664	Bike helmet	Helmets	22.00
1665	Motorcycle helmet	Helmets	30.00
1666	Bike gloves	Gloves	15.00
1667	Motorcycle gloves	Gloves	19.00
1668	Sport socks	Footwear	10.00

TIP

Because there is only one such row, only one is changed. If there is a possibility that more than one product might have the same name, you might erroneously update a row that you did not intend, along with the one that you did. To avoid this problem, assuming you know the ProductID of the item you want to change, you should use the ProductID in your WHERE clause. In a well-designed database, ProductID would be the primary key and thus guaranteed to be unique.

```
UPDATE PRODUCT
   SET Cost = 22.00
   WHERE ProductID = 1664 ;
```

You may want to update a select group of rows in a table. To do that, you specify a condition in the WHERE clause of your update, that applies to the rows you want to update and only the rows you want to update. For example, suppose management decides that the Helmets category should be renamed as Headgear, to include hats and bandannas. Because their wish is your command, you duly change the category names of all the Helmet rows in the table to Headgear by doing the following:

```
UPDATE PRODUCT
    SET Category = 'Headgear'
    WHERE Category = 'Helmets' ;
```

This would give you what is shown in Table 5-3.

TABLE 5-3

PRODUCT Table

ProductID	Name	Category	Cost
1664	Bike helmet	Headgear	22.00
1665	Motorcycle helmet	Headgear	30.00
1666	Bike gloves	Gloves	15.00
1667	Motorcycle gloves	Gloves	19.00
1668	Sport socks	Footwear	10.00

Now suppose management decides it would be more efficient to lump headgear and gloves together into a single category named Accessories. Here's the UPDATE statement that will do that:

```
UPDATE PRODUCT
    SET Category = 'Accessories'
    WHERE Category = 'Headgear' OR Category = 'Gloves' ;
```

The result would be what is shown in Table 5-4.

TABLE 5-4

PRODUCT Table

ProductID	Name	Category	Cost
1664	Bike helmet	Accessories	22.00
1665	Motorcycle helmet	Accessories	30.00
1666	Bike gloves	Accessories	15.00
1667	Motorcycle gloves	Accessories	19.00
1668	Sport socks	Footwear	10.00

All the headgear and gloves items are now considered accessories, but other categories, such as footwear, are left unaffected.

Now suppose management sees that considerable savings have been achieved by merging the headgear and gloves categories. The decision is made that the company is actually in the active-wear business. To convert all company products to the new Active-wear category, a really simple UPDATE statement will do the trick:

```
UPDATE PRODUCT
    SET Category = 'Active-wear' ;
```

This produces the table shown in Table 5-5.

TABLE 5-5

PRODUCT Table

ProductID	Name	Category	Cost
1664	Bike helmet	Active-wear	22.00
1665	Motorcycle helmet	Active-wear	30.00
1666	Bike gloves	Active-wear	15.00
1667	Motorcycle gloves	Active-wear	19.00
1668	Sport socks	Active-wear	10.00

Deleting data from a table

After you become really good at collecting data, your database starts to fill up with the stuff. With hard disk capacities getting bigger all the time, this may not seem like much of a problem. However, although you may never have to worry about filling up your new 6TB (that's 6,000,000,000,000 bytes) hard disk, the larger your database gets, the slower retrievals become. If much of that data consists of rows that you'll probably never need to access again, it makes sense to get rid of it. Financial information from the previous fiscal year after you've gone ahead and closed the books does not need to be in your active database. You may have to keep such data for a period of years to meet government regulatory requirements, but you can always keep it in an offline archive instead of burdening your active database with it. Additionally, data of a confidential nature may present a legal liability if compromised.

If you no longer need it, get rid of it. With SQL, this is easy to do. First, decide whether you need to archive the data that you are about to delete, and save it in that location. After that is taken care of, deletion can be as simple as this:

```
DELETE FROM TRANSACTION
    WHERE TransDate < '2019-01-01' ;
```

Poof! All of 2018's transaction records are gone, and your database is speedy again. You can be as selective as you need to be with the WHERE clause and delete all the records you want to delete — and only the records you want to delete.

Updating views doesn't make sense

Although ANSI/ISO standard SQL makes it possible to update a view, it rarely makes sense to do so. Recall that a view is a virtual table. It does not have any existence apart from the table or tables that it draws columns from. If you want to update a view, updating the underlying table will accomplish your intent and avoid problems in the process. Problems? What problems? Consider a view that draws salary and commission data from the SALESPERSON table:

```
CREATE VIEW TOTALPAY (EmployeeName, Pay)
    AS SELECT EmployeeName, Salary + Commission AS Pay
    FROM SALESPERSON ;
```

The view TOTALPAY has two columns, EmployeeName and Pay. The virtual Pay column is created by adding the values in the Salary and the Commission columns in the SALESPERSON table. This is fine, as long as you don't ever need to update the virtual Pay column, like this:

```
UPDATE TOTALPAY SET Pay = Pay + 100
```

You may think you are giving all the salespeople a hundred dollar raise. Instead, you are just generating an error message. The data in the TOTALPAY view isn't stored as such on the system. It is stored in the SALESPERSON table, and the SALESPERSON table does not have a Pay column. Salary + Commission is an expression, and you cannot update an expression.

You've seen expressions a couple of times earlier in this minibook. In this case, the expression Salary + Commission is a combination of the values in two columns in the SALESPERSON table. In this case, you don't really want to update Pay. You probably want to update Salary, since Commission is based on actual sales.

Another source of potential problems can be views that draw data from more than one table. If you try to update such a view, even if expressions are not involved, the database engine may get confused about which of the underlying tables to apply the update to.

REMEMBER

The lesson here is that although it is possible to update views, it is generally not a good practice to do so. Update the underlying tables instead, even if it causes you to make a few more keystrokes. You'll have fewer problems in the long run.

Maintaining Security in the Data Control Language (DCL)

The third major component of SQL performs a function just as important as the functions performed by the DDL and the DML. The Data Control Language consists of statements that protect your precious data from misuse, misappropriation, corruption, and destruction. It would be a shame to go to all the trouble of creating a database and filling it with data critical to your business, and then have the whole thing end up being destroyed. It would be even worse to have the data end up in the possession of your fiercest competitor. The DCL gives you the tools to address all those concerns. I discuss the DCL in detail in Book 4, Chapter 3. For now, here's an overview of how you can grant people access to a table, revoke those privileges, and find out how to protect your operations with transactions.

Granting access privileges

Most organizations have several different kinds of data with several different levels of sensitivity. Some data, such as the retail price list for your company's products, doesn't cause any problems even if everyone in the world can see it. In fact, you probably want everyone out there to see your retail price list. Somebody might buy something. On the other hand, you don't want unauthorized people to make changes to your retail price list. You might find yourself giving away product for under your cost. Data of a more confidential nature, such as personal information about your employees or customers, should be accessible to only those who have a legitimate need to know about it. Finally, some forms of access, such as the ability to erase the entire database, should be restricted to a very small number of highly trusted individuals.

You have complete control over who has access to the various elements of a database, as well as what level of access they have, by using the GRANT statement, which gives you a fine-grained ability to grant specific privileges to specific individuals or to well-defined groups of individuals.

One example might be

```
GRANT SELECT ON PRICELIST TO PUBLIC ;
```

The PUBLIC keyword means everyone. No one is left out when you grant access to the public. The particular kind of access here, SELECT, enables people to retrieve the data in the price list, but not to change it in any way.

Revoking access privileges

If it is possible to grant access to someone, it better be possible to revoke those privileges too. People's jobs change within an organization, requiring different access privileges than those that were appropriate before the change. An employee may even leave the company and go to a competitor. Privilege revocation is especially important in such cases. The REVOKE statement does the job. Its syntax is almost identical to the syntax of the GRANT statement. Only its action is reversed.

```
REVOKE SELECT ON PRICELIST FROM PUBLIC ;
```

Now the pricelist is no longer accessible to the general public.

Preserving database integrity with transactions

Two problems that can damage database integrity are

>> **System failures:** Suppose you are performing a complex, multistep operation on a database when the system goes down. Some changes have been made to the database and others have not. After you get back on the air, the database is no longer in the condition it was in before you started your operation, and it is not yet in the condition you hoped to achieve at the end of your operation. It is in some unknown intermediate state that is almost surely wrong.

>> **Interactions between users:** When two users of the database are operating on the same data at the same time, they can interfere with each other. This interference can slow them both down or, even worse, the changes each makes to the database can get mixed up, resulting in incorrect data being stored.

The common solution to both these problems is to use transactions. A *transaction* is a unit of work that has both a beginning and an end. If a transaction is interrupted between the beginning and the end, after operation resumes, all the changes to the database made during the transaction are reversed in a ROLLBACK operation, returning the database to the condition it was in before the transaction started. Now the transaction can be repeated, assuming whatever caused the interruption has been corrected.

Transactions can also help eliminate harmful interactions between simultaneous users. If one user has access to a resource, such as a row in a database table, other users cannot access that row until the first user's transaction has been completed with a COMMIT operation. In Book 4, Chapter 2, I discuss these important issues in considerable detail.

Chapter **6**

Drilling Down to the SQL Nitty-Gritty

n this chapter, I get into the nitty-gritty of SQL. This is knowledge you need to master before you embark on actually writing SQL statements. SQL has some similarities to computer languages you may already be familiar with, and some important differences. I touch on some of these similarities and differences right here in this chapter, but will discuss others later when I get to the appropriate points in a complete discussion of SQL.

Executing SQL Statements

SQL is not a complete language, but a data sublanguage. As such, you cannot write a program in the SQL language like you can with C or Java. That doesn't mean SQL is useless, though. There are several ways that you *can* use SQL. Say you have a query editor up on your screen and all you want is the answer to a simple question. Just type an SQL query, and the answer, in the form of one or more lines of data, appears on your screen. This mode of operation is called *interactive SQL*.

If your needs are more complex, you have two additional ways of making SQL queries:

>> You can write a program in a host language, such as C or Java, and embed single SQL statements here and there in the program as needed. This mode of operation is called *embedded SQL*.

>> You can write a module containing SQL statements in the form of procedures, and then call these procedures from a program written in a language such as C or Java. This mode of operation is called *module language*.

Interactive SQL

Interactive SQL consists of entering SQL statements into a database management system such as SQL Server, Oracle, or DB2. The DBMS then performs the commands specified by the statements. You could build a database from scratch this way, starting with a CREATE DATABASE statement, and building everything from there. You could fill it with data, and then type queries to selectively pull information out of it.

Although it's possible to do everything you need to do to a database with interactive SQL, this approach has a couple of disadvantages:

>> It can get awfully tedious to enter everything in the form of SQL statements from the keyboard.

>> Only people fluent in the SQL language can operate on the database, and most people have never even heard of SQL, let alone are able to use it effectively.

SQL *is* the only language that most relational databases understand, so there is no getting around using it. However, the people who interact with databases the most — those folks that ask questions of the data — do not need to be exposed to naked SQL. They can be protected from that intimidating prospect by wrapping the SQL in a blanket of code written in another language. With that other language, a programmer can generate screens, forms, menus, and other familiar objects for the user to interact with. Ultimately, those things translate the user's actions to SQL code that the DBMS understands. The desired information is retrieved, and the user sees the result.

Challenges to combining SQL with a host language

SQL has these fundamental differences from host languages that you might want to combine it with:

>> **SQL is nonprocedural.** One basic feature of all common host languages is that they are *procedural*, meaning that programs written in those languages execute procedures in a step-by-step fashion. They deal with data the same way, one row at a time. Because SQL is nonprocedural, it does whatever it is going to do all at once and deals with data a set of rows at a time. Procedural programmers coming to SQL for the first time need to adjust their thinking in order to use SQL effectively as a data manipulation and retrieval tool.

>> **SQL recognizes different data types than does whatever host language you are using with it.** Because there are a large number of languages out there that could serve as host languages for SQL, and the data types of any one of them do not necessarily agree with the data types of any other, the committee that created the ANSI/ISO standard defined the data types for SQL that they thought would be most useful, without referring to the data types recognized by any of the potential host languages. This data type incompatibility presents a problem if you want to perform calculations with your host language on data that was retrieved from a database with SQL. The problem is not serious; you just need to be aware of it. (It helps that SQL provides the CAST statement for translating one data type into another.)

Embedded SQL

Until recently, the most common form of SQL has been embedded SQL. This method uses a general-purpose computer language such as C, C++, or COBOL to write the bulk of an application. Such languages are great for creating an application's user interface. They can create forms with buttons and menus, format reports, perform calculations, and basically do all the things that SQL cannot do. In a database application, however, sooner or later, the database must be accessed. That's a job for SQL.

It makes sense to write the application in a host language and, when needed, drop in SQL statements to interact with the data. It is the best of both worlds. The host language does what it's best at, and the embedded SQL does what *it's* best at. The only downside to the cooperative arrangement is that the host language compiler will not recognize the SQL code when it encounters it and will issue an error message. To avoid this problem, a precompiler processes the SQL before the host language compiler takes over. When everything works, this is a great arrangement. Before everything works, however, debugging can be tough because a host language debugger doesn't know how to handle any SQL that it encounters. Nevertheless, embedded SQL remains the most popular way to create database applications.

For example, look at a fragment of C code that contains embedded SQL statements. This particular fragment is written in Oracle's Pro*C dialect of the C language and is code that might be found in an organization's human resources department. This particular code block is designed to authenticate and log on a user, and then enable the user to change the salary and commission information for an employee.

```
EXEC SQL BEGIN DECLARE SECTION;
    VARCHAR uid[20];
    VARCHAR pwd[20];
    VARCHAR ename[10];
    FLOAT salary, comm;
    SHORT salary_ind, comm_ind;
EXEC SQL END DECLARE SECTION;
main()
{
    int sret;           /* scanf return code */
    /* Log in */
    strcpy(uid.arr,"Mary");    /* copy the user name */
    uid.len=strlen(uid.arr);
    strcpy(pwd.arr,"Bennett");   /* copy the password */
    pwd.len=strlen(pwd.arr);
    EXEC SQL WHENEVER SQLERROR STOP;
    EXEC SQL WHENEVER NOT FOUND STOP;
    EXEC SQL CONNECT :uid;
    printf("Connected to user: percents \n",uid.arr);
    printf("Enter employee name to update:  ");
    scanf("percents",ename.arr);
    ename.len=strlen(ename.arr);
    EXEC SQL SELECT SALARY,COMM INTO :salary,:comm
                FROM EMPLOY
                WHERE ENAME=:ename;
    printf("Employee: percents salary: percent6.2f
            comm: percent6.2f \n", ename.arr, salary, comm);
    printf("Enter new salary:  ");
    sret=scanf("percentf",&salary);
    salary_ind = 0;
    if (sret == EOF !! sret == 0)    /* set indicator */
        salary_ind =-1;    /* Set indicator for NULL */
```

```
        printf("Enter new commission:  ");
        sret=scanf("percentf",&comm);
        comm_ind = 0;    /* set indicator */
        if (sret == EOF !! sret == 0)
            comm_ind=-1;          /* Set indicator for NULL */
        EXEC SQL UPDATE EMPLOY
                SET SALARY=:salary:salary_ind
                SET COMM=:comm:comm_ind
                WHERE ENAME=:ename;
        printf("Employee percents updated. \n",ename.arr);
        EXEC SQL COMMIT WORK;
        exit(0);
}
```

Here's a closer look at what the code does:

>> First comes an SQL declaration section, where variables are declared.

>> Next, C code accepts a username and password.

>> A couple of SQL error traps follow, and then a connection to the database is established. (If an SQL error code or Not Found code is returned from the database, the run is aborted before it begins.)

>> C code prints out some messages and accepts the name of the employee whose record will be changed.

>> SQL retrieves that employee's salary and commission data.

>> C displays the salary and commission data and solicits new salary and commission data.

>> SQL updates the database with the new data.

>> C displays a successful completion message.

>> SQL commits the transaction.

>> C terminates the program.

In this implementation, every SQL statement is introduced with an EXEC SQL directive. This is a clue to the compiler not to try to compile what follows, but instead to pass it directly to the DBMS's database engine.

REMEMBER

Some implementations have deprecated embedded SQL or discontinued it entirely. For example, embedded SQL was deprecated in SQL Server 2008, meaning it was still present, but may not be in a subsequent version. Software vendors recommend that deprecated features not be included in new development efforts.

Embedded SQL is now absent from MySQL and SAP SQL Anywhere, although an independently developed preprocessor is available for MySQL.

Module language

Module language is similar to embedded SQL in that it combines the strengths of SQL with those of a host language. However, it does it in a slightly different way. All the SQL code is stored — as procedures — in a module separate from the host language program. Whenever the host language program needs to perform a database operation, it calls a procedure from the SQL module to do the job. With this arrangement, all your SQL is kept out of the main program, so the host language compiler has no problem, and neither does the debugger. All they see is host language code, including the procedure calls. The procedures themselves cause no difficulty because they are in a separate module, and the compiler and debugger just skip over them.

Another advantage of module language over embedded SQL is that the SQL code is separated from the host language code. Because high skill in *both* SQL and any given host language is rare, it is difficult to find good people to program embedded SQL applications. Because a module language implementation separates the languages, you can hire the best SQL programmer to write the SQL, and the best host language programmer to write the host language code. Neither one has to be an expert in the other language.

To see how this would work, check out the following module definition, which shows you the syntax you'd use to create a module that contains SQL procedures:

```
MODULE [module-name]
    [NAMES ARE character-set-name]
    LANGUAGE {ADA|C|COBOL|FORTRAN|MUMPS|PASCAL|PLI|SQL}
    [SCHEMA schema-name]
    [AUTHORIZATION authorization-id]
    [temporary-table-declarations...]
    [cursor-declarations...]
    [dynamic-cursor-declarations...]
    procedures...
```

The MODULE declaration is mandatory, but the module name is not. (It's a good idea to name your modules anyway, just to reduce the confusion.) With the optional NAMES ARE clause, you can specify a character set — Hebrew, for example, or Cyrillic. The default character set will be used if you don't include a NAMES ARE clause.

The next line lets you specify a host language — something you definitely have to do. Each language has different expectations about what the procedure will look like, so the LANGUAGE clause determines the format of the procedures in the module.

Although the SCHEMA clause and the AUTHORIZATION clause are both optional, you must specify at least one of them. The AUTHORIZATION clause is a security feature. If your authorization ID does not carry sufficient privileges, you won't be allowed to use the procedures in the module.

REMEMBER

If any of the procedures use temporary tables, cursors, or dynamic cursors, they must be declared before they are used. I talk about cursors in Book 3, Chapter 5.

Using Reserved Words Correctly

Given the fact that SQL makes constant use of command words such as CREATE and ALTER, it stands to reason that it would probably be unwise to use these same words as the names of tables or variables. To do so is a guaranteed way to confuse your DBMS. In addition to such command words, a number of other words also have a special meaning in SQL. These *reserved words* should also not be used for any purpose other than the one for which they are designed. Consider the following SQL statement:

```
SELECT CustomerID, FirstName, LastName
    FROM Customer
    WHERE CustomerID < 1000;
```

SELECT is a command word, and FROM and WHERE are reserved words. SQL has hundreds of reserved words, and you must be careful not to inadvertently use any of them as the names of objects or variables. Appendix A of this book contains a list of reserved words in ISO/IEC SQL:2016.

SQL's Data Types

SQL is capable of dealing with data of many different types — as this aptly named section will soon make clear. From the beginning, SQL has been able to handle the common types of numeric and character data, but more recently, new types have been added that enable SQL to deal with nontraditional data types, such as BLOB, CLOB, BINARY, and just recently added as part of SQL:2023, the JSON data type.

At present, there are 12 major categories of data types: exact numerics, approximate numerics, character strings, binary strings, Booleans, datetimes, intervals, XML type, collection types, REF types, JSON types, and user-defined types. Within each category, one or more specific types may exist.

REMEMBER

Some implementations of SQL may include data types not mentioned here. These additional types are not mentioned in the ANSI/ISO standard and thus are not guaranteed to be available in other implementations. To maximize portability for your applications, stick to the standard types.

REMEMBER

Your SQL implementation may not support all the data types that I describe in this section. Furthermore, your implementation may support nonstandard data types that I don't describe here.

With that proviso out of the way, read on to find brief descriptions of each of the categories as well as enumerations of the standard types they include.

Exact numerics

Because computers store numbers in registers of finite size, there is a limit to how large or small a number can be and still be represented exactly. There is a range of numbers centered on zero that can be represented exactly. The size of that range depends on the size of the registers that the numbers are stored in. Thus a machine with 64-bit registers can exactly represent a range of numbers that is wider than the range that can be exactly represented on a machine with 32-bit registers.

After doing all the complex math, you're left with six standard exact numeric data types. They are

>> INTEGER

>> SMALLINT

>> BIGINT

>> NUMERIC

>> DECIMAL

>> DECFLOAT

The next few sections drill down deeper into each type.

INTEGER

Data of the INTEGER type is numeric data that has no fractional part. Any given implementation of SQL will have a limit to the number of digits that an integer can have. If, for some reason, you want to specify a maximum size for an integer that is less than the default maximum, you can restrict the maximum number of digits by specifying a *precision* argument. By declaring a variable as having type INTEGER (10), you are saying numbers of this type can have no more than ten digits, even if the system you are running on is capable of handling more digits. Of course, if you specify a precision that exceeds the maximum capacity of the system, you're not gonna get it no matter how much you whine. You cannot magically expand the sizes of the hardware registers in a machine with an SQL declaration.

TIP

If there is a possibility that sometime in the near or distant future, your application may be ported to a system that has a different default precision for exact numeric numbers, you should specify a precision. That way, the precision you have planned on will carry over to the new system. If you rely on the default precision, and the default precision of the system you port to is different, your operations may produce different results from those produced by your original system. On the other hand, you may be fine. For example, both Microsoft SQL Server and MySQL reserve the same amount of space for a number of the INTEGER type and thus the precision is the same for both.

SMALLINT

The SMALLINT data type is similar to the INTEGER type, but how it differs from the INTEGER type is implementation-dependent. It may not differ from the INTEGER type at all. The only constraint on the SMALLINT type is that its precision may be no larger than the precision of the INTEGER type.

For systems where the precision of the SMALLINT type actually is less than the precision of the INTEGER type, it may be advantageous to specify variables as being of the SMALLINT type if you can be sure that the values of those variables will never exceed the precision of the SMALLINT type. This saves you some storage space. If storage space is not an issue, or if you cannot be absolutely sure that the value of a variable will never exceed the precision of the SMALLINT type, you may be better off specifying it as being of the INTEGER type.

BIGINT

The BIGINT type is similar to the SMALLINT type. The only difference is that the precision of the BIGINT type can be no *smaller* than the precision of the INTEGER type. As is the case with SMALLINT, the precision of the BIGINT type could be the same as the precision of the INTEGER type.

If the precision of the BIGINT type for any given implementation is actually larger than the precision of the INTEGER type, a variable of the BIGINT type will take up more storage space than a variable of the INTEGER type. Only use the BIGINT type if there is a possibility that the size of a variable may exceed the precision of the INTEGER type.

NUMERIC

Data of the NUMERIC type *does* have a fractional part. This means the number contains a decimal point and zero or more digits to the right of the decimal point. For NUMERIC data, you can specify both precision and scale. The *scale* of a number is the number of digits to the right of the decimal point. For example, a variable declared as of type NUMERIC (10, 2) would have a maximum of ten digits, with two of those digits to the right of the decimal point. The largest number you can represent with this type is 99,999,999.99. If the system you are running on happens to be able to handle numbers with precision greater than ten, only the precision you specify will be used.

DECIMAL

Data of the DECIMAL type is similar to data of the NUMERIC type with one difference. For data of the DECIMAL type, if the system you are running on happens to be able to handle numbers with larger precision than what you have specified, the extra precision will be used.

TIP

The NUMERIC data type is better if portability is a possibility. When you use the NUMERIC type, you can be sure the precision you specify will be the precision that is used, regardless of the capabilities of the system. This ensures consistent results across diverse platforms.

DECFLOAT

DECFLOAT is a new exact numeric data type in SQL:2016. It was added to ISO/IEC standard SQL specifically for business applications that deal with exact decimal values. Floating point data types, such as REAL and DOUBLE, can handle larger numbers than exact numerics such as NUMERIC and DECIMAL. However, they cannot be counted upon to produce exact decimal values. DECFLOAT can handle larger numbers than other exact numeric data types, and retain the exactness of an exact numeric type.

Approximate numerics

The approximate numeric types (all three of them) exist so that you can represent numbers either too large or too small to be represented by an exact numeric type.

If, for example, a system has 32-bit registers, then the largest number that can be represented with an *exact* numeric type is the largest number that can be represented with 32 binary digits — which happens to be 4,294,967,295 in decimal. If you have to deal with numbers larger than that, you must move to *approximate* numerics or buy a computer with 64-bit registers. Using approximate numerics may not be much of a hardship: For most applications, after you get above four billion, approximations are good enough.

Similarly, values very close to zero cannot be represented with exact numerics either. The smallest number that can be represented exactly on a 32-bit machine has a one in the least significant bit position and zeros everywhere else. This is a very small number, but there are a lot of numbers of interest, particularly in science, that are smaller. For such numbers, you must also rely on approximate numerics.

With that intro out of the way, it's time to meet the three approximate numeric types: REAL, DOUBLE PRECISION, and FLOAT.

REAL

The REAL data type is what you would normally use for single-precision floating-point numbers. The exact meaning of the term *single precision* depends on the implementation. This is hardware-dependent and a machine with 64-bit registers will, in general, have a larger precision than a machine with 32-bit registers. How much larger may vary from one implementation to another.

REMEMBER

A *floating-point number* is a number that contains a radix point. In the case of decimal numbers, that means a decimal point. The decimal point could appear anywhere in the number, which is why it is called floating. 2.7, 2.73, 27.3, and 2735.53894 are all examples of floating-point numbers. Although we humans are accustomed to seeing numbers expressed in this form, approximate numerics are expressed as a combination of a mantissa and an exponent. This form is a little less user friendly, but enables the approximate representation of very large and very small numbers in a compact form. 6.626×10^{-34}, for example, is a very small number, being as it is an approximation of Planck's constant, also a very small number. 6.626 is the mantissa, and -34 is the exponent. It would not be possible to represent a number that small exactly with any currently existing hardware.

DOUBLE PRECISION

A double-precision number, which is the basis for the double precision (DOUBLE) data type, on any given system has greater precision than a real number on the same system. However, despite the name, a double-precision number does not necessarily have twice the precision of a real number. The most that can be said in general is that a double-precision number on any given system has greater precision than does a real number on the same system. On some systems, a double-precision number may have a larger mantissa than does a real number. On other systems, a double-precision number may support a larger exponent (absolute value). On yet other systems, both mantissa and exponent of a double-precision number may be larger than for a real number. You will have to look at the specifications for whatever system you are using to find out what is true for you.

FLOAT

The FLOAT data type is very similar to the REAL data type. The difference is that with the FLOAT data type you can specify a precision. With the REAL and DOUBLE PRECISION data types, the default precision is your only option. Because the default precision of these data types can vary from one system to another, porting your application from one system to another could be a problem. With the FLOAT data type, specifying the precision of an attribute on one machine guarantees that the precision will be maintained after porting the application to another machine. If a system's hardware supports double-precision operations and the application requires double-precision operations, the FLOAT data type automatically uses the double-precision circuitry. If single-precision is sufficient, it uses that.

Character strings

After numbers, the next most common thing to be stored is strings of alphanumeric characters. SQL provides several character string types, each with somewhat different characteristics from the others. The three main types are CHARACTER, CHARACTER VARYING, and CHARACTER LARGE OBJECT. These three types are mirrored by NATIONAL CHARACTER, NATIONAL CHARACTER VARYING, and NATIONAL CHARACTER LARGE OBJECT, which deal with character sets other than the default character set, which is usually the character set of the English language.

CHARACTER

A column defined as being of type CHARACTER or CHAR can contain any of the normal alphanumeric characters of the language being used. A column definition also includes the maximum length allowed for an item of the CHAR type. Consider this example:

```
Name CHAR (15)
```

This field can hold a name up to 15 characters long. If the name is less than 15 characters long, the remaining spaces are filled with blank characters to bring the total length up to 15. Thus a CHARACTER field always takes up the same amount of space in memory, regardless of how long the actual data item in the field is.

CHARACTER VARYING

The CHARACTER VARYING or VARCHAR data type is like the CHARACTER type in all respects except that short entries are not padded out with blanks to fill the field to the stated maximum.

```
Name VARCHAR (15)
```

The VARCHAR data type doesn't add blanks on the end of a name. Thus if the Name field contains Joe, the length of the field that is stored will be only 3 characters rather than 15.

TIP

The new SQL:2023 standard now allows you to define a VARCHAR data type without specifying the maximum length. In that case, the default maximum length allowed by the specific SQL implementation is used.

CHARACTER LARGE OBJECT (CLOB)

Any implementation of SQL has a limit to the number of characters that are allowed in a CHARACTER or CHARACTER VARYING field. For example, the maximum length of a character string in Oracle 11g is 1,024 characters. If you want to store text that goes beyond that limit, you can use the CHARACTER LARGE OBJECT data type. The CLOB type, as it is affectionately known, is much less flexible than either the CHAR or VARCHAR types in that it does not allow you to do many of the fine-grained manipulations that you can do in those other types. You can compare two CLOB items for equality, but that's about all you can do. With CHARACTER type data you can, for example, scan a string for the first occurrence of the letter W, and display where in the string it occurs. This type of operation is not possible with CHARACTER LARGE OBJECT data.

Here's an example of the declaration of a CHARACTER LARGE OBJECT:

```
Dream CLOB (8721)
```

Another restriction on CLOB data is that a CLOB data item may not be used as a primary key or a foreign key. Furthermore, you cannot apply the UNIQUE constraint to an item of the CLOB type. The bottom line is that the CLOB data type enables you to store and retrieve large blocks of text, but it turns out you can't do much with them beyond that.

NATIONAL CHARACTER, NATIONAL CHARACTER VARYING, and NATIONAL CHARACTER LARGE OBJECT

Different languages use different character sets. For example, Spanish and German have letters with diacritical marks that change the way the letter is pronounced. Other languages, such as Russian, have an entirely different character set. To store character strings that contain these different character sets, the various national character types have been added to SQL. If the English character type is the default on your system, as it is for most people, you can designate a different character set as your national character set. From that point on, when you specify a data type as NATIONAL CHARACTER, NATIONAL CHARACTER VARYING, or NATIONAL CHARACTER LARGE OBJECT, items in columns so specified use the chosen national character set rather than the default character set.

In addition to whatever national character set you specify, you can use multiple other character sets in a table definition, by specifying them explicitly. Here's an example where the national character set is Russian, but you explicitly add Greek and Kanji (Japanese) to the mix:

```
CREATE TABLE BOOK_TITLE_TRANSLATIONS (
    English      CHARACTER (40),
    Greek        VARCHAR (40)           CHARACTER SET GREEK,
    Russian      NATIONAL CHARACTER (40),
    Japanese     CHARACTER (40)         CHARACTER SET KANJI
) ;
```

Some implementations may not support all the character sets. For example, MySQL does not currently support Kanji.

Binary strings

The various binary string data types were added to SQL:2008. Binary strings are like character strings except that the only characters allowed are 1 and 0. There are three different types of binary strings, BINARY, BINARY VARYING, and BINARY LARGE OBJECT.

BINARY

A string of binary characters of the BINARY type must be some multiple of eight bits long. You can specify such a string with BINARY (x), where x is the number of bytes of binary data contained in the string. For example, if you specify a binary string with BINARY (2), then the string will be two bytes, or 16 bits long. Byte one is defined as the first byte of the string.

BINARY VARYING

The BINARY VARYING or VARBINARY type is like the BINARY type except the string length need not be x bytes long. A string specified as VARBINARY (x) can be a minimum of zero bytes long and a maximum of x bytes long.

BINARY LARGE OBJECT (BLOB)

The BINARY LARGE OBJECT (BLOB) type is used for a really large binary number. That large binary number may represent the pixels in a graphical image, or something else that doesn't seem to be a number. However, at the most fundamental level, it is a number.

The BLOB type, like the CLOB type, was added to the SQL standard to reflect the reality that more and more of the things that people want to store in databases do not fall into the classical categories of being either numbers or text. You cannot perform arithmetic operations on BLOB data, but at least you can store it in a relational database and perform some elementary operations on it.

Booleans

A column of the BOOLEAN data type, named after 19th-century English mathematician George Boole, will accept any one of three values: TRUE, FALSE, and UNKNOWN. The fact that SQL entertains the possibility of NULL values expands the traditional restriction of Boolean values from just TRUE and FALSE to TRUE, FALSE, and UNKNOWN. If a Boolean TRUE or FALSE value is compared to a NULL value, the result is UNKNOWN. Of course, comparing a Boolean UNKNOWN value to any value also gives an UNKNOWN result.

Datetimes

You often need to store either dates, times, or both, in addition to numeric and character data. ISO/IEC standard SQL defines five datetime types. Because considerable overlap exists among the five types, not all implementations of SQL include all five types. This could cause problems if you try to migrate a database from a platform that uses one subset of the five types to a platform that uses a different subset. There is not much you can do about this except deal with it when the issue arises.

DATE

The DATE data type is the one to use if you care about the date of something but could not care less about the time of day within a date. The DATE data type stores a year, month, and day in that order, using ten character positions in the form yyyy-mm-dd. If you were recording the dates that humans first landed on the Moon, the entry for Apollo 11 would be 1969-07-20.

TIME WITHOUT TIME ZONE

Suppose you want to store the time of day, but don't care which day, and furthermore, don't even care which time zone the time refers to? In that case, the TIME WITHOUT TIME ZONE data type is just the ticket. It stores hours, minutes, and seconds. The hours and minutes data occupies two digits apiece. The seconds data also occupies two digits, but in addition may include a fractional part for fractions of a second. If you specify a column as being of TIME WITHOUT TIME ZONE type, with no parameter, it will hold a time that has no fractional seconds. An example is 02:56:31, which is 56 minutes and 31 seconds after 2 in the morning.

For greater precision in storing a time value, you can use a parameter to specify the number of digits beyond the decimal point that will be stored for seconds. Here's an example of such a definition:

```
Smallstep TIME WITHOUT TIME ZONE (2),
```

In this example, there are two digits past the decimal point, so time is measured down to a hundredth of a second. It would take the form of 02:56:31.17.

TIME WITH TIME ZONE

The TIME WITH TIME ZONE data type gives you all the information that you get in the TIME WITHOUT TIME ZONE data type, and adds the additional fact of what time zone the time refers to. All time zones around the Earth are referenced to Coordinated Universal Time (UTC), formerly known as Greenwich Mean Time (GMT). Coordinated Universal Time is the time in Greenwich, U.K., which was the place where people first started being concerned with highly accurate time-keeping. Of course, the United Kingdom is a fairly small country, so UTC is in effect throughout the entire U.K. In fact, a huge "watermelon slice" of the Earth, running from the North Pole to the South Pole, is also in the same time zone as Greenwich. There are 24 such slices that girdle the Earth. Times around the earth range from 11 hours and 59 minutes behind UTC to 12 hours ahead of UTC (not counting Daylight Saving Time). If Daylight Saving Time is in effect, the offset from UTC could be as much as −12:59 or +13:00. The International Date Line is theoretically exactly opposite Greenwich on the other side of the world, but is offset in spots so as to keep some countries in one time zone.

TIMESTAMP WITHOUT TIME ZONE

Just as sometimes you will need to record dates, and other times you will need to record times, it's certain that there will also be times when you need to store both times and dates. That is what the TIMESTAMP WITHOUT TIME ZONE data type is for. It is a combination of the DATE type and the TIME WITHOUT TIMEZONE type. The one difference between this data type and the TIME WITHOUT TIMEZONE type is that the default value for fractions of a second is six digits rather than zero. You can, of course, specify zero fractional digits, if that is what you want. Suppose you specified a database table column as follows:

```
Smallstep TIMESTAMP WITHOUT TIME ZONE (0),
```

A valid value for Smallstep would be 1969-07-21 02:56:31. That was the date and time in Greenwich when Neil Armstrong's foot first touched the lunar soil. It consists of ten date characters, a blank space separator, and eight time characters.

TIMESTAMP WITH TIME ZONE

If you have to record the time zone that a date and time refers to, use the TIMESTAMP WITH TIME ZONE data type. It's the same as the TIMSESTAMP WITHOUT TIME ZONE data type, with the addition of an offset that shows the time's relationship to Coordinated Universal Time. Here's an example:

```
Smallstep TIMESTAMP WITH TIME ZONE (0),
```

In this case, Smallstep might be recorded as 1969-07-20 21:56:31-05:00. That is the date and time in Houston when Neil Armstrong's foot first touched the lunar soil. Houston time is normally six hours ahead of Greenwich time, but in July, it is only five hours ahead due to Daylight Saving Time.

Intervals

An *interval* is the difference between two dates, two times, or two datetimes. There are two different kinds of intervals, the year-month interval and the day-hour-minute-second interval. A day always has 24 hours. An hour always has 60 minutes. A minute always has 60 seconds. However, a month may have 28, 29, 30, or 31 days. Because of that variability, you cannot mix the two kinds of intervals. A field of the INTERVAL type can store the difference in time between two instants in the same month, but cannot store an interval such as 2 years, 7 months, 13 days, 5 hours, 6 minutes, and 45 seconds.

XML type

The SQL/XML:2003 update to the ISO/IEC SQL standard introduced the XML data type. Values in the XML type are XML values, meaning you can now manage and query XML data in an SQL database.

With SQL/XML:2006, folks moved to the XQuery Data Model, which means that any XML value is also an XQuery sequence. The details of the XQuery Data Model are beyond the scope of this book. Refer to *Querying XML*, by Jim Melton and Stephen Buxton (published by Morgan Kaufmann), for detailed coverage of this topic.

With the introduction of SQL/XML:2006, three specific subtypes of the XML type were defined. They are XML(SEQUENCE), XML(CONTENT), and XML(DOCUMENT). The three subtypes are related to each other hierarchically. An XML(SEQUENCE) is any sequence of XML nodes, XML values, or both. An XML(CONTENT) is an XML(SEQUENCE) that is an XML fragment wrapped in a document node. An XML(DOCUMENT) is an XML(CONTENT) that is a well-formed XML document.

Every XML value is at least an XML(SEQUENCE). An XML(SEQUENCE) that is a document node is an XML(CONTENT). An XML(CONTENT) that has legal document children is an XML(DOCUMENT).

XML types may be associated with an XML schema. There are three possibilities:

>> UNTYPED: There is no associated XML schema.

>> XMLSCHEMA: There is an associated XML schema.

>> ANY: There may or may not be an associated XML schema.

So a document of type XML(DOCUMENT(ANY)) may or may not have an associated XML schema. If you specify a column as being of type XML with no modifiers, it must be either XML(SEQUENCE), XML(CONTENT(ANY)), or XML(CONTENT(UNTYPED)). Which of those it is depends on the implementation.

ROW type

The ROW type, introduced in the 1999 version of the ISO/IEC SQL standard (SQL:1999), represents the first break of SQL away from the relational model, as defined by its creator, Dr. E.F. Codd. With the introduction of this type, SQL databases can no longer be considered pure relational databases. One of the defining characteristics of Codd's First Normal Form (1NF) is the fact that no field in a table row may be multivalued. Multivalued fields are exactly what the ROW type introduces. The ROW type enables you to place a whole row's worth of data into a single field, effectively nesting a row within a row. To see how this works, create a ROW type.

Note: The normal forms constrain the structure of database tables as a defense against anomalies, which are inconsistencies in table data or even outright wrong values. 1NF is the least restrictive of the normal forms, and thus the easiest to satisfy. Notwithstanding that, a table that includes a ROW type fails the test of First Normal Form. According to Dr. Codd, such a table is not a relation, and thus cannot be present in a relational database. I give extensive coverage to normalization and the normal forms in Book 2, Chapter 2.

```
CREATE ROW TYPE address_type (
    Street      VARCHAR (25),
    City        VARCHAR (20),
    State       CHAR (2),
    PostalCode  VARCHAR (9)
    ) ;
```

This code effectively compresses four attributes into a single type. After you have created a ROW type — such as address_type in the preceding example — you can then use it in a table definition.

```
CREATE TABLE VENDOR (
    VendorID    INTEGER PRIMARY KEY,
    VendorName  VARCHAR (25),
    Address     address_type,
    Phone       VARCHAR (15)
) ;
```

If you have tables for multiple groups, such as vendors, employees, customers, stockholders, or prospects, you have to declare only one attribute rather than four. That may not seem like much of a savings, but you're not limited to putting just four attributes into a ROW type. What if you had to type in the same 40 attributes into a 100 tables?

REMEMBER

The ROW type, like many other aspects of SQL that have been added relatively recently, has not yet been included into many of the most popular implementations of SQL. Even Oracle, which is one of the closest implementations to the SQL:2016 standard, does not currently support the ROW type. Instead, it supports object types, which perform a similar function.

Collection types

The introduction of ROW types in SQL:1999 was not the only break from the iron-clad rules of relational database theory. In that same version of the standard, the ARRAY type was introduced, and in SQL:2003, the MULTISET type was added. Both of these collection types violate the ol' First Normal Form (1NF) and thus take SQL databases a couple of steps further away from relational purity.

ARRAY

The ARRAY type violates 1NF, but not in the same way that the ROW type does. The ARRAY type enables you to enhance a field of an existing type by putting more than one entry into it. This creates a repeating group, which was demonized in Codd's original formulation of the relational model, but now reappears as a desirable feature. Arrays are ordered in the sense that each element in the array corresponds to exactly one ordinal position in the array.

You might ask how a repeating group of the ARRAY type differs from the ROW type's ability to put "a whole row's worth of data into a single field." The distinction is subtle. The ROW type enables you to compress multiple *different* attributes into a single field, such as a street, city, state, and postal code. The repeating group of the ARRAY type enables you to put multiple instances of the *same* attribute into a single field, such as a phone number and three alternate phone numbers.

As an example, suppose you want to have alternative ways of contacting your vendors in case the main telephone number does not work for you. Perhaps you would like the option of storing as many as four telephone numbers, just to be safe. A slight modification to the code shown previously will do the trick.

```
CREATE TABLE VENDOR (
    VendorID    INTEGER PRIMARY KEY,
    VendorName  VARCHAR (25),
    Address     address_type,
    Phone       VARCHAR (15)  ARRAY [4]
) ;
```

When he created the relational model, Dr. Codd made a conscious decision to sacrifice some functional flexibility in exchange for enhanced data integrity. The addition of the ARRAY type, along with the ROW type and later the MULTISET type, takes back some of that flexibility in exchange for added complexity. That added complexity could lead to data integrity problems if it is not handled correctly. The more complex a system is, the more things that can go wrong, and the more opportunities there are for people to make mistakes.

Multiset

Whereas an *array* is an ordered collection of elements, a *multiset* is an unordered collection. You cannot reference individual elements in a multiset because you don't know where they are located in the collection. If you want to have multiples of an attribute, such as phone numbers, but don't care what order they are listed in, you can use a multiset rather than an array.

REF types

REF types are different from distinct data types such as INTEGER or CHAR. They are used in obscure circumstances by highly skilled SQL wizards, and just about nobody else. Instead of holding values, an REF type references a user-defined structured type associated with a typed table. Typed tables are beyond the scope of this book, but I mention REF type here for the sake of completeness.

REF types are not a part of core SQL. This means that database vendors can claim compliance with the SQL standard without implementing REF types.

The REF type is an aspect of the object-oriented nature of SQL since the SQL:1999 standard. If object-oriented programming seems obscure to you, as it does to many programmers of a more traditional bent, you can probably survive quite well without ever needing the REF type.

JSON types

The SQL:2016 standard introduced JavaScript Object Notation (JSON) operations, but JSON data itself still had to be stored in character data type fields. The SQL:2023 standard adds a new JSON data type specifically for storing JSON-formatted data.

Originally designed as a way for JavaScript programs to send data to web hosts (thus, the *J* in the name), JSON has quickly become a popular way to store and transmit data in web-based applications. JSON has similar features to XML, but it's somewhat more streamlined, combining the data values with the data names in a more straightforward manner:

```
{
    "userid": "rblum",
    "name": "Richard Blum",
    "contact": "312-555-1234"
}
```

At the time of this writing, not all database servers have implemented the JSON data type yet, but with its increasing popularity, I expect that will change very soon.

User-defined types

User-defined types (UDTs) are another addition to SQL imported from the world of object-oriented programming. If the data types that I have enumerated here are not enough for you, you can define your own data types. To do so, use the principles of abstract data types (ADTs) that are major features of such object-oriented languages as C++.

REMEMBER

SQL is not a complete programming language, and as such must be used with a host language that is complete, such as C. One of the problems with this arrangement is that the data types of the host language often do not match the data types of SQL. User-defined types come to the rescue here. You can define a type that matches the corresponding type in the host language.

The object-oriented nature of UDTs becomes evident when you see that a UDT has attributes and methods encapsulated within it. The attribute definitions and the results of the methods are visible to the outside world, but the ways the methods are actually implemented are hidden from view. In this object-oriented world, you can declare attributes and methods to be public, private, or protected. A *public* attribute or method is available to anyone who uses the UDT. A *private* attribute or method may be used only by the UDT itself. A *protected* attribute or method may be used only by the UDT itself and its subtypes. (If this sounds familiar to you, don't be surprised — an SQL UDT is much like a class in object-oriented programming.)

There are two kinds of UDTs: distinct types and structured types. The next sections take a look at each one in turn.

Distinct types

A *distinct* type is very similar to a regular predefined SQL type. In fact, a distinct type is derived directly from a predefined type, called the *source* type. You can create multiple distinct types from a single source type, each one distinct from all the others and from the source type. Here's how to create a distinct type from a predefined type:

```
CREATE DISTINCT TYPE USdollar AS DECIMAL (10,2) ;
```

This definition (USdollar) creates a new data type for (wait for it) U.S. dollars, based on the predefined DECIMAL type. You can create additional distinct types in the same way:

```
CREATE DISTINCT TYPE Euro AS DECIMAL (10,2) ;
```

Now you can create tables that use the new types:

```
CREATE TABLE USinvoice (
    InvoiceNo    INTEGER PRIMARY KEY,
    CustomerID   INTEGER,
    SalesID      INTEGER,
    SaleTotal    USdollar,
    Tax          USdollar,
    Shipping     USdollar,
    GrandTotal   USdollar
    ) ;
```

```
CREATE TABLE Europeaninvoice (
    InvoiceNo    INTEGER PRIMARY KEY,
    CustomerID   INTEGER,
    SalesID      INTEGER,
    SaleTotal    Euro,
    Tax          Euro,
    Shipping     Euro,
    GrandTotal   Euro
    ) ;
```

The USdollar type and the Euro type are both based on the DECIMAL type, but you cannot directly compare a USdollar value to a Euro value, nor can you directly compare either of those to a DECIMAL value. This is consistent with reality because one U.S. dollar is not equal to one euro. However, it is possible to exchange dollars for euros and vice versa when traveling. You can make that exchange with SQL too, but not directly. You must use a CAST operation, which I describe in Book 3, Chapter 1.

Structured types

Structured types are not based on a single source type as are the distinct types. Instead, they are expressed as a list of attributes and methods. When you create a structured UDT, the DBMS automatically creates a constructor function, a mutator function, and an observer function. The *constructor* for a UDT is given the same name as the UDT. Its job is to initialize the UDT's attributes to their default values. When you invoke a *mutator* function, it changes the value of an attribute of a structured type. You can then use an *observer* function to retrieve the value of an attribute of a structured type. If you include an observer function in a SELECT statement, it will retrieve values from the database.

SUBTYPES AND SUPERTYPES

A hierarchical relationship can exist between two structured types. One structured type can be a "child" or subtype of a "parent" or supertype. Consider an example involving books, as shown in Figure 6-1.

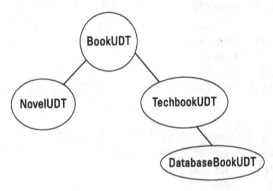

FIGURE 6-1:
Defining subtypes
and supertypes
of books.

Suppose you have a UDT named BookUDT, which has a subtype named NovelUDT and another subtype named TechBookUDT. BookUDT is a supertype of both subtypes. Suppose further that TechBookUDT has a subtype named DatabaseBookUDT. DatabaseBookUDT is not only a subtype of TechBookUDT, but also a subtype of BookUDT. Because DatabaseBookUDT is a direct child of TechBookUDT it is considered a *proper subtype* of TechBookUDT. Since DatabaseBookUDT is not a direct child of BookUDT, but rather a grandchild, it is not considered a proper subtype of BookUDT.

A structured type that has no supertype is considered a *maximal supertype*, and a structured type that has no subtypes is considered a *leaf subtype*.

STRUCTURED TYPE EXAMPLE

Here's how you can create structured UDTs:

```
/* Create a UDT named BookUDT */
CREATE TYPE BookUDT AS
/* Specify attributes */
    Title        CHAR (40),
    Author       CHAR (40),
```

```
    MyCost        DECIMAL (9,2),
    ListPrice     DECIMAL (9.2)
/* Allow for subtypes */
    NOT FINAL ;


/* Create a subtype named TechBookUDT */
CREATE TYPE TechBookUDT UNDER BookUDT NOT FINAL ;


/* Create a subtype named DatabaseBookUDT */
CREATE TYPE DatabaseBookUDT UNDER TechBookUDT FINAL ;
```

Note: In this code, comments are enclosed within /* comment */ pairs. The NOT FINAL keywords indicate that even though a semicolon is closing out the statement, there is more to come. Subtypes are about to be defined under the supertype. The lowest level subtype closes out with the keyword FINAL.

Now that the types are defined, you can create tables that use them.

```
CREATE TABLE DATABASEBOOKS (
    StockItem    DatabaseBookUDT,
    StockNumber INTEGER
    ) ;
```

Now that the table exists, you can add data to it.

```
BEGIN
    /* Declare a temporary variable x */
    DECLARE x = DatabaseBookUDT;
    /* Execute the constructor function */
    Set x = DatabaseBookUDT() ;
    /* Execute the first mutator function */
    SET x = x.Title('SQL For Dummies') ;
    /* Execute the second mutator function */
    SET x = x.Author('Allen G. Taylor') ;
    /* Execute the third mutator function */
    SET x = x.MyCost(23.56) ;
    /* Execute the fourth mutator function */
    SET x = x.ListPrice(29.99) ;
    INSERT INTO DATABASEBOOKS VALUES (x, 271828) ;
END
```

Data type summary

Table 6-1 summarizes the SQL data types and gives an example of each.

TABLE 6-1   Data Types

Data Type	Example Value
CHARACTER (20)	'Amateur Radio'
VARCHAR (20)	'Amateur Radio'
CLOB (1000000)	'This character string is a million characters long... '
SMALLINT, BIGINT, or INTEGER	7500
NUMERIC or DECIMAL	3425.432
REAL, FLOAT, or DOUBLE PRECISION	6.626E-34
BINARY	'1011001110101010'
BINARY VARYING	'10110'
BLOB (1000000)	'1001001110101011010101010101... '
BOOLEAN	'true'
DATE	1957-08-14
TIME WITHOUT TIME ZONE (2)*	12:46:02.43
TIME WITH TIME ZONE (3)	12:46:02.432-08:00
TIMESTAMP WITHOUT TIME ZONE (0)	1957-08-14 12:46:02
TIMESTAMP WITH TIME ZONE (0)	1957-08-14 12:46:02-08:00
INTERVAL DAY	INTERVAL '4' DAY
ROW	ROW (Street VARCHAR (25), City VARCHAR (20), State CHAR (2), PostalCode VARCHAR (9))
ARRAY	INTEGER ARRAY [15]
MULTISET	Phone VARCHAR (15) MULTISET [4]
REF	Not an ordinary type, but a pointer to a referenced type
JSON	{ "product": "Oranges", "price": "2.00"}
USER DEFINED TYPE	Currency type based on DECIMAL

Argument specifies number of fractional digits.

Handling Null Values

SQL is different from practically any computer language that you may have encountered up to this point in that it allows null values. Other languages don't. Allowing null values gives SQL a flexibility that other languages lack, but also contributes to the impedance mismatch between SQL and host languages that it must work with in an application. If an SQL database contains null values that the host language does not recognize, you have to come up with a plan that handles that difference in a consistent way.

I'm borrowing the term *impedance mismatch* from the world of electrical engineering. If, for example, you've set up your stereo system using speaker cable with a characteristic impedance of 50 ohms feeding speakers with an impedance of 8 ohms, you've got yourself a case of impedance mismatch and you'll surely get fuzzy, noisy sound — definitely low fidelity. If a data type of a host language does not exactly match the corresponding data type of SQL, you have a similar situation, bad communication across the interface between the two.

A *null value* is a nonvalue. If you are talking about numeric data, a null value is not the same as zero, which is a definite value. It is one less than one. If you are talking about character data, a null value is not the same as a blank space. A blank space is also a definite value. If you are talking about Boolean data, a null value is not the same as FALSE. A false Boolean value is a definite value too.

A null value is the absence of a value. It reminds me of the Buddhist concept of emptiness. I almost feel that if I ever come to understand null values completely, I will have transcended the illusions of this world and achieved a state of enlightenment.

A field may contain a null value for several reasons:

>> A field may have a definite value, but the value is currently unknown.

>> A field may not yet have a definite value, but it may gain one in the future.

>> For some rows in a table, a particular field in that row may not be applicable.

>> The old value of a field has been deleted, but it has not yet been replaced with a new value.

In any situation where knowledge is incomplete, null values are possible. Because in most application areas, knowledge is never complete, null values are very likely to appear in most databases.

Applying Constraints

Constraints are one of the primary mechanisms for keeping the contents of a database from turning into a misleading or confusing mess. By applying constraints to tables, columns, or entire databases, you prevent the addition of invalid data or the deletion of data that is required to maintain overall consistency. A constraint can also identify invalid data that already exists in a database. If an operation that you perform in a transaction causes a constraint to be violated, the DBMS will prevent the transaction from taking effect (being *committed*). This protects the database from being put into an inconsistent state.

Column constraints

You can constrain the contents of a table column. In some cases, that means constraining what the column *must* contain, and in other cases, what it *may not* contain. There are three kinds of column constraints: the NOT NULL, UNIQUE, and CHECK constraints.

NOT NULL

Although SQL allows a column to contain null values, there are times when you want to be sure that a column always has a distinct value. In order for one row in a table to be distinguished from another, there must be some way of telling them apart. This is usually done with a primary key, which must have a unique value in every row. Because a null value in a column could be anything, it might match the value for that column in any of the other rows. Thus it makes sense to disallow a null value in the column that is used to distinguish one row from the rest. You can do this with a NOT NULL constraint, as shown in the following example:

```
CREATE TABLE CLIENT (

    ClientName      CHAR (30)     NOT NULL,
    Address1        CHAR (30),
    Address2        CHAR (30),
    City            CHAR (25),
    State           CHAR (2),
    PostalCode      CHAR (10),
    Phone           CHAR (13),
    Fax             CHAR (13),
    ContactPerson   CHAR (30)
    ) ;
```

When entering a new client into the CLIENT table, you must make an entry in the ClientName column.

UNIQUE

The NOT NULL constraint is a fairly weak constraint. You can satisfy the constraint as long as you put anything at all into the field, even if what you put into it would allow inconsistencies into your table. For example, suppose you already had a client named David Taylor in your database, and someone tried to enter another record with the same client name. If the table was protected only by a NOT NULL constraint, the entry of the second David Taylor would be allowed. Now when you go to retrieve David Taylor's information, which one will you get? How will you tell whether you have the one you want? A way around this problem is to use the stronger UNIQUE constraint.

TIP

Previous versions of the SQL standard were a little ambiguous on how the UNIQUE constraint handled NULL values, but the new SQL:2023 standard specifies that you can define the UNIQUE constraint to either allow duplicate NULL values or disallow them by adding the DISTINCT clause.

CHECK

Use the CHECK constraint for preventing the entry of invalid data that goes beyond maintaining uniqueness. For example, you can check to make sure that a numeric value falls within an allowed range. You can also check to see that a particular character string is not entered into a column.

Here's an example that ensures that the charge for a service falls within the acceptable range. It ensures that a customer is not mistakenly given a credit rather than a debit, and that she is not charged a ridiculously high amount either.

```
CREATE TABLE TESTS (
    TestName         CHARACTER (30)      NOT NULL,
    StandardCharge   NUMERIC (6,2)
        CHECK (StandardCharge >= 0.00
          AND StandardCharge <= 200.00)
    ) ;
```

The constraint is satisfied only if the charge is positive and less than or equal to $200.

Table constraints

Sometimes a constraint applies not just to a column, but to an entire table. The `PRIMARY KEY` constraint is the principal example of a table constraint; it applies to an entire table.

Although a primary key *may* consist of a single column, it could also be made up of a combination of two or more columns. Because a primary key must be guaranteed to be unique, multiple columns may be needed if one column is not enough to guarantee uniqueness.

To see what I mean, check out the following, which shows a table with a single-column primary key:

```
CREATE TABLE PROSPECT (
    ProspectName    CHAR (30)    PRIMARY KEY,
    Address1        CHAR (30),
    Address2        CHAR (30),
    City            CHAR (25),
    State           CHAR (2),
    PostalCode      CHAR (10),
    Phone           CHAR (13),
    Fax             CHAR (13)
    ) ;
```

The primary key constraint in this case is listed with the ProspectName column, but it is nonetheless a table constraint because it guarantees that the table contains no duplicate rows. By applying the primary key constraint to ProspectName, you are guaranteeing that ProspectName cannot have a null value, and no entry in the ProspectName column may duplicate another entry in the ProspectName column. Because ProspectName is guaranteed to be unique, every row in the table must be distinguishable from every other row.

ProspectName may not be a particularly good choice for a proposed primary key. Some people have rather common names— Joe Wilson or Jane Adams. It is quite possible that two people with the same name might both be prospects of your business. You could overcome that problem by using more than one column for the primary key. Here's one way to do that:

```
CREATE TABLE PROSPECT (
    ProspectName    CHAR (30)    NOT NULL,
    Address1        CHAR (30)    NOT NULL,
    Address2        CHAR (30),
    City            CHAR (25),
```

```
        State               CHAR (2),
        PostalCode          CHAR (10),
        Phone               CHAR (13),

        CONSTRAINT prospect_pk PRIMARY KEY
                (ProspectName, Address1)
        ) ;
```

A composite primary key is made up of both ProspectName and Address1.

You might ask, "What if a father and son have the same name and live at the same address?" The more such scenarios you think up, the more complex things tend to get. In many cases, it's best to make up a unique ID number for every row in a table and let that be the primary key. If you use an autoincrementer to generate the keys, you can be sure they are unique. This keeps things relatively simple. You can also program your own unique ID numbers by storing a value in memory and incrementing it by one after each time you add a new record that uses the stored value as its primary key.

```
CREATE TABLE PROSPECT (
        ProspectID          INTEGER             PRIMARY KEY,
        ProspectName        CHAR (30),
        Address1            CHAR (30),
        Address2            CHAR (30),
        City                CHAR (25),
        State               CHAR (2),
        PostalCode          CHAR (10),
        Phone               CHAR (13)
        ) ;
```

Many database management systems automatically create autoincrementing primary keys for you as you enter new rows into a table.

Foreign key constraints

Relational databases are categorized as they are because the data is stored in tables that are *related* to each other in some way. The relationship occurs because a row in one table may be directly related to one or more rows in another table.

Figure 6-2 demonstrates an example of a retail database. The record in the CUSTOMER table for customer Lisa Mazzone is directly related to the records in the INVOICE table for purchases that Ms. Mazzone has made. To establish this relationship, one or more columns in the CUSTOMER table must have corresponding columns in the INVOICE table.

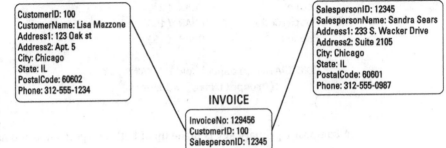

CustomerID: 100
CustomerName: Lisa Mazzone
Address1: 123 Oak st
Address2: Apt. 5
City: Chicago
State: IL
PostalCode: 60602
Phone: 312-555-1234

SALESPERSON

SalespersonID: 12345
SalespersonName: Sandra Sears
Address1: 233 S. Wacker Drive
Address2: Suite 2105
City: Chicago
State: IL
PostalCode: 60601
Phone: 312-555-0987

INVOICE

InvoiceNo: 129456
CustomerID: 100
SalespersonID: 12345

FIGURE 6-2:
An example
of foreign key
constraints
in tables.

The primary key of the CUSTOMER table uniquely identifies each customer. The primary key of the INVOICE table uniquely identifies each invoice. In addition, the primary key of the CUSTOMER table acts as a foreign key in INVOICE to link the two tables. In this setup, the foreign key in each row of the INVOICE table identifies the customer who made this particular purchase. Here's an example:

```
CREATE TABLE CUSTOMER (
    CustomerID        INTEGER           PRIMARY KEY,
    CustomerName      CHAR (30),
    Address1          CHAR (30),
    Address2          CHAR (30),
    City              CHAR (25),
    State             CHAR (2),
    PostalCode        CHAR (10),
    Phone             CHAR (13)
    ) ;

CREATE TABLE SALESPERSON (
    SalespersonID     INTEGER           PRIMARY KEY,
    SalespersonName   CHAR (30),
    Address1          CHAR (30),
    Address2          CHAR (30),
    City              CHAR (25),
    State             CHAR (2),
    PostalCode        CHAR (10),
    Phone             CHAR (13)
    ) ;

CREATE TABLE INVOICE (
    InvoiceNo         INTEGER PRIMARY KEY,
    CustomerID        INTEGER,
    SalespersonID     INTEGER,
```

```
    CONSTRAINT customer_fk FOREIGN KEY (CustomerID)
        REFERENCES CUSTOMER (CustomerID),
    CONSTRAINT salesperson_fk FOREIGN KEY (SalespersonID)
        REFERENCES SALESPERSON (SalespersonID)
    ) ;
```

Each invoice is related to the customer who made the purchase and the salesperson who made the sale.

Using constraints in this way is what makes relational databases relational. This is the core of the whole thing right here! How do the tables in a relational databases relate to each other? They relate by the keys they hold in common. The relationship is established, but also constrained by the fact that a column in one table has to match a corresponding column in another table. The only relationships present in a relational database are those where there is a key-to-key link mediated by a foreign key constraint.

Assertions

Sometimes a constraint may apply not just to a column or a table, but to multiple tables or even an entire database. A constraint with such broad applicability is called an *assertion*.

Suppose a small bookstore wants to control its exposure to dead inventory by not allowing total inventory to grow beyond 20,000 items. Suppose further that stocks of books and DVDs are maintained in different tables — the BOOKS and DVD tables. An assertion can guarantee that the maximum is not exceeded.

```
CREATE TABLE BOOKS (
    ISBN        INTEGER,
    Title       CHAR (50),
    Quantity    INTEGER ) ;

CREATE TABLE DVD (
    BarCode     INTEGER,
    Title       CHAR (50),
    Quantity    INTEGER ) ;

CREATE ASSERTION
    CHECK ((SELECT SUM (Quantity)
            FROM BOOKS)
        + (SELECT SUM (Quantity)
            FROM DVD)
        < 20000) ;
```

This assertion adds up all the books in stock, then adds up all the DVDs in stock, and finally adds those two sums together. It then checks to see that the sum of them all is less than 20,000. Whenever an attempt is made to add a book or DVD to inventory, and that addition would push total inventory to 20,000 or more, the assertion is violated and the addition is not allowed.

Most popular implementations do not support assertions. For example, SQL Server 2016, DB2, Oracle Database 18c, SAP SQL Anywhere, MySQL, and PostgreSQL do not. Assertions may become available in the future, since they are a part of SQL:2003, but it would not be wise to hold your breath until this functionality appears. Although a feature that would be nice to have, assertions are far down on the list of features to add for most DBMS vendors.

2

Developing Relational Databases

Contents at a Glance

Chapter **1**

System Development Overview

SQL is the international standard language used by practically everybody to communicate with relational databases. This book is about SQL, but in order for you to truly understand SQL, it must be placed in the proper context — in the world of relational databases. In this minibook, I cover the ground necessary to prepare you to exercise the full power of SQL.

Databases don't exist in isolation. They are part of a system designed to perform some needed function. To create a useful and reliable database system, you must be aware of all the parts of the system and how they work together. You must also follow a disciplined approach to system development if you're to have any hope at all of delivering an effective and reliable product on time and on budget. In this chapter, I lay out the component parts of such a system, and then break down the steps you must go through to successfully complete a database system development project.

The Components of a Database System

A database containing absolutely critical information would not be of much use if there was no way to operate on the data or retrieve the particular information that you wanted. That's why several intermediate components (the database engine, DBMS front end, and database application) take their place between the database and the user in order to do these two things:

>> **Translate the user's requests into a form that the database understands.**

>> **Return the requested information to the user in a form that the user understands.**

Figure 1-1 shows the information flow from the user to the database and back again, through the intermediate components.

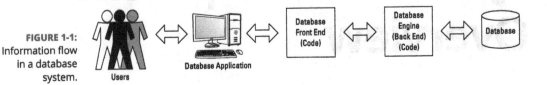

FIGURE 1-1:
Information flow
in a database
system.

I examine each of these components one by one, starting with the database itself.

The database

The core component of a database system is — no surprise here — the database itself. The salient features of a database are as follows:

>> The database is the place where data is stored.

>> Data is stored there in a structured way, which is what makes it a database rather than a random pile of data items.

>> The structure of a database enables the efficient retrieval of specific items.

>> A database may be stored in one place or it could be distributed across multiple locations.

>> Regardless of its physical form, logically a database behaves as a single, unified repository of data.

The database engine

The database engine, also called the *back end* of a database management system (DBMS), is where the processing power of the database system resides. The *database engine* is that part of the system that acts upon the database. It responds to commands in the form of SQL statements and performs the requested operations on the database.

In addition to its processing functions, the database engine functions as a two-way communications channel, accepting commands from the DBMS front end (see the next section) and translating them into actions on the database. Results of those actions are then passed back to the front end for further processing by the database application and ultimate presentation to the user.

The DBMS front end

Whereas the back end is that portion of a DBMS that interfaces directly with the database, the *front end* is the portion that communicates with the database application or directly with the user. It translates instructions it receives from the user or the user's application into a form that the back end can understand. On the return path, it translates the results it receives from the back end into a form the user or the user's application can understand.

The front end is what you see after you click an icon to launch a DBMS such as Access, SQL Server, or Oracle. Despite appearances, what you see is not the database. It is not even the database management system. It is just a translator, designed to make it easier for you to communicate with the database.

The database application

Although it is possible for a person to interact directly with the DBMS front end, this is not the way database systems are normally used. Most people deal with databases indirectly through an application. An application is a program, written in a combination of a host language such as C or Java, and SQL, which performs actions that are required on a repeating basis. The *database application* provides a friendly environment for the user, with helpful screens, menus, command buttons, and instructive text, to make the job of dealing with the database more understandable and easier.

Although it may take significant time and effort to build a database application, after it's built, it can be used multiple times. It also makes the user's job much easier, so that high-level understanding of the database is not needed in order to effectively maintain and use it.

The user

The user is a human being, but one who is typically not you, dear reader. Because you are reading this book, I assume that your goal is to learn to use SQL effectively. The user in a database system typically does not use SQL at all and may be unaware that it even exists. The user deals with the screens, menus, and command buttons of the database applications that you write. Your applications shield the user from the complexities of SQL. The user may interact directly with the application you write or, if your application is web-based, may deal with it through a browser.

It is possible for a user, in interactive SQL mode, to enter SQL statements directly into a DBMS and receive result sets or other feedback from the DBMS. This, however, is not the normal case. Usually a database application developer such as you operates in this manner, rather than the typical user.

The System Development Life Cycle

Producing both a reliable database and an easy-to-use application that fills a real need is a complex task. If you take the task too lightly and build a system without careful preparation, you're likely to produce something that is neither reliable nor adequately functional.

The best way to accomplish a large, complex task is to break it down into steps, each one of which you can do and do well. To develop a robust and reliable database system, you must go through the seven phases of the System Development Life Cycle (SDLC):

>> Definition

>> Requirements

>> Evaluation

>> Design

>> Implementation

>> Final Documentation and Testing

>> Maintenance

Each one of these phases is important. Sometimes schedule pressure may tempt you to shortchange or even skip one of the phases. To do so invites costly errors or a final product that does not meet the needs of the users.

With that last word to the wise out of the way, read on to find out more about each phase of the System Development Life Cycle.

Definition phase

At the beginning of a project, the person who assigns you the task of building a system — the client — has some idea of what is needed. That idea may be very specific, sharp, and concise, or it may be vague, nebulous, and ill-defined. Your first task is to generate and put into writing a detailed description of exactly what the end result of the project, called *the deliverables*, should be. This is the primary task of the Definition phase, but this phase also includes the following tasks:

>> **Define the task to be performed.** Define the problem to be solved by your database and associated application as accurately as possible. Do this by listening carefully to your client as she describes what she envisions the system to be. Ask questions to clarify vague points. Often, the client will not have thought things through completely. She will have a general idea of what she wants, but no clear idea of the specifics. You must come to an agreement with her on the specifics before you can proceed.

>> **Determine the project's scope.** How big a job will it be? What will it require in terms of systems analyst time, programmer time, equipment, and other cost items? What is the deadline?

>> **Perform a feasibility analysis.** Ask yourself, "Is it possible to do this job within the time and cost constraints placed on it by the client?" To answer this question, you must do a *feasibility analysis* — a determination of the time and resources it will take to do the job. After you complete the analysis, you may decide that the project is not feasible as currently defined, and you must either decline it or convince the client to reduce the scope to something more manageable.

>> **Form a project team.** Decide who will work on the project. You may be able to do a small job all by yourself, but most development efforts require a team of several individuals. Finding people who have the requisite skills and who are also available to work on the project when you need them can be just as challenging as any other part of the total development effort.

>> **Document the task definition, the project scope, the feasibility analysis, and the membership of the project team.** Carefully document the project definition, its scope, the feasibility analysis, and the development team membership. This documentation will be a valuable guide for everything that follows.

>> **Get the client to approve the Definition phase document.** Make sure the client sees and agrees with everything recorded in the Definition phase document. It is best to have her sign the document, signifying that she understands and approves of your plan for the development effort.

Requirements phase

In the Definition phase, you talk with the client. This is the person who has the authority to hire you or, if you are already an employee, assign you to this development task. This person is not, however, the only one with an interest in the project. Chances are, someone other than the client will use the system on a daily basis. Even more people may depend on the results generated by the system. It is important to find out what these people need and what they prefer because your primary client may not have a complete understanding of what would serve them best.

The amount of work you must do in the Requirements phase depends on the client. It can be quick and easy if you are dealing with a client who has prior experience with similar database development projects. Such a client has a clear idea of what he wants and, equally important, what is feasible within the time and budget constraints that apply.

On the other hand, this phase can be difficult and drawn-out if the client has no experience with this kind of development, only a vague idea of what he wants, and an even vaguer idea of what can reasonably be done within the allotted time and budget.

ESTABLISHING REQUIREMENTS: AN EXAMPLE

I once created a database application for an adoption agency. First I talked to the manager who had overall charge of the agency. She had very definite ideas about how she wanted the system to perform. The agency already had a computerized adoption application, but it was becoming progressively less satisfactory as their business grew. The agency needed to keep track of quite a few facts in order to match children with the best prospective adoptive parents and to meet stringent government requirements.

The manager wanted a system with expanded capacity, additional features, and higher performance compared to her existing system. However, she wanted the user interface to be as close as possible to that of their current system to minimize the confusion of users and the retraining time that a different user interface would require.

After talking to the manager, I talked to the users, each one specializing on a specific segment of the overall process. These people, who would be using the system every day, each had their own perspective on what was needed for them to do their jobs most effectively. I had to find a way to come up with a set of requirements that met the needs of the users and the desires of the manager, and at the same time one that specified a system that was feasible to build.

After considerable dialog with all concerned, I crafted a set of requirements that everyone could endorse. At every succeeding stage of development, I went back to the same people and kept them informed of my progress. This way, they all felt they had a personal stake in the final product. These follow-up meetings also helped me to be sure that I had a good understanding of what they had in mind when they told me what they wanted.

As I mention previously, aside from your primary client — the one who hired you — other stakeholders in the project, such as various users, managers, executives, and board members, also have ideas of what they need. These ideas often conflict with each other. Your job at this point is to come up with a set of requirements that everyone can agree on. This will probably not meet everyone's needs completely. It will represent a compromise between conflicting desires, but will be the solution that gives the most important functions to the people who need them.

The users' data model

After you have consensus among the stakeholders, you can use their requirements to construct a users' data model, which includes all the items of interest and how they relate to each other. It also incorporates any business rules that you may have been able to infer from people's comments. Business rules place restrictions on the items that can be included in a database and on what can be done with those items. See Chapter 2 of Book 1 for a fuller description of the users' data model.

Statement of Requirements

After you have constructed the users' data model and verified its accuracy with your client, you can write a formal Statement of Requirements, which is an explicit statement of the database application's display, update, and control mechanisms. It will answer such questions as

>> What will the display look like? What arrangement of items? What color scheme?

>> What items will need to be updated, and how will that be done?

>> How will users navigate between screens?

>> Will selections be made by key depressions? If so, which keys will do what? If not, how will users make selections?

>> Will operations be initiated by mouse clicks? If so, which operations? If not, how will users initiate operations?

>> What will the maximum acceptable response time to a query be?

REMEMBER

The Statement of Requirements must be as detailed as possible because it is essentially a contract between you and your client. You are agreeing on exactly what will be delivered and when it will be delivered. To seal the arrangement, both you and your client should sign the Statement of Requirements, signifying agreement on what you'll be responsible for delivering. This step may seem rather formal, but it protects both parties. There can never be any question later as to what was agreed upon.

Here's a summary of what you must do in the Requirements phase:

>> Interview typical members of all classes of stakeholders in the project.

>> Provide leadership in getting stakeholders to agree on what is needed.

>> Create a users' data model of the proposed system.

>> Create the Statement of Requirements, which describes in detail what the system will look like and what it will do.

>> Obtain client approval of the Statement of Requirements, indicated by a signature and date.

Evaluation phase

Upon completion of the Requirements phase (see the preceding section), it's a good idea to do some serious thinking about what you'll need to do in order to meet the requirements. This thinking is the main task of the Evaluation phase, in which you address the issues of scope and feasibility more carefully than you have up to this point.

Here are some important considerations for the Evaluation phase:

>> **Determine the project's scope.** This step includes several tasks, including

- *Selecting the best DBMS for the job, based on all relevant considerations.*

- *Selecting the best host language.*

- *Writing job descriptions for all team members.*

>> **Reassess the feasibility of the project and adjust project scope, deadlines, or budget if needed.**

>> **Document all the decisions made in this phase and the reasoning for them.**

Determining project scope

Now that you know what you need to do, it's time to decide on exactly how you're going to do it. First and foremost, you'll have to choose what development tools you'll use. In other words, decide on the best DBMS to accomplish this particular project. To determine this, you need to consider these several factors:

» All DBMS products have limitations in terms of number of tables and records they'll support, supported data types, and number of users. Considering the size and complexity of the task, which DBMS products will support the current project and any reasonable extensions to it that might be required in the years to come? (Chapter 3 of Book 1 provides some information on the capabilities of several of the most popular DBMS products currently available.)

» Does the client have an institutional standard DBMS that is used for all development? If so, will it work for the current project?

» Is your development team proficient with the selected DBMS? If not, what will it take for them to climb the learning curve and become proficient?

» Is the DBMS you choose supported by a strong company or developer community that will be able to provide upgrades and other services in the coming years?

» Is the best DBMS, from a performance standpoint, affordable to the client from a financial standpoint?

» Does the DBMS have a track record of reliable operation in applications similar to the one you're planning?

Another consideration is the language that you'll use to develop the application. You can develop some database applications without writing a single line of program code. These tend to be simple applications that are useful in small organizations. More complex applications require at least some programming. For those more complex applications, you must choose the computer language in which you'll write it. Some of the same considerations that apply to the selection of a DBMS apply here, including the following:

» Languages have limitations. Choose one that has all the functionality you need.

» Clients sometimes have a language standard. Is their standard language adequate?

» Is your development team familiar with the chosen language?

» Is the language popular enough to have a large number of practitioners? Ongoing maintenance of your code depends on the availability of people who understand it.

With a clear idea of your task and the tools you'll use to perform it, you can now write detailed job descriptions for everyone who will have a part in the development effort. This important step eliminates any confusion and finger-pointing about who is responsible for what.

Reassessing feasibility

At this stage in the process, you probably have a clearer idea than ever of the assigned task and what it will take to accomplish it. This is a good time to reassess the feasibility of the project. Is it really doable, or are both you and your client too optimistic in thinking that you can achieve everything in the Statement of Requirements, given the DBMS, language, team, budget, and time that you have decided upon?

If the job is not really feasible, it is much better to speak up now than to plunge ahead, burn through your budget and your scheduled time, only to fail to deliver a satisfactory product. At this point, when not much has been invested, you still have some flexibility. You may be able to reduce the scope of the project by deferring until later or even eliminating elements of the project that are not crucial. You may be able to negotiate for a schedule that is not quite so tight, or for a larger budget. You may even decide that the best course for all concerned would be to abandon the project.

At this point, you can bow out relatively gracefully. It will not cost either you or the client very much. If instead, you push ahead with a project that is doomed from the start, you could both suffer substantial loss, both monetarily and in terms of reputation. Making the correct decision here is of critical importance.

Documenting the Evaluation phase

As you should do for every phase, document the steps you took in evaluating development tools such as DBMSs and languages. Place the job descriptions you wrote up with the documentation. Document the feasibility analysis, the conclusions you came to, and the adjustments to the task scope, budget, and schedule that you made, if any.

Design phase

Up until this point, the project has primarily been analysis. Now you can make the transition from analysis to design. You most likely know everything you need to know about the problem and can now start designing the solution.

Here's an overview of what you do in the Design phase:

>> Translate the users' data model into an ER model. (Remember, the ER model is described in Chapter 2 of Book 1.)

>> Convert the ER model into a relational model.

>> Design the user interface.

>> Design the logic that performs the database application's functions.

>> Determine what might go wrong and include safeguards in the design to avoid problems.

>> Document the database design and the database application design thoroughly.

>> Obtain client signoff of the complete design.

Designing the database

Database design is all about models. Right now, you have the users' data model, which captures the users' concept of the structure of the database. It includes all the major types of objects, as well as the characteristics of those objects, and how the objects are related to one another. This is great as far as it goes. However, it's not sufficiently structured to be the basis for a database design. For that, you need to convert the users' data model into a model that conforms to one of the formal database modeling systems that have been developed over the past few decades.

The most popular of the formal modeling systems is the entity-relationship model, commonly referred to as the ER model, which I introduced in Book 1, Chapter 2. In the next chapter of this minibook, I describe the ER model in greater detail. With this model, you can capture what the users have told you into a well-defined form that you can then easily translate into a relational database.

As you convert the users' data model into an ER model, you need to make decisions that affect how that conversion is made. Make sure you document your reasoning for why you do things the way you do. At some later time, someone is going to have to modify, update, or add to the database you're building. That person will need all possible information about why the system is designed the way it is. Take the time to document your reasoning as well as documenting the model itself.

After you have the system in the form of an ER model, it's easy to convert into a relational model. The relational model is something that your DBMS understands, and you can create the database directly from it.

The database application

After you have designed the database, the design task is only half done. You have a structure that you can now fill with data, but you do not yet have a tool for operating on that data. The tool you must design now is the database application.

The database application is the part of the total system that interacts with the user. It creates everything that the user sees on the screen. It senses and responds to every time the user presses a key or uses the mouse. It prints every report that is read by the user's coworkers. From the standpoint of the user, the database application *is* the system.

In designing the database application, you must ensure that it enables the users to do everything that the Statement of Requirements promises that they'll be able to do. It must also present a user interface that is understandable and easy to use. The functions of the system must appear in logical positions on the screen, and the user must easily grasp how to perform all the functions that the application provides.

What functions must the application perform, pray tell? Using the DBMS and language that you chose — or that was chosen for you by the client — how will you implement those functions? At this point, you must conceive of and map out the logical flow of the application. Make sure you know exactly how each function will be performed.

REMEMBER

Aside from mapping out all the functions that the application will perform, you must also think about protecting the database from inadvertent or intentional harm. People make mistakes. Sometimes they press the wrong key and perform an operation they really didn't want to perform. Sometimes they enter incorrect data. Sometimes they even want to mess up the database on purpose. You need to design the application in such a way that minimizes the damage that such actions cause. Anticipate that someone might make an inappropriate keystroke, or enter a wrong value, or delete something that should not be deleted. If you anticipate such problems, you can incorporate recovery procedures that will restore things to their proper state.

Documenting the Design phase

The final part of the Design phase is — you guessed it — to document everything carefully and completely. The documentation should be so complete that a new development team could come in and implement the system without asking you a single question about the analysis and design efforts that you have just completed. Take the completed design document to the client and get him to sign it, signifying that he understands your design and authorizes you to build it.

REMEMBER

It is critically important to keep the client informed of what you are doing, every step of the way. This gives the client a sense of ownership in the decisions that are made, and makes it less likely that the client will experience an unpleasant surprise when you deliver the final product. The client will know in advance what you intend to deliver and will feel as if he had a major part in shaping its development and its final form.

Implementation phase

Many nondevelopers believe that developing a database and application is synonymous with writing the code to implement them. By now, you should realize that there is much more to developing a database system than that. In fact, writing the code is only a minor fraction of the total effort. However, it is a very important minor fraction! The best planning and design in the world would not be of much use if they did not lead to the building of an actual database and its associated application.

In the Implementation phase, you

>> **Build the database structure.** In the following chapters of Book 2, I describe how to create a relational model, based on the ER model that you derive from the users' data model. The relational model consists of major elements called *relations*, which have properties called *attributes* and are linked to other relations in the model. You build the structure of your database by converting the model's relations to tables in the database, whose columns correspond to the relation's attributes. You implement the links between tables that correspond to the links between the model's relations. Ultimately, those tables and the links between them are constructed with SQL.

>> **Build the database application.** Building the database application consists of constructing the screens that the user will see and interact with. It also involves creating the formats for any printed reports and writing program code to make any calculations or perform database operations such as adding data to a table, changing the data in a table, deleting data from a table, or retrieving data from a table.

>> **Generate user documentation and maintenance programmer documentation.** I'm repeating myself, but I can't emphasize enough the importance of creating and updating documentation at each phase.

Final Documentation and Testing phase

Documenting the database is relatively easy because most DBMS products do it for you. You can retrieve the documentation that the DBMS creates at any time, or print it out to add to the project records. You definitely need to print at least one copy for that purpose.

Documenting a database application calls for some real work on your part. Application documentation comes in two forms, aimed at two potential audiences:

>> You must create user documentation that describes all the functions the application is capable of and how to perform them.

>> You must create maintenance documentation aimed at the developers who will be supporting the system in the future. Typically, those maintenance programmers will be people other than the members of your team. You must make your documentation so complete that a person completely unfamiliar with the development effort will be able to understand what you did and why you did it that way. Program code must be heavily documented with comments in addition to the descriptions and instructions that you write in documents separate from the program code.

The testing and documentation phase includes the following tasks:

>> Giving your completed system to an independent testing entity to test it for functionality, ease of use, bugs, and compatibility with all the platforms it's supposed to run on.

>> Generating final documentation.

>> Delivering the completed (and tested) system to the client and receiving signed acceptance.

>> Celebrating!

Testing the system with sample data

After you have built and documented a database system, it may seem like you are finished and you can enjoy a well-deserved vacation. I'm all in favor of vacations, but you're not quite finished yet. The system needs to be rigorously tested, and that testing needs to be done by someone who does not think the same way you do. After the system becomes operational, users are sure to do things to it that you never imagined, including making combinations of selections that you didn't foresee, entering values into fields that make no sense, and doing things backward and upside down. There is no telling what they will do. Whatever unexpected thing the user does, you want the system to respond in a way that protects the database and guides the user into making appropriate input actions.

It is hard to build into a system protections against problems that you can't foresee. For that reason, before you turn the system over to your client, you must have an independent tester try to make it fail. The tester performs a functional test to see that the system does everything it is supposed to do. Also, the tester runs it on all the types of computers and all the operating systems that it is supposed to run on. If it is a web-based application, it needs to be tested for compatibility with all popular browsers. In addition, the tester needs to do illogical things that a user might do to see how the system reacts. If it crashes, or responds in some other unhelpful way, you'll have to modify your implementation so it will prompt the user with helpful responses.

Quite often, when you modify a database or application to fix a problem, the modification will cause another problem. So after such a modification, the entire system must be retested to make sure that no new problems have been introduced. You might have to go through several iterations of testing and modification before you have a system that you can be very confident will operate properly under all possible conditions.

Finalizing the documentation

While the independent tester is trying everything conceivable (and several things inconceivable) to make your product fail, you and your team still aren't ready to take that well-deserved vacation. Now is the time for you to put your documentation into final form. You have been carefully documenting every step along the way of every phase. At this time, you need to organize all that documentation because it is an important part of what you'll deliver to the client.

User documentation will probably consist of both context-sensitive help that is part of the application and a printed user's manual. The context-sensitive help is best for answers to quick questions that arise when a person is in the middle of trying to perform a function. The printed manual is best as a general reference and as an overview of the entire system. Both are important and deserve your full attention.

Delivering the results (and celebrating)

When the testing and documentation phase is complete, all that is left to do is formally deliver the system, complete with full documentation, to your client. This usually triggers the client's final payment to you if you are an independent contractor. If you are an employee, it will most likely result in a favorable entry in your personnel file that may help you get a raise at your next review.

Now you and your team can celebrate!

Maintenance phase

Just because you've delivered the system on time and on budget, have celebrated, and have collected your final payment for the job does not mean that your responsibilities are over. Even if the independent tester has done a fantastic job of trying to make the system fail, after delivery it may still harbor latent bugs that show up weeks, months, or even years later. You may be obligated to fix those bugs at no charge, depending on your contractual agreement with the client.

Even if no bugs are found, you may still have some ongoing responsibility. After all, no one understands the system as well as you do. As time goes on, your client's needs will change. Perhaps she'll need additional functions. Perhaps she'll want to migrate to newer, more powerful hardware. Perhaps she'll want to upgrade to a newer operating system. All of these possibilities may require modifications to the database application, and you're in the best position to do those modifications, based on your prior knowledge.

This kind of maintenance can be good because it is revenue that you don't have to go out hunting for. It can also be bad because it ties you down to technology that, over time, you may consider obsolete and no longer of interest. Be aware that you may have at least an ethical obligation to provide this kind of ongoing support.

Every software development project that gets delivered has a Maintenance phase. You may be required to provide the following services during that phase:

>> Fix latent bugs discovered after the client has accepted the system. Often the client doesn't pay extra for this work, on the assumption that the bugs are your responsibility. However, if you write your contract correctly, their signoff at acceptance protects you from perpetual bug fixing.

>> Provide enhancements and updates requested by the client. This is a good, recurring income source.

Chapter **2**

Building a Database Model

A successful database system must satisfy the needs of a diverse group of people. This group includes the folks who'll actually enter data and retrieve results, but it also includes a host of others. People at various levels of management, for example, may rely on reports generated by the system. People in other functional areas, such as sales or manufacturing, may use the products of the system, such as reports or bar code labels. The information technology (IT) people who set overall data processing standards for the organization may also weigh in on how the system is constructed and the form of the outputs it will produce. When designing a successful database system, consider the needs of all these groups — and possibly quite a few others as well. You'll have to combine all these inputs into a consensus that database creators call the *users' data model*.

Back in Book 1, I mention how important it is to talk to all the possible stakeholders in a project so you can discover for yourself what is important to them. In this chapter, I revisit that topic and go into a bit more depth by discussing specific cases typical of the kinds of concerns that stakeholders might have. The ultimate goal in all this talking is to have the stakeholders arrive at a consensus that they can all support. If you're going to develop a database system, you want everybody to be in agreement about what that system should be and what it should do, as well as what it should *not* be and not do.

Finding and Listening to Interested Parties

When you're assigned the task of building a database system, one of the first things that you must do is determine who all the interested parties are and what their level of involvement is.

Human relations is an important part of your job here. When the views of different people in the organization conflict with each other, as they often do, you have to decide on a path to follow. You cannot simply take the word of the person with the most impressive title. Often unofficial lines of authority in an organization (which are the ones that really count) differ significantly from what the official organization chart might show.

Take into account the opinions and ideas of the person you report to, the database users, the IT organization that governs database projects at the company where you're doing the project, and the bigwigs who have a stake in the database system.

Your immediate supervisor

Generally, if you are dealing with a medium- to large-sized organization, the person who contacts you about doing the development project is a middle manager. This person typically has the authority to find and recommend a developer for a needed application, but may not have the budget authority to approve the total development cost.

The person who hired you is probably your closest ally in the organization. She wants you to succeed because it will reflect badly on her if you don't. Be sure that you have a good understanding of what she wants and how important her stated desires are to her. It could be that she has merely been tasked with obtaining a developer and does not have strong opinions about what is to be developed. On the other hand, she may be directly responsible for what the application delivers and may have a very specific idea of what is needed. In addition to hearing what she tells you, you must also be able to read between the lines and determine how much *importance* she ascribes to what she is saying.

The users

After the manager who hires you, the next group of people you are likely to meet are the future hands-on users of the system you will build. They enter the data that populates the database tables. They run the queries that answer questions that they and others in the organization may have. They generate the reports that are circulated to coworkers and managers. They are the ones who come into closest contact with what you have built.

In general, these people are already accustomed to dealing with the data that will be in your system, or data very much like it. They are either using a manual system, based on paper records, or a computer-based system that your system will replace. In either case, they have become comfortable with a certain look and feel for forms and reports.

TIP

To ease the transition from the old system to the new one you are building, you'll probably want to make your forms and reports look as much like the old ones as possible. Your system may present new information, but if it's presented in a familiar way, the users may accept it more readily and start making effective use of it sooner.

The people who'll use your system probably have very definite ideas about what they like and what they don't like about the system they are currently using. In your new system, you'll want to eliminate the aspects of the old system that they don't like, and retain the things they do like. It is critical for the success of your system that the hands-on users like it. Even if your system does everything that the Statement of Requirements (which I tell you about in Chapter 1 of this minibook) specifies, it will surely be a failure if the everyday users just don't like it. Aside from providing them with what they want, it is also important to build rapport with these people during the development effort. Make sure they agree with what you are doing, every step along the way.

The standards organization

Large organizations with existing software applications have probably standardized on a particular hardware platform and operating system. These choices can constrain which database management system you use because not all DBMSs are available on all platforms. The standards organization may even have a preferred DBMS. This is almost certain to be true if they already support other database applications.

Supporting database applications on an ongoing basis requires a significant infrastructure. That infrastructure includes DBMS software, periodic DBMS software upgrades, training of users, and training of support personnel. If the organization already supports applications based on one DBMS, it makes sense to leverage that investment by mandating that all future database applications use the same DBMS. If the application you have been brought in to create would best be built upon a foundation of a different DBMS, you're going to have to justify the increased support burden. Often this can be done only if the currently supported DBMS is downright incapable of doing the job.

Aside from your choice of DBMS, the standards people might also have something to say about your coding practices. They might have standards requiring structured programming and modular development, as well as very specific documentation guidelines. Where such standards and guidelines exist, they are usually all to the good. You just have to make sure that you comply with all of them. Your product will doubtless be better for it anyway.

Smaller organizations probably will *not* have any IT people enforcing data processing standards and guidelines. In those cases, you must act as if *you* were the IT people. Try to understand what would be best for the client organization in the long term. Make your selection of DBMS, coding style, and documentation with those long-term considerations in mind, rather than what would be most expedient for the current project. Be sure that your clients are aware of why you make the choices you do. They may want to participate in the decision, and at any rate, will appreciate the fact that you have their long-term interests at heart.

Upper management

Unless you're dealing with a very small organization, the manager who hired you for this project is not the highest-ranking person who has an interest in what you'll be producing. It's likely that the manager with whom you are dealing must carry your proposals to a higher level for approval. It's important to find out who that higher-up is and get a sense of what he wants your application to accomplish for the organization. Be aware that this person may not carry the most prestigious title in the organization, and may not even be on a direct line on the company organization chart to the person who hired you. Talk to the troops on the front line, the people who'll actually be using your application. They can tell you where the real power resides. After you find out what is most important to this key person, make sure that it's included in the final product.

Building Consensus

The interested parties in the application you are developing are called *stakeholders*, and you must talk to at least one representative of each group.

Just so you know: After you talk to them, you're likely to be confused. Some people insist that one feature is crucial and they don't care about a second feature. Others insist that the second feature is very important and won't even mention the first. Some will want the application to look and act one way, and others will want an entirely different look and feel. Some people consider one particular report to be the most important thing about the application, and other people don't care about reports at all, but only about the application's *ad hoc* query ability. It's just not practical to expect everyone in the client organization to want the same things and to ascribe the same levels of importance to those things.

Your job is to bring some order out of this chaos. You'll have to transform all these diverse points of view into a consensus that everyone can agree upon. This requires compromise on the part of the stakeholders. You want to build an application that meets the needs of the organization in the best possible way.

THE THREE-OPTION PROPOSAL

Sometimes, it's not easy to get all the stakeholders to agree on what they want. Some might want more features, and others might want lower cost. One way to break this logjam is to come up with three proposals for the project rather than just one. Present the three proposals to your clients and let them decide which one they want. Here's what the three proposals should be:

- A **minimal project** that includes all the elements that everyone agrees are absolutely mandatory. This is also the lowest-cost option in terms of time and dollars.

- A **medium project** that includes everything in the first option, plus additional features that most of the stakeholders believe would be valuable. This is a medium-cost option in terms of time and dollars.

- A **maximum project** that includes everything that everyone wants.

Typically, the third option is rejected immediately because it is too expensive and takes too long to complete. Next, the first option is usually rejected because it is not really satisfactory to anybody. The stakeholders will then most likely agree to go ahead with the medium project, perhaps with some minor modifications. Be sure to recalculate the time and cost estimates for any such changes to your original proposal.

Gauging what people want

As the developer, it should not be your job to resolve conflicts among the stakeholders regarding what the proposed system should do. However, as the technical person who is building it and has no vested interest in exactly what it should look like or what it should do, you may be the only person who can break the gridlock. This means that negotiating skills are a valuable addition to your toolkit of technical know-how.

Find out who cares passionately about what the system will provide, and whose opinions carry the most weight. The decisions that are ultimately made about project scope, functionality, and appearance will affect the amount of time and budget that will be needed to complete development.

Arriving at a consensus

Somehow, the conflicting input you receive from all the stakeholders must be combined into a uniform vision of what the proposed system should be and do. You may need to ask disagreeing groups of people to sit down together and arrive at a compromise that is at least satisfactory to all, if not everything they had wished for.

To specify a system that can be built within the time and budget constraints that have been set out for the project, some people may have to give up features they would like to have, but which are not absolutely necessary. As an interested but impartial outsider, you may be able to serve as a facilitator in the discussion.

After the stakeholders have agreed upon what they want the new database system to do for them, you need to transform this consensus into a model that represents their thinking. The model should include all the items of interest. It should describe how these items relate to each other. It should also describe in detail the attributes of the items of interest. This users' data model will be the basis for a more formal Entity-Relationship (ER) model that you will then convert into a relational model. I cover both the users' data model and the ER model in Chapter 2 of Book 1.

Building a Relational Model

Newcomers to database design sometimes get confused when listening to old-timers talk. This is due to the historical fact that those old-timers come out of three distinct traditions, each with its own set of terms for things. The three traditions are the relational tradition, the flat file tradition, and the personal computer tradition.

Reviewing the three database traditions

The relational tradition had its beginnings in a paper published in 1970 by Dr. E.F. Codd, who was at that time employed by IBM. In that paper, Dr. Codd gave names to the major constituents of the relational model. The major elements of the relational model correspond closely to the major elements of the ER model (see Book 1, Chapter 2), making it fairly easy to translate one into the other.

In the relational model, items that people can identify and that they consider important enough to track are called *relations*. (For those of you keeping score, *relations* in the relational model are similar to *entities* in the ER model. Relations have certain properties, called *attributes*, which correspond to the attributes in the ER model.)

Relations can be represented in the form of two-dimensional tables. Each column in the table holds the information about a single attribute. The rows of the table are called *tuples*. Each tuple corresponds to an individual instance of a relation. Figure 2-1 shows an example of a relation, with attributes and tuples. Attributes are the columns: Title, Author, ISBN, and Pub. Date. The tuples are the rows.

Title	Author	ISBN	Pub. Date
The Road To Reality	Roger Penrose	0679454438	2004
Saturn Rukh	Robert L. Forward	0312863217	1997
Red Mars	Kim Stanley Robinson	0553092049	1993
The Artful Universe	John D. Barrow	0198539967	1995

FIGURE 2-1:
The BOOK
relation.

I mentioned that current database practitioners come out of three different traditions, the relational tradition being one of them. A second group consists of people who were dealing with flat files before the relational model became popular. Their terms *files, fields,* and *records* correspond to what Dr. Codd called *relations, attributes,* and *tuples*. The third group, the PC community, came to databases by way of the electronic spreadsheet. They used the spreadsheet terms *tables, columns,* and *rows,* to mean the same things as *files, fields,* and *records*. Table 2-1 shows how to translate terminology from the three segments of the database community.

TABLE 2-1

Describing the Elements of a Database

Relational community says . . .	Relation	Attribute	Tuple
Flat-file community says . . .	File	Field	Record
PC community says . . .	Table	Column	Row

Don't be surprised if you hear database veterans mix these terms in the course of explaining or describing something. They may use them interchangeably within a single sentence. For example, one might say, "The value of the TELEPHONE attribute in the fifth record of the CUSTOMER table is Null."

Knowing what a relation is

Despite the casual manner in which database old-timers use the words *relation*, *file*, and *table* interchangeably, a relation is not exactly the same thing as a file or table. Relations were defined by a database theoretician, and thus the definition is very precise. The words *file* and *table*, on the other hand, are in general use and are often much more loosely defined. When I use these terms in this book, I mean them in the strict sense, as alternates for relation. That said, what's a relation? A *relation* is a two-dimensional table that must satisfy all the following criteria:

>> Each cell in the table must contain a single value, if it contains a value at all.

>> All the entries in any column must be of the same kind. For example, if a column contains a telephone number in one row, it must contain telephone numbers in all rows that contain a value in that column.

>> Each column has a unique name.

>> The order of the columns is not significant.

>> The order of the rows is not significant.

>> No two rows can be identical.

REMEMBER

A table qualifies as a relation if and only if it meets all the above criteria. A table that fails to meet one or more of them might still be considered a table in the loose sense of the word, but it is not a relation, and thus not a table in the strict sense of the word.

Functional dependencies

Functional dependencies are relationships between or among attributes. For example, two attributes of the VENDOR relation are State and Zipcode. If you know a vendor's zip code, you can determine the vendor's state by a simple table lookup because each zip code appears in only one state. Therefore, State is *functionally dependent* on Zipcode. Another way of describing this situation is to say that Zipcode *determines* State, thus Zipcode is a *determinant* of State. Functional dependencies are shown diagrammatically as follows:

Zipcode ⇨ State (Zipcode determines State)

Sometimes, a single attribute may not be a determinant, but when it is combined with one or more other attributes, the group of them collectively *is* a determinant. Suppose you receive a bill from your local department store. It would list the bill number, your customer number, what you bought, how many you bought, the unit price, and the extended price for all of them. The bill you receive represents a row in the BILLS table of the store's database. It would be of the form

```
BILL(BillNo, CustNo, ProdNo, ProdName, UnitPrice, Quantity, ExtPrice)
```

The combination of UnitPrice and Quantity determines ExtPrice.

(UnitPrice, Quantity) ⇨ ExtPrice

Thus, ExtPrice is functionally dependent upon UnitPrice and Quantity.

Keys

A *key* is a group of one or more attributes that uniquely identifies a tuple in a relation. For example, VendorID is a key of the VENDOR relation. VendorID determines all the other attributes in the relation. All keys are determinants, but not all determinants are keys. In the BILL relation, (UnitPrice, Quantity) is a determinant because it determines ExtPrice. However, (UnitPrice, Quantity) is not a key. It does not uniquely identify its tuple because another line in the relation might have the same values for Price and Quantity. The key of the BILL relation is BillNo, which identifies one particular bill.

Sometimes it is hard to tell whether a determinant qualifies as a key. In the BILL case, I consider BillNo to be a key, based on the assumption that bill numbers are not duplicated. If this assumption is valid, BillNo is a unique identifier of a bill and qualifies as a key. When you are defining the keys for the relations that you build, you must make sure that your keys uniquely identify each tuple (row) in the relation. Often you don't have to worry about this because your DBMS will automatically assign a unique key to each row of the table as it is added.

Being Aware of the Danger of Anomalies

Just because a database table meets the qualifications to be a relation does not mean that it is well designed. In fact, bad relations are incredibly easy to create. By a bad relation, I mean one prone to errors or confusing to users. The best way to illustrate a bad relation is to show you an example.

Suppose an automotive service shop specializes in transmissions, brakes, and suspension systems. Let's say that Tyson is the lead mechanic for transmissions, Dave is the lead mechanic for brakes, and Keith is the lead mechanic for suspension systems. Tyson works out of the Alabama Avenue location, Dave works at the Perimeter Road shop, and Keith operates out of the Main Street garage. You could summarize this information with a relation MECHANICS, as shown in Figure 2-2.

Mechanic	Specialty	Location
Tyson	Transmissions	Alabama Avenue
Dave	Brakes	Perimeter Road
Keith	Suspensions	Main Street

FIGURE 2-2:
The MECHANICS
relation.

This table qualifies as a relation, for the following reasons. Each cell contains only one value. All entries in each column are of the same kind — all names, or all specialties, or all locations. Each column has a unique name. The order of the columns and rows is not significant. If the order were changed, no information would be lost. And finally, no two rows are identical.

So what's the problem? Problems can arise when things change, and things always change, sooner or later. Problems caused by changes are known as *modification anomalies* and come in different types, two of which I describe here:

>> **Deletion anomaly:** You lose information that you don't want to lose, as a result of a deletion operation. Suppose that Dave decides to go back to school and study computer science. When he quits his job, you can delete the second row in the table shown in Figure 2-2. If you do, however, you lose more than the fact that Dave is the brakes mechanic. You also lose the fact that brake service takes place at the Perimeter Road location.

>> **Insertion anomaly:** You can insert new data only when other data is included with it. Suppose you want to start working on engines at the Alabama Avenue facility. You cannot record that fact until an engine mechanic is hired to work there. This is an *insertion anomaly*. Because Mechanic is the key to this relation, you cannot insert a new tuple into the relation unless it has a value in the Mechanic column.

REMEMBER

If modification anomalies are even remotely possible in a database, more than likely they're going to occur. If they occur, they can seriously degrade a database's usefulness. They may even cause users to draw incorrect conclusions from the results of queries they pose to the database.

Eliminating anomalies

When Dr. Codd created the relational model, he recognized the possibility of data corruption due to modification anomalies. To address this problem, he devised the concept of *normal forms*. Each normal form is defined by a set of rules, similar to the rules stated previously for qualification as a relation. Anything that follows *those* particular rules is a relation, and by definition is in First Normal Form (1NF). Subsequent normal forms add progressively more qualifications. As I discuss in the preceding section, tables in 1NF are subject to certain modification anomalies. Codd's Second Normal Form (2NF) removes these anomalies, but the possibility of others still remains. Codd foresaw some of those anomalies and defined Third Normal Form (3NF) to deal with them. Subsequent research uncovered the possibility of progressively more obscure anomalies, and a succession of normal forms was devised to eliminate them. Boyce–Codd Normal Form (BCNF), Fourth Normal Form (4NF), Fifth Normal Form (5NF), and Domain/Key Normal Form (DKNF) provide increasing levels of protection against modification anomalies.

It is instructive to look at the normal forms to gain an insight into the kinds of anomalies that can occur, and how normalization eliminates the possibility of such anomalies.

REMEMBER

For a relation to be in Second Normal Form, every nonkey attribute must be dependent on the entire key.

To start, consider the Second Normal Form. Suppose Tyson receives certification to repair brakes and spends some of his time at the Perimeter Road garage fixing brakes as well as continuing to do his old job repairing transmissions at the Alabama Avenue shop. This leads to the table shown in Figure 2-3.

FIGURE 2-3:
The modified
MECHANICS
relation.

Mechanic	Specialty	Location
Tyson	Transmissions	Alabama Avenue
Tyson	Brakes	Perimeter Road
Dave	Brakes	Perimeter Road
Keith	Suspensions	Main Street

This table still qualifies as a relation, but the Mechanic column no longer is a key because it does not uniquely determine a row. However, the combination of Mechanic and Specialty does qualify as a determinant and as a key.

(Mechanic, Specialty) ⇨ Location

This looks fine, but there is a problem. What if Tyson decides to work full time on brakes, and not fix transmissions any longer. If I delete the Tyson/Transmissions/ Alabama row, I not only remove the fact that Tyson works on transmissions, but also lose the fact that transmission work is done at the Alabama shop. This is a deletion anomaly. This problem is caused by the fact that Specialty is a determinant, but is not a key. It is only part of a key.

Specialty ⇨ Location

I can meet the requirement of every nonkey attribute depending on the entire key by breaking up the MECHANICS relation into two relations, MECH–SPEC and SPEC–LOC. This is illustrated in Figure 2-4.

FIGURE 2-4:
The MECHANICS relation has been broken into two relations, MECH-SPEC and SPEC-LOC.

Table MECH-SPEC

Mechanic	Specialty
Tyson	Transmissions
Tyson	Brakes
Dave	Brakes
Keith	Suspensions

Table SPEC-LOC

Specialty	Location
Transmissions	Alabama Avenue
Brakes	Perimeter Road
Suspensions	Main Street

The old MECHANICS relation had problems because it dealt with more than one idea. It dealt with the idea of the specialties of the mechanics, and it also dealt with the idea of where various specialties are performed. By breaking the MECHANICS relation into two, each one of which deals with only one idea, the modification anomalies disappear. Mechanic and Specialty together comprise a composite key of the MECH–SPEC relation, and all the nonkey attributes depend on the entire key because there *are* no nonkey attributes. Specialty is the key of the SPEC–LOC relation, and all of the nonkey attributes (Location) depend on the entire key, which in this case is Specialty. Now if Tyson decides to work full time on brakes, the Tyson/Transmissions row can be removed from the MECH–SPEC relation. The fact that transmission work is done at the Alabama garage is still recorded in the SPEC–LOC relation.

To qualify as being in second normal form, a relation must qualify as being in first normal form, plus all non-key attributes must depend on the entire key. MECH-SPEC and SPEC-LOC both qualify as being in 2NF.

A relation in Second Normal Form could still harbor anomalies. Suppose you are concerned about your cholesterol intake and want to track the relative levels of cholesterol in various foods. You might construct a table named LIPIDLEVEL such as the one shown in Figure 2-5.

FoodItem	FoodType	Cholesterol
apple	fruit	none
beefsteak	red meat	high
hen's egg	egg	very high
salmon	fish	medium

FIGURE 2-5:
The LIPIDLEVEL
relation.

This relation is in First Normal Form because it satisfies the requirements of a relation. And because it has a single attribute key (FoodItem), it is automatically in Second Normal Form also — all nonkey attributes are dependent on the entire key.

Nonetheless, there is still the chance of an anomaly. What if you decide to eliminate all beef products from your diet? If you delete the Beefsteak row from the table, you not only eliminate beefsteak, but you also lose the fact that red meat is high in cholesterol. This fact might be important to you if you are considering substituting some other red meat such as pork, bison, or lamb for the beef you no longer eat. This is a deletion anomaly. There is a corresponding insertion anomaly. You cannot add a FoodType of Poultry, for example, and assign it a Cholesterol value of High until you actually enter in a specific FoodItem of the Poultry type.

The problem this time is once again a matter of keys and dependencies. FoodType depends on FoodItem. If the FoodItem is Apple, the FoodType must be Fruit. If the FoodItem is Salmon, the FoodType must be Fish. Similarly, Cholesterol depends on FoodType. If the FoodType is Egg, the Cholesterol value is Very High. This is a *transitive dependency* — called thus because one item depends on a second, which in turn depends on a third.

FoodItem ⇨ FoodType ⇨ Cholesterol

Transitive dependencies are a source of modification anomalies. You can eliminate the anomalies by eliminating the transitive dependency. Breaking the table into two tables, each one of which embodies a single idea, does the trick.

Figure 2-6 shows the resulting tables, which are now in Third Normal Form (3NF). A relation is in 3NF if it qualifies as being in 2NF and in addition has no transitive dependencies.

Table ITEM-TYPE

FoodItem	FoodType
apple	fruit
beefsteak	red meat
hen's egg	egg
salmon	fish

Table TYPE-CHOL

FoodType	Cholesterol
fruit	none
red meat	high
egg	very high
fish	medium

FIGURE 2-6: The ITEM-TYPE relation and the TYPE-CHOL relation.

Now if you delete the Beefsteak row from the ITEM-TYPE relation, the fact that red meat is high in cholesterol is retained in the TYPE-CHOL relation. You can add poultry to the TYPE-CHOL relation, even though you don't have a specific type of poultry in the ITEM-TYPE relation.

Examining the higher normal forms

Boyce-Codd Normal Form (BCNF), Fourth Normal Form (4NF), and Fifth Normal Form (5NF) each eliminate successively more obscure types of anomalies. In all likelihood, you might never encounter the types of anomalies they remove. There is one higher normal form, however, that is worth discussing: the Domain/Key Normal Form (DKNF), which is the only normal form that *guarantees* that a database contains no modification anomalies. If you want to be absolutely certain that your database is anomaly-free, put it into DKNF.

Happily, Domain/Key Normal Form is easier to understand than most of the other normal forms. You need to understand only three things: constraints, keys, and domains.

REMEMBER

A relation is in Domain/Key Normal Form if every constraint on the relation is a logical consequence of the definition of keys and domains:

>> A *constraint* is a rule that restricts the static values that attributes may assume. The rule must be precise enough for you to tell whether the attribute follows the rule. A static value is one that does not vary with time.

>> A *key* is a unique identifier of a tuple.

>> The *domain* of an attribute is the set of all values that the attribute can take.

If enforcing key and domain restrictions on a table causes all constraints to be met, the table is in DKNF. It is also guaranteed to be free of all modification anomalies.

As an example of putting a table into DKNF, look again at the LIPIDLEVEL relation in Figure 2-5. You can analyze it as follows:

LIPIDLEVEL(FoodItem, FoodType, Cholesterol)

Key: FoodItem

Constraints: FoodItem ⇨ FoodType

FoodType ⇨ Cholesterol

Cholesterol level may be (None, Low, Medium, High, Very High)

This relation is not in DKNF. It is not even in 3NF. However, you can put it into DKNF by making all constraints a logical consequence of domains and keys. You can make the Cholesterol constraint a logical consequence of domains by defining the domain of Cholesterol to be (None, Low, Medium, High, Very High). The constraint FoodItem ⇨ FoodType is a logical consequence of keys because Food-Item is a key. Those were both easy. One more constraint to go! You can handle the third constraint by making FoodType a key. The way to do this is to break the LIPIDLEVEL relation into two relations, one having FoodItem as its key and the other having FoodType as its key. This is exactly what I did in Figure 2-6. Putting LIPIDLEVEL into 3NF put it into DKNF at the same time.

REMEMBER

Every relation in DKNF is, by necessity, also in 3NF. However, the reverse is not true. A relation can be in 3NF and not satisfy the criteria for DKNF.

Here is the new description for this system:

Domain Definitions:

FoodItem in CHAR(30)

FoodType in CHAR(30)

Cholesterol level may be (None, Low, Medium, High, Very High)

CHAR(30) defines the domain of FoodItem and also of FoodType, stating that they may be character strings up to 30 characters in length. The domain of cholesterol has exactly five values, which are None, Low, Medium, High, and Very High.

Relation and Key Definitions:

ITEM-TYPE (FoodItem, FoodType)

Key: FoodItem

TYPE-CHOL (FoodType, Cholesterol)

Key: FoodType

All constraints are a logical consequence of keys and domains.

The Database Integrity versus Performance Tradeoff

In the previous section, I talk about some of the problems that can arise with database relations, and how they can be solved through normalization. I point out that the ultimate in normalization is Domain/Key Normal Form, which provides solid protection from the data corruption that can occur due to modification anomalies. It might seem that whenever you create a database, you should always put all its tables into DKNF. This, however, is not true.

When you guarantee a database's freedom from anomalies by putting all its tables into DKNF, you do so at a cost. Why? When you make your original unnormalized design, you group attributes together into relations because they have something in common. If you normalize some of those tables by breaking them into multiple tables, you are separating attributes that would normally be grouped together. This can degrade your performance on retrievals if you want to use those attributes together. You'll have to combine these now-separated attributes again before proceeding with the rest of the retrieval operation.

Consider an example. Suppose you are the secretary of a club made up of people located all around the United States who share a hobby. It is your job to send them a monthly newsletter as well as notices of various sorts. You have a database consisting of a single relation, named MEMBERS.

MEMBERS(MemID, Fname, Lname, Street, City, State, Zip)

Key: MemID

Functional Dependencies:

MemID ⇨ all nonkey attributes

Zip ⇨ State

This relation is not in DKNF because State is dependent on Zip and Zip is not a key. If you know a person's zip code, you can do a simple table lookup and you'll know what state that person lives in.

You could put the database into DKNF by breaking the MEMBERS table into two tables as follows:

MEM-ZIP(MemID, Fname, Lname, Street, City, Zip)

ZIP-STATE(Zip, State)

MemID is the key of MEM–ZIP and Zip is the key of ZIP–STATE. The database is now in DKNF, but consider what you have gained and what you have lost:

>> **What you have gained:** In MEMBERS, if I delete the last club member in zip code 92027, I lose the fact that zip code 92027 is in California. However, in the normalized database, that information is retained in ZIP-STATE when the last member with that zip code is removed from MEM-ZIP.

In MEMBERS, if you want to add the fact that zip code 07110 is in New Jersey, you can't, until you have a member living in that zip code. The normalized database handles this nicely by allowing you to add that state and zip code to ZIP-STATE, even though no members in the MEM-ZIP table live there.

>> **What you have lost:** Because the primary purpose of this database is to facilitate mailings to members, every time a mailing is made, the MEM-ZIP table and the ZIP-STATE table have to be joined together to generate the mailing labels. This is an extra operation that would not be needed if the data were all kept in a single MEMBERS table.

>> **What you care about:** Considering the purpose of this database, the club secretary probably doesn't care what state a particular zip code is in if the club has no members in that zip code. She also probably doesn't care about adding zip codes where there are no members. In this case, both of the gains from normalization are of no value to the user. However, the cost of normalization is a genuine penalty. It will take longer for the address labels to print out based on the data in the normalized database than it would if they were stored in the unnormalized MEMBERS table. For this case, and others like it, normalization to DKNF does not make sense.

Chapter **3**

Balancing Performance and Correctness

There's a natural conflict between the performance of a database and its correctness. If you want to minimize the chance that incorrect or inappropriate data ends up in a database, you must include safeguards against it. These safeguards take time and thus slow down operation.

Configuring a database to bypass data checks to achieve the highest possible performance may make the data it contains unreliable to the point of being unacceptable. Conversely, making the database as immune to corruption as possible by checking every byte of data could reduce performance to the point of being unacceptable. A database designer must aim for that sweet spot somewhere in the middle where performance is high enough to be acceptable, and the few data errors that occur do not significantly affect the conclusions drawn from information retrieved. Some applications put the sweet spot closer to the performance end;

others put it closer to the reliability end. Each situation is potentially different and depends on what is most important to the stakeholders. To illustrate the considerations that apply when designing a database system, in this chapter I show you a fictional example, as well as discuss other factors you must consider when you're navigating the delicate balance between correctness and performance.

Designing a Sample Database

Suppose you have gone through all the steps to construct an efficient and reliable ER model for a database. The next step is to convert that ER model, which is a logical model, into a relational model, which maps to the physical structure of the database. Probably the easiest way to show this process is to use a fictional example.

Imagine a local auto repair business located in the small town of Springfield, owned and operated by the fictional Abraham "Abe" Hanks. Abe employs mechanics who perform repairs on the automobiles in the fleets of Abe's corporate customers. All of Abe's customers are corporations. Repair jobs are recorded in invoices, which include charges for parts and labor. Charges are itemized on separate lines on the invoices. The mechanics hold certifications in such specialty areas as brakes, transmissions, electrical systems, and engines. Abe buys parts from multiple suppliers. Multiple suppliers could potentially supply the same part.

The ER model for Honest Abe's

Figure 3-1 shows the Entity-Relationship (ER) model for Honest Abe's Fleet Auto Repair. (ER models — and their important role in database design — are covered in great detail in Book 1, Chapter 2.)

Take a look at the relationships.

>> A customer can make purchases on multiple invoices, but each invoice deals with one and only one customer.

>> An invoice can have multiple invoice lines, but each invoice line appears on one and only one invoice.

>> A mechanic can work on multiple jobs, each one represented by one invoice, but each invoice is the responsibility of one and only one mechanic.

>> A mechanic may have multiple certifications, but each certification belongs to one and only one mechanic.

>> Multiple suppliers can supply a given standard part, and multiple parts can be sourced by a single supplier.

>> One and only one part can appear on a single invoice line, and one and only one invoice line on an invoice can contain a given part.

>> One and only one standard labor charge can appear on a single invoice line, but a particular standard labor charge may apply to multiple invoice lines.

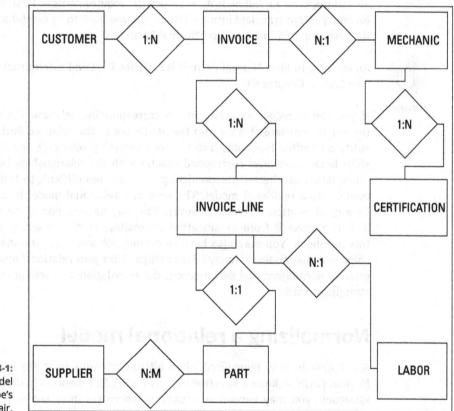

FIGURE 3-1:
The ER model
for Honest Abe's
Fleet Auto Repair.

After you have an ER model that accurately represents your target system, the next step is to convert the ER model into a relational model. The relational model is the direct precursor to a relational database.

Converting an ER model into a relational model

The first step in converting an ER model into a relational model is to understand how the terminology used for one relates to the terminology used for the other. In the ER model, we speak of *entities*, *attributes*, *identifiers*, and *relationships*. In the relational model, the primary items of concern are *relations*, *attributes*, *keys*, and *relationships*. How do these two sets of terms relate to each other?

In the ER model, entities are physical or conceptual objects that you want to keep track of. This sounds a lot like the definition of a relation. The difference is that for something to be a relation, it must satisfy the requirements of First Normal Form. An entity might translate into a relation, but you have to be careful to ensure that the resulting relation is in First Normal Form (1NF).

REMEMBER

An entity is in First Normal Form if it satisfies Dr. Codd's definition of a relation (see Book 1, Chapter 6).

If you can translate an entity into a corresponding relation, the attributes of the entity translate directly into the attributes of the relation. Furthermore, an entity's *identifier* translates into the corresponding relation's *key*. The relationships between entities correspond exactly with the relationships between relations. Based on these correspondences, it's not too difficult to translate an ER model into a relational model. The resulting relational model is not necessarily a good relational model, however. You may have to normalize the relations in it to protect it from modification anomalies, as spelled out in Chapter 2 of this minibook. You may also have to decompose any many-to-many relationships to simpler one-to-many relationships. After your relational model is appropriately normalized and decomposed, the translation to a relational database is straightforward.

Normalizing a relational model

A database is fully *normalized* when all the relations in it are in Domain/Key Normal Form — known affectionately as DKNF. As I mention in Chapter 2 of this minibook, you may encounter situations where you may not want to normalize all the way to DKNF. As a rule, however, it is best to normalize to DKNF and then check performance. Only if performance is unacceptable should you consider selective *denormalization* — going down the ladder from DKNF to a lower normal form — in order to speed things up.

REMEMBER

For a review of how normalization works, check out Chapter 2 in this minibook.

Consider the example system shown back in Figure 3-1, and then focus on one of the entities in the model. An important entity in the Honest Abe model is the CUSTOMER entity. Figure 3-2 shows a representation of the CUSTOMER entity (top) and the corresponding relation in the relational model (bottom).

The attributes of the CUSTOMER entity are listed in Figure 3-2. Figure 3-2 also shows the standard way of listing the attributes of a relation. The CustID attribute is underlined to signify that it is the key of the CUSTOMER relation. Every customer has a unique CustID number.

```
CUSTOMER
     CustID
     CustName
     StreetAddr
     City
     State
     PostalCode
     ContactName
     ContactPhone
     ContactEmail
```

CUSTOMER (CustID, CustName, Street Addr, City, State, PostalCode, ContactName, ContactPhone, ContactEmail)

One way to determine whether CUSTOMER is in DKNF is to see whether all constraints on the relation are the result of the definitions of domains and keys. An easier way, one that works well most of the time, is to see if the relation deals with more than one idea. It does, and thus cannot be in DKNF. One idea is the customer itself. CustID, CustName, StreetAddr, and City are primarily associated with this idea. Another idea is the geographic idea. As I mention back in Chapter 2 of this minibook, if you know the postal code of an address, you can find the state or province that contains that postal code. Finally, there is the idea of the customer's contact person. ContactName, ContactPhone, and ContactEmail are the attributes that cluster around this idea.

You can normalize the CUSTOMER relation by breaking it into three relations as follows:

CUSTOMER (CustID, CustName, StreetAddr, City, PostalCode, ContactName)

POSTAL (PostalCode, State)

CONTACT (ContactName, ContactPhone, ContactEmail)

These three relations are in DKNF. They also demonstrate a new idea about keys. The three relations are closely related to each other because they share attributes. The PostalCode attribute is contained in both the CUSTOMER and the POSTAL relations. The ContactName attribute is contained in both the CUSTOMER and the CONTACT relations. CustID is called the *primary key* of the CUSTOMER relation because it uniquely identifies each tuple in the relation. Similarly, PostalCode is the primary key of the POSTAL relation and ContactName is the primary key of the CONTACT relation.

In addition to being the primary key of the POSTAL relation, PostalCode is a *foreign key* in the CUSTOMER relation. A foreign key in a relation is an attribute that, although it is not the primary key of that relation, *does* match the primary key of another relation in the model. It provides a link between the two relations. In the same way, ContactName is a foreign key in the CUSTOMER relation as well as being the primary key of the CONTACT relation. An attribute need not be unique in a relation where it is serving as a foreign key, but it must be unique on the other end of the relationship where it is the primary key.

After you have normalized a relation into DKNF, as I did here with the original CUSTOMER relation, you should ask yourself whether full normalization makes sense in this specific case. Depending on how you plan to use the relations, you may want to denormalize somewhat to improve performance. In this example, you may want to fold the POSTAL relation back into the CUSTOMER relation if you frequently need to access your customers' complete address. On the other hand, it might make sense to keep CONTACT as a separate relation if you frequently refer to customer address information without specifically needing your primary contact at that company.

Handling binary relationships

In Book 1, Chapter 2, I describe the three kinds of binary relationships: one-to-one, one-to-many, and many-to-many. The simplest of these is the one-to-one relationship. In the Honest Abe model earlier in this chapter, I use the relationship between a part and an invoice line to illustrate a one-to-one relationship. Figure 3-3 shows the ER model of this relationship.

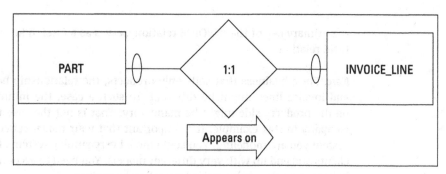

FIGURE 3-3:
The ER model of
PART: INVOICE_
LINE relationship.

The maximum cardinality diamond explicitly shows that this is a one-to-one relationship. The relationship is this: One PART connects to one INVOICE_LINE. The minimum cardinality oval at both ends of the PART:INVOICE_LINE relationship shows that it is possible to have a PART without an INVOICE_LINE, and it is also possible to have an INVOICE_LINE without an associated PART. A part on the shelf has not yet been sold, so it would not appear on an invoice. In addition, an invoice line could hold a labor charge rather than a part.

A relational model corresponding to the ER model shown in Figure 3-3 might look something like the model in Figure 3-4, which is an example of a *data structure diagram*.

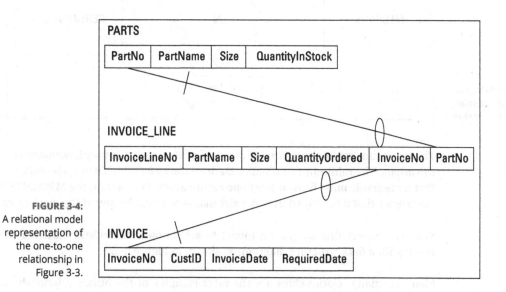

FIGURE 3-4:
A relational model
representation of
the one-to-one
relationship in
Figure 3-3.

PartNo is the primary key of the PART relation and InvoiceLineNo is the primary key of the INVOICE_LINE relation. PartNo also serves as a foreign key in the INVOICE_LINE relation, binding the two relations together. Similarly, InvoiceNo, the primary key of the INVOICE relation, serves as a foreign key in the INVOICE_ LINE relation.

Note: For a business that sells only products, the relationship between products and invoice lines might be different. In such a case, the minimum cardinality on the products side might be mandatory. That is not the case for the fictitious company in this example. It is important that your model reflect accurately the system you are modeling. You could model very similar systems for two different clients and end up with very different models. You need to account for differences in business rules and standard operating procedure.

A one-to-many relationship is somewhat more complex than a one-to-one relationship. One instance of the first relation corresponds to multiple instances of the second relation. An example of a one-to-many relationship in the Honest Abe model would be the relationship between a mechanic and his or her certifications. A mechanic can have multiple certifications, but each certification belongs to one and only one mechanic. The ER diagram shown in Figure 3-5 illustrates that relationship.

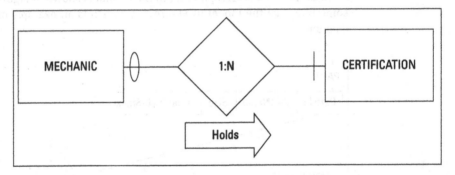

FIGURE 3-5: An ER diagram of a one-to-many relationship.

The maximum cardinality diamond shows that one mechanic may have many certifications. The minimum cardinality slash on the CERTIFICATIONS side indicates that a mechanic must have at least one certification. The oval on the MECHANICS side shows that a certification may exist that is not held by any of the mechanics.

You can convert this simple ER model to a relational model and illustrate the result with a data structure diagram, as shown in Figure 3-6.

Many-to-many relationships are the most complex of the binary relationships. Two relations connected by a many-to-many relationship can have serious integrity problems, even if both relations are in DKNF. To illustrate the problem and then the solution, consider a many-to-many relationship in the Honest Abe model.

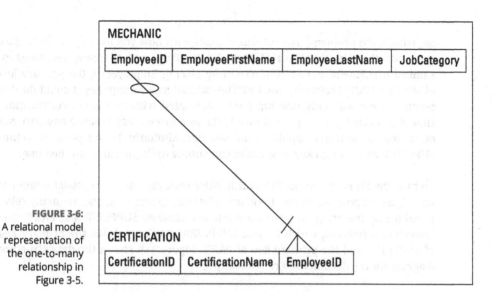

FIGURE 3-6:
A relational model
representation of
the one-to-many
relationship in
Figure 3-5.

The relationship between suppliers and parts is a many-to-many relationship. A supplier may be a source for multiple different parts, and a specific part may be obtainable from multiple suppliers. Figure 3-7 is an ER diagram that illustrates this relationship.

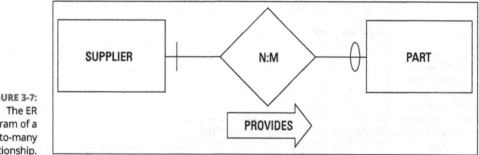

FIGURE 3-7:
The ER
diagram of a
many-to-many
relationship.

The maximum cardinality diamond shows that one supplier can supply different parts, and one specific part can be supplied by multiple suppliers. The fact that N is different from M shows that the number of suppliers that can supply a part does not have to be equal to the number of different parts that a single supplier can supply. The minimum cardinality slash on the SUPPLIER side of the relationship indicates that a part must come from a supplier. Parts don't materialize out of thin air. The oval on the PART side of the relationship means that a company could have qualified a supplier before it has supplied any parts.

So, what's the problem? The difficulty arises with how you use keys to link relations together. In the MECHANIC:CERTIFICATION one-to-many relationship, I linked MECHANIC to CERTIFICATION by placing EmployeeID, the primary key of the MECHANIC relation, into CERTIFICATION as a foreign key. I could do this because there was only one mechanic associated with any given certification. However, I can't put SupplierID into PART as a foreign key because any part can be sourced by multiple suppliers, not just one. Similarly, I can't put PartNo into SUPPLIER as a foreign key. A supplier can supply multiple parts, not just one.

To turn the ER model of the SUPPLIER:PART relationship into a robust relational model, decompose the many-to-many relationship into two, one-to-many relationships by inserting an *intersection relation* between SUPPLIER and PART. The intersection relation, which I name SUPPLIER_PART, contains the primary key of SUPPLIER and the primary key of PART. Figure 3-8 shows the data structure diagram for the decomposed relationship.

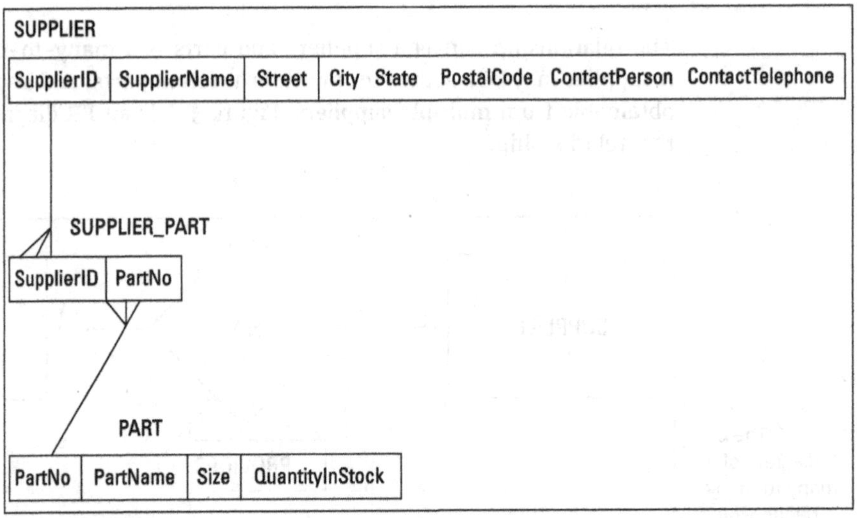

FIGURE 3-8: The relational model representation of the decomposition of the many-to-many relationship in Figure 3-7.

The SUPPLIER relation has a record (row, tuple) for every qualified supplier. The PART relation has a record for every part that Honest Abe uses. The SUPPLIER_ PART relation has a record for every part supplied by every supplier. Thus there are multiple records in the SUPPLIER_PART relation for each supplier, depending on the number of different parts supplied by that supplier. Similarly, there are multiple records in the SUPPLIER_PART relation for each part, depending on the number of suppliers that supply each different part. If five suppliers are supplying N2457 alternators, there are five records in SUPPLIER_PART corresponding to the N2457 alternator. If Roadrunner Distribution supplies 15 different parts, 15 records in SUPPLIER_PART will relate to Roadrunner Distribution.

A sample conversion

Figure 3-9 shows the ER diagram constructed earlier for Honest Abe's Fleet Auto Repair. I'd like you to look at it again because now you're going to convert it to a relational model.

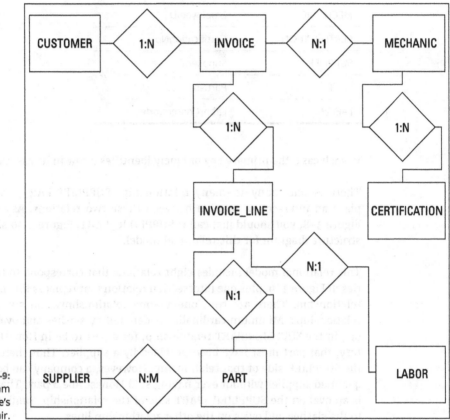

FIGURE 3-9:
The ER diagram
for Honest Abe's
Fleet Auto Repair.

The many-to-many relationship (SUPPLIER:PART) tells you that you have to decompose it by creating an intersection relation. First, however, look at the relations that correspond to the pictured entities and their primary keys, shown in Table 3-1.

TABLE 3-1

Primary Keys for Sample Relations

Relation	Primary Key
CUSTOMER	CustomerID
INVOICE	InvoiceNo
INVOICE_LINE	Invoice_Line_No
MECHANIC	EmployeeID
CERTIFICATION	CertificationNo
SUPPLIER	SupplierID
PART	PartNo
LABOR	LaborChargeCode

In each case, the primary key uniquely identifies a row in its associated table.

There is one many-to-many relationship, SUPPLIER:PART, so you need to place an intersection relation between these two relations. As shown back in Figure 3-8, you should just call it SUPPLIER_PART. Figure 3-10 shows the data structure diagram for this relational model.

This relational model includes eight relations that correspond to the eight entities in Figure 3-9, plus one intersection relation that replaces the many-to-many relationship. There are two, one-to-one relationships and six, one-to-many relationships. Minimum cardinality is denoted by slashes and ovals. For example, in the SUPPLIER:PART relationship, for a part to be in Honest Abe's inventory, that part must have been provided by a supplier. Thus there is a slash on the SUPPLIER side of that relationship. However, a company can be considered a qualified supplier without ever having sold Honest Abe a part. That is why there is an oval on the SUPPLIER_PART side of the relationship. Similar logic applies to the slashes and ovals on the other relationship lines.

When you have a relational model that accurately reflects the ER model and contains no many-to-many relationships, construction of a relational database is straightforward. You have identified the relations, the attributes of those relations, the primary and foreign keys of those relations, and the relationships between those relations.

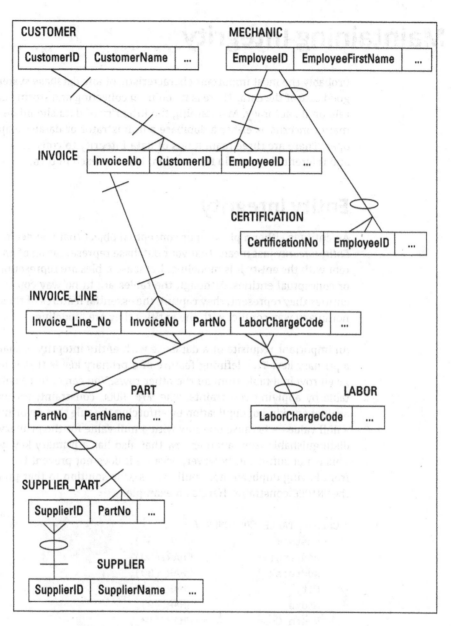

FIGURE 3-10:
The relational
model
representation
of the Honest
Abe's model in
Figure 3-9.

Maintaining Integrity

Probably the most important characteristic of any database system is that it takes good care of the data. There is no point in collecting and storing data if you cannot rely on its accuracy. Maintaining the integrity of data should be one of your primary concerns as either a database administrator or database application developer. There are three main kinds of data integrity to consider — entity, domain, and referential — and in this section, I look at each in turn.

Entity integrity

An entity is either a physical or conceptual object that you deem to be important. *Entity integrity* just means that your database representation of an entity is consistent with the entity it is modeling. Database tables are representations of physical or conceptual entities. Although the tables are in no way copies or clones of the entities they represent, they capture the essential features of those entities and do not in any way conflict with the entities they are modeling.

An important requisite of a database with entity integrity is that every table has a primary key. The defining feature of a primary key is that it distinguishes any given row in a table from all the other rows. You can enforce entity integrity in a table by applying constraints. The NOT NULL constraint, for example, protects against one kind of duplication by enforcing the rule that no primary key can have a null value — because one row with a null value for the primary key may not be distinguishable from another row that also has a primary key with a null value. This is not sufficient, however, because it does not prevent two rows in the table from having duplicate non-null values. One solution to that problem is to apply the UNIQUE constraint. Here's an example:

```
CREATE TABLE CUSTOMER (
    CustName        CHAR (30),
    Address1        CHAR (30),
    Address2        CHAR (30),
    City            CHAR (25),
    State           CHAR (2),
    PostalCode      CHAR (10),
    Telephone       CHAR (13),
    Email           CHAR (30),
    UNIQUE (CustName) ) ;
```

The UNIQUE constraint prevents two customers with the exact same name from being entered into the database. In some businesses, it is likely that two customers will have the same name. In that case, using an auto-incrementing integer as the primary key is the best solution: It leaves no possibility of duplication. The details of using an auto-incrementing integer as the primary key will vary from one DBMS to another. Check the documentation for the system you are using.

Although the UNIQUE constraint guarantees that at least one column in a table contains no duplicates, you can achieve the same result with the PRIMARY KEY constraint, which applies to the entire table rather than just one column of the table. Below is an example of the use of the PRIMARY KEY constraint:

```
CREATE TABLE CUSTOMER (
    CustName        CHAR (30)    PRIMARY KEY,
    Address1        CHAR (30),
    Address2        CHAR (30),
    City            CHAR (25),
    State           CHAR (2),
    PostalCode      CHAR (10),
    Telephone       CHAR (13),
    Email           CHAR (30) ) ;
```

A primary key is an attribute of a table. It could comprise a single column or a combination of columns. In some cases, every column in a table must be part of the primary key to guarantee that there are no duplicate rows. If, for example, you have added the PRIMARY KEY constraint to the CustName attribute, and you already have a customer named John Smith in the CUSTOMER table, the DBMS will not allow users to add a second customer named John Smith.

Domain integrity

The set of values that an attribute of an entity can have is that attribute's *domain*. For example, say that a manufacturer identifies its products with part numbers that all start with the letters *GJ*. Any time a person tries to enter a new part number that doesn't start with GJ into the system, a violation of domain integrity occurs. *Domain integrity* in this case is maintained by adding a constraint to the system that all part numbers must start with the letters GJ. You can specify a domain with a domain constraint, as follows:

```
CREATE DOMAIN PartNoDomain CHAR (15)
    CHECK (SUBSTRING (PartNo FROM 1 FOR 2) = 'GJ') ;
```

After a domain has been created, you can use it in a table definition:

```
CREATE TABLE PRODUCT (
    PartNo          PartNoDomain          PRIMARY KEY,
```

```
   PartName          CHAR (30),
   Cost              Numeric,
   QuantityStocked   Integer;
```

The domain is specified instead of the data type.

Referential integrity

Entity integrity and domain integrity apply to individual tables. Relational data-bases depend not only on tables but also on the relationships *between* tables. Those relationships are in the form of one table referencing another. Those references must be consistent for the database to have *referential integrity*. Problems can arise when data is added to or changed in a table, and that addition or alteration is not reflected in the related tables. Consider the sample database created by the following code:

```
CREATE TABLE CUSTOMER (
   CustomerName    CHAR (30)    PRIMARY KEY,
   Address1        CHAR (30),
   Address2        CHAR (30),
   City            CHAR (25)    NOT NULL,
   State           CHAR (2),
   PostalCode      CHAR (10),
   Phone           CHAR (13),
   Email           CHAR (30)
   ) ;

CREATE TABLE PRODUCT (
   ProductName     CHAR (30)    PRIMARY KEY,
   Price           CHAR (30)
   ) ;

CREATE TABLE EMPLOYEE (
   EmployeeName    CHAR (30)    PRIMARY KEY,
   Address1        CHAR (30),
   Address2        CHAR (30),
   City            CHAR (25),
   State           CHAR (2),
   PostalCode      CHAR (10),
   HomePhone       CHAR (13),
   OfficeExtension CHAR (4),
   HireDate        DATE,
   JobClassification CHAR (10),
```

```
        HourSalComm              CHAR (1)
        ) ;

CREATE TABLE ORDERS (
        OrderNumber              INTEGER            PRIMARY KEY,
        ClientName               CHAR (30),
        TestOrdered              CHAR (30),
        Salesperson              CHAR (30),
        OrderDate                DATE,
        CONSTRAINT NameFK FOREIGN KEY (ClientName)
            REFERENCES CUSTOMER (CustomerName)
                ON DELETE CASCADE,
        CONSTRAINT ProductFK FOREIGN KEY (TestOrdered)
            REFERENCES PRODUCT (ProductName)
                ON DELETE CASCADE,
        CONSTRAINT SalesFK FOREIGN KEY (Salesperson)
            REFERENCES EMPLOYEE (EmployeeName)
                ON DELETE CASCADE
        ) ;
```

In this system, the ORDERS table is directly related to the CUSTOMER table, the PRODUCT table, and the EMPLOYEE table. One of the attributes of ORDERS serves as a foreign key by corresponding to the primary key of CUSTOMER. The ORDERS table is linked to PRODUCT and to EMPLOYEE by the same mechanism.

The ON DELETE CASCADE clause is included in the definition of the constraints on the ORDERS table to prevent deletion anomalies, which I cover in the next section.

TIP

Some implementations do not yet support the ON DELETE CASCADE syntax, so don't be surprised if it doesn't work for you. In such cases, you'll have to cascade the deletes to the child tables with code.

REMEMBER

Child records depend for their existence on parent records. For example, a membership organization may have a MEMBERS table and an ACTIVITIES table that records all the activities participated in by members. If a person's membership ends and she is deleted from the MEMBERS table, all the records in the ACTIVITIES table that refer to that member should be deleted too. Deleting those child records is a cascade deletion operation.

Avoiding Data Corruption

Databases are susceptible to corruption. It is possible, but extremely rare, for data in a database to be altered by some physical event, such as the flipping of a one to a zero by a cosmic ray. In general, though, aside from a disk failure or cosmic ray strike, only three occasions cause the data in a database to be corrupted:

>> Adding data to a table

>> Changing data in a table

>> Deleting data from a table

If you don't allow changes to be made to a database (in other words, if you make it a read-only database), it can't be modified in a way that adds erroneous and misleading information (although it can still be destroyed completely). However, read-only databases are of limited use. Most things that you want to track do tend to change over time, and the database needs to change too. Changes to the database can lead to inconsistencies in its data, called *anomalies*. By careful design, you can minimize the impact of these anomalies, or even prevent them from ever occurring.

As discussed in Chapter 2 of this minibook, anomalies can be largely prevented by normalizing a database. This can be done by ensuring that each table in the database deals with only one idea. The ER model of the Honest Abe database shown earlier in Figures 3-1 and 3-9 is a good example of a model where each entity represents a single idea. The only problem with it is the presence of a many-to-many relationship. As in the relational model shown in Figure 3-10, you can eliminate that problem in the ER model by inserting an intersection relation between one entity — the SUPPLIERS entity in my example — and the other entity — PARTS, in my example — to convert the many-to-many relationship to two one-to-many relationships. Figure 3-11 shows the result.

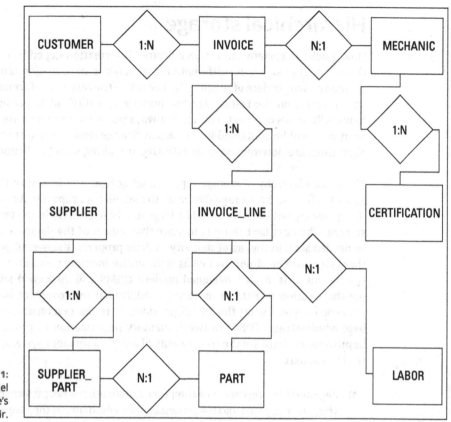

FIGURE 3-11:
Revised ER model
for Honest Abe's
Fleet Auto Repair.

Speeding Data Retrievals

Clearly, maintaining the integrity of a database is of vital importance. A database is worthless, or even worse than worthless, if erroneous data in it leads to bad decisions and lost opportunities. However, the database must also allow needed information to be retrieved in a reasonable amount of time. Sometimes late information causes just as much harm as bad information. The speed with which information is retrieved from a database depends on a number of factors. The size of the database and the speed of the hardware it is running on are obvious factors. Perhaps most critical, however, is the method used to access table data, which depends on the way the data is structured on the storage medium.

Hierarchical storage

How quickly a system can retrieve desired information depends on the speed of the device that stores it. Different storage devices have a wide range of speeds, spanning many orders of magnitude. For fast retrievals, the information you want should reside on the fastest devices. Because it is difficult to predict which data items will be needed next, you can't always make sure the data you are going to want next will be contained in the fastest storage device. Some storage allocation algorithms are nonetheless quite effective at making such predictions.

There is a hierarchy of storage types, ranging from the fastest to the slowest. In general, the faster a storage device is, the smaller its capacity. As a consequence, it is generally not possible to hold a large database entirely in the fastest available storage. The next best thing is to store that subset of the database most likely to be needed soon in the faster memory. If done properly, the overall performance of the system will be almost as fast as if the entire memory was as fast as the fastest component of it. A well-designed modern DBMS will do a good job of optimizing the location of data in memory. If additional improvement in performance is needed beyond what the DBMS provides, it is the responsibility of the database administrator (DBA) to tweak memory organization to provide the needed improvement. Here are the components of a typical memory system, starting with the fastest part:

>> **Registers:** The registers in a computer system are the fastest form of storage. They are integrated into the processor chip, which means they are implemented with the fastest technology, and the delay for transfers between the processing unit and the registers is minimal. It is not feasible to store any portion of a database in the registers, which are limited in number and in size. Instead, registers hold the operands that the processor is currently working on.

>> **L1 cache:** Level 1 cache is typically also located in the processor chip, but is not as intimately integrated with the processor as are the registers. Consisting of static RAM devices, it is the fastest form of storage that can store a significant fraction of a database.

>> **L2 cache:** Level 2 cache is generally located on a separate chip from the processor. It uses the same static RAM technology as L1 cache but has greater capacity and is usually somewhat slower than the L1 cache.

>> **Main memory:** Main memory is implemented with solid state dynamic RAM devices, which are slower than static RAM, but cheaper and less power-hungry.

>> **Solid state disk (SSD):** Solid state disk is really not a disk at all. It is an array of solid-state devices built out of flash technology. Locations in a SSD are

addressed in exactly the same way as locations on hard disk, which is why solid-state disks are called solid-state disks.

>> **Hard disk:** Hard disk storage has more capacity than does cache or SSD, and it's orders of magnitude slower. However, due to its larger capacity, this is where databases are stored. Registers, L1 cache, and L2 cache are all volatile forms of memory; the data is lost when power is removed. SSD is nonvolatile, but more expensive per byte than hard disk storage. Hard disk storage, like SSD, is nonvolatile. With both SSD and hard disks, the data is retained even when the system is turned off. Because hard disk systems can hold a large database and retain it when power is off or interrupted, such systems are the normal home of all databases.

>> **Offline storage:** It is not necessary to have immediate access to databases that are not in active use. They can be retained on storage media that are slower than hard disk drives. A sequential storage medium such as magnetic tape is fine for such use. Data access is exceedingly slow, but acceptable for data that is rarely if ever needed. Huge quantities of data can be stored on tape. Tape is the ideal home for archives of obsolete data that nevertheless need to be retained against the day when they might be called upon again.

Full table scans

The simplest data retrieval method is the *full table scan*, which entails reading a table sequentially, one row after another. Sooner or later, all the rows that satisfy the retrieval criteria will be reached, and a result set can be returned to the database application. If you are retrieving just a few rows from a large table, this method can waste a lot of time accessing rows that you don't want. If a table is so large that most of it does not fit into cache, this retrieval method can be so slow as to make retrievals impractical. The alternative is to use an index.

Working with Indexes

Indexes speed access to table rows. An *index* is a data structure consisting of pointers to the rows in a data table. Data tables are typically not maintained in sorted order. Re-sorting a table every time it is modified is time-consuming, and sorting for fast retrieval by one retrieval key guarantees that the table is not sorted for all other retrieval keys. For example, if a CUSTOMER table is sorted by customer last name, you will be able to zero in on a particular customer quickly by last name, because you can reach the desired record after just a few steps, using a divide and conquer strategy. However, the postal codes of the customers, for example, will be in some random order. If you want to retrieve all the customers living in a particular zip code, the sort on last name will not help you. In contrast to sorting, you can have an index for every potential retrieval key, keeping each index sorted by its associated retrieval key. For example, in a CUSTOMER table, one index might be sorted in CustID order and another index sorted in PostalCode order. This would enable rapid retrieval of selected records by CustID or all the records with a given range of postal codes.

REMEMBER

Modern database management systems include a facility called a *query optimizer*. The optimizer examines queries as they come in and, if their performance would be improved by an index, the optimizer will create one and use it. Performance is improved without the database application developer even realizing why.

Creating the right indexes

A major factor in maximizing performance is choosing the best columns to index in a table. Because all the indexes on a table must be updated every time a row in the table is added or deleted, maintaining an index creates a definite performance penalty. This penalty is negligible compared to the performance improvement provided by the index if it is frequently used, but is a significant drain on performance if the index is rarely or never used to locate rows in the data table. Indexes help the most when tables are frequently queried but infrequently subjected to insertions or deletions of records. They are least helpful in tables that are rarely queried but frequently subjected to insertions or deletions of records.

Analyze the way the tables in your database will be used, and build indexes accordingly. Primary keys should always be indexed. Other columns should be indexed if you plan on frequently using them as retrieval keys. Columns that will not be frequently used as retrieval keys should not be indexed. Removing unneeded indexes from a database can often significantly improve performance.

Indexes and the ANSI/ISO standard

The ANSI/ISO SQL standard does not specify how indexes should be constructed. This leaves the implementation of indexes up to each DBMS vendor. That means that the indexing scheme of one vendor may differ from that of another. If you want to migrate a database system from one vendor's DBMS to another's, you'll have to re-create all the indexes.

Index costs

There are costs to excessive indexing that go beyond updating them whenever changes are made to their associated tables. If a database has multiple indexes, the DBMS's optimizer may choose the wrong one when making a retrieval. This could impact performance in a major way. Updates to indexed columns are particularly hard on performance because the old index value must be deleted and the new one added. The bottom line is that you should index only columns that will frequently be used as retrieval keys or used to enforce uniqueness, such as primary keys.

Query type dictates the best index

For a typical database, the number of possible queries that could be run is huge. In most cases, however, a few specific types of queries are run frequently, others are run infrequently, and many are not run at all. You want to optimize your indexes so that the queries you run frequently gain the most benefit. There is no point in adding indexes to a database to speed up query types that are never run. This just adds system overhead and results in no benefit. To help you understand which indexes work best with which query types, check out the next few sections where I examine the most frequently used query types.

Point query

A *point query* returns at most one record. The query includes an equality condition.

```
SELECT FirstName FROM EMPLOYEE
    WHERE EmployeeID = 31415 ;
```

There is only one record in the database where EmployeeID is equal to 31415 because EmployeeID is the primary key of the EMPLOYEE table. If this is an example of a query that might be run, then indexing on EmployeeID is a good idea.

Multipoint query

A *multipoint query* may return more than one record, using an equality condition.

```
SELECT FirstName FROM EMPLOYEE
    WHERE Department = 'Advanced Research' ;
```

There are probably multiple people in the Advanced Research department. The first names of all of them will be retrieved by this query. Creating an index on Department makes sense if there are a large number of departments and the employees are fairly evenly spread across them.

Range query

A *range query* returns a set of records whose values lie within an interval or half interval. A range where both lower and upper bounds are specified is an interval. A range where only one bound is specified is a half interval.

```
SELECT FirstName, LastName FROM EMPLOYEE
    WHERE AGE >= 55
    AND < 65 ;

SELECT FirstName, LastName FROM EMPLOYEE
    WHERE AGE >= 65 ;
```

Indexing on AGE could speed retrievals if an organization has a large number of employees and retrievals based on age are frequent.

Prefix match query

A *prefix match query* is one in which only the first part of an attribute or sequence of attributes is specified.

```
SELECT FirstName, LastName FROM EMPLOYEE
    WHERE LastName LIKE 'Sm%' ;
```

This query returns all the Smarts, Smetanas, Smiths, and Smurfs. LastName is probably a good field to index.

Extremal query

An *extremal query* returns the extremes, the minima and maxima.

```
SELECT FirstName, LastName FROM EMPLOYEE
    WHERE Age = MAX(SELECT Age FROM EMPLOYEE) ;
```

This query returns the name of the oldest employee.

Ordering query

An *ordering query* is one that includes an ORDER BY clause. The records returned are sorted by a specified attribute.

```
SELECT FirstName, LastName FROM EMPLOYEE
    ORDER BY LastName, FirstName ;
```

This query returns a list of all employees in ascending alphabetical order, sorted first by last name and within each last name, by first name. Indexing by LastName would be good for this type of query. An additional index on FirstName would probably not improve performance significantly, unless duplicate last names are common.

Grouping query

A *grouping query* is one that includes a GROUP BY clause. The records returned are partitioned into groups.

```
SELECT FirstName, LastName FROM EMPLOYEE
    GROUP BY Department ;
```

This query returns the names of all employees, with the members of each department listed together as a group.

Equi-join query

Equi-join queries are common in normalized relational databases. The condition that filters out the rows you don't want to retrieve is based on an attribute of one table being equal to a corresponding attribute in a second table.

```
SELECT EAST.EMP.FirstName, EAST.EMP.LastName
    FROM EAST.EMP, WEST.EMP
    WHERE EAST.EMP.EmpID = WEST.EMP.EMPID ;
```

One schema (EAST) holds the tables for the eastern division of a company, and another schema (WEST) holds the tables for the western division. Only the names of the employees who appear in both the eastern and western schemas are retrieved by this query.

Data structures used for indexes

Closely related to the types of queries typically run on a database is the way the indexes are structured. Because of the huge difference in speed between semiconductor cache memory and online hard disk storage, it makes sense to keep the indexes you are most likely to need soon in cache. The less often you must go out to hard disk storage, the better.

A variety of data structures are possible. Some of these structures are particularly efficient for some types of queries, whereas other structures work best with other types of queries. The best data structure for a given application depends on the types of queries that will be run against the data.

With that in mind, take a look at the two most popular data structure variants:

>> **B+ trees:** Most popular data structures for indexes have a tree-like organization where one master node (the root) connects to multiple nodes, each of which in turn connects to multiple nodes, and so on. The B+ tree, where B stands for *balanced,* is a good index structure for queries of a number of types. B+ trees are particularly efficient in handling range queries. They also are good in databases where insertions of new records are frequently made.

>> **Hash structures:** Hash structures use a key and a pseudo-random hash function to find a location. They are particularly good at making quick retrievals of point queries and multipoint queries, but perform poorly on range, prefix, and extremal queries. If a query requires a scan of all the data in the target tables, hash structures are less efficient than B+ tree structures.

Pseudo-random hash function? This sounds like mumbo-jumbo doesn't it? I'm not sure how the term originated but it reminds me of corned beef hash. Corned beef hash is a smooshed-up combination of corned beef, finely diced potatoes, and maybe a few spices. You put all these different things into a pan, stir them up, and cook them. Pretty tasty!

And yet, what does that have to do with finding a record quickly in a database table? It is the idea of putting together things which are dissimilar, but nevertheless related in some way. In a database, instead of putting everything into a frying pan, the items are placed into logical buckets. For the speediest retrievals you want all your buckets to contain about the same number of items. That's where the pseudo-random part comes in. Genuine random number generators are practically impossible to construct, so computer scientists use pseudo-random number generators instead. They produce a good approximation of a set of random numbers. The use of pseudo-random numbers for assigning hash buckets assures that the buckets are more or less evenly filled. When you want to retrieve a data item, the hash structure enables you to find the bucket it is in quickly. Then, if the bucket holds relatively few items, you can scan through them and find the item you want without spending too much time.

Indexes, sparse and dense

The best choice of indexes depends largely on the types of queries to be supported and on the size of the cache available for data, compared to the total size of the database.

Data is shuttled back and forth between the cache and the disk storage in chunks called *pages.* In one table, a page may hold many records; in another, it may contain few. Indexes are pointers to the data in tables, and if there is at most one such pointer per page, it is called a *sparse index*. At the other end of the scale, a *dense index* is one that points to every record in the table. A sparse index entails less overhead than a dense index does, and if there are many records per page, for certain types of queries, it can perform better. Whether that performance improvement materializes depends on *clustering* — which gets its day in the sun in the next section.

Index clustering

The rationale for maintaining indexes is that it is too time-consuming to maintain data tables in sorted order for rapid retrieval of desired records. Instead, you keep the *index* in sorted order. Such an index is said to be *clustered*. A clustered index is organized in a way similar to the way a telephone book is organized. In a telephone book, the entries are sorted alphabetically by a person's last name, and secondarily by his or her first name. This means that all the Smiths are together and so are all the Taylors. This organization is good for partial match, range, point, multipoint, and general join queries. If you pull up a page that contains one of the target records into cache, it's likely that other records that you want are on the same page and are pulled into cache at the same time.

A database table can have multiple indexes, but only one of them can be clustered. The same is true of a telephone book. If the entries in the book are sorted by last name, the order of the telephone numbers is a random jumble. This means that if you must choose one table attribute to assign a clustered index, choose the attribute most likely to be used as a retrieval key. Building unclustered indexes for other attributes is still of value, but isn't as beneficial as the clustered index.

Composite indexes

Composite indexes are, as the name implies, based on a combination of attributes. In certain situations, a composite index can give better performance than can a combination of single attribute indexes. For example, a composite index on last name and first name zeroes in on the small number of records that match both criteria. Alternatively, if last name and first name are separately indexed, first all the records with the desired last name are retrieved, and then these are scanned to find the ones with the correct first name. The extra operation takes extra time and makes extra demands on the bandwidth of the path between the database and the database engine.

Although composite indexes can be helpful, you must be careful when you craft your query to call for the components of the index in the same order that they exist in the index itself. For example, if you have an index on LastName, First-Name, the following query would perform well:

```
SELECT * FROM CUSTOMER
    WHERE LastName = 'Smith'
    AND FirstName = 'Bob' ;
```

This efficiently retrieves the records for all the customers named Bob Smith. However, the following seemingly equivalent query doesn't perform as well:

```
SELECT * FROM CUSTOMER
    WHERE FirstName = 'Bob'
    AND LastName = 'Smith' ;
```

The same rows are retrieved, but not as quickly. If you have a clustered index on LastName, FirstName, all the Smiths will be together. If you search for Smith first, once you have found one, you have found them all, including Bob. However, if you search for Bob first, you will compile a list containing Bob Adams, Bob Beaman, Bob Coats, and so on, and finally Bob Zappa. Then you will look through that list to find Bob Smith. Doing things in the wrong order can make a big difference.

TIP

A DBMS with an intelligent query optimizer would examine the query and reverse the order of retrieval to deliver the best performance. You can check how smart your optimizer is by coding a sample retrieval both ways and noting the retrieval time. If it is the same in both instances, your query optimizer has passed the test.

Index effect on join performance

As a rule, joins are expensive in terms of the time it takes to construct them. If the join attribute in both tables is indexed, the amount of time needed is dramatically reduced. (I discuss joins in Book 3, Chapter 4.)

Table size as an indexing consideration

The amount of time it takes to scan every row in a table becomes an issue as the table becomes large. The larger the table is, the more time indexes can save you. The corollary to this fact is that indexes of small tables don't do much good. If a table has no more than a few hundred rows, it doesn't make sense to create indexes for it. The overhead involved with maintaining the indexes overshadows any performance gain you might get from having them.

Indexes versus full table scans

The point of using indexes is to save time in query and join operations by enabling you to go directly to the records you want instead of having to look at every record in a table to see whether it satisfies your selection conditions. If you can anticipate the types of queries likely to be run, you can configure indexes accordingly to maximize performance. There will still likely be queries of a type that you did not anticipate. For those, full table scans are run. Hopefully, these queries won't be run often and thus won't have a major effect on overall performance. Full table scans are the preferred retrieval method for small tables that are likely to be completely contained in cache.

You might wonder how to create an index. Interestingly enough, for such an important function, the ISO/IEC international SQL standard does not specify how to do it. Thus each implementation is free to do it its own way. Most use some form of CREATE INDEX statement, but consult the documentation for whatever DBMS you are using to determine what is right for your situation.

Reading SQL Server Execution Plans

When you enter an SQL query into a database, the DBMS decides how to execute it by developing an execution plan. In most cases, the execution plan the DBMS develops is the best possible, but sometimes it could do with a little tuning to make it better. In this section, I look at how one particular DBMS (Microsoft SQL Server, to be precise) develops an execution plan, and then I apply SQL Server's Database Engine Tuning Advisor to determine whether the plan can be improved.

Robust execution plans

Any nontrivial query draws data from multiple tables. How you reach those tables, how you join them, and the order in which you join them determines, to a large extent, how efficient your retrieval will be. The order in which you do these things is called an *execution plan*. For any given retrieval, there is a myriad of possible execution plans. One of them is optimal, a small number are near-optimal, and others are not good at all.

The optimal plan may be hard to find, but in many cases the near-optimal plans, called *robust execution plans*, are quite adequate. You can identify a robust execution plan by noting its characteristics. All major DBMS products include a query optimizer that takes in your SQL and comes up with an execution plan to implement it. In many cases, plans derived in this manner are satisfactory. Sometimes, however, for complex queries involving many joins, manual tuning significantly improves performance.

TIP

Query performance largely depends on the number of rows touched by the query — the fewer the better. This means that with a query involving multi-table joins, it is a good practice for the execution plan to start with the table with the best filter ratio. A table's *filter ratio* is the number of rows remaining after a condition is applied divided by the total number of rows in the table. The lower the filter ratio, the fewer rows that are joined to the next table in line in a join. For best performance in most cases, construct the join from the many side to the one side of one-to-many relationships, choosing the table on the one side that has the lowest filter ratio.

A sample database

The AdventureWorks2022 database is a sample database that Microsoft supplies for use with its SQL Server product. You can download both the free Microsoft SQL Server 2022 Express Edition, as well as the AdventureWorks2022 database from the Microsoft website.

There are a lot of data tables in the AdventureWorks2022 database. To get a bird's-eye view of all the tables and how they're related, you can create a database diagram following these steps:

1. **Open the SQL Server Management Studio application and connect to your SQL server.**

2. **Expand the Databases entry in the left-hand pane.**

3. **Expand the AdventureWorks2022 database entry.**

4. **Right-click the Database Diagrams entry, and select New Database Diagram.**

    This produces a list of the tables in the AdventureWorks2022 database.

5. **Add all the tables to the new data diagram.**

6. **Click the first table in the list, scroll down to the bottom of the list, hold the Shift key down, and click the last table in the list.**

    All the tables are selected.

7. **Click the Add button.**

After you've created the database diagram, you can maneuver around the map, looking at all the tables and their relationships. Figure 3-12 shows just a small section of the diagram.

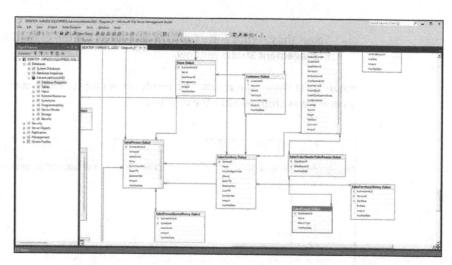

FIGURE 3-12:
Tables and relationships in the Adventure Works2022 database.

You can move the tables around in the diagram to help organize things and view specific relations. There is a one-to-many relationship between SalesTerritory and Customer, a one-to-many relationship between SalesTerritory and SalesPerson, and a one-to-many relationship between SalesPerson and SalesPersonQuotaHistory. The AdventureWorks2022 database is fairly large and contains multiple schemas. All the tables in Figure 3-12, plus quite a few more, are contained in the Sales schema. You might have questions about the AdventureWorks business, as modeled by this database. In the following section, I build a query to answer one of those questions.

A typical query

Suppose you want to know if any of AdventureWorks's salespeople are promising more than AdventureWorks can deliver. You can get an indication of this by seeing which salespeople took orders where the ShipDate was later than the DueDate. To do that, follow these steps:

1. With the AdventureWorks2022 database selected in the left-hand panel, click the New Query entry in the toolbar at the top of the SQL Server Management Studio window.

2. In the new tab, enter the query:

```
SELECT SalesOrderID
FROM AdventureWorks.Sales.Salesperson, AdventureWorks.
   Sales.SalesOrderHeader
WHERE SalesOrderHeader.SalesPersonID = SalesPerson.
   BusinessEntityID
     AND ShipDate > DueDate ;
```

3. **Select the Execute entry from the toolbar at the top of the SQL Server Management Studio window.**

Figure 3-13 shows the result. The result set is empty. There were no cases where an order was shipped after the due date.

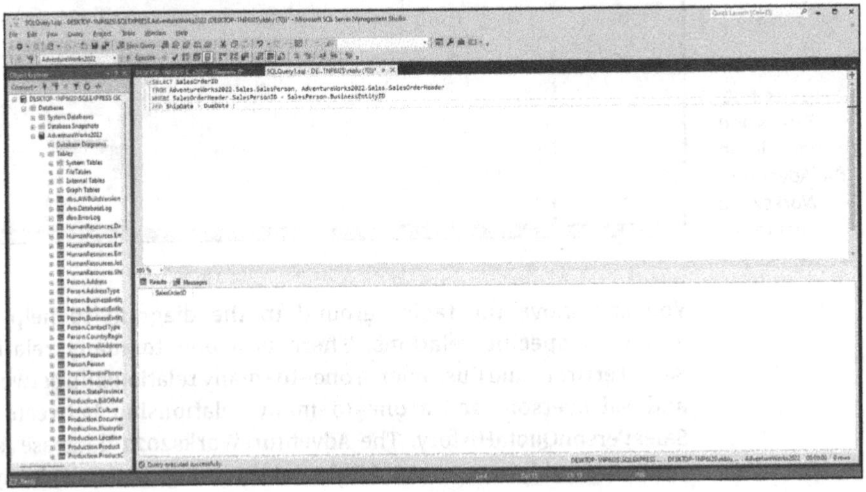

FIGURE 3-13:
SQL Server 2022
Management
Studio execution
of an SQL query.

> **TIP**
> Feel free to experiment with the query, such as changing the > to a < to see a list of the orders that were delivered before their due date.

The execution plan

Click the Display Estimated Execution Plan icon (three icons over from the Execute icon) to show what you see in Figure 3-14. An index scan, a clustered index scan, and a hash match consumed processor cycles, with the clustered index scan on SalesOrderHeader taking up 85 percent of the total time used. This shows that a lot more time is spent dealing with the SalesOrderHeader table than with the SalesPerson table. This makes sense, as I would expect there to be a lot more sales orders than there are sales people. This plan gives you a baseline on performance. If performance is not satisfactory, you can rewrite the query, generate a new execution plan, and compare results. If the query will be run many times, it is worth it to spend a little time here optimizing the way the query is written.

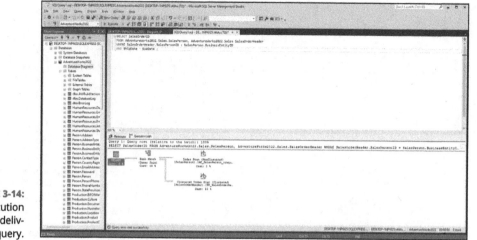

FIGURE 3-14:
The execution
plan for the deliv-
ery time query.

Chapter **4**

Creating a Database with SQL

s I stated way back in Book 1, Chapter 5, SQL is functionally divided into three components: the Data Definition Language (DDL), the Data Manipulation Language (DML), and the Data Control Language (DCL). The DDL consists of three statements: CREATE, ALTER, and DROP. You can use these statements to create database objects (such as tables), change the structure of an existing object, or delete an object. After you have designed a database, the first step in bringing it into reality is to build a table with the help of the DDL. After you have built the tables, the next step is to fill them with data. That's the job of the DML. As for the DCL, you call on it to help you preserve data integrity. In this chapter, I discuss the functions of the DDL. The aspects of the DML that were not covered in Book 1 — namely queries — will be discussed in Book 3. I discuss the DCL in Book 4.

First Things First: Planning Your Database

Before you can start constructing a database, you need to have a clear idea of the real-world or conceptual system that you are modeling. Some aspects of the system are of primary importance. Other aspects are subsidiary to the ones you have identified as primary. Additional aspects may not be important at all, depending on what you are using the database for. Based on these considerations, you'll build an ER model of the system, with primary aspects identified as *entities* and subsidiary aspects identified as *attributes* of those entities. Unimportant aspects don't appear in the model at all.

After you have finalized your ER model, you can translate it into a normalized relational model. The relational model is your guide for creating database tables and establishing the relationships between them.

Building Tables

The fundamental object in a relational database is the table. Tables correspond directly to the relations in a normalized relational model. Table creation can be simple or quite involved. In either case, it is accomplished with a CREATE TABLE statement.

In Chapter 3 of this minibook, I take you through the creation of a relational model for Honest Abe's Fleet Auto Repair. Using that sample design, you can take it to the next level by creating database tables based on the model. Table 4-1 shows the tables (and their attributes) that correspond to the relational model I came up with for Ol' Honest Abe.

You can construct the DDL statements required to build the database tables directly from the enumeration of tables and columns in Table 4-1, but first you should understand the important topic of *keys*, which I discuss in the next section.

Locating table rows with keys

Keys are the main tool used to locate specific rows within a table. Without a *key* — that handy item that guarantees that a row in a table is not a duplicate of any other row in the table — ambiguities can arise. The row you want to retrieve may be indistinguishable from one or more other rows in the table, meaning you wouldn't be able to tell which one was the right one.

TABLE 4-1

Tables for Honest Abe

Table	Column
CUSTOMER	CustomerID
	CustomerName
	StreetAddr
	City
	State
	PostalCode
	ContactName
	ContactPhone
	ContactEmail
MECHANIC	EmployeeID
	FirstName
	LastName
	StreetAddr
	City
	State
	PostalCode
	JobTitle
CERTIFICATION	CertificationNo
	CertName
	Expires
INVOICE	InvoiceNo
	Date
	CustomerID
	EmployeeID
	Tax
	TotalCharge

(continued)

Creating a Database
with SQL

TABLE 4-1 *(continued)*

Table	Column
INVOICE_LINE	Invoice_Line_No
	PartNo
	UnitPrice
	Quantity
	Extended Price
	LaborChargeCode
LABOR	LaborChargeCode
	TaskDescription
	StandardCharge
PART	PartNo
	Name
	Description
	CostBasis
	ListPrice
	QuantityInStock
SUPPLIER	SupplierID
	SupplierName
	StreetAddr
	City
	State
	PostalCode
	ContactName
	ContactPhone
	ContactEmail
SUPPLIER_PART	SupplierID
	PartNo

There are several different terms you may see in discussions of keys that you can use to uniquely identify rows in a table:

>> **Candidate key:** Ideally, at least one column or combination of columns within a table contains a unique entry in every row. Any such column or combination of columns is a candidate key. Perhaps your table has more than one such candidate. If your table has multiple candidate keys, select one of them to be the table's primary key.

>> **The primary key:** A table's primary key has the characteristic of being a unique identifier of all the rows in the table. It is specifically chosen from among the candidate keys to serve as the primary identifier of table rows.

>> **Composite key:** Sometimes no single column uniquely identifies every row in a table, but a combination of two or more columns does. Together, those columns comprise a composite key, which can collectively serve as a table's primary key.

Using the CREATE TABLE statement

Once you understand the function of keys (see the preceding bulleted list), you can create tables using the CREATE TABLE statement. Whatever database development environment you are using will have a facility that enables you to enter SQL code. This is an alternative to using the form-based tools that the environment also provides. In general, it is a lot easier to use the provided form-based tool, but using SQL gives you the finest control over what you are doing. The code examples that follow are written in ISO/IEC standard SQL. That means they should run without problems, regardless of the development environment you are using. However, because no implementation conforms to the standard 100 percent, you may have to consult your documentation if the tables are not created as you expect them to be.

```
CREATE TABLE CUSTOMER (
    CustomerID        INTEGER      PRIMARY KEY,
    CustomerName      CHAR (30),
    StreetAddr        CHAR (30),
    City              CHAR (25),
    State             CHAR (2),
    PostalCode        CHAR (10),
    ContactName       CHAR (30),
    ContactPhone      CHAR (13),
    ContactEmail      CHAR (30) ) ;
```

```
CREATE TABLE MECHANIC (
    EmployeeID          INTEGER         PRIMARY KEY,
    FirstName           CHAR (15),
    LastName            CHAR (20),
    StreetAddr          CHAR (30),
    City                CHAR (25),
    State               CHAR (2),
    PostalCode          CHAR (10),
    JobTitle            CHAR (30) ) ;

CREATE TABLE CERTIFICATION (
    CertificationNo     INTEGER         PRIMARY KEY,
    CertName            CHAR (30),
    Expires             Date ) ;

CREATE TABLE INVOICE (
    InvoiceNo           INTEGER         PRIMARY KEY,
    Date                DATE,
    CustomerID          INTEGER,
    EmployeeID          INTEGER,
    Tax                 NUMERIC (9,2),
    TotalCharge         NUMERIC (9,2) ) ;

CREATE TABLE INVOICE_LINE (
    Invoice_Line_No     INTEGER         PRIMARY KEY,
    PartNo              INTEGER,
    UnitPrice           NUMERIC (9,2),
    Quantity            INTEGER,
    ExtendedPrice       NUMERIC (9,2),
    LaborChargeCode     INTEGER ) ;

CREATE TABLE LABOR (
    LaborChargeCode     INTEGER         PRIMARY KEY,
    TaskDescription     CHAR (40),
    StandardCharge      NUMERIC (9,2) ) ;

CREATE TABLE PART (
    PartNo              INTEGER         PRIMARY KEY,
    Name                CHAR (30),
    Description         CHAR (40),
    CostBasis           NUMERIC (9,2),
    ListPrice           NUMERIC (9,2),
    QuantityInStock     INTEGER ) ;
```

```
CREATE TABLE SUPPLIER (
    SupplierID          INTEGER         PRIMARY KEY,
    SupplierName        CHAR (30),
    StreetAddr          CHAR (30),
    City                CHAR (25),
    State               CHAR (2),
    PostalCode          CHAR (10),
    ContactName         CHAR (30),
    ContactPhone        CHAR (13),
    ContactEmail        CHAR (30) ) ;

CREATE TABLE SUPPLIER_PART (
    SupplierID          INTEGER,
    PartNo              INTEGER,
    UNIQUE (SupplierID, PartNo) ) ;
```

All the tables except SUPPLIER_PART have a single attribute as their primary key. In the SUPPLIER_PART table, no single attribute uniquely identifies a row, so the table has a composite key made up of both SupplierID and PartNo. (That's the UNIQUE (SupplierID, PartNo) business.) Those two attributes together *do* uniquely identify each row in the table. Not all suppliers supply all parts, but there is a row in SUPPLIER_PART for every case where a specific supplier supplies a specific part. The UNIQUE constraint guarantees that no two rows in SUPPLIER_PART are identical.

TIP

The data types used to define each of the data fields are discussed in Book 1, Chapter 6.

Setting Constraints

One way to protect the integrity of your data is to add constraints to your table definitions. There are several different kinds of constraints, including column constraints, table constraints, check constraints, and foreign key constraints. In this section, I cover column constraints and table constraints. Other types of constraints will pop up here and there in the book as I go along.

Column constraints

Column constraints determine what may or may not appear in a column of a table. For example, in the SUPPLIER_PART table, NOT NULL is a constraint on the SupplierID column. It guarantees that the SupplierID column must contain a value. It doesn't say what that value must be, as long as it is *some* value.

Table constraints

A table constraint is not restricted to a particular column, but applies to an entire table. The PRIMARY KEY constraint is an example of a table constraint. A primary key may consist of one column, multiple columns, or even all the columns in the table — whatever it takes to uniquely identify every row in the table. Regardless of how many columns are included in the primary key, the primary key is a characteristic of the entire table.

Keys and Indexes

Because primary keys uniquely identify each row in a table, they are ideal for indexes. The purpose of an index is to point to a row or set of rows that satisfies a condition. Because a primary key identifies one and only one row in a table, an index on a table's primary key provides the fastest, most direct access to the row it points to. Less selective indexes give access to multiple rows that all satisfy the selection condition. Thus, although CustomerID may take you directly to the record of the customer you want, you may not remember every customer's CustomerID. A search on LastName might return several records, but you can probably determine pretty quickly which one is the one you want. In such a case, you may want to create an index on the LastName column as well as on CustomerID. Any column that you frequently use as a retrieval condition should probably be indexed. If a table's primary key is a composite key, the index would be on the combination of all the columns that make up the key. Composite keys that are not a table's primary key can also be indexed. (I talk about creating indexes in Chapter 3 of this minibook.)

Ensuring Data Validity with Domains

Although you, as a database creator, can't guarantee that the data entry operator always enters the correct data, at least you can ensure that the data entered is *valid* — that it excludes values that cannot possibly be correct. Do this with a CREATE DOMAIN statement. For example, in the LABOR table definition given in the earlier "Using the CREATE TABLE statement" section, the StandardCharge field holds currency values of the NUMERIC type. Suppose you want to ensure that a negative value is never entered for a StandardCharge. You can do so by creating a domain, as in the following example:

```
CREATE DOMAIN CurrencyDom NUMERIC (9,2)
   CHECK (VALUE >= 0);
```

You should now delete the old LABOR table and redefine it as shown below:

```
CREATE TABLE LABOR (
    LaborChargeCode    INTEGER  PRIMARY KEY,
    TaskDescription    CHAR (40),
    StandardCharge     CurrencyDom ) ;
```

The data type of StandardCharge is replaced by the new domain. With a domain, you can constrain an attribute to assume only those values that are valid.

Establishing Relationships between Tables

After you have created tables for a database, the next step is to establish the relationships between the tables. A normalized relational database has multiple tables, perhaps hundreds of them. Most queries or reports require data from more than one table. To pull the correct data from the tables, you must have a way of relating the rows in one table to corresponding rows in another table. This is accomplished with links consisting of columns in one table that correspond to columns in a related table.

Earlier in this chapter, I talk about primary keys and composite keys (which can be primary keys). Another important kind of key is the *foreign key*. Unlike primary keys, foreign keys do not uniquely identify a row in a table. Instead, they serve as links to other tables.

Relational databases are characterized by having multiple tables that are related to each other. Those relationships are established by columns that are shared between two tables. In a one-to-one relationship, one row in the first table corresponds to one and only one row in the second table. For a given row, one or more columns in the first table match a corresponding column or set of columns in the second table. In a one-to-many relationship, one row in the first table matches multiple rows in the second table. Once again, the match is made by columns in the first table that correspond to columns in the second table.

Consider the Honest Abe sample database in the previous chapter. It has a one-to-many link between CUSTOMER and INVOICE, mediated by the shared CustomerID column, and also a one-to-many link between MECHANIC and INVOICE mediated by the EmployeeID column. To create these links, you have to add a little more SQL code to the definition of the INVOICE table. Here's the new definition:

```
CREATE TABLE INVOICE (
    InvoiceNo          INTEGER     PRIMARY KEY,
    Date               DATE,
    CustomerID         INTEGER,
    EmployeeID         INTEGER,
    CONSTRAINT CustFK FOREIGN KEY (CustomerID)
        REFERENCES CUSTOMER (CustomerID),
    CONSTRAINT MechFK FOREIGN KEY (EmployeeID)
        REFERENCES MECHANIC (EmployeeID)
) ;
```

TIP

Adding the foreign key constraints to the table on the many side of a one-to-many relationship creates the links. For a one-to-one relationship, it doesn't matter which of the two tables you add the foreign key constraint to.

To tie the Honest Abe database together, add foreign key constraints to establish all the relationships. Here's the result:

```
CREATE TABLE CUSTOMER (
    CustomerID         INTEGER        PRIMARY KEY,
    CustomerName       CHAR (30),
    StreetAddr         CHAR (30),
    City               CHAR (25),
    State              CHAR (2),
    PostalCode         CHAR (10),
    ContactName        CHAR (30),
    ContactPhone       CHAR (13),
    ContactEmail       CHAR (30) ) ;

CREATE TABLE MECHANIC (
    EmployeeID         INTEGER PRIMARY KEY,
    FirstName          CHAR (15),
    LastName           CHAR (20),
    StreetAddr         CHAR (30),
    City               CHAR (25),
    State              CHAR (2),
    PostalCode         CHAR (10),
    Specialty          CHAR (30),
    JobTitle           CHAR (30) ) ;
```

```
CREATE TABLE CERTIFICATION (
    CertificationNo    INTEGER  PRIMARY KEY,
    CertName           CHAR (30),
    MechanicID         INTEGER,
    Expires            Date,
    CONSTRAINT CertMechFK FOREIGN KEY (MechanicID)
        REFERENCES MECHANIC (EmployeeID)
) ;

CREATE TABLE INVOICE (
    InvoiceNo          INTEGER  PRIMARY KEY,
    Date               DATE,
    CustomerID         INTEGER,
    EmployeeID         INTEGER,
    Tax                NUMERIC (9,2),
    TotalCharge        NUMERIC (9,2),
    CONSTRAINT CustFK FOREIGN KEY (CustomerID)
        REFERENCES CUSTOMER (CustomerID),
    CONSTRAINT MechFK FOREIGN KEY (EmployeeID)
        REFERENCES MECHANIC (EmployeeID)
) ;

CREATE TABLE INVOICE_LINE (
    Invoice_Line_No    INTEGER        PRIMARY KEY,
    InvoiceNo          INTEGER,
    LaborChargeCode    INTEGER,
    PartNo             INTEGER,
    UnitPrice          NUMERIC (9,2),
    Quantity           INTEGER,
    ExtendedPrice      NUMERIC (9,2),
    LaborChargeCode    INTEGER,
    CONSTRAINT InvFK FOREIGN KEY (InvoiceNo)
        REFERENCES INVOICE (InvoiceNo),
    CONSTRAINT LaborFK FOREIGN KEY (LaborChargeCode)
        REFERENCES LABOR (LaborChargeCode),
    CONSTRAINT PartFK FOREIGN KEY (PartNo)
        REFERENCES PART (PartNo)
) ;

CREATE DOMAIN CurrencyDom NUMERIC (9,2)
    CHECK (VALUE >= 0);
```

```
CREATE TABLE LABOR (
    LaborChargeCode     INTEGER  PRIMARY KEY,
    TaskDescription     CHAR (40),
    StandardCharge      CurrencyDom ) ;

CREATE TABLE PART (
    PartNo              INTEGER          PRIMARY KEY,
    Name                CHAR (30),
    Description         CHAR (40),
    CostBasis           NUMERIC (9,2),
    ListPrice           NUMERIC (9,2),
    QuantityInStock     INTEGER ) ;

CREATE TABLE SUPPLIER (
    SupplierID          INTEGER          PRIMARY KEY,
    SupplierName        CHAR (30),
    StreetAddr          CHAR (30),
    City                CHAR (25),
    State               CHAR (2),
    PostalCode          CHAR (10),
    ContactName         CHAR (30),
    ContactPhone        CHAR (13),
    ContactEmail        CHAR (30) ) ;

CREATE TABLE SUPPLIER_PART (
    SupplierID          INTEGER      NOT NULL,
    PartNo              INTEGER      NOT NULL,
    CONSTRAINT SuppFK FOREIGN KEY (SupplierID)
        REFERENCES SUPPLIER (SupplierID),
    CONSTRAINT PartSuppFK FOREIGN KEY (PartNo)
        REFERENCES PART (PartNo)
) ;
```

Foreign key constraints need to be added to only one side of a relationship. In a one-to-many relationship, they are added to the many side.

Note that the CERTIFICATION table has a column named MechanicID, which corresponds to the column named EmployeeID in the MECHANIC table. This is to show that a foreign key need not have the same name as the corresponding column in the table that it links to. Note also that additional columns that serve as foreign keys have been added to some of the tables on the many sides of relationships. These are required in addition to the constraint clauses.

A database properly linked together using foreign keys is said to have *referential integrity*. The key to assuring referential integrity is to make sure that the ER diagram of the database is accurate and properly translated into a relational model, which is then converted into a relational database.

Altering Table Structure

In the real world, requirements tend to change. Sooner or later, this is bound to affect the databases that model some aspect of that world. SQL's Data Definition Language provides a means to change the structure of a database that has already been created. Structural changes can involve adding a new column to a table or deleting an existing one. The SQL to perform these tasks is pretty straightforward. Here is an example of adding a column:

```
ALTER TABLE MECHANIC
    ADD COLUMN Birthday DATE ;
```

Here's an example of deleting a column:

```
ALTER TABLE MECHANIC
    DROP COLUMN Birthday ;
```

I guess Honest Abe decided not to keep track of employee birthdays after all.

Deleting Tables

It's just as easy to delete an entire table as it is to delete a column in a table. Here's how:

```
DROP TABLE CUSTOMER ;
```

Uh-oh. Be really careful about dropping tables. When it's gone, it's gone, along with all its data. Because of this danger, sometimes a DBMS will not allow you to drop a table. If this happens, check to see whether a referential integrity constraint is preventing the drop operation. When two tables are linked with a primary key/foreign key relationship, you may be prevented from deleting the table on the primary key side, unless you first break that link by deleting the table on the foreign key side.

3
Writing SQL Queries

Contents at a Glance

Chapter **1**

Values, Variables, Functions, and Expressions

This chapter describes the tools that ISO/IEC standard SQL provides to operate on data. In addition to specifying the value of a data item, you can slice and dice an item in a variety of ways. Instead of just retrieving raw data as it exists in the database, you can preprocess it to deliver just the information you want, in the form that you want it.

Entering Data Values

After you've created a database table, the next step is to enter data into it. SQL supports a number of different data types. (Refer to Book 1, Chapter 6 for coverage of those types.) Within any specific data type, the data can take any of several forms. The five different forms that can appear in table rows are

» Row values

» Column references

- ➤ Literal values
- ➤ Variables
- ➤ Special variables

I discuss each in turn throughout this section.

Row values have multiple parts

A *row value* includes the values of all the data in all the columns in a row in a table. It is actually multiple values rather than just one. The intersection of a row and a column, called a *field*, contains a single, so-called "atomic" value. All the values of all the fields in a row, taken together, are that single row's row value.

Identifying values in a column

Just as you can specify a row value consisting of multiple values, you can specify the value contained in a single column. For illustration, consider this example from the Honest Abe database shown back in Book 2, Chapter 3:

```
SELECT * FROM CUSTOMER
    WHERE CustomerName = 'John Smith' ;
```

This query returns all the rows in the CUSTOMER table where the value in the CustomerName column is John Smith.

Literal values don't change

In SQL, a value can either be a constant or it can be represented by a variable. Constant values are called *literals*. Table 1-1 shows sample literals for each of the SQL data types.

REMEMBER

Numeric literals are just the values that they represent. Nonnumeric literals are enclosed in single quotes.

TIP

The SQL:2023 standard adds a couple of new features to use with numeric literal values. For large integer values, you can add underscores to make the value more readable (for example, 1_000_000). You can also now specify nondecimal numeric literal values as binary, octal, or hexadecimal values. Binary values are preceded with 0b (for example, 0b1011), octal values with 0o (for example, 0o672), and hexadecimal values with 0x (for example, 0xA0FF).

TABLE 1-1   Sample Literals of Various Data Types

Data Type	Sample Literal
BIGINT	8589934592
INTEGER	186282
SMALLINT	186
NUMERIC	186282.42
DECIMAL	186282.42
DECFLOAT (16)	1234567890123456
REAL	6.02257E23
DOUBLE PRECISION	3.1415926535897E00
FLOAT	6.02257E23
BINARY (2)	'0110011111101010'
VARBINARY (1)	'10011'
CHARACTER(15)	'GREECE '
Note: Fifteen total characters and spaces are between the quote marks above.	
VARCHAR (CHARACTER VARYING)	'lepton'
NATIONAL CHARACTER(15)	'ΕΛΛΑΣ ' [1]
Note: Fifteen total characters and spaces are between the quote marks above.	
NATIONAL CHARACTER VARYING	'λεπτον' [2]
CHARACTER LARGE OBJECT (CLOB)	(A really long character string)
BINARY LARGE OBJECT (BLOB)	(A really long string of ones and zeros)
DATE	DATE '1969-07-20'
TIME(2)	TIME '13.41.32.50'
TIMESTAMP(0)	TIMESTAMP '2007-07-25-13.03.16.000000'
TIME WITH TIMEZONE(4)	TIME '13.41.32.5000-08.00'
TIMESTAMP WITH TIMEZONE(0)	TIMESTAMP '2007-07-25-13.03.16.0000+02.00'
INTERVAL DAY	INTERVAL '7' DAY

[1]This term is the word that Greeks use to name their own country in their own language. (The English equivalent is Hellas.)
[2]This term is the word lepton in Greek national characters.

Variables vary

Literals, which explicitly hold a single value, are fine if that value appears only once or twice in an application. However, if a value appears multiple times, and if there is any chance that value might change in the future, you should represent it with a variable. That way, if changes are necessary, you have to change the code in one place only, where the value is assigned to the variable, rather than in all the places in the application where that value appears.

For example, suppose an application dealing with a table containing the archives of a magazine retrieves information from various sections of the current issue. One such retrieval might look like this:

```
SELECT Editorial FROM PENGUINLIFE
    WHERE Issue = 47 ;
```

Another could be

```
SELECT LeadStory FROM PENGUINLIFE
    WHERE Issue = 47 ;
```

There could be many more like these two in the application. When next week rolls around and you want to run the application again for the latest issue, you must go through the program by hand and change all the instances of 47 to 48. Computers are supposed to rescue us from such boring, repetitive tasks, and they do. Instead of using literals in such cases, use variables instead, like this:

```
SET @IssueNumber = 48;
SELECT Editorial FROM PENGUINLIFE
    WHERE Issue = @IssueNumber ;
SELECT LeadStory FROM PENGUINLIFE
    WHERE Issue = @IssueNumber ;
```

You have to change the IssueNumber variable in one place only, and the change affects all the places in the application where the variable appears.

Special variables hold specific values

SQL has a few special variables that hold information about system usage. In multiuser systems, you often need to know who is using the system at any given time. This information can be captured in a log file, using the special variables. The special variables are

>> SESSION_USER, which holds a value that's equal to the user authorization identifier of the current SQL session. If you write a program that performs a monitoring function, you can interrogate SESSION_USER to find out who is executing SQL statements.

>> CURRENT_USER, which stores a user-specified authorization identifier. If a module has no such identifier, CURRENT_USER has the same value as SESSION_USER.

>> SYSTEM_USER, which contains the operating system's user identifier. This identifier may differ from that user's identifier in an SQL module. A user may log onto the system as ANDREW, for example, but identify himself to a module as DIRECTOR. The value in SESSION_USER is DIRECTOR. If he makes no explicit specification of the module identifier, and CURRENT_USER also contains DIRECTOR, SYSTEM_USER holds the value ANDREW.

One use of the SYSTEM_USER, SESSION_USER, and CURRENT_USER special variables is to track who is using the system. You can maintain a log table and periodically insert into that table the values that SYSTEM_USER, SESSION_USER, and CURRENT_USER contain. The following example shows how:

```
INSERT INTO USAGELOG (SNAPSHOT)
    VALUES ('User ' || SYSTEM_USER ||
        ' with ID ' || SESSION_USER ||
        ' active at ' || CURRENT_TIMESTAMP) ;
```

This statement produces log entries similar to the following example:

```
User ANDREW with ID DIRECTOR active at 2019-01-03-23.50.00
```

Working with Functions

Functions perform computations or operations that are more elaborate than what you would expect a simple command statement to do. SQL has two kinds of functions: set functions and value functions. *Set functions* are so named because they operate on a set of rows in a table rather than on a single row. *Value functions* operate on the values of fields in a table row.

Summarizing data with set functions

When dealing with a set of table rows, often what you want to know is some aggregate property that applies to the whole set. SQL has five such aggregate or set functions: COUNT, AVG, MAX, MIN, and SUM. To see how these work, consider the example data for a table named PAPERS in Table 1-2. It is a price table for photographic papers of various sizes and characteristics.

TABLE 1-2 **Photographic Paper Price List per 20 Sheets**

Paper Type	Size8	Size11
Dual-sided matte	8.49	13.99
Card stock dual-sided matte	9.49	16.95
Professional photo gloss	10.99	19.99
Glossy HW 9M	8.99	13.99
Smooth silk	10.99	19.95
Royal satin	10.99	19.95
Dual-sided semigloss	9.99	17.95
Dual-sided HW semigloss	--	--
Universal two-sided matte	--	--
Transparency	29.95	--

The fields that contain dashes do not have a value. The dash in the table represents a null value.

COUNT

The COUNT function returns the number of rows in a table, or the number of rows that meet a specified condition. In the simplest case, you have

```
SELECT COUNT (*)
   FROM PAPERS ;
```

This returns a value of 10 because there are ten rows in the PAPERS table. You can add a condition to see how many types of paper are available in Size 8:

```
SELECT COUNT (Size8)
   FROM PAPERS ;
```

This returns a value of 8 because, of the ten types of paper in the PAPERS table, only eight are available in size 8. You might also want to know how many different prices there are for papers of size 8. That is also easy to determine:

```
SELECT COUNT (DISTINCT Size8)
   FROM PAPERS ;
```

This returns a value of 6 because there are six distinct values of Size 8 paper. Null values are ignored.

AVG

The AVG function calculates and returns the average of the values in the specified column. It works only on columns that contain numeric data.

```
SELECT AVG (Size8)
   FROM PAPERS ;
```

This returns a value of 12.485. If you wonder what the average price is for the Size 11 papers, you can find out this way:

```
SELECT AVG (Size11)
   FROM PAPERS ;
```

This returns a value of 17.539.

MAX

As you might expect, the MAX function returns the maximum value found in the specified column. Find the maximum value in the Size8 column:

```
SELECT MAX (Size8)
   FROM PAPERS ;
```

This returns 29.95, the price for 20 sheets of Size 8 transparencies.

MIN

The MIN function gives you the minimum value found in the specified column.

```
SELECT MIN (Size8)
   FROM PAPERS ;
```

Here the value returned is 8.49.

SUM

In the case of the photographic paper example, it doesn't make much sense to calculate the sum of all the prices for the papers being offered for sale, but in other applications, this type of calculation can be valuable. Just in case you want to know what it would cost to buy 20 sheets of every Size 11 paper being offered, you could make the following query:

```
SELECT SUM (Size11)
   FROM PAPERS ;
```

It would cost 122.77 to buy 20 sheets of each of the 7 kinds of Size 11 paper that are available.

LISTAGG

LISTAGG is a set function, defined in the SQL:2016 ISO/IEC specification. Its purpose is to transform the values from a group of rows into a list of values delimited by a character that does not occur within the data. An example would be to transform a group of table rows into a string of comma-separated values (CSV).

```
SELECT LISTAGG(LastName, ', ')
          WITHIN GROUP (ORDER BY LastName) "Customer"
  FROM CUSTOMER
  WHERE Zipcode = 97201;
```

This statement will return a list of all customers residing in the 97201 zip code, in ascending order of their last names. This will work as long as there are no commas in the LastName field of any customer.

ANY_VALUE

The ANY_VALUE function, new in SQL:2023, returns any non-null value from the specified data set.

```
SELECT ANY_VALUE(Size8)
   FROM PAPERS;
```

This function will return a randomly selected value from the data values stored in the Size8 column of the data records.

Dissecting data with value functions

A number of data manipulation operations occur fairly frequently. SQL provides value functions to perform these tasks. There are four types of value functions:

>> String value functions

>> Numeric value functions

>> Datetime value functions

>> Interval value functions

In the following subsections, I look at the functions available in each of these categories.

String value functions

String value functions take one character string as input and produce another character string as output. There are 12 string value functions:

>> SUBSTRING (FROM)

>> SUBSTRING (SIMILAR)

>> UPPER

>> LOWER

>> TRIM

>> LTRIM

>> RTRIM

>> LPAD

>> RPAD

>> TRANSLATE

>> CONVERT

>> OVERLAY

SUBSTRING (FROM)

The operation of SUBSTRING (FROM) is similar to substring operations in many other computer languages. Here's an example:

```
SUBSTRING ('manual transmission' FROM 8 FOR 4)
```

This returns tran, the substring that starts in the eighth character position and continues for four characters. You want to make sure that the starting point and substring length you specify locate the substring entirely within the source string. If part or all of the substring falls outside the source string, you could receive a result you are not expecting.

REMEMBER

Some implementations do not adhere strictly to the ANSI/ISO standard syntax for the SUBSTRING function, or for the other functions that follow. Check the documentation of the implementation you are using if the code samples given here do not work for you.

SUBSTRING (SIMILAR)

SUBSTRING (SIMILAR) is a regular expression substring function. It divides a string into three parts and returns the middle part. Formally, a regular expression is a string of legal characters. A substring is a particular designated part of that string. Consider this example:

```
SUBSTRING ('antidisestablishmentarianism'
           SIMILAR 'antidis\"[:ALPHA:]+\"arianism'
           ESCAPE '\' )
```

The original string is the first operand. The operand following the SIMILAR keyword is a character string literal that includes a regular expression in the form of another character string literal, a separator (\"), a second regular expression that means "one or more alphabetic characters," a second separator (\"), and a third regular expression in the form of a different character string literal. The value returned is

```
establishment
```

UPPER

The UPPER function converts its target string to all uppercase.

```
UPPER ('ChAoTic')                    returns 'CHAOTIC'
```

The UPPER function has no effect on character sets, such as Hebrew, that do not distinguish between upper- and lowercase.

LOWER

The LOWER function converts its target string to all lowercase.

```
LOWER ('INTRUDER ALERT!')        returns 'intruder alert!'
```

As is the case for UPPER, LOWER has no effect on character sets that do not include the concept of case.

TRIM

In the SQL:2023 standard, the TRIM function enables you to crop a string, shaving off one character at the front or the back of the string — or both. Here are a few examples:

```
TRIM (LEADING ' ' FROM ' ALERT ')     returns 'ALERT '
TRIM (TRAILING ' ' FROM ' ALERT ')    returns ' ALERT'
TRIM (BOTH ' ' FROM ' ALERT ')        returns 'ALERT'
TRIM (LEADING 'A' FROM 'ALERT')       returns 'LERT'
```

If you don't specify what to trim, the blank space (' ') is the default.

WARNING

Many current SQL implementations don't follow this standard behavior for the TRIM function. Instead, the TRIM function they implement behaves similar to the new LTRIM and RTRIM functions (described in the following section).

LTRIM AND RTRIM

Because of the disparate behavior of the TRIM function implemented by various database packages, the SQL:2023 standard tries to accommodate the different implementations by adding the LTRIM and RTRIM functions. These functions expand on the standard TRIM function by allowing you to shave off multiple instances of the specified character left (LTRIM) or right (RTRIM) of the specified string.

```
LTRIM('    ALERT ', ' ')    returns 'ALERT '
RTRIM(' ALERT    ', ' ')    returns ' ALERT'
```

As with the TRIM function, if you don't specify what to trim, the blank space (' ') is the default.

TIP

Unfortunately, there is no function for trimming multiple characters off of both the left *and* right sides of the string. To do that, you'll need to use both functions on the same string.

LPAD AND RPAD

The SQL:2023 standard adds the LPAD and RPAD functions, which allow you to pad a string value to a specific size.

```
LPAD('Rich', 10, ' ')    returns '      Rich'
RPAD('Rich', 10, ' ')    returns 'Rich      '
```

As with the TRIM function, if you don't specify what to pad, the padding character is the blank space (' ') by default.

TRANSLATE AND CONVERT

The TRANSLATE and CONVERT functions take a source string in one character set and transform the original string into a string in another character set. Examples might be Greek to English or Katakana to Norwegian. The conversion functions that specify these transformations are implementation-specific, so I don't give any details here.

These functions do not really translate character strings from one language to another. All they do is translate a character from the first character set to the corresponding character in the second character set. In going from Greek to English, it would convert Ελλασ to Ellas instead of translating it as Greece. ("Ελλασ" is what the Greeks call their country. I have no idea why English speakers call it Greece.)

OVERLAY

The OVERLAY function is a SUBSTRING function with a little extra functionality. As with SUBSTRING, it finds a specified substring within a target string. However, instead of returning the string that it finds, it replaces it with a different string. For example:

```
OVERLAY ('I Love Paris' PLACING 'Tokyo' FROM 8 FOR 5)
```

This changes the string to

```
I Love Tokyo
```

This won't work if you want to change I Love Paris to I Love London. The number of letters in London does not match the number in Paris.

Numeric value functions

Numeric value functions can take a variety of data types as input, but the output is always a numeric value. SQL has 14 types of numeric value functions. The defining characteristic of a function is that it returns a value of some sort. Numeric value functions always return a numeric value. Thus, the square root function will return a value that is the square root of the input; the natural logarithm function will return a value that is the natural logarithm of the input, and so on.

>> Position expression (POSITION)

>> Extract expression (EXTRACT)

>> Length expression (CHAR_LENGTH, CHARACTER_LENGTH, OCTET_LENGTH)

>> Cardinality expression (CARDINALITY)

>> Absolute value expression (ABS)

>> Modulus expression (MOD)

>> Trigonometric functions (SIN, COS, TAN, ASIN, ACOS, ATAN, SINH, COSH, TANH)

>> Logarithmic functions (LOG, LOG10, LN)

>> Exponential function (EXP)

>> Power function (POWER)

>> Square root (SQRT)

>> Floor function (FLOOR)

>> Ceiling function (CEIL, CEILING)

>> Greatest function (GREATEST)

>> Least function (LEAST)

>> Width bucket function (WIDTH_BUCKET)

POSITION

POSITION searches for a specified target string within a specified source string and returns the character position where the target string begins. The syntax is as follows:

```
POSITION (target IN source)
```

Table 1-3 shows a few examples.

TABLE 1-3   ## Sample Uses of the POSITION Statement

This Statement	Returns
POSITION ('T' IN 'Transmission, automatic')	1
POSITION ('Tra' IN 'Transmission, automatic')	1
POSITION ('au' IN 'Transmission, automatic')	15
POSITION ('man' IN 'Transmission, automatic')	0
POSITION ('' IN 'Transmission, automatic')	1

If the function doesn't find the target string, the POSITION function returns a zero value. If the target string has zero length (as in the last example), the POSITION function always returns a value of 1. If any operand in the function has a null value, the result is a null value.

EXTRACT

The EXTRACT function extracts a single field from a datetime or an interval. The following statement, for example, returns 12:

```
EXTRACT (MONTH FROM DATE '2018-12-04')
```

CHARACTER_LENGTH

The CHARACTER_LENGTH function returns the number of characters in a character string. The following statement, for example, returns 20:

```
CHARACTER_LENGTH ('Transmission, manual')
```

REMEMBER

As you can see, commas and even blank spaces count as characters. Note that this function is not particularly useful if its argument is a literal like 'Transmission, manual'. I can write 20 just as easily as I can write CHARACTER_LENGTH ('Transmission, manual'). In fact, writing 20 is easier. This function is more useful if its argument is an expression rather than a literal value.

OCTET_LENGTH

In music, a vocal ensemble made up of eight singers is called an *octet*. Typically, the parts that the ensemble represents are first and second soprano, first and second alto, first and second tenor, and first and second bass. In computer terminology, an ensemble of eight data bits is called a *byte*. The word *byte* is clever in that the term clearly relates to *bit* but implies something larger than a bit. A nice wordplay — but unfortunately, nothing in the word *byte* conveys the concept of "eightness." By borrowing the musical term, a more apt description of a collection of eight bits becomes possible.

Practically all modern computers use eight bits to represent a single alphanumeric character. More complex character sets (such as Chinese) require 16 bits to represent a single character. The OCTET_LENGTH function counts and returns the number of octets (bytes) in a string. If the string is a bit string, OCTET_LENGTH returns the number of octets you need to hold that number of bits. If the string is an English-language character string (with one octet per character), the function returns the number of characters in the string. If the string is a Chinese character string, the function returns a number that is twice the number of Chinese characters. The following string is an example:

```
OCTET_LENGTH ('Brakes, disc')
```

This function returns 12 because each character takes up one octet.

Some character sets use a variable number of octets for different characters. In particular, some character sets that support mixtures of Kanji and Latin characters use *escape* characters to switch between the two character sets. A string that contains both Latin and Kanji may have, for example, 30 characters and require 30 octets if all the characters are Latin; 62 characters if all the characters are Kanji (60 characters plus a leading and trailing shift character); and 150 characters if the characters alternate between Latin and Kanji (because each Kanji character needs two octets for the character and one octet each for the leading and trailing shift characters). The OCTET_LENGTH function returns the number of octets you need for the current value of the string.

CARDINALITY

Cardinality deals with collections of elements such as arrays or multisets, where each element is a value of some data type. The cardinality of the collection is the number of elements that it contains. One use of the CARDINALITY function is something like this:

```
CARDINALITY (TeamRoster)
```

This function would return 12, for example, if there were 12 team members on the roster. TeamRoster, a column in the TEAM table, can be either an array or a multiset. An *array* is an ordered collection of elements, and a *multiset* is an unordered collection of elements. For a team roster, which changes frequently, a multiset makes more sense. (You can find out more about arrays and multisets in Book 1, Chapter 6.)

ABS

The ABS function returns the absolute value of a numeric value expression.

```
ABS (-273)
```

This returns 273.

TRIGONOMETRIC FUNCTIONS SIN, COS, TAN, ASIN, ACOS, ATAN, SINH, COSH, TANH

The trig functions give you the values you would expect, such as the sine of an angle or the hyperbolic tangent of one.

LOGARITHMIC FUNCTIONS LOG10, LN, LOG (<BASE>, <VALUE>)

The logarithmic functions enable you to generate the logarithm of a number, either a base-10 logarithm, a natural logarithm, or a logarithm to a base that you specify.

MOD

The MOD function returns the *modulus* — the remainder of division of one number by another — of two numeric value expressions.

```
MOD (6,4)
```

This function returns 2, the modulus of six divided by four.

EXP

This function raises the base of the natural logarithms *e* to the power specified by a numeric value expression:

```
EXP (2)
```

This function returns something like 7.389056. The number of digits beyond the decimal point is implementation-dependent.

POWER

This function raises the value of the first numeric value expression to the power of the second numeric value expression:

```
POWER (3,7)
```

This function returns 2187, which is three raised to the seventh power.

SQRT

This function returns the square root of the value of the numeric value expression:

```
SQRT (9)
```

This function returns 3, the square root of nine.

FLOOR

This function rounds the numeric value expression to the largest integer not greater than the expression:

```
FLOOR (2.73)
```

This function returns 2.0.

CEIL OR CEILING

This function rounds the numeric value expression to the smallest integer not less than the expression.

```
CEIL (2.73)
```

This function returns 3.0.

GREATEST

Because the set functions already use the MAX function, the SQL:2023 standard defines the GREATEST function to use for numeric values.

```
GREATEST(1.0,2.0,3.5)
```

This functions returns 3.5.

LEAST

Because the set functions already use the MIN function, the SQL:2023 standard defines the LEAST function to use for numeric values.

```
LEAST(1.0, 2.0, 3.5)
```

This function returns 1.0.

WIDTH_BUCKET

The WIDTH_BUCKET function, used in online application processing (OLAP), is a function of four arguments, returning an integer between the value of the second (minimum) argument and the value of the third (maximum) argument. It assigns the first argument to an equiwidth partitioning of the range of numbers between the second and third arguments. Values outside this range are assigned to either the value of zero or one more than the fourth argument (the number of buckets).

For example:

```
WIDTH_BUCKET (PI, 0, 10, 5)
```

Suppose PI is a numeric value expression with a value of 3.141592. The example partitions the interval from zero to ten into five equal *buckets*, each with a width of two. The function returns a value of 2 because 3.141592 falls into the second bucket, which covers the range from two to four.

Datetime value functions

SQL includes three functions that return information about the current date, current time, or both. CURRENT_DATE returns the current date; CURRENT_TIME returns the current time; and CURRENT_TIMESTAMP returns both the current date and the current time. CURRENT_DATE doesn't take an argument, but CURRENT_TIME and CURRENT_TIMESTAMP both take a single argument. The argument specifies the precision for the seconds part of the time value that the function returns. Datetime data types and the precision concept are described in Book 1, Chapter 6.

The following table offers some examples of these datetime value functions.

This Statement	Returns
CURRENT_DATE	2019-01-23
CURRENT_TIME (1)	08:36:57.3
CURRENT_IMESTAMP (2)	2019-01-23 08:36:57.38

The date that CURRENT_DATE returns is DATE type data. The time that CURRENT_TIME (*p*) returns is TIME type data, and the timestamp that CURRENT_TIMESTAMP (*p*) returns is TIMESTAMP type data. The precision (*p*) specified is the number of digits beyond the decimal point, showing fractions of a second. Because SQL retrieves date and time information from your computer's system clock, the information is correct for the time zone in which the computer resides.

In some applications, you may want to deal with dates, times, or timestamps as character strings to take advantage of the functions that operate on character data. You can perform a type conversion by using the CAST expression, which I describe later in this chapter.

Polymorphic table functions

A table function is a user-defined function that returns a table as a result. A polymorphic table function, first described in SQL:2016, is a table function whose row type is not declared when the function is created. Instead, the row type may depend on the function arguments used when the function is invoked.

Using Expressions

An *expression* is any combination of elements that reduces to a single value. The elements can be numbers, strings, dates, times, intervals, Booleans, or more complex things. What they are doesn't matter, as long as after all operations have taken place, the result is a single value.

Numeric value expressions

The operands in a numeric value expression can be numbers of an exact numeric type or of an approximate numeric type. (Exact and approximate numeric types are discussed in Book 1, Chapter 6.) Operands of different types can be used within a single expression. If at least one operand is of an approximate type, the result is of an approximate type. If all operands are of exact types, the result is of an exact type. The SQL specification does not specify exactly what type the result of any given expression will be, due to the wide variety of platforms that SQL runs on.

Here are some examples of valid numeric value expressions:

>> -24

>> 13+78

» 4*(5+8)

» Weight/(Length*Width*Height)

» Miles/5280

String value expressions

String value expressions can consist of a single string or a concatenation of strings. The concatenation operator (||) joins two strings together and is the only one you can use in a string value expression. Table 1-4 shows some examples of string value expressions and the strings that they produce.

TABLE 1-4 **Examples of String Value Expressions**

String Value Expression	Resulting String
`'nanotechnology'`	`'nanotechnology'`
`'nano' || 'technology'`	`'nanotechnology'`
`'nano' || '' || 'technology'`	`'nanotechnology'`
`'Isaac' || '' || 'Newton'`	`'Isaac Newton'`
`FirstName || ' ' || LastName`	`'Isaac Newton'`
`B'10101010' || B'01010101'`	`B'1010101001010101'`

From the first two rows in Table 1-4, you see that concatenating two strings produces a result string that has seamlessly joined the two original strings. The third row shows that concatenating a null value with two source strings produces the same result as if the null were not there. The fourth row shows concatenation of two strings while retaining a blank space in between. The fifth row shows the concatenation of two variables with a blank space in between produces a string consisting of the values of those variables separated by a blank space. Finally, the last line of Table 1-4 shows the concatenation of two binary strings. The result is a single binary string that is a seamless combination of the two source strings.

Datetime value expressions

Datetime value expressions perform operations on dates and times. Such data is of the DATE, TIME, TIMESTAMP, or INTERVAL type. The result of a datetime value expression is always of the DATE, TIME, or TIMESTAMP type. Intervals are not one of the datetime types, but an interval can be added to or subtracted from a datetime to produce another datetime. Here's an example datetime value expression that makes use of an added interval:

```
CURRENT_DATE + INTERVAL '2' DAY
```

This expression evaluates to the day after tomorrow.

Datetimes can also include time zone information. The system maintains times in Coordinated Universal Time (UTC), which until recently was known as Greenwich Mean Time (GMT). (I guess the feeling was that Greenwich was too provincial, and a more general name for world time was called for.) You can specify a time as being either at your local time, or as an offset from UTC. An example is

```
TIME '13:15:00' AT LOCAL
```

for 1:15 p.m. local time. Another example is

```
TIME '13:15:00' AT TIME ZONE INTERVAL '-8:00' HOUR TO MINUTE
```

for 1:15 p.m. Pacific Standard Time. (Pacific Standard Time is eight hours earlier than UTC.)

Interval value expressions

An *interval* is the difference between two datetimes. If you subtract one datetime from another, the result is an interval. It makes no sense to add two datetimes, so SQL does not allow you to do it.

There are two kinds of intervals: year-month and day-time. This situation is a little messy, but necessary because not all months contain the same number of days. Because a month can be 28, 29, 30, or 31 days long, there is no direct translation from days to months. As a result, when using an interval, you must specify which kind of interval it is. Suppose you expect to take an around-the-world cruise after you retire, starting on June 1, 2045. How many years and months is that from now? An interval value expression gives you the answer.

```
(DATE '2045-06-01' - CURRENT_DATE) YEAR TO MONTH
```

You can add two intervals to obtain an interval result.

```
INTERVAL '30' DAY + INTERVAL '14' DAY
```

However, you cannot do the following:

```
INTERVAL '30' DAY + INTERVAL '14' MONTH
```

The two kinds of intervals do not mix. Besides addition and subtraction, multiplication and division of intervals also are allowed. The expression

```
INTERVAL '7' DAY * 3
```

is valid and gives an interval of 21 days. The expression

```
INTERVAL '12' MONTH / 2
```

is also valid and gives an interval of 6 months. Intervals can also be negative.

```
INTERVAL '-3' DAY
```

gives an interval of -3 days. Aside from the literals I use in the previous examples, any value expression or combination of value expressions that evaluates to an interval can be used in an interval value expression.

Boolean value expressions

Only three legal Boolean values exist: TRUE, FALSE, and UNKNOWN. The UNKNOWN value becomes operative when a NULL is involved. Suppose the Boolean variable Signal1 is TRUE and the Boolean variable Signal2 is FALSE. The following Boolean value expression evaluates to TRUE:

```
Signal1 IS TRUE
```

So does this one:

```
Signal1 IS TRUE OR Signal2 IS TRUE
```

However, the following Boolean value expression evaluates to FALSE.

```
Signal1 IS TRUE AND Signal2 IS TRUE
```

The AND operator means that both predicates must be true for the result to be true. (A *predicate* is an expression that asserts a fact about values.) Because Signal2 is false, the entire expression evaluates to a FALSE value.

Array value expressions

You can use a couple of types of expressions with arrays. The first has to do with cardinality. The maximum number of elements an array can have is called the array's *maximum cardinality*. The actual number of elements in the array at a given time is called its *actual cardinality*. You can combine two arrays by concatenating them, summing their maximum cardinalities in the process. Suppose you want to know the actual cardinality of the concatenation of two array-type columns in a table, where the first element of the first column has a given value. You can execute the following statement:

```
SELECT CARDINALITY (FirstColumn || SecondColumn)
   FROM TARGETTABLE
WHERE FirstColumn[1] = 42 ;
```

The CARDINALITY function gives the combined cardinality of the two arrays, where the first element in the first array has a value of 42.

Note: The first element of an SQL array is considered to be element 1, rather than element 0 as is true for some other languages.

Conditional value expressions

The value of a conditional value expression depends on a condition. SQL offers three variants of conditional value expressions: CASE, NULLIF, and COALESCE. I look at each of these separately.

Handling different cases

The CASE conditional expression was added to SQL to give it some of the functionality that all full-featured computer languages have, the ability to do one thing if a condition holds and another thing if the condition does not hold. Originally conceived as a data sublanguage that was concerned only with managing data, SQL has gradually gained features that enable it to take on more of the functions needed by application programs.

SQL actually has two different CASE structures: the CASE expression described here, and a CASE statement. The CASE expression, like all expressions, evaluates to a single value. You can use a CASE expression anywhere where a value is legal. The CASE statement, on the other hand, doesn't evaluate to a value. Instead, it executes a block of statements.

The CASE expression searches a table, one row at a time, taking on the value of a specified result whenever one of a list of conditions is TRUE. If the first condition is not satisfied for a row, the second condition is tested, and if it is TRUE, the result specified for it is given to the expression, and so on until all conditions are processed. If no match is found, the expression takes on a NULL value. Processing then moves to the next row.

SEARCHING FOR TABLE ROWS THAT SATISFY VARIOUS CONDITIONS

You can specify the value to be given to a CASE expression, based on which of several conditions is satisfied. Here's the syntax:

```
CASE
    WHEN condition1 THEN result1
    WHEN condition2 THEN result2
    . . .
    WHEN conditionN THEN resultN
    ELSE resultx
END
```

If, in searching a table, the CASE expression finds a row where condition1 is true, it takes on the value of result1. If condition1 is not true, but condition2 is true, it takes on the value of result2. This continues for all conditions. If none of the conditions are met and there is no ELSE clause, the expression is given the NULL value. Here's an example of usage:

```
UPDATE MECHANIC
    Set JobTitle = CASE
                    WHEN Specialty = 'Brakes'
                        THEN 'Brake Fixer'
                    WHEN Specialty = 'Engines'
                        THEN 'Motor Master'
                    WHEN Specialty = 'Electrical'
                        THEN 'Wizard'
                    ELSE 'Apprentice'
                END ;
```

THE EQUALITY CONDITION ALLOWS A COMPACT CASE VALUE EXPRESSION

A shorthand version of the CASE statement can be used when the condition, as in the previous example, is based on one thing being equal (=) to one other thing. The syntax is as follows:

```
CASE valuet
```

```
        WHEN value1 THEN result1
        WHEN value2 THEN result2
        ...
        WHEN valueN THEN resultN
        ELSE resultx
END
```

For the preceding example, this translates to

```
UPDATE MECHANIC
     Set JobTitle = CASE Specialty
                         WHEN 'Brakes' THEN 'Brake Fixer'
                         WHEN 'Engines' THEN 'Motor Master'
                         WHEN 'Electrical' THEN 'Wizard'
                         ELSE 'Apprentice'
                    END ;
```

If the condition involves anything other than equality, the first, nonabbreviated form must be used.

The NULLIF special CASE

SQL databases are unusual in that NULL values are allowed. A NULL value can represent an unknown value, a known value that has just not been entered into the database yet, or a value that does not exist. Most other languages that deal with data do not support nulls, so whenever a situation arises in such databases where a value is not known, not yet entered, or nonexistent, the space is filled with a value that would not otherwise occur, such as –1 in a field that never holds a negative value, or ∗∗∗ in a character field in which asterisks are not valid characters.

To migrate data from a database that does not support nulls to an SQL database that does, you can use a CASE statement such as

```
UPDATE MECHANIC
     SET Specialty = CASE Specialty
                         WHEN '***' THEN NULL
                         ELSE Specialty
                    END ;
```

You can do the same thing in a shorthand manner, using a NULLIF expression, as follows:

```
UPDATE MECHANIC
     SET Specialty = NULLIF(Specialty, '***') ;
```

Admittedly, this looks more cryptic than the CASE version, but it does save some tedious typing. You could interpret it as, "Update the MECHANIC table by setting the value of Specialty to NULL if its current value is '***'".

Bypassing null values with COALESCE

The COALESCE expression is another shorthand version of CASE that deals with NULL values. It examines a series of values in a table row and assumes the value of the first one that is not NULL. If all the listed values are NULL, the COALESCE expression takes on the NULL value. Here's the syntax for a CASE expression that does this:

```
CASE
    WHEN value1 IS NOT NULL
        THEN value1
    WHEN value2 IS NOT NULL
        THEN value2
    ...
    WHEN valueN is NOT NULL
        THEN valueN
    ELSE NULL
END
```

Here's the syntax for the equivalent COALESCE expression:

```
COALESCE(value1, value2, ..., valueN)
```

If you are dealing with a large number of cases, the COALESCE version can save you quite a bit of typing.

Converting data types with a CAST expression

In Book 1, Chapter 6, I describe the data types that SQL recognizes. The host languages that SQL statements are often embedded in also recognize data types, and those host language data types are never an exact match for the SQL data types. This could present a problem, except for the fact that, with a CAST expression, you can convert data of one type into data of another type. Whereas the first type might not be compatible with the place you want to send the data, the second type is. Of course, not all conversions are possible. If you have a character string such as '2019-02-14', you can convert it to the DATE type with a CAST expression. However, SQL doesn't let you convert a character string such as 'rhinoceros' to the DATE type. The data to be converted must be compatible with the destination type.

Casting one SQL data type to another

The simplest kind of cast is from one SQL data type to another SQL data type. Even for this operation, however, you cannot indiscriminately make any conversion you want. The data you are converting must be compatible with the target data type. For example, suppose you have a table named ENGINEERS with a column named SSN, which is of the NUMERIC type. Perhaps you have another table, named MANAGERS, that has a column named SocSecNo, which is of the CHAR (9) type. A typical entry in SSN might be 987654321. To find all the engineers who are also managers, you can use the following query. The CAST expression converts the CHAR (9) type to the NUMERIC type so that the operation can proceed.

```
SELECT * FROM ENGINEER
    WHERE ENGINEER.SSN = CAST(MANAGER.SocSecNo AS INTEGER) ;
```

This returns all the rows from the ENGINEER table that have Social Security Numbers that match Social Security Numbers in the MANAGERS table. To do so, it changes the Social Security Number from the MANAGER table from the CHAR (9) type to the INTEGER type, for the purposes of the comparison.

Using CAST to overcome data type incompatibilities between SQL and its host language

Problems arise when you want to send data between SQL and its host language. For example, SQL has the DECIMAL and NUMERIC types, but some host languages, such as FORTRAN and Pascal, do not. One way around this problem is to use CAST to put a numeric value into a character string, and then put the character string into a host variable that the host language can take in and deal with.

Suppose you maintain salary information as REAL type data in the EMPLOYEE table. You want to make some manipulations on that data that SQL is not well-equipped to perform, but your host language is. You can cast the data into a form the host language can accept, operate on it at the host level, and then cast the result back to a form acceptable to the SQL database.

```
SELECT CAST(Salary AS CHAR (10)) INTO :salary_var
    FROM EMPLOYEE
    WHERE EmpID = :emp_id_var ;
```

That puts the salary value where the host language can grab it, and in a form that the host language understands. After the host language is finished operating on the data item, it can return to the SQL database via a similar path:

```
UPDATE EMPLOYEE
    SET Salary = CAST(:salary_var AS DECIMAL(10,2))
        WHERE EmpID = :emp_id_var ;
```

In addition to these conversions, you can do a number of other conversions, including the following:

>> Any numeric type to any other numeric type

>> Any exact numeric type to a single-component interval, such as INTERVAL DAY

>> Any DATE to a TIMESTAMP

>> Any TIME to a TIME with a different fractional seconds precision or a TIMESTAMP

>> Any TIMESTAMP to a DATE, a TIME, or a TIMESTAMP with a different fractional seconds precision

>> Any year-month INTERVAL to an exact numeric type

>> Any day-time INTERVAL to an exact numeric type

>> Any character string to any other type, where the data makes sense

>> Any bit string to a character string

>> A Boolean to a character string

Row value expressions

Row value expressions (as distinct from mere row values, which are covered at the beginning of this chapter) enable you to deal with the data in an entire table row or a subset of a row. The other expressions that I've shown deal only with a single field in a row at a time. Row value expressions are useful for adding new data to a table a row at a time, or to specify the retrieval of multiple fields from a table row. Here's an example of a row value expression used to enter a new row of data to a table:

```
INSERT INTO CERTIFICATIONS
  (CertificationNo, CertName, MechanicID, Expires)
  VALUES
  (1, 'V8 Engines', 34, 2021-07-31) ;
```

One advantage of using row value expressions is that many SQL implementations can process them faster than the equivalent one-field-at-a-time operations. This could make a significant difference in performance at runtime.

Chapter **2**

SELECT Statements and Modifying Clauses

T he main purpose of storing data on a computer is to be able to retrieve specific elements of the data when you need them. As databases grow in size, the proportion that you are likely to want on any given occasion becomes smaller. As a result, SQL provides tools that enable you to make retrievals in a variety of ways. With these tools — SELECT statements and modifying clauses — you can zero in on the precise pieces of information that you want, even though they may be buried among megabytes of data that you're not interested in at the moment.

Finding Needles in Haystacks withthe SELECT Statement

SQL's primary tool for retrieving information from a database is the SELECT statement. In its simplest form, with one modifying clause (a FROM clause), it retrieves everything from a table. By adding more modifying clauses, you can whittle down what it retrieves until you are getting exactly what you want, no more and no less.

Suppose you want to display a complete list of all the customers in your CUSTOMER table, including every piece of data that the table stores about each one. That is the simplest retrieval you can do. Here's the syntax:

```
SELECT * FROM CUSTOMER ;
```

The asterisk (*) is a wildcard character that means *all columns*. This statement returns all the data held in all the rows of the CUSTOMER table. Sometimes that is exactly what you want. At other times, you may only want *some* of the data on *some* of the customers: those that satisfy one or more conditions. For such refined retrievals, you must use one or more modifying clauses.

WARNING

Returning more data fields than you actually need may sound trivial, but it can drastically decrease the performance of a query. It's usually best to avoid using the asterisk unless you really do use all the data.

Modifying Clauses

In any SELECT statement, the FROM clause is mandatory. You *must* specify the source of the data you want to retrieve. Other modifying clauses are optional. They serve several different functions:

>> The WHERE clause specifies a condition. Only those table rows that satisfy the condition are returned.

>> The GROUP BY clause rearranges the order of the rows returned by placing rows together that have the same value in a grouping column.

>> The HAVING clause filters out groups that do not meet a specified condition.

>> The ORDER BY clause sorts whatever is left after all the other modifying clauses have had a chance to operate.

The next few sections look at these clauses in greater detail.

FROM clauses

The FROM clause is easy to understand if you specify only one table, as in the previous example.

```
SELECT * FROM CUSTOMER ;
```

This statement returns all the data in all the rows of every column in the CUSTOMER table. You can, however, specify more than one table in a FROM clause. Consider the following example:

```
SELECT *
  FROM CUSTOMER, INVOICE ;
```

This statement forms a virtual table that combines the data from the CUSTOMER table with the data from the INVOICE table. Each row in the CUSTOMER table combines with every row in the INVOICE table to form the new table. The new virtual table that this combination forms contains the number of rows in the CUSTOMER table multiplied by the number of rows in the INVOICE table. If the CUSTOMER table has 10 rows and the INVOICE table has 100, the new virtual table has 1,000 rows.

This operation is called the *Cartesian product* of the two source tables. The Cartesian product is a type of JOIN. I cover JOIN operations in detail in Chapter 4 of this minibook.

In most applications, the majority of the rows that form as a result of taking the Cartesian product of two tables are meaningless. In the case of the virtual table that forms from the CUSTOMER and INVOICE tables, only the rows where the CustomerID from the CUSTOMER table matches the CustomerID from the INVOICE table would be of any real interest. You can filter out the rest of the rows by using a WHERE clause.

Row pattern recognition is a new capability that was added to the FROM clause in SQL:2016. It enables you to find patterns in a data set. The capability is particularly useful in finding patterns in time series data, such as stock market quotes or any other data set where it would be helpful to know when a trend reverses direction. The row pattern recognition operation is accomplished with a MATCH_RECOGNIZE clause within an SQL statement's FROM clause. The syntax of the row pattern recognition operation is more complex than I want to get into in this overview of modifying clauses. It is described in detail in ISO/IEC TR 19075-5:2016(E), Section 3, which is available for free from ISO. As of this writing, of the major RDBMS products, only Oracle implements row pattern recognition.

WHERE clauses

I use the WHERE clause many times throughout this book without really explaining it because its meaning and use are obvious: A statement performs an operation (such as a SELECT, DELETE, or UPDATE) only on table rows where a stated condition is TRUE. The syntax of the WHERE clause is as follows:

```
SELECT column_list
   FROM table_name
   WHERE condition ;

DELETE FROM table_name
   WHERE condition ;

UPDATE table_name
   SET column₁=value₁, column₂=value₂, ..., columnₙ=valueₙ
   WHERE condition ;
```

The condition in the WHERE clause may be simple or arbitrarily complex. You may join multiple conditions together by using the logical connectives AND, OR, and NOT (which I discuss later in this chapter) to create a single condition.

The following statements show you some typical examples of WHERE clauses:

```
WHERE CUSTOMER.CustomerID = INVOICE.CustomerID
WHERE MECHANIC.EmployeeID = CERTIFICATION.MechanicID
WHERE PART.QuantityInStock < 10
WHERE PART.QuantityInStock > 100 AND PART.CostBasis > 100.00
```

The conditions that these WHERE clauses express are known as predicates. A *predicate* is an expression that asserts a fact about values.

The predicate PART.QuantityInStock < 10, for example, is True if the value for the current row of the column PART.QuantityInStock is less than 10. If the assertion is True, it satisfies the condition. An assertion may be True, False, or UNKNOWN. The UNKNOWN case arises if one or more elements in the assertion are null. The *comparison predicates* (=, <, >, <>, <=, and >=) are the most common, but SQL offers several others that greatly increase your capability to distinguish, or filter out, a desired data item from others in the same column. The following list notes the predicates that give you that filtering capability:

» Comparison predicates

» BETWEEN

» IN [NOT IN]

» LIKE [NOT LIKE]

» NULL

- » ALL, SOME, and ANY
- » EXISTS
- » UNIQUE
- » DISTINCT
- » OVERLAPS
- » MATCH

The mechanics of filtering can get a bit complicated, so let me take the time to go down this list and explain the mechanics of each predicate.

Comparison predicates

The examples in the preceding section show typical uses of comparison predicates in which you compare one value to another. For every row in which the comparison evaluates to a True value, that value satisfies the WHERE clause, and the operation (SELECT, UPDATE, DELETE, or whatever) executes upon that row. Rows that the comparison evaluates to FALSE are skipped. Consider the following SQL statement:

```
SELECT * FROM PART
    WHERE QuantityInStock < 10 ;
```

This statement displays all rows from the PART table that have a value of less than 10 in the QuantityInStock column.

Six comparison predicates are listed in Table 2-1.

TABLE 2-1

SQL's Comparison Predicates

Comparison	Symbol
Equal	=
Not equal	<>
Less than	<
Less than or equal	<=
Greater than	>
Greater than or equal	>=

SELECT Statements
and Modifying Clauses

BETWEEN

Sometimes, you want to select a row if the value in a column falls within a specified range. One way to make this selection is by using comparison predicates. For example, you can formulate a WHERE clause to select all the rows in the PART table that have a value in the QuantityInStock column greater than 10 and less than 100, as follows:

```
WHERE PART.QuantityInStock > 10 AND PART.QuantityInStock < 100
```

This comparison doesn't include parts with a quantity in stock of exactly 10 or 100 — only those values that fall in between these two numbers. To include the end points, you can write the statement as follows:

```
WHERE PART.QuantityInStock >= 10 AND PART.QuantityInStock <= 100
```

Another (potentially simpler) way of specifying a range that includes the end points is to use a BETWEEN predicate, like this:

```
WHERE PART.QuantityInStock BETWEEN 10 AND 100
```

This clause is functionally identical to the preceding example, which uses comparison predicates. This formulation saves some typing and is a little more intuitive than the one that uses two comparison predicates joined by the logical connective AND.

WARNING

The BETWEEN keyword may be confusing because it doesn't tell you explicitly whether the clause includes the end points. In fact, the clause *does* include these end points. BETWEEN also fails to tell you explicitly that the first term in the comparison must be equal to or less than the second. If, for example, PART. QuantityInStock contains a value of 50, the following clause returns a TRUE value:

```
WHERE PART.QuantityInStock BETWEEN 10 AND 100
```

However, a clause that you may think is equivalent to the preceding example returns the opposite result, False:

```
WHERE PART.QuantityInStock BETWEEN 100 AND 10
```

REMEMBER

If you use BETWEEN, you must be able to guarantee that the first term in your comparison is always equal to or less than the second term.

You can use the BETWEEN predicate with character, bit, and datetime data types as well as with the numeric types. You may see something like the following example:

```
SELECT FirstName, LastName
   FROM CUSTOMER
   WHERE CUSTOMER.LastName BETWEEN 'A' AND 'Mzzz' ;
```

This example returns all customers whose last names are in the first half of the alphabet.

IN and NOT IN

The IN and NOT IN predicates deal with whether specified values (such as GA, AL, and MS) are contained within a particular set of values (such as the states of the United States). You may, for example, have a table that lists suppliers of a commodity that your company purchases on a regular basis. You want to know the phone numbers of those suppliers located in the southern United States. You can find these numbers by using comparison predicates, such as those shown in the following example:

```
SELECT Company, Phone
   FROM SUPPLIER
   WHERE State = 'GA' OR State = 'AL' OR State = 'MS' ;
```

You can also use the IN predicate to perform the same task, as follows:

```
SELECT Company, Phone
   FROM SUPPLIER
   WHERE State IN ('GA', 'AL', 'MS') ;
```

This formulation is more compact than the one using comparison predicates and logical OR.

The NOT IN version of this predicate works the same way. Say that you have locations in New York, New Jersey, and Connecticut, and to avoid paying sales tax, you want to consider using suppliers located anywhere except in those states. Use the following construction:

```
SELECT Company, Phone
   FROM SUPPLIER
   WHERE State NOT IN ('NY', 'NJ', 'CT') ;
```

Using the IN keyword this way saves you a little typing. Saving a little typing, however, isn't that great an advantage. You can do the same job by using comparison predicates, as shown in this section's first example.

You may have another good reason to use the IN predicate rather than comparison predicates, even if using IN doesn't save much typing. Your DBMS probably implements the two methods differently, and one of the methods may be significantly faster than the other on your system. You may want to run a performance comparison on the two ways of expressing inclusion in (or exclusion from) a group and then use the technique that produces the quicker result. A DBMS with a good optimizer will probably choose the more efficient method, regardless of which kind of predicate you use. A performance comparison gives you some idea of how good your DBMS's optimizer is. If a significant difference between the run times of the two statements exists, the quality of your DBMS's optimizer is called into question.

The IN keyword is valuable in another area, too. If IN is part of a subquery, the keyword enables you to pull information from two tables to obtain results that you can't derive from a single table. I cover subqueries in detail in Chapter 3 of this minibook, but following is an example that shows how a subquery uses the IN keyword.

Suppose that you want to display the names of all customers who've bought the flux capacitor product in the last 30 days. Customer names are in the CUSTOMER table, and sales transaction data is in the PART table. You can use the following query:

```
SELECT FirstName, LastName
  FROM CUSTOMER
  WHERE CustomerID IN
    (SELECT CustomerID
      FROM INVOICE
      WHERE SalesDate >= (CurrentDate - 30) AND InvoiceNo IN
        (SELECT InvoiceNo
          FROM INVOICE_LINE
          WHERE PartNo IN
            (SELECT PartNo
              FROM PART
              WHERE NAME = 'flux capacitor' ) ;
```

The inner SELECT of the INVOICE table nests within the outer SELECT of the CUSTOMER table. The inner SELECT of the INVOICE_LINE table nests within the outer SELECT of the INVOICE table. The inner select of the PART table nests within the outer SELECT of the INVOICE_LINE table. The SELECT on the INVOICE table finds the CustomerID numbers of all customers who bought the flux capacitor product in the last 30 days. The outermost SELECT (on the CUSTOMER table) displays the first and last names of all customers whose CustomerID is retrieved by the inner SELECT statements.

LIKE and NOT LIKE

You can use the LIKE predicate to compare two character strings for a partial match. Partial matches are valuable if you don't know the exact form of the string for which you're searching. You can also use partial matches to retrieve multiple rows that contain similar strings in one of the table's columns.

To identify partial matches, SQL uses two wildcard characters. The percent sign (%) can stand for any string of characters that have zero or more characters. The underscore (_) stands for any single character. Table 2-2 provides some examples that show how to use LIKE.

TABLE 2-2

SQL's LIKE Predicate

Statement	Values Returned
WHERE String LIKE 'auto%'	auto
	automotive
	automobile
	automatic
	autocracy
WHERE String LIKE '%ode%'	code of conduct
	model citizen
WHERE String LIKE '_o_e'	mope
	tote
	rope
	love
	cone
	node

The NOT LIKE predicate retrieves all rows that don't satisfy a partial match, including one or more wildcard characters, as in the following example:

```
WHERE Email NOT LIKE '%@databasecentral.info'
```

This example returns all the rows in the table where the email address is not hosted at www.databasecentral.info.

TIP

You may want to search for a string that includes a percent sign or an underscore. In this case, you want SQL to interpret the percent sign as a percent sign and not as a wildcard character. You can conduct such a search by typing an escape character just prior to the character you want SQL to take literally. You can choose any character as the escape character, as long as that character doesn't appear in the string that you're testing, as shown in the following example:

```
SELECT Quote
    FROM BARTLETTS
    WHERE Quote LIKE '20#%'
       ESCAPE '#' ;
```

The % character is escaped by the preceding # sign, so the statement interprets this symbol as a percent sign rather than as a wildcard. You can escape an underscore or the escape character itself, in the same way. The preceding query, for example, would find the following quotation in *Bartlett's Familiar Quotations*:

```
20% of the salespeople produce 80% of the results.
```

The query would also find the following:

```
20%
```

NULL

The NULL predicate finds all rows where the value in the selected column is null. In the photographic paper price list table I describe in Chapter 1 of this minibook, several rows have null values in the Size11 column. You can retrieve their names by using a statement such as the following:

```
SELECT (PaperType)
    FROM PAPERS
    WHERE Size11Price IS NULL ;
```

This query returns the following values:

```
Dual-sided HW semigloss
Universal two-sided matte
Transparency
```

As you may expect, including the NOT keyword reverses the result, as in the following example:

```
SELECT (PaperType)
  FROM PAPERS
  WHERE Size11Price IS NOT NULL ;
```

This query returns all the rows in the table except the three that the preceding query returns.

WARNING

The statement Size11Price IS NULL is not the same as Size11Price = NULL. To illustrate this point, assume that, in the current row of the PAPERS table, both Size11Price and Size8Price are null. From this fact, you can draw the following conclusions:

» Size11Price IS NULL is True.

» Size8Price IS NULL is True.

» (Size11Price IS NULL AND Size8Price IS NULL) is True.

» Size11Price = Size8Price is unknown.

Size11Price = NULL is an illegal expression. Using the keyword NULL in a comparison is meaningless because the answer always returns as *unknown*.

Why is Size11Price = Size8Price defined as unknown, even though Size11Price and Size8Price have the same (null) value? Because NULL simply means, "I don't know." You don't know what Size11Price is, and you don't know what Size8Price is; therefore, you don't know whether those (unknown) values are the same. Maybe Size11Price is 9.95, and Size8Price is 8.95; or maybe Size11Price is 10.95, and Size8Price is 10.95. If you don't know both the Size11 value and the Size8 value, you can't say whether the two are the same.

ALL, SOME, and ANY

Thousands of years ago, the Greek philosopher Aristotle formulated a system of logic that became the basis for much of Western thought. The essence of this logic is to start with a set of premises that you know to be true, apply valid operations to these premises, and thereby arrive at new truths. The classic example of this procedure is as follows:

Premise 1: All Greeks are human.

Premise 2: All humans are mortal.

Conclusion: All Greeks are mortal.

Another example:

Premise 1: Some Greeks are women.

Premise 2: All women are human.

Conclusion: Some Greeks are human.

Another way of stating the same logical idea of this second example is as follows:

If any Greeks are women and all women are human, then some Greeks are human.

The first example uses the universal quantifier ALL in both premises, enabling you to make a sound deduction about all Greeks in the conclusion. The second example uses the existential quantifier SOME in one premise, enabling you to make a deduction about some, but not all, Greeks in the conclusion. The third example uses the existential quantifier ANY, which is a synonym for SOME, to reach the same conclusion you reach in the second example.

Look at how SOME, ANY, and ALL apply in SQL.

ANY CAN BE AMBIGUOUS

The original SQL used the word ANY for existential quantification. This usage turned out to be confusing and error-prone because the English language connotations of *any* are sometimes universal and sometimes existential:

- "Do any of you know where Wilbur Street is?"
- "I can eat more pizza than any of you."

The first sentence is probably asking whether at least one person knows where Wilbur Street is. *Any* is used as an existential quantifier. The second sentence, however, is a boast that's stating that I can eat more pizza than the biggest eater among all you people can eat. In this case, *any* is used as a universal quantifier.

Thus, for the SQL-92 standard, the developers retained the word ANY for compatibility with early products but added the word SOME as a less confusing synonym. SQL continues to support both existential quantifiers.

Consider an example in baseball statistics. Baseball is a physically demanding sport, especially for pitchers. A pitcher must throw the baseball from the pitcher's mound, at speeds up to 100 miles per hour, to home plate between 90 and 150 times during a game. This effort can be very tiring, and many times, the starting pitcher becomes ineffective, and a relief pitcher must replace him before the game ends. Pitching an entire game is an outstanding achievement, regardless of whether the effort results in a victory.

Suppose that you're keeping track of the number of complete games that all Major League pitchers pitch. In one table, you list all the American League pitchers, and in another table, you list all the National League pitchers. Both tables contain the players' first names, last names, and number of complete games pitched.

The American League permits a designated hitter (DH) (who isn't required to play a defensive position) to bat in place of any of the nine players who play defense. Usually, the DH bats for the pitcher because pitchers are notoriously poor hitters. (Pitchers must spend so much time and effort on perfecting their pitching that they do not have as much time to practice batting as the other players do.)

Say that you speculate that, on average, American League starting pitchers throw more complete games than do National League starting pitchers. This is based on your observation that designated hitters enable hard-throwing, but weak-hitting, American League pitchers to stay in close games. Because the DH is already batting for them, the fact that they are poor hitters is not a liability. In the National League, however, a pinch hitter would replace a comparable National League pitcher in a close game because he would have a better chance at getting a hit. To test your idea, you formulate the following query:

```
SELECT FirstName, LastName
    FROM AMERICAN_LEAGUER
    WHERE CompleteGames > ALL
        (SELECT CompleteGames
            FROM NATIONAL_LEAGUER) ;
```

The subquery (the inner SELECT) returns a list, showing for every National League pitcher, the number of complete games he pitched. The outer query returns the first and last names of all American Leaguers who pitched more complete games than ALL of the National Leaguers. In other words, the query returns the names of those American League pitchers who pitched more complete games than the pitcher who has thrown the most complete games in the National League.

Consider the following similar statement:

```
SELECT FirstName, LastName
   FROM AMERICAN_LEAGUER
   WHERE CompleteGames > ANY
      (SELECT CompleteGames
         FROM NATIONAL_LEAGUER) ;
```

In this case, you use the existential quantifier ANY rather than the universal quantifier ALL. The subquery (the inner, nested query) is identical to the subquery in the previous example. This subquery retrieves a complete list of the complete game statistics for all the National League pitchers. The outer query returns the first and last names of all American League pitchers who pitched more complete games than ANY National League pitcher. Because you can be virtually certain that at least one National League pitcher hasn't pitched a complete game, the result probably includes all American League pitchers who've pitched at least one complete game.

If you replace the keyword ANY with the equivalent keyword SOME, the result is the same. If the statement that at least one National League pitcher hasn't pitched a complete game is a true statement, you can then say that SOME National League pitcher hasn't pitched a complete game.

EXISTS

You can use the EXISTS predicate in conjunction with a subquery to determine whether the subquery returns any rows. If the subquery returns at least one row, that result satisfies the EXISTS condition, and the outer query executes. Consider the following example:

```
SELECT FirstName, LastName
   FROM CUSTOMER
   WHERE EXISTS
      (SELECT DISTINCT CustomerID
        FROM INVOICE
        WHERE INVOICE.CustomerID = CUSTOMER.CustomerID);
```

The INVOICE table contains all your company's sales transactions. The table includes the CustomerID of the customer who makes each purchase, as well as other pertinent information. The CUSTOMER table contains each customer's first and last names, but no information about specific transactions.

The subquery in the preceding example returns a row for every customer who has made at least one purchase. The DISTINCT keyword assures you that you retrieve only one copy of each CustomerID, even if a customer has made more than one purchase. The outer query returns the first and last names of the customers who made the purchases that the INVOICE table records.

UNIQUE

As you do with the EXISTS predicate, you use the UNIQUE predicate with a subquery. Although the EXISTS predicate evaluates to TRUE only if the subquery returns at least one row, the UNIQUE predicate evaluates to TRUE only if no two rows that the subquery returns are identical. In other words, the UNIQUE predicate evaluates to TRUE *only* if all rows that its subquery returns are unique. Consider the following example:

```
SELECT FirstName, LastName
   FROM CUSTOMER
   WHERE UNIQUE
      (SELECT CustomerID FROM INVOICE
          WHERE INVOICE.CustomerID = CUSTOMER.CustomerID);
```

This statement retrieves the names of all first time customers for whom the INVOICE table records only one sale. Two null values are considered to be not equal to each other and thus unique. When the UNIQUE keyword is applied to a result table that only contains two null rows, the UNIQUE predicate evaluates to True.

DISTINCT

The DISTINCT predicate is similar to the UNIQUE predicate, except in the way it treats nulls. If all the values in a result table are UNIQUE, they're also DISTINCT from each other. However, unlike the result for the UNIQUE predicate, if the DISTINCT keyword is applied to a result table that contains only two null rows, the DISTINCT predicate evaluates to False. By default, two null values are *not* considered distinct from each other, while at the same time they are considered to be unique. This strange situation seems contradictory, but there's a reason for it. In some situations, you may want to treat two null values as different from each other, whereas in other situations, you want to treat them as if they're the same. In the first case, use the UNIQUE predicate. In the second case, use the DISTINCT predicate. However, you can combine the UNIQUE and DISTINCT predicates to treat null values as also being distinct. The UNIQUE NULLS NOT DISTINCT predicate combination considers two null values as being distinct as well as unique.

OVERLAPS

You use the OVERLAPS predicate to determine whether two time intervals overlap each other. This predicate is useful for avoiding scheduling conflicts. If the two intervals overlap, the predicate returns a True value. If they don't overlap, the predicate returns a False value.

You can specify an interval in two ways: either as a start time and an end time or as a start time and a duration. Following are a few examples:

```
(TIME '2:55:00', INTERVAL '1' HOUR)
OVERLAPS
(TIME '3:30:00', INTERVAL '2' HOUR)
```

The preceding example returns a True because 3:30 is less than one hour after 2:55.

```
(TIME '9:00:00', TIME '9:30:00')
OVERLAPS
(TIME '9:29:00', TIME '9:31:00')
```

The preceding example returns a True because you have a one-minute overlap between the two intervals.

```
(TIME '9:00:00', TIME '10:00:00')
OVERLAPS
(TIME '10:15:00', INTERVAL '3' HOUR)
```

The preceding example returns a False because the two intervals don't overlap.

```
(TIME '9:00:00', TIME '9:30:00')
OVERLAPS
(TIME '9:30:00', TIME '9:35:00')
```

This example returns a False because even though the two intervals are contiguous, they don't overlap.

MATCH

In Book 2, Chapter 3, I discuss referential integrity, which involves maintaining consistency in a multitable database. You can lose integrity by adding a row to a child table that doesn't have a corresponding row in the child's parent table. You can cause similar problems by deleting a row from a parent table if rows corresponding to that row exist in a child table.

Say that your business has a CUSTOMER table that keeps track of all your customers and a TRANSACT table that records all sales transactions. You don't want to add a row to TRANSACT until after you enter the customer making the purchase into the CUSTOMER table. You also don't want to delete a customer from the CUSTOMER table if that customer made purchases that exist in the TRANSACT table. Before you perform an insertion or deletion, you may want to check the candidate row to make sure that inserting or deleting that row doesn't cause integrity problems. The MATCH predicate can perform such a check.

To examine the MATCH predicate, I use an example that employs the CUSTOMER and TRANSACT tables. CustomerID is the primary key of the CUSTOMER table and acts as a foreign key in the TRANSACT table. Every row in the CUSTOMER table must have a unique, nonnull CustomerID. CustomerID isn't unique in the TRANSACT table because repeat customers buy more than once. This situation is fine and does not threaten integrity because CustomerID is a foreign key rather than a primary key in that table.

TIP

Seemingly, CustomerID can be null in the TRANSACT table because someone can walk in off the street, buy something, and walk out before you get a chance to enter his name and address into the CUSTOMER table. This situation can create a row in the child table with no corresponding row in the parent table. To overcome this problem, you can create a generic customer in the CUSTOMER table and assign all such anonymous sales to that customer.

Say that a customer steps up to the cash register and claims that she bought a flux capacitor on January 15, 2019. She now wants to return the device because she has discovered that her DeLorean lacks time circuits, and so the flux capacitor is of no use. You can verify her claim by searching your TRANSACT database for a match. First, you must retrieve her CustomerID into the variable vcustid; then you can use the following syntax:

```
... WHERE (:vcustid, 'flux capacitor', '2019-01-15')
        MATCH
        (SELECT CustomerID, ProductName, Date
            FROM TRANSACT)
```

If a sale exists for that customer ID for that product on that date, the MATCH predicate returns a True value. Take back the product and refund the customer's money. (*Note:* If any values in the first argument of the MATCH predicate are null, a True value always returns.)

TECHNICAL
STUFF

SQL's developers added the MATCH predicate and the UNIQUE predicate for the same reason — to provide a way to explicitly perform the tests defined for the implicit referential integrity (RI) and UNIQUE constraints. (See the next section for more on referential integrity.)

The general form of the MATCH predicate is as follows:

```
Row_value MATCH   [UNIQUE] [SIMPLE| PARTIAL | FULL ] Subquery
```

The UNIQUE, SIMPLE, PARTIAL, and FULL options relate to rules that come into play if the row value expression R has one or more columns that are null. The rules for the MATCH predicate are a copy of corresponding referential integrity rules.

The MATCH predicate and referential integrity

Referential integrity rules require that the values of a column or columns in one table match the values of a column or columns in another table. You refer to the columns in the first table as the *foreign key* and the columns in the second table as the *primary key* or *unique key*. For example, you may declare the column EmpDeptNo in an EMPLOYEE table as a foreign key that references the DeptNo column of a DEPT table. This matchup ensures that if you record an employee in the EMPLOYEE table as working in department 123, a row appears in the DEPT table, where DeptNo is 123.

This situation is fairly straightforward if the foreign key and primary key both consist of a single column. The two keys can, however, consist of multiple columns. The DeptNo value, for example, may be unique only within a Location; therefore, to uniquely identify a DEPT row, you must specify both a Location and a DeptNo. If both the Boston and Tampa offices have a department 123, you need to identify the departments as ('Boston', '123') and ('Tampa', '123'). In this case, the EMPLOYEE table needs two columns to identify a DEPT. Call those columns EmpLoc and EmpDeptNo. If an employee works in department 123 in Boston, the EmpLoc and EmpDeptNo values are 'Boston' and '123'. And the foreign key declaration in EMPLOYEE is as follows:

```
FOREIGN KEY (EmpLoc, EmpDeptNo)
    REFERENCES DEPT (Location, DeptNo)
```

Drawing valid conclusions from your data is complicated immensely if the data contains nulls. Sometimes you want to treat null-containing data one way, and sometimes you want to treat it another way. The UNIQUE, SIMPLE, PARTIAL, and FULL keywords specify different ways of treating data that contains nulls. If your data does not contain any null values, you can save yourself a lot of head-scratching by merely skipping to the section called "Logical connectives" later in this chapter. If your data *does* contain null values, drop out of Evelyn Wood speed-reading mode now and read the following paragraphs slowly and carefully. Each paragraph presents a different situation with respect to null values and tells how the MATCH predicate handles it.

If the values of EmpLoc and EmpDeptNo are both nonnull or both null, the referential integrity rules are the same as for single-column keys with values that are null or nonnull. But if EmpLoc is null and EmpDeptNo is nonnull — or EmpLoc is nonnull and EmpDeptNo is null — you need new rules. What should the rules be if you insert or update the EMPLOYEE table with EmpLoc and EmpDeptNo values of (NULL, '123') or ('Boston', NULL)? You have six main alternatives: SIMPLE, PARTIAL, and FULL, each either with or without the UNIQUE keyword. The UNIQUE keyword, if present, means that a matching row in the subquery result table must be unique in order for the predicate to evaluate to a True value. If both components of the row value expression R are null, the MATCH predicate returns a True value regardless of the contents of the subquery result table being compared.

If neither component of the row value expression R is null, SIMPLE is specified, UNIQUE is not specified, and at least one row in the subquery result table matches R, the MATCH predicate returns a True value. Otherwise, it returns a False value.

If neither component of the row value expression R is null, SIMPLE is specified, UNIQUE is specified, and at least one row in the subquery result table is both unique and matches R, the MATCH predicate returns a True value. Otherwise, it returns a False value.

If any component of the row value expression R is null and SIMPLE is specified, the MATCH predicate returns a True value.

If any component of the row value expression R is nonnull, PARTIAL is specified, UNIQUE is not specified, and the nonnull parts of at least one row in the subquery result table matches R, the MATCH predicate returns a True value. Otherwise, it returns a False value.

If any component of the row value expression R is nonnull, PARTIAL is specified, UNIQUE is specified, and the nonnull parts of R match the nonnull parts of at least one unique row in the subquery result table, the MATCH predicate returns a True value. Otherwise, it returns a False value.

If neither component of the row value expression R is null, FULL is specified, UNIQUE is not specified, and at least one row in the subquery result table matches R, the MATCH predicate returns a True value. Otherwise, it returns a False value.

If neither component of the row value expression R is null, FULL is specified, UNIQUE is specified, and at least one row in the subquery result table is both unique and matches R, the MATCH predicate returns a True value. Otherwise, it returns a False value.

If any component of the row value expression R is null and FULL is specified, the MATCH predicate returns a False value.

Logical connectives

Often, as a number of previous examples show, applying one condition in a query isn't enough to return the rows that you want from a table. In some cases, the rows must satisfy two or more conditions. In other cases, if a row satisfies any of two or more conditions, it qualifies for retrieval. On other occasions, you want to retrieve only rows that don't satisfy a specified condition. To meet these needs, SQL offers the logical connectives AND, OR, and NOT.

AND

If multiple conditions must all be True before you can retrieve a row, use the AND logical connective. Consider the following example:

```
SELECT InvoiceNo, SaleDate, SalesPerson, TotalSale
    FROM SALES
    WHERE SaleDate >= '2019-01-16'
        AND SaleDate <= '2019-01-22' ;
```

The WHERE clause must meet the following two conditions:

» SaleDate must be greater than or equal to January 16, 2019.

» SaleDate must be less than or equal to January 22, 2019.

Only rows that record sales occurring during the week of January 16 meet both conditions. The query returns only these rows.

Notice that the AND connective is strictly logical. This restriction can sometimes be confusing because people commonly use the word *and* with a looser meaning. Suppose, for example, that your boss says to you, "I'd like to see the sales for Acheson and Bryant." She said, "Acheson and Bryant," so you may write the following SQL query:

```
SELECT *
  FROM SALES
  WHERE Salesperson = 'Acheson'
    AND Salesperson = 'Bryant';
```

Well, don't take that answer back to your boss. The following query is more like what she had in mind:

```
SELECT *
  FROM SALES
  WHERE Salesperson IN ('Acheson', 'Bryant') ;
```

The first query won't return anything, because none of the sales in the SALES table were made by *both* Acheson and Bryant. The second query returns the information on all sales made by either Acheson or Bryant, which is probably what the boss wanted.

OR

If any one of two or more conditions must be True to qualify a row for retrieval, use the OR logical connective, as in the following example:

```
SELECT InvoiceNo, SaleDate, Salesperson, TotalSale
  FROM SALES
    WHERE Salesperson = 'Bryant'
      OR TotalSale > 200 ;
```

This query retrieves all of Bryant's sales, regardless of how large, as well as all sales of more than $200, regardless of who made the sales.

NOT

The NOT connective negates a condition. If the condition normally returns a True value, adding NOT causes the same condition to return a False value. If a condition normally returns a False value, adding NOT causes the condition to return a True value. Consider the following example:

```
SELECT InvoiceNo, SaleDate, Salesperson, TotalSale
    FROM SALES
        WHERE NOT (Salesperson = 'Bryant') ;
```

This query returns rows for all sales transactions completed by salespeople other than Bryant.

WARNING

When you use AND, OR, or NOT, sometimes the scope of the connective isn't clear. To be safe, use parentheses to make sure that SQL applies the connective to the predicate you want. In the preceding example, the NOT connective applies to the entire predicate (Salesperson = 'Bryant').

GROUP BY clauses

Sometimes, instead of retrieving individual records, you want to know something about a group of records. The GROUP BY clause is the tool you need. I use the AdventureWorks2022 sample database designed to work with Microsoft SQL Server 2022 for the following examples.

REMEMBER

SQL Server Express is a version of Microsoft SQL Server that you can download for free from www.microsoft.com.

Suppose you're the sales manager and you want to look at the performance of your sales force. You could do a simple SELECT such as the following:

```
SELECT SalesOrderId, OrderDate, LastName, TotalDue
    FROM Sales.SalesOrderHeader, Person.Person
    WHERE BusinessEntityID = SalesPersonID
        AND OrderDate >= '2011-07-01'
        AND OrderDate <= '2011-07-31'
```

You would receive a result similar to that shown in Figure 2-1. In this database, SalesOrderHeader is a table in the Sales schema and Person is a table in the Person schema. BusinessEntityID is the primary key of the SalesOrderHeader table, and SalesPersonID is the primary key of the Person table. SalesOrderID, OrderDate, and TotalDue are rows in the SalesOrderHeader table, and LastName is a row in the Person table.

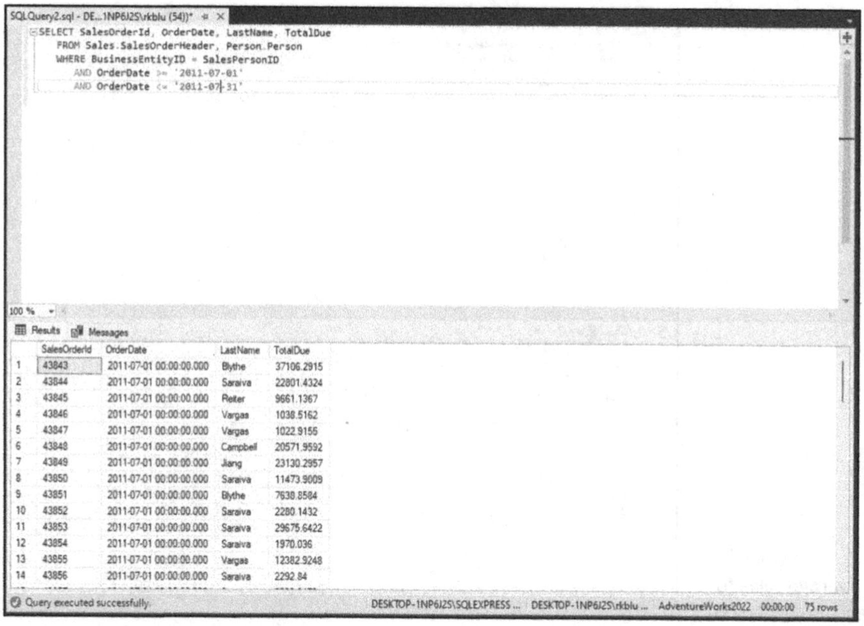

FIGURE 2-1:
The result set for
retrieval of sales
for July 2011.

This result gives you some idea of how well your salespeople are doing because relatively few sales are involved. Seventy-five rows were returned. However, in real life, a company would have many more sales, and it wouldn't be as easy to tell whether sales objectives were being met. To do that, you can combine the GROUP BY clause with one of the *aggregate* functions (also called *set* functions) to get a quantitative picture of sales performance. For example, you can see which salesperson is selling more of the profitable high-ticket items by using the average (AVG) function as follows:

```
SELECT LastName, AVG(TotalDue)
    FROM Sales.SalesOrderHeader, Person.Person
    WHERE BusinessEntityID = SalesPersonID
        AND OrderDate >= '2011-07-01'
        AND OrderDate <= '2011-07-31'
    GROUP BY LastName;
```

You would receive a result similar to that shown in Figure 2-2. The GROUP BY clause causes records to be grouped by LastName and the groups to be sorted in ascending alphabetical order.

SELECT Statements
and Modifying Clauses

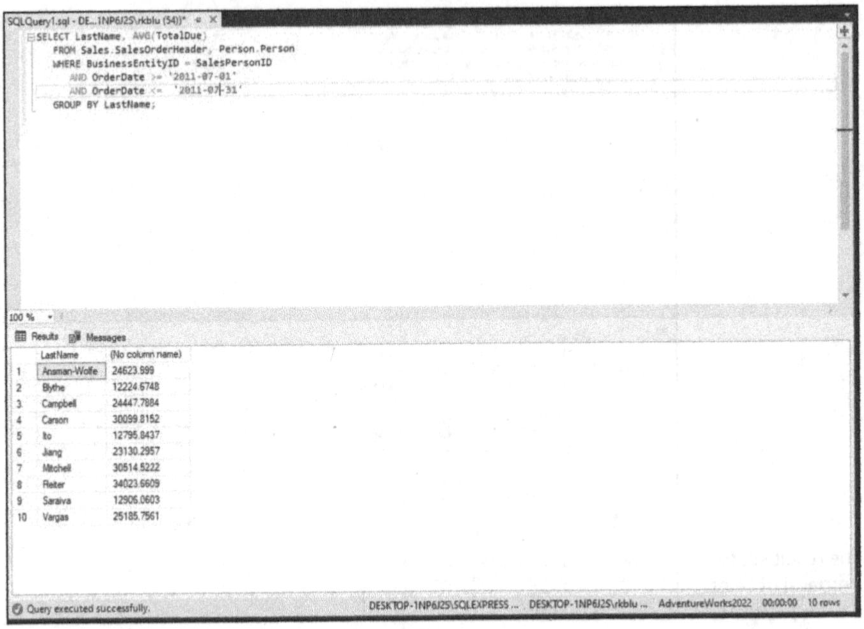

FIGURE 2-2:
Average sales for
each salesperson.

As shown in Figure 2-2, Reiter has the highest average sales. You can compare total sales with a similar query — this time using SUM:

```
SELECT LastName, SUM(TotalDue)
    FROM Sales.SalesOrderHeader, Person.Person
    WHERE BusinessEntityID = SalesPersonID
        AND OrderDate >= '2011-07-01'
        AND OrderDate <= '2011-07-31'
    GROUP BY LastName;
```

This gives the result shown in Figure 2-3. As in the previous example, the GROUP BY clause causes records to be grouped by LastName and the groups to be sorted in ascending alphabetical order.

Reiter also has the highest total sales for the month.

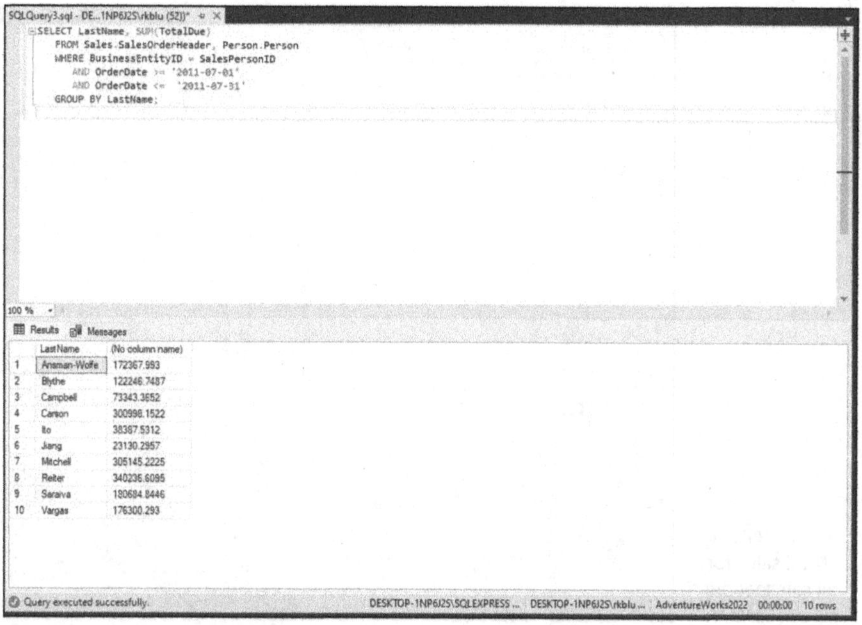

FIGURE 2-3:
Total sales for
each salesperson.

HAVING clauses

You can analyze the grouped data further by using the HAVING clause. The HAVING clause is a filter that acts similar to a WHERE clause, but the filter acts on groups of rows rather than on individual rows. To illustrate the function of the HAVING clause, suppose Saraiva has just resigned, and the sales manager wants to display the overall data for the other salespeople. You can exclude Saraiva's sales from the grouped data by using a HAVING clause as follows:

```
SELECT LastName, SUM(TotalDue)
    FROM Sales.SalesOrderHeader, Person.Person
    WHERE BusinessEntityID = SalesPersonID
        AND OrderDate >= '2011-07-01'
        AND OrderDate <= '2011-07-31'
    GROUP BY LastName
    HAVING LastName <> 'Saraiva';
```

This gives the result shown in Figure 2-4. Only rows where the salesperson is *not* Saraiva are returned. As before, the GROUP BY clause causes records to be grouped by LastName and the groups to be sorted in ascending alphabetical order.

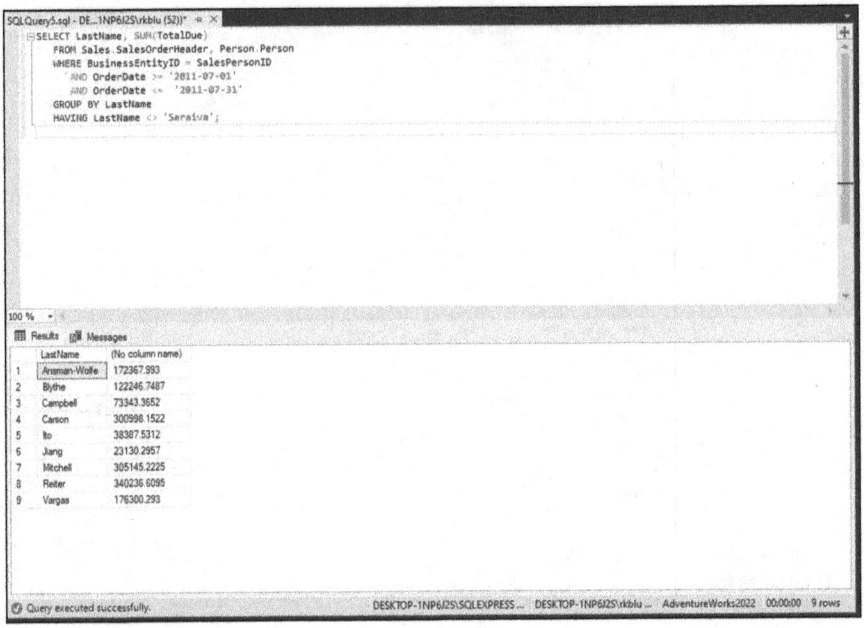

FIGURE 2-4:
Total sales for
all salespeople
except Saraiva.

ORDER BY clauses

You can use the ORDER BY clause to display the output table of a query in either ascending or descending alphabetical order. Whereas the GROUP BY clause gathers rows into groups and sorts the groups into alphabetical order, ORDER BY sorts individual rows. The ORDER BY clause must be the last clause that you specify in a query. If the query also contains a GROUP BY clause, the clause first arranges the output rows into groups. The ORDER BY clause then sorts the rows within each group. If you have no GROUP BY clause, the statement considers the entire table as a group, and the ORDER BY clause sorts all its rows according to the column (or columns) that the ORDER BY clause specifies.

To illustrate this point, consider the data in the SalesOrderHeader table. The SalesOrderHeader table contains columns for SalesOrderID, OrderDate, DueDate, ShipDate, and SalesPersonID, among other things. If you use the following example, you see all the SALES data:

```
SELECT * FROM Sales.SalesOrderHeader ;
```

Theoretically, the order in which the records are listed is arbitrary. If you're using the Microsoft SQL Server Management Studio, it orders the result records by SalesOrderID, because that's the primary key of the table. This practice is not standard, though. In one implementation, the order may be the one in which you inserted the rows in the table, and in another implementation, the order may be that of the most recent updates.

The order can also change unexpectedly if anyone physically reorganizes the database. Usually, you want to specify the order in which you want to display the rows. You may, for example, want to see the rows in order by the OrderDate, as follows:

```
SELECT * FROM Sales.SalesOrderHeader ORDER BY OrderDate ;
```

This example returns all the rows in the SalesOrderHeader table, in ascending order by OrderDate.

For rows with the same OrderDate, the default order depends on the implementation. You can, however, specify how to sort the rows that share the same OrderDate. You may want to see the orders for each OrderDate in order by SalesOrderID, as follows:

```
SELECT * FROM Sales.SalesOrderHeader ORDER BY OrderDate,
    SalesOrderID ;
```

This example first orders the sales by OrderDate; then for each OrderDate, it orders the sales by SalesOrderID. But don't confuse that example with the following query:

```
SELECT * FROM Sales.SalesOrderHeader ORDER BY SalesOrderID,
    OrderDate ;
```

This query first orders the sales by SalesOrderID. Then for each different SalesOrderID, the query orders the sales by OrderDate. This probably won't yield the result you want because it is unlikely that multiple order dates exist for a single sales order number.

The following query is another example of how SQL can return data:

```
SELECT * FROM Sales.SalesOrderHeader ORDER BY SalesPersonID,
    OrderDate ;
```

This example first orders by salesperson and then by order date. After you look at the data in that order, you may want to invert it, as follows:

```
SELECT * FROM Sales.SalesPersonID ORDER BY OrderDate,
    SalesPersonID ;
```

This example orders the rows first by order date and then by salesperson.

All these ordering examples are ascending (ASC), which is the default sort order. In the AdventureWorks2017 sample database, this last SELECT would show earlier sales first and, within a given date, shows sales for 'Ansman-Wolfe' before 'Blythe'. If you prefer descending (DESC) order, you can specify this order for one or more of the order columns, as follows:

```
SELECT * FROM Sales.SalesPersonID ORDER BY OrderDate DESC,
    SalesPersonID ASC;
```

This example specifies a descending order for order date, showing the more recent orders first, and an ascending order for salespeople.

TIP

SQL:2023 has cleared up one bit of confusion with how the ORDER BY clause works. Prior to SQL:2023, the standard specified that a SELECT query was not allowed to use a data field in the ORDER BY clause that wasn't included as part of the SELECT data fields. However, almost all SQL implementations ignored that rule and allowed you to order the result set by a data field not included in the result set. SQL:2023 has incorporated that behavior as part of the standard, so if you order the result set using a data field that isn't contained in the result set, you're staying within the SQL:2023 standard.

Tuning Queries

Performance is always a top priority for any organizational database system. As usage of the system goes up, if resources such as processor speed, cache memory, and hard disk storage do not go up proportionally, performance starts to suffer and users start to complain. Clearly, one thing that a system administrator can do is increase the resources — install a faster processor, add more cache, buy more hard disks. These solutions may give the needed improvement, and may even be necessary, but you should try a cheaper solution first: improving the efficiency of the queries that are loading down the system.

Generally, there are several different ways that you can obtain the information you want from a database; in other words, there are several different ways that you can code a query. Some of those ways are more efficient than others. If one or more queries that are run on a regular basis are bogging down the system, you may be able to bring your system back up to speed without spending a penny on additional hardware. You may just have to recode the queries that are causing the bottleneck.

Popular database management systems have query optimizers that try to eliminate bottlenecks for you, but they don't always do as well as you could do if you tested various alternatives and picked the one with the best performance.

Unfortunately, no general rules apply across the board. The way a database is structured and the columns that are indexed have definite effects. In addition, a coding practice that would be optimal if you use Microsoft SQL Server might result in the worst possible performance if you use Oracle. Because the different DBMSs do things in different ways, what is good for one is not necessarily good for another. There are some things you can do, however, that enable you to find good query plans. In the following sections, I show you some common situations where sometimes just adding common SQL clauses to a query can help with performance.

SELECT DISTINCT

You use SELECT DISTINCT when you want to make sure there are no duplicates in records you retrieve. However, the DISTINCT keyword potentially adds overhead to a query that could impact system performance. The impact it may or may not have depends on how it is implemented by the DBMS. Furthermore, including the DISTINCT keyword in a SELECT operation may not even be needed to ensure there are no duplicates. If you are doing a select on a primary key, the result set is guaranteed to contain no duplicates anyway, so adding the DISTINCT keyword provides no advantage.

Instead of relying on general rules such as, "Avoid using the DISTINCT keyword if you can," if you suspect that a query that includes a DISTINCT keyword is inefficient, test it to see. First, make a typical query into Microsoft's AdventureWorks2022 sample database. The AdventureWorks2017 database contains records typical of a commercial enterprise. There is a Customer table and a SalesOrderHeader table, among others. One thing you might want to do is see what companies in the Customer table have actually placed orders, as recorded in the Orders table. Because a customer may place multiple orders, it makes sense to use the DISTINCT keyword so that only one row is returned for each customer. Here's the code for the query:

```
SELECT DISTINCT SalesOrderHeader.CustomerID, Customer.StoreID, SalesOrderHeader.
   TotalDue
  FROM Sales.Customer, Sales.SalesOrderHeader
  WHERE Customer.CustomerID = SalesOrderHeader.CustomerID ;
```

Before executing this query, click on the Include Client Statistics icon to select it. Then click the Execute button.

The result is shown in Figure 2-5, which shows the first few customer ID numbers of the 31,349 companies that have placed at least one order.

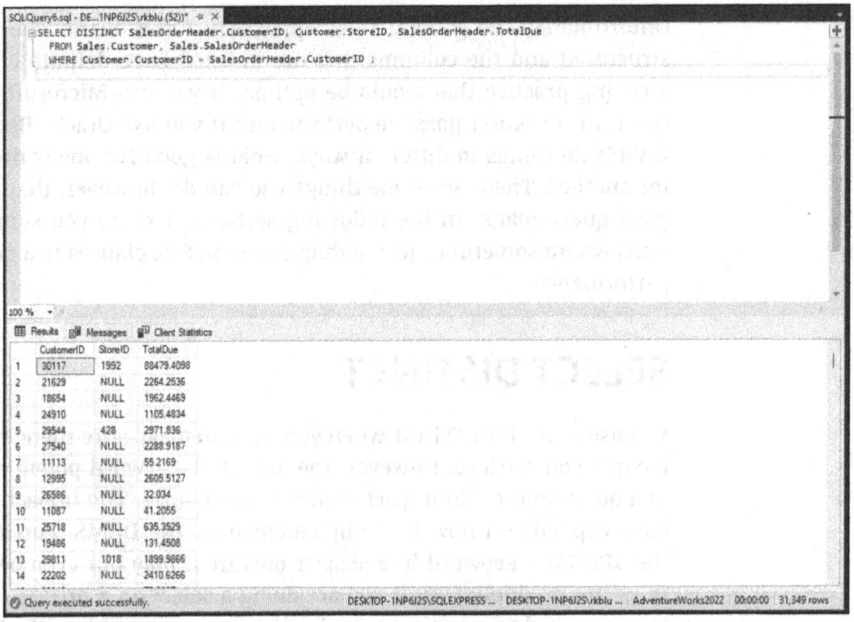

	CustomerID	StoreID	TotalDue
1	30117	1992	88479.4098
2	21629	NULL	2264.2536
3	18654	NULL	1962.4469
4	24910	NULL	1105.4834
5	29544	428	2971.836
6	27540	NULL	2288.9187
7	11113	NULL	55.2169
8	12995	NULL	2605.5127
9	26586	NULL	32.034
10	11087	NULL	41.2055
11	25718	NULL	635.3529
12	19486	NULL	131.4508
13	29811	1018	1899.9866
14	22202	NULL	2410.6266

FIGURE 2-5: Customers who have placed at least one order.

In this query, I used CustomerID to link the Customer table to the SalesOrderHeader table so that I could pull information from both.

It would be interesting to see how efficient this query is. Use Microsoft SQL Server 2022's tools to find out. First, look at the execution plan that was followed to run this query in Figure 2-6. To see the execution plan, click the Estimated Execution Plan icon in the toolbar.

The execution plan shows that a hash match on an aggregation operation takes 49 percent of the execution time, and a hash match on an inner join takes another 20 percent. A clustered index scan on the primary key of the customer table takes 5 percent of the time, and a clustered index scan on the primary key of the SalesOrderHeader table takes 26 percent. To see how well or how poorly I'm doing, I look at the client statistics (Figure 2-7), by clicking the Include Client Statistics icon in the toolbar.

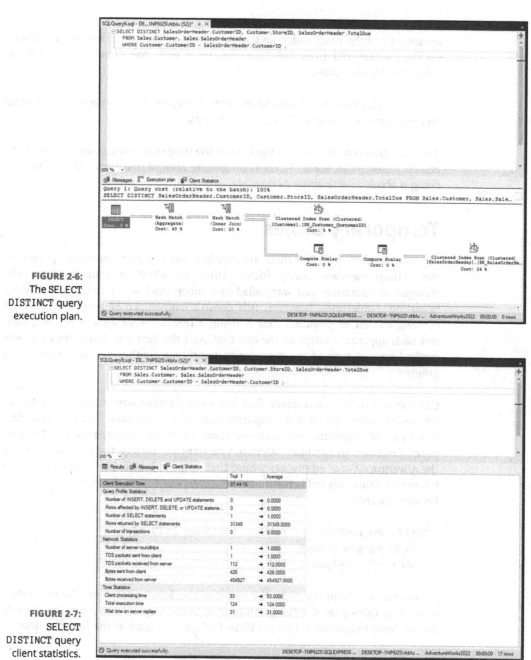

FIGURE 2-6:
The SELECT
DISTINCT query
execution plan.

FIGURE 2-7:
SELECT
DISTINCT query
client statistics.

I cover *inner joins* in Chapter 4 of this minibook. A *clustered index scan* is a row-by-row examination of the index on a table column. In this case, the index of SalesOrderHeader.CustomerID is scanned. The hash match on the aggregation operation and the hash match on the inner join are the operations used to match up the CustomerID from the Customer table with the CustomerID from the SalesOrderHeader table.

Total execution time is 124 time units, with client processing time at 93 time units and wait time on server replies at 31 time units.

The execution plan shows that the bulk of the time consumed is due to hash joins and clustered index scans. There is no getting around these operations, and it is doing it about as efficiently as possible.

Temporary tables

SQL is so feature-rich that there are multiple ways to perform many operations. Not all those ways are equally efficient. Often, the DBMS's optimizer dynamically changes an operation that was coded in a suboptimal way into a more efficient operation. Sometimes, however, this doesn't happen. To be sure your query is running as fast as possible, code it using a few different approaches and then test each approach. Settle on the one that does the best job. Sometimes the best method on one type of query performs poorly on another, so take nothing for granted.

One method of coding a query that has multiple selection conditions is to use temporary tables. Think of a temporary table as a scratchpad. You put some data in it as an intermediate step in an operation. When you are done with it, it disappears. Consider an example. Suppose you want to retrieve the last names of all the AdventureWorks employees whose first name is Janice. First you can create a temporary table that holds the information you want from the Person table in the Person schema:

```
SELECT PersonType, FirstName, LastName INTO #Temp
   FROM Person.Person
   WHERE PersonType = 'EM' ;
```

As you can see from the code, the result of the select operation is placed into a temporary table named #Temp rather than being displayed in a window. In SQL Server, local temporary tables are identified with a # sign as the first character.

Now you can find the Janices in the #Temp table:

```
SELECT FirstName, LastName
   FROM #Temp
   WHERE FirstName = 'Janice' ;
```

Running these two queries consecutively gives the result shown in Figure 2-8.

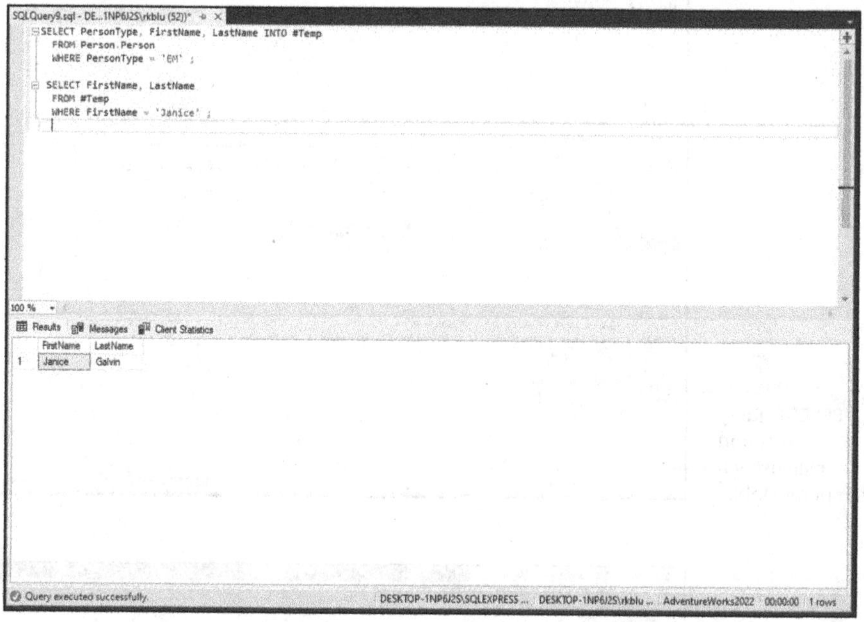

FIGURE 2-8:
Retrieve all
employees
named Janice
from the
Person table.

The summary at the bottom of the screen shows that AdventureWorks has only one employee named Janice. Look at the execution plan (see Figure 2-9) to see how I did this retrieval.

Creation of the temporary table to separate the employees is one operation, and finding all the Janices is another. In the Table Creation query, creating the temporary table took up only 1 percent of the time used. A clustered index scan on the primary key of the Person table took up the other 99 percent. Also notice that a missing index was flagged, with an impact of over 97, followed by a recommendation to create a nonclustered index on the PersonType column. Considering the huge impact on runtime due to the absence of that index, if you were to run queries such as this frequently, you should consider creating an index on PersonType. Indexing PersonType in the Person table provides a big performance boost in this case because the number of employees in the table is a relatively small number out of over 31,000 total records.

The table scan of the temporary table took up all the time of the second query. How did you do performance-wise? Figure 2-10 gives the details from the Client Statistics tab.

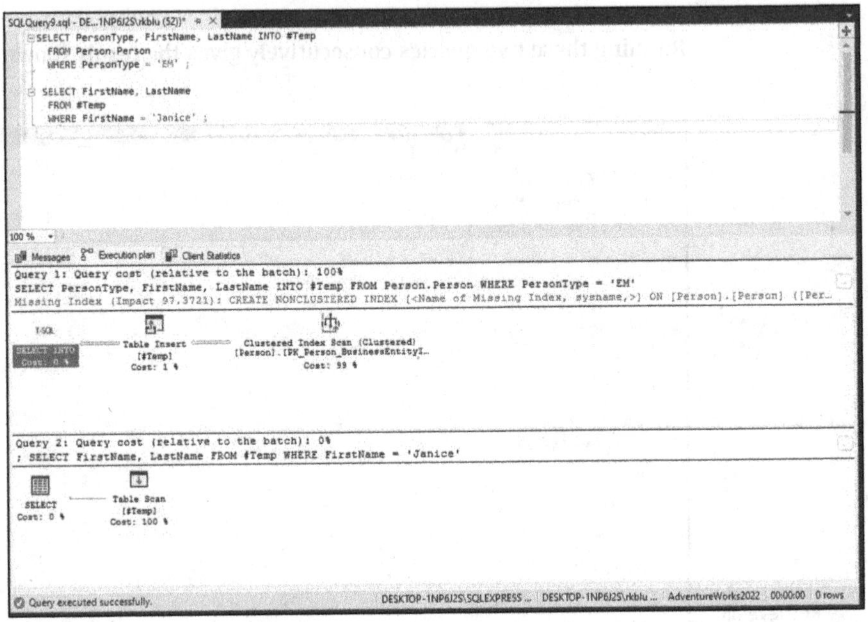

FIGURE 2-9:
SELECT query execution plan using a temporary table.

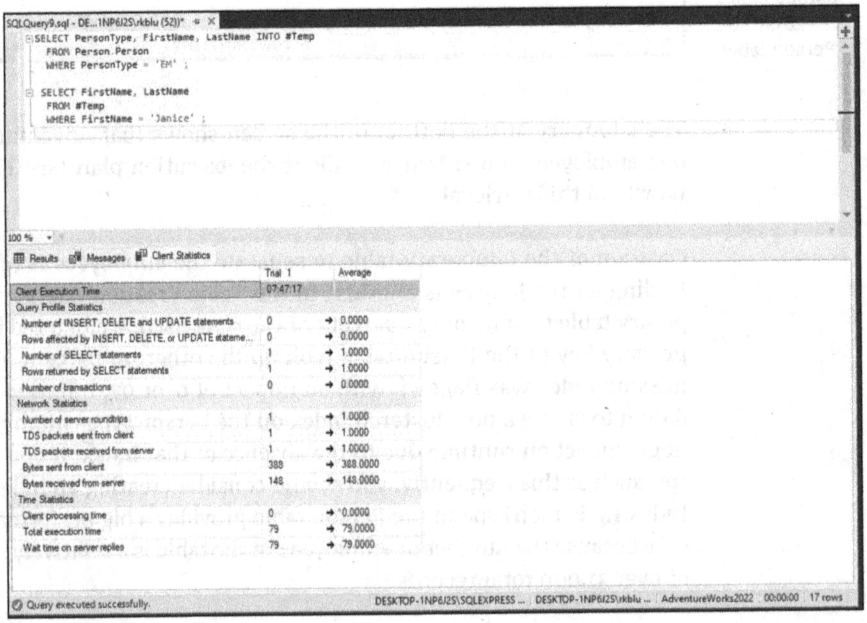

FIGURE 2-10:
SELECT query execution client statistics using a temporary table.

As you see in the Client Statistics tab, total execution time was 79 time units, with no units going to client processing time (as rounded to the nearest integer value) and all 79 units waiting for server replies. A total of 388 bytes were sent from the client, and 148 bytes were returned by the server. These figures will vary from one run to the next due to caching and other factors.

Now suppose you performed the same operation without using a temporary table. You could do so with the following code:

```
SELECT FirstName, LastName
  FROM Person.Person
  WHERE PersonType = 'EM'
  AND FirstName = 'Janice';
```

EM is AdventureWorks' code for a PersonType of employee. You get the same result (shown in Figure 2-11) as in Figure 2-8. Janice Galvin is the only employee with a first name of Janice.

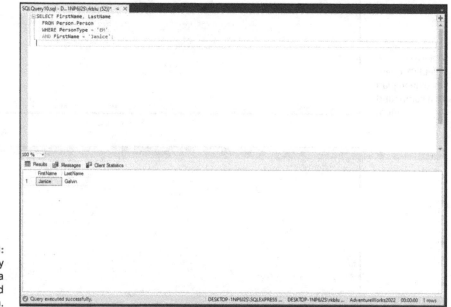

FIGURE 2-11: SELECT query result with a compound condition.

How does the execution plan (shown in Figure 2-12) compare with the one in Figure 2-9?

As you can see, the same result was obtained by a completely different execution plan. A nonclustered index scan took up 56 percent of the total execution time, a key lookup took 39 percent, and the remaining 5 percent was consumed by an inner join. Once again, a recommendation for a nonclustered index has been made, this time on the combined PersonType and FirstName columns. The real

SELECT Statements
and Modifying Clauses

story, however, is revealed in the client statistics (shown in Figure 2-13). How does performance compare with the temporary table version?

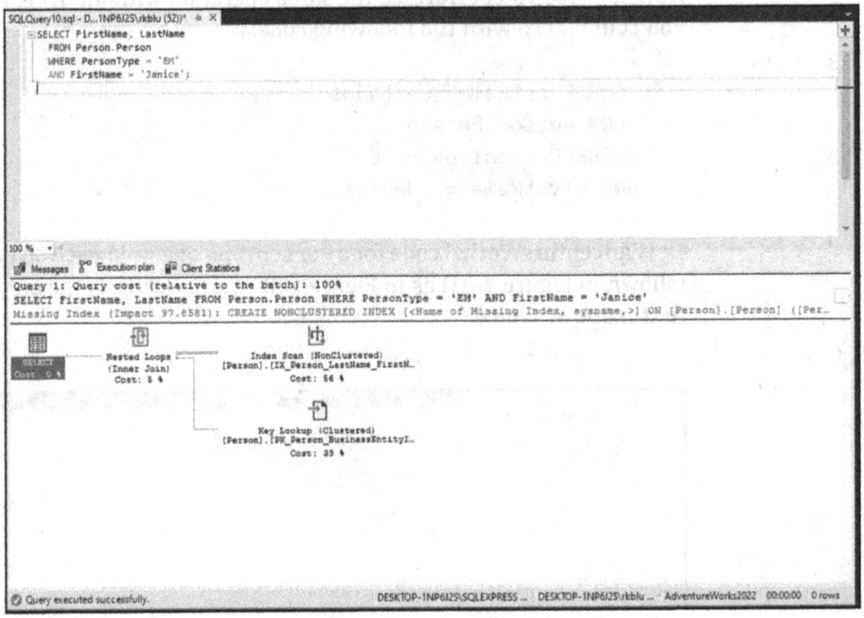

FIGURE 2-12:
SELECT query
execution plan
with a compound
condition.

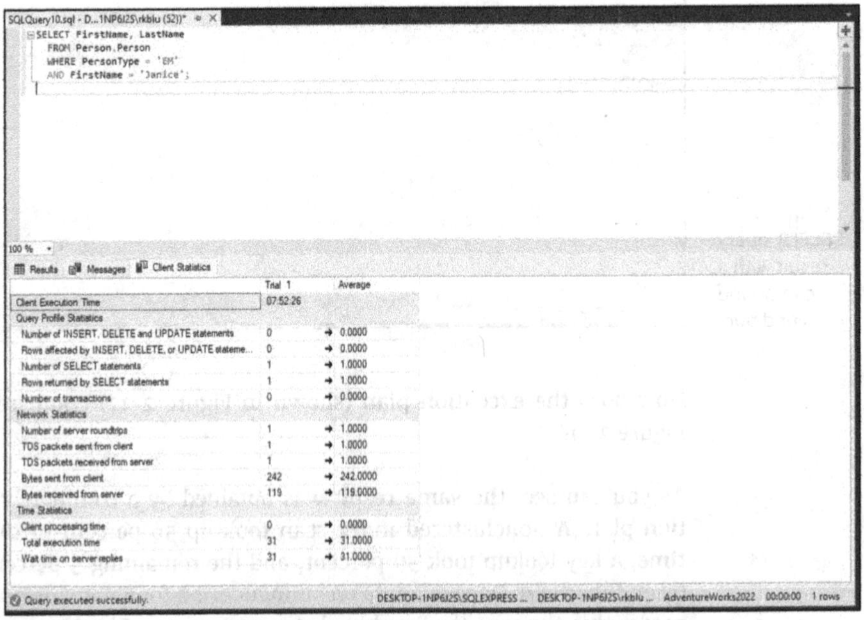

FIGURE 2-13:
SELECT query
client statistics,
with a compound
condition.

Hmmm. Total execution time is 31 time units, all of which is due to wait time for server replies. That's significantly less than the 79 time units consumed by the temporary table formulation. A total of 242 bytes were sent from the client, which is less than the upstream traffic in the temporary table case. In addition, just 119 bytes were sent from the server down to the client. That's comparable to the 148 bytes that were downloaded using the temporary table. All things considered, the performance of both methods turns out to be about a wash. There may be situations where using one or the other is better, but creating a nonclustered index on [PersonType] in the first case, or on [PersonType, FirstName] in the second case will have a much bigger impact.

The ORDER BY clause

The ORDER BY clause can be expensive in terms of both bandwidth between the server and the client and execution time simply because ORDER BY initiates a sort operation, and sorts consume large amounts of both time and memory. If you can minimize the number of ORDER BY clauses in a series of queries, you may save resources. This is one place where using a temporary table might perform better. Consider an example. Suppose you want to do a series of retrievals on your Products table, in which you see which products are available in several price ranges. For example, you want one list of products priced between 10 dollars and 20 dollars, ordered by unit price. Then you want a list of products priced between 20 dollars and 30 dollars, similarly ordered, and so on. To cover four such price ranges, you could make four queries, all four with an ORDER BY clause. Alternatively, you could create a temporary table with a query that uses an ORDER BY clause, and then draw the data for the ranges in separate queries that do not have ORDER BY clauses. Compare the two approaches. Here's the code for the temporary table approach:

```
SELECT Name, ListPrice INTO #Product
  FROM Production.Product
  WHERE ListPrice > 10
  AND ListPrice <= 50
  ORDER BY ListPrice;
SELECT Name, ListPrice
  FROM #Product
  WHERE ListPrice > 10
  AND ListPrice <= 20;
SELECT Name, ListPrice
  FROM #Product
  WHERE ListPrice > 20
  AND ListPrice <= 30;
```

```
SELECT Name, ListPrice
   FROM #Product
   WHERE ListPrice > 30
   AND ListPrice <= 40;
SELECT Name, ListPrice
   FROM #Product
   WHERE ListPrice > 40
   AND ListPrice <= 50;
```

The execution plan for this series of queries is shown in Figure 2-14.

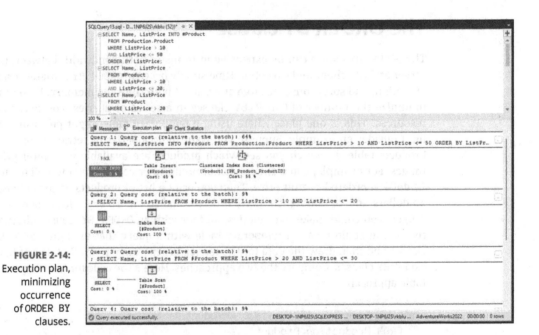

FIGURE 2-14:
Execution plan,
minimizing
occurrence
of ORDER BY
clauses.

The first query, the one that creates the temporary table, has the most complex execution plan. By itself, it takes up 64 percent of the allotted time, and the other four queries take up the remaining 36 percent. Figure 2-15 shows the client statistics, measuring resource usage.

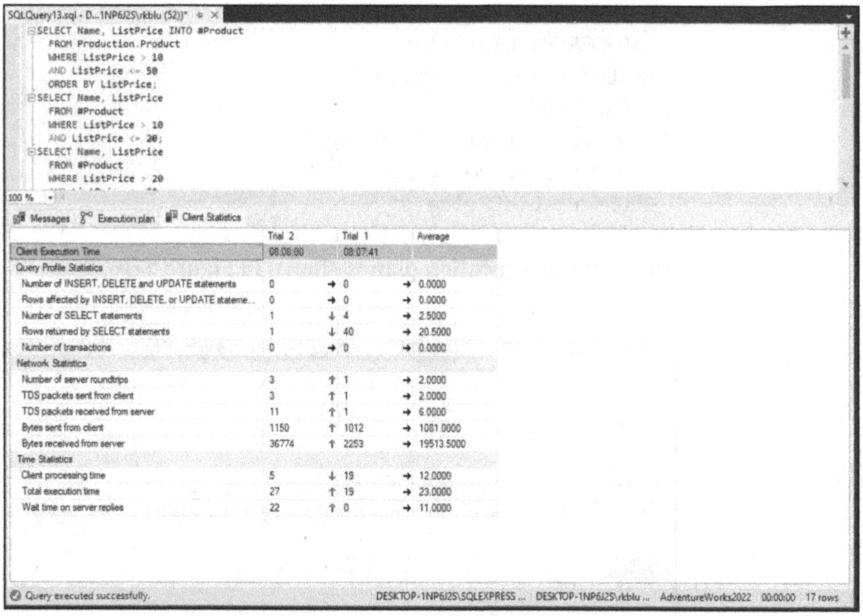

FIGURE 2-15:
Client statistics,
minimizing
occurrence
of ORDER BY
clauses.

Total execution time varies from run to run because of variances in the time spent waiting to hear back from the server, and an average of 19,513 bytes were received from the server. Now compare that with no temporary table, but four separate queries, each with its own ORDER BY clause. Here's the code:

```
SELECT Name, ListPrice INTO #Product
  FROM Production.Product
  WHERE ListPrice > 10
  AND ListPrice <= 50
  ORDER BY ListPrice;
SELECT Name, ListPrice
  FROM #Product
  WHERE ListPrice > 10
  AND ListPrice <= 20
  ORDER BY ListPrice ;
SELECT Name, ListPrice
  FROM #Product
  WHERE ListPrice > 20
  AND ListPrice <= 30
  ORDER BY ListPrice ;
SELECT Name, ListPrice
  FROM #Product
  WHERE ListPrice > 30
  AND ListPrice <= 40
```

SELECT Statements
and Modifying Clauses

```
    ORDER BY ListPrice ;
SELECT Name, ListPrice
  FROM #Product
  WHERE ListPrice > 40
  AND ListPrice <= 50
ORDER BY ListPrice ;
```

The resulting execution plan is shown in Figure 2-16.

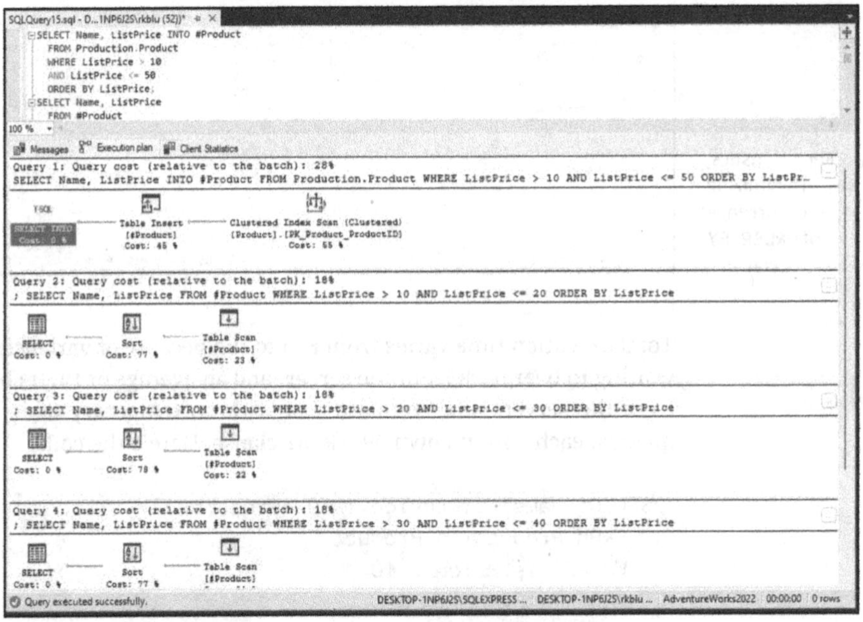

FIGURE 2-16:
Execution
plan, queries
with separate
ORDER BY
clauses.

Each of the four queries involves a sort, which consumes about 77 percent of the total time of the query. This could be costly. Figure 2-17 shows what the client statistics look like.

Total execution time varies from one run to the next, primarily due to the client processing time. The number of bytes returned by the server also varies. A cursory look at the statistics does not determine whether this latter method is slower than the temporary table method; averages over multiple independent runs will be required. At any rate, as table sizes increase, the time it takes to sort them goes up exponentially. For larger tables, the performance advantage tips strongly to the temporary table method.

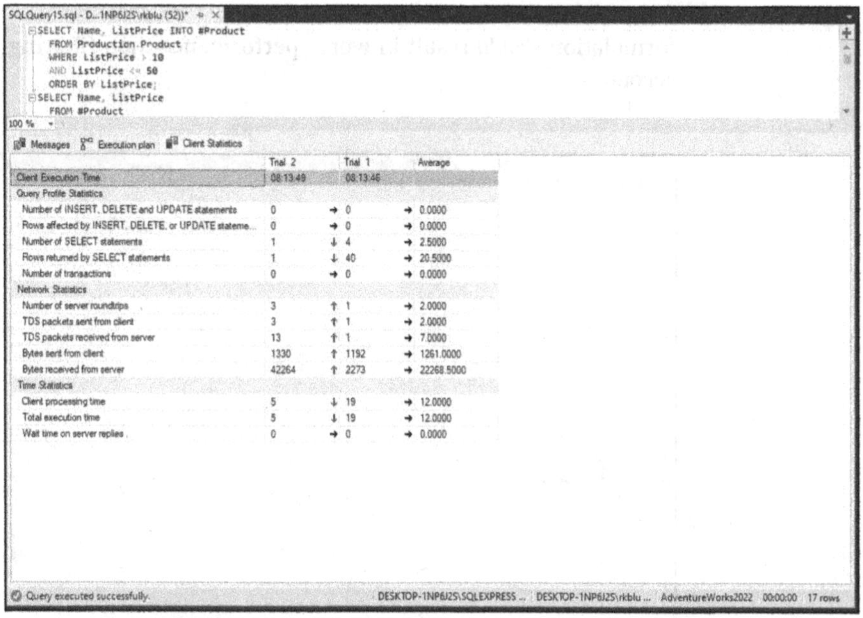

FIGURE 2-17: Client statistics, queries with separate ORDER BY clauses.

The HAVING clause

Think about the order in which you do things. Performing operations in the correct order can make a big difference in how long it takes to complete those operations. Whereas the WHERE clause filters out rows that don't meet a search condition, the HAVING clause filters out entire groups that don't meet a search condition. It makes sense to filter first (with a WHERE clause) and group later (with a GROUP BY clause) rather than group first and filter later (with a HAVING clause). If you group first, you perform the grouping operation on everything. If you filter first, you perform the grouping operation only on what is left after the rows you don't want have been filtered out.

This line of reasoning sounds good. To see if it is borne out in practice, consider this code:

```
SELECT AVG(ListPrice) AS AvgPrice, ProductLine
  FROM Production.Product
  GROUP BY ProductLine
  HAVING ProductLine = 'T' ;
```

It finds the average price of all the products in the T product line by first grouping the products into categories and then filtering out all except those in product line T. The AS keyword is used to give a name to the average list price — in this case the name is AvgPrice. Figure 2-18 shows what SQL Server returns. This formulation *should* result in worse performance than filtering first and grouping second.

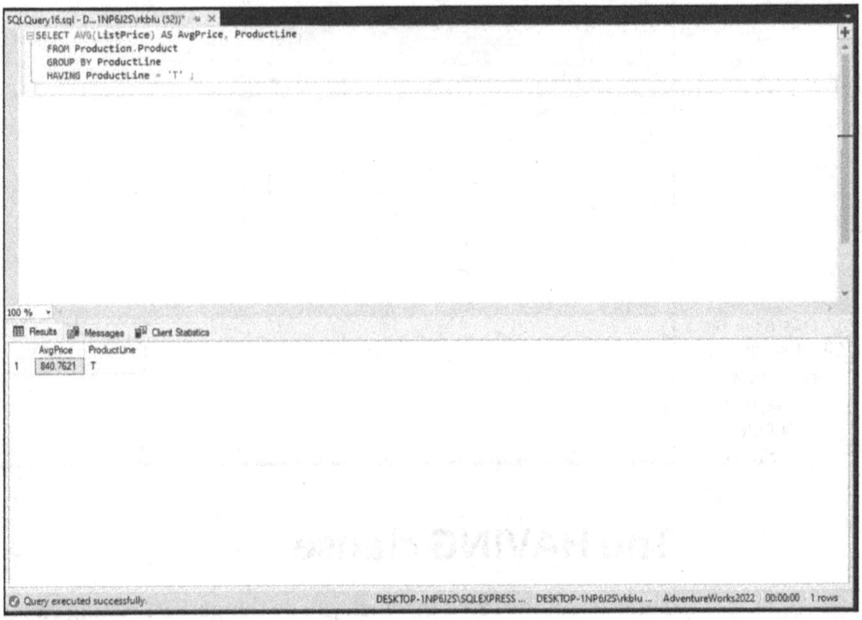

FIGURE 2-18:
Retrieval with a
HAVING clause.

The average price for the products in product line T is $840.7621. Figure 2-19 shows what the execution plan tells us.

A clustered index scan takes up most of the time. This is a fairly efficient operation. The client statistics are shown in Figure 2-20.

Client execution time is about 15 time units. Now, try filtering first and grouping second.

```
SELECT AVG(ListPrice) AS AvgPrice, ProductLine
   FROM Production.Product
   WHERE ProductLine = 'T' ;
```

There is no need to group because all product lines except product line T are filtered out by the WHERE clause. Figure 2-21 shows that the result is the same as in the previous case, $840.7621.

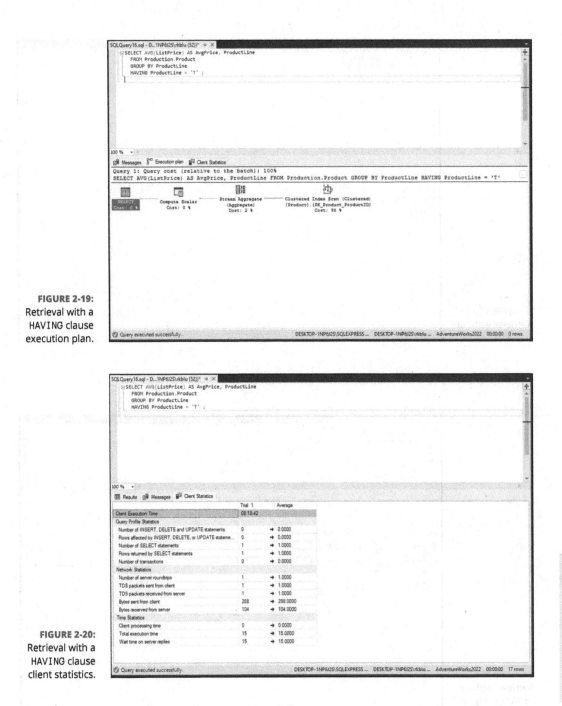

FIGURE 2-19:
Retrieval with a
HAVING clause
execution plan.

FIGURE 2-20:
Retrieval with a
HAVING clause
client statistics.

Figure 2-22 shows how the execution plan differs.

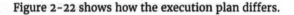

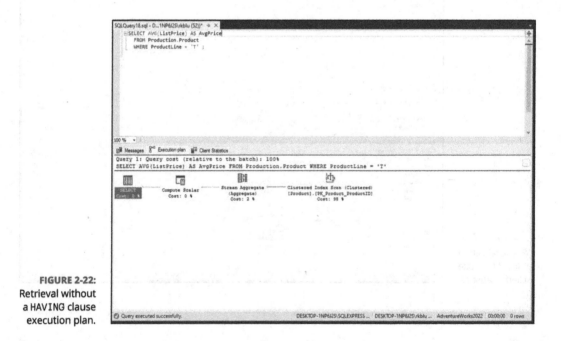

Interesting! The execution plan is exactly the same. SQL Server's optimizer has done its job and optimized the less efficient case. Are the client statistics the same too? Check Figure 2-23 to find out.

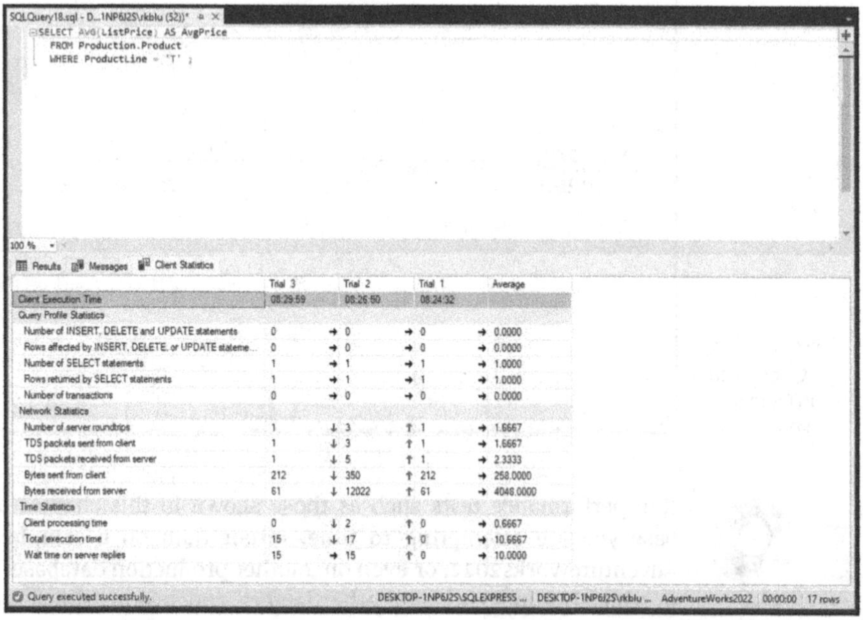

FIGURE 2-23: Retrieval without a HAVING clause client statistics.

Running the query multiple times shows that basically the client execution time is essentially the same.

The OR logical connective

Some systems never use indexes when expressions in a WHERE clause are connected by the OR logical connective. Check your system to see if it does. See how SQL Server handles it.

```
SELECT ProductID, Name
  FROM Production.Product
  WHERE ListPrice < 20
  OR SafetyStockLevel < 30 ;
```

Check the execution plan to see if SQL Server uses an index (like the one shown in Figure 2-24). SQL Server *does* use an index in this situation, so there is no point in looking for alternative ways to code this type of query.

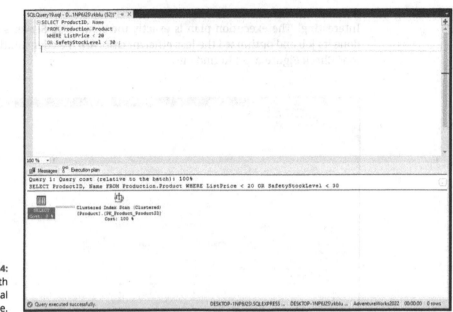

```
SQLQuery19.sql - D...1NP6J2S\rkblu (52))* + X
□SELECT ProductID, Name
    FROM Production.Product
    WHERE ListPrice < 20
    OR SafetyStockLevel < 30 ;
```

```
100 %  ▾ ◂
Messages  Execution plan
Query 1: Query cost (relative to the batch): 100%
SELECT ProductID, Name FROM Production.Product WHERE ListPrice < 20 OR SafetyStockLevel < 30
```

```
SELECT          Clustered Index Scan (Clustered)
Cost: 0 %       [Product].[PK_Product_ProductID]
                        Cost: 100 %
```

Query executed successfully.   DESKTOP-1NP6J2S\SQLEXPRESS ...   DESKTOP-1NP6J2S\rkblu ...   AdventureWorks2022   00:00:00   0 rows

FIGURE 2-24:
Query with
an OR logical
connective.

TIP

Run performance tests such as those shown in this chapter on the exact database you are attempting to tune, rather than on a sample database such as AdventureWorks2022, or even on another production database. Due to differences in table size, indexing, and other factors, conclusions you come to, based on one database, don't necessarily apply to another.

Chapter **3**

Querying Multiple Tables with Subqueries

Relational databases have multiple tables. That's where the word *relational* comes from — multiple tables that relate to each other in some way. One consequence of the distribution of data across multiple tables is that most queries need to pull data from more than one of them. There are a couple of ways to do this. One is to use relational operators, which I cover in the next chapter. The other method is to use subqueries, which is the subject of this chapter.

What Is a Subquery?

A *subquery* is an SQL statement embedded within another SQL statement. It's possible for a subquery to be embedded within another subquery, which is in turn embedded within an outermost SQL statement. Theoretically, there is no limit to the number of levels of subquery that an SQL statement may include, although any given implementation has a practical limit. A key feature of a subquery is that the table or tables that it references need not be the same as the table or tables referenced by its enclosing query. This has the effect of returning results based on the information in multiple tables.

What Subqueries Do

Subqueries are located within the WHERE clause of their enclosing statement. Their function is to set the search conditions for the WHERE clause. The combination of a subquery and its enclosing query is called a *nested query*. Different kinds of nested queries produce different results. Some subqueries produce a list of values that is then used as input by the enclosing statement. Other subqueries produce a single value that the enclosing statement then evaluates with a comparison operator. A third kind of subquery, called a *correlated subquery*, operates differently, and I discuss it in the upcoming "Correlated subqueries" section.

Subqueries that return multiple values

A key concern of many businesses is inventory control. When you are building products that are made up of various parts, you want to make sure that you have an adequate supply of all the parts. If just one part is in short supply, it could bring the entire manufacturing operation to a screeching halt. To see how many products are impacted by the lack of a part they need, you can use a subquery.

Subqueries that retrieve rows satisfying a condition

Suppose your company (Penguin Electronics, Inc.) manufactures a variety of electronic products, such as audio amplifiers, FM radio tuners, and handheld metal detectors. You keep track of inventory of all your products — as well as all the parts that go into their manufacture — in a relational database. The database has a PRODUCTS table that holds the inventory levels of finished products and a PARTS table that holds the inventory levels of the parts that go into the products.

A part could be included in multiple products, and each product is made up of multiple parts. This means that there is a many-to-many relationship between the PRODUCTS table and the PARTS table. Because this could present problems (see Book 2, Chapter 3 for a rundown of the kinds of problems I mean), you decide to insert an intersection table between PRODUCTS and PARTS, transforming the problematical many-to-many relationship into two easier-to-deal-with one-to-many relationships. The intersection table, named PROD_PARTS, takes the primary keys of PRODUCTS and PARTS as its only attributes. You can create these three tables with the following code:

```
CREATE TABLE PRODUCTS (
    ProductID          INTEGER       PRIMARY KEY,
    ProductName        CHAR (30),
    ProductDescription CHAR (50),
```

```
    ListPrice               NUMERIC (9,2),
    QuantityInStock         INTEGER ) ;

CREATE TABLE PARTS (
    PartID                  INTEGER      PRIMARY KEY,
    PartName                CHAR (30),
    PartDescription         CHAR (50),
    QuantityInStock         INTEGER ) ;

CREATE TABLE PROD_PARTS (
    ProductID               INTEGER      NOT NULL,
    PartID                  INTEGER      NOT NULL ) ;
```

Suppose some of your products include an APM-17 DC analog panel meter. Now you find to your horror that you are completely out of the APM-17 part. You can't complete the manufacture of any product that includes it. It is time for management to take some emergency actions. One is to check on the status of any outstanding orders to the supplier of the APM-17 panel meters. Another is to notify the sales department to stop selling all products that include the APM-17, and switch to promoting products that do not include it.

To discover which products include the APM-17, you can use a nested query such as the following:

```
SELECT ProductID
  FROM PROD_PARTS
  WHERE PartID IN
    (SELECT PartID
       FROM PARTS
      WHERE PartDescription = 'APM-17') ;
```

SQL processes the innermost query first, so it queries the PARTS table, returning the PartID of every row in the PARTS table where the PartDescription is APM-17. There should be only one such row. Only one part should have a description of APM-17. The outer query uses the IN keyword to find all the rows in the PROD_PARTS table that include the PartID that appears in the result set from the inner query. The outer query then extracts from the PROD_PARTS table the ProductIDs of all the products that include the APM-17 part. These are the products that the Sales department should stop selling.

Subqueries that retrieve rows that don't satisfy a condition

Because sales are the lifeblood of any business, it is even more important to determine which products the Sales team can continue to sell than it is to tell them what not to sell. You can do this with another nested query. Use the query just executed in the preceding section as a base, add one more layer of query to it, and return the ProductIDs of all the products not affected by the APM-17 shortage.

```
SELECT ProductID
  FROM PROD_PARTS
  WHERE ProductID NOT IN
    (SELECT ProductID
      FROM PROD_PARTS
      WHERE PartID IN
        (SELECT PartID
          FROM PARTS
          WHERE PartDescription = 'APM-17') ;
```

The two inner queries return the ProductIDs of all the products that include the APM-17 part. The outer query returns all the ProductIDs of all the products that are not included in the result set from the inner queries. This final result set is the list of ProductIDs of products that do not include the APM-17 analog panel meter.

Subqueries that return a single value

Introducing a subquery with one of the six comparison operators (=, <>, <, <=, >, >=) is often useful. In such a case, the expression preceding the operator evaluates to a single value, and the subquery following the operator must also evaluate to a single value. An exception is the case of the *quantified comparison operator*, which is a comparison operator followed by a quantifier (ANY, SOME, or ALL).

To illustrate a case in which a subquery returns a single value, look at another piece of Penguin Electronics' database. It contains a CUSTOMER table that holds information about the companies that buy Penguin products. It also contains a CONTACT table that holds personal data about individuals at each of Penguin's customer organizations. The following code creates Penguin's CUSTOMER and CONTACT tables.

```
CREATE TABLE CUSTOMER (
  CustomerID        INTEGER        PRIMARY KEY,
  Company           CHAR (40),
  Address1          CHAR (50),
  Address2          CHAR (50),
  City              CHAR (25),
  State             CHAR (2),
  PostalCode        CHAR (10),
  Phone             CHAR (13) ) ;
```

```
CREATE TABLE CONTACT (
  CustomerID              INTEGER     PRIMARY KEY,
  FirstName               CHAR (15),
  LastName                CHAR (20),
  Phone                   CHAR (13),
  Email                   CHAR (30),
  Fax                     CHAR (13),
  Notes                   CHAR (100),
  CONSTRAINT ContactFK FOREIGN KEY (CustomerID)
    REFERENCES CUSTOMER (CustomerID) ) ;
```

Say that you want to look at the contact information for the customer named Baker Electronic Sales, but you don't remember that company's CustomerID. Use a nested query like this one to recover the information you want:

```
SELECT *
    FROM CONTACT
        WHERE CustomerID =
            (SELECT CustomerID
                FROM CUSTOMER
                    WHERE Company = 'Baker Electronic Sales') ;
```

The result looks something like this:

CustomerID	FirstName	LastName	Phone	Notes
787	David	Lee	555-876-3456	Likes to visit El Pollo Loco when in Cali.

You can now call Dave at Baker and tell him about this month's special sale on metal detectors.

When you use a subquery in an "=" comparison, the subquery's SELECT list must specify a single column (CustomerID in the example). When the subquery is executed, it must return a single row in order to have a single value for the comparison.

In this example, I assume that the CUSTOMER table has only one row with a Company value of Baker Electronic Sales. If the CREATE TABLE statement for CUSTOMER specified a UNIQUE constraint for Company, such a statement guarantees that the subquery in the preceding example returns a single value (or no value). Subqueries like the one in the example, however, are commonly used on columns not specified to be UNIQUE. In such cases, you are relying on some other reasons for believing that the column has no duplicates.

If more than one CUSTOMER has a value of Baker Electronic Sales in the Company column (perhaps in different states), the subquery raises an error.

If no Customer with such a company name exists, the subquery is treated as if it were null, and the comparison becomes unknown. In this case, the WHERE clause returns no row (because it returns only rows with the condition True and filters rows with the condition False or Unknown). This would probably happen, for example, if someone misspelled the COMPANY as Baker Electronics Sales.

Although the equals operator (=) is the most common, you can use any of the other five comparison operators in a similar structure. For every row in the table specified in the enclosing statement's FROM clause, the single value returned by the subquery is compared to the expression in the enclosing statement's WHERE clause. If the comparison gives a True value, a row is added to the result table.

You can guarantee that a subquery returns a single value if you include a set function in it. Set functions, also known as *aggregate* functions, always return a single value. (I describe set functions in Chapter 1 of this minibook.) Of course, this way of returning a single value is helpful only if you want the result of a set function.

Say that you are a Penguin Electronics salesperson and you need to earn a big commission check to pay for some unexpected bills. You decide to concentrate on selling Penguin's most expensive product. You can find out what that product is with a nested query:

```
SELECT ProductID, ProductName, ListPrice
    FROM PRODUCT
        WHERE ListPrice =
            (SELECT MAX(ListPrice)
                FROM PRODUCT) ;
```

This is an example of a nested query where both the subquery and the enclosing statement operate on the same table. The subquery returns a single value: the maximum list price in the PRODUCTS table. The outer query retrieves all rows from the PRODUCTS table that have that list price.

The next example shows a comparison subquery that uses a comparison operator other than =:

```
SELECT ProductID, ProductName, ListPrice
    FROM PRODUCTS
```

```
WHERE ListPrice <
    (SELECT AVG(ListPrice)
        FROM PRODUCTS) ;
```

The subquery returns a single value: the average list price in the PRODUCTS table. The outer query retrieves all rows from the PRODUCTS table that have a list price less than the average list price.

In the original SQL standard, a comparison could have only one subquery, and it had to be on the right side of the comparison. SQL:1999 allowed either or both operands of the comparison to be subqueries, and later versions of SQL retain that expanded capability.

Quantified subqueries return a single value

One way to make sure a subquery returns a single value is to introduce it with a quantified comparison operator. The universal quantifier ALL, and the existential quantifiers SOME and ANY, when combined with a comparison operator, process the result set returned by the inner subquery, reducing it to a single value.

Look at an example. From the 1960s through the 1980s, there was fierce competition between Ford and Chevrolet to produce the most powerful cars. Both companies had small-block V-8 engines that went into Mustangs, Camaros, and other performance-oriented vehicles.

Power is measured in units of horsepower. In general, a larger engine delivers more horsepower, all other things being equal. Because the displacements (sizes) of the engines varied from one model to another, it's unfair to look only at horsepower. A better measure of the efficiency of an engine is horsepower per displacement. Displacement is measured in cubic inches (CID). Table 3-1 shows the year, displacement, and horsepower ratings for Ford small-block V-8s between 1960 and 1980.

The Shelby GT350 was a classic muscle car — not a typical car for the weekday commute. Emission regulations taking effect in the early 1970s halved power output and brought an end to the muscle car era. Table 3-2 shows what Chevy put out during the same timeframe.

Here again you see the effect of the emission regulations that kicked in circa 1971 — a drastic drop in horsepower per displacement.

TABLE 3-1 **Ford Small-Block V-8s, 1960–1980**

Year	Displacement (CID)	Maximum Horsepower	Notes
1962	221	145	
1963	289	225	4bbl carburetor
1965	289	271	289HP model
1965	289	306	Shelby GT350
1969	351	290	4bbl carburetor
1975	302	140	Emission regulations

TABLE 3-2 **Chevy Small-Block V-8s, 1960–1980**

Year	Displacement (CID)	Maximum Horsepower	Notes
1960	283	315	
1962	327	375	
1967	350	295	
1968	302	290	
1968	307	200	
1969	350	370	Corvette
1970	400	265	
1975	262	110	Emission regulations

Use the following code to create tables to hold these data items:

```
CREATE TABLE Ford (
    EngineID            INTEGER         PRIMARY KEY,
    ModelYear           CHAR (4),
    Displacement        NUMERIC (5,2),
    MaxHP               NUMERIC (5,2),
    Notes               CHAR (30) ) ;

CREATE TABLE Chevy (
    EngineID            INTEGER         PRIMARY KEY,
    ModelYear           CHAR (4),
    Displacement        NUMERIC (5,2),
    MaxHP               NUMERIC (5,2),
    Notes               CHAR (30) ) ;
```

After filling these tables with the data in Tables 3-1 and 3-2, you can run some queries. Suppose you are a dyed-in-the-wool Chevy fan and are quite certain that the most powerful Chevrolet has a higher horsepower-to-displacement ratio than any of the Fords. To verify that assumption, enter the following query:

```
SELECT *
  FROM Chevy
  WHERE (MaxHP/Displacement) > ALL
    (SELECT (MaxHP/Displacement) FROM Ford) ;
```

This returns the result shown in Figure 3-1.

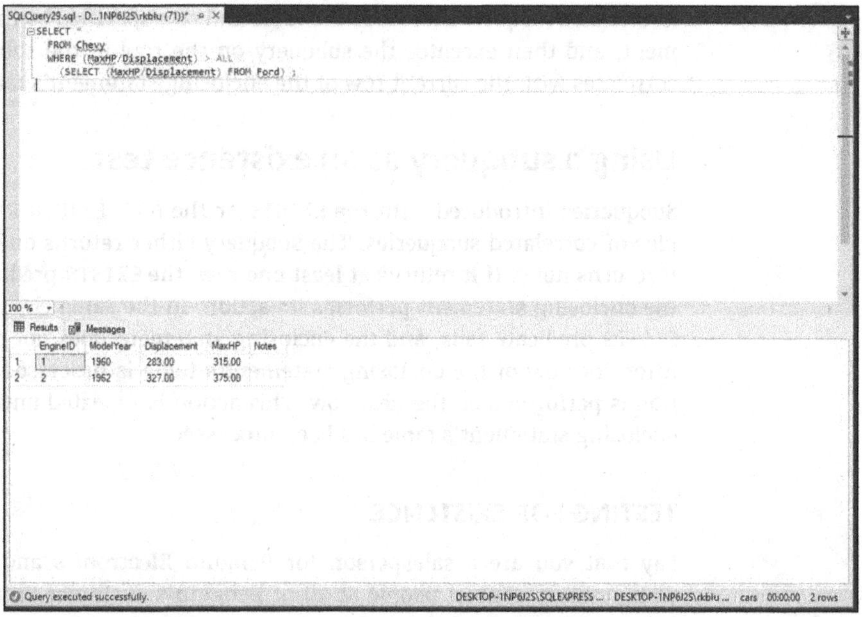

FIGURE 3-1:
Chevy muscle cars with horsepower to displacement ratios higher than any of the Fords listed.

The subquery (SELECT (MaxHP/Displacement) FROM Ford) returns the horsepower-to-displacement ratios of all the Ford engines in the Ford table. The ALL quantifier says to return only those records from the Chevy table that have horsepower-to-displacement ratios higher than all the ratios returned for the Ford engines. Two different Chevy engines had higher ratios than any Ford engine of that era, including the highly regarded Shelby GT350. Ford fans should not be bothered by this result, however. There's more to what makes a car awesome than just the horsepower-to-displacement ratio.

What if you had made the opposite assumption? What if you had entered the following query?

```
SELECT *
  FROM Ford
  WHERE (MaxHP/Displacement) > ALL
    (SELECT (MaxHP/Displacement) FROM Chevy) ;
```

Because none of the Ford engines has a higher horsepower-to-displacement ratio than *all* of the Chevy engines, the query doesn't return any rows.

Correlated subqueries

In all the nested queries I show in the previous sections, the inner subquery is executed first, and then its result is applied to the outer enclosing statement. A *correlated subquery* first finds the table and row specified by the enclosing statement, and then executes the subquery on the row in the subquery's table that correlates with the current row of the enclosing statement's table.

Using a subquery as an existence test

Subqueries introduced with the EXISTS or the NOT EXISTS keyword are examples of correlated subqueries. The subquery either returns one or more rows, or it returns none. If it returns at least one row, the EXISTS predicate succeeds, and the enclosing statement performs its action. In the same circumstances, the NOT EXISTS predicate fails, and the enclosing statement does not perform its action. After one row of the enclosing statement's table is processed, the same operation is performed on the next row. This action is repeated until every row in the enclosing statement's table has been processed.

TESTING FOR EXISTENCE

Say that you are a salesperson for Penguin Electronics and you want to call your primary contact people at all of Penguin's customer organizations in New Hampshire. Try the following query:

```
SELECT *
  FROM CONTACT
  WHERE EXISTS
    (SELECT *
       FROM CUSTOMER
       WHERE State = 'NH'
         AND CONTACT.CustomerID = CUSTOMER.CustomerID) ;
```

Notice the reference to CONTACT.CustomerID, which is referencing a column from the outer query and comparing it with another column, CUSTOMER.CustomerID, from the inner query. For each candidate row of the outer query, you evaluate the inner query, using the CustomerID value from the current CONTACT row of the outer query in the WHERE clause of the inner query.

The CustomerID column links the CONTACT table to the CUSTOMER table. SQL looks at the first record in the CONTACT table, finds the row in the CUSTOMER table that has the same CustomerID, and checks that row's State field. If CUSTOMER.State = 'NH', the current CONTACT row is added to the result table. The next CONTACT record is then processed in the same way, and so on, until the entire CONTACT table has been processed. Because the query specifies SELECT * FROM CONTACT, all the CONTACT table's fields are returned, including the contact's name and phone number.

TESTING FOR NONEXISTENCE

In the previous example, the Penguin salesperson wants to know the names and numbers of the contact people of all the customers in New Hampshire. Imagine that a second salesperson is responsible for all of the United States except New Hampshire. She can retrieve her contacts by using NOT EXISTS in a query similar to the preceding one:

```
SELECT *
    FROM CONTACT
    WHERE NOT EXISTS
        (SELECT *
            FROM CUSTOMER
            WHERE State = 'NH'
                AND CONTACT.CustomerID = CUSTOMER.CustomerID) ;
```

Every row in CONTACT for which the subquery does not return a row is added to the result table.

Introducing a correlated subquery with the IN keyword

As I note in a previous section of this chapter, subqueries introduced by IN or by a comparison operator need not be correlated queries, but they can be. In the "Subqueries that retrieve rows satisfying a condition" section, I give examples of how a noncorrelated subquery can be used with the IN predicate. To show how a correlated subquery may use the IN predicate, ask the same question that came up with the EXISTS predicate: What are the names and phone numbers of the contacts at all of Penguin's customers in New Hampshire? You can answer this question with a correlated IN subquery:

```
SELECT *
   FROM CONTACT
   WHERE 'NH' IN
      (SELECT State
          FROM CUSTOMER
          WHERE CONTACT.CustomerID = CUSTOMER.CustomerID) ;
```

The statement is evaluated for each record in the CONTACT table. If, for that record, the CustomerID numbers in CONTACT and CUSTOMER match, the value of CUSTOMER.State is compared to 'NH'. The result of the subquery is a list that contains, at most, one element. If that one element is 'NH', the WHERE clause of the enclosing statement is satisfied, and a row is added to the query's result table.

Introducing a correlated subquery with a comparison operator

A correlated subquery can also be introduced by one of the six comparison operators, as shown in the next example.

Penguin pays bonuses to its salespeople based on their total monthly sales volume. The higher the volume, the higher the bonus percentage. The bonus percentage list is kept in the BONUSRATE table:

MinAmount	MaxAmount	BonusPct
0.00	24999.99	0.
25000.00	49999.99	0.01
50000.00	99999.99	0.02
100000.00	249999.99	0.03
250000.00	499999.99	0.04
500000.00	749999.99	0.05
750000.00	999999.99	0.06

If a person's monthly sales total is between $100,000.00 and $249,999.99, the bonus is 3 percent of sales.

Sales are recorded in a transaction master table named TRANSMASTER, which is created as follows:

```
CREATE TABLE TRANSMASTER (
   TransID       INTEGER              PRIMARY KEY,
```

```
CustID        INTEGER        FOREIGN KEY,
EmpID         INTEGER        FOREIGN KEY,
TransDate     DATE,
NetAmount     NUMERIC,
Freight       NUMERIC,
Tax           NUMERIC,
InvoiceTotal  NUMERIC) ;
```

Sales bonuses are based on the sum of the NetAmount field for all of a person's transactions in the month. You can find any person's bonus rate with a correlated subquery that uses comparison operators:

```
SELECT BonusPct
   FROM BONUSRATE
      WHERE MinAmount <=
         (SELECT SUM(NetAmount)
            FROM TRANSMASTER
               WHERE EmpID = 133)
         AND MaxAmount >=
            (SELECT SUM(NetAmount)
               FROM TRANSMASTER
                  WHERE EmpID = 133) ;
```

This query is interesting in that it contains two subqueries, making use of the logical connective AND. The subqueries use the SUM aggregate operator, which returns a single value: the total monthly sales of employee 133. That value is then compared against the MinAmount and the MaxAmount columns in the BONUSRATE table, producing the bonus rate for that employee.

If you had not known the EmpID but had known the person's name, you could arrive at the same answer with a more complex query:

```
SELECT BonusPct
   FROM BONUSRATE
      WHERE MinAmount <=
         (SELECT SUM(NetAmount)
            FROM TRANSMASTER
               WHERE EmpID =
                  (SELECT EmployeeID
                      FROM EMPLOYEE
                         WHERE EmplName = 'Thornton'))
         AND MaxAmount >=
            (SELECT SUM(NetAmount)
               FROM TRANSMASTER
```

```
                    WHERE EmpID =
                    (SELECT EmployeeID
                     FROM EMPLOYEE
                     WHERE EmplName = 'Thornton'));
```

This example uses subqueries nested within subqueries, which in turn are nested within an enclosing query, to arrive at the bonus rate for the employee named Thornton. This structure works only if you know for sure that the company has one, and only one, employee whose name is Thornton. If you know that more than one employee is named Thornton, you can add terms to the WHERE clause of the innermost subquery until you're sure that only one row of the EMPLOYEE table is selected.

Correlated subqueries in a HAVING clause

You can have a correlated subquery in a HAVING clause just as you can in a WHERE clause. As I mention in Chapter 2 of this minibook, a HAVING clause is normally preceded by a GROUP BY clause. The HAVING clause acts as a filter to restrict the groups created by the GROUP BY clause. Groups that don't satisfy the condition of the HAVING clause are not included in the result. When used in this way, the HAVING clause is evaluated for each group created by the GROUP BY clause. In the absence of a GROUP BY clause, the HAVING clause is evaluated for the set of rows passed by the WHERE clause, which is considered to be a single group. If neither a WHERE clause nor a GROUP BY clause is present, the HAVING clause is evaluated for the entire table:

```
SELECT TM1.EmpID
    FROM TRANSMASTER TM1
        GROUP BY TM1.EmpID
        HAVING MAX(TM1.NetAmount) >= ALL
            (SELECT 2 * AVG (TM2.NetAmount)
                FROM TRANSMASTER TM2
                WHERE TM1.EmpID <> TM2.EmpID) ;
```

This query uses two aliases for the same table, enabling you to retrieve the EmpID number of all salespeople who had a sale of at least twice the average value of all the other salespeople. Short aliases such as TM1 are often used to eliminate excessive typing when long table names such as TRANSMASTER are involved. But in this case, aliases do more than just save some typing. The TRANSMASTER table is used for two different purposes, so two different aliases are used to distinguish between them. The query works as follows:

1. The outer query groups TRANSMASTER rows by the EmpID. This is done with the SELECT, FROM, and GROUP BY clauses.

2. The HAVING clause filters these groups. For each group, it calculates the MAX of the NetAmount column for the rows in that group.

3. The inner query evaluates twice the average NetAmount from all rows of TRANSMASTER whose EmpID is different from the EmpID of the current group of the outer query. Each group contains the transaction records for an employee whose biggest sale had at least twice the value of the average of the sales of all the other employees. Note that in the last line, you need to reference two different EmpID values, so in the FROM clauses of the outer and inner queries, you use different aliases for TRANSMASTER.

4. You then use those aliases in the comparison of the query's last line to indicate that you're referencing both the EmpID from the current row of the inner subquery (TM2.EmpID) and the EmpID from the current group of the outer subquery (TM1.EmpID).

Using Subqueries in INSERT, DELETE, and UPDATE Statements

In addition to SELECT statements, UPDATE, DELETE, and INSERT statements can also include WHERE clauses. Those WHERE clauses can contain subqueries in the same way that SELECT statement WHERE clauses do.

For example, Penguin has just made a volume purchase deal with Baker Electronic Sales and wants to retroactively provide Baker with a 10 percent credit for all its purchases in the last month. You can give this credit with an UPDATE statement:

```
UPDATE TRANSMASTER
   SET NetAmount = NetAmount * 0.9
   WHERE CustID =
      (SELECT CustID
         FROM CUSTOMER
         WHERE Company = 'Baker Electronic Sales') ;
```

You can also have a correlated subquery in an UPDATE statement. Suppose the CUSTOMER table has a column LastMonthsMax, and Penguin wants to give the same 10 percent credit for purchases that exceed LastMonthsMax for the customer:

```
UPDATE TRANSMASTER TM
   SET NetAmount = NetAmount * 0.9
   WHERE NetAmount >
      (SELECT LastMonthsMax
```

```
        FROM CUSTOMER C
        WHERE C.CustID = TM.CustID) ;
```

Note that this subquery is correlated: The WHERE clause in the last line references both the CustID of the CUSTOMER row from the subquery and the CustID of the current TRANSMASTER row that is a candidate for updating.

A subquery in an UPDATE statement can also reference the table being updated. Suppose that Penguin wants to give a 10 percent credit to customers whose purchases have exceeded $10,000:

```
UPDATE TRANSMASTER TM1
    SET NetAmount = NetAmount * 0.9
    WHERE 10000 < (SELECT SUM(NetAmount)
                   FROM TRANSMASTER TM2
                        WHERE TM1.CustID = TM2.CustID);
```

The inner subquery calculates the SUM of the NetAmount column for all TRANSMASTER rows for the same customer. What does this mean? Suppose that the customer with CustID = 37 has four rows in TRANSMASTER with values for NetAmount: 3000, 5000, 2000, and 1000. The SUM of NetAmount for this CustID is 11000.

REMEMBER

The order in which the UPDATE statement processes the rows is defined by your implementation and is generally not predictable. The order may differ depending on how the rows are arranged on the disk. Assume that the implementation processes the rows for this CustID in this order: first the TRANSMASTER row with a NetAmount of 3000, and then the one with NetAmount = 5000, and so on. After the first three rows for CustID 37 have been updated, their NetAmount values are 2700 (90 percent of 3000), 4500 (90 percent of 5000), and 1800 (90 percent of 2000). Then when you process the last TRANSMASTER row for CustID 37, whose NetAmount is 1000, the SUM returned by the subquery would seem to be 10000 — that is, the SUM of the *new* NetAmount values of the first three rows for CustID 37 and the *old* NetAmount value of the last row for CustID 37. Thus it would seem that the last row for CustID 37 isn't updated because the comparison with that SUM is not True, since 10000 is not less than SELECT SUM (NetAmount). But that is not how the UPDATE statement is defined when a subquery references the table being updated. All evaluations of subqueries in an UPDATE statement reference the *old* values of the table being updated. In the preceding UPDATE for CustID 37, the subquery returns 11000 — the original SUM.

The subquery in an UPDATE statement WHERE clause operates the same as it does in a SELECT statement WHERE clause. The same is true for DELETE and INSERT. To delete all of Baker's transactions, use this statement:

```
DELETE FROM TRANSMASTER
   WHERE CustID =
      (SELECT CustomerID
         FROM CUSTOMER
         WHERE Company = 'Baker Electronic Sales') ;
```

As with UPDATE, DELETE subqueries can also be correlated and can also reference the table whose rows are being deleted. The rules are similar to the rules for
UPDATE subqueries. Suppose you want to delete all rows from TRANSMASTER for
customers whose total NetAmount is larger than $10,000:

```
DELETE FROM TRANSMASTER TM1
   WHERE 10000 < (SELECT SUM(NetAmount)
      FROM TRANSMASTER TM2
         WHERE TM1.CustID = TM2.CustID) ;
```

This query deletes all rows from TRANSMASTER referencing customers with
purchases exceeding $10,000 — including the aforementioned customer with
CustID 37. All references to TRANSMASTER in the subquery denote the contents of
TRANSMASTER before any deletes by the current statement. So even when you
are deleting the last TRANSMASTER row, the subquery is evaluated on the original
TRANSMASTER table, identified by TM1.

REMEMBER

When you update, delete, or insert database records, you risk making a table's data
inconsistent with other tables in the database. Such an inconsistency is called a
modification anomaly, discussed in Book 2, Chapter 2. If you delete TRANSMASTER
records and a TRANSDETAIL table depends on TRANSMASTER, you must delete
the corresponding records from TRANSDETAIL too. This operation is called a
cascading delete because the deletion of a parent record cascades to its associated child records. Otherwise, the undeleted child records become orphans. In this
case, they would be invoice detail lines that are in limbo because they are no longer connected to an invoice record. Your database management system will give
you the option to either specify a cascading delete or not.

INSERT can include a SELECT clause. One use for this statement is filling
snapshot tables — tables that take a snapshot of another table at a particular moment
in time. For example, to create a table with the contents of TRANSMASTER for
October 27, do this:

```
CREATE TABLE TRANSMASTER_1027
   (TransID INTEGER, TransDate DATE,
   ...) ;
```

```
INSERT INTO TRANSMASTER_1027
    (SELECT * FROM TRANSMASTER
          WHERE TransDate = 2018-10-27) ;
```

The CREATE TABLE statement creates an empty table; the INSERT INTO statement fills it with the data that was added on October 27. Or you may want to save rows only for large NetAmounts:

```
INSERT INTO TRANSMASTER_1027
    (SELECT * FROM TRANSMASTER
          WHERE TRANSMASTER.NetAmount > 10000
              AND TransDate = 2018-10-27) ;
```

Tuning Considerations for Statements Containing Nested Queries

How do you tune a nested query? In some cases, there is no need because the nested query is about as efficient as it can be. In other cases, nested queries are not particularly efficient. Depending on the characteristics of the database management system you're using, you may want to recode a nested query for higher performance. I mentioned at the beginning of this chapter that many tasks performed by nested queries could also be performed using relational operators. In some cases, using a relational operator yields better performance than a nested query that produces the same result. If performance is an issue in a given application and a nested query seems to be the bottleneck, you might want to try a statement containing a relational operator instead and compare execution times. I discuss relational operations extensively in the next chapter, but for now, take a look at an example.

As I mention earlier in this chapter, there are two kinds of subqueries, noncorrelated and correlated. Using the AdventureWorks2022 database, let's look at a noncorrelated subquery without a set function.

```
SELECT SalesOrderID
    FROM Sales.SalesOrderDetail
    WHERE ProductID IN
        (SELECT ProductID
            FROM Production.ProductInventory
            WHERE Quantity = 0) ;
```

This query takes data from both the ProductInventory table and the SalesOrderDetail table. It returns the SalesOrderIDs of all orders that include out-of-stock products. Figure 3-2 shows the result of the query. Figure 3-3 shows the execution plan, and Figure 3-4 shows the client statistics.

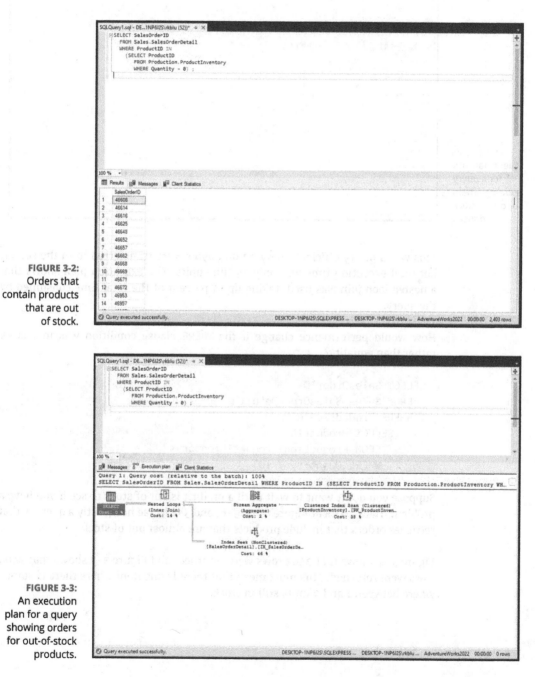

FIGURE 3-2:
Orders that
contain products
that are out
of stock.

FIGURE 3-3:
An execution
plan for a query
showing orders
for out-of-stock
products.

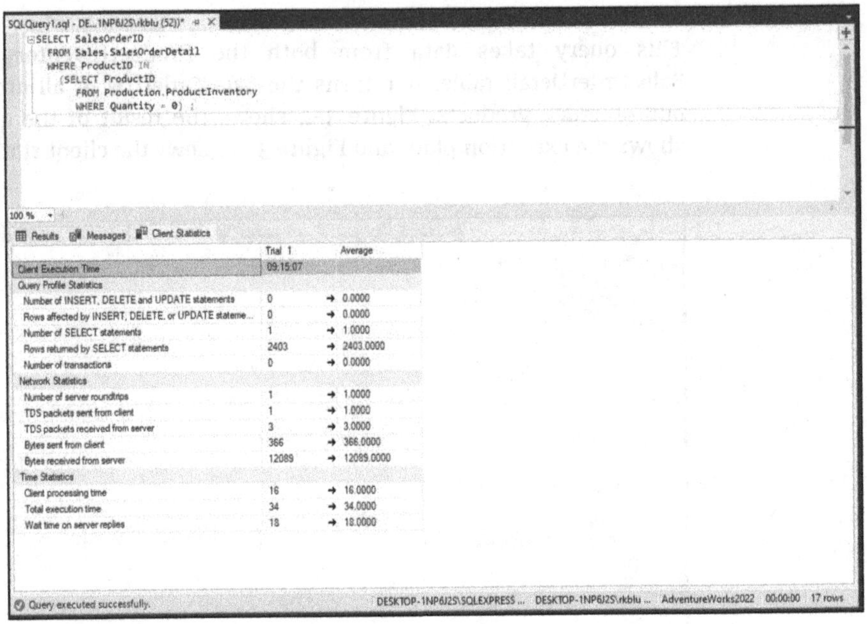

FIGURE 3-4:
Client statistics
for a query
showing orders
for out-of-stock
products.

This was a pretty efficient query. 12,089 bytes were transferred from the server, but total execution time was only 34 time units. The execution plan shows that a nested loop join was used, taking up 14 percent of the total time consumed by the query.

How would performance change if the WHERE clause condition was inequality rather than equality?

```
SELECT SalesOrderID
  FROM Sales.SalesOrderDetail
  WHERE ProductID IN
    (SELECT ProductID
      FROM Production.ProductInventory
      WHERE Quantity < 10) ;
```

Suppose you don't want to wait until a product is out of stock to see if you have a problem. Take a look at Figures 3-5, 3-6, and 3-7 to see how costly a query is that retrieves orders that include products that are almost out of stock.

Figure 3-4 shows that 2403 rows were returned, and Figure 3-7 shows that 2404 rows were returned. This must mean that there is one item where there is somewhere between 1 and 9 units still in stock.

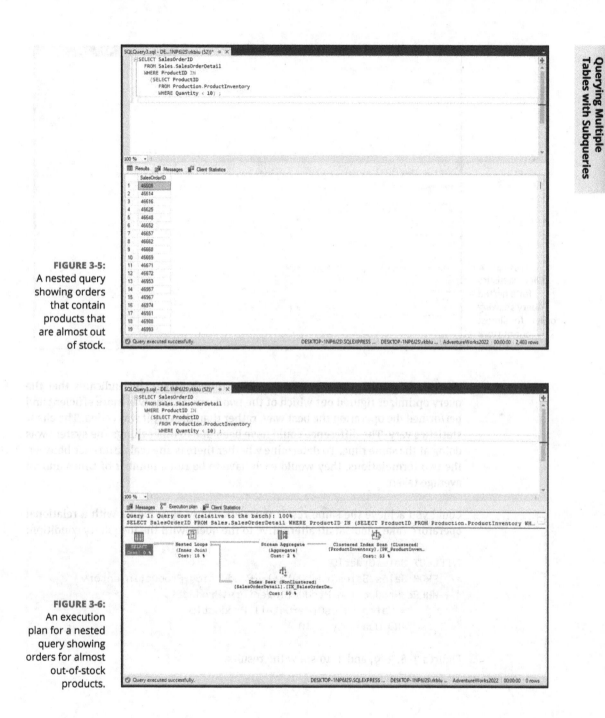

FIGURE 3-5:
A nested query
showing orders
that contain
products that
are almost out
of stock.

FIGURE 3-6:
An execution
plan for a nested
query showing
orders for almost
out-of-stock
products.

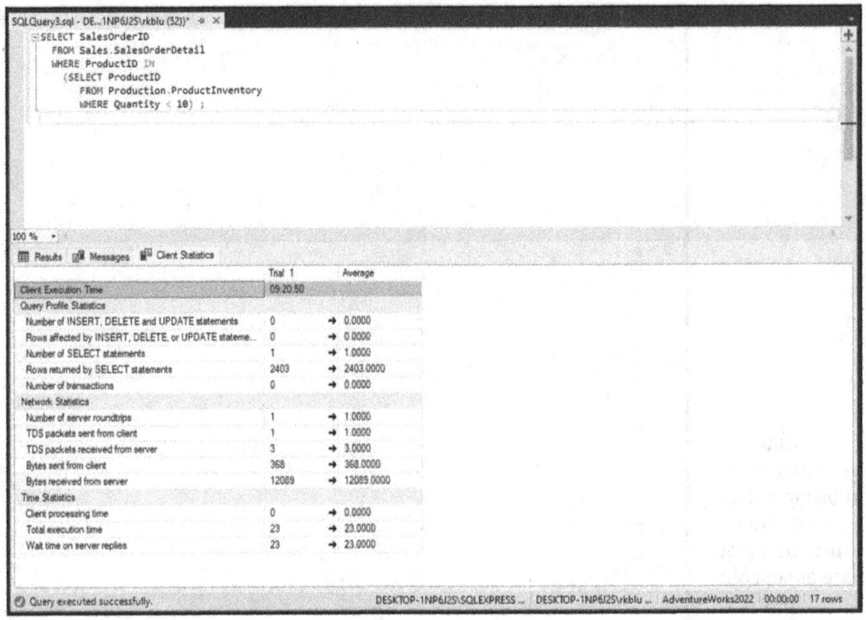

FIGURE 3-7:
Client statistics for a nested query showing orders for almost out-of-stock products.

The execution plan times are pretty close in both cases. This indicates that the query optimizer figured out which of the two formulations was more efficient and performed the operation the best way, rather than the way it was coded. The client statistics vary. The difference could have been due to other things the system was doing at the same time. To determine whether there is any real difference between the two formulations, they would each have to be run a number of times and an average taken.

Could you achieve the same result more efficiently by recoding with a relational operator? Take a look at an alternative to the query with the inequality condition:

```
SELECT SalesOrderID
  FROM Sales.SalesOrderDetail, Production.ProductInventory
  WHERE Production.ProductInventory.ProductID
     = Sales.SalesOrderDetail.ProductID
     AND Quantity < 10 ;
```

Figures 3-8, 3-9, and 3-10 show the results.

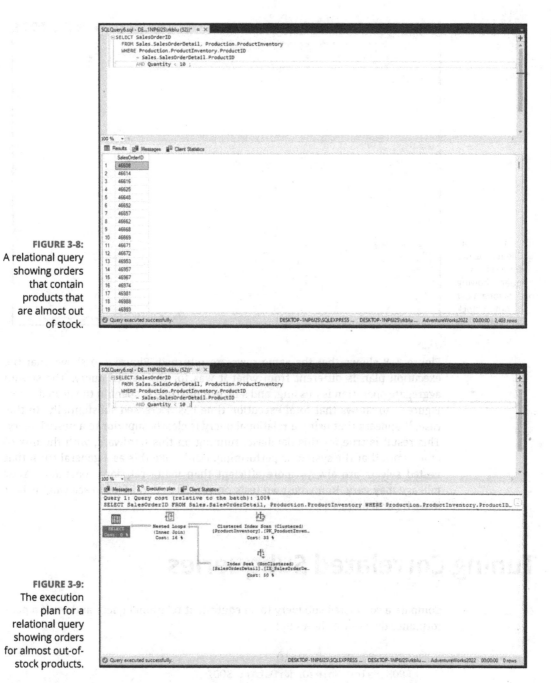

FIGURE 3-8:
A relational query showing orders that contain products that are almost out of stock.

FIGURE 3-9:
The execution plan for a relational query showing orders for almost out-of-stock products.

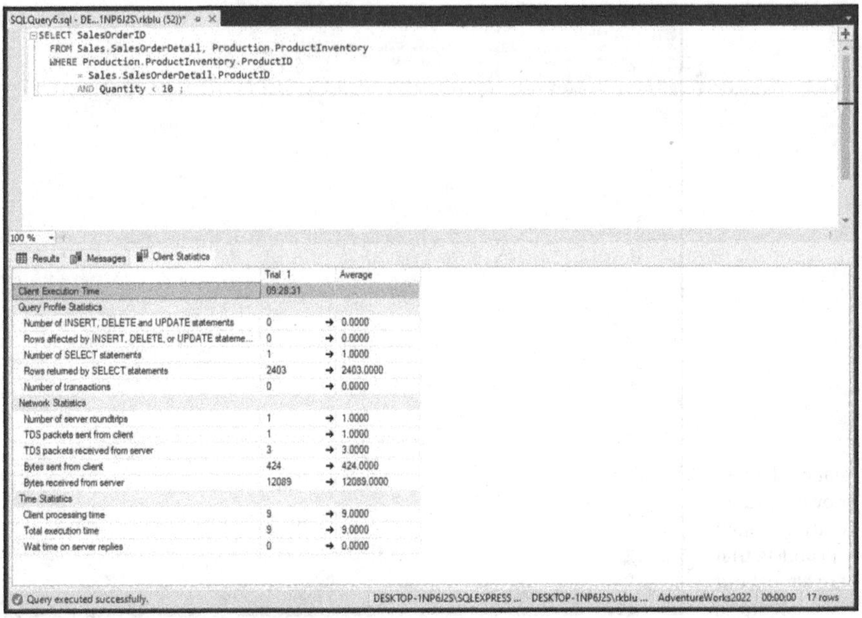

FIGURE 3-10:
Client statistics
for a relational
query showing
orders for almost
out-of-stock
products.

Figure 3-8 shows that the same rows are returned. Figure 3-9 shows that the execution plan is different from what it was for the nested query. The stream aggregate operation is missing, and a little more time is spent in the nested loops. Figure 3-10 shows that total execution time has decreased substantially. In this case, it appears that using a relational query is clearly superior to a nested query. This result is true for this database, running on this hardware, with the mix of other work that the system is performing. Don't take this as a general truth that nested selects are always more efficient than using relational operators. Your mileage may vary. Run your own tests on your own databases to see what is best in each particular case.

Tuning Correlated Subqueries

Compare a correlated subquery to an equivalent relational query and see if a performance difference shows up:

```
SELECT SOD1.SalesOrderID
    FROM Sales.SalesOrderDetail SOD1
        GROUP BY SOD1.SalesOrderID
        HAVING MAX (SOD1.UnitPrice) >= ALL
            (SELECT 2 * AVG (SOD2.UnitPrice)
                FROM Sales.SalesOrderDetail SOD2
                WHERE SOD1.SalesOrderID <> SOD2.SalesOrderID) ;
```

This query into the AdventureWorks2022 database extracts from the SalesOrderDetail table the order numbers of all the rows that contain a product whose unit price is greater than or equal to twice the average unit price of all the other products in the table. Because of the complexity of this query, it may take some time to return the result, depending on your workstation or server speed. Figures 3-11, 3-12, and 3-13 show the result of the query.

As shown in the lower right corner of Figure 3-11, 13,831 orders contained a product whose unit price is greater than or equal to twice the average unit price of all the other products in the table.

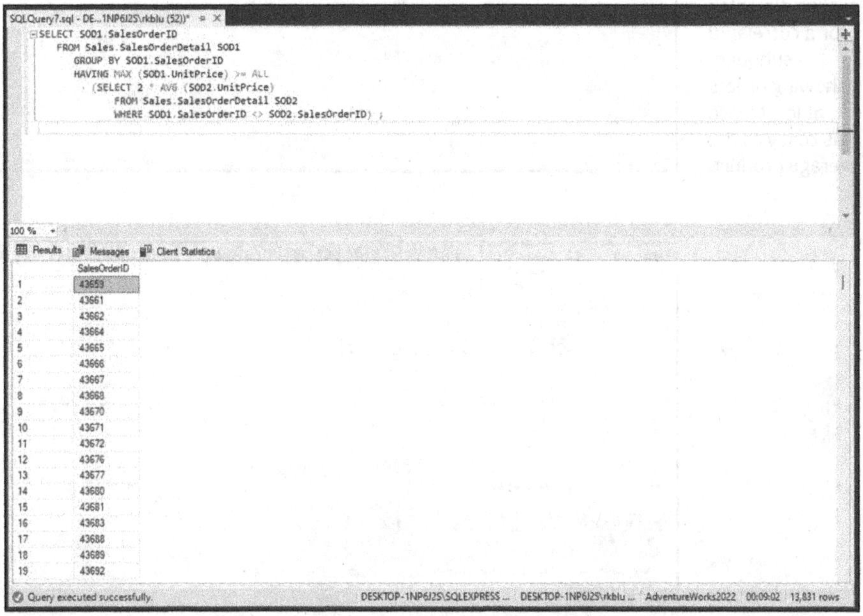

FIGURE 3-11:
A correlated
subquery
showing orders
that contain
products at least
twice as costly
as the average
product.

Figure 3-12 shows the most complex execution plan in this book. Correlated subqueries are intrinsically more complex than are the noncorrelated variety. Many parts of the plan have minimal cost, but the clustered index seek takes up 70 percent of the total, and the stream aggregate due to the MAX set function takes up 30 percent. The query took much longer to run than any of the queries discussed so far in this chapter.

The client statistics table in Figure 3-13 shows that 69,341 bytes were returned by the server and that the total execution time was 542,375 time units. As shown in the bottom right corner of the statistics panel, the query took just a little over nine minutes to execute, whereas all the previous queries in this chapter executed in such a small fraction of a second that the result seemed to appear instantaneously. This is clearly an example of a query that anyone would like to perform more efficiently.

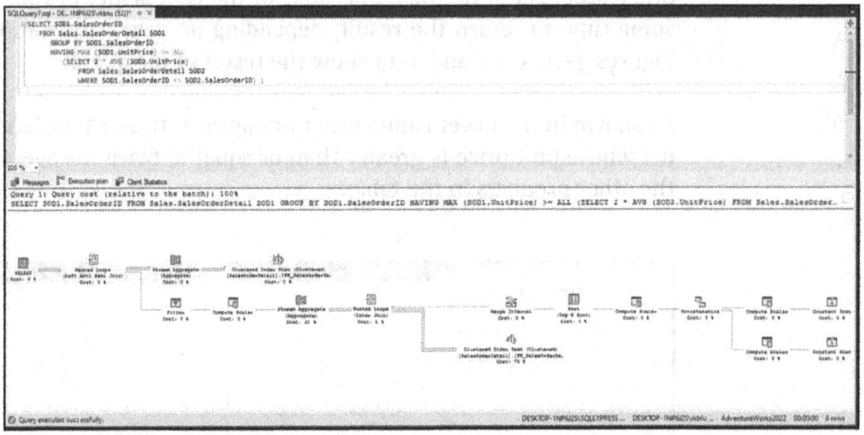

FIGURE 3-12:
An execution plan for a correlated subquery showing orders at least twice as costly as the average product.

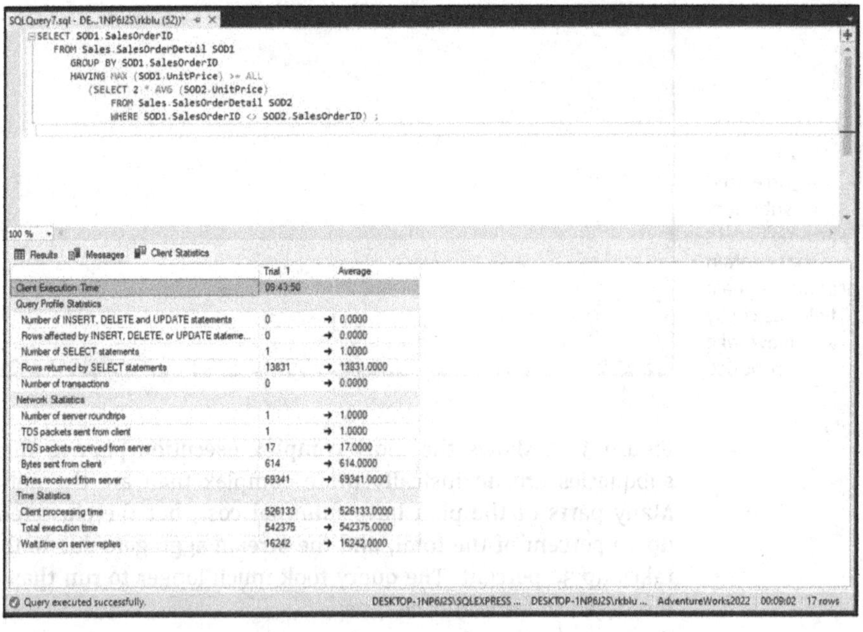

FIGURE 3-13:
Client statistics for a correlated subquery showing orders at least twice as costly as the average product.

Would a relational query do better? You can formulate one, using a temporary table:

```
SELECT 2 * AVG(UnitPrice) AS TwiceAvgPrice INTO #TempPrice
  FROM Sales.SalesOrderDetail ;

SELECT DISTINCT SalesOrderID
  FROM Sales.SalesOrderDetail, #TempPrice
  WHERE UnitPrice >= twiceavgprice ;
```

When you run this two-part query, you get the results shown in Figures 3-14, 3-15, and 3-16.

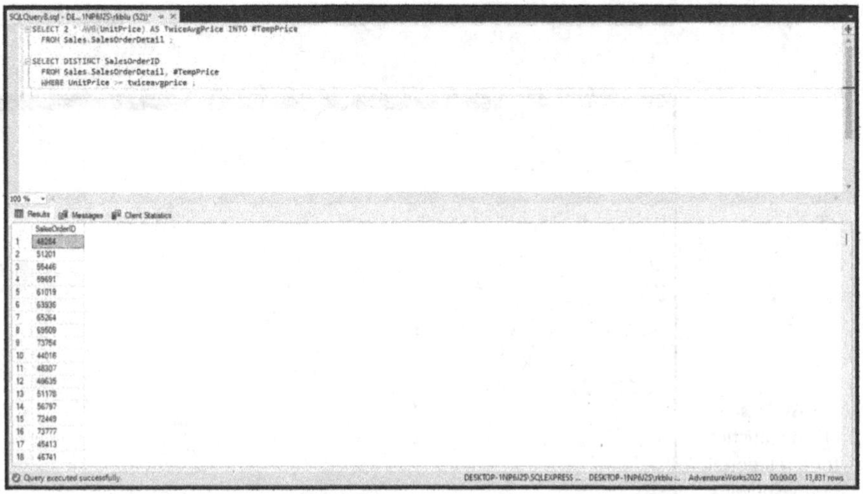

FIGURE 3-14: Relational query showing orders that contain products at least twice as costly as the average product.

This query returns the same result as the previous one, but the difference in execution time is astounding. This query ran almost instantly, rather than over nine minutes.

Figure 3-15 shows the execution plans for the two parts of the relational query. In the first part, a clustered index scan takes up most of the time (93 percent). In the second part, a clustered index scan and an inner join consume most of the time.

Figure 3-16 shows a tremendous difference in performance with the correlated subquery in Figure 3-13, which produced exactly the same result. The total execution time is reduced to 188 time units compared to the 542,375 time units shown in Figure 3-13.

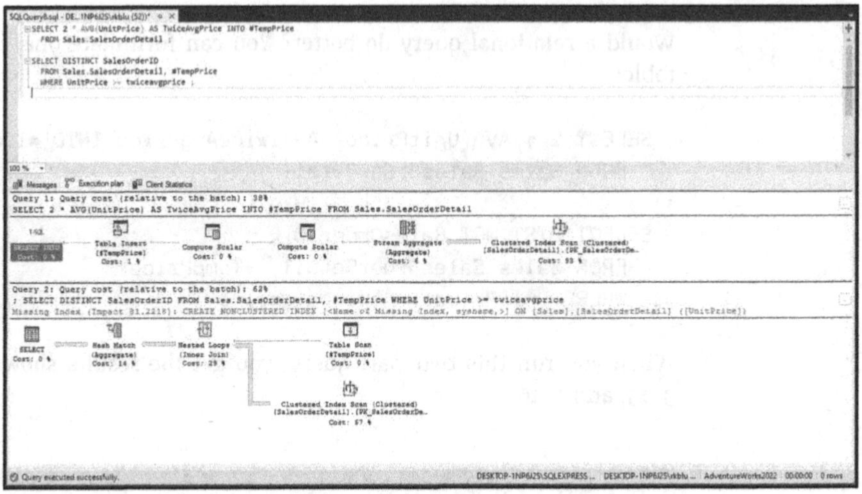

FIGURE 3-15:
An execution plan for a relational query showing orders for almost out-of-stock products.

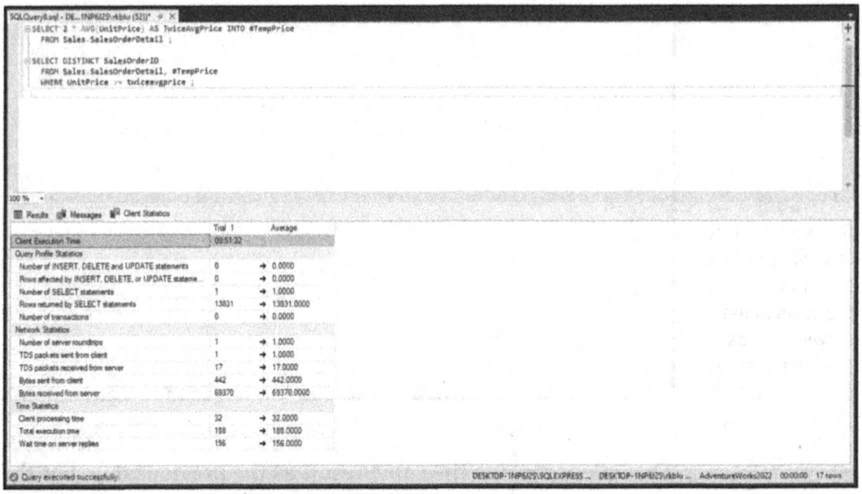

FIGURE 3-16:
Client statistics for a relational query showing orders for almost out-of-stock products.

> **TIP** If you have a similar query that will be run repeatedly, give serious consideration to performing a relational query rather than a correlated subquery if performance is an issue and if an equivalent relational query can be composed. It is worth running a couple of tests.

Chapter **4**

Querying Multiple Tables with Relational Operators

I n Chapter 3 of this minibook, I show you how, by using nested queries, data can be drawn from multiple tables to answer a question that involves different ideas. Another way to collect information from multiple tables is to use the relational operators UNION, INTERSECT, EXCEPT, and JOIN. SQL's UNION, INTERSECT, and EXCEPT operators are modeled after the union, intersect, and except operators of relational algebra. Each one performs a very specific combining operation on the data in two or more tables. The JOIN operator, on the other hand, is considerably more flexible. A number of different joins exist, and each performs a somewhat different operation. Depending on what you want in terms of information retrieved from multiple tables, one or another of the joins or the other relational operators is likely to give it to you. In this chapter, I show you each of SQL's relational operators, cover how it works, and discuss what you can use it for.

UNION

The UNION operator is the SQL implementation of the union operator used in relational algebra. SQL's UNION operator enables you to draw information from two or more tables that have the same structure. *Same structure* means

>> The tables must all have the same number of columns.

>> Corresponding columns must all have identical data types and lengths.

When these criteria are met, the tables are *union-compatible*. The union of two tables returns all the rows that appear in either table and eliminates duplicates.

Suppose you have created a database for a business named Acme Systems that sells and installs computer products. Acme has two warehouses that stock the products, one in Fort Deposit, Alabama, and the other in East Kingston, New Hampshire. It contains two union-compatible tables, named DEPOSIT and KINGSTON. Both tables have two columns, and corresponding columns are of the same type. In fact, corresponding columns have identical column names (although this condition isn't required for union compatibility).

DEPOSIT lists the names and quantity in stock of products in the Fort Deposit warehouse. KINGSTON lists the same information about the East Kingston warehouse. The UNION of the two tables gives you a virtual result table containing all the rows in the first table plus all the rows in the second table. For this example, I put just a few rows in each table to illustrate the operation:

```
SELECT * FROM DEPOSIT ;

ProductName     QuantityInStock
-----------     ---------------
185_Express           12
505_Express            5
510_Express            6
520_Express            2
550_Express            3

SELECT * FROM KINGSTON ;

ProductName     QuantityInStock
-----------     ---------------
185_Express           15
505_Express            7
510_Express            6
```

```
520_Express          2
550_Express          1

SELECT * FROM DEPOSIT
UNION
SELECT * FROM KINGSTON ;

ProductName      QuantityInStock
-----------      ---------------
185_Express          12
185_Express          15
505_Express          5
505_Express          7
510_Express          6
520_Express          2
550_Express          3
550_Express          1
```

The UNION DISTINCT operator functions identically to the UNION operator without the DISTINCT keyword. In both cases, duplicate rows are eliminated from the result set. In this example, because both warehouses had the same number of 510_Express and 520_Express products, those rows in both tables were exact duplicates, only one of which was returned.

This example shows how UNION works, but it isn't very practical. In most cases, I imagine Acme's manager would not care which products were stocked in exactly the same numbers at both warehouses, and thus partially removed from the result set. All the information is present, but the user must be savvy enough to realize that the total number of units of 510_Express is actually 12 rather than 6, and the total number of units of 520_Express is 4 rather than 2.

WARNING

I use the asterisk (*) as shorthand for all the columns in a table. This shortcut is fine most of the time, but it can get you into trouble when you use relational operators in embedded or module-language SQL. What if you add one or more new columns to one table and not to another, or you add different columns to the two tables? The two tables are then no longer union-compatible, and your program is invalid the next time it's recompiled. Even if the same new columns are added to both tables so that they are still union-compatible, your program is probably not prepared to deal with this additional data. So, explicitly listing the columns that you want rather than relying on the * shorthand is generally a good idea. When you're entering ad hoc SQL from the console, the asterisk will probably work fine because you can quickly display table structure to verify union compatibility if your query isn't successful.

UNION ALL

As mentioned previously, the UNION operation normally eliminates any duplicate rows that result from its operation, which is the desired result most of the time. Sometimes, however, you may want to preserve duplicate rows. On those occasions, use UNION ALL.

The following code shows you what UNION ALL produces when it's used with the DEPOSIT and KINGSTON tables:

```
SELECT * FROM DEPOSIT
UNION ALL
SELECT * FROM KINGSTON ;

ProductName      QuantityInStock
------------     ---------------

185_Express            12
505_Express             5
510_Express             6
520_Express             2
550_Express             3
185_Express            15
505_Express             7
510_Express             6
520_Express             2
550_Express             1
```

UNION CORRESPONDING

You can sometimes form the union of two tables even if they are not union-compatible. If the columns you want in your result set are present and compatible in both source tables, you can perform a UNION CORRESPONDING operation. Only the specified columns are considered, and they are the only columns displayed in the result set.

Suppose ACME Systems opens a third warehouse, in Jefferson, Maine. A new table named JEFFERSON is added to the database, which includes Product and QuantityInStock columns (as the DEPOSIT and KINGSTON tables do), but also has an additional column named QuantityOnHold. A UNION or UNION ALL of JEFFERSON with either DEPOSIT or KINGSTON would not return any rows because there is not a complete match between all the columns of JEFFERSON and all the columns of the other two tables. However, you can still add the JEFFERSON data to that of either DEPOSIT or KINGSTON by specifying only the columns in JEFFERSON that correspond with the columns in the other table. Here's a sample query:

```
SELECT *
    FROM JEFFERSON
UNION CORRESPONDING BY
    (ProductName, QuantityInStock)
SELECT *
    FROM KINGSTON ;
```

The result table holds the products and the quantities in stock at both warehouses. As with the simple UNION, duplicates are eliminated. Thus, if the Jefferson warehouse happens to have the same quantity of a particular product that the Kingston warehouse has, the UNION CORRESPONDING operation loses one of those rows. To avoid this problem, use UNION ALL CORRESPONDING.

TIP

Each column name in the list following the CORRESPONDING keyword must be a name that exists in both unioned tables. If you omit this list of names, an implicit list of all names that appear in both tables is used. But this implicit list of names may change when new columns are added to one or both tables. Therefore, explicitly listing the column names is better than omitting them.

INTERSECT

The UNION operation produces a result table containing all rows that appear in at least one of the source tables. If you want only rows that appear in all the source tables, you can use the INTERSECT operation, which is the SQL implementation of relational algebra's intersect operation. I illustrate INTERSECT by returning to the Acme Systems warehouse table:

```
SELECT * FROM DEPOSIT ;

ProductName         QuantityInStock
-----------         ---------------
185_Express                12
505_Express                 5
510_Express                 6
520_Express                 2
550_Express                 3
```

```
SELECT * FROM KINGSTON ;

ProductName        QuantityInStock
-----------        ---------------
185_Express              15
505_Express               7
510_Express               6
520_Express               2
550_Express               1
```

Only rows that appear in all source tables show up in the INTERSECT operation's result table:

```
SELECT *
   FROM DEPOSIT
INTERSECT
SELECT *
   FROM KINGSTON;

ProductName        QuantityInStock
-----------        ---------------
510_Express               6
520_Express               2
```

The result table shows that the Fort Deposit and East Kingston warehouses both have exactly the same number of 510_Express and 520_Express products in stock, a fact of dubious value. Note that, as was the case with UNION, INTERSECT DISTINCT produces the same result as the INTERSECT operator used alone. In this example, only one of the identical rows displaying each of two products is returned.

The ALL and CORRESPONDING keywords function in an INTERSECT operation the same way they do in a UNION operation. If you use ALL, duplicates are retained in the result table. If you use CORRESPONDING, the intersected tables need not be union-compatible, although the corresponding columns need to have matching types and lengths.

Consider another example: A municipality keeps track of the phones carried by police officers, firefighters, parking enforcement officers, and other city employees. A database table called PHONES contains data on all phones in active use. Another table named OUT, with an identical structure, contains data on all phones that have been taken out of service. No cellphone should ever exist in both tables.

With an INTERSECT operation, you can test to see whether such an unwanted duplication has occurred:

```
SELECT *
    FROM PHONES
INTERSECT CORRESPONDING BY (PhoneID)
SELECT *
    FROM OUT ;
```

If the result table contains any rows, you know you have a problem. You should investigate any PhoneID entries that appear in the result table. The corresponding phone is either active or out of service; it can't be both. After you detect the problem, you can perform a DELETE operation on one of the two tables to restore database integrity.

EXCEPT

The UNION operation acts on two source tables and returns all rows that appear in *either* table. The INTERSECT operation returns all rows that appear in *both* the first and the second table. In contrast, the EXCEPT (or EXCEPT DISTINCT) operation returns all rows that appear in the first table but that *do not* also appear in the second table.

Returning to the municipal phone database example, say that a group of phones that had been declared out of service and returned to the vendor for repairs have now been fixed and placed back into service. The PHONES table was updated to reflect the returned phones, but the returned phones were not removed from the OUT table as they should have been. You can display the PhoneID numbers of the phones in the OUT table, with the reactivated ones eliminated, using an EXCEPT operation:

```
SELECT *
    FROM OUT
EXCEPT CORRESPONDING BY (PhoneID)
SELECT *
    FROM PHONES;
```

This query returns all the rows in the OUT table whose PhoneID is not also present in the PHONES table. These are the phones still out of service.

JOINS

The UNION, INTERSECT, and EXCEPT operators are valuable in multitable databases in which the tables are union-compatible. In many cases, however, you
want to draw data from multiple tables that have very little in common. JOINs are
powerful relational operators that combine data from multiple tables into a single
result table. The source tables may have little (or even nothing) in common with
each other.

SQL supports a number of types of JOINs. The best one to choose in a given situation depends on the result you're trying to achieve.

Cartesian product or cross join

Any multitable query is a type of JOIN. The source tables are joined in the sense
that the result table includes information taken from all the source tables. The
simplest JOIN is a two-table SELECT that has no WHERE clause qualifiers. Every
row of the first table is joined to every row of the second table. The result table is
referred to as the *Cartesian product* of the two source tables — the direct product
of the two sets. (The less fancy name for the same thing is *cross join*.) The number
of rows in the result table is equal to the number of rows in the first source table
multiplied by the number of rows in the second source table.

For example, imagine that you're the personnel manager for a company, and that
part of your job is to maintain employee records. Most employee data, such as
home address and telephone number, is not particularly sensitive. But some data,
such as current salary, should be available only to authorized personnel. To maintain security of the sensitive information, you'd probably keep it in a separate
table that is password protected. Consider the following pair of tables:

EMPLOYEE	COMPENSATION
EmpID	Employ
FName	Salary
LName	Bonus
City	
Phone	

Fill the tables with some sample data:

EmpID	FName	LName	City	Phone
1	Jenny	Smith	Orange	555-1001

```
2      Bill     Jones     Newark     555-3221
3      Val      Brown     Nutley     555-6905
4      Justin   Time      Passaic    555-8908

Employ   Salary   Bonus
------   ------   -----
     1    63000   10000
     2    48000    2000
     3    54000    5000
     4    52000    7000
```

Create a virtual result table with the following query:

```
SELECT *
   FROM EMPLOYEE, COMPENSATION ;
```

which can also be written

```
SELECT *
   FROM EMPLOYEE CROSS JOIN COMPENSATION ;
```

Both of the above formulations do exactly the same thing. This query produces

```
EmpID FName  LName  City     Phone      Employ Salary Bonus
----- -----  -----  ----     -----      ------ ------ -----
    1 Jenny  Smith  Orange   555-1001        1  63000 10000
    1 Jenny  Smith  Orange   555-1001        2  48000  2000
    1 Jenny  Smith  Orange   555-1001        3  54000  5000
    1 Jenny  Smith  Orange   555-1001        4  52000  7000
    2 Bill   Jones  Newark   555-3221        1  63000 10000
    2 Bill   Jones  Newark   555-3221        2  48000  2000
    2 Bill   Jones  Newark   555-3221        3  54000  5000
    2 Bill   Jones  Newark   555-3221        4  52000  7000
    3 Val    Brown  Nutley   555-6905        1  63000 10000
    3 Val    Brown  Nutley   555-6905        2  48000  2000
    3 Val    Brown  Nutley   555-6905        3  54000  5000
    3 Val    Brown  Nutley   555-6905        4  52000  7000
    4 Justin Time   Passaic  555-8908        1  63000 10000
    4 Justin Time   Passaic  555-8908        2  48000  2000
    4 Justin Time   Passaic  555-8908        3  54000  5000
    4 Justin Time   Passaic  555-8908        4  52000  7000
```

The result table, which is the Cartesian product of the EMPLOYEE and
COMPENSATION tables, contains considerable redundancy. Furthermore, it

doesn't make much sense. It combines every row of EMPLOYEE with every row of COMPENSATION. The only rows that convey meaningful information are those in which the EmpID number that came from EMPLOYEE matches the Employ number that came from COMPENSATION. In those rows, an employee's name and address are associated with that same employee's compensation.

When you're trying to get useful information out of a multitable database, the Cartesian product produced by a cross join is almost never what you want, but it's almost always the first step toward what you want. By applying constraints to the JOIN with a WHERE clause, you can filter out the unwanted rows. The most common JOIN that uses the WHERE clause filter is the equi-join.

Equi-join

An *equi-join* is a cross join with the addition of a WHERE clause containing a condition specifying that the value in one column in the first table must be equal to the value of a corresponding column in the second table. Applying an equi-join to the example tables from the previous section brings a more meaningful result:

```
SELECT *
   FROM EMPLOYEE, COMPENSATION
   WHERE EMPLOYEE.EmpID = COMPENSATION.Employ ;
```

This produces the following:

EmpID	FName	LName	City	Phone	Employ	Salary	Bonus
1	Jenny	Smith	Orange	555-1001	1	63000	10000
2	Bill	Jones	Newark	555-3221	2	48000	2000
3	Val	Brown	Nutley	555-6905	3	54000	5000
4	Justin	Time	Passaic	555-8908	4	52000	7000

In this result table, the salaries and bonuses on the right apply to the employees named on the left. The table still has some redundancy because the EmpID column duplicates the Employ column. You can fix this problem by specifying in your query which columns you want selected from the COMPENSATION table:

```
SELECT EMPLOYEE.*,COMPENSATION.Salary,COMPENSATION.Bonus
   FROM EMPLOYEE, COMPENSATION
   WHERE EMPLOYEE.EmpID = COMPENSATION.Employ ;
```

This produces the following result:

EmpID	FName	LName	City	Phone	Salary	Bonus
1	Jenny	Smith	Orange	555-1001	63000	10000
2	Bill	Jones	Newark	555-3221	48000	2000
3	Val	Brown	Nutley	555-6905	54000	5000
4	Justin	Time	Passaic	555-8908	52000	7000

This table tells you what you want to know, but doesn't burden you with any extraneous data. The query is somewhat tedious to write, however. To avoid ambiguity, it makes good sense to qualify the column names with the names of the tables they came from. However, writing those table names repeatedly can be tiresome.

You can cut down on the amount of typing by using aliases (or *correlation names*). An *alias* is a short name that stands for a table name. If you use aliases in recasting the preceding query, it comes out like this:

```
SELECT E.*, C.Salary, C.Bonus
   FROM EMPLOYEE E, COMPENSATION C
   WHERE E.EmpID = C.Employ ;
```

In this example, E is the alias for EMPLOYEE, and C is the alias for COMPENSATION. The alias is local to the statement it's in. After you declare an alias (in the FROM clause), you must use it throughout the statement. You can't use both the alias and the long form of the table name.

Mixing the long form of table names with aliases creates confusion. Consider the following example, which is confusing:

```
SELECT T1.C, T2.C
   FROM T1 T2, T2 T1
   WHERE T1.C > T2.C ;
```

In this example, the alias for T1 is T2, and the alias for T2 is T1. Admittedly, this isn't a smart selection of aliases, but it isn't forbidden by the rules. If you mix aliases with long-form table names, you can't tell which table is which.

The preceding example with aliases is equivalent to the following SELECT with no aliases:

```
SELECT T2.C, T1.C
   FROM T1, T2
   WHERE T2.C > T1.C ;
```

SQL enables you to join more than two tables. The maximum number varies from one implementation to another. The syntax is analogous to the two-table case:

```
SELECT E.*, C.Salary, C.Bonus, Y.TotalSales
   FROM EMPLOYEE E, COMPENSATION C, YTD_SALES Y
   WHERE E.EmpID = C.Employ
      AND C.Employ = Y.EmpNo ;
```

This statement performs an equi-join on three tables, pulling data from corresponding rows of each one to produce a result table that shows the salespeople's names, the amount of sales they are responsible for, and their compensation. The sales manager can quickly see whether compensation is in line with production.

TIP

Storing a salesperson's year-to-date sales in a separate YTD_SALES table ensures better performance and reliability than keeping that data in the EMPLOYEE table. The data in the EMPLOYEE table is relatively static. A person's name, address, and telephone number don't change very often. In contrast, the year-to-date sales change frequently. (You hope.) Because the YTD_SALES table has fewer columns than EMPLOYEE, you may be able to update it more quickly. If, in the course of updating sales totals, you don't touch the EMPLOYEE table, you decrease the risk of accidentally modifying EMPLOYEE information that should stay the same.

Natural join

The *natural join* is a special case of an equi-join. In the WHERE clause of an equi-join, a column from one source table is compared with a column of a second source table for equality. The two columns must be the same type and length and must have the same name. In fact, in a natural join, *all* columns in one table that have the same names, types, and lengths as corresponding columns in the second table are compared for equality.

Imagine that the COMPENSATION table from the preceding example has columns EmpID, Salary, and Bonus rather than Employ, Salary, and Bonus. In that case, you can perform a natural join of the COMPENSATION table with the EMPLOYEE table. The traditional JOIN syntax looks like this:

```
SELECT E.*, C.Salary, C.Bonus
   FROM EMPLOYEE E, COMPENSATION C
   WHERE E.EmpID = C.EmpID ;
```

This query is a natural join. An alternate syntax for the same operation is the following:

```
SELECT E.*, C.Salary, C.Bonus
    FROM EMPLOYEE E NATURAL JOIN COMPENSATION C ;
```

Condition join

A *condition join* is like an equi-join, except the condition being tested doesn't have to be equality (although it can be). It can be any well-formed predicate. If the condition is satisfied, the corresponding row becomes part of the result table. The syntax is a little different from what you have seen so far, in that the condition is contained in an ON clause rather than a WHERE clause.

Suppose Acme Systems wants to know which products the Fort Deposit warehouse has in larger numbers than does the East Kingston warehouse. This question is a job for a condition join:

```
SELECT *
    FROM DEPOSIT JOIN KINGSTON
    ON DEPOSIT.QuantityInStock > KINGSTON.QuantityInStock ;
```

Within the predicate of a condition join, ON syntax is used in place of WHERE syntax.

Column-name join

The *column-name join* is like a natural join, but it's more flexible. In a natural join, all the source table columns that have the same name are compared with each other for equality. With the column-name join, you select which same-name columns to compare. You can choose them all if you want, making the column-name join effectively a natural join. Or you may choose fewer than all same-name columns. In this way, you have a great degree of control over which cross product rows qualify to be placed into your result table.

Suppose you are Acme Systems, and you have shipped the exact same number of products to the East Kingston warehouse that you have shipped to the Fort Deposit warehouse. So far, nothing has been sold, so the number of products in inventory in East Kingston should match the number in Fort Deposit. If there are mismatches, it means that something is wrong. Either some products were never delivered to the warehouse, or they were misplaced or stolen after they arrived. With a simple query, you can retrieve the inventory levels at the two warehouses.

```
SELECT * FROM DEPOSIT ;

ProductName        QuantityInStock
-----------        ---------------
185_Express              12
505_Express               5
510_Express               6
520_Express               2
550_Express               3


SELECT * FROM KINGSTON ;

ProductName        QuantityInStock
-----------        ---------------
185_Express              15
505_Express               7
510_Express               6
520_Express               2
550_Express               1
```

For such small tables, it is fairly easy to see which rows don't match. However, for a table with thousands of rows, it's not so easy. You can use a column-name join to see whether any discrepancies exist. I show only two columns of the DEPOSIT and KINGSTON tables, to make it easy to see how the various relational operators work on them. In any real application, such tables would have additional columns, and the contents of those additional columns would not necessarily match. With a column-name join, the join operation considers only the columns specified.

```
SELECT *
    FROM DEPOSIT JOIN KINGSTON
    USING (ProductName, QuantityInStock) ;
```

Note the USING keyword, which tells the DBMS which columns to use.

The result table shows only the rows for which the number of products in stock at Fort Deposit equals the number of products in stock at East Kingston:

ProductName	QuantityInStock	ProductName	QuantityInStock
510_Express	6	510_Express	6
520_Express	2	520_Express	2

Wow! Only two products match. There is a definite "shrinkage" problem at one or both warehouses. Acme needs to get a handle on security.

Inner join

By now, you're probably getting the idea that joins are pretty esoteric and that it takes an uncommon level of spiritual discernment to deal with them adequately. You may have even heard of the mysterious *inner join* and speculated that it probably represents the core or essence of relational operations. Well, ha! The joke is on you: There's nothing mysterious about inner joins. In fact, all the joins covered so far in this chapter are inner joins. I could have formulated the column-name join in the last example as an inner join by using the following syntax:

```
SELECT *
    FROM DEPOSIT INNER JOIN KINGSTON
    USING (ProductName, QuantityInStock) ;
```

The result is the same.

The inner join is so named to distinguish it from the outer join. An *inner join* discards all rows from the result table that don't have corresponding rows in both source tables. An *outer join* preserves unmatched rows. That's the difference. Nothing metaphysical about it.

Outer join

When you're joining two tables, the first one (call it the one on the left) may have rows that don't have matching counterparts in the second table (the one on the right). Conversely, the table on the right may have rows that don't have matching counterparts in the table on the left. If you perform an inner join on those tables, all the unmatched rows are excluded from the output. *Outer joins*, however, don't exclude the unmatched rows. Outer joins come in three types: the left outer join, the right outer join, and the full outer join.

Left outer join

In a query that includes a join, the left table is the one that precedes the keyword JOIN, and the right table is the one that follows it. The *left outer join* preserves unmatched rows from the left table but discards unmatched rows from the right table.

To understand outer joins, consider a corporate database that maintains records of the company's employees, departments, and locations. Tables 4-1, 4-2, and 4-3 contain the database's sample data.

TABLE 4-1

LOCATION

LocationID	CITY
1	Boston
3	Tampa
5	Chicago

TABLE 4-2

DEPT

DeptID	LocationID	NAME
21	1	Sales
24	1	Admin
27	5	Repair
29	5	Stock

TABLE 4-3

EMPLOYEE

EmpID	DeptID	NAME
61	24	Kirk
63	27	McCoy

Now suppose that you want to see all the data for all employees, including department and location. You get this with an equi-join:

```
SELECT *
   FROM LOCATION L, DEPT D, EMPLOYEE E
   WHERE L.LocationID = D.LocationID
      AND D.DeptID = E.DeptID ;
```

This statement produces the following result:

```
1    Boston    24    1    Admin     61    24    Kirk
5    Chicago   27    5    Repair    63    27    McCoy
```

This results table gives all the data for all the employees, including their location and department. The equi-join works because every employee has a location and a department.

Suppose now that you want the data on the locations, with the related department and employee data. This is a different problem because a location without any associated departments may exist. To get what you want, you have to use an outer join, as in the following example:

```
SELECT *
    FROM LOCATION L LEFT OUTER JOIN DEPT D
        ON (L.LocationID = D.LocationID)
    LEFT OUTER JOIN EMPLOYEE E
        ON (D.DeptID = E.DeptID);
```

This join pulls data from three tables. First, the LOCATION table is joined to the DEPT table. The resulting table is then joined to the EMPLOYEE table. Rows from the table on the left of the LEFT OUTER JOIN operator that have no corresponding row in the table on the right are included in the result. Thus, in the first join, all locations are included, even if no department associated with them exists. In the second join, all departments are included, even if no employee associated with them exists. The result is as follows:

1	Boston	24	1	Admin	61	24	Kirk
5	Chicago	27	5	Repair	63	27	McCoy
3	Tampa	NULL	NULL	NULL	NULL	NULL	NULL
5	Chicago	29	5	Stock	NULL	NULL	NULL
1	Boston	21	1	Sales	NULL	NULL	NULL

The first two rows are the same as the two result rows in the previous example. The third row (3 Tampa) has nulls in the department and employee columns because no departments are defined for Tampa and no employees are stationed there. (Perhaps Tampa is a brand new location and has not yet been staffed.) The fourth and fifth rows (5 Chicago and 1 Boston) contain data about the Stock and the Sales departments, but the employee columns for these rows contain nulls because these two departments have no employees. This outer join tells you everything that the equi-join told you plus the following:

>> All the company's locations, whether or not they have any departments

>> All the company's departments, whether or not they have any employees

The rows returned in the preceding example aren't guaranteed to be in the order you want. The order may vary from one implementation to the next. To make sure that the rows returned are in the order you want, add an ORDER BY clause to your SELECT statement, like this:

```
SELECT *
    FROM LOCATION L LEFT OUTER JOIN DEPT D
        ON (L.LocationID = D.LocationID)
    LEFT OUTER JOIN EMPLOYEE E
        ON (D.DeptID = E.DeptID)
    ORDER BY L.LocationID, D.DeptID, E.EmpID;
```

TIP

You can abbreviate the left outer join language as LEFT JOIN because there's no such thing as a left inner join.

Right outer join

I'm sure you have figured out by now how the right outer join behaves. It preserves unmatched rows from the right table but discards unmatched rows from the left table. You can use it on the same tables and get the same result by reversing the order in which you present tables to the join:

```
SELECT *
    FROM EMPLOYEE E RIGHT OUTER JOIN DEPT D
        ON (D.DeptID = E.DeptID)
    RIGHT OUTER JOIN LOCATION L
        ON (L.LocationID = D.LocationID) ;
```

In this formulation, the first join produces a table that contains all departments, whether they have an associated employee or not. The second join produces a table that contains all locations, whether they have an associated department or not.

TIP

You can abbreviate the right outer join language as RIGHT JOIN because there's no such thing as a right inner join.

Full outer join

The *full outer join* combines the functions of the left outer join and the right outer join. It retains the unmatched rows from both the left and the right tables. Consider the most general case of the company database used in the preceding examples. It could have

>> Locations with no departments

>> Locations with no employees

>> Departments with no locations

>> Departments with no employees

>> Employees with no locations

>> Employees with no departments

REMEMBER

Whereas the preceding named conditions are unusual, they can happen, particularly in a startup situation, and when they do, you'll be glad you have outer joins to deal with them. As soon as you say that a certain situation is not possible, reality will conk you on the head with an example of that very situation.

To show all locations, departments, and employees, regardless of whether they have corresponding rows in the other tables, use a full outer join in the following form:

```
SELECT *
    FROM LOCATION L FULL OUTER JOIN DEPT D
        ON (L.LocationID = D.LocationID)
    FULL OUTER JOIN EMPLOYEE E
        ON (D.DeptID = E.DeptID) ;
```

TIP

You can abbreviate the full outer join language as FULL JOIN because there's no such thing as a full inner join.

ON versus WHERE

The function of the ON and WHERE clauses in the various types of joins is potentially confusing. These facts may help you keep things straight:

>> The ON clause is part of the inner, left, right, and full joins. The cross join and UNION join don't have an ON clause because neither of them does any filtering of the data.

>> The ON clause in an inner join is logically equivalent to a WHERE clause; the same condition could be specified either in the ON clause or a WHERE clause.

>> The ON clauses in outer joins (left, right, and full joins) are different from WHERE clauses. The WHERE clause simply filters the rows returned by the FROM clause. Rows rejected by the filter are not included in the result. The ON clause in an outer join first filters the rows of a cross product and then includes the rejected rows, extended with nulls.

Join Conditions and Clustering Indexes

The performance of queries that include joins depends, to a large extent, on which columns are indexed, and whether the index is clustering or not. A table can have only one clustering index, where data items that are near each other logically, such as 'Smith' and 'Smithson', are also near each other physically on disk. Using a clustering index to sequentially step through a table speeds up hard disk retrievals and thus maximizes performance.

REMEMBER

An index is a separate table that corresponds to a data table, but is sorted in some order. A clustering index is an index sorted in the same order that items are stored in memory and thus provides the fastest retrievals.

A clustering index works well with multipoint queries, which look for equality in nonunique columns. This is similar to looking up names in a telephone book. All the Smiths are listed together on consecutive pages. Most or all of them are located on the same hard disk cylinder. You can access multiple Smiths with a single disk seek operation. A nonclustering index, on the other hand, would not have this advantage. Each record typically requires a new disk seek, greatly slowing down operation. Furthermore, you probably have to touch every index to be sure you have not missed one. This is analogous to searching the greater Los Angeles telephone book for every instance of Area Code 626. Most of the numbers are in Area 213, but there will be instances of 626 sprinkled throughout the book.

Consider the following sample query:

```
SELECT Employee.FirstName, Employee.LastName, Student.Major
  FROM Employee, Students
  WHERE Employee.IDNum = Student.IDNum ;
```

This query returns the first and last names and the majors of university employees who are also students. How long it takes to run the query depends on how the tables are indexed. If Employee has a clustering index on IDNum, records searched are on consecutive pages. If Employee and Student both have clustering indexes on IDNum, the DBMS will likely use a merge join, which reads both tables in sorted order, minimizing the number of disk accesses needed. Such clustering often eliminates the need for a costly ORDER BY clause because the records are already sorted in the desired order.

The one disadvantage of clustered indexes is that they can become "tired" after a number of updates have been performed, causing the generation of overflow pages, which require additional disk seeks. Rebuilding the index corrects this problem. By tired, I mean less helpful. Every time you add or delete a record, the index loses some of its advantage. A deleted record must be skipped over, and added records must be put on an overflow page, which will usually require a couple of extra disk seeks.

Some modern DBMS products perform automatic clustered index maintenance, meaning they rebuild clustered indexes without having to be told to do so. If you have such a product, then the disadvantage that I just noted goes away.

Chapter **5**

Cursors

SQL differs from most other computer languages in one important respect: Other languages, such as C, Java, or Basic, are *procedural languages* because programs written in those languages set out a specified series of operations that need to be carried out in the same manner and in the same order — *procedures*, in other words. That means procedural languages first execute one instruction, and then the next one, then the next, and so on. The pertinent point here is that they can do only one thing at a time, so that when they are asked to deal with data, they operate on one table row at a time. SQL is a *nonprocedural language*, and thus is not restricted to operating on a single table row at a time. Its natural mode of operation is to operate on a set of rows. For example, an SQL query may return 42 rows from a database containing thousands of rows. That operation is performed by a single SQL SELECT statement.

REMEMBER

Because SQL is a data sublanguage, it does not contain all the features needed to create a database application. It must be used in combination with a procedural language. The SQL portion operates on the data, and the procedural language takes care of the other aspects of the task.

The fact that SQL normally operates on data a set at a time rather than a row at a time constitutes a major incompatibility between SQL and the most popular application development languages. A *cursor* enables SQL to retrieve (or update, or delete) a single row at a time so that you can use SQL in combination with an application written in any of the procedural languages.

REMEMBER

A cursor is like a pointer that locates a specific table row. When a cursor is active, you can SELECT, UPDATE, or DELETE the row at which the cursor is pointing.

Cursors are valuable if you want to retrieve selected rows from a table, check their contents, and perform different operations based on those contents. SQL can't perform this sequence of operations by itself. SQL can retrieve the rows, but procedural languages are better at making decisions based on field contents. Cursors enable SQL to retrieve rows from a table one at a time and then feed the result to procedural code for processing. By placing the SQL code in a loop, you can process the entire table row by row.

In a pseudocode representation of how embedded SQL meshes with procedural code, the most common flow of execution looks like this:

```
EXEC SQL DECLARE CURSOR statement
EXEC SQL OPEN statement
Test for end of table
Procedural code
Start loop
    Procedural code
    EXEC SQL FETCH
    Procedural code
    Test for end of table
End loop
EXEC SQL CLOSE statement
Procedural code
```

The SQL statements in this listing are DECLARE, OPEN, FETCH, and CLOSE. Each of these statements is discussed in detail in this chapter.

TIP

If you can perform the operation that you want with normal SQL statements — which operate on data a set at a time — do so. Declare a cursor, retrieve table rows one at a time, and use your system's host language only when normal SQL can't do what you want.

Declaring a Cursor

To use a cursor, you first must declare its existence to the database management system (DBMS). You do this with a DECLARE CURSOR statement. The DECLARE CURSOR statement doesn't actually cause anything to happen; it just announces the cursor's name to the DBMS and specifies what query the cursor will operate on. A DECLARE CURSOR statement has the following syntax:

```
DECLARE cursor-name [<cursor sensitivity>]
[<cursor scrollability>]
CURSOR [<cursor holdability>] [<cursor returnability>]
FOR query expression
    [ORDER BY order-by expression]
    [FOR updatability expression] ;
```

Note: The cursor name uniquely identifies a cursor, so it must be unlike that of any other cursor name in the current module or compilation unit.

TIP

To make your application more readable, give the cursor a meaningful name. Relate it to the data that the query expression requests or to the operation that your procedural code performs on the data.

Cursor sensitivity may be SENSITIVE, INSENSITIVE, or ASENSITIVE. Cursor scrollability may be either SCROLL or NO SCROLL. Cursor holdability may be either WITH HOLD or WITHOUT HOLD. Cursor returnability may be either WITH RETURN or WITHOUT RETURN. All these terms are explained in the following sections.

The query expression

REMEMBER

The *query expression* can be any legal SELECT statement. The rows that the SELECT statement retrieves are the ones that the cursor steps through one at a time. These rows are the scope of the cursor.

The query is not actually performed when the DECLARE CURSOR statement given in the previous pseudocode is read. You can't retrieve data until you execute the OPEN statement. The row-by-row examination of the data starts after you enter the loop that encloses the FETCH statement.

Ordering the query result set

You may want to process your retrieved data in a particular order, depending on what your procedural code does with the data. You can sort the retrieved rows before processing them by using the optional ORDER BY clause. The clause has the following syntax:

```
ORDER BY sort-specification [ , sort-specification]...
```

You can have multiple sort specifications. Each has the following syntax:

```
(column-name) [COLLATE BY collation-name] [ASC|DESC]
```

You sort by column name, and to do so, the column must be in the select list of the query expression. Columns that are in the table but not in the query select list do not work as sort specifications. For example, say you want to perform an operation that is not supported by SQL on selected rows of the CUSTOMER table. You can use a DECLARE CURSOR statement like this:

```
DECLARE cust1 CURSOR FOR
    SELECT CustID, FirstName, LastName, City, State, Phone
        FROM CUSTOMER
    ORDER BY State, LastName, FirstName ;
```

In this example, the SELECT statement retrieves rows sorted first by state, then by last name, and then by first name. The statement retrieves all customers in New Jersey (NJ) before it retrieves the first customer from New York (NY). The statement then sorts customer records from Alaska by the customer's last name (*Aaron* before *Abbott*). Where the last name is the same, sorting then goes by first name (*George Aaron* before *Henry Aaron*).

Have you ever made 40 copies of a 20-page document on a photocopier without a collator? What a drag! You must make 20 stacks on tables and desks, and then walk by the stacks 40 times, placing a sheet on each stack. This process is called *collation*. A similar process plays a role in SQL.

A *collation* is a set of rules that determines how strings in a character set compare. A character set has a default collation sequence that defines the order in which elements are sorted. But you can apply a collation sequence other than the default to a column. To do so, use the optional COLLATE BY clause. Your implementation probably supports several common collations. Pick one and then make the collation ascending or descending by appending an ASC or DESC keyword to the clause.

In a DECLARE CURSOR statement, you can specify a calculated column that doesn't exist in the underlying table. In this case, the calculated column doesn't have a name that you can use in the ORDER BY clause. You can give it a name in the DECLARE CURSOR query expression, which enables you to identify the column later. Consider the following example:

```
DECLARE revenue CURSOR FOR
    SELECT Model, Units, Price,
            Units * Price AS ExtPrice
        FROM TRANSDETAIL
    ORDER BY Model, ExtPrice DESC ;
```

In this example, no COLLATE BY clause is in the ORDER BY clause, so the default collation sequence is used. Notice that the fourth column in the select list comes from a calculation on the data in the second and third columns. The fourth column is an extended price named ExtPrice. In the ORDER BY clause, I first sort by model name and then by ExtPrice. The sort on ExtPrice is descending, as specified by the DESC keyword; transactions with the highest dollar value are processed first.

REMEMBER

The default sort order in an ORDER BY clause is ascending. If a sort specification list includes a DESC sort and the next sort should also be in descending order, you must explicitly specify DESC for the next sort. For example:

```
ORDER BY A, B DESC, C, D, E, F
```

is equivalent to

```
ORDER BY A ASC, B DESC, C ASC, D ASC, E ASC, F ASC
```

Updating table rows

Sometimes, you may want to update or delete table rows that you access with a cursor. Other times, you may want to guarantee that such updates or deletions can't be made. SQL gives you control over this issue with the updatability clause of the DECLARE CURSOR statement. If you want to prevent updates and deletions within the scope of the cursor, use this clause:

```
FOR READ ONLY
```

For updates of specified columns only — leaving all others protected — use

```
FOR UPDATE OF column-name [ , column-name]...
```

REMEMBER

Any columns listed must appear in the DECLARE CURSOR's query expression. If you don't include an updatability clause, the default assumption is that all columns listed in the query expression are updatable. In that case, an UPDATE statement can update all the columns in the row to which the cursor is pointing, and a DELETE statement can delete that row.

Sensitive versus insensitive cursors

The query expression in the DECLARE CURSOR statement determines the rows that fall within a cursor's scope. Consider this possible problem: What if a statement in your program, located between the OPEN and CLOSE statements, changes the contents of some of those rows so that they no longer satisfy the query? What if such a statement deletes some of those rows entirely? Does the cursor continue to process all the rows that originally qualified, or does it recognize the new situation and ignore rows that no longer qualify or that have been deleted?

REMEMBER

Changing the data in columns that are part of a DECLARE CURSOR query expression after some — but not all — of the query's rows have been processed results in a big mess. Your results are likely to be inconsistent and misleading. To avoid this problem, make your cursor insensitive to any changes that statements within its scope may make. Add the INSENSITIVE keyword to your DECLARE CURSOR statement. As long as your cursor is open, it is insensitive to table changes that otherwise affect rows qualified to be included in the cursor's scope. A cursor can't be both insensitive and updatable. An insensitive cursor must be read-only.

Think of it this way: A normal SQL statement, such as UPDATE, INSERT, or DELETE, operates on a set of rows in a database table (perhaps the entire table). While such a statement is active, SQL's transaction mechanism protects it from interference by other statements acting concurrently on the same data. If you use a cursor, however, your window of vulnerability to harmful interaction is wide open. When you open a cursor, you are at risk until you close it again. If you open one cursor, start processing through a table, and then open a second cursor while the first is still active, the actions you take with the second cursor can affect what the statement controlled by the first cursor sees. For example, suppose that you write these queries:

```
DECLARE C1 CURSOR FOR SELECT * FROM EMPLOYEE
    ORDER BY Salary ;
DECLARE C2 CURSOR FOR SELECT * FROM EMPLOYEE
    FOR UPDATE OF Salary ;
```

Now, suppose you open both cursors and fetch a few rows with C1 and then update a salary with C2 to increase its value. This change can cause a row that you have already fetched with C1 to appear again on a later fetch that uses C1.

REMEMBER

The peculiar interactions possible with multiple open cursors, or open cursors and set operations, are the sort of concurrency problems that transaction isolation avoids. If you operate this way, you're asking for trouble. If you have multiple open cursors, that means that you are performing more than one operation at a time. If those concurrent operations happen to interact with each other, you may get unpredictable results. This is similar to the kind of harmful interaction that enclosing your operations within a transaction protects you from. The difference is that using transactions protects you from harmful interference by other users. Having only one cursor open at a time protects you from harmful interactions with yourself. So remember: Don't operate with multiple open cursors.

The default condition of cursor sensitivity is ASENSITIVE. The meaning of ASENSITIVE is implementation-dependent. For one implementation, it could be equivalent to SENSITIVE and, for another, it could be equivalent to INSENSITIVE. Check your system documentation for its meaning in your own case.

Scrolling a cursor

Scrollability is a capability that cursors didn't have prior to SQL-92. In implementations adhering to SQL-86 or SQL-89, the only allowed cursor movement was sequential, starting at the first row retrieved by the query expression and ending with the last row. SQL-92's SCROLL keyword in the DECLARE CURSOR statement gives you the capability to access rows in any order you want. The current version of SQL retains this capability. The syntax of the FETCH statement controls the cursor's movement. I describe the FETCH statement later in this chapter. (See the "Operating on a Single Row" section.)

Holding a cursor

Previously, I mention that a cursor could be declared either WITH HOLD or WITHOUT HOLD (you're probably wondering what *that's* all about), that it is a bad idea to have more than one cursor open at a time, and that transactions are a mechanism for preventing two users from interfering with each other. All these ideas are interrelated.

In general, it is a good idea to enclose any database operation consisting of multiple SQL statements in a transaction. This is fine most of the time, but whenever a transaction is active, the resources it uses are off limits to all other users. Furthermore, results are not saved to permanent storage until the transaction is closed. For a very lengthy transaction, where a cursor is stepping through a large table, it may be beneficial to close the transaction in order to flush results to disk, and then reopen it to continue processing. The problem with this is that the cursor will lose its place in the table. To avoid this problem, use the WITH HOLD syntax. When WITH HOLD is declared, the cursor will not be automatically closed when the transaction closes, but will be left open. When the new transaction is opened, the still open cursor can pick up where it left off and continue processing. WITHOUT HOLD is the default condition, so if you don't mention HOLD in your cursor declaration, the cursor closes automatically when the transaction that encloses it is closed.

Declaring a result set cursor

A procedure invoked from another procedure or function may need to return a result set to the invoking procedure or function. If this is the case, the cursor must be declared with the WITH RETURN syntax. The default condition is WITHOUT RETURN.

Opening a Cursor

Although the DECLARE CURSOR statement specifies which rows to include in the cursor, it doesn't actually cause anything to happen because DECLARE is a declaration and not an executable statement. The OPEN statement brings the cursor into existence. It has the following form:

```
OPEN cursor-name ;
```

To open the cursor that I use in the discussion of the ORDER BY clause (earlier in this chapter), use the following:

```
DECLARE revenue CURSOR FOR
    SELECT Model, Units, Price,
            Units * Price AS ExtPrice
        FROM TRANSDETAIL
    ORDER BY Model, ExtPrice DESC ;
OPEN revenue ;
```

THE FIX IS IN (FOR DATETIMES)

A fixing of datetime values — similar to what happens when a cursor is opened — exists in set operations. Consider this example:

```
UPDATE ORDERS SET RecheckDate = CURRENT_DATE WHERE....;
```

Now suppose that you have a bunch of orders. You begin executing this statement at a minute before midnight. At midnight, the statement is still running, and it doesn't finish executing until five minutes after midnight. It doesn't matter. If a statement has any reference to CURRENT_DATE (or TIME or TIMESTAMP), the value is fixed when the statement begins, so all the ORDERS rows in the statement get the same RecheckDate. Similarly, if a statement references TIMESTAMP, the whole statement uses only one timestamp value, no matter how long the statement runs.

Here's an interesting example of an implication of this rule:

```
UPDATE EMPLOYEE SET KEY=CURRENT_TIMESTAMP;
```

You may expect that statement to set a unique value in the key column of each EMPLOYEE because time advances while the statement is executing. You'd be disappointed; it sets the same value in every row.

So when the OPEN statement fixes datetime values for all statements referencing the cursor, it treats all these statements like an extended statement.

You can't fetch rows from a cursor until you open the cursor. When you open a cursor, the values of variables referenced in the DECLARE CURSOR statement become fixed, as do all current datetime functions. Consider the following example of SQL statements embedded in a host language program:

```
EXEC SQL DECLARE CURSOR C1 FOR SELECT * FROM ORDERS
        WHERE ORDERS.Customer = :NAME
        AND DueDate < CURRENT_DATE ;
NAME := 'Acme Co';     //A host language statement
EXEC SQL OPEN C1;
NAME := 'Omega Inc.';  //Another host statement
...
EXEC SQL UPDATE ORDERS SET DueDate = CURRENT_DATE;
```

The OPEN statement fixes the value of all variables referenced in the DECLARE CURSOR statement and also fixes a value for all current datetime functions. Thus the second assignment to the name variable (NAME := 'Omega Inc.') has no effect on the rows that the cursor fetches. (That value of NAME is used the next time you open C1.) And even if the OPEN statement is executed a minute before midnight and the UPDATE statement is executed a minute after midnight, the value of CURRENT_DATE in the UPDATE statement is the value of that function at the time the OPEN statement executed. This is true even if DECLARE CURSOR doesn't reference the datetime function.

Operating on a Single Row

Whereas the DECLARE CURSOR statement specifies the cursor's name and scope, and the OPEN statement collects the table rows selected by the DECLARE CURSOR query expression, the FETCH statement actually retrieves the data. The cursor may point to one of the rows in the cursor's scope, or to the location immediately before the first row in the scope, or to the location immediately after the last row in the scope, or to the empty space between two rows. You can specify where the cursor points with the orientation clause in the FETCH statement.

FETCH syntax

The syntax for the FETCH statement is

```
FETCH [[orientation] FROM] cursor-name
   INTO target-specification [, target-specification]... ;
```

Seven orientation options are available:

» NEXT

» PRIOR

» FIRST

» LAST

» ABSOLUTE

» RELATIVE

» <simple value specification>

The default option is NEXT, which was the only orientation available in versions of SQL prior to SQL-92. It moves the cursor from wherever it is to the next row in the set specified by the query expression. If the cursor is located before the first record, it moves to the first record. If it points to record n, it moves to record n+1. If the cursor points to the last record in the set, it moves beyond that record, and notification of a no data condition is returned in the SQLSTATE system variable. (Book 4, Chapter 4 details SQLSTATE and the rest of SQL's error-handling facilities.)

The target specifications are either host variables or parameters, respectively, depending on whether embedded SQL or module language is using the cursor. The number and types of the target specifications must match the number and types of the columns specified by the query expression in the DECLARE CURSOR statement. So in the case of embedded SQL, when you fetch a list of five values from a row of a table, five host variables must be there to receive those values, and they must be the right types.

Absolute versus relative fetches

Because the SQL cursor is scrollable, you have other choices besides NEXT. If you specify PRIOR, the pointer moves to the row immediately preceding its current location. If you specify FIRST, it points to the first record in the set, and if you specify LAST, it points to the last record.

An integer value specification must accompany ABSOLUTE and RELATIVE. For example, FETCH ABSOLUTE 7 moves the cursor to the seventh row from the beginning of the set. FETCH RELATIVE 7 moves the cursor seven rows beyond its current position. FETCH RELATIVE 0 doesn't move the cursor.

FETCH RELATIVE 1 has the same effect as FETCH NEXT. FETCH RELATIVE −1 has the same effect as FETCH PRIOR. FETCH ABSOLUTE 1 gives you the first record in the set, FETCH ABSOLUTE 2 gives you the second record in the set, and so on. Similarly, FETCH ABSOLUTE −1 gives you the last record in the set, FETCH ABSOLUTE −2 gives you the next-to-last record, and so on. Specifying FETCH ABSOLUTE 0 returns the no data exception condition code, as does FETCH ABSOLUTE 17 if only 16 rows are in the set. FETCH <simple value specification> gives you the record specified by the simple value specification.

Deleting a row

You can perform delete and update operations on the row that the cursor is currently pointing to. The syntax of the DELETE statement is as follows:

```
DELETE FROM table-name WHERE CURRENT OF cursor-name ;
```

If the cursor doesn't point to a row, the statement returns an error condition. No deletion occurs.

Updating a row

The syntax of the UPDATE statement is as follows:

```
UPDATE table-name
    SET column-name = value [,column-name = value]...
    WHERE CURRENT OF cursor-name ;
```

The value you place into each specified column must be a value expression or the keyword DEFAULT. If an attempted positioned update operation returns an error, the update isn't performed. (A *positioned* update operation, as distinct from an ordinary set-oriented update operation, is an update of the row the cursor is currently pointing to.)

Closing a Cursor

TIP

After you finish with a cursor, make a habit of closing it immediately. Leaving a cursor open as your application goes on to other issues may cause harm. Someone may open another cursor on the same table, and you may forget it is open and perform an operation that you do not intend to. Also, open cursors use system resources.

If you close a cursor that was insensitive to changes made while it was open, when you reopen it, the reopened cursor reflects any such changes.

The syntax for closing cursor C1 is

```
CLOSE C1 ;
```

4

Securing Your Data

Contents at a Glance

Chapter **1**

Protecting Against Hardware Failure and External Threats

D atabase applications are complex pieces of software that interact with databases, which in turn are complex collections of data that run on computer systems, which in their own right are complex assemblages of hardware components. The more complex something is, the more likely it is to have unanticipated failures. That being the case, a database application is an accident waiting to happen. With complexity piled upon complexity, not only is something sure to go wrong, but also, when it does, you'll have a hard time telling where the problem lies.

Fortunately, you can do some things to protect yourself against these threats. The protections require you to spend time and money, of course, but you must evaluate the trade-off between protection and expense to find a level of protection you are comfortable with at a cost you can afford.

What Could Possibly Go Wrong?

Problems can arise in several areas. Here are a few:

>> Your database could be structured incorrectly, making modification anomalies inevitable. Modification anomalies, remember, are inconsistencies introduced when changes are made to the contents of a database.

>> Data-entry errors could introduce bad data into the database.

>> Users accessing the same data at the same time could interfere with one another.

>> Changes in the database structure could "break" existing database applications.

>> Upgrading to a new operating system could create problems with existing database applications.

>> Upgrading system hardware could "break" existing database applications.

>> Posing a query that has never been asked before could expose a hidden bug.

>> An operator could accidentally destroy data.

>> A malicious person could intentionally destroy or steal data.

>> Hardware could age or wear out and fail permanently.

>> An environmental condition such as overheating or a stray cosmic ray could cause a "soft" error that exists long enough to alter data and then disappear. (These types of errors are maddening.)

>> A virus or worm could arrive over the Internet and corrupt data.

From the preceding partial list, you can clearly see that protecting your data can require a significant effort, which you should budget for adequately while planning a database project. In this chapter, I highlight hardware issues and malicious threats that arrive over the Internet. I address the other concerns in the next chapter.

Equipment failure

Great strides have been made in recent years toward improving the reliability of computer hardware, but we're still a long way from perfect hardware that will never fail. Anything with moving parts is subject to wear and tear. As a consequence, such devices fail more often than do devices that have no moving parts. Hard drives, CD-ROM drives, and DVD-ROM drives all depend on mechanical movement and, thus, are possible points of failure. So are cooling fans and even on/off switches. Cables and connectors — such as USB ports and audio or video jacks that are frequently inserted and extracted — are also liable to fail before the nonmoving parts do.

Even devices without moving parts, such as solid state drives (SSDs) or processor chips can fail due to overheating or carrying electrical current for too long. Also, anything can fail if it's physically abused (dropped, shaken, or drenched with coffee, for example).

You can do several things to minimize, if not eliminate, problems caused by equipment failure. Here are a few ideas:

>> Check the specifications of components with moving parts, such as hard drives and DVD-ROM drives, and pick components with a high mean time between failures (MTBF).

>> Check the read and write limits on SSDs, as well as any USB storage devices you use. These drives don't have unlimited read and write capabilities, but the values are usually fairly high.

TIP

Do some comparison shopping. You'll find a range of values. When you're shopping for a hard drive, for example, the number of gigabytes per dollar shouldn't be the only thing you look at.

>> Make sure that your computer system has adequate cooling. It's especially important that the processor chips have sufficient cooling, because they generate enormous amounts of heat.

>> Buy memory chips with a high MTBF.

>> Control the environment where your computer is located. Make sure that the computer gets adequate ventilation and is never subjected to high temperatures. If you cannot control the ambient temperature, turn the system off when the weather gets too hot. Humans can tolerate extreme heat better than computers can.

>> Isolate your system from shock and vibration.

>> Establish a policy that prohibits liquids such as coffee, or even water, from being anywhere near the computer.

>> Restrict access to the computer so that only those people who agree to your protection rules can come near it.

Platform instability

What's a platform? A *platform* is the system your database application is running on. It includes the operating system, the basic input/output subsystem (either BIOS for older systems, or the Unified Extensible Firmware Interface [UEFI] for newer systems), the processor, the memory, and all the ancillary and peripheral devices that make up a functioning computer system.

Platform instability is a fancy way of saying that you cannot count on your platform to operate the way it is supposed to. Sometimes, this instability is due to an equipment failure or an impending equipment failure. At other times, instability is due to an incompatibility introduced when one or another element in the system is changed.

Because of the danger of platform instability, many database administrators (DBAs) are extremely reluctant to upgrade when a new release of the operating system or a larger, higher-capacity hard drive becomes available. The person who coined the phrase "If it ain't broke, don't fix it" must have been a database administrator. Any change in a happily functioning system is liable to cause platform instability. However, in this day and age, it's impossible to avoid changes to the system. Operating system and application security patches are released on a regular basis, and installing them is not optional. So how do you protect against platform instability, aside from forbidding any changes in the platform? Here are a few things you can do to protect yourself:

>> Install the upgrade or patch when nothing important is running and nothing important is scheduled to be run for several days. (Yes, this means either staying late into the evening after normal business hours or coming in on the weekend.)

>> Change only one thing at a time, and deal with any issues that arise before making another change that could interact with the first change.

>> Warn users before you make a configuration change so that they can protect themselves from any possible adverse consequences.

>> If you can afford to do so, bring up the new environment on a parallel system, and switch over your production work only when it's clear that the new system has stabilized.

>> Make sure everything is backed up before making any configuration change.

Database design flaws

The design of robust, reliable, and high-performing databases is a topic that goes beyond SQL and is worthy of a book in its own right. I recommend my *Database Development For Dummies* (published by Wiley). Many problems that show up long after a database has been placed in service can be traced back to faulty design at the beginning. It's important to get database design right from the start. Give the design phase of every development project the time and consideration it deserves.

Data-entry errors

It's really hard to draw valid conclusions from information retrieved from a database if faulty data was entered in the database to begin with. Book 1, Chapter 5 describes how to enter data into a database with SQL's INSERT statement, and how to modify the data in an existing database record with the UPDATE statement. If a person is entering a series of such statements, keyboarding errors are a real possibility. Even if you're entering records through a form that does validation checks on what you enter, mistypes are still a concern. Entered data can be valid but nonetheless incorrect. Although 0 through 9 are all valid decimal digits, if a field is supposed to contain 7, 6 is just as wrong as Tuesday. The best defense against data-entry errors is to have someone other than the person who entered the data check it against the source document.

Operator error

People make mistakes. You can try to minimize the impact of such mistakes by making sure that only intelligent, highly trained, and well-meaning people can get their hands on the database, but even the most intelligent, highly trained, and well-meaning people make mistakes from time to time, and sometimes those mistakes destroy data or alter it in a way that makes it unusable.

Your best defense against such an eventuality is a robust and active backup policy, which I discuss in "Backing Up Your System," later in this chapter.

Taking Advantage of RAID

Equipment failure is one of the things that can go wrong with your database. Of all the pieces of equipment that make up a computer system, the one piece that's most likely to fail is the hard drive. A motor is turning a spindle at 7,000 to 10,000 revolutions per minute. Platters holding data are attached to the spindle and spinning with it. Read/write heads on cantilevers are moving in and out across the platter surfaces. Significant heat is generated by the motor and the moving parts. Sooner or later, wear takes its toll, and the hard drive fails. When it does, whatever information it contained becomes unrecoverable.

Disk failures are inevitable; you just don't know when they will occur. You can do a couple of things, however, to protect yourself from the worst consequences of disk failure:

>> Maintain a regular backup discipline that copies production data at intervals and stores it in a safe place offline.

>> Put some redundancy in the storage system by using RAID (Redundant Array of Independent Disks).

RAID technology has two main advantages: redundancy and low cost. The redundancy aspect gives the system a measure of fault tolerance. The low-cost aspect comes from the fact that several disks with smaller capacities are generally cheaper than a single disk of the same capacity, because the large single disk is using the most recent, most advanced technology and is operating on the edge of what is possible. In fact, a RAID array can be configured to have a capacity larger than that of the largest disk available at any price.

In a RAID array, two or more disks are combined to form a logical disk drive. To the database, the logical disk drive appears to be a single unit, although physically, it may be made up of multiple disk drives.

Striping

A key concept of RAID architecture is *striping* — spreading data in chunks across multiple disks. One chunk is placed on the first disk, the next chunk is placed on the next disk, and so on. After a chunk is placed on the last disk in the array, the next chunk goes on the first disk, and the cycle starts over. In this way, the data is evenly spread across all the disks in the array, and no single disk contains anything meaningful. In a five-disk array, for example, each disk holds one fifth of the data. If the chunks are words in a text file, one disk holds every fifth word in the document. You need all of the disks to put the text back together again in readable form.

Figure 1-1 illustrates the idea of striping.

In Figure 1-1, chunks 1, 2, 3, and 4 constitute one stripe; chunks 5, 6, 7, and 8 constitute the next stripe, and so on. A *stripe* is made up of contiguous chunks on the logical drive, but physically, each chunk is on a different hard drive.

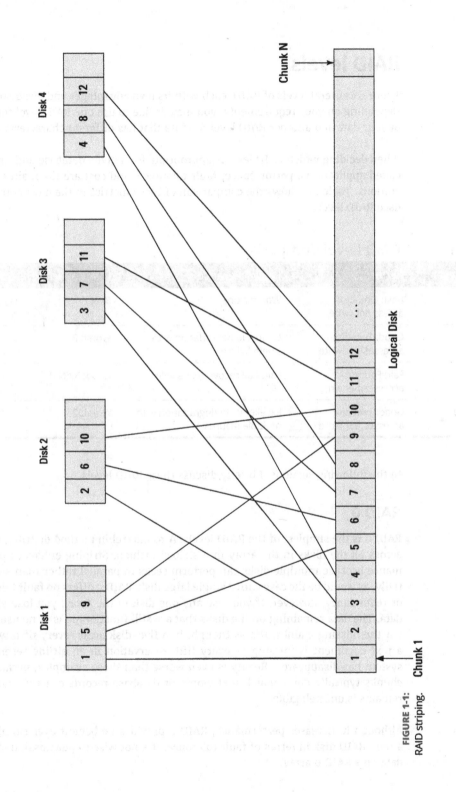

FIGURE 1-1:
RAID striping.

RAID levels

There are several levels of RAID, each with its own advantages and disadvantages. Depending on your requirements, you may decide to use one RAID level for some of your data and another RAID level for data that has different characteristics.

When deciding which RAID level is appropriate for a given database and its associated applications, performance, fault tolerance, and cost are the main considerations. Table 1-1 shows the comparison of these metrics in the most commonly used RAID levels.

TABLE 1-1   ## RAID Level Comparison

RAID Level	Performance	Fault Tolerance	Disk Capacity/Data Size
RAID 0	Best: One disk access per write	Worst: None	Best: 1
RAID 1	Good: Two disk accesses per write	Good: No degradation with single failure	Worst: 2
RAID 5	Fair: Four disk accesses per write	Fair: Full recovery possible	Good: N/(N–1)
RAID 10	Good: Two disk accesses per write	Excellent: No degradation with multiple failures	Worst: 2

In the following sections, I briefly discuss these RAID levels.

RAID 0

RAID 0 is the simplest of the RAID levels. A round-robin method distributes data across all the disks in the array in a striped fashion. Striping enhances performance because multiple disks can perform seeks in parallel rather than sequentially, as would be the case with a single large disk. RAID 0 offers no fault tolerance or redundancy, however. If you lose any one disk in the array, you lose *all* your data. The data remaining on the disks that are still functioning is of no use without the missing chunks. It's as though, in a five-disk array, every fifth word of a text document is missing or every fifth reservation in an airline reservation system has disappeared. Reality is even worse than these examples, because the chunks typically don't match text words or database records exactly, and what remains is unintelligible.

Although it increases performance, RAID 0 provides no benefit over running on a non-RAID disk in terms of fault tolerance. It's not wise to put mission-critical data on a RAID 0 array.

RAID 1

RAID 1 is the simplest of the fault-tolerant RAID levels. It doesn't employ striping. Also known as *disk mirroring*, RAID 1 duplicates the content of one disk on a second disk. Performance is somewhat worse than the performance of a non-RAID disk because every write operation has to go to two disks rather than one. A second disadvantage is that you use two hard disks to hold one hard disk's worth of data, which doubles your disk cost.

The benefit of RAID 1 is in the area of fault tolerance. If either of the mirrored disks fails, the other one contains all the data, and performance is unaffected. You can replace the failed disk and fill it with data to match the surviving disk and return to the same level of fault tolerance you had at the beginning.

RAID 1 is a good choice when both fault tolerance and performance are important, when all your data will fit on a single disk drive, and when cost is not a primary concern.

RAID 5

RAID 5 uses parity rather than data duplication to achieve fault tolerance. In an array of, say, six physical disks, each stripe consists of five data chunks and one parity chunk. If any of the physical drives fails, its contents can be deduced from the information on the other five drives. The advantage of RAID 5 is that the space available to hold data is $N-1$, where N is the number of disk drives. This compares favorably with RAID 1, where the space available to hold data is N/2. A six-drive RAID 5 array holds up to five disks full of data. Three two-drive RAID 1 arrays hold only up to three disks full of data. You pay a performance penalty for the additional capacity. In a RAID 5 system, every write operation requires four disk accesses: two reads and two writes. Both the target disk stripe and the parity stripe must be read and the parity calculated, and then both stripes must be written.

Because of the performance penalty RAID 5 exacts on writes, RAID 5 isn't a good choice for disks that are written to often. RAID 5 is fine for databases that are read-only or read-mostly. If more than 10 percent of disk operations are writes, RAID 5 probably isn't the best choice.

RAID 10

RAID 10 combines aspects of RAID 0 and RAID 1. Like RAID 1, RAID 10 mirrors disks. Each disk has an exact duplicate. Like RAID 0, the disks in the array are striped. RAID 10 provides the fault tolerance of RAID 1 and the performance of RAID 0. A RAID 10 array can consist of a large number of disks, so it's a good level to use when a large amount of data is being stored. It's also good from a fault-tolerance point of view because it can tolerate the loss of more than one disk, although it cannot handle the loss of both members of a mirror pair.

Backing Up Your System

Fault tolerance, as described in the preceding section on RAID and also as implemented with redundant hardware that goes beyond RAID, responds to some — but not all — of the threats listed at the beginning of this chapter. The most effective defense you have against the full spectrum of potential problems is an effective backup procedure. *Backing up* means making copies of all your important programs and data as often as necessary so that you can easily and quickly regain full functionality after some misfortune corrupts or destroys your system. The means you employ to protect your assets depend on how critical your application is.

Preparation for the worst

On September 11, 2001, a terrorist attack destroyed the twin towers of the World Trade Center in lower Manhattan. Along with the lives of thousands of people, the financial hub of the American economy was snuffed out. Virtually all of America's major financial institutions, including the New York Board of Trade (NYBOT), had their center of operations in the World Trade Center. The lives that were lost that day were gone for good. Within hours, however, the NYBOT was up and running again, hardly missing a beat. This was possible because the NYBOT had prepared for the worst. It had implemented the most effective (and most expensive) form of backup. It continuously sent its information offsite to a hot site in Queens. (A hot site, as compared to one at a lower "temperature," is always powered up and on standby, ready to take over if the need arises.) The hot site was close enough so that employees who had evacuated the World Trade Center could get to it quickly and start the recovery effort, yet far enough away that it wasn't affected by the disaster.

Many companies and government entities can justify the investment in the level of backup employed by the NYBOT. That investment was made because analysis showed that downtime would cost the NYBOT and its clients close to $4 million a day. For enterprises in which downtime isn't so costly, a lesser investment in backup is justified, but if loss of your data or programs would cause you any pain at all, some level of backup is called for. This backup may be no more than copying your active work onto a thumb drive every night after work and taking it home with you. It could mean putting removable hard disks in a fireproof safe in another building. It could mean distributing copies of your data to remote sites over your corporate network.

In choosing a backup method, think carefully about what your threats are; what losses are possible; what the consequences of those losses are; and what investment in backup is justified in light of those threats, losses, and consequences.

Full or incremental backup

Perhaps only 1MB or 2MB of data that you're actively working with would cause pain if you were to lose them. Alternatively, you may have a critical database in the terabyte (TB) range. In the first case, it won't take much time for you to back up the entire database and remove the backup copy to a safe place. On the other hand, you probably don't want to back up a 10TB database completely several times a day or even once a day.

The size of your database, the speed of your backup procedure, and the cost of your backup medium dictate whether you implement a full backup procedure or back up only the changes that have been made since the last backup. Backing up only the changes is called *incremental backup*. When a failure occurs, you can go back to your last full backup and then restore all the incremental backups that followed it one by one.

Frequency

A big question about backup is "How often should I do it?" I answer that question with another question: "How much pain are you willing to endure if you were to suddenly and unexpectedly lose your data?" If you don't mind redoing a couple of hours of work, there's no point in backing up more frequently than every couple of hours. Many organizations perform backups at night, after the workers have gone home for the day. These organizations run the risk of losing no more than a day's work.

Think carefully about your total situation and what effect data loss could have on you; then choose an appropriate backup interval.

REMEMBER

Be sure to adhere to your backup schedule without fail. Long intervals without a failure shouldn't weaken your resolve to maintain your schedule. You're defending against the unexpected.

Backup maintenance

When your latest backup is sent to offsite storage or your hot site, don't recycle the backup media from the previous backup immediately. Sometimes, problems in the data aren't noticed right away, and several backup generations can be made before anyone recognizes that the data is corrupted.

TIP

One good discipline, if you're backing up on a daily basis, is to keep a whole week of daily backups, as well as a month's worth of weekly backups and a year's worth of monthly backups. That should cover most possibilities.

The important point is to maintain the number of backups you need for as long as you need them to ensure that you will be able to continue operating, with minimum downtime, regardless of what might happen.

Another thing you should do is restore a backup occasionally, just to see whether you recover all the data that you backed up. I once went into a company (which shall remain nameless) as a database consultant. The employees very proudly showed me their backup disks and the fireproof safe they kept those disks in. There was only one problem: The backup disks were all empty! The employee who dutifully did the backups every night didn't have a full understanding of the backup procedure and was actually recording nothing. Luckily, I asked the employee to do a test restore, and the problem was discovered before the company had to do a restoration for real.

Coping with Internet Threats

In addition to all the bad things that can happen to your hardware due to random failures and human mistakes, the Internet is a potential source of major problems. People with malicious intent (called *crackers)* don't have to get anywhere near your hardware to do great damage to your computer system and your organization. The Internet is your connection to your customers, clients, suppliers, friends, news organizations, and entertainment providers. It's also a connection to people who either want to harm you or to steal the resources of your computer.

Attacks on your system can take a variety of forms. I briefly discuss a few of the most common ones in the following sections. Most of these attacks are carried out by *malware* — any kind of software that has a malicious intent. Examples are viruses, Trojan horses, and worms.

Viruses

A *virus* is a self-replicating piece of software that spreads by attaching itself to other programs or to documents. When a human launches the host program or performs some other action on it, the virus is activated. After it's activated, the virus can propagate by copying itself to other programs. The virus's payload can perform other actions, such as erasing disk files; crashing the computer; displaying mocking messages on the user's screen; or commandeering system resources to perform a computation for, and send results back to, the attacker who originated the virus.

Initially, virus writers created and released viruses to show off their knowledge and skill to their peers. They would cause their viruses to display a message on a computer screen, along with their signatures. Nowadays, viruses have evolved in a much more destructive direction. Criminal enterprises, political groups, and even national governments release viruses that can steal critical data, resulting in millions of dollars in losses. Aside from data theft, considerable damage can be done by modifying or destroying data.

At any given time, hundreds of viruses of varying virulence are circulating on the Internet. If one happens to infect your computer, you may experience an annoyance or a disaster. Consider these options to protect yourself:

» **Never connect your computer to the Internet.** This technique is very effective. It's a viable idea if none of the work you intend to do on that computer relies on the Internet's resources, and the computer never exchanges files with any computers that *are* connected to the Internet.

» **Install antivirus software on your computer, and keep it up to date by maintaining a subscription.** New viruses are emerging all the time. To thwart them, you need the latest antivirus protection.

» **Make sure users are aware of virus threats and know how to recognize suspicious emails.** Awareness is an important defense against viruses. Caution users not to open email attachments from unknown sources and to be careful about visiting websites of unknown character. Set their browser settings at a high security level.

» **Disable USB ports so that thumb drives cannot be connected.** Some of the most serious security breaches have been caused by viruses or worms placed on a system with a thumb drive.

Even if you take all the preceding recommended actions, your computer still may become infected with a virus. Be on the lookout for any change in the way your computer operates. A sudden slowdown in performance could be a sign that a virus has taken over your system, which is now doing the bidding of some unknown attacker rather than doing what you want it to do.

CONNECTING TO THE INTERNET IS RISKY

Attackers are becoming more sophisticated all the time. You could be hit by a virus by opening an email that appears to come from someone you know and trust. This type of attack is called *spoofing*. A spoofed email contains a virus that comes from an attacker, even though it looks like it's coming from your trusted friend.

As soon as you go on the web, there's no such thing as privacy anymore. Any sufficiently clever person can find out enough about you and your friends to create a spoofed email. Actually, people don't even have to be very clever to do it. Amateur virus creators, called *script kiddies,* can obtain virus software freely on the Internet and use it to launch an attack. These attacks can be annoying.

More dangerous are attacks by people who really know what they want and how to get it. Professional virus writers are masters of *social engineering* — the act of telling a plausible story (that is, lying) in such a way as to cause the unsuspecting target to do something that helps the attacker penetrate the target's defenses.

Trojan horses

In an ancient legend recounting the war between the Greeks and the city of Troy, after a 10-year siege, the Greek commander, Odysseus, thought of a trick to beat the Trojans. He ordered a huge wooden horse to be built, knowing that the Trojans considered the horse to be the symbol of their city, and hid 30 soldiers inside it. Then he loaded the rest of his army onto ships and sailed away. The Trojans were jubilant, figuring the Greeks had finally given up. They pulled the horse within the walls of their city as a trophy of war. That night, the Greek soldiers climbed out of the horse and opened the city gates to the waiting Greek army, which had sailed back under cover of darkness. Troy was conquered and destroyed, never again to challenge the Greeks.

Today, malware creators can create a different kind of Trojan horse: a program that has some useful purpose but that has a secret payload. When the program is activated inside the target computer, it does what the malware writer wants rather than what the computer owner wants. It may steal data and send it out over the computer's Internet connection, or it may have some other destructive effect. Making the useful purpose of the program seem desirable is a form of social engineering.

It always pays to bear Trojan horses in mind. If you do download a program from the web or even from a CD-ROM or DVD, make sure that you're getting it from a reputable source.

REMEMBER

WARNING

I know that *you* would never be tempted to download pornographic images from the web, but you may know someone who could be so tempted. Be aware that a very high percentage of such material contains malicious Trojan horses that can do a lot of damage.

Worms

Worms are similar to viruses in some respects and different in others. The defining characteristic of a virus is that it spreads by attaching itself to other programs. The defining characteristic of a worm is that it spreads via networks. Both viruses and worms are self-replicating, but viruses typically need some action by a human to become active, whereas worms have no such limitation. They can enter an unsuspecting computer via a network connection at any time of day or night without any action by a human.

Worms can take over thousands of computers in a matter of hours, as an exponentially expanding wave of infection flows out from a single infected computer. An infected computer can send a copy of the worm to every address in the computer's email address book, for example. Each of those computers, which are now infected too, sends the worm on to all the computers in their respective address books. It doesn't take long for the infection to spread around the world. The worm clogs communication channels as bandwidth is consumed by thousands of copies of the worm, which are sent from one computer to another. Depending on the worm's payload, infected computers may start performing a computation (such as password cracking) for the originator of the worm, or they may start erasing files or causing other damage.

You can do a few things to protect yourself from being infected or, failing that, from passing on the infection:

>> **Employ all patches from the vendors of your software as soon as possible.** Worms generally take advantage of some weakness in your operating system or some other program on your computer. As soon as such a vulnerability becomes known, the software vendor responsible for that program will develop a modification of the program called a *patch*. The patch closes the window of vulnerability without degrading the performance of the software.

>> **Harden your system to prevent bad stuff from getting in.** This precaution may involve closing ports that are normally open.

>> **Block arbitrary outbound connections.** When you do so, if your computer does get infected, it won't pass on the infection.

If everyone did these things, worms would fizzle out before they got very far.

Denial-of-service attacks

Worms need not actively perform computations or cause damage to the systems they infect. Instead, they can lie dormant, in stealth mode, waiting for a specific time and date or some other trigger to occur. At the appointed time, thousands of infected computers, now under the control of a malicious cracker, can simultaneously launch what is referred to as a *denial-of-service* attack on some target website. The thousands of incoming messages from the worms completely overwhelm the ability of the target site to handle the traffic, preventing legitimate messages from getting through and bringing the website down.

Ransomware

Ransomware attacks are particularly dangerous in database environments. With ransomware, the attacker specifically looks for data files stored on the server and encrypts them. The attacker then sends a ransom email to the organization demanding payment in return for the key required to decrypt the files. The database files are still on the server, but because they're encrypted, the database server can't read or write to them until someone manually decrypts the files. This is a good example of where it comes in handy to have current database backups stored on another server separate from the main database server (ransomware attacks often look for even backup database files stored on the same server). Without the ability to restore the entire database, the organization either must pay the ransom or accept defeat and rebuild the database from scratch.

SQL injection attacks

SQL injection attacks, like denial-of-service attacks, are attacks carried out on websites. If your website takes input from site visitors, such as their names and contact information, you could be vulnerable to an SQL injection attack. The information that visitors enter goes into an SQL database on your server. Everything is fine as long as people enter the information that they are supposed to enter in the appropriate text boxes. Attackers, however, will attempt to take control of your database and all the information in it by entering things that are *not* appropriate for the text boxes in which they enter data.

Chipping away at your wall of protection

Unlike what you may see in a movie or on TV, breaching database security isn't a simple matter of making an educated guess and then typing a few keystrokes. Breaking into an online database can be a laborious and tedious process. To a sufficiently motivated attacker, however, the prize is worth the effort. The goal is to find the smallest chink in the armor of your application. The attacker can poke into that chink and discover another small opening. Through a series of small actions that reveal progressively more about your installation — and, thus, more about its vulnerabilities — your adversary can penetrate farther into your sanctuary, ultimately gaining system administrator privileges. At this point, your opponent can destroy all your data or, even worse, alter it subtly and undetectably in a way that benefits him, perhaps bankrupting you in the process.

Database hacking through SQL injection is a serious threat, not only to the database you are exposing on the web, but also to all the other databases that may reside on your database server.

Understanding SQL injection

Any database application that solicits input from the user is potentially susceptible to an SQL injection attack. You expect users to enter the asked-for data in the text boxes that your database application uses to accept input. An SQL injection attack occurs when a cracker fools your application into accepting and executing an SQL command that has been entered in the text box rather than the expected data. This attack isn't a simple matter of entering an SQL statement in the text box that asks for the user's first name. These days plenty of input validation options are in place so doing that probably will net the attacker nothing more than an error message. Ironically, however, that error message itself is the first chink in your armor. It could tell the attacker what to do next to gain the next bit of information that will extend her penetration of your defenses.

An SQL injection attack is an incremental process in which attackers gain one bit of information after another until it becomes clear what to do to escalate their privilege level to the point where they can do whatever they want. When a database application fails to properly handle parameters that are passed to dynamically created SQL statements, it becomes possible for an attacker to modify those SQL statements. Then the attacker has the same privileges as the application user. When the database server executes commands that interact with the operating system, the attacker gains the privilege level of the database server, which in many cases is very high.

Using a GET parameter

Typically, parameters are passed from a web application to a database server with a GET or a POST command. GET is usually used to retrieve something from the database server, and POST is usually used to write something to the database server. Either command can provide an avenue for an SQL injection attack. In the following sections, I look at some ways that GET can be dangerous.

THE DANGERS OF DYNAMIC STRING BUILDING

If a user is entering a parameter in a text box, it must be true that the application doesn't already know which of several possibilities the user will enter. That means that the complete syntax of the SQL statement that the user wants to execute wasn't known when the application was written; thus, that data couldn't be hard-coded into the application. SQL statements that are hard-coded into an application are called *static* SQL. SQL statements that aren't put together until runtime are called *dynamic* SQL. By necessity, any SQL that includes parameters passed from user input in a text box to the DBMS is dynamic SQL. Because the SQL being generated is incorporating user input, it's susceptible to being co-opted by an SQL injection attack.

You have two ways to incorporate user input into an SQL query, one of which is much more secure than the other:

>> The safer alternative is to pass a parameter containing validated user input from your host language application code to an SQL procedure that will incorporate the parameter, treating it as data.

>> The less-safe alternative is to use dynamic SQL to build an SQL statement at runtime that incorporates the user input. This dynamic method of handling user input is susceptible to an SQL injection attack. When you build an SQL statement at runtime with dynamic SQL, an SQL injection attack can piggyback a malicious SQL statement on top of the benign one your application is building.

Suppose that your application has a feature in which the user enters a customer name in a text box, and in response, the database returns that customer's full record. The SQL would be of the following form:

```
SELECT * FROM CUSTOMER WHERE LastName = 'Ferguson';
```

When you wrote the application, you didn't know that the information desired was for customer Ferguson. You wrote it so that the user could enter a customer name at runtime. One way to do that is to create a dynamic SQL statement on the fly at runtime. Here's how to do that when your host language is PHP, which is the host language most commonly used with MySQL:

```
$query = "SELECT * FROM CUSTOMER WHERE LastName = '$_GET["lastname"]'";
```

This example assumes that the user enters the last name of the person desired in a text box named lastname. If the user enters Ferguson in the text box, Ferguson's full record will be returned.

A similar dynamic SQL string can be built in a .NET environment, as follows:

```
query = "SELECT * FROM CUSTOMER WHERE LastName = '" +
    request.getParameter("lastname") + "'";
```

A parameterized query is safer than a query built from a dynamic string because the database engine isn't expecting to build an SQL statement. It expects only a parameter, which isn't executable; thus, it won't be fooled by an SQL injection.

Here's an ADO.NET example of a parameterized query equivalent to the query above:

```
sqlConnection con = new SqlConnection (ConnectionString);
string Sql = "SELECT * FROM CUSTOMER WHERE LastName=@lastname" ;
cmd = new SqlCommand(Sql, con) ;
// Add parameter
cmd.Parameters.Add("@lastname",          //name
                    SqlDbType.NvarChar,   //data type
                    20) ;                 //length
cmd.Parameters.Value["@lastname"] = LastName ;
reader = cmd.ExecuteReader () ;
```

MISHANDLING ESCAPE CHARACTERS

An *escape character* is a character that has a special meaning in a text string. A text string, for example, may be delimited by quote characters at the beginning and the end of the string. The quote characters aren't part of the string. They indicate to the database management system (DBMS) that the characters between the beginning and the ending quote characters are to be treated as a text string. What happens, however, if the text string *contains* a quote character? There must be a way to tell the DBMS that the quote character located within the string is part of the string rather than a delimiter for the string. You typically do this by preceding the character that you want to be treated as a text character with an escape character. In this context, the escape character tells the DBMS to interpret the following character as a text character.

Some of the most devastating SQL injection attacks, in which millions of credit-card records have been stolen, have resulted from inadequately filtered escape characters. Mishandling an escape character can lead to a successful SQL injection attack.

Suppose that you have a database that only authorized users can access. To gain database access, a user must enter a username and a password in text boxes.

Protecting Against Hardware
Failure and External Threats

Assuming that the authorized user GoodGuy enters his name and password (Secret), the following SQL statement is built dynamically:

```
SELECT UserID
FROM USERS
WHERE User = 'GoodGuy' AND Password = 'Secret';
```

The single quotes mark the beginning and the end of a text string.

Now suppose that an attacker has deduced, from previous probes of your system, that the names of authorized users are contained in a table named USERS, that usernames are contained in the User column of that table, and that user passwords are contained in the Password column. Now the attacker can enter anything — ABC in the User text box and XYZ' OR 'V' = 'V in the Password text box, for example. The DBMS will dutifully incorporate this data into the following dynamic SQL statement:

```
SELECT UserID
FROM USERS
WHERE user = 'ABC' AND password = 'XYZ' OR 'V' = 'V';
```

It doesn't matter that the attacker doesn't know any valid usernames or passwords. The compound predicate partitioned by the OR keyword requires only one of the two predicates to be true. Because V is always equal to V, the condition of the WHERE clause is satisfied, and all the UserIDs in the USERS table are returned. Furthermore, the attacker is logged in, probably with the privileges of the first user in the USERS table. The DBMS assumes that because more than zero records have been returned, a valid authentication credential must have been entered.

Now that the attacker is logged in, it's relatively easy for him to discover that sensitive information about users is contained in a table named USERINFO. Stealing the information in that table is easy, as follows:

```
SELECT * FROM USERINFO;
```

At this point, the attacker can slink out with his ill-gotten gains, and you won't even know that you've been compromised.

Alternatively, on the way out, the attacker could issue this command:

```
DROP TABLE USERS; DROP TABLE USERINFO;
```

Your USERS and USERINFO tables are toast. Now you *know* that you've been compromised. I hope you have a recent backup of your database.

As long as an SQL statement is syntactically correct, a DBMS will execute it. That being the case, how can you protect yourself from an SQL injection attack? The only surefire way is to validate every input that you accept and revalidate it every step along the way from the client to the database. Don't depend on checks at the client end to protect you. An attacker skillful enough to bypass your client will have a field day in your unprotected back end.

Check every input to ensure the following:

>> The input is of the expected type (text, numeric, and so on).

>> Values fall within the expected range.

>> The number of characters falls within the expected range.

>> Only allowed (whitelisted) characters are present.

REMEMBER

Comparing input against a whitelist of allowed entries is safer than comparing it against a blacklist of nonallowed entries. If you leave a vulnerability off your blacklist, you're wide open to exploitation. On the other hand, if you leave a valid entry off your whitelist, you may hear some complaining from your users, but nothing terrible will happen. All you need to do to remedy the situation is add the forgotten entry to your whitelist and move on.

Test the adequacy of your checks by violating them and noting what happens. Error messages should be returned to the user, but those messages shouldn't be too helpful. Overly helpful error messages end up giving clues to attackers on how to penetrate your defenses.

MISHANDLING TYPES

An attacker doesn't need a mishandled escape character to gain control of a database. Whereas character strings use the single-quote character as a delimiter, numeric data has no such delimiter. Suppose that you want to allow users to view the information you have on file for them in your USERINFO table. They can access their information by entering their UserID, which is a number, in a numeric variable named NumVar. You could accept their input in the following SQL statement:

```
userinfo := "SELECT * FROM USERINFO
            WHERE UserID = " + NumVar + ";"
```

The expectation, of course, is that the user will enter a valid UserID number. What if a malicious user entered the following instead?

```
1; DROP TABLE USERINFO;
```

Protecting Against Hardware Failure and External Threats

This entry would generate the following SQL statements:

```
SELECT * FROM USERINFO WHERE UserID = 1; DROP TABLE USERINFO;
```

After reading the contents of a record in the table, the attacker can destroy the entire table.

You can protect yourself from a data-type-based attack the same way that you protect yourself from an escape-character attack: by validating the input. If you expect the variable NumVar to be a number, check it to make sure that it *is* a number, with nothing extra added.

THE DANGER OF PUTTING USER INPUT DIRECTLY IN A DYNAMIC SQL STATEMENT

Some applications really do require dynamic SQL. Sometimes, you want to retrieve data from a table that didn't even exist when you wrote your application. If you use GET without validation to place user input directly in the dynamic SQL statement that you're building, you are wide open to exploitation. Consider an example in which a new table is created every month to hold records of transactions during that month. You want authorized users to be able to display the data in selected columns for all the records in this table, but not necessarily the contents of any other tables in the database. A mishandled escape character is one way that attackers can become authorized users. What more could they do, beyond seeing what's in the transaction table?

They can do a lot. They could hijack the dynamic SQL statement you're building, for example, and use it to penetrate a table that you don't want them to see.

Take a look at the following PHP and MySQL code, which builds a dynamic SQL statement to display the transaction number and dollar amount from the transactions table for last month:

```
// Build statement to pull transaction amounts from table for specified month
$SQL = "SELECT $_GET["ColumnA"], $_GET["ColumnB"] FROM $_GET["MonthlyTrans"];

// Execute statement
$result = mysql_query($SQL);

// Count rows returned
$rowcount = mysql_num_rows($result);

// Display each record
$row = 1;
while ($db_field = mysql_fetch_assoc($result)) {
```

```
    if ($row <= $rowcount) {
       print $db_field[$row] . "<BR>";
       $row++;
    }
}
```

You expect the user to make reasonable inputs, such as a customer name (which is the first column), transaction amount (which is the second column), and Trans-For022019 (which is the table name for the month desired). That's not what an attacker will do, however.

Taking user input and placing it directly in a dynamic SQL statement is like sending formal invitations to thieves to come visit your house while you're away on vacation. Instead of entering a customer name and transaction amount for the TransFor022019 table, an attacker might enter a user and password for the USERS table, thereby gaining access to anything that any user, including the system administrator, can access.

The solution to this problem is (again) quite simple: Validate user input before incorporating it into a dynamic SQL statement. You'd be surprised to see how many developers don't do this.

GIVING TOO MUCH AWAY IN ERROR MESSAGES

Error messages are important parts of any computer program. Legitimate users sometimes make mistakes or get confused about the right way to interact with the system. Error messages are designed to give helpful hints to users when they get off track. That's good. Those messages can also give helpful hints to attackers. That's not so good.

One way to help attackers penetrate a database application is to tell them which DBMS you are using. SQL Server has a lot of standard names for things that differ from those of Oracle, MySQL, or PostgreSQL. Often, an attacker can gain a critical piece of information just by entering illegal characters in a text box and noting what the error message says.

Microsoft SQL Server is particularly "helpful" in this regard. Consider a dynamic SQL query in the AdventureWorks database. The application expects a user who wants to know about sales to customer number 1 to enter 1 in a text box onscreen. This entry would generate the following SQL statement:

```
SELECT * FROM Sales.Customer WHERE CustomerID=1;
```

An attacker, however, instead of entering 1, enters the following:

```
1 and 1 in (SELECT AccountNumber) --
```

This creates the following erroneous SQL statement:

```
SELECT * FROM Sales.Customer WHERE CustomerID=1 and 1 in (SELECT version) --
```

Instead of returning all the information about Customer 1, SQL Server 2017 returns the following error message:

```
Msg 207, Level 16, State 1, Line 1
Invalid column name 'version'.
```

Thankfully, this does not reveal too much to a hacker. However, if you are using an earlier version of SQL Server than SQL Server 2017, the hacker might be a lot luckier. Take note of what SQL Server 2008 R2 returned for this same input.

```
Msg 245, Level 16, State 1, Line 1
Conversion failed when converting the nvarchar value 'Microsoft SQL Server 2008
    R2 (RTM) - 10.50.1600.1 (X64)
    Apr  2 2010 15:48:46
    Copyright (c) Microsoft Corporation
    Web Edition (64-bit) on Windows NT 6.0 <X64> (Build 6002: Service Pack 2)
' to data type int.
```

Talk about giving away the store! SQL Server helpfully provided full details on the version of DBMS that was running. I suspect Microsoft read my coverage of this issue in an earlier edition of this book and performed a major overhaul of their error messages as a result. With the older error message, the attacker knows exactly what dialect of SQL to use, as well as what helpful functions are available, which will aid her in prying more secrets from the database.

DEPENDING ON NORMAL FLOW OF EXECUTION

There is a tendency for a software developer to follow a logical path in code development and to expect the user to follow a similar logical path. The expectation is that the user will make entries in form 1 and move on to form 2, finally interacting with form 3. Based on that flow, the developer will validate an input made in form 1 and not bother to revalidate it in the code behind form 2. That's logical. If the input is validated in the code of form 1 and assigned to a parameter, surely there's no point in validating it again when it's used by the code of form 2.

Don't count on it. An attacker could bypass form 1, along with all its validation checks, jumping directly to form 2. As a result, malicious code can enter the system. The bottom line is that any data derived from user input should be validated every time it crosses a trust boundary, such as the boundary between the code behind form 1 and the code behind form 2.

Recognizing unsafe configurations

If the code you have behind your data-entry screens doesn't have adequate validation checks for everything that's entered, your database could be taken over by an attacker co-opting your SQL statements. Even if your data-entry screens do have validation checks, the very error messages that these checks produce could give the attacker the information he needs to complete a penetration. When the attacker has broken through, your database and everything in it is laid bare.

The most popular DBMS products have some pretty serious vulnerabilities after you do a default installation. These vulnerabilities have to do with highly privileged user accounts. If an attacker can gain access to one of these accounts, she can operate without restriction on everything on your server. Nothing is safe.

Microsoft SQL Server comes with a system administrator account named sa. Clearly, somebody needs to have system administrator privileges, but it would be wise for a new system's system administrator to log in as sa but then immediately create a new system administrator account under a different name and then delete the sa account. That will at least cause the attacker to work a little harder to take over your system.

Other products have similar vulnerabilities. MySQL's root account, for example, is highly privileged and created by default. Oracle has several highly privileged default accounts, preconfigured with well-known passwords, including SYS, SYSTEM, DBSNMP, and OUTLN. In the case of Oracle running under Windows, at least, you cannot summarily delete these accounts, because doing so can prevent Oracle from running at all.

The best precaution is to create each user account with the minimum privileges needed for the user to do his or her job. This way, if an account is compromised, the damage done will be the minimum possible.

Finding vulnerabilities on your site

SQL injection vulnerabilities are relatively easy to spot when you can examine the source code of an application. Look for cases in which the code places user input directly or indirectly in dynamic SQL statements. Often, however, you don't have access to the source code of a web-based application that you're testing for such vulnerabilities. In such cases, you must infer the presence of a vulnerability from the responses you get from inputs that you send to the application. This is exactly what an attacker does. To test for vulnerabilities, you would approach a site the same way that an attacker would.

TESTING BY INFERENCE

From the way that a database application responds to inputs, you can infer things about the details of that application. Based on these inferences, you can try additional inputs that may enable you to penetrate the system.

The first order of business is discovering which inputs the system considers to be legal. You can determine this by making reasonable entries, such as numbers in a numeric field and character strings in a text field. Assuming that you don't hit the jackpot by making an actual valid entry, the system should return a generic error message. When you know the normal response to a legal but incorrect entry, you can probe further by making entries that are illegal and unexpected. If you receive an error message for one of these entries that's different from the message you received for a legal but incorrect input, you've made progress. Often, you can infer what to do next, based on how one error message differs from another.

USING VULNERABILITY TESTING TOOLS

Some developers try to protect their sites from SQL injection attacks by using a drop-down menu to restrict data entry to legal values. Others place size limits on what can be entered in a data-entry field. These measures prevent a legitimate user from accidentally entering invalid data but don't inconvenience an attacker. This client-side functionality can be bypassed easily, and you can send what you want to the database back end. Most modern browser clients allow you to look at the HTML, CSS, and JavaScript code in a web page just by pressing the F12 key. This displays the developer window, which allows you to poke around in the code looking for vulnerabilities.

More advanced tools are also available, such as add-ons to the Mozilla Firefox browser that expand its capabilities. Many tools are available to help you scan your site for vulnerabilities. Here are a few of these tools:

>> **Web Developer:** Web Developer is a Firefox add-on that you can download from https://addons.mozilla.org/en-US/firefox/addon/60. This add-on has a lot of functionality that doesn't relate directly to website security. You can display the contents of all the cookies that the site being tested has set, for example. You can display the contents of the associated cascading style sheet and even edit it. More helpful to both website testers and

attackers, you can view the source code behind a form, display details on entry fields, display hidden fields, show passwords, convert GET to POST or POST to GET, and remove the maximum length restriction on a data-entry field. You can also change a drop-down list to a field in which you can enter what you want.

>> **SQL Map:** The SQL Map tool is an open-source penetration testing tool that automates the ability to detect and exploit SQL injection flaws in websites. It's available at https://sqlmap.org. It has the ability to test for several different types of SQL injection attacks, including Boolean-based blind, time-based blind, error-based, UNION query-based, stacked queries, and out-of-band attacks.

WARNING

Be careful when using the SQL Map tool. There are severe criminal penalties for computer crime, which your actions could be construed to be. Make sure you have permission to test a site for vulnerabilities — preferably in writing — before you use SQL Map to discover weaknesses in a site.

>> **HP WebInspect:** Whereas the Firefox and open-source tools described in this list are available for free download, you can buy commercial products to test your websites for vulnerabilities. HP WebInspect is one such product. It scans a website and provides more extensive information about vulnerabilities than SQL Inject Me does — and appears to find more of them, too. You can generate a variety of reports giving the results of a scan, explanations of the vulnerabilities, and suggestions for eliminating those vulnerabilities.

Figure 1-2 shows the HP WebInspect screen after a scan has finished. The website shown is a sample site that deliberately displays a variety of vulnerabilities. Contact Hewlett-Packard at www.hp.com for prices for HP WebInspect.

>> **IBM Security AppScan:** IBM provides a family of security products to accommodate the needs of organizations of different sizes. These products come with 12 months of support and consequently are pretty spendy. In addition to identifying SQL injection attacks, IBM Rational AppScan discovers and identifies problems such as cross-site scripting and even predictable login credentials — "weak" logins that are too easily predicted by hackers. Figure 1-3 shows the result of a scan of a test site deliberately salted with vulnerabilities.

>> **HP Scrawlr:** HP Scrawlr is a free scan tool from Hewlett-Packard that does only a cursory scan of a website. It catches only a small fraction of the vulnerabilities revealed by its "big brother" product HP WebInspect or by IBM Rational AppScan. However, if it *does* detect a vulnerability in your site, you would be wise to address it immediately.

FIGURE 1-2:
HP WebInspect
scan result.

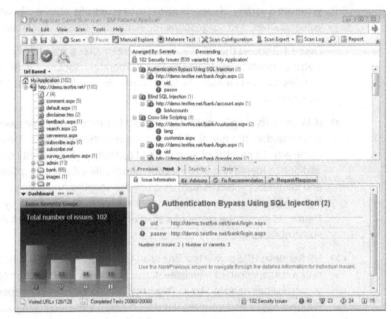

FIGURE 1-3:
IBM Security
AppScan scan
result.

Much more can be said about SQL injection attacks than I have room to cover here. My objective with this brief overview is to alert you to the potential damage to your organization from a successful attack. As with other types of malware, you have defenses against SQL injection attacks. Make sure, however, that your site is created and maintained by experienced and security-conscious web database developers. Testing for vulnerabilities is a must for anything that will be exposed to the world on the web. A lot of people can build database applications that function well, but not nearly as many know how to protect those applications well. Many programmers have never even heard of SQL injection attacks. These attacks generally aren't covered in computer science classes.

Phishing scams

Experienced fisherfolk will get a bite sooner or later, if they cast their lures into a lake enough times. Phishing is like fishing, but in this case, the victims are people rather than fish. Scammers send out emails to thousands or even millions of people, purporting to be from a legitimate bank or business such as eBay, saying that your account has shown unusual activity and you must update your information. These messages can look very legitimate. After you enter your financial information, the scammer has access to your bank or business account and can transfer your funds to his offshore account in a country that doesn't monitor financial transactions. The next time you access your account, you receive an unpleasant surprise.

The best defense against a phishing attack is to never respond to an email with sensitive information. Even though the email sends you to a site that looks for all the world like the official website of your bank, it's a fake, specifically designed to induce you to surrender your account information and, along with it, all the money in the account.

Zombie spambots

Zombie spambots are similar to the worms that engage in denial-of-service attacks, but instead of launching an attack on a single website, they spew unsolicited advertising messages to lists of email addresses that the spammers have acquired. Instead of being from a single, relatively easy-to-trace source, the spam is produced by thousands of computers that have been taken over by worms to mindlessly pump out spam to their address lists. If you happen to be one of the people whose computer has been taken over, you see an unexplained drop in performance, as a significant fraction of your computational capacity and Internet bandwidth is dedicated to sending spam to unlucky recipients around the world. Such distributed spam attacks are devilishly difficult to trace to their source.

Installing Layers of Protection

The creators of viruses, worms, and bots have become increasingly sophisticated and are perpetually one or two steps ahead of the guys in the white hats who are trying to stamp them out. As a user, you should do everything you can to protect your computers and the sensitive information they contain. Because no one type of protection is totally effective, your best hope is to put several layers of protection between your valuable files and programs and the outside world.

Network-layer firewalls

Communication on the Internet consists of packets of data that conform to the TCP/IP protocol. A *network-layer firewall* is a packet filter, operating on a low level, that resides on a computer situated between the Internet and a local area network (LAN), in what is called the DMZ (demilitarized zone). The computer that's running the firewall in the DMZ doesn't contain any sensitive information. Its sole purpose is to protect the LAN. Rules set up by the network administrator (or default values) determine which packets are allowed to pass from the Internet to the LAN and which are rejected.

Application-layer firewalls

An *application-layer firewall* operates at a higher (more abstract) level than the network-layer firewall. It can inspect the contents of network traffic and block traffic that the firewall administrator deems to be inappropriate, such as traffic from known-malicious websites, recognized viruses, or attempts to exploit known vulnerabilities in software running on the LAN.

Antivirus software

Considering the hundreds of viruses and worms circulating in the wild, up-to-date antivirus software is a necessity for any computer directly or indirectly connected to the Internet. Even computers that aren't connected to the Internet are susceptible to infection if they can receive software from CD-ROMs, DVDs, or flash (thumb) drives. Be sure to buy a subscription to one of the popular antivirus programs, such as McAfee or Norton, and then keep the subscription current with regular downloads of updates.

Vulnerabilities, exploits, and patches

Antivirus software can protect you from viruses, worms, and other malware that crackers have created to serve their own nefarious purposes. Such software, however, can't protect you from malware that hasn't yet been released into the wild and detected by the antivirus software vendors.

Existing software may have vulnerabilities that haven't yet been exploited by malware developers. New software is almost certain to contain vulnerabilities just waiting to be exploited. When exploits for these vulnerabilities appear, all computers are at risk until the vulnerabilities have been patched.

Sometimes, exploits (called *zero-day exploits)* are released into the wild on the same day that the vulnerability becomes known. In such cases, the time between the release of the exploit and the release of the patch that shuts it down is a period during which there is no effective defense against the exploit.

When a patch *does* become available, install it immediately on all susceptible machines. An ongoing problem is the huge number of naive users who are unaware of either the danger (and the associated patch) or who don't realize the importance of hardening their systems against attack. By remaining vulnerable, they endanger not only their own systems, but also others that could be attacked if their machine is compromised.

Education

One of the best defenses against malicious attacks on your systems is for all users to be educated about the threats and the countermeasures available to eliminate those threats. Regular training on security should be part of every organization's defensive arsenal.

Alertness

If you ever sit down at your computer and see something that just strikes you as odd, beware. You could be seeing evidence that your computer has been compromised. Run some checks. If you don't know what checks to run, ask someone who does know for help. The problem could be nothing, but then again, maybe a stranger is sucking value out of your system. It doesn't hurt to be a little paranoid.

Chapter **2**

Protecting Against User Errors and Conflicts

After you have done everything you can do to minimize the possibility of problems due to hardware faults and Internet threats (which I discuss in Book 4, Chapter 1), you still have to worry about yet other things that can damage the data in your database or degrade performance.

Several additional potential sources of error exist. Here are a few of the most important:

» The database design could be faulty, leading to modification anomalies or poor performance.

» The database application written to access the data in the database could be buggy, leading to database corruption, erroneous results, poor performance, or all of the above.

» The data entered into the database could be wrong.

>> Users accessing the same (or nearby) data at the same time could interfere with one another, affecting performance or even corrupting the data.

Reducing Data-Entry Errors

All the things you do to protect your database from harm are to no avail if bad data is entered in the first place. Even though nowadays quite a bit of data is recorded automatically by instrumentation and delivered to databases electronically, much of the data stored in the world's databases was initially entered by hand by a fallible human at a computer keyboard. Humans are notorious for making typing errors, even if they are very conscientious and are excellent spellers. Even data collected automatically could contain errors produced by electronic noise or a thousand other unpredictable causes. You can't eliminate all these problems before they put bad data in a database, but you can discover and eliminate some of them. This section shows the features of a database that can help reduce data errors in your application.

Data types: The first line of defense

SQL is a strongly typed language. That means that if a data entry is supposed to be of a particular type, the database engine will not accept any entry that does not conform to the rules of that type. The BOOLEAN type, for example, accepts only values of TRUE and FALSE; it rejects any and all other entries. The INTEGER type accepts only integers, the CHAR type accepts only valid alphanumeric characters, and so on. The strongly typed nature of SQL prevents a lot of bad stuff from being added to databases accidentally. Strong typing, however, does not prevent data of the correct type but with an incorrect value from being entered.

Constraints: The second line of defense

By applying constraints to your database tables, you can prevent incorrect data of the correct type from being accepted. (I cover constraints in Book 1, Chapter 5.) Several kinds of constraints exist, each of which prevents a certain class of problems. Probably the most flexible is the CHECK constraint because it enables you to specify exactly what values are acceptable for entry in a specific database field.

Here's another look at an example of the use of a CHECK constraint that first appears in Book 1, Chapter 5:

```
CREATE TABLE TESTS (
   TestName          CHARACTER (30)        NOT NULL,
   StandardCharge    NUMERIC (6,2)
      CHECK (StandardCharge >= 0.00
         AND StandardCharge <= 200.00)
   ) ;
```

This code guarantees that any entry in the StandardCharge field is of the NUMERIC type, with two decimal places, and that the value entered in the StandardCharge field must be no less than 0 and no more than 200.00. This kind of protection can prevent many errors due to a slip of the finger or the slip of a decimal point.

Sharp-eyed humans: The third line of defense

Strong typing can ensure that data being entered is of the proper type, and constraints can ensure that it is in the proper range of values. These defenses cannot ensure that the data is *right*, however. The only way to make sure that the data entered is indeed the data that is supposed to be entered is to have it checked by a human who knows what the data should be. In most cases, human checking is too costly and time-consuming, so it is not done. We accept a certain amount of bad data because having a human check it is not feasible in all but the most critical cases.

Coping with Errors in Database Design

In Book 1, I talk quite a bit about modeling a database before you start creating its tables. People who don't put in a full effort at modeling are likely to build databases with inherent design flaws. People who *do* put in a full effort at modeling, however, still may have problems if their models are not normalized adequately. Unnormalized or incompletely normalized models are susceptible to modification anomalies that introduce inconsistencies into the data. Those inconsistencies ultimately lead to incorrect results, which could snowball into disastrous executive decisions. Database design is a topic worthy of a book of its own, and many books have been written on the subject. I give a brief introduction to normalization in Book 2, Chapter 2. I cover the topic more extensively in my *SQL For Dummies* (Wiley).

Handling Programming Errors

Even if a database is carefully modeled and designed in such a way that it accurately and efficiently structures the data, and even if the data entered in is 100 percent correct, you still could draw incorrect conclusions based on information you retrieve from that database. How is that so?

Although you can certainly retrieve the information you want from a relational database by entering SQL statements at the system console, this is not the way retrieval is usually done. It is too tedious, time-consuming, and boring — not to mention error-prone — to think up complex SQL queries and enter them on the fly while you sit in front of your computer. Instead, database owners hire people like you to write database applications that manage and query their databases for them. Those database applications are other potential sources of error.

People who write database applications must not only be masters of SQL, but also be experts in the procedural languages in which they embed their SQL statements. Unfortunately, many people who don't have the requisite background are drafted into writing such applications, with predictable results. The applications never really do all the things that the database owner expected them to do, and even worse, the applications may provide misleading results. In recent years, business intelligence (BI) tools that query databases have become widespread. If not used properly, these tools can produce misleading results.

TIP

Although you can't completely eliminate the chance that your database may have design flaws or that your database application may contain hidden bugs, you can do one thing to minimize the chance that such problems will do you significant harm: Hire experienced professionals who understand solid database design and database application design, and who have a good understanding of the system that you want to build. People with this kind of expertise do not come cheap, but in the long run, they are worth what they cost. You get a system that does what you want it to do — and does it reliably and expeditiously.

Solving Concurrent-Operation Conflicts

Suppose that your database is well designed and contains correct data, and that all the applications that access it are bug-free. You still may have a problem. Databases are typically central repositories of important data for businesses, government agencies, and academic institutions, and as such, they are likely to be accessed by multiple people at the same time. If two people attempt to access the same database record at the same time, one could be given precedence, locking out the other. The users could even interfere with each other in such a way that both are locked out and neither gets the job done. Even more problematic, both users could be given access, and their operations could be mixed, corrupting the database.

Protecting the database from corruption is the number-one priority. After that, making sure that people are able to get their jobs done, even when traffic to and from the database is heavy, is very important. In the following paragraphs, I take a look at some of the problems involved here and suggest ways to solve them.

Here's a look at how two perfectly legitimate operations by two authorized users can cause a major problem. Suppose that you and your friend Calypso have a joint savings account at Medieval Savings and Loan. Currently, the account has a balance of $47.17. To meet upcoming expenses, you decide to deposit $100 into the account. Calypso has the same thought at about the same time. You go to the nearest ATM machine, and Calypso, who works in another part of the city, goes to a different ATM machine. A problem arises because two operations are being performed on the same account at the same time. Here's what happens:

1. You insert your ATM card into your ATM.

2. Your ATM pulls up your account and notes that you have a balance of $47.17.

3. Calypso inserts her ATM card into her ATM.

4. Calypso's ATM pulls up your account and notes that you have a balance of $47.17.

5. You insert $100 in cash into your ATM.

6. Your ATM adds $100 to the balance it originally read, producing a total of $147.17.

7. Calypso inserts $100 in cash into her ATM.

8. Calypso's ATM adds $100 to the balance it originally read, producing a total of $147.17.

If you don't compare notes with Calypso at a later time, you have just been victimized to the tune of $100. The write of Calypso's transaction wiped out the fact that you previously deposited $100.

What is the root cause of this problem? The bank tried to handle two operations at the same time and mixed them up. In this case, the mistake was to the bank's advantage, but it could just as easily have gone the other way. At any rate, any bank that loses its customers' money doesn't keep those customers very long.

Problems such as the lost-update scenario described here caused database architects to introduce the idea of a transaction. A *transaction* is an indivisible unit of work that cannot be mixed up with anything else the database might be doing.

Well-designed transaction architectures have four essential characteristics. You find out all about this quartet in the next section.

Passing the ACID Test: Atomicity, Consistency, Isolation, and Durability

The four characteristics of an effective transaction — atomicity, consistency, isolation, and durability — are commonly known by the acronym ACID. To ensure that a transaction will protect your data, no matter what unlucky event might occur, it should have ACID. What do those four magic words mean?

>> **Atomicity:** Database transactions should be atomic, in the classic sense of the word: The entire transaction is treated as an indivisible unit. Either it is executed in its entirety (committed), or the database is restored (rolled back) to the state it would have been in if the transaction had not been executed.

>> **Consistency:** Oddly enough, the meaning of *consistency* is not consistent; it varies from one application to another. When you transfer funds from one account to another in a banking application, for example, you want the total amount of money in both accounts at the end of the transaction to be the same as it was at the beginning of the transaction. In a different application, your criterion for consistency may be different.

>> **Isolation:** Ideally, database transactions should be isolated from other transactions that execute at the same time. If the transactions are serializable, total isolation is achieved. A serializable set of transactions produces the same results as though they were executed serially, one after another. Serializable transactions do not need to be executed serially; they just need to give the same results that they would give if they had been executed serially. Insisting on serializability can cause performance problems, so if a system has to process transactions at top speed, lower levels of isolation are sometimes used. If you serialize two transactions, it is as if a two lane highway suddenly merges into one lane. You are not going to be able to go as fast.

>> **Durability:** After a transaction has either committed or rolled back, you should be able to count on the database to be in the proper state: well stocked with uncorrupted, reliable, up-to-date data. Even if your system suffers a hard crash after a commit — but before the transaction is stored

to disk — a durable database management system (DBMS) can guarantee that upon recovery from the crash, the database can be restored to its proper state.

Operating with Transactions

Any operation that reads data from or writes data to a database should be enclosed in a transaction. As a result, whenever the database engine encounters an SQL statement that either reads or writes, it automatically starts a transaction, called the *default transaction*. Thus, you do not have to explicitly tell the database engine to start a transaction, but you can do so if you want to modify the default parameters. After you start a transaction, it either completes successfully or it does not. What happens in either case is discussed in the following sections.

Using the SET TRANSACTION statement

Whatever DBMS you are using has default settings for how the transaction will be run. Although the default settings are perfectly fine most of the time, you can override them, if you want, with a SET TRANSACTION statement. Here's the syntax:

```
<set transaction statement> ::=
    SET [ LOCAL ] TRANSACTION <mode> [ , <mode> ] ...

<mode> ::=
   <isolation level>
|  <access mode>
|  <diagnostics size>

<isolation level> ::=
    READ UNCOMMITTED
|   READ COMMITTED
|   REPEATABLE READ
|   SERIALIZABLE

<access mode> ::=
    READ ONLY
|   READ WRITE

<diagnostics size> ::=
    DIAGNOSTICS SIZE <simple value expression>
```

With the SET TRANSACTION statement, you can set the isolation level, the access mode, and the diagnostics size. Any one of the modes that you do not specify assumes the default value for that mode. If you specify the READ ONLY access mode, for example, any statements that change the database — such as UPDATE, INSERT, and DELETE — cannot execute. The default access mode is READ WRITE unless the isolation level is READ UNCOMMITTED. When you are running at the READ UNCOMMITTED isolation level, the default access mode is READ ONLY. The default isolation level is SERIALIZABLE. (I cover isolation levels in more detail in the next section. I defer discussion of DIAGNOSTICS SIZE to Book 4, Chapter 4.)

REMEMBER

You can't start a new transaction while an existing transaction is still active. If you *do* execute a SET TRANSACTION statement while a transaction is active, the modes specified in the statement apply only to the *next* transaction, not the current one. The LOCAL keyword restricts the mode settings specified to the local transaction included in a transaction that encompasses multiple databases.

Starting a transaction

As I mention earlier in this section, a transaction is started automatically when the database engine senses that the next statement to execute either reads from or writes to the database. Default modes are assumed unless a SET TRANSACTION statement has been executed. If one has, the modes specified in it are used rather than the default modes. The modes specified by a SET TRANSACTION statement are active only for the next transaction to execute. Any following transactions once again use the default modes unless another SET TRANSACTION statement is executed or a START TRANSACTION statement is executed.

With a START TRANSACTION statement, you can specify modes the same way you can with a SET TRANSACTION statement. The difference is that a START TRANSACTION statement starts a transaction, whereas a SET TRANSACTION statement sets up the modes for a transaction but does not actually start one.

Access modes

There is not much mystery about the access modes, READ ONLY and READ WRITE. In either mode, you can read the contents of database records by using the SELECT statement. You can make changes to the database only in READ WRITE mode, however.

Isolation levels

In the Medieval Savings and Loan example (refer to "Solving Concurrent-Operation Conflicts," earlier in this chapter), I outline one of the potential problems when two database operations are not sufficiently isolated from each other and interact in an undesirable way. Transactions provide four levels of protection from such harmful interactions, ranging from the fairly weak protection of READ UNCOMMITTED to the level of protection you would get if transactions never ran concurrently (SERIALIZABLE).

READ UNCOMMITTED

The weakest level of isolation is called READ UNCOMMITTED, which allows the sometimes-problematic *dirty read* — a situation in which a change made by one user can be read by a second user before the first user commits (that is, finalizes) the change. The problem arises when the first user aborts and rolls back his transaction. Now the second user's subsequent operations are based on an incorrect value.

The classic example of this foul-up can appear in an inventory application: One user decrements inventory, and a second user reads the new (lower) value. The first user rolls back her transaction (restoring the inventory to its initial value), but the second user, thinking that inventory is low, orders more stock and possibly creates a severe overstock. And that's if you're lucky.

WARNING

Don't use the READ UNCOMMITTED isolation level unless you don't care about accurate results.

You *can* use READ UNCOMMITTED if you want to generate approximate statistical data, such as the following:

» Maximum delay in filling orders

» Average age of salespeople who don't make quota

» Average age of new employees

In many such cases, approximate information is sufficient; the extra (performance) cost of the concurrency control required to produce an exact result may not be worthwhile.

READ COMMITTED

The next-highest level of isolation is READ COMMITTED. At this level, a change made by another transaction isn't visible to your transaction until the other user has committed the other transaction. This level gives you a better result than you can get from READ UNCOMMITTED, but it's still subject to a *nonrepeatable read* — a serious problem that creates a comedy of errors.

To illustrate, consider the classic inventory example. User 1 queries the database to see how many items of a particular product are in stock. That number is 10. At almost the same time, User 2 starts — and then commits — a transaction that records an order for 10 units of that same product, decrementing the inventory and leaving none. Now User 1, having seen that 10 units are available, tries to order 5 of them — but 5 units are no longer left, because User 2 has in effect raided the pantry. User 1's initial read of the quantity available is not repeatable. The quantity has changed out from under User 1; any assumptions made on the basis of the initial read are not valid.

REPEATABLE READ

An isolation level of REPEATABLE READ guarantees that the nonrepeatable-read problem doesn't happen. When running at this isolation level, the DBMS simply will not allow a change by a second user to take place after the first user has read a set of records but has not completed the transaction. This isolation level, however, is still haunted by the *phantom read* — a problem that arises when the data a user is reading changes in response to another transaction (and does not show the change onscreen) *while the user is reading it.*

Suppose that User 1 issues a command whose search condition (the WHERE clause or HAVING clause) selects a set of rows, and immediately afterward, User 2 performs and commits an operation that changes the data in some of those rows while User 1's read operation is still running. Those data items met User 1's search condition at the start of this snafu, but now they no longer do. Maybe some other rows that first did not meet the original search condition now do meet it. User 1, whose transaction is still active, has no inkling of these changes; the application behaves as though nothing has happened. The hapless User 1 issues another SQL statement with the same search conditions as the original one, expecting to retrieve the same rows. Instead, the second operation is performed on rows other than those used in the first operation. Reliable results go out the window, spirited away by the phantom read.

SERIALIZABLE

An isolation level of SERIALIZABLE is not subject to any of the problems that beset the other three levels. At this level, concurrent transactions can (in principle) be run serially — one after the other — rather than in parallel, and the results come out the same. If you're running at this isolation level, hardware or software problems can still cause your transaction to fail, but at least you don't have to worry about the validity of your results if you know that your system is functioning properly.

Superior reliability may come at the price of slower performance, of course, so you're back in Trade-Off City. Table 2-1 sums up the trade-off terms, showing the four isolation levels and the problems they solve.

TABLE 2-1

Isolation Levels and Problems Solved

Isolation Level	Problems Solved
READ UNCOMMITTED	None
READ COMMITTED	Dirty read
REPEATABLE READ	Dirty read
	Nonrepeatable read
SERIALIZABLE	Dirty read
	Nonrepeatable read
	Phantom read

Committing a transaction

Although SQL doesn't require an explicit transaction-starting keyword, it has two that terminate a transaction: COMMIT and ROLLBACK. Use COMMIT when you have come to the end of the transaction and want to make permanent the changes that you have made in the database (if any). You may include the optional keyword WORK (COMMIT WORK), if you want. If an error is encountered or the system crashes while a COMMIT is in progress, you may have to roll the transaction back and try it again.

Rolling back a transaction

When you come to the end of a transaction, you may decide that you don't want to make permanent the changes that have occurred during the transaction. In fact, you want to restore the database to the state it was in before the transaction began. To do this, issue a ROLLBACK statement. ROLLBACK is a fail-safe mechanism. Even if the system crashes while a ROLLBACK is in progress, you can restart the ROLLBACK after the system is restored, and it restores the database to its pre-transaction state.

Why roll back a transaction?

It may be necessary to roll back a transaction if some kind of system failure occurs while the transaction is active. Such a failure has several possible causes, including the following:

>> Power failure

>> Application crash

>> Operating-system crash

>> Failed peripheral device

>> Failed processor

>> System shutdown due to overheating

>> Hurricane, wildfire, or other weather damage

>> Electromagnetic storms due to solar coronal mass ejections

>> Bit flips due to cosmic rays

>> Terrorist attack

In most of the cases cited, although system operation is interrupted and everything in volatile main memory is lost, information stored on a nonvolatile hard disk is still intact, particularly if it's stored in a RAID array physically removed from the main system box. (For details on RAID, see Book 4, Chapter 1.) The good information on your hard disk forms the basis for a rollback operation that takes the system back to the condition it was in before the start of any of the transactions that were active when the service interruption occurred.

How can you roll back changes that have already been made? How can you undelete records that you have deleted? How can you restore fields that you have overwritten with new data? How can you remove new records that you have added? The answers to all these questions lie in the log file.

The log file

Because volatile semiconductor memory is so much faster than hard disk storage, when changes are made to a data file, they are not immediately written to hard disk, which is a relatively slow process. Instead, they are written to a page buffer in semiconductor memory. If those same logical memory locations must be accessed again fairly soon, the retrieval is much quicker from the page buffer than it would be from hard disk.

Eventually, the page buffer fills, and when a new page is needed, one of the existing pages in the buffer must be swapped out to make room for the new page. During the period when information has been written to memory but is still in the page buffer, it is vulnerable to a failure of the volatile page buffer memory. When a power failure occurs, everything in the page buffer is lost, as well as everything in the system's main memory. The log file is the primary tool for recovering what has been lost and rendering the system able to redo the incomplete transactions.

The log file, primarily located on disk but also necessarily partly in the page buffer, records every change made to the database. Log-file entries pertaining to a transaction are always flushed from the page buffer to disk before the actual changes themselves are flushed. If a failure occurs between the time the log-file entries are flushed to disk and the time the changes themselves would have been flushed, the changes can be reconstructed from the log-file entries. The main idea is to make the window of vulnerability as small as possible. When log-file entries are frequently flushed to disk, that window is open only a crack. For all but the most ill-timed and severe failures, a minimum of data is lost, and it can be re-entered without too much trouble.

The write-ahead log protocol

The entries in the log file are made according to a formula known as the *write-ahead log protocol*. When a transaction prepares to write to a page containing some target record, it obtains an exclusive lock on the page. (I discuss locks extensively in the next section of this chapter.) Before the transaction makes the modification to a record, it writes a log record containing the contents of the record both before and after the change. After the log record has been successfully written, the modification itself is written. Now the change is sitting in the page buffer, where it is vulnerable to a power outage or other mischance that may require a reboot that erases all volatile storage.

If a failure occurs before the log record and modification are flushed to disk, they are lost. In that case, you must go back to the last good version on disk and redo everything from that point on. If a failure occurs after the log file has been written to disk but before the modification has been, the data in the log file enables full reconstitution of the change.

After a failure, the log file may contain information on the following:

>> Transactions that were committed but not yet written to disk

>> Transactions that were rolled back

>> Transactions that were still active and (of course) not yet written to disk

Transactions that were committed and not yet written to disk need to be redone. Transactions that were rolled back need to be undone. Transactions that were still active need to be restarted. You can figure out which of these three actions to take by scanning the log file backward in time, undoing actions as you go. When you come to a COMMIT statement, put that transaction in the redo list. When you come to a ROLLBACK statement, put that transaction in the undo list. Put the rest of the transactions in the restart list.

When you reach the beginning of the log, you have undone all the transactions. Now scan forward to redo all the transactions in the redo list. Skip the transactions in the undo list, because you have already undone them. Finally, submit the restart list to the DBMS to start those transactions from scratch.

Checkpoints

A log file may accumulate records of transactions for months or years, becoming quite large in the process. Scanning back through the log file can be time-consuming. There is no point in scanning back beyond a point at which all transactions are guaranteed to have been safely stored on disk. To shorten the portion of the log that must be scanned, checkpoints are established at intervals. These intervals may be fixed units of time, such as 15 minutes, or they may come after a specific number of entries have been made in the log. In either case, at a checkpoint, all log entries in the page buffer are flushed to disk. This checkpoint establishes a point beyond which you can be assured that all log entries and all committed transactions are safely on disk.

When a problem occurs that requires recovery, you need concern yourself only with transactions that were active at, or that started later than, the checkpoint. Transactions that were committed before the checkpoint will have been flushed to disk at the checkpoint, if not before. The same is true for transactions that were rolled back. Transactions that were active at the checkpoint have to be undone back to the point at which they started and then restarted.

Implementing deferrable constraints

Ensuring the validity of the data in your database means doing more than just making sure that the data is of the right type. Perhaps some columns, for example, should never hold a null value — and maybe others should hold only values that fall within a certain range. Such restrictions are *constraints*, as discussed in Book 1, Chapter 5.

Constraints are relevant to transactions because they can conceivably prevent you from doing what you want. Suppose that you want to add data to a table that contains a column with a NOT NULL constraint. One common method of adding a record is to append a blank row to your table and then insert values into it later. The NOT NULL constraint on one column, however, causes the append operation to fail. SQL doesn't allow you to add a row that has a null value in a column with a NOT NULL constraint, even though you plan to add data to that column before your transaction ends. To address this problem, SQL enables you to designate constraints as DEFERRABLE or NOT DEFERRABLE.

Constraints that are NOT DEFERRABLE are applied immediately. You can set DEFERRABLE constraints to be initially DEFERRED or IMMEDIATE. If a DEFERRABLE constraint is set to IMMEDIATE, it acts like a NOT DEFERRABLE constraint: It is applied immediately. If a DEFERRABLE constraint is set to DEFERRED, it is not enforced.

To append blank records or perform other operations that may violate constraints, ISO/IEC standard SQL allows you to use a statement similar to the following:

```
SET CONSTRAINTS ALL DEFERRED ;
```

This statement puts all DEFERRABLE constraints in the DEFERRED condition. It does not affect the NOT DEFERRABLE constraints. After you have performed all operations that could violate your constraints, and the table reaches a state that doesn't violate them, you can reapply them. The statement that reapplies your constraints looks like this:

```
SET CONSTRAINTS ALL IMMEDIATE ;
```

If you made a mistake, and any of your constraints are still being violated, you find out as soon as this statement takes effect.

If you do not explicitly set your DEFERRED constraints to IMMEDIATE, SQL does it for you when you attempt to COMMIT your transaction. If a violation is still present at that time, the transaction does not COMMIT; instead, SQL gives you an error message.

SQL's handling of constraints protects you from entering invalid data (or an invalid *absence* of data, which is just as important) while giving you the flexibility to violate constraints temporarily while a transaction is still active.

Consider a payroll example to see why being able to defer the application of constraints is important.

Assume that an EMPLOYEE table has columns EmpNo, EmpName, DeptNo, and Salary. EMPLOYEE.DeptNo is a foreign key referencing the DEPT table. Assume also that the DEPT table has columns DeptNo and DeptName. DEPT.DeptNo is the primary key.

In addition, you want to have a table like DEPT that also contains a Payroll column that holds the sum of the Salary values for employees in each department.

You can create the equivalent of this table with the following view:

```
CREATE VIEW DEPT2 AS
    SELECT D.*, SUM(E.Salary) AS Payroll
        FROM DEPT D, EMPLOYEE E
        WHERE D.DeptNo = E.DeptNo
        GROUP BY D.DeptNo ;
```

You can also define this same view as follows:

```
CREATE VIEW DEPT3 AS
    SELECT D.*,
        (SELECT SUM(E.Salary)
            FROM EMPLOYEE E
            WHERE D.DeptNo = E.DeptNo) AS Payroll
    FROM DEPT D ;
```

But suppose that for efficiency, you don't want to calculate the sum every time you reference DEPT3.Payroll. Instead, you want to store an actual Payroll column in the DEPT table. Then you will update that column every time you change a salary.

To make sure that the Salary column is accurate, you can include a CONSTRAINT in the table definition, as follows:

```
CREATE TABLE DEPT
    (DeptNo CHAR(5),
    DeptName CHAR(20),
    Payroll DECIMAL(15,2),
    CHECK (Payroll = (SELECT SUM(Salary)
                FROM EMPLOYEE E WHERE E.DeptNo= DEPT.DeptNo)));
```

Now suppose that you want to increase the salary of employee 123 by 100. You can do it with the following update:

```
UPDATE EMPLOYEE
    SET Salary = Salary + 100
    WHERE EmpNo = '123' ;
```

You must remember to do the following as well:

```
UPDATE DEPT D
   SET Payroll = Payroll + 100
   WHERE D.DeptNo = (SELECT E.DeptNo
                     FROM EMPLOYEE E
                     WHERE E.EmpNo = '123') ;
```

(You use the subquery to reference the DeptNo of employee 123.)

But there's a problem: Constraints are checked after each statement. In principle, *all* constraints are checked. In practice, implementations check only the constraints that reference the values modified by the statement.

After the first preceding UPDATE statement, the implementation checks all constraints that reference values that the statement modifies. This check includes the constraint defined in the DEPT table, because that constraint references the Salary column of the EMPLOYEE table, and the UPDATE statement is modifying that column. After the first UPDATE statement, that constraint is violated. You assume that before you execute the UPDATE statement, the database is correct, and each Payroll value in the DEPT table equals the sum of the Salary values in the corresponding columns of the EMPLOYEE table. When the first UPDATE statement increases a Salary value, this equality is no longer true. The second UPDATE statement corrects this problem and again leaves the database values in a state for which the constraint is True. Between the two updates, the constraint is False.

The SET CONSTRAINTS DEFERRED statement lets you temporarily disable or suspend all constraints or only specified constraints. The constraints are deferred until you execute a SET CONSTRAINTS IMMEDIATE statement or a COMMIT or ROLLBACK statement. So you surround the previous two UPDATE statements with SET CONSTRAINTS statements. The code looks like this:

```
SET CONSTRAINTS DEFERRED ;
UPDATE EMPLOYEE
   SET Salary = Salary + 100
   WHERE EmpNo = '123' ;
UPDATE DEPT D
   SET Payroll = Payroll + 100
   WHERE D.DeptNo = (SELECT E.DeptNo
                     FROM EMPLOYEE E
      WHERE E.EmpNo = '123') ;
SET CONSTRAINTS IMMEDIATE ;
```

This procedure defers all constraints. If you insert new rows into DEPT, the primary keys won't be checked; you have removed protection that you may want to keep. Specifying the constraints that you want to defer is preferable. To do this, name the constraints when you create them, as follows:

```
CREATE TABLE DEPT
    (DeptNo     CHAR(5),
    DeptName    CHAR(20),
    Payroll     DECIMAL(15,2),
    CONSTRAINT PayEqSumSal
    CHECK       (Payroll = SELECT SUM(Salary)
    FROM EMPLOYEE E
    WHERE E.DeptNo = DEPT.DeptNo)) ;
```

With constraint names in place, you can reference your constraints individually, as follows:

```
SET CONSTRAINTS PayEqSumSal DEFERRED;
UPDATE EMPLOYEE
    SET Salary = Salary + 100
    WHERE EmpNo = '123' ;
UPDATE DEPT D
    SET Payroll = Payroll + 100
    WHERE D.DeptNo = (SELECT E.DeptNo
                        FROM EMPLOYEE E
                        WHERE E.EmpNo = '123') ;
SET CONSTRAINTS PayEqSumSal IMMEDIATE;
```

Without a constraint name in the CREATE statement, SQL generates one implicitly. That implicit name is in the schema information (catalog) tables, but specifying the names explicitly is more straightforward.

Now suppose that in the second UPDATE statement, you mistakenly specified an increment value of 1000. This value is allowed in the UPDATE statement because the constraint has been deferred. But when you execute SET CONSTRAINTS IMMEDIATE, the specified constraints are checked. If they fail, SET CONSTRAINTS raises an exception. If, rather than a SET CONSTRAINTS IMMEDIATE statement, you execute COMMIT, and the constraints are found to be false, COMMIT instead performs a ROLLBACK.

Bottom line: You can defer the constraints only *within* a transaction. When the transaction is terminated by a ROLLBACK or a COMMIT, the constraints are both enabled and checked. The SQL capability of deferring constraints is meant to be used within a transaction. If used properly, it doesn't create any data that violates a constraint available to other transactions.

Getting Familiar with Locking

The gold standard for maintaining database integrity is to operate on it with only serializable transactions. You have two major approaches for providing serializability: locking and timestamps. In this section, I look at locking. I cover timestamps in "Enforcing Serializability with Timestamps," later in this chapter.

If a transaction is granted a lock on a particular resource, access to that resource by competing transactions is restricted. There are two main kinds of locks:

>> **Shared locks:** Two or more transactions, each with a shared lock, can concurrently read the contents of a memory location without interfering with one another. As long as none of the transactions attempts to change the data at that location, all the transactions can proceed without delay. The lock manager portion of the DBMS can grant shared locks to all transactions that want to perform only read operations. Shared locks are sometimes called *read locks*.

>> **Exclusive locks:** To perform a write operation on a memory location, a transaction must acquire an *exclusive lock,* which grants to its holder the exclusive right to access the resource being locked. If one transaction holds an exclusive lock on a resource, no competing transaction may acquire either a shared lock or an exclusive lock on that resource until the first transaction releases its lock. Exclusive locks are sometimes called *write locks*.

Two-phase locking

Two-phase locking is a protocol designed to guarantee serializability. In the first phase, a transaction can acquire shared and exclusive locks, and may also upgrade a shared lock to an exclusive lock. It may not release any locks or downgrade an exclusive lock to a shared lock, however. In the second phase, the transaction may release shared and exclusive locks, as well as downgrade an exclusive lock to a shared lock, but it may not acquire a new shared or exclusive lock, or upgrade a shared lock to an exclusive lock.

In the strictest form of two-phase locking, the second phase, in which locks are released or downgraded, cannot occur until the transaction either commits or rolls back. This restriction protects a competing transaction from acquiring a lock on, and reading a value from, a resource that the original transaction released before aborting. In such a case, the second transaction would potentially read a value that no longer existed in the resource. In fact, after a rollback, it is as though that value never existed.

Granularity

The *granularity* of a lock determines the size of the resource being locked. Locks that are coarse-grained take rather large resources out of circulation. Fine-grained locks sequester relatively small resources. Course-grained locks deny access to big things, such as tables. Fine-grained locks protect smaller things, such as rows in a table.

This list describes four types of locks and the granularity of each type:

>> **Database locks:** The database lock is the ultimate in coarse-grained locks. If a transaction puts an exclusive lock on a database, no other transaction can access the database at all until the lock is released. As you might imagine, database locks have a disastrous effect on overall productivity and should be avoided if at all possible. Sometimes, a database administrator must apply a database lock to prevent other transactions from corrupting the database while she is making alterations in the database structure.

>> **Table locks:** Table locks, by locking an entire database table, are not as restrictive as database locks but are still pretty coarse. Generally, you would impose a table lock only if you were altering the structure of the table or if you were changing data in most or all of the rows in the table.

>> **Row locks:** Row locks are fine-grained in that they lock only a single row in a table. If you're changing only a value in a single row, there is no point in locking any rows other than that one target row. The only transactions that are affected by a row lock are those that want to do something to the very same row of the very same table.

>> **Page locks:** A page lock — which has an intermediate granularity between a table lock and a row lock — locks an entire page in the page buffer. Because information gets transferred between the page buffer and disk a page at a time, some DBMSs provide locks at the page level. As processing proceeds, requiring pages currently residing in the page buffer to be swapped out in favor of pages on disk that are currently needed, the DBMS will resist, if possible, the urge to swap out any page locked by an active transaction. Swapping it out and then swapping it back in again soon would waste a tremendous amount of time.

Deadlock

A deadlock is not a type of lock or an example of granularity, but a problem that can arise in even a well-designed system that uses locking for concurrency control. To illustrate how a deadlock can happen, look again at the example in which you and your friend Calypso share a bank account (refer to "Solving Concurrent-Operation Conflicts," earlier in this chapter). Now that you are using transactions with two-phase locking, you don't have to worry about the lost-update problem anymore. A potential problem still exists, however. Once again, you and Calypso arrive at two different ATM machines at about the same time.

1. You insert your ATM card into your ATM.

2. The DBMS's lock manager grants you a shared lock on your account record, enabling you to read your balance of $47.17.

3. Calypso inserts her ATM card into her ATM.

4. The DBMS's lock manager grants Calypso a shared lock on your account record, enabling her to read the balance of $47.17.

5. You insert $100 in cash into your ATM.

6. The DBMS's lock manager attempts to upgrade your shared lock to an exclusive lock but cannot because of Calypso's shared lock. It goes into a wait loop, waiting for Calypso's lock to be released.

7. Calypso inserts $100 in cash into her ATM.

8. The DBMS's lock manager attempts to upgrade Calypso's shared lock to an exclusive lock but cannot because of your shared lock. It goes into a wait loop, waiting for your lock to be released.

9. The machine is deadlocked. Neither you nor Calypso can complete the transaction.

10. After some period of time, the DBMS recognizes the deadlock situation and aborts one or both of the deadlocked transactions.

Ideally, instances such as this don't occur too often. By putting your account update in a transaction, you have traded the lost-update problem for the deadlock problem. This situation is an improvement. At least you don't end up with incorrect data in your database. It's a hassle to have to redo your ATM transaction, however. If all goes well, you and Calypso don't try to redo your transactions at the same time.

Tuning Locks

Locks perform an important function in preserving the integrity of transactions. They prevent database corruption by making sure that changes by one transaction do not affect the results of another transaction that is operating concurrently.

They do so at a cost, however. Locks consume memory and also affect performance because it takes time to acquire a lock, and it takes time to release one. Additional performance is lost while transactions wait for resources that have been locked by another. In some cases, such lockouts prevent data corruption; in other cases, locks are needlessly placed when harmful interactions cannot occur.

You can do some things to reduce the overhead burden of locking. Generally, you apply these measures only if performance becomes unsatisfactory. For some of the tuning interventions that I discuss in this section, you may have to trade off some accuracy in exchange for improved performance.

Measuring performance with throughput

What is performance, anyway? There are many ways of thinking about performance and many system parameters that you can measure to glean information about one aspect of performance or another. In this book, when I talk about *performance*, I am referring to *throughput* — a measure of the amount of work that gets completed per unit time. It is an overall measure that takes into account all the jobs running on a system. If one job is running really fast, but its locks are slowing all the other jobs running at the same time, throughput may well be lower than it would be if the first job were reconfigured so that it did not run quite so fast and held its locks for a shorter period.

Eliminating unneeded locks

Locks are designed to prevent concurrently running transactions from interfering with one another. They are applied automatically by the DBMS, so the application programmer does not have to worry about whether he should apply a lock. At times, however, such interference is not possible. In those cases, the locking overhead is a burden on the system, but no corresponding benefit in data integrity occurs.

This is true when only one transaction is running at a time, such as when a database is loading. It is also true when all queries are guaranteed to be read-only — when mining archived information, for example. In such cases, it makes sense to take advantage of the option to suppress the acquisition of locks.

Shortening transactions

Long transactions, which do a lot of things, tend to hold locks for a long time. This situation, of course, has a negative effect on the performance of all the other transactions running at the same time. If everyone followed the discipline of making transactions as short as possible, everyone would benefit by being able to acquire needed locks sooner.

Albert Einstein once said, with regard to physics, "Make everything as simple as possible, but not simpler." The same logic applies here. Make transactions as short as possible, but not shorter. If you chop up transactions too finely, you could lose serializability, which means that you could lose accuracy. To continue the lost-update example (refer to "Solving Concurrent-Operation Conflicts," earlier in this chapter), if you acquired a shared lock on your bank account, viewed your bank balance, and then dropped your shared lock before acquiring an exclusive lock to make a withdrawal, Calypso could have sneaked in while your locks were down and cleaned out your account. This situation would have been both surprising and disappointing, because you would just have read that there was plenty of money in your account.

Weakening isolation levels (ver-r-ry carefully)

If you weaken your isolation level from SERIALIZABLE to REPEATABLE READ or perhaps READ COMMITTED, you can increase your throughput. A good chance exists that in doing so, however, bad data will creep into your database. In most cases, weakening your isolation level in that way isn't worthwhile.

In a few scenarios, perfect accuracy in data is not required, and system response time is very important. In such cases, weakening the isolation level may be appropriate.

Consider an airline's reservation system. Suppose that a traveler goes to an airline's online website, which is running at the READ COMMITTED isolation level, to look up a particular flight. Checking available seats is a read-only operation that puts a shared lock on the entire airplane. As soon as the cabin image is transmitted, the shared lock is dropped. The traveler decides that she would like to sit in seat 10-C, which the website shows as available. She clicks that seat on her screen image to indicate that she wants to reserve that seat. The database attempts to put an exclusive lock on the record for seat 10-C but fails. In the small interval of time between the database read and the attempted database write, someone else has reserved that seat, and it is no longer available.

This scenario could clearly happen with READ COMMITTED isolation. Is this a problem? Many airlines would think that it is not. Although such a sequence of events is possible, it also tends to be extremely rare. When it does occur, it is not a big deal. The traveler just directs a few choice words at the computer (the universal scapegoat) and successfully selects another seat. In exchange, all the travelers who use the reservation system benefit from faster response to their actions, which might be considered to be a reasonable trade-off.

WARNING

Be sure to think through the possible problems that could occur if you weaken the isolation level of your database and the consequences that follow from those problems. If you do decide to weaken the isolation level, it should be with full knowledge of the consequences.

Controlling lock granularity

In most systems, row-level locking, which is fine-grained, is the default. This is the best choice for maximizing throughput in an online transaction environment, such as an airline reservation system or a banking system. It's not necessarily best in a system that runs long transactions that involve most of the rows in a table, however. In that kind of environment, a table lock — one with lower overhead than a large number of row locks — could well deliver better overall throughput. Concurrent transactions could be delayed to a lesser extent than they would be with row-level locking.

REMEMBER

Don't assume that the finest-grained locking setting is the best. Consider the types of jobs that are typically run, and choose lock granularity accordingly.

Scheduling DDL statements correctly

Data Definition Language (DDL) statements such as CREATE TABLE, DROP INDEX, and ALTER TABLE operate on the system catalog. Because these operations are of such a fundamental nature, ordinary traffic comes to a standstill while they are active. In any normal installation, you are going to need to run some DDL statements from time to time. Just keep in mind the way that they monopolize system resources, and schedule them at a time when your normal transaction volume is light.

Partitioning insertions

Sequential insertion of records can be a bottleneck. If multiple transactions are inserting records sequentially into the tail end of a table, all of them will be hitting the same buffer page at about the same time and running into page locks. One way to relieve the congestion is to partition insertions into the table across different pages or even different disks. One way to achieve this result is to set up a clustering index based on something other than the time of insertion. This method spreads out the inserted records to different pages. I define clustered indexes in Book 2, Chapter 3, and will discuss their effect on performance in Book 7, Chapter 1.

Cooling hot spots

Hot spots are those records, pages, or tables that everybody wants access to at the same time. When a lengthy transaction acquires a lock on a hot item, everybody else suffers.

You can do a couple of things to lower the "temperature" of chronic hot spots:

>> Partition transactions as described in the preceding section.

>> Access hot spots as late as possible in a long transaction. Within a transaction, you have some control over the order in which you do things. When possible, place a lock on a hot resource as late as possible. This method makes the overheated resource unavailable for the shortest amount of time.

Tuning the deadlock interval

Earlier in this chapter, in the section titled "Deadlock," I mention deadlock as being a possible problem, even when you are running with a serializable isolation level. The common solution to the deadlock problem starts when the system senses that two or more transactions have not made any progress for an extended period. To break the deadlock, the system forces the abort and rollback of one or perhaps all of the transactions involved. The *deadlock interval* is the period that the system waits before allowing an aborted transaction to restart. Clearly, you don't want to give all the aborted transactions the same deadlock interval. Doing so would just be asking for another deadlock. Even if only one transaction is aborted, restarting it too soon could conflict with a lengthy transaction that is still running.

So how do you choose a good deadlock interval? There is no one good answer, although the interval should have an element of randomness so that you don't assign the same interval to both participants in a deadlock. Make an educated guess based on the types of transactions that you are running. If excessive deadlocks ensue, try changing the interval or the average difference between the deadlock interval of one aborted transaction and the deadlock interval of the other participant in the deadly embrace that started the whole mess.

Enforcing Serializability with Timestamps

Locks aren't the only effective mechanisms for keeping concurrent transactions from interfering with one another. Another method involves timestamps. A *timestamp* is a centrally dispensed number assigned to each transaction in strictly increasing order. A timestamp could be based on the computer's real-time clock, or it could just be a counter that is continually counting up. This method enables the system to determine which active transaction is the oldest and which is the youngest, as well as the relative positions of all transactions in between. In a conflict situation, the timestamp solution works by designating the younger transaction as the winner.

To demonstrate this method, look again at the bank-account update example (introduced in "Solving Concurrent-Operation Conflicts," earlier in this chapter):

1. The system sets the timestamp to 0, which is the timestamp for a creating or updating operation.

2. You insert your ATM card into your ATM.

3. Your ATM pulls up your account and notes that you have a balance of $47.17. It sets the timestamp for your transaction to 1 and checks that 1 is greater than or equal to the timestamp of the youngest operation in the system (0). Because 1 is greater than 0, everything is fine.

4. Calypso inserts her ATM card into her ATM.

5. Calypso's ATM pulls up your account and notes that you have a balance of $47.17. It sets the timestamp for her transaction to 2 and checks that 2 is greater than or equal to the youngest operation in the system (1). Because 2 is greater than 1, everything is fine.

6. You insert $100 in cash into your ATM.

7. Calypso inserts $100 in cash into her ATM.

8. Calypso's ATM checks whether her timestamp (2) is equal to or greater than the most recent timestamp. It is, so everything is fine. Calypso's transaction commits and the ATM registers a balance of $147.17.

9. Your ATM checks your timestamp (1) against the youngest timestamp in the system (2). Because 1 is not greater than or equal to 2, you lose. There are no changes in the database to undo, so a new transaction is started for you with timestamp 3.

10. Your ATM notes that your timestamp (3) is equal to or greater than the timestamp of the most recent create or update operation (2).

11. Your update is accomplished; your transaction commits, and the account balance goes to $247.17.

There was a little hitch in the proceedings, but you probably didn't even notice it while you were standing there at the ATM machine. The account updates were performed properly.

The preceding scenario sounds great, but problems could occur if the timing is just a little bit off. Consider the following example:

1. The system sets the timestamp to 0, which is the timestamp for a creating or updating operation.

2. You insert your ATM card into your ATM.

3. Your ATM pulls up your account and notes that you have a balance of $47.17. It sets the timestamp for your transaction to 1 and checks that 1 is greater than or equal to the youngest timestamp in the system (0). It is, so everything is fine.

4. Calypso inserts her ATM card into her ATM.

5. Calypso's ATM pulls up your account and notes that you have a balance of $47.17. It sets the timestamp for her transaction to 2 and checks that 2 is greater than or equal to the youngest timestamp in the system (1). It is, so everything is fine.

6. You insert $100 in cash into your ATM.

7. Your ATM checks your timestamp (1) against the timestamp of the youngest read in the system (2). Because 1 is not greater than or equal to 2, you lose. There are no changes in the database to undo, so a new transaction is started for you with timestamp 3.

8. Your new transaction checks your timestamp (3) against the timestamp of the youngest update in the system (2). Because 3 is equal to or greater than 2, everything is fine. Your transaction reads a balance of $47.17.

9. Calypso inserts $100 in cash into her ATM.

10. Calypso's ATM checks whether her timestamp (2) is equal to or greater than the most recent timestamp (3). It is not, so her transaction is aborted, and a new transaction with timestamp 4 is started for her.

11. Calypso's ATM checks whether her timestamp (4) is equal to or greater than the most recent (3). It is, so everything is fine. Her transaction reads a balance of $47.17.

12. Your ATM checks your timestamp (3) against the timestamp of the youngest create or update operation in the system (4). Because 3 is not greater than or equal to 4, you lose. There are no changes in the database to undo, so a new transaction is started for you with timestamp 5.

13. And so on, ad infinitum.

Your ATM has eaten $100 of your money and Calypso's ATM has eaten $100 of her money. This situation is called a *livelock* as opposed to a *deadlock*. In a *deadlock*, two or more transactions are stuck in wait states because they cannot continue without a resource that has been acquired by another one of the dead-locked transactions. A *livelock* differs in that the participating transactions are continually processing but are moving no closer to completion; they are stuck in a loop.

One way out of this situation is for the DBMS to keep a list of transactions that have been aborted some fixed number of times. When a transaction goes over the threshold, the DBMS can halt the normal flow of execution and execute the livelocked transactions serially. Your account will finally show the correct balance.

Tuning the Recovery System

One thing you can do to maximize performance is to put your database log on a different disk from the disks that contain data. The log is continuously updated with every command performed. It just pours its information onto the log disk sequentially. This minimizes the amount of time that the disk drive spends seeking because data is written sequentially to a single track and then to other tracks on the same cylinder, after which a short seek is made to an adjacent cylinder and the operation continues. By contrast, the data disks are constantly doing random seeks from one track to another. Mixing that operation with the sequential writing of the log would cause a severe hit on performance.

Tuning the recovery system is always a balance between maximizing performance and maintaining system integrity. Although disk failures are rare, they do happen occasionally. Even if your system is protected with a RAID system, you should take a copy of your database offline at intervals. This copy, called a *database dump*, has an effect on performance because it uses resources while it is being run. The dump gives you a starting point if your hard disk system fails catastrophically. You must decide how often to perform database dumps by weighing the performance hit you take while it is running against the pain you would suffer if you didn't run it and a disk failure occurred.

Similar considerations apply to checkpoints (refer to "Checkpoints," earlier in this chapter). At a checkpoint, all committed transactions are flushed to disk. This method is a significant time consumer, because disk operations are orders of magnitude slower than data transfers to solid-state memory. Balanced against this situation is the time that checkpoints save you when that inevitable failure does occur. A checkpoint limits the distance you have to go back in the log to resynchronize the system after a failure.

How frequently should you force a checkpoint? It's a tradeoff. Compare the overhead cost of a checkpoint with the time it saves you when you have to go to the log to recover consistency after a failure. Set the checkpoint interval at that sweet spot where you save more time in a recovery operation than the overhead of implementing the checkpoints is costing you.

Chapter **3**

Assigning Access Privileges

ecause databases are among the most valuable assets that any organization has, you must be able to control who has access to them, as well as
what level of access to grant. SQL handles access management with the
third of its main components, the Data Control Language (DCL). Whereas the
Data Definition Language (DDL) is used to create and maintain the structure of a
database, and the Data Manipulation Language (DML) is used to fill the database
structure with data and then operate on that data, the DCL protects the database
from unauthorized access and other potential problems.

Working with the SQL Data Control Language

The DCL consists of four SQL statements, and two of them — COMMIT and
ROLLBACK — are discussed in Book 4, Chapter 2. The other two DCL statements —
GRANT and REVOKE — control who may access various parts of the database. Before
you can grant database access to someone, you must have some way of identifying that person. Some parts of user identification, such as issuing passwords and

taking other security measures, are implementation-specific. SQL has a standard way of identifying and categorizing users, however, so granting and revoking privileges can be handled relatively easily.

Identifying Authorized Users

Users may be identified individually with a unique identifier, or they may be identified as a member of a group. Individually identified users can be given a customized array of access privileges, whereas all group members receive the same suite of privileges. Groups are defined by the roles that the people in them play. People who all perform the same role have the same access privileges.

Understanding user identifiers

SQL doesn't specify how a user identifier is assigned. In many cases, the operating system's login ID serves the purpose. A user identifier is one of two forms of authorization identifier that enable access to a database system. The other form is a role name, which I discuss in the next section.

Every SQL session is started by a user. That user's user identifier is called the *SQL-session user identifier.* The privileges associated with the SQL-session user identifier determine what privileges that user has and what actions she may perform during the session. When your SQL session starts, your SQL-session user identifier is also the *current user identifier.* The identity of the current user is kept in a special value named CURRENT_USER, which can be queried to find out who is currently in charge of a session.

Getting familiar with roles

In a small company, identifying users individually doesn't present any problem. In a larger organization, however, with hundreds of employees doing a variety of jobs, identifying users individually can become a burden. Every time someone leaves or joins a company or changes job responsibilities, database privileges have to be adjusted. This adjustment is where roles come in.

Although a company may have hundreds or thousands of employees, these employees do a limited number of jobs. If everyone who plays the same role in the company requires the same database access privileges, you can assign those privileges to that group of people based on the roles they play in the organization. One role might be SALES_CLERK. All the sales clerks require the same privileges. All the warehouse workers require different privileges, which is fine, because they play a different role in the company. In this way, the job of maintaining authorizations for everyone is made much simpler. A new sales clerk is added to the SALES_CLERK role name and immediately gains the privileges assigned to that role. A sales clerk leaving the company is deleted from the SALES_CLERK role name and immediately loses all database privileges. An employee changing from one job category to another is deleted from one role name and added to another.

Just as a session initiated by a user is associated with an SQL-session user identifier, it is also associated with an SQL-session role name. The value of the current role name is available in the CURRENT_ROLE special value. When an SQL session is created, the current role name has a null value. At any given instant, either a user identifier is specified, and the associated role name has a null value, or a role name is specified, and the associated user identifier has a null value. A SET ROLE statement can create a situation in which both the user identifier for a session and a role name are non-null. In such a case, the privileges assigned to both the user identifier and to the role name are available to the user.

Creating roles

You can create a role with a single SQL statement. Here is the syntax:

```
CREATE ROLE <role name>
  [WITH ADMIN {CURRENT_USER | CURRENT_ROLE}] ;
```

When you create a role, the role is automatically granted to you. You are also granted the right to pass the role-creation privilege on to others. When creating a role, you may identify yourself as either the current user or the current role. If you identify yourself as the current user, you're the only one who can operate on the new role. If you identify yourself as the current role, anyone who shares your current role is also able to operate on the new role.

Destroying roles

The syntax for destroying a role is easy to understand, as follows:

```
DROP ROLE <role name> ;
```

Classifying Users

Aside from the fact that users may be members of a group identified as a role, there are four classes of users. Each of these classes has associated privileges that may supersede the privileges accorded to a user by virtue of his role. The four classes are

» **Database administrator (DBA):** Every database has at least one DBA and possibly multiple DBAs. It's the responsibility of the DBA to maintain the database, making sure that it's protected from harm and operating at peak efficiency. DBAs have full rights to all the objects in the database. They can create, modify, or destroy any object in the database, including tables and indexes. They can also decide what privileges other users may have.

» **Database object owners:** Users who create database objects such as tables and views are automatically the owners of those objects. A database object owner possesses all privileges related to that object. A database object owner's privileges are equal to those of a DBA, but only with respect to the object in question.

» **Grantees:** *Grantees* are users who have been granted selected privileges by a DBA or database object owner. A grantee may or may not be given the right to grant her privileges to others, who thus also become grantees.

» **The public:** All users are considered to be part of the public, regardless of whether they have been specifically granted any privileges. Thus, privileges granted to PUBLIC may be exercised by any user.

Granting Privileges

The GRANT statement is the tool you use to grant privileges to users. A fairly large number of privileges may be granted, and they may apply to a fairly large number of objects. As a result, the syntax of the GRANT statement is lengthy. Don't let the length intimidate you! The syntax is very logical and fairly simple when you become familiar with it. Here's the syntax:

```
GRANT <privilege list>
  ON <privilege object>
  TO <user list> [WITH GRANT OPTION]
  [GRANTED BY {CURRENT_USER | CURRENT_ROLE}] ;
```

```
<privilege list> ::= privilege [ , privilege]...

<privilege> ::=
    SELECT [(<column name> [ , <column name>]...)]
  | SELECT (<method designator> [ , <method designator]...)
  | DELETE
  | INSERT [(<column name> [ , <column name>]...)]
  | UPDATE [(<column name> [ , <column name>]...)]
  | REFERENCES [(<column name> [ , <column name>]...)]
  | USAGE
  | TRIGGER
  | UNDER
  | EXECUTE

<privilege object> ::=
    [TABLE] <table name>
  | <view name>
  | DOMAIN <domain name>
  | CHARACTER SET <character set name>
  | COLLATION <collation name>
  | TRANSLATION <translation name>
  | TYPE <user-defined type name>
  | <specific routine designator>

<user list> ::=
    authorizationID [ , authorizationID]...
  | PUBLIC
```

Whew! That's a lot of syntax. Look at it piece by piece so that it's a little more comprehensible.

Not all privileges apply to all privilege objects. The SELECT, DELETE, INSERT, UPDATE, and REFERENCES privileges apply to the table privilege object. The SELECT privilege also applies to views. The USAGE privilege applies to the DOMAIN, CHARACTER SET, COLLATION, and TRANSLATION objects. The TRIGGER privilege applies, logically enough, to triggers. The UNDER privilege applies to user-defined types, and the EXECUTE privilege applies to specific routines.

Looking at data

The first privilege in the privilege list is the privilege of looking at a database object. The SELECT statement retrieves data from database tables and views.

To enable a user to execute the SELECT statement, issue a GRANT SELECT statement, like this example:

```
GRANT SELECT
  ON CUSTOMER
  TO SALES_MANAGER ;
```

This statement enables the sales manager to query the CUSTOMER table.

Deleting data

In a similar fashion, the GRANT DELETE statement enables a user to delete specified rows from a table, as follows:

```
GRANT DELETE
  ON CUSTOMER
  TO SALES_MANAGER ;
```

This statement enables the sales manager to prune inactive customers from the customer table.

Adding data

With the INSERT statement, you can add a new row of data to a table. The GRANT INSERT statement determines who has the right to perform this operation, as follows:

```
GRANT INSERT
  ON CUSTOMER
  TO SALES_MANAGER ;
```

Now the sales manager can add a new customer record to the CUSTOMER table.

Changing data

You can change the contents of a table row with the UPDATE statement. GRANT UPDATE determines who can do it, as in this example:

```
GRANT UPDATE
  ON RETAIL_PRICE_LIST
  TO SALES_MANAGER ;
```

Now the sales manager can update the retail price list with new pricing information.

Referencing data in another table

You may think that if you can control who does the seeing, creating, modifying, and deleting functions on a table, you're well protected. Against most threats, you are. A knowledgeable hacker, however, can still break in by using an indirect method.

A correctly designed relational database has *referential integrity,* which means that the data in one table in the database is consistent with the data in all the other tables. To ensure referential integrity, database designers apply constraints to tables that restrict what someone can enter into the tables. If you have a database with referential-integrity constraints, a user can possibly create a new table that uses a column in your confidential table as a foreign key. Then that column serves as a link through which someone could steal confidential information.

Suppose that you're a famous Wall Street stock analyst. Many people believe in the accuracy of your stock picks, so whenever you recommend a stock to your subscribers, many people buy that stock, and its price goes up. You keep your analysis in a database that contains a table named FOUR_STAR. Your top recommendations for your next newsletter are in that table. Naturally, you restrict access to FOUR_STAR so that word doesn't leak out to the investing public before your paying subscribers receive the newsletter.

You're still vulnerable, however, if anyone other than you can create a new table that uses the stock-name field of FOUR_STAR as a foreign key, as shown in the following command example:

```
CREATE TABLE HOT_STOCKS (
    Stock CHARACTER (4) REFERENCES FOUR_STAR
    );
```

The hacker can try to insert the symbol for every stock on the New York Stock Exchange, American Stock Exchange, and NASDAQ into the table. Those inserts that succeed tell the hacker which stocks match the stocks that you name in your confidential table. It doesn't take long for the hacker to extract your entire list of stocks.

You can protect yourself from hacks such as the one in the preceding example by being very careful about entering statements similar to the following:

```
GRANT REFERENCES (Stock)
```

```
ON FOUR_STAR
  TO SECRET_HACKER;
```

Your hacker will not have a user identifier of SECRET_HACKER, of course. More likely, it'll be something like JOHN_SMITH. Beneath that innocent exterior, however, lies a profiteer or agent of a competitor.

TIP

Avoid granting privileges to people who may abuse them. True, people don't come with guarantees printed on their foreheads, but if you wouldn't lend your new car to a person, you probably shouldn't grant him the REFERENCES privilege on an important table, either.

The preceding example offers one good reason for maintaining careful control of the REFERENCES privilege. Here are two other reasons for carefully controlling REFERENCES, even if the other person is totally innocent:

» If the other person specifies a constraint in HOT STOCKS by using a RESTRICT option, and you try to delete a row from your table, the database management system (DBMS) tells you that you can't because doing so violates a referential constraint.

» If you want to use the DROP command to destroy your table, you find that you must get the other person to first drop his constraint (or his table).

REMEMBER

The bottom line is that enabling another person to specify integrity constraints on your table not only introduces a potential security breach, but also means that the other person may prevent you from doing your normal database administrator job.

Using certain database facilities

The USAGE privilege applies to domains and user-defined types (UDTs). I've talked about domains before; UDTs are exactly what the name implies, data types that users have defined. I'll describe them in a minute. To use or even see a domain or UDT, a user must have the USAGE privilege for that domain or UDT. Suppose that Major League Baseball has a domain named MLBTEAMS that consists of the names of all the Major League Baseball teams. A user holding the role of team owner could be granted use of that domain, as follows:

```
GRANT USAGE
  ON MLBTEAMS
  TO TEAM_OWNER ;
```

Responding to an event

You can grant a user or a role the privilege of creating a trigger that fires when a specified change takes place to a table, such as the renaming of a Major League Baseball team, as in this example:

```
GRANT TRIGGER
   ON MLBTEAMS
   TO TEAM_OWNER ;
```

Defining new data types

One advanced feature that was added to SQL in the SQL:1999 version enables users to create structured user-defined types. Naturally, the creator of a UDT has all privileges attached to that UDT. Among those privileges is the USAGE privilege, which allows the type to be used to define columns, routines, and other schema objects. Also included is the UNDER privilege, which permits subtypes of the type to be defined, as follows:

```
GRANT UNDER
   ON MLBTEAMS
   TO LEAGUE_VICE_PRESIDENT ;
```

Executing an SQL statement

The EXECUTE privilege enables the grantee to use SQL-invoked routines. By restricting the ability to invoke routines, you keep those routines in the hands of those who are authorized to run them, as in this example:

```
GRANT EXECUTE
   ON PRICECHANGE
   TO SALES_MANAGER ;
```

Doing it all

For a highly trusted person who has just been given major responsibility, instead of issuing a whole series of GRANT statements, you can take care of everything with just one statement, GRANT ALL. Here's an example:

```
GRANT ALL PRIVILEGES
   ON MLBTEAMS
   TO LEAGUE_VICE_PRESIDENT ;
```

`GRANT ALL PRIVILEGES` is a pretty dangerous statement, however. In the wrong hands, it could cause a lot of damage. For this reason, SQL Server 2005 deprecated this syntax. Although it's still supported in SQL Server 2008 R2, in SQL Server 2017 you get a message that it is deprecated when you try to use it.

Passing on the power

To keep your system secure, you must severely restrict the access privileges you grant and the people to whom you grant these privileges. People who can't do their work because they lack access, however, are likely to hassle you. To preserve your sanity, you probably need to delegate some of the responsibility for maintaining database security.

SQL provides for such delegation through the `WITH GRANT OPTION` clause. Consider the following example:

```
GRANT UPDATE
  ON RETAIL_PRICE_LIST
  TO SALES_MANAGER WITH GRANT OPTION ;
```

This statement is similar to the `GRANT UPDATE` example (refer to "Changing data," earlier in this chapter) in that the statement enables the sales manager to update the retail price list. The statement also gives her the right to grant the update privilege to anyone she wants. If you use this form of the `GRANT` statement, you must not only trust the grantee to use the privilege wisely, but also trust her to choose wisely in granting the privilege to others.

Revoking Privileges

If it's possible to grant database privileges to users and roles, it had better be possible to revoke those privileges, too. Things change. People's jobs change, and their need for data changes. Sometimes, people leave the company and go to work for a competitor. You certainly want to revoke privileges in a case like that.

The syntax for revoking privileges is similar to the `GRANT` syntax, as follows:

```
REVOKE [GRANT OPTION FOR] <privilege list>
  ON <privilege object>
  FROM <user list>
  [GRANTED BY {CURRENT_USER | CURRENT_ROLE}]
  {RESTRICT | CASCADE} ;
```

The privilege list, privilege object, and user list are the same as they are for GRANT. The major difference from the GRANT syntax is the addition of the RESTRICT and CASCADE keywords. Note that {RESTRICT | CASCADE} isn't enclosed in square brackets, meaning that it isn't optional. One of the two keywords is required in any REVOKE statement.

REMEMBER

In SQL Server's T-SQL, the CASCADE keyword *is* optional, and the RESTRICT sense is assumed if CASCADE is not present.

If a REVOKE statement includes the RESTRICT keyword, the DBMS checks to see whether the privilege being revoked was passed on to one or more other users. If it was, the privilege isn't revoked, and you receive an error message instead. If a REVOKE statement includes the CASCADE keyword, the DBMS revokes the privilege, as well as any dependent instances of this privilege that were granted by the instance you're revoking.

With the optional GRANT OPTION FOR clause, you can revoke a user's ability to grant a privilege without revoking his ability to use the privilege himself. If you specify GRANT OPTION FOR along with CASCADE, not only is the grant option taken away, but also, everyone who obtained the privilege through that grant loses the privilege. If you specify GRANT OPTION FOR along with RESTRICT, and anyone was granted the privilege under consideration, you get an error message, and the grant option isn't revoked.

If the optional GRANTED BY clause is present, only those privileges granted by the current user or current role (whichever is specified) are revoked.

If none of the privileges you're trying to revoke exists, you get an error message, and nothing changes. If some of the privileges you're trying to revoke exist, but others don't, you get a warning.

REMEMBER

Revoking a user's privileges may not remove those privileges from the user. If you granted the SELECT privilege to Alice WITH GRANT OPTION, and Alice granted the privilege to Bob, Bob has the SELECT privilege. If you later grant the SELECT privilege to Bob, now he has that privilege from two sources. If you revoke the SELECT privilege from Bob, he still has SELECT access to the table in question because of the GRANT SELECT he received from Alice. This situation complicates revocation. If you want to truly be sure that a person no longer has access to a resource, you must make sure that all grants have been revoked.

Granting Roles

Just as you can grant a privilege to a user, you can grant a role to a user. Granting a role is a more significant action: When you grant a role to a person, you're granting all the privileges that go along with that role in one action. Here's the syntax:

```
GRANT <role name> [{ , <role name>}...]
   TO <user list>
   [WITH ADMIN OPTION]
   [GRANTED BY {CURRENT_USER | CURRENT_ROLE}] ;
```

As you can see from the syntax, you can grant any number of roles to the names in a list of users with a single GRANT statement. The optional WITH ADMIN OPTION clause is similar to the WITH GRANT OPTION clause that may be a part of a grant of privileges. If you want to grant a role and extend to the grantee the right to grant the same role to others, you do so with the WITH ADMIN OPTION clause. The optional GRANTED BY clause specifies whether you want to record that this GRANT was granted by the current user or by the current role. This distinction may become meaningful when the time comes to revoke the role granted here.

Revoking Roles

The command for revoking a role is very similar to the command for revoking a privilege. Here's what it looks like:

```
REVOKE [ADMIN OPTION FOR] <role name> [{ , <role name>}...]
   FROM <user list>
   [GRANTED BY {CURRENT_USER | CURRENT_ROLE}]
   {RESTRICT | CASCADE}
```

Here, you revoke one or more roles from the users in the user list. You can revoke the admin option from a role without revoking the role itself.

The GRANTED BY clause requires a little explanation. If a role was specified as being granted by the current user, revoking it with a GRANTED BY CURRENT_USER clause works, but revoking it with GRANTED BY CURRENT_ROLE clause doesn't. The RESTRICT or CASCADE keywords apply only if the admin option has been used to grant the specified role to other users or roles. If RESTRICT is specified, and this role or list of roles has been granted to a subgrantee, an error message is returned, and the revocation doesn't take effect. If CASCADE is specified, and this role or list of roles has been granted to a subgrantee, the role and all the subgrantee roles are revoked.

Chapter **4**

Error Handling

Wouldn't it be great if every application you wrote worked perfectly every time? Yeah, and it would also be really cool to win $210 million in the Powerball lottery. Unfortunately, both possibilities are equally unlikely to happen. Error conditions of one sort or another are inevitable, so it's helpful to know what causes them.

SQL's mechanism for returning error information to you is the *status parameter* (or *host variable*) SQLSTATE. Based on the contents of SQLSTATE, you can take different actions to remedy the error condition. The WHENEVER directive, for example, enables you to take a predetermined action whenever a specified condition is met — if SQLSTATE has a nonzero value, to take one example. You can also find detailed status information about the SQL statement that you just executed in the diagnostics area.

In this chapter, I explain these helpful error-handling facilities and how to use them. First, however, I show you the conditions that may cause those error-handling facilities to be invoked.

Identifying Error Conditions

When people say that a person has a *condition*, they usually mean that something is wrong with that person; he's sick or injured. People usually don't bother to mention that a person is in *good* condition; rather, we talk about people who are in serious condition or, even worse, in critical condition. This idea is similar to the way that programmers talk about the condition of an SQL statement. The execution of an SQL statement can lead to a successful result, to a questionable result, or to an outright erroneous result. Each of these possible results corresponds to a condition.

Getting to Know SQLSTATE

Every time an SQL statement executes, the database server places a value in the status parameter SQLSTATE. SQLSTATE is a five-character field, accepting the 26 uppercase letters and the numerals 0 through 9. The value placed in SQLSTATE indicates whether the preceding SQL statement executed successfully. If it didn't execute successfully, the value of SQLSTATE provides some information about the error.

The first two of the five characters of SQLSTATE (the class value) give you the major news about whether the preceding SQL statement executed successfully, returned a result that may or may not have been successful, or produced an error. Table 4-1 shows the four possible results.

TABLE 4-1 SQLSTATE Class Values

Class	Description
00	Successful completion
01	Warning
02	Not found
Other	Exception

The following list further explains the class values:

» **00**: Indicates that the preceding SQL statement executed successfully. This is a very welcome result — most of the time.

» **01**: Indicates a warning, meaning that something unusual happened during the execution of the SQL statement. This occurrence may or may not be an error; the database management system (DBMS) can't tell. The warning is a heads-up to the developer, suggesting that perhaps she should check the preceding SQL statement carefully to ensure that it's operating correctly.

» **02**: Indicates that no data was returned as a result of the execution of the preceding SQL statement. This result may or may not be good news, depending on what the developer was trying to do with the statement. Sometimes an empty result set is exactly what the developer wanted the SQL statement to return.

» **Any class code other than 00, 01, or 02**: Indicates an error condition. An indication of the nature of the error appears in the three characters that hold the subclass value. The two characters of the class code, plus the three characters of the subclass code, together comprise the five characters of SQLSTATE.

The SQL standard defines any class code that starts with the letters *A* through *H* or the numerals 0 through 4; therefore, these class codes mean the same thing in any implementation. Class codes that start with the letters *I* through *Z* or the numerals 5 through 9 are left open for *implementers* (the people who build DBMSs) to define because the SQL specification can't anticipate every condition that may occur in every implementation. Implementers should use these nonstandard class codes as little as possible, however, to prevent migration problems from one DBMS to another. Ideally, implementers should use the standard codes most of the time and the nonstandard codes only under the most unusual circumstances.

Because SQLSTATE updates after every SQL operation, you can check it after every statement executes. If SQLSTATE contains 00000 (successful completion), you can proceed with the next operation. If it contains anything else, you may want to branch out of the main line of your code to handle the situation. The specific class code and subclass code that an SQLSTATE contains determines which of several possible actions you should take.

To use SQLSTATE in a module language program, in which SQL statements are called from a module by a host program written in a procedural language such as C, include a reference to it in your procedure definitions, as in the following example:

```
PROCEDURE POWERPLANT
    (SQLSTATE, :enginename CHAR (20), :displacement SMALLINT,
        :hp INTEGER, :cylinders INTEGER, :valves INTEGER
INSERT INTO ENGINES
    (EngineName, Displacement, Horsepower, Cylinders, Valves)
    VALUES
    (:enginename, :displacement, :hp, :cylinders, :valves) ;
```

At the appropriate spot in your procedural language program, you can make values available for the parameters (perhaps by soliciting them from the user) and then call up the procedure. The syntax of this operation varies from one language to another but looks something like this:

```
enginename = "289HP" ;
displacement = 289 ;
hp = 271 ;
cylinders = 8 ;
valves = 16 ;
POWERPLANT(state, enginename, displacement, hp, cylinders, valves);
```

The state of SQLSTATE is returned in the variable state. Your program can examine this variable and then take the appropriate action based on the variable's contents.

Handling Conditions

You can have your program look at SQLSTATE after the execution of every SQL statement. The question then is what to do with the knowledge that you gain. Depending on the contents of SQLSTATE, you may want your program to branch to a procedure that handles the existing situation. Examples here would be along the lines of the following:

>> **If you find a class code of 00, you probably don't want to do anything.** You want execution to proceed as you originally planned.

>> **If you find a class code of 01 or 02, you may or may not want to take special action.** If you expected a "warning" or "not found" indication, you probably want to let execution proceed normally. If you didn't expect either of these class codes, you probably want to have execution branch to a

procedure specifically designed to handle the unexpected, but not totally unanticipated, warning or not-found result.

>> **If you receive any other class code, something is wrong.** You should branch to an exception-handling procedure. The specific procedure that you choose to branch to depends on the contents of the three subclass characters, as well as the two class characters of SQLSTATE. If multiple different exceptions are possible, there should be an exception-handling procedure for each one because different exceptions often require different responses. Some errors may be correctable, or you may find a workaround. Other errors may be fatal, calling for termination of the application.

Handler declarations

You can put a condition handler within a compound statement. To create a condition handler, you must first declare the condition that it will handle. The condition declared can be some sort of exception, or it can just be something that is true. Table 4-2 lists the possible conditions and includes a brief description of what causes each type of condition.

TABLE 4-2

Conditions That May Be Specified in a Condition Handler

Condition	Description
SQLSTATE VALUE 'xxyyy'	Specific SQLSTATE value
SQLEXCEPTION	SQLSTATE class other than 00, 01, or 02
SQLWARNING	SQLSTATE class 01
NOT FOUND	SQLSTATE class 02

Following is an example of a condition declaration:

```
DECLARE constraint_violation CONDITION
        FOR SQLSTATE VALUE '23000' ;
```

Handler actions and handler effects

If a condition occurs that invokes a handler, the action specified by the handler executes. This action is an SQL statement, which can be a compound statement.

If the handler action completes successfully, the handler effect executes. Following is a list of the three possible handler effects:

>> CONTINUE: Continues execution immediately after the statement that caused the handler to be invoked.

>> EXIT: Continues execution after the compound statement that contains the handler.

>> UNDO: Undoes the work of the preceding statements in the compound statement and continues execution after the statement that contains the handler.

If the handler was able to correct whatever problem invoked the handler, the CONTINUE effect may be appropriate. The EXIT effect may be appropriate if the handler didn't fix the problem but the changes made to the compound statement don't need to be undone. The UNDO effect is appropriate if you want to return the database to the state it was in before the compound statement started execution. Consider the following example:

```
BEGIN ATOMIC
    DECLARE constraint_violation CONDITION
        FOR SQLSTATE VALUE '23000' ;
    DECLARE UNDO HANDLER
        FOR constraint_violation
        RESIGNAL ;
    INSERT INTO students (StudentID, Fname, Lname)
        VALUES (:sid, :sfname, :slname) ;
    INSERT INTO roster (ClassID, Class, StudentID)
        VALUES (:cid, :cname, :sid) ;
END ;
```

If either of the INSERT statements causes a constraint violation, such as adding a record with a primary key that duplicates an existing primary key in the table, SQLSTATE assumes a value of 23000, thus setting the constraint_violation condition to a TRUE value. This action causes the handler to undo any changes that have been made to any tables by either INSERT command. The RESIGNAL statement transfers control back to the procedure that called the currently executing procedure.

If both INSERT statements execute successfully, execution continues with the statement following the END keyword.

REMEMBER

The ATOMIC keyword is mandatory whenever a handler's effect is UNDO. This is not the case for handlers whose effect is either CONTINUE or EXIT. An ATOMIC transaction treats everything in the transaction as a unit. If the handler effect is UNDO, you want to undo the entire transaction. In the cases of CONTINUE and EXIT, this doesn't matter.

Conditions that aren't handled

In the preceding example, consider this possibility: What if an exception occurred that returned an SQLSTATE value other than 23000? Something is definitely wrong, but the exception handler that you coded can't handle it. What happens now? Because the current procedure doesn't know what to do, a RESIGNAL occurs, bumping the problem up to the next-higher level of control. If the problem isn't handled at that level, it continues to be elevated to higher levels until it is handled or causes an error condition in the main application.

TIP

The idea that I want to emphasize here is that if you write an SQL statement that may cause exceptions, you should write exception handlers for all such possible exceptions. If you don't, you'll have more difficulty isolating the source of the problem when it inevitably occurs.

Dealing with Execution Exceptions: The WHENEVER Clause

What's the point of knowing that an SQL operation didn't execute successfully if you can't do anything about it? If an error occurs, you don't want your application to continue executing as though everything is fine. You need to be able to acknowledge the error and do something to correct it. If you can't correct the error, at the very least you want to inform the user of the problem and bring the application to a graceful termination.

The WHENEVER directive is the SQL mechanism for dealing with execution exceptions. WHENEVER is actually a declaration and, therefore, is located in your application's SQL declaration section, before the executable SQL code. The syntax is as follows:

```
WHENEVER <condition> <action> ;
```

The condition may be either SQLERROR or NOT FOUND. The action may be either CONTINUE or GOTO address. SQLERROR is TRUE if SQLSTATE has a class code other than 00, 01, or 02. NOT FOUND is TRUE if SQLSTATE is 02000.

If the action is CONTINUE, nothing special happens, and the execution continues normally. If the action is GOTO address (or GO TO address), execution branches to the designated address in the program. At the branch address, you can put a conditional statement that examines SQLSTATE and takes different actions based on what it finds. Here are two examples of this scenario:

```
WHENEVER SQLERROR GO TO error_trap ;
```

or

```
WHENEVER NOT FOUND CONTINUE ;
```

The GO TO option is simply a macro. The implementation (that is, the embedded language precompiler) inserts the following test after every EXEC SQL statement:

```
IF SQLSTATE <> '00000'
   AND SQLSTATE <> '00001'
   AND SQLSTATE <> '00002'
THEN GOTO error_trap;
```

The CONTINUE option is essentially a NO-OP that says "ignore this."

Getting More Information: The Diagnostics Area

Although SQLSTATE can give you some information about why a particular statement failed, the information is pretty brief, so SQL provides for the capture and retention of additional status information in diagnostics areas. Multiple diagnostics areas are maintained in the form of a last-in-first-out (LIFO) stack. Information on the most recent error appears at the top of the stack. The additional status information in a diagnostics area can be particularly helpful in cases in which the execution of a single SQL statement generates multiple warnings followed by an error. SQLSTATE reports the occurrence of only one error, but the diagnostics area has the capacity to report on multiple errors — ideally, all errors.

The diagnostics area is a DBMS-managed data structure that has two components:

>> **Header:** The header contains general information about the last SQL statement executed.

>> **Detail area:** The detail area contains information about each code (error, warning, or success) that the statement generated.

The diagnostics header area

In the SET TRANSACTION statement (described in Book 4, Chapter 2), you can specify DIAGNOSTICS SIZE. The SIZE that you specify is the number of detail areas allocated for status information. If you don't include a DIAGNOSTICS SIZE clause in your SET TRANSACTION statement, your DBMS assigns its default number of detail areas, whatever that happens to be.

The header area contains ten items, as listed in Table 4-3.

TABLE 4-3

Diagnostics Header Area

Fields	Data Type
NUMBER	Exact numeric with no fractional part
ROW_COUNT	Exact numeric with no fractional part
COMMAND_FUNCTION	VARCHAR (>=128)
COMMAND_FUNCTION_CODE	Exact numeric with no fractional part
DYNAMIC_FUNCTION	VARCHAR (>=128)
DYNAMIC_FUNCTION_CODE	Exact numeric with no fractional part
MORE	Exact numeric with no fractional part
TRANSACTIONS_COMMITTED	Exact numeric with no fractional part
TRANSACTIONS_ROLLED_BACK	Exact numeric with no fractional part
TRANSACTION_ACTIVE	Exact numeric with no fractional part

The following list describes these items in more detail:

>> The NUMBER field is the number of detail areas that have been filled with diagnostic information about the current exception.

- >> The ROW_COUNT field holds the number of rows affected if the preceding SQL statement was an INSERT, UPDATE, or DELETE statement.

- >> The COMMAND_FUNCTION field describes the SQL statement that was just executed.

- >> The COMMAND_FUNCTION_CODE field gives the code number for the SQL statement that was just executed. Every command function has an associated numeric code.

- >> The DYNAMIC_FUNCTION field contains the dynamic SQL statement.

- >> The DYNAMIC_FUNCTION_CODE field contains a numeric code corresponding to the dynamic SQL statement.

- >> The MORE field may be either Y or N. Y indicates that there are more status records than the detail area can hold. N indicates that all the status records generated are present in the detail area. Depending on your implementation, you may be able to expand the number of records you can handle by using the SET TRANSACTION statement.

- >> The TRANSACTIONS_COMMITTED field holds the number of transactions that have been committed.

- >> The TRANSACTIONS_ROLLED_BACK field holds the number of transactions that have been rolled back.

- >> The TRANSACTION_ACTIVE field holds 1 if a transaction is currently active and 0 otherwise. A transaction is deemed to be active if a cursor is open or if the DBMS is waiting for a deferred parameter.

The diagnostics detail area

The detail areas contain data on each individual error, warning, or success condition. Each detail area contains 28 items, as Table 4-4 shows.

I give brief descriptions of some of the entries in Table 4-4 next, and more detailed coverage of other entries in later sections of this chapter.

CONDITION_NUMBER holds the sequence number of the detail area. If a statement generates five status items that fill five detail areas, the CONDITION_NUMBER for the fifth detail area is 5. To retrieve a specific detail area for examination, use a GET DIAGNOSTICS statement (described in "Interpreting SQLSTATE Information," later in this chapter) with the desired CONDITION_NUMBER. RETURNED_SQLSTATE holds the SQLSTATE value that caused this detail area to be filled.

TABLE 4-4

Diagnostics Detail Area

Fields	Data Type
CONDITION_NUMBER	Exact numeric with no fractional part
RETURNED_SQLSTATE	CHAR (6)
MESSAGE_TEXT	VARCHAR (>=128)
MESSAGE_LENGTH	Exact numeric with no fractional part
MESSAGE_OCTET_LENGTH	Exact numeric with no fractional part
CLASS_ORIGIN	VARCHAR (>=128)
SUBCLASS_ORIGIN	VARCHAR (>=128)
CONNECTION_NAME	VARCHAR (>=128)
SERVER_NAME	VARCHAR (>=128)
CONSTRAINT_CATALOG	VARCHAR (>=128)
CONSTRAINT_SCHEMA	VARCHAR (>=128)
CONSTRAINT_NAME	VARCHAR (>=128)
CATALOG_NAME	VARCHAR (>=128)
SCHEMA_NAME	VARCHAR (>=128)
TABLE_NAME	VARCHAR (>=128)
COLUMN_NAME	VARCHAR (>=128)
CURSOR_NAME	VARCHAR (>=128)
CONDITION_IDENTIFIER	VARCHAR (>=128)
PARAMETER_NAME	VARCHAR (>=128)
PARAMETER_ORDINAL_POSITION	Exact numeric with no fractional part
PARAMETER_MODE	Exact numeric with no fractional part
ROUTINE_CATALOG	VARCHAR (>=128)
ROUTINE_SCHEMA	VARCHAR (>=128)
ROUTINE_NAME	VARCHAR (>=128)
SPECIFIC_NAME	VARCHAR (>=128)
TRIGGER_CATALOG	VARCHAR (>=128)
TRIGGER_SCHEMA	VARCHAR (>=128)
TRIGGER_NAME	VARCHAR (>=128)

Error Handling

CLASS_ORIGIN tells you the source of the class code value returned in SQLSTATE. If the SQL standard defines the value, the CLASS_ORIGIN is ISO 9075. If your DBMS implementation defines the value, CLASS_ORIGIN holds a string identifying the source of your DBMS. SUBCLASS_ORIGIN tells you the source of the subclass code value returned in SQLSTATE.

CLASS_ORIGIN is important. If you get an SQLSTATE of 22012, for example, the values indicate that it's in the range of standard SQLSTATEs, so you know that it means the same thing in all SQL implementations. If the SQLSTATE is 22500, however, the first two characters are in the standard range and indicate a data exception, but the last three characters are in the implementation-defined range. Finally, if SQLSTATE is 90001, it's completely in the implementation-defined range. SQLSTATE values in the implementation-defined range can mean different things in different implementations, even though the code itself may be the same.

So how do you find out the detailed meaning of 22500 or the meaning of 90001? You must look in the implementer's documentation. Which implementer? If you're using CONNECT to connect to data sources, you could be connecting to several products at once. To determine which one produced the error condition, look at CLASS_ORIGIN and SUBCLASS_ORIGIN: They have values that identify each implementation. You can test CLASS_ORIGIN and SUBCLASS_ORIGIN to see whether they identify implementers for which you have the SQLSTATE listings. The actual values placed in CLASS_ORIGIN and SUBCLASS_ORIGIN are implementer-defined, but they also are expected to be self-explanatory company names.

If the error reported is a constraint violation, the CONSTRAINT_CATALOG, CONSTRAINT_SCHEMA, and CONSTRAINT_NAME fields identify the constraint being violated.

Examining an Example Constraint Violation

The constraint violation information is probably the most important information that GET DIAGNOSTICS provides. I discuss GET DIAGNOSTICS in "Interpreting SQLSTATE Information," later in this chapter.

Consider the following EMPLOYEE table:

```
CREATE TABLE EMPLOYEE (
    ID      CHAR(5)   CONSTRAINT EmpPK PRIMARY KEY,
    Salary  DEC(8,2)  CONSTRAINT EmpSal CHECK Salary > 0,
```

```
   Dept   CHAR(5)  CONSTRAINT EmpDept,
   REFERENCES DEPARTMENT) ;
```

Now consider this DEPARTMENT table:

```
CREATE TABLE DEPARTMENT (
  DeptNo CHAR(5),
  Budget DEC(12,2) CONSTRAINT DeptBudget
  CHECK(Budget >= SELECT SUM(Salary) FROM EMPLOYEE,
        WHERE EMPLOYEE.Dept=DEPARTMENT.DeptNo),
  ...);
```

Consider an INSERT as follows:

```
INSERT INTO EMPLOYEE VALUES(:ID_VAR, :SAL_VAR, :DEPT_VAR);
```

Suppose that you get an SQLSTATE of 23000. You look it up in your SQL documentation, and it says "integrity constraint violation." Now what? That SQLSTATE value means that one of the following situations is true:

>> **The value in** ID_VAR **is a duplicate of an existing ID value:** You have violated the PRIMARY KEY constraint.

>> **The value in** SAL_VAR **is negative:** You have violated the CHECK constraint on Salary.

>> **The value in** DEPT_VAR **isn't a valid key value for any existing row of** DEPARTMENT: You have violated the REFERENCES constraint on Dept.

>> **The value in** SAL_VAR **is large enough that the sum of the employees' salaries in this department exceeds the budget:** You have violated the CHECK constraint in the Budget column of DEPARTMENT. (Recall that if you change the database, all constraints that may be affected are checked, not just those defined in the immediate table.)

Under normal circumstances, you would need to do a great deal of testing to figure out what's wrong with that INSERT, but you can find out what you need to know by using GET DIAGNOSTICS as follows:

```
DECLARE ConstNameVar CHAR(18) ;
GET DIAGNOSTICS EXCEPTION 1
   ConstNameVar = CONSTRAINT_NAME ;
```

Assuming that SQLSTATE is 23000, this GET DIAGNOSTICS sets ConstNameVar to EmpPK, EmpSal, EmpDept, or DeptBudget. Notice that in practice, you may also want to obtain the CONSTRAINT_SCHEMA and CONSTRAINT_CATALOG to uniquely identify the constraint given by CONSTRAINT_NAME.

Adding Constraints to an Existing Table

This use of GET DIAGNOSTICS — determining which of several constraints has been violated — is particularly important when ALTER TABLE is used to add constraints that didn't exist when you wrote the program, as in this example:

```
ALTER TABLE EMPLOYEE
    ADD CONSTRAINT SalLimit CHECK(Salary < 200000) ;
```

Now if you insert data into EMPLOYEE or update the Salary column of EMPLOYEE, you get an SQLSTATE of 23000 if Salary exceeds 200000. You can program your INSERT statement so that if you get an SQLSTATE of 23000 and don't recognize the particular constraint name that GET DIAGNOSTICS returns, you can display a helpful message, such as Invalid INSERT: Violated constraint SalLimit.

Interpreting SQLSTATE Information

CONNECTION_NAME and ENVIRONMENT_NAME identify the connection and environment to which you are connected at the time the SQL statement is executed.

If the report deals with a table operation, CATALOG_NAME, SCHEMA_NAME, and TABLE_NAME identify the table. COLUMN_NAME identifies the column within the table that caused the report to be made. If the situation involves a cursor, CURSOR_NAME gives its name.

Sometimes, a DBMS produces a string of natural-language text to explain a condition. The MESSAGE_TEXT item is for this kind of information. The contents of this item depend on the implementation; the SQL standard doesn't define them explicitly. If you do have something in MESSAGE_TEXT, its length in characters is recorded in MESSAGE_LENGTH, and its length (in octets) is recorded in MESSAGE_OCTET_LENGTH. If the message is in normal ASCII characters, MESSAGE_LENGTH equals MESSAGE_OCTET_LENGTH. If, on the other hand, the message is in Kanji or some other language whose characters require more than an octet to express, MESSAGE_LENGTH differs from MESSAGE_OCTET_LENGTH.

To retrieve diagnostic information from a diagnostics area header, use the following:

```
GET DIAGNOSTICS status1 = item1 [, status2 = item2]... ;
```

status*n* is a host variable or parameter; item*n* can be any of the keywords NUMBER, MORE, COMMAND_FUNCTION, DYNAMIC_FUNCTION, or ROW_COUNT.

To retrieve diagnostic information from a diagnostics detail area, the syntax is as follows:

```
GET DIAGNOSTICS EXCEPTION <condition number>
    status1 = item1 [, status2 = item2]... ;
```

Again, status*n* is a host variable or parameter, and item*n* is any of the 28 keywords for the detail items listed in Table 4-4 (refer to "The diagnostics detail area," earlier in this chapter). The condition number is — surprise! — the detail area's CONDITION_NUMBER item.

Handling Exceptions

When SQLSTATE indicates an exception condition by holding a value other than 00000, 00001, or 00002, you may want to handle the situation by taking one of the following actions:

» Returning control to the parent procedure that called the subprocedure that raised the exception.

» Using a WHENEVER clause to branch to an exception-handling routine or perform some other action.

» Handling the exception on the spot with a compound SQL statement. A *compound* SQL statement consists of one or more simple SQL statements, sandwiched between BEGIN and END keywords.

Following is an example of a compound-statement exception handler:

```
BEGIN
    DECLARE ValueOutOfRange EXCEPTION FOR SQLSTATE '74001' ;
    INSERT INTO ENGINES
        (Displacement)
        VALUES
```

```
      (:displacement) ;
   SIGNAL ValueOutOfRange ;
   MESSAGE 'Process the next displacement value.'
   EXCEPTION
      WHEN ValueOutOfRange THEN
         MESSAGE 'Handling the displacement range error' ;
      WHEN OTHERS THEN
         RESIGNAL ;
END
```

With one or more DECLARE statements, you can give names to specific SQLSTATE values that you suspect may arise. The INSERT statement is the one that may cause an exception to occur. If the value of :displacement exceeds the maximum value for a SMALLINT data item, SQLSTATE is set to 74001. The SIGNAL statement signals an exception condition. It clears the top diagnostics area. It sets the RETURNED_SQLSTATE field of the diagnostics area to the SQLSTATE for the named exception. If no exception has occurred, the series of statements represented by the MESSAGE 'Process the next displacement value' statement is executed. If an exception has occurred, however, that series of statements is skipped, and the EXCEPTION statement is executed.

If the exception was a ValueOutOfRange exception, the series of statements represented by the MESSAGE 'Handling the displacement range error' statement is executed. If any other exception occurred, the RESIGNAL statement is executed. RESIGNAL merely passes control of execution to the calling parent procedure. That procedure may have additional error-handling code to deal with exceptions other than the expected ValueOutOfRange error.

5
Programming with SQL

Contents at a Glance

Chapter **1**

Database Development Environments

A side from organizations that locked themselves into a database environment before about 1985, for most applications, any organization that's using a database system now is probably using a relational database system. Any relational database system that's still around today uses a version of SQL for communication between users and data. Although several specialty database products serve specific niche markets, for general use, a relatively small number of database management system (DBMS) products have significant market share. These products are Access and SQL Server from Microsoft, DB2 from IBM, Oracle and MySQL from Oracle, SQL Anywhere from SAP, and PostgreSQL from PostgreSQL Global Development Group.

In this chapter, I take a brief look at the popular relational DBMS products and how they implement SQL.

Microsoft Access

Microsoft Access, like all relational DBMS products today, uses SQL for communication between the user and the database, but it does a really good job of hiding that fact. Access comes with a procedural language called Visual Basic for

Applications (VBA). The normal way of writing a data-driven application is to write it in VBA and use a library of classes for dealing with the data. The tools for doing that have undergone a massive upheaval in recent years. The back-end database engine part of Access, called the Jet engine, has undergone changes and expanded in flexibility. In addition, the recommended method of talking to the Jet engine has gone through one change after another.

Over the years, Access has evolved and expanded in its capabilities. As part of the evolution, the way of connecting to the database itself has changed several times. The following sections give brief descriptions of those different ways.

The Jet engine

The Jet engine originated in 1992 as the back end of Access 1.0. Initially, it didn't support data access via SQL, but a later version implemented a subset of SQL-92 functionality. In the early days, connecting to native Access .mdb files was done exclusively with Data Access Objects (DAO). Indexed Sequential Access Method (ISAM) drivers enabled connecting to xBase, Paradox, FoxPro, and Btrieve databases. Later, Open Database Connectivity (ODBC) made it possible to connect to SQL Server databases, Oracle databases, and any other ODBC-compliant database.

The Jet engine has evolved over the years and is no longer included with Access; now, in fact, it's integrated into all Windows operating systems from Windows 2000 onward.

DAO

The DAO interface to the Jet database engine is an object-oriented Dynamic Link Library (DLL) that creates a workspace object, which acts as a container within which all database operations are performed. The DAO DLL, which for years was used with products in addition to Access, has been superseded and deprecated for those other uses. It remains in the playbook for Access, however, including Microsoft Office Access 2016.

ADO

Microsoft introduced ActiveX Data Objects (ADO) in 1996 as a successor to DAO and as yet another alternative to SQL. Developers can create database applications with ADO without any knowledge of SQL. High-level procedural languages such as Visual Basic, VBScript, Embarcadero Delphi, and Embarcadero C++ Builder support the ADO interface.

ODBC

Open Database Connectivity (ODBC) is a procedural application programming interface (API) that connects an SQL query to a database. Developed and released by Microsoft in 1992, ODBC has come to be used in many programming environments to access many databases. Hundreds of ODBC drivers exist. Microsoft's version of ODBC ships with every supported version of Windows. Open-source implementations are widely used by Unix and Unix-derived operating systems.

OLE DB

Object Linking and Embedding Database (OLE DB) is a Microsoft API — designed as a successor to ODBC — for accessing a wide variety of data stores, including but not limited to SQL-compliant relational databases. OLE DB interfaces also work with such diverse data sources as object databases, text files, and spreadsheets.

Files with the .mdb extension

One of the unusual characteristics of Access databases is that they're entirely contained in a single file. All versions of Access (up to and including Access build 2309, which is currently available in Office 365) are capable of storing data, metadata, and everything else in a single file with a .mdb extension.

The Access Database Engine

Back with Access Office 2007, a new database engine (now called the Access Database Engine) was introduced that operates on a new file format, with a .accdb extension, although it continues to support .mdb files. This new format enables new features, chief among which is interoperability with Microsoft Office SharePoint Server. The .accdb format isn't usable by earlier versions of Access, so if you read in a .mdb file but then write it out in .accdb format, it will no longer run on older versions of Access.

Microsoft SQL Server

SQL Server is Microsoft's primary entry in the database arena. Ranging from the entry-level SQL Server Express 2022 to the unlimited-class SQL Server 2022 Enterprise Edition, SQL Server is based on Microsoft's Transact-SQL, which, in contrast to the SQL in Access, is a full-featured robust implementation of the SQL:2016 international standard that also includes numerous proprietary extensions to the standard syntax. Because Microsoft was actively involved with the development of the SQL:2023 standard, you can assume that the next release of SQL Server will incorporate all the SQL:2023 changes. SQL Server runs only under Microsoft operating systems. You can connect to an SQL Server 2022 database via the SQL native client. Transact-SQL is also compatible with ODBC, OLE DB, and ADO.NET.

REMEMBER

ADO.NET is a set of data access application programming interfaces (APIs) that evolved from ADO, but it has changed so much that it is essentially a different product. It is a part of the base class library included with the Microsoft .NET framework.

IBM Db2

Db2 is IBM's full-range relational DBMS. Scaling from a single user to an unlimited-class enterprise DBMS, Db2 also features a robust implementation of SQL. Db2 operates in a variety of environments, including Microsoft Windows, IBM mainframe z/OS, Unix, Linux, and cloud environments. Db2 supports a wide variety of interfaces, including the following:

- » ODBC
- » OLE DB
- » ADO
- » JDBC (Java-based DataBase Connectivity)
- » SQLJ (Java-based embedded SQL)
- » SQL
- » DRDA (X/Open Distributed Database Standard)
- » CLI (X/Open Database Access Standard)
- » EDA/SQL (IBI's EDA SQL Standard)
- » DAL (Apple Relational Database Standard APIs)
- » Net.Data (Internet Database Access)

Oracle 23c

Oracle 23c is the current version of Oracle's full-range DBMS. Oracle Version 2 was the first commercial relational database product when it hit the market in 1979, and Oracle has retained a leading position in the marketplace ever since. Oracle's implementation of SQL, called PL/SQL, is a very complete implementation with a high degree of conformance to the SQL:2016 ANSI/ISO standard, as well as useful proprietary extensions. Oracle 23c supports many of the new features added in the SQL:2023 standard, but at the time of this writing, it's not quite fully compatible. As with Microsoft, Oracle was involved with the development of the SQL:2023 standard, so you can safely assume the next release of the Oracle database will be fully compatible.

Oracle Database 23c supports all standard relational data types and can be connected to in many ways, such as with PL/SQL, JDBC, SQLJ, ODBC.NET, OLE.NET, ODP.NET, XML, XQUERY, and WebDAV. You can write stored procedures in Java or PL/SQL. You can also use .NET CLR support.

SQL Anywhere

SQL Anywhere is a DBMS developed by Sybase, and now marketed by SAP. The product is a powerful, full-featured database product that has been optimized for connecting mobile devices to a central database server. SQL Anywhere is operated via Sybase Transact-SQL.

The sharp-eyed person will notice that Sybase's implementation of SQL has a very similar name to the version of SQL used by Microsoft's SQL Server. This similarity is no accident; Microsoft's SQL Server was based on a Sybase product. After several years of cooperation, the two companies parted ways, and product development diverged.

PostgreSQL

PostgreSQL is a full-featured open source object-relational DBMS. It is used by a diverse array of organizations, ranging from Yahoo! to the International Space Station. The version of SQL used by PostgreSQL, PL/pgSQL, resembles Oracle's PL/SQL. At the time of this writing, the current version of PostgreSQL is version 16, which supports many of the new features defined in the SQL:2023 standard, though sometimes with differing syntax or function.

MySQL

MySQL is an open source DBMS owned by Oracle. The product has grown in capability over the years to the point where it's competitive with the other DBMS products mentioned in this chapter in terms of the SQL functionality that it supports.

MySQL 8.0.2 is a full-featured implementation of SQL and the most widely used open source DBMS in the world. It gained popularity in the web development world mostly due to it being free and fast. It offers ODBC, JDBC, and OLE DB connectivity, as well as APIs for most popular languages, including C, C++, Python, Tcl, Perl, PHP, and Eiffel.

TIP

When Oracle obtained ownership of MySQL, the original developers of MySQL branched off to create a new open-source MySQL clone called MariaDB. MariaDB supports most of the SQL syntax used in MySQL, making it easy for developers to port existing MySQL applications to the MariaDB environment. MariaDB is quickly gaining popularity in the open-source world, especially in Linux server environments.

Chapter **2**

Interfacing SQL to a Procedural Language

Y ou can't build a user-friendly database application with SQL alone. SQL is a data sublanguage and as such lacks many of the facilities required to build a user interface or even execute a sequence of steps. Building a moderately sophisticated application that uses the data in a database requires a procedural language in addition to SQL. Most database management systems (DBMSs) offer compatibility with several procedural languages. Which ones are offered depends on the source of the DBMS and its history, as well as considerations of what capabilities users are most likely to need. In this chapter, I discuss the most common ways of connecting and interfacing to the most popular DBMS products: Access, SQL Server, MySQL, Oracle 23c, and IBM Db2.

Building an Application with SQL and a Procedural Language

Although languages such as C, Java, and Visual Basic don't intrinsically support database operations, you can use those languages to write procedures that perform such operations. To make their products more usable, DBMS vendors offer libraries of such procedures. Some of these procedures perform operations that SQL can't perform; others work with SQL to perform a needed function. As a result, in some environments, you can create quite complex database operations without ever having to resort to SQL. Read on to find out how this issue is addressed by the popular database platforms.

Access and VBA

Visual Basic for Applications (VBA) is a subset of Microsoft's Visual Basic language, specifically designed to be the procedural language to go along with Microsoft Access. Hundreds of libraries are available to the VBA database programmer. Figure 2-1 shows a small subset of these libraries. The figure depicts the References dialog box, which is accessible from the Visual Basic for Applications Tools menu, which in turn is accessible from the Access Database Tools ⇨ Macro menu.

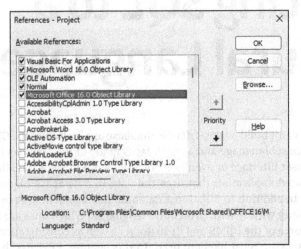

FIGURE 2-1:
Visual Basic for Applications References dialog box enables you to select libraries to include with your program.

Two of the most important libraries for most applications are ADOdb and ADOX. The next sections tell you why they're so important.

The ADOdb library

The ADOdb library is a data abstraction library for PHP and Python modeled after the ADO object model. It has a small memory footprint and contains only basic procedures that just about every application needs. Programs that use this library aren't burdened with having to carry along a bunch of procedures that they never use.

In keeping with the object-oriented nature of the ActiveX Data Objects (ADO) object model, the library contains objects that perform basic functions, including the following:

>> Making connections

>> Issuing commands

>> Retrieving recordsets

>> Navigating a recordset

>> Performing basic maintenance tasks

Clearly, any application that deals with a database has to connect to it before it can do anything else. The ADOdb library gives you that capability with the connection object. In addition, the library contains procedures for retrieving data from a data source, specifying a location in the database, and setting the type of locking that will be in force. The command object works with the SQL Data Manipulation Language (DML) commands to perform SELECT, UPDATE, INSERT, and DELETE operations. (For more information on DML commands, see Book 1, Chapter 5.)

The ADOX library

ADOX is short for *ADO Extensions for DDL and Security*. DDL, of course, is SQL's Data Definition Language, which is that part of SQL used to create and destroy database objects. With the ADOX library, you can create tables, indexes, keys, groups, user identities, and views. You can also delete any of those things.

Other libraries

In addition to the general-purpose libraries with broad applicability, many specialty libraries may be of value to your application. Be sure to check on what's available from your DBMS vendor or independent third parties before you go about reinventing the wheel.

SQL Server and the .NET languages

Microsoft's .NET initiative introduced the idea of managed code as a way of eliminating several of the most common sources of programming bugs, as well as eliminating the chaos and lack of portability that results when each language has its own application programming interface (API) that isn't compatible with any other. All the .NET languages, such as Visual Basic.NET and C#, create code that runs under the control of the Common Language Runtime (CLR). The CLR provides just-in-time compilation, memory management, type safety enforcement, exception handling, thread management, and security.

Regardless of what .NET language you write in, your code is compiled down to Common Intermediate Language (CIL). As a result, all the .NET languages are essentially equivalent, so anything that you can do with any of them, you can do with all of them. If you feel more comfortable writing in Visual Basic.NET, go for it. You can do everything that the people writing in C# or C++.NET can do. When you're programming in the .NET world, you can use the thousands of classes, structs, interfaces, enumerations, and delegates in the .NET Framework class library. Because every language uses the same API, after you learn the .NET Framework as it applies to one language, you've learned it as it applies to any other language.

How does this relate to SQL? Microsoft's implementation of SQL, Transact-SQL, runs on the database server to operate on data stored there. The managed code you write in VB.NET, C#, or any of the other .NET languages can run on either the server or the client. This flexibility is welcome when you want to minimize the computational load on the server. Many of the functions that have tradition-ally been performed by Transact-SQL can be performed by managed code — in many cases, more efficiently. The net result (no pun intended) is a reduction in the overall use of SQL in applications written in a .NET language.

MySQL and C++.NET or C#

Although .NET technology was developed by Microsoft, it works with non-Microsoft products, such as the open source database MySQL. You can access MySQL from C++.NET or C# via an Open Database Connectivity (ODBC) data provider or the MySQL.Data.dll connector. In either case, you have the advantages of managed code but don't need to use a proprietary DBMS such as SQL Server. All the resources of the .NET Framework are available for you to use on a MySQL database. This situation may well enable you to do some data manipulations with MySQL that you couldn't do by using MySQL's implementation of SQL in conjunc-tion with other languages.

MySQL and C

MySQL provides a client library written in C. The library enables you to access a MySQL database from within an application program written in C. The library provides an API that defines how clients establish contact with the database server and how communication is handled. Other languages — such as Perl, PHP, Java, Python, C++, and Tcl — all have client APIs that are built on top of the C library.

MySQL and Perl

Perl scripts connect to MySQL databases through the Perl interpreter. The Perl interpreter comprises two levels: the database interface (DBI) level and the database driver (DBD) level. The DBI is generic and can direct commands to a MySQL driver, but also to a PostgreSQL driver or drivers that connect to other kinds of databases. Just download the DBI and the DBD::mysql modules for your Perl library.

MySQL and Python

Python scripts connect to MySQL databases through the MySQL connector. After you download the MySQLdb driver into your installed Python libraries, you can import the `mysql.connector` library into your program and then use the MySQL library functions to connect to the database and submit SQL statements.

MySQL and PHP

PHP, like Perl, is an interpreted scripting language, but unlike Perl, it's especially designed for the development of web applications. It provides a means of embedding executable scripts in web pages. The web page is processed by PHP before being sent to the client for display, which enables the script to generate dynamic content. Use the `php_mysqli` library functions to connect to a MySQL database and submit SQL statements directly from your PHP programs.

MySQL and Java

MySQL connects to programs written in the Java language through the Java DataBase Connectivity (JDBC) protocol. MySQL/J is a native Java driver that converts JDBC calls into the network protocol used by the MySQL database.

Oracle SQL and Java

You can connect to an Oracle 23c database from a Java program by using either of two technologies:

>> **Java-based embedded SQL (SQLJ):** SQLJ statements may appear anywhere in a Java program where a Java statement may appear. All SQLJ statements begin with #sql to distinguish them from other Java statements. Two kinds of SQLJ statements exist:

- **Declarations:** With a declaration, you can establish a connection to a database. You can also use a declaration to store result sets that come back from the database.

- **Executable statements:** Executable statements execute embedded SQL statements and PL/SQL blocks. PL/SQL includes extensions to SQL for performing procedural operations. Executable expressions may also be used to exchange information between the Java program and the database, using variables.

>> **Java-based DataBase Connectivity (JDBC):** JDBC is an API for connecting Java programs to a wide variety of database back ends. In this respect, it's similar to ODBC.

Db2 and Java

IBM's Db2 database is accessible to Java application programs via SQLJ and JDBC. JDBC drivers of various types are available on platforms that include Linux, Unix, and Windows, as well as IBM proprietary operating systems such as OS/390, z/OS, and iSeries. SQLJ applets and applications contain embedded SQL statements that are precompiled and bound to a Db2 database. The SQLJ driver translates the embedded SQL code into Java code.

SQL user-defined functions (UDFs) can be in the form of Java modules. Stored procedures can also be created from Java classes. With UDFs, you can extend the functionality of the "plain vanilla" SQL provided by DB2. Putting program logic in stored procedures that reside on the server improves performance by reducing traffic between the client and the server. Instead of the client's issuing a command and receiving a response for each operation, the client merely calls the stored procedure, which performs all the operations and returns the result to the client.

Chapter 3

Using SQL in an Application Program

SQL was conceived and implemented with one objective in mind: to create and maintain a structure for data to be stored in a relational database. It was never intended to be a complete language that you could use to create application programs. Application programming was — and is — the domain of procedural languages such as C, C++, C#, Java, Python, and Visual Basic.

Clearly, a need exists for application programs that deal with databases. Such programs require a combination of the features of a procedural language such as C and a data sublanguage such as SQL. Fundamental differences between the architectures and philosophies of procedural languages and of SQL make combining them a challenge.

In this chapter, I look at the characteristics of — and differences between — those two very different worlds.

Comparing SQL with Procedural Languages

First, I look at SQL, which is strong in data retrieval. If important information is buried somewhere in a single-table or multitable database, SQL gives you the tools you need to retrieve it. You don't need to know the order of the table's rows or columns, because SQL doesn't deal with rows or columns individually. The SQL transaction-processing facilities also ensure that your database operations are unaffected by any other users who may be simultaneously accessing the same tables that you are — another plus.

A major weakness of SQL is its rudimentary user interface. It has no provision for formatting screens or reports. It accepts command lines from the keyboard and sends retrieved values to the terminal one row at a time.

Sometimes, a strength in one context is a weakness in another. One strength of SQL is that it can operate on an entire table at the same time. Whether the table has 1 row, 100 rows, or 100,000 rows, a single SELECT statement can extract the data you want. SQL can't easily operate on one row of a multi-row table at a time, however, and sometimes, you do want to deal with each row individually. In such cases, you can use SQL's cursor facility (described in Book 3, Chapter 5), or you can use a procedural host language.

Speaking of procedural host languages, what are their strengths and weaknesses? In contrast to SQL, procedural languages are designed for one-row-at-a-time operation, which allows the application developer precise control of the way a table is processed. This detailed control is a great strength of procedural languages. A corresponding weakness, however, is the fact that the application developer must have detailed knowledge of the way data is stored in the database tables. The order of the database's columns and rows is significant and must be taken into account.

Because of the step-by-step nature of procedural languages, they have the flexibility to produce user-friendly screens for data entry and viewing. You can also produce sophisticated printed reports with any desired layout.

Classic procedural languages

Classic procedural languages are the first languages used to program computers and their descendants. The very first languages were machine languages, in which both instructions and data were represented as ones and zeros. Digital computers are binary machines, and ones and zeros are the only things they understand. Unfortunately, long sequences of ones and zeros aren't particularly easy for humans to understand, so it wasn't long before machine language was superseded — first by assembly language and then by compiled high-level languages such as Fortran and COBOL. C and Basic are examples of more recent classic procedural languages.

Classic procedural languages such as C and Basic are complete programming languages. They can implement any procedure that can be represented in algorithmic form. They operate primarily by executing one command after another in sequence, although they also have flow of control structures that enable them to branch, either unconditionally or depending on the value of a condition. They also support loops, which enable a program to execute a section of code repeatedly. SQL, as defined by the SQL-92 international standard, didn't have these capabilities. Additions to the standard that became part of SQL:1999 have added some of these capabilities, but not all implementations of SQL have been upgraded yet to support them.

Object-oriented procedural languages

Object-oriented programming, the first incarnation of which was Simula-67 in 1967, came into its own in the 1990s, when it became the predominant programming paradigm. Large, complex software projects that would have been very difficult to build with one of the classical procedural languages were easier to accomplish with one or another of the object-oriented languages, such as C++, Java, C#, Python, or Visual Basic.NET.

The fundamental unit of a program written in an object-oriented language is the *object,* whereas the *instruction* is the fundamental unit of a classic procedural language program. Each object in an object-oriented program can receive messages sent by other objects, process data, and send messages to other objects.

Object-oriented code is intrinsically modular, which makes object-oriented programs easier to develop, understand, and maintain than programs generated according to the earlier classic paradigm. Objects are instances of classes. A class has associated attributes and methods. Attributes are characteristics of a class, and methods are actions that members of the class can perform.

Nonprocedural languages

SQL is an example of a nonprocedural language. Rather than deal with the data in a table one row at a time, it deals with data a set at a time, which means that a query may return a result set containing multiple rows. By contrast, procedural languages (both classic and object-oriented) process tables one row at a time and return data to the application the same way: one row at a time.

In the early days of relational databases, other nonprocedural languages competed with SQL. Among these competitors were QUEL and RDML. QUEL was the data sublanguage of the Ingres database management system (DBMS) that was developed at the University of California at Berkeley and later commercialized. Now it's sold as an open source product by Ingres Corp. Due to the overwhelming acceptance of SQL in the marketplace, SQL syntax has been added to QUEL. RDML is the data sublanguage for Digital Equipment Corp.'s Rdb relational database products. Alas, both Rdb and Digital Equipment itself have passed into history.

Although SQL was developed by IBM, it was adopted at a very early stage by the company that was to become Oracle Corp. Other DBMS vendors followed suit, and SQL became a de facto standard that was codified into a recognized official standard in 1986. SQL didn't beat out QUEL and RDML because of its technical superiority, which was debatable. It won because of IBM's market clout and because Oracle's early adoption of it started a domino effect of DBMS vendors joining the club and supporting SQL.

Difficulties in Combining SQL with a Procedural Language

Any time the database and the programming language addressing it use different data models, problems are going to arise. Beyond data models, differences in data types add to the problems. SQL's data types don't match the data types of any of the languages that try to communicate with SQL databases. Despite these challenges, SQL and procedural languages must be made to work together, because neither by itself can do the complete job.

Challenges of using SQL with a classical procedural language

It makes sense to try to combine SQL and procedural languages in such a way that you can benefit from their combined strengths and not be penalized by their combined weaknesses. As valuable as such a combination may be, some challenges must be overcome before it can be achieved practically.

Contrasting operating modes

A big problem in combining SQL with a procedural language is that SQL operates on tables a set at a time, whereas procedural languages work on them a row at a time. Sometimes, this difference isn't a big deal. You can separate set operations from row operations, doing each with the appropriate tool. If, however, you want to search a table for records that meet certain conditions and perform different operations on the records depending on whether they meet the conditions, you may have a problem. Such a process requires both the retrieval power of SQL and the branching capability of a procedural language. Embedded SQL gives you this combination of capabilities by enabling you to embed SQL statements at strategic locations within a program that you've written in a conventional procedural language. Other solutions to this problem include proprietary application programming interfaces (APIs) and the use of module language. Module language, described later in this chapter in the section titled "Using SQL Modules with an Application," puts SQL statements in a separate module instead of embedding them in the procedural language code.

Data type incompatibilities

Another hurdle to the smooth integration of SQL with any procedural language is that SQL's data types are different from those of all major procedural languages. This circumstance shouldn't be surprising, because the data types defined for any procedural language are different from the types for the other procedural languages. No standardization of data types exists across languages. In releases of SQL before SQL-92, data type incompatibility was a major concern. In SQL-92 (and also in subsequent releases of the SQL standard), the CAST statement addresses the problem. Book 3, Chapter 1 explains how you can use CAST to convert a data item from the procedural language's data type to one that SQL recognizes, as long as the data item itself is compatible with the new data type.

Challenges of using SQL with an object-oriented procedural language

The challenges mentioned in the preceding section with regard to using SQL with classic procedural languages apply equally to using SQL with object-oriented procedural languages. Added to those challenges are incompatibilities often called the *impedance mismatch* between SQL and object-oriented languages.

The original context of the term *impedance mismatch* comes from electrical engineering. Different parts of an electrical circuit may have different impedance values, and connecting two such circuit elements can cause problems. As a simple example, suppose that an audio speaker with an intrinsic impedance of 8 ohms is connected to a line with a 50-ohm impedance value. The result will sound attenuated, distorted, and noisy. In the context of SQL and object-oriented procedural languages, similar problems occur. The row and column organization of relational tables doesn't mesh well with the hierarchical class/object paradigm of object-oriented programming.

Database vendors have addressed the impedance-mismatch problem by adding object-oriented features to their relational database products, turning their hybrid products into *object-relational* DBMSs. The object-oriented features added to such products as Db2, Oracle, and SQL Server were codified in the SQL:1999 international standard.

SQL:1999 notwithstanding, the marriage of SQL with object-oriented languages such as C++, C#, and Visual Basic.NET isn't a perfect one. Difficulties remain, but these difficulties are manageable.

Embedding SQL in an Application

In the past, the most common method of mixing SQL with procedural languages was embedded SQL. The name is descriptive: SQL statements are dropped into the middle of a procedural program, wherever they're needed. Support for embedded SQL, however, has recently been deprecated or dropped completely by one database vendor after another.

Microsoft deprecated embedded SQL for C in SQL Server 2008, although COBOL-IT currently distributes an embedded SQL precompiler for its open source COBOL implementation, designed to work with SQL Server. SAP has discontinued embedded SQL support for its SQL Anywhere product. MySQL has never supported embedded SQL, but COBOL-IT is distributing an embedded SQL precompiler designed to work with MySQL.

PostgreSQL does support embedded SQL for C and C++, and COBOL-IT distributes a COBOL precompiler for PostgreSQL. IBM Db2 still supports embedded SQL for C, C++, and COBOL. Oracle is probably the biggest remaining supporter of embedded SQL.

It may seem like everybody is in the process of either deprecating or outright abandoning embedded SQL. It's not quite that bad. There is still quite a lot of support for embedded SQL out there, as I describe in the following sections. For those implementations that don't offer embedded SQL, there are alternatives that accomplish the same thing. Some pass the SQL statements to the database as strings and others encapsulate the SQL statements in modules. Both of these methods are described later in this chapter.

REMEMBER

As you may expect, an SQL statement that suddenly appears in the middle of a C program, for example, can present a challenge for a compiler that isn't expecting it. For that reason, programs containing embedded SQL are usually passed through a preprocessor before being compiled or interpreted. The preprocessor is warned of the imminent appearance of SQL code by a preprocessor directive such as EXEC SQL.

Embedding SQL in an Oracle Pro*C application

As an example of embedded SQL, look at a program written in Oracle's Pro*C version of the C language. The program, which accesses a company's employee table, prompts the user for an employee name and then displays that employee's salary and commission. Then it prompts the user for new salary and commission data, and updates the employee table with it, as follows:

```
EXEC SQL BEGIN DECLARE SECTION;
    VARCHAR uid[20];
    VARCHAR pwd[20];
    VARCHAR ename[10];
    FLOAT salary, comm;
    SHORT salary_ind, comm_ind;
EXEC SQL END DECLARE SECTION;
main()
{
    int sret;                          /* scanf return code */
    /* Log in */
    strcpy(uid.arr,"FRED");            /* copy the user name */
    uid.len=strlen(uid.arr);
    strcpy(pwd.arr,"TOWER");           /* copy the password */
    pwd.len=strlen(pwd.arr);
    EXEC SQL WHENEVER SQLERROR STOP;
    EXEC SQL WHENEVER NOT FOUND STOP;
    EXEC SQL CONNECT :uid;
    printf("Connected to user: percents \n",uid.arr);
    printf("Enter employee name to update:  ");
    scanf("percents",ename.arr);
    ename.len=strlen(ename.arr);
    EXEC SQL SELECT SALARY,COMM INTO :salary,:comm
                FROM EMPLOY
                WHERE ENAME=:ename;
    printf("Employee: percents salary: percent6.2f comm:
percent6.2f \n",
```

```
                ename.arr, salary, comm);
      printf("Enter new salary:   ");
      sret=scanf("percentf",&salary);
      salary_ind = 0;
      if (sret == EOF !! sret == 0)         /* set indicator */
            salary_ind =-1;           /* set indicator for NULL */
      printf("Enter new commission:   ");
      sret=scanf("percentf",&comm);
      comm_ind = 0;                            /* set indicator */
      if (sret == EOF !! sret == 0)
            comm_ind=-1;                 /* set indicator for NULL */
      EXEC SQL UPDATE EMPLOY
                  SET SALARY=:salary:salary_ind
                  SET COMM=:comm:comm_ind
                  WHERE ENAME=:ename;
      printf("Employee percents updated. \n",ename.arr);
      EXEC SQL COMMIT WORK;
      exit(0);
}
```

You don't have to be an expert in C to understand the essence of what this program is doing and how the program does it. Here's a rundown of the order in which the statements execute:

1. SQL declares host variables.

2. C code controls the user login procedure.

3. SQL sets up error handling and connects to the database.

4. C code solicits an employee name from the user and places it in a variable.

5. An SQL SELECT statement retrieves the named employee's salary and commission data, and stores it in the host variables :salary and :comm.

6. C takes over again, displaying the employee's name, salary, and commission data, and then soliciting new values for salary and commission. It also checks whether an entry has been made, and if an entry hasn't been made, it sets an indicator.

7. SQL updates the database with the new values.

8. C displays an "operation complete" message.

9. SQL commits the transaction, and C exits the program.

TIP

You can mix the commands of two languages this way because of the preprocessor. The preprocessor separates the SQL statements from the host language commands, placing the SQL statements in a separate external routine. Each SQL statement is replaced by a host-language call of the corresponding external routine, and then the language compiler can do its job. The way that the SQL part is passed to the database is implementation-dependent. You, as the application developer, don't have to worry about any of this process; the preprocessor takes care of it. You should be concerned, however, about a few things that don't appear in interactive SQL — things such as host variables and incompatible data types.

REMEMBER

Interactive SQL is a conversation that takes place between a user entering SQL statements by hand at a terminal and a DBMS responding to those statements. SQL statements embedded in a procedural language program have some complications that go beyond what you encounter with interactive SQL.

Declaring host variables

REMEMBER

The procedural language that SQL is embedded in is considered the host language, and the SQL is considered the guest. Some information must be passed between the host language program and the SQL segments. You do this with *host variables* — which are variables originally defined in the host language program. For SQL to recognize the host variables, you must declare them before you use them. Declarations are included in a declaration segment that precedes the program segment. The declaration segment is announced by the following directive:

```
EXEC SQL BEGIN DECLARE SECTION ;
```

The end of the declaration segment is signaled by the following:

```
EXEC SQL END DECLARE SECTION ;
```

When you use embedded SQL with Pro*C, every SQL statement must be preceded by an EXEC SQL directive. The end of an SQL segment may or may not be signaled by a terminator directive. In COBOL, the terminator directive is END-EXEC; in FORTRAN, it's the end of a line; and in Ada, C, Pascal, and PL/I, it's a semicolon (;).

Converting data types

Depending on the compatibility of the data types supported by the host language and those supported by SQL, you may have to use CAST to convert certain types. You can use host variables that have been declared in the DECLARE SECTION.

Remember to prefix host variable names with a colon (:) when you use them in SQL statements, as in the following example:

```
EXEC SQL INSERT INTO ENGINES
    (EngineName, Displacement, Horsepower, Cylinders, Valves)
    VALUES
    (:engname, :cid, :hp, :cyl, :valves) ;
```

Embedding SQL in a Java application

SQLJ is the tool to use to embed SQL in a Java program. The process is similar to the way that SQL statements are embedded in an Oracle Pro*C application but with a slight syntactical difference. Here's an example:

```
#sql (INSERT INTO ENGINES
    (EngineName, Displacement, Horsepower, Cylinders, Valves)
    VALUES
    (:engname, :cid, :hp, :cyl, :valves)) ;
```

#sql, rather than EXEC SQL, is the signal to the preprocessor that what follows is an SQL statement.

Using SQL in a Perl application

In a Perl application, the SQL statement is passed to the DBMS as a string rather than as an embedded executable statement in the Perl code, as follows:

```
my $sql = "INSERT INTO ENGINES
    (EngineName,Displacement,Horsepower,Cylinders, Valves) " .
    "values('$engname','$cid','$hp','$cyl','valves')";
        print "SQL => $sql\n" if $DEBUG;
        my $sth = $dbh->prepare($sql);
        $sth->execute();
```

This code uses the Perl database interface (DBI), which I mention in Book 5, Chapter 2. If an error is encountered, the offending SQL statement is printed out. If no error is detected, the SQL statement is prepared and then the last line actually executes it.

Embedding SQL in a PHP application

Once again, with PHP and a MySQL database, the operation is basically the same as with Perl, except that the syntax has been changed to protect the innocent, as in this example:

```
$con = mysqli_connect("hostname", "userid", "password", "database");
$query = "INSERT INTO ENGINES
    (EngineName, Displacement, Horsepower, Cylinders, Valves)
    VALUES
    ('engname', 'cid', 'hp', 'cyl', 'valves')" ;
$result = mysqli_query($con, $query) or die('Error, insert query
    failed');
```

The last line checks whether the insert was performed successfully. If not, an error message is displayed.

Using SQL with a Visual Basic .NET application

Unlike Oracle's Pro*C, and Java, but like Perl and PHP, Visual Basic .NET doesn't support embedded SQL. Instead, it passes a string containing the SQL statement to the ADO.NET data provider to accomplish the same effect as embedded SQL.

Here's an example of an SQL operation as Oracle's Pro*C would do it with embedded SQL, followed by the Visual Basic .NET equivalent using ADO.NET. First, here's the Pro*C:

```
EXEC SQL UPDATE VENDOR
SET VendorName = :vendorname
WHERE VendorID = 'PENGUIN';
```

Here's the ADO.NET equivalent:

```
Dim strSQL As String
strSQL = "UPDATE VENDOR SET VendorName = @vendorname "& _
"WHERE VendorID = 'PENGUIN'"
Dim cmd As New SqlCommand(strSQL, cn)
Dim par As SqlParameter
Par = cmd.Parameters.Add("@vendorname",SqlDbType.VarChar, 10)
Par.Value = "VendorName"
Dim InsertRecordsAffected As Integer = cmd.ExecuteNonQuery()
```

ADO.NET is a library of data access procedures in the .NET Framework.

Using SQL with other .NET languages

All .NET languages other than Visual Basic .NET — C#, C++.NET, COBOL.NET, Perl.NET, and so on — use ADO.NET in the same way that Visual Basic .NET does to provide data access to relational databases. ADO.NET eliminates the need to embed SQL code within a procedural application program.

Using SQL Modules with an Application

Module language provides another method of using SQL with a procedural programming language. With module language, you explicitly put all the SQL statements in a separate SQL module.

REMEMBER

An SQL module is simply a list of SQL statements. Each SQL statement is included in an SQL procedure and is preceded by a specification of the procedure's name and the number and types of parameters.

Each SQL procedure contains only one SQL statement. In the host program, you explicitly call an SQL procedure at whatever point in the host program you want to execute the SQL statement in that procedure. You call the SQL procedure as though it were a host language subprogram.

Thus, an SQL module and the associated host program are essentially a way of explicitly doing what the SQL preprocessor for embedded syntax does.

REMEMBER

Embedded SQL is much more common than module language. Most vendors offer some form of module language, but few emphasize it in their documentation.

Module language does have several advantages:

>> Because the SQL is completely separated from the procedural language, you can hire the best SQL programmers available to write your SQL modules, whether or not they have any experience with your procedural language. In fact, you can even defer deciding which procedural language to use until after your SQL modules are written and debugged.

>> You can hire the best programmers who work in your procedural language, even if they know nothing about SQL.

>> Most important, no SQL is mixed with the procedural code, so your procedural language debugger works — which can save you considerable development time.

Once again, what can be looked at as an advantage from one perspective may be a disadvantage from another. Because the SQL modules are separated from the procedural code, following the flow of the logic isn't as easy as it is in embedded SQL when you're trying to understand how the program works.

Module declarations

The syntax for the declarations in a module is as follows:

```
MODULE [module-name]
   [NAMES ARE character-set-name]
   LANGUAGE {ADA|C|COBOL|FORTRAN|MUMPS|PASCAL|PLI|SQL|JAVA}
   [SCHEMA schema-name]
   [AUTHORIZATION authorization-id]
   [temporary-table-declarations...]
   [cursor-declarations...]
   [dynamic-cursor-declarations...]
   procedures...
```

As indicated by the square brackets, the module name is optional. Naming it anyway is a good idea, however, to help keep things from getting too confusing.

The optional NAMES ARE clause specifies a character set. If you don't include a NAMES ARE clause, the default set of SQL characters for your implementation is used.

The LANGUAGE clause tells the module which language it will be called from. The compiler must know what the calling language is, because it will make the SQL statements appear to the calling program to be subprograms in that program's language.

Although both the SCHEMA clause and the AUTHORIZATION clause are optional, you must specify at least one of them, or you can specify both. The SCHEMA clause specifies the default schema, and the AUTHORIZATION clause specifies the authorization identifier. The authorization identifier establishes the privileges you have. If you don't specify an authorization ID, the DBMS uses the authorization ID associated with your session to determine the privileges your module is allowed. If you don't have the privilege to perform the operation your procedure calls for, your procedure isn't executed.

TIP

If your procedure requires temporary tables, declare them with the temporary table declaration clause. Declare cursors and dynamic cursors before any procedures that use them. Declaring a cursor after a procedure is permissible as long as that particular procedure doesn't use the cursor. Doing this for cursors used by later procedures may make sense. You can find more in-depth information on cursors in Book 3, Chapter 5.

Module procedures

Finally, after all these declarations, the functional parts of the module are the procedures. An SQL module language procedure has a name, parameter declarations, and executable SQL statements. The procedural language program calls the procedure by its name and passes values to it through the declared parameters. Procedure syntax is as follows:

```
PROCEDURE procedure-name
    (parameter-declaration [, parameter-declaration ]... )
    SQL statement ;
    [SQL statements] ;
```

The parameter declaration should take the following form:

```
parameter-name data-type
```

or

```
SQLSTATE
```

The parameters you declare may be input parameters, output parameters, or both. SQLSTATE is a status parameter through which errors are reported. SQLSTATE is covered extensively in Book 4, Chapter 4.

Modules in Oracle

Oracle's implementation of module language, named SQL*Module, is specifically designed to overcome the impedance mismatch (refer to "Challenges of using SQL with an object-oriented procedural language," earlier in this chapter) between SQL and application programs written in the Ada programming language. SQL*Module compiles SQL module language files. A module language file contains parameterized procedures that encapsulate SQL statements. The SQL*Module compiler translates these procedures into calls to the SQL runtime library on the Oracle server. All the SQL code resides in a separate module. SQL*Module defines the interface between the SQL module and the host program written in Ada.

A module is composed of three parts:

» A *preamble,* containing introductory material

» *Cursor declarations* that queries use to return multiple rows of data

» Definitions of *procedures* that will be called by the host application

The SQL code that you can put in a module is somewhat restricted. Statements that aren't supported by SQL*Module include the following:

» Data Definition Language (DDL) statements

» Data Manipulation Language (DML) statements other than SELECT, UPDATE, DELETE, and INSERT

» Data Control Language (DCL) statements other than COMMIT, ROLLBACK, CONNECT, and DISCONNECT

The fact that SQL*Module doesn't support DDL statements means that you can't create database objects such as tables with SQL*Module. You can't even alter the structure of an existing table. Thus, the database must exist and be in its final form before you try to operate on it with an application program that uses SQL*Module.

» Taking a first run at the problem

» Deciding on the deliverables

» Creating and transforming an Entity-Relationship model

» Creating, changing, and deleting tables

» Building the user interface

Chapter **4**

Designing a Sample Application

The whole point of knowing SQL is being able to apply that knowledge to solve some problem. Individuals and organizations need information to conduct their businesses, whatever they may be. At any given time, the information they need is buried within a huge collection of data, the vast majority of which they don't need right now. The key to being able to retrieve information that you *do* need is to make sure that it's organized in a way that facilitates retrieval, regardless of your specific needs today.

In this chapter, I go through the steps of creating an application that gives one (fictitious) organization the information it needs. You can adapt the ideas explained here to your own situation.

Understanding the Client's Problem

After several decades of relatively little activity, interest in the exploration of deep space is heating up. Half a dozen nations, and even some private companies, have expressed interest in or made concrete plans to send spacecraft to the Moon, either to study it from lunar orbit or to land and establish bases.

The Google Lunar X PRIZE drew the interest of more than 20 teams, which planned to land a spacecraft on the Moon and deploy a rover to explore the area. Alas, none of the competing teams were able to launch a spacecraft before the prize deadline. However, imagine that someday in the not too distant future, a fictitious not for profit organization named The Oregon Lunar Society (OLS) in Portland, Oregon will take up the challenge. The OLS has members who may or may not be members of one or more of the society's research teams. The research teams do research and produce scholarly papers, which they deliver at conferences and submit to prestigious scientific journals. Members of the teams serve as authors of the papers. The OLS leadership would like to keep track of members, research teams, papers, and the authors of the papers.

Approaching the Problem

The first thing you need to do, as a developer, when starting a project is find out what problem needs to be solved. There must be a problem; otherwise, you wouldn't have been called in to solve it.

For the example scenario in this chapter, you were called in by the president of the OLS, a small, independent research organization. Because the president is the person who hired you, she's your primary client and probably your best source of information initially. She reveals that the organization currently has two research teams, one focusing on the Moon and the other on Mars. (Since it was founded, the organization has broadened its focus to include bodies in the solar system other than Earth's Moon.) The president is most interested in keeping up-to-date records on the members of the society and the projects in which they are involved.

Interviewing the stakeholders

After telling you her perspective on what is needed, the president of the OLS suggests that you talk to the leaders of the research teams, as well as several members whose papers have been delivered at conferences or published in scholarly journals. You need to get the perspectives of all those people, because they may know aspects of the problem that are unknown to the president, who initially gave you the assignment. These people are *stakeholders* — people who may use your application or make decisions based on the results it produces.

REMEMBER

You need to identify and carefully listen to all the stakeholders in the project. Your client, the users, the information technology people (if any), and the recipients of reports all have perspectives and opinions that must be factored into your design.

Your job in drawing out these people is very important. Because the system will be performing a new function, the stakeholders probably don't have a well-defined idea of what it should do, as they would in the case of an upgrade of an existing system. They don't have any reference point on which to base their design ideas. They're also more likely to disagree with one another about what is needed. After a first round of interviews, you may have to go back to these people a second time to build a consensus on what is needed.

Drafting a detailed statement of requirements

After you interview all the stakeholders and feel that you have a clear idea of what you need to deliver, when you need to deliver it, and what delivering it in that time frame will cost, you need to draft a formal statement of requirements. The statement of requirements document describes in detail exactly what you will deliver, along with a projected delivery date.

Meet with your client, and obtain agreement on the statement of requirements. If the client wants to revise what you've drafted, make sure that the requested revisions are feasible, considering the resources that you're able to apply to the project. Generate a revised statement of requirements document, and have the client sign it, signifying agreement with its contents.

Following up with a proposal

Now that you know exactly what the client wants and when she wants it, decide whether you want to do the job. If you feel that the project isn't feasible, given the time and budget constraints and the resources you can devote to it, politely decline, and move on to other things. If the time and budget are adequate, but you don't have the expertise required to do the job, consider hiring a subcontractor that has the expertise. This arrangement has the benefit of meeting the client's needs while giving you at least a portion of the income that you would have realized had you done the job all by yourself.

If you decide to take the job, write a proposal that takes from the statement of requirements the things you agree to deliver and when you'll deliver them. If you're an outside contractor, include what you'll charge to do the job. If you're an employee of the client, include your estimate of the number of hours it will take to complete the job, along with any materials and personnel required.

If the client accepts your proposal, that acceptance forms the basis of a contract between the two of you. This contract protects both parties. It protects the client by guaranteeing that she'll receive the functionality and performance from the system that she expects, and it protects you, the developer, by specifying exactly what you've agreed to deliver.

All too often, after a project is under way, a client thinks of additional features that would enhance the value of the system. She asks you to add them to the project, usually with a statement that the new features won't add significantly to the work. This phenomenon is called *feature creep.* The first time this happens, you may agree that the added feature wouldn't be much of a burden. After you acknowledge that new features can be added to the scope of the project, however, additional requests are sure to follow. These additional features soak up your time and mental energy, and may even cause you to miss the delivery date on the original project.

WARNING

Avoid feature creep like the plague! Don't let it get started. When the client comes to you with the first small, innocent-seeming request, refer her to the contract that you both signed. If she wants additional work, it should be considered to be a separate job, with a separate budget and a separate schedule for completion. This practice significantly lowers your stress level and protects your bottom line. Giving away add-ons to a project can turn a profitable job into a losing proposition.

Determining the Deliverables

The proposal that you create in response to the statement of requirements should specify exactly what you'll deliver; when you'll deliver it; and what it will cost, either in dollars or in manpower and resources.

Keep a few things in mind when you're developing your proposal. These things have to do with what the client organization needs now and what it will need in the future.

Finding out what's needed now and later

After interviewing all the stakeholders, you should go back to your client and tell her what you have found. She may be able to give you some important perspective, and tell you which items brought up by stakeholders are the most important.

When you discuss the assignment with your client after interviewing the stakeholders but before formulating the statement of requirements, both you and the client are aware of the current needs of the organization. The project you're planning should meet those needs. It should also provide some of the features that have been identified as being valuable, if not absolutely necessary, assuming that sufficient time and budget are available to include them.

Sometimes, clients are so focused on their current challenges that they don't think about what their needs may be five years, three years, or even one year from now. One thing that has become clear in recent years is that the business environment is changing rapidly. An organization may succeed and grow beyond its expectations. Alternatively, the demand for an organization's products or services may diminish drastically or even disappear. In that case, a rapid shift to new products or services may be necessary. In either case, the organization's data handling needs are likely to change. An appreciation of the potential for those changing needs can affect the way you design your system and the particular database management system (DBMS) that you choose to build it with.

Planning for organization growth

Small organizations generally have a relatively informal management structure. The company's chief executive officer probably knows all the employees by name. Company meetings are held on a regular basis, and everybody has a voice in decisions that are made. Most transactions are handled verbally. As an organization grows, however, this "high touch" environment becomes harder and harder to maintain. Gradually, more and more organizational structure must be put into place. Communication becomes more formal and documented, and more things need to be tracked in company databases. If you're developing for a small organization that has expansion potential, you should design flexibility into your system so that additional functions can be added later without requiring major alterations of the existing system.

Greater database needs

Growth in an organization's business volume can have a major effect on its database needs. If sales increase, more sales and customers need to be tracked. An expanded product line means that more products must be tracked, and more employees are needed to manufacture, sell, and ship them. Those employees need to be tracked as well. Also, many of these employees need to access the database at the same time during the workday, increasing contention for database access and other system resources.

Increased need for data security

As an organization grows, the value of its databases also grows, and protecting them from corruption, loss, and misuse becomes more and more important. A small organization with growth potential should have a database system based on a DBMS with strong data protection features.

When a company has hundreds or thousands of employees, it's difficult for managers to have the same level of trust in every one of them. Some files containing sensitive data need to be restricted so that only those employees who have a legitimate need to access them can do so.

If the organization you're developing for has the potential to expand significantly, you need to consider using a DBMS that has more robust security than may be warranted by the organization as it currently exists.

Growth in the example scenario

Even a not-for-profit organization such as the OLS could have similar growing pains. Research activity could expand dramatically as surprising findings increase government interest and funding. Membership could expand as the public becomes more interested in space exploration. As the developer of the OLS system, you should design it in such a way that it has a reasonable amount of reserve capacity and will be easy to expand after that reserve is used up.

For this example, you'll base your application on one of the commercially available DBMSs. Some of these products are more robust than others under heavy load conditions. An idea of the extent of possible organizational growth may guide you in your choice of DBMS for the project. If substantial growth is possible within the next few years, you should choose a DBMS that can handle the increased load.

Nailing down project scope

One of the most important things that you must do as a developer is accurately determine the scope of the project that you're planning. Several factors enter into project scope, some obvious and some not so obvious. The obvious factors are these:

>> How many things need to be tracked?

>> What are those things?

>> How much time will development require?

Some not-so-obvious factors are

>> How complex are the relationships between the things that are being tracked?

>> What level of expertise is needed to finish the job on time and on budget?

>> What development tools are needed, and what do they cost?

>> Where should development be done: at the client's site or your own facility?

>> What about travel expenses? Will travel be required? If so, to where and how frequently?

>> How available is the client to answer questions?

TIP

More nonobvious factors will probably appear after you start the project. It's wise to build a contingency factor into your proposed price to cover those factors.

For an independent developer, accurate project scoping is critical. If you underestimate project scope and underbid the project, you may be forced to spend weeks or months working on a project that's guaranteed to lose you money. If you overestimate project scope, a competing developer with better estimating skill will underbid you and land the job.

If you're an employee of the client organization, accurate scoping is equally important. If you underestimate project scope, you can't deliver what you promised when you promised to deliver it. If you overestimate project scope, your management may decide to give the project to someone else, and your ability may be called into question. Whether you're an independent developer or an employee of a client organization, your ability to scope projects accurately is crucial to your success.

Building an Entity-Relationship Model

In Book 1, Chapter 2, I explain the Entity-Relationship (ER) model. In this section, I show you how to apply that model, based on what you found out by interviewing the stakeholders of the OLS database. The first step is determining what major entities need to be tracked. Then you must determine how these entities relate to one another.

Determining what the entities are

After talking to all the stakeholders you can find, you come to some conclusions about what the database should contain. Clearly, you want to track certain things:

» OLS members and some personal information on each one

» Research teams

» Scholarly papers, both conference and journal

» Authors of papers, whether they're OLS members or not

Relating the entities to one another

Interviews with society leaders and other members lead you to construct an ER diagram like the one shown in Figure 4-1.

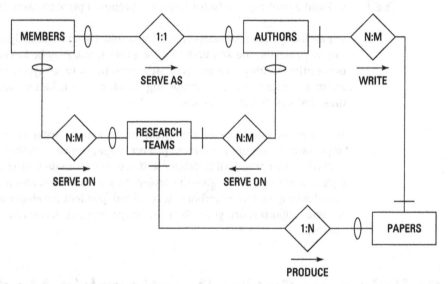

FIGURE 4-1:
An ER diagram of
OLS research.

This diagram probably seems confusing at first sight, but a little explanation should make it clearer. In the following sections, I first address the relationships, then the maximum cardinality, and finally the minimum cardinality. I also discuss business rules.

Relationships

The relationships define how the important elements of the system are related to one another, as follows:

- » Members serve as authors.
- » Members serve on research teams.
- » Research teams produce papers.
- » Authors write papers.
- » Authors serve on research teams.

Maximum cardinality

Recall from Book 1, Chapter 2 that the *maximum cardinality* of a side of a relationship is the largest number of entity instances that can exist on that side. The relationship between members and authors is one-to-one because a member can be one (and only one) author, and an author can be one (and only one) member. An author may or may not be a member, but if she's a member, she's only one member.

The relationship between members and research teams is many-to-many because a member can serve on multiple research teams, and a research team can be composed of multiple members.

The relationship between research teams and papers is one-to-many because a research team can produce multiple papers, but each paper is produced by one (and only one) research team.

The relationship between authors and papers is many-to-many because an author may write multiple papers, and a paper may have multiple authors.

The relationship between authors and research teams is many-to-many because an author may serve on multiple research teams, and a research team may include multiple people who are authors.

Minimum cardinality

Minimum cardinality of a side of a relationship is the smallest number of entity instances that can exist on that side. The relationship between members and authors is optional-to-optional because an author of an OLS paper need not be a member of OLS, and a member of OLS need not be an author of a paper.

The relationship between members and research teams is optional-to-optional because not all research-team members need to be members of OLS, and a member of OLS doesn't need to be a member of a research team.

The relationship between research teams and papers is mandatory-to-optional because all papers must be produced by a research team, but a research team may exist that has not yet produced any papers.

The relationship between authors and papers is mandatory-to-mandatory because a paper must have at least one author, and a person is not considered to be an author until he has participated in the writing of a paper.

The relationship between authors and research teams is optional-to-mandatory because for an author to serve on a research team, the research team must exist, but a research team can exist that doesn't include any authors.

Business rules

To model a system accurately, you must do more than determine the relevant entities, the attributes and identifiers of those entities, and the relationships among the entities. You must also capture the business rules that the organization follows for that system. Business rules vary from one organization to another, and they can make a big difference in how you model a system. In an educational context, one school may have a rule that at least eight students must sign up for a class for it to be offered. Another school may allow a class to proceed if as few as four students enroll. This would make a difference in the minimum cardinality of the relationship relating courses to students. One airline might cancel a scheduled flight if fewer than five people have bought tickets. Another airline might go ahead with the flight, even if no passengers are aboard. These are differences in business rules.

As a database developer, your job is to find out what your client's business rules are. You have to ask probing questions of the people you interview. Their business rules are so much a part of their lives that they probably won't think to mention them to you unless you ask detailed questions about them. Every stakeholder in the client organization has a different perspective on the database system you're building and is likely to be aware of different business rules, too. For that reason, it's important to talk to everyone involved and make sure that you flush out all the rules.

With regard to OLS, investigation uncovers several business rules:

» Papers may have multiple coauthors, some of whom may not be members of OLS.

>> An OLS member may be a member of multiple research teams.

>> Any given paper may be associated with one (and only one) research team.

REMEMBER

The OLS example is simple, but it illustrates the depth of thinking you must do about the entities in a system and how they relate to one another.

Transforming the Model

The first step in converting an ER model to a relational model is understanding how the terminology used with one relates to the terminology used with the other. In the ER model, we speak of entities, attributes, identifiers, and relationships. In the relational model, the primary items of concern are relations, attributes, keys, and relationships. How do these two sets of terms relate?

In the ER model, an *entity* is something identified as being important. Entities are physical or conceptual objects that you want to keep track of. This definition sounds a lot like the definition of a relation. The difference is that for something to be a relation, it must satisfy the requirements of First Normal Form (1NF; see Book 2, Chapter 2). An entity may translate into a relation, but you have to be careful to ensure that the resulting relation is in 1NF.

If you can translate an entity into a corresponding relation, the attributes of the entity translate directly into the attributes of the relation. Furthermore, an entity's identifier translates into the corresponding relation's primary key. The relationships among entities correspond exactly with the relationships among relations. Based on these correspondences, it isn't too difficult to translate an ER model into a relational model. The resulting relational model isn't necessarily a good relational model, however. You may have to normalize the relations in it to protect it from modification anomalies. You also may have to decompose any many-to-many relationships to simpler one-to-many relationships. After your relational model is appropriately normalized and decomposed, the translation to a relational database is straightforward.

Eliminating any many-to-many relationships

The ER model of the OLS database shown in Figure 4-1 (refer to "Relating the entities to one another," earlier in this chapter) contains many-to-many relationships. Such relationships can be problematic when you're trying to create a reliable database, so the usual practice is to decompose a single many-to-many relationship into two equivalent one-to-many relationships. This decomposition involves creating an intersection entity located between the two entities that were originally joined by a many-to-many relationship.

To prepare for the decomposition, first look at the entities involved and their identifiers, as follows:

Entity	Identifier
MEMBERS	MemberID
AUTHORS	AuthorID
RESEARCHTEAMS	TeamID
PAPERS	PaperID

MemberID uniquely identifies a member, and AuthorID uniquely identifies an author. TeamID uniquely identifies each of the research teams, and PaperID uniquely identifies each of the papers written under the auspices of the OLS.

Three many-to-many relationships exist:

MEMBERS:RESEARCHTEAMS

AUTHORS:RESEARCHTEAMS

AUTHORS:PAPERS

You need to place an intersection entity between the two entities of each of these pairs. You could call the intersection entities MEM-RES, AUTH-RES, and AUTH-PAP. Figure 4-2 shows the data structure diagram for this relational model.

This relational model includes four entities that correspond to the four entities in Figure 4-1, plus three intersection entities that replace the many-to-many relationships. There is one one-to-one relationship and seven one-to-many relationships. Minimum cardinality is denoted by slashes and ovals. In the MEMBERS:AUTHORS relationship, for example, an oval, meaning optional, appears on the MEMBERS side of that relationship because an author need not be a member of OLS. Furthermore, a person can be a member of OLS without ever writing a society paper, so an oval appears on the AUTHORS side of the relationship. A slash means mandatory. Similar logic to what is shown for the relationship between MEMBERS and AUTHORS applies to the slashes and ovals on the other relationship lines.

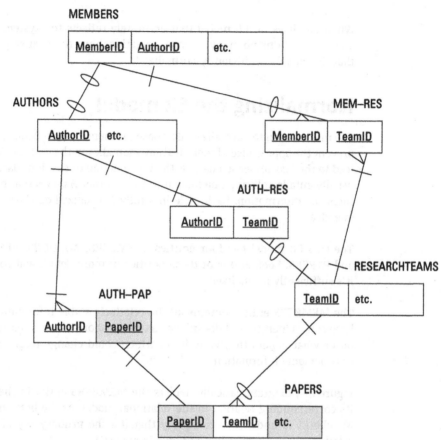

FIGURE 4-2:
An ER model
representation of
the OLS system
in Figure 4-1.

The relations are

```
MEMBERS (MemberID, FirstName, LastName, OfficeHeld, Email,
    Phone, Street, City, State, ZIP)
AUTHORS (AuthorID, FirstName, LastName)
RESEARCHTEAMS (TeamID, TeamName, TeamLeaderFirstName,
    TeamLeaderLastName, ResearchFocus, MeetingLocation,
    MeetingSchedule)
PAPERS (PaperID, TeamID, PaperTitle, PrincipalAuthorID,
    Abstract, WherePublished)
MEM-RES (MemberID, TeamID)
AUTH-RES (AuthorID, TeamID)
AUTH-PAP (AuthorID, PaperID)
```

Note: The underlines in the list indicate that the underlined attribute is the key of the relation or part of the key.

When you have an ER model that accurately reflects the system being modeled and that contains no many-to-many relationships, the next step is making sure that the model is sufficiently normalized.

Normalizing the ER model

The main reason to normalize a database (as mentioned in Book 2, Chapter 2) is to prevent the appearance of modification anomalies in the data. Such anomalies can lead to the loss of needed data or the introduction of spurious data. *Normalization* usually entails splitting one table into two (or more) tables that together contain the same information. Each table in a fully normalized database deals with only one idea.

The OLS ER model has four entities: MEMBERS, AUTHORS, RESEARCHTEAMS, and PAPERS. Look at one of these entities in more detail, and consider whether it's sufficiently normalized.

The MEMBERS entity contains all the relatively stable information that the OLS keeps on its members. It doesn't say anything about which research teams they're on or what papers they've written, which could change frequently; it contains only personal information.

Figure 4-3 diagrammatically depicts the MEMBERS entity in the ER model and its corresponding relation in the relational model. At the bottom in Figure 4-3, MemberID is underlined to signify that it's the primary key of the MEMBERS relation. Every member has a unique MemberID.

```
MEMBERS
 MemberID
 FirstName
 LastName
 OfficeHeld
 E-mail
 Phone
 Street
 City
 State
 PostalCode
```

FIGURE 4-3:
The MEMBERS entity (top) and the MEMBERS relation.

MEMBERS (MemberID, FirstName, LastName, OfficeHeld, Email, Phone, Street, City, PostalCode)

The MEMBERS entity maps exactly to the MEMBERS relation. It's natural to ask whether the MEMBERS relation is in Domain-Key Normal Form (DKNF) (see Book 2, Chapter 2). Clearly, it isn't. It isn't even in Second Normal Form (2NF). State is functionally dependent on PostalCode, which isn't a key.

You could normalize the MEMBERS relation by breaking it into two relations, as follows:

```
MEMBERS (MemberID, FirstName, LastName, OfficeHeld, Email,
   Phone, Street, City, PostalCode)
POSTAL (PostalCode, State)
```

These two relations are in 2NF and also in DKNF. They also demonstrate a new idea about keys. The two relations are closely related because they share attributes. The PostalCode attribute is contained in both the MEMBERS and the POSTAL relations. MemberID is called the primary key of the MEMBERS relation. It must uniquely identify each *tuple* — the ER model equivalent of a row in a database table — in the relation. Similarly, PostalCode is the primary key of the POSTAL relation.

In addition to being the primary key of the POSTAL relation, PostalCode is a foreign key in the MEMBERS relation. It provides a link between the two relations. An attribute need not be unique in a relation in which it serves as a foreign key, but it must be unique at the other end of the relationship, where it serves as the primary key.

After you normalize a relation into DKNF, as I did with the original MEMBERS relation, it's wise to ask yourself whether full normalization makes sense in this specific case. Depending on how you plan to use the relations, you may want to denormalize somewhat to improve performance. In this example, you probably want to fold the POSTAL relation back into the MEMBERS relation. Generally, if you need any part of a person's address, you need all of it.

Creating Tables

You can create a database (including all its tables) by typing SQL statements into your computer using tools provided by the DBMS, such as MySQL's MySQL Workbench or SQL Server's Management Studio; by including embedded CREATE statements in a host language program; or by putting the CREATE statements in a module from which they can be called by a procedural language program.

Using interactive SQL, you can start building your OLS database by creating the MEMBERS table. Here's the Data Definition Language (DDL) code to do it:

```
CREATE TABLE MEMBERS (
    MemberID   Integer      PRIMARY KEY,
    FirstName  Char (15),
    LastName   Char (20)    NOT NULL,
    OfficeHeld Char (20),
    Email      Char (50),
    Phone      Char (20),
    Street     Char (25),
    City       Char (20),
    State      Char (2),
    Zip        Char (10) );
```

Note: Each line within the outer parentheses (except the last one) in the preceding statement above is terminated by a comma. The comma tells the DBMS where one field ends and the next one starts. The DBMS doesn't pay any attention to what line something is printed on. The separation of this single statement on multiple lines is for the convenience of human readers, not for the DBMS.

The preceding SQL code creates a MEMBERS table. MemberID is the primary key of the table. Applying the NOT NULL constraint to the LastName attribute ensures that you know at least a member's last name even when you may not have complete information on that member. For each Character field, you must explicitly specify the maximum length of an entry in that field. The NOT NULL constraint is an example of a *column constraint*, which applies only to a single column. By contrast, a *table constraint* applies to an entire table. In the following code, I create the AUTHORS table and illustrate the use of a table constraint in the process:

```
CREATE TABLE AUTHORS (
    AuthorID        Integer       PRIMARY KEY,
    MemberID        Integer,
    FirstName       Char (15),
    LastName        Char (20) NOT NULL,
    CONSTRAINT MemFK FOREIGN KEY (MemberID)
        REFERENCES MEMBERS (MemberID)
        ON DELETE NO ACTION );
```

Note: In the preceding code, no comma appears at the end of the CONSTRAINT line because the REFERENCES clause is part of that line. No comma appears at the end of the REFERENCES line because ON DELETE NO ACTION is also part of the CONSTRAINT line.

The PRIMARY KEY constraint is a table constraint. It applies to the entire table. In this case, it says that AuthorID is the primary key of the AUTHORS table.

MemFK is a foreign key constraint and another example of a table constraint. It links the MemberID field in the AUTHORS table to the MemberID field in the MEMBERS table. The ON DELETE NO ACTION clause means that if a person is ever deleted from the AUTHORS table, she isn't also deleted from the MEMBERS table. If for any reason a paper is retracted by the journal that published it, a supposed author may suddenly become a nonauthor, but this change wouldn't necessarily affect that person's membership in the OLS.

Note: I used the convention of naming foreign key constraints by taking the first several letters of the key field and appending *FK* to them (for example, MemFK). This convention makes it immediately obvious that I'm discussing a foreign key.

You can create the rest of the tables in a similar manner. Here's the SQL statement that creates the RESEARCHTEAMS table:

```
CREATE TABLE RESEARCHTEAMS (
    TeamID                Integer         PRIMARY KEY,
    TeamName              Char (30),
    TeamLeaderFirstName   Char (15),
    TeamLeaderLastName    Char (20),
    ResearchFocus         Char (50),
    MeetingLocation       Char (50),
    MeetingSchedule       Char (30) );
```

The PAPERS table is defined in a similar fashion:

```
CREATE TABLE PAPERS (
    PaperID            Integer         PRIMARY KEY,
    TeamID             Integer,
    PaperTitle         Char (50),
    PrincipalAuthorID  Integer,
    Abstract           Char (300),
    WherePublished     Char (30) );
```

The linking tables MEM-RES, AUTH-RES, and AUTH-PAP, derived from the intersection relations with the same names in the relational model, are also defined the same way but also include foreign key constraints, as follows:

```
CREATE TABLE MEM-RES (
    MemberID           Integer         NOT NULL,
    Team ID            Integer         NOT NULL,
```

```
    CONSTRAINT MemFK FOREIGN KEY (MemberID)
       REFERENCES MEMBERS (MemberID)
       ON DELETE CASCADE,
    CONSTRAINT TeamFK FOREIGN KEY (TeamID)
       REFERENCES RESEARCHTEAMS (TeamID)
       ON DELETE CASCADE );
```

The foreign key constraint MemFK establishes the fact that the MemberID field
in the MEM-RES table corresponds to the MemberID field in the MEMBERS tables.
Corresponding fields need not have the same names, but it reduces confusion if
they do. The ON DELETE CASCADE clause has the effect of removing a person from
all research teams when his membership in the OLS expires and he is removed
from the MEMBERS table.

The TeamFK constraint operates in a similar manner. When a research team is
disbanded, all references to that team in MEM-RES are deleted. This deletion has
the effect of updating members' information so that they're no longer shown
as being members of the disbanded team. The members' other team memberships
are unaffected.

The final two linking tables, AUTH-RES and AUTH-PAP, are defined in the same
way that MEM-RES was defined, as follows:

```
CREATE TABLE AUTH-RES (
    AuthorID           Integer           NOT NULL,
    Team ID            Integer           NOT NULL,
    CONSTRAINT AuthFK FOREIGN KEY (AuthorID)
       REFERENCES AUTHORS (AuthorID)
       ON DELETE CASCADE,
    CONSTRAINT TeamFK FOREIGN KEY (TeamID)
       REFERENCES RESEARCHTEAMS (TeamID)
       ON DELETE CASCADE );
```

```
CREATE TABLE AUTH-PAP (
    AuthorID           Integer           NOT NULL,
    Paper ID           Integer           NOT NULL,
    CONSTRAINT AuthFK FOREIGN KEY (AuthorID)
       REFERENCES AUTHORS (AuthorID)
       ON DELETE CASCADE,
    CONSTRAINT PapFK FOREIGN KEY (PaperID)
       REFERENCES PAPERS (PaperID)
       ON DELETE CASCADE );
```

AuthFK is a table constraint, so the fact that a constraint in AUTH-RES has the same name as a constraint in AUTH-PAP doesn't matter. The DBMS won't confuse the two constraints.

At this point, all the tables have been defined, and they're ready to accept data.

Changing Table Structure

Suppose that after you create a table, you decide that you need to add a new column to it or perhaps remove an existing column that serves no purpose. The DDL ALTER statement is included in SQL for these purposes. If you want to add a Fax column to the MEMBERS table, for example, you could do so with the following SQL statement:

```
ALTER TABLE MEMBERS
    ADD COLUMN Fax Char (20) ;
```

You can remove columns by using a similar statement, as follows:

```
ALTER TABLE MEMBERS
    DROP COLUMN Fax ;
```

Removing Tables

It's really easy to get rid of tables you no longer want — perhaps too easy. For that reason, maintaining a rigorous backup discipline is important. To remove a table from your database, the DROP statement is all you need:

```
DROP TABLE PAPERS ;
```

There's no going back after you use the DROP statement. SQL doesn't ask you whether you *really* want to perform such a drastic act; it just blows away the table and then waits for your next instruction.

Designing the User Interface

Every database application has a user interface, which consists of what the user sees on her screen and the key presses, mouse movements, and clicks that she performs to interact with the application. The screen presents the user options for actions to perform, queries to process, or reports to view. SQL isn't designed to perform any of these user interface tasks. In any relational database application, the part created by the procedural language takes care of these tasks. Your job as application developer is to make sure that the user interface is intuitive and easy to use — and, of course, that it provides access to all the functionality that the application possesses. Book 5, Chapter 5 provides an example of user interface design.

Chapter **5**

Building an Application

I n Book 5, Chapter 4, I take the idea of a database system for the Oregon Lunar
Society (OLS) from an entity-relationship (ER) model to a relational model to
a relational database. Just as important as the database itself is the user interface. If users can't get the information they need out of the database, the database isn't of much value. For a simple application such as the one that the OLS
needs, after you've designed the user interface, for all intents and purposes you've
designed the whole application. So because the database itself is done, all that's
left is designing the user interface and connecting it to the database.

To make sure that you don't miss anything important, consider the project as a
whole. Imagine that you're looking down on the project from 20,000 feet. This
way, you view not only the project itself, but also the context in which it operates. Taking this view often brings to the surface concerns that you may not have
thought of otherwise.

Designing from the Top Down

When you take a top-down approach to design, you consider all the elements of
the system and how they relate to one another. You also consider elements external to the system that interact with it. In the case of the OLS system, the primary
external element is the users. The user interface should be designed with the users
in mind. How familiar are they with computers in general and with the kinds of

data stored in the OLS database? If they're fairly sophisticated and comfortable with computers and with the OLS, you would design the user interface differently from the way you would if the users were computer novices who were largely unaware of the type of work that the OLS does. Placing considerations of the user interface aside for the moment, the first order of business is deciding what the application should include.

Determining what the application should include

At this point in the process, determining what the application should include is easy. Just look at the proposal that the client signed (refer to Book 5, Chapter 4), which specifies exactly what the deliverables are. Here's a list of deliverables taken directly from a signed and agreed-on proposal:

>> Entry/update/view form for members

>> Membership list

>> Entry/update/view form for authors

>> Author list

>> Entry/update/view form for research teams

>> Research team roster

>> Entry/update/view form for papers

>> Complete papers report

>> Query: Show all papers by a specified author

>> Query: Show all papers by a specified research team

Designing the user interface

After you determine the forms, reports, and queries that you must support, you can decide how to arrange things so that users can quickly specify what they want and ask the application to deliver it. At this point, you should create some mock-ups of screens and present them to the users for feedback. Present two or three alternatives — perhaps one with a background image and a second without. The users feel a greater sense of ownership of the project if they get to choose what it looks like, which helps you tremendously in gaining user acceptance.

Figure 5-1 shows a mock-up of the main screen, using command buttons.

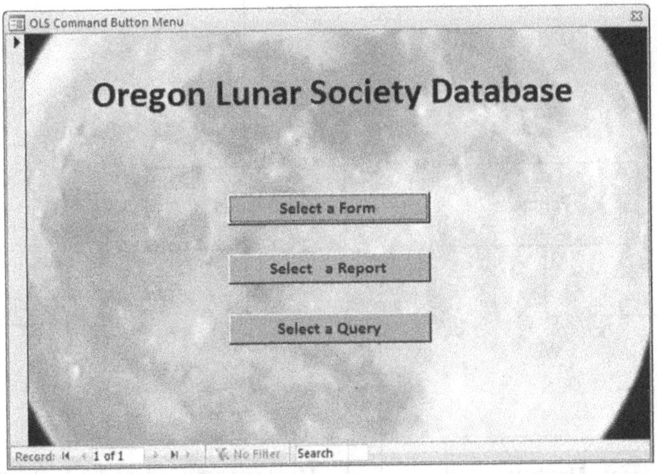

FIGURE 5-1:
The OLS application main screen with command buttons.

One key design criterion is to keep the screen simple. Sometimes, designers err by cluttering screens with too many confusing options.

After you show the alternatives for the main screen to the users and obtain their feedback, you can proceed to connect the user interface to the database.

Connecting the user interface to the database

Design a menu hierarchy that makes it easy for users to get to the functions they want to perform. Figure 5-2 shows an example of such a hierarchy for the OLS application.

The tools for building forms, reports, and queries vary from one database management system to another, so I won't go into detail on how to do it here. As an example of what one of the forms on the second level of the hierarchy might look like, Figure 5-3 shows one possible form for selecting one of the four forms used to view, enter, modify, or delete records from the MEMBERS, AUTHORS, RESEARCHTEAMS, and PAPERS tables.

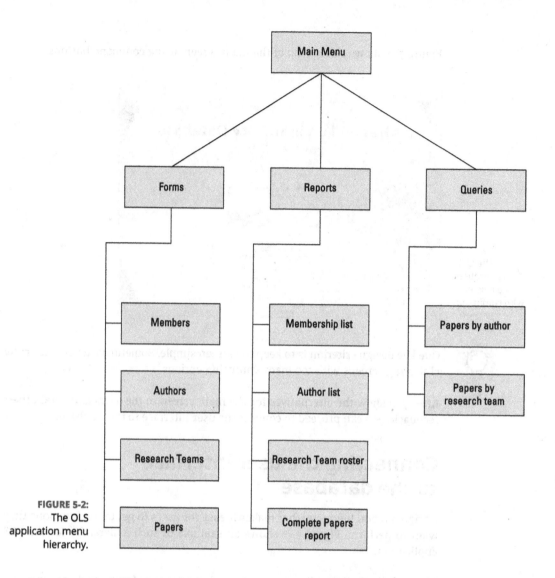

FIGURE 5-2:
The OLS application menu hierarchy.

Similar forms for reports and queries would also be on the second level.

The third level consists of forms for viewing or editing table information. Figure 5-4 shows an example of such a form for the MEMBERS table. You're free to lay out the form any way you want, put your company logo on it, or follow whatever stylistic conventions are standard in your organization.

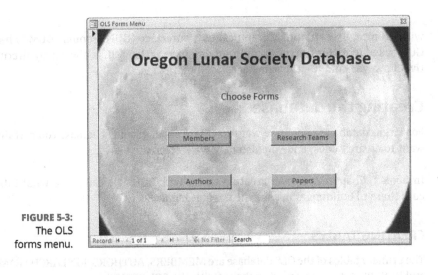

FIGURE 5-3:
The OLS
forms menu.

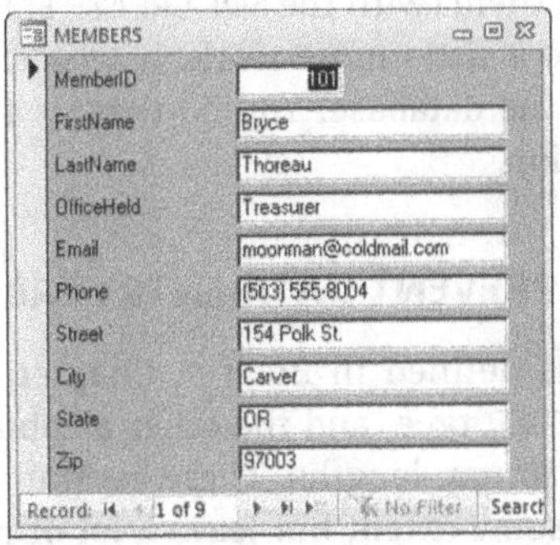

FIGURE 5-4:
The OLS
Members form.

Coding from the Bottom Up

After you develop mock-ups of all the forms in the menu hierarchy, all the reports, and the query result sets, and you obtain approval from the stakeholders (refer to Book 5, Chapter 4), the real work can begin. You've created the *appearance* of an application. Now you must build the substance.

Preparing to build the application

The first thing you must do is build the database itself. The easiest and best way to do this varies from one database management system (DBMS) to another. Probably the easiest way will turn out *not* to use SQL. Now, SQL is the ultimate tool for creating and maintaining databases in that anything you can do with any other tool, you can do with SQL. And, there are things you can do with SQL that you can't do with anything else. However, SQL is a computer language with no nice, user-friendly, graphical user interface (GUI). Popular DBMSs have GUI-based tools for the most common database tasks. SQL is always an alternative, however, and it's the same across all platforms.

Creating the database

For larger databases, you may want to create catalogs and schemas. You certainly want to create tables, and you also may want to create views.

In Book 2, Chapter 4, I cover creating tables with SQL. You can apply what I discuss there to building tables for the Oregon Lunar Society.

CREATING TABLES

The primary tables of the OLS database are MEMBERS, AUTHORS, RESEARCHTEAMS, and PAPERS. I describe creating them (with the SQL CREATE statement) in Book 5, Chapter 4. You may want to do a little more work, however, in the interest of keeping erroneous data out of the database. You do that by adding constraints, which I discuss in the next section.

ADDING CONSTRAINTS TO PREVENT DATA-ENTRY ERRORS

When the MEMBERS table was defined in Book 5, Chapter 4, the MemberID attribute was assigned the INTEGER type, and the other attributes were assigned the CHAR type, with various maximum lengths. These assignments constrain the data entered in those fields to some extent but leave a lot of room for the entry of erroneous data. You can do a better job by applying some constraints to the attributes, as follows:

>> At this time, OLS leadership cannot imagine a membership of more than 1,000 members, so MemberID could be capped at that level. Any larger number entered must be an error.

>> Only five offices exist: president, vice president, secretary, treasurer, and archivist. Any entry in OfficeHeld other than one of those five must be an error.

>> The State field may contain only the two-letter abbreviations for Oregon (OR) and the three adjacent states: Washington (WA), Idaho (ID), and California (CA). Membership is restricted to residents of those four states.

>> All zip codes for Oregon, Washington, Idaho, and California start with either 8 or 9.

Applying these constraints to the MEMBERS table eliminates at least some, if not all, data-entry errors. If you had thought ahead, you could have applied these constraints when you created MEMBERS with the CREATE statement. If the table has already been created, but data hasn't yet been entered in it, you can drop the existing empty table and then re-create it, this time applying the constraints. Here's an example:

```
CREATE TABLE MEMBERS (
    MemberID    Integer     PRIMARY KEY,
    FirstName   Char (15),
    LastName    Char (20)   NOT NULL,
    OfficeHeld  Char (20),
    Email       Char (50),
    Phone       Char (20),
    Street      Char (25),
    City        Char (20),
    State       Char (2),
    Zip         Char (10),
    CONSTRAINT max_size
       CHECK (MemberID BETWEEN 1 AND 1000),
    CONSTRAINT offices
       CHECK (OfficeHeld IN ('President', 'Vice President',
               'Secretary', 'Treasurer', 'Archivist')),
    CONSTRAINT valid_states
       CHECK (State IN ('OR','WA','ID','CA')),
    CONSTRAINT valid_zip
       CHECK (SUBSTRING (Zip FROM 1 FOR 1) = 8
           OR SUBSTRING (Zip FROM 1 FOR 1) = 9)
);
```

If the table has already been created and data has already been added to it, you can't add constraints after the fact, because they could conflict with data that's already in the database.

By examining all the table designs before creating them, you can add appropriate constraints and thereby minimize the problems that inevitably arise when erroneous data enters the database.

Filling database tables with sample data

Every database table starts out empty. After you create a table, either by using SQL's CREATE statement or a DBMS's forms-based tools, that table is nothing but a structured shell containing no data. To make the table useful, you must put some data in it. You may or may not have that data already stored in digital form.

>> If your data isn't already in digital form, someone probably has to enter the data manually, one record at a time. You can also enter data by using optical scanners and voice recognition systems, but the use of such devices for data entry is still relatively rare and error-prone.

>> If your data is already in digital form but perhaps not in the format of the database tables that you use, you need to translate the data into the appropriate format and then insert the data into the database.

>> If your data is already in digital form and in the correct format, it's ready to be transferred to a new database.

Depending on the current form of the data, you may be able to transfer it to your database in one operation by using a bulk loading utility (or by taking a series of steps before a bulk loading operation), or you may need to enter the data one record at a time. Each data record that you enter corresponds to a single row in a database table.

ADDING DATA WITH FORMS

Most DBMSs support form-based data entry. This feature enables you to create a screen form that has a field for every column in a database table. Field labels in the form enable you to determine easily what data goes into each field. The data-entry operator enters all the data for a single row in the form. After the DBMS accepts the new row, the system clears the form to accept another row. In this way, you can easily add data to a table one row at a time.

Form-based data entry is easy and less susceptible to data-entry errors than is a list of comma-delimited values. The main problem with form-based data entry is that it's nonstandard; each DBMS has its own method of creating forms. This diversity, however, isn't a problem for the data-entry operator. You can make the form look generally the same from one DBMS to another. Although this practice is great for the data-entry operator, the application developer must return to the bottom of the learning curve every time he changes development tools. Another possible problem with form-based data entry is that some implementations may not permit a full range of validity checks on the data that you enter.

REMEMBER

The best way to maintain a high level of data integrity in a database is to keep bad data out of the database in the first place. You can prevent the entry of some bad data by applying constraints to the fields on a data-entry form. This approach enables you to make sure that the database accepts only data values of the correct type, which fall within a predefined range. Applying such constraints can't prevent all possible errors, but it does catch some of them.

TIP

If the form-design tool in your DBMS doesn't enable you to apply all the validity checks that you need to ensure data integrity, you may want to build your own screen, accept data entries in variables, and check the entries by using application program code. After you're sure that all the values entered for a table row are valid, you can add that row by using the SQL INSERT command.

ENTERING DATA WITH SQL

If you enter the data for a single row in a database table, the INSERT command uses the following syntax:

```
INSERT INTO table_1 [(column_1, column_2, ..., column_n)]
    VALUES (value_1, value_2, ..., value_n) ;
```

As indicated by the square brackets ([ ]), the listing of column names is optional. The default column list order is the order of the columns in the table. If you put the VALUES in the same order as the columns in the table, these elements go in the correct columns — whether you explicitly specify those columns or not. If you want to specify the VALUES in some order other than the order of the columns in the table, you must list the column names, putting the columns in an order that corresponds to the order of the VALUES.

To enter a record in the MEMBERS table, for example, use the following syntax:

```
INSERT INTO MEMBERS (MemberID, FirstName, LastName, OfficeHeld, Email, Phone,
    Street, City, State, Zip)
    VALUES (:vmemid, 'Linda', 'Nguyen', '235 Ion Drive',
    'Titania', 'OR', '97110', '(503) 555-1963') ;
```

The first VALUE, vmemid, is a variable that you increment with your program code after you enter each new row of the table. This approach guarantees that you have no duplication of the MemberID, which is the primary key for this table and, therefore, must be unique.

The rest of the values are data items rather than variables that contain data items. You can hold the data for these columns in variables, too, if you want. The INSERT statement works equally well with variables or with an explicit copy of the data itself as arguments of the VALUES keyword.

ADDING DATA ONLY TO SELECTED COLUMNS

Sometimes, you want to note the existence of an object, even if you don't have all the facts on it yet. If you have a database table for such objects, you can insert a row for the new object without filling in the data in all the columns. If you want the table to be in First Normal Form (1NF), you must insert enough data to distinguish the new row from all the other rows in the table. (For a discussion of 1NF, see Book 2, Chapter 2.) Inserting the new row's primary key is sufficient for this purpose. In addition to the primary key, insert any other data that you have about the object. Columns in which you enter no data contain nulls.

The following example shows such a partial row entry:

```
INSERT INTO MEMBERS (MemberID, FirstName, LastName)
    VALUES (:vmemid, 'Linda', 'Nguyen') ;
```

You insert only the customer's unique identification number and name into the database table. The other columns in this row contain null values.

ADDING A BLOCK OF ROWS TO A TABLE

Loading a database table one row at a time by using INSERT statements can be tedious, particularly if that's all you do. Even entering the data in a carefully human-engineered ergonomic screen form gets tiring after a while. Clearly, if you have a reliable way to enter the data automatically, you'll find occasions in which automatic entry is better than having a person sit at a keyboard and type.

Automatic data entry is feasible, for example, if the data already exists in electronic form because somebody has already entered the data manually. If so, you have no reason to repeat history. The transfer of data from one data file to another is a task that a computer can perform with minimum human involvement. If you know the characteristics of the source data and the desired form of the destination table, a computer can (in principle) perform the data transfer automatically.

COPYING FROM A FOREIGN DATA FILE

Suppose that you're building a database for a new application. Some data that you need already exists in a computer file. The file may be a flat file or a table in a database created by a DBMS different from the one you use. The data may be in ASCII or EBCDIC code or in some arcane proprietary format. What do you do?

The first thing you do is hope and pray that the data you want is in a widely used format. If the data is in a popular format, you have a good chance of finding a format conversion utility that can translate the data into one or more other popular formats. Your development environment probably can import at least one of these formats. If you're really lucky, your development environment can handle the data's current format directly. On personal computers, the Access, xBASE, and Paradox formats are probably the most widely used. If the data that you want is in one of these formats, conversion should be easy. If the format of the data is less common, you may need to go through a two-step conversion. Just about any environment you're likely to encounter will support the comma-separated value (csv) format. Translating from your source format to csv and then from csv to your destination format should work in most cases.

As a last resort, you can turn to one of the professional data-translation services. These businesses specialize in translating computer data from one format to another. They have the capability of dealing with hundreds of formats — most of which nobody has ever heard of. Give one of these services a tape or disk containing the data in its original format, and you get back the same data translated into whatever format you specify.

TRANSFERRING ALL ROWS BETWEEN TABLES

A less severe problem than dealing with foreign data is taking data that already exists in one table in your database and combining that data with compatible data in another table. This process works great if the structure of the second table is identical to the structure of the first table — that is, if every column in the first table has a corresponding column in the second table, and the data types of the corresponding columns match. If so, you can combine the contents of the two tables by using the UNION relational operator. The result is a virtual table containing data from both source tables. I discuss the relational operators, including UNION, in Book 3, Chapter 4.

TRANSFERRING SELECTED COLUMNS AND ROWS BETWEEN TABLES

Generally, the structure of the data in the source table isn't identical to the structure of the table into which you want to insert the data. Perhaps only some of the columns match — and these are the columns that you want to transfer. By combining SELECT statements with a UNION, you can specify which columns from the source tables to include in the virtual result table. By including WHERE clauses in the SELECT statements, you can restrict the rows that you place in the result table to those that satisfy specific conditions. I cover WHERE clauses extensively in Book 3, Chapter 2.

Suppose that you have two tables — MEMBERS and PROSPECTS — and you want to list everyone living in the state of Idaho who appears in either table. You can create a virtual result table with the desired information by using the following command:

```
SELECT FirstName, LastName
    FROM MEMBERS
```

```
      WHERE State = 'ID'
UNION
SELECT FirstName, LastName
      FROM PROSPECTS
      WHERE State = 'ID' ;
```

Here's a closer look:

>> The SELECT statements specify that the columns included in the result table are FirstName and LastName.

>> The WHERE clauses restrict the rows included to those with the value 'ID' in the State column.

>> The State column isn't included in the results table but is present in both the MEMBERS and PROSPECTS tables.

>> The UNION operator combines the results from the SELECT on MEMBERS with the results of the SELECT on PROSPECTS, deletes any duplicate rows, and then displays the result.

Another way to copy data from one table in a database to another is to nest a SELECT statement within an INSERT statement. This method (a subselect) doesn't create a virtual table but instead duplicates the selected data. You can take all the rows from the MEMBERS table, for example, and insert those rows into the PROSPECTS table. This method works only if the structures of the MEMBERS and PROSPECTS tables are identical, of course. If you want to place only those customers who live in Idaho in the PROSPECTS table, a simple SELECT with one condition in the WHERE clause does the trick, as shown in the following example:

```
INSERT INTO PROSPECTS
   SELECT * FROM MEMBERS
   WHERE State = 'ID' ;
```

WARNING

Even though this operation creates redundant data (now you're storing member data in both the PROSPECTS and MEMBERS tables), you may want to do it anyway to improve the performance of retrievals. Be aware of the redundancy, however, and to maintain data consistency, make sure that you don't insert, update, or delete rows in one table without inserting, updating, or deleting the corresponding rows in the other table. Another potential problem is the possibility that the INSERT might generate duplicate primary keys. If even one preexisting prospect has a primary key called ProspectID that matches the corresponding primary key, MemberID, of a member that you're trying to insert into the PROSPECTS table, the insert operation will fail.

Creating the application's building blocks

Although you may use SQL INSERT statements to enter a few rows of sample data to validate that your tables were created correctly, the application that your production people use must be easier to use and less error-prone. Similarly, although you can obtain meaningful results to questions about the data by using SQL SELECT statements, doing so isn't particularly easy or error-resistant.

You need to build a user-friendly application that features screen forms for data entry, viewing, modification, and deletion. You also need predesigned reports that can be run at regular intervals or whenever desired.

Developing screen forms

Design your screen forms so that users can quickly and easily understand them. Here are a few tips:

>> Make the placement of items in the forms logical and visible.

>> Group related items.

>> Make sure that the navigation from one form to another is easy and logical.

>> Create a navigation map similar to Figure 5-3 (refer to "Connecting the user interface to the database," earlier in this chapter) that shows how forms are linked.

>> Because user communities can differ widely, have typical users try out your forms and give you feedback on how easy the forms are to use and whether they provide all the functionality needed.

Developing reports

The discipline required for generating reports is similar to that required for generating screen forms. SQL isn't equipped to handle either function. You have to write code in Visual Basic, C, or some other procedural language to create the forms and reports, depending on the tools available in whatever DBMS environment you are operating in, or use a third-party report writer such as Crystal Reports from SAP. In any case, when you've completed all the forms and reports that your application needs to provide, the next step is placing them in an integrated structure that gives the users a unified tool that meets their needs in a convenient way.

Building an Application

Gluing everything together

Some development environments, such as Microsoft Access, give you the integrated structure you need, complete with navigation from one screen to another, without the need for any procedural programming. These applications have limited flexibility, however, and can't handle requirements even slightly out of the ordinary. In most cases, you end up having to write some procedural code.

If you're developing in the .NET environment, Visual Studio is the tool you use to write the needed procedural code. If you're developing in another environment, you use other tools, but your task is essentially the same. Any analysis of the data beyond what SQL can do requires programming, as do responses to events such as button clicks or error conditions.

Testing, Testing, Testing

After you finish all your forms, reports, and queries, and write all the code needed to bind the application together, you're still not done. In fact, you may be less than halfway to completion of the project. In most large projects, testing is the most time-consuming part of the entire task — more time-consuming than the design phase or the creation of all the forms, reports, queries, and program code. You need to test your application with the volume and diversity of data that it's likely to encounter after it goes into production. This test typically reveals problems that didn't show up when you were working with a few rows of sample data in each of your tables.

You need to deliberately try to break the application by making erroneous inputs, because you can be sure that after the system goes into production, someone will make data-entry mistakes sooner or later. If dates and times are involved, try entering some nonsensical ones to see how the system responds. See what happens if you say, for example, that a product has been delivered before it was ordered. How does the system handle that entry? How do you *want* the system to handle it?

In the more challenging world that we find ourselves in today, you need to make sure that your application is not only resistant to mistakes, but also resistant to deliberate attempts to penetrate it or even destroy it. In Book 4, Chapter 1, I mention SQL injection attacks as threats to databases that are exposed to the Internet. Such attacks can be harmful to any system, regardless of whether it's connected to the Internet. Any database application that accepts input from the user is potentially vulnerable to an SQL injection attack. Your attempts to break an application that you've just created should include SQL injection attacks in your test mix.

Fixing the bugs

In the course of testing, you inevitably find things that aren't as they should be, such as program bugs or inelegancies that, now that you look at them, you know that you can improve. Fix them all.

REMEMBER

After you have fixed a group of bugs, go back and test the entire application again. If you discover more bugs in this second round of testing, fix them and then test everything again. Don't just test whatever it was that you fixed; test *everything*. Bugs and fixes have a way of interacting in unanticipated ways. Often, what you do to fix one bug creates three or four other problems in what you would swear are unrelated areas. The only way to make sure that you haven't created additional problems in the course of fixing one is to test everything again every time you fix anything. This discipline is called *regression testing* because you regress to square one every time you fix a bug.

Turning naive users loose

After you can go through your entire suite of tests without encountering a single problem, you're ready to go to the next phase of testing, which is generally called *beta testing*. In a beta test, you give the application to users who are no more technically sophisticated than the end users you're targeting. Actually, the less technically sophisticated your beta testers are, the better. They use your application in ways that you'd never think of in a million years. In the process, they uncover bugs that you never came close to finding.

Bringing on the hackers

Another good class of beta testers is made up of people with a hacker mentality. These people feel challenged to find the weak spots in your application. They try things that they *know* they're not supposed to do, just to see what happens. In the process, they may find problems that neither you nor your unsophisticated beta testers encountered.

Fixing the newly found bugs

As new bugs crop up in the course of beta testing, fix them one by one as they appear. After each fix, run a regression test (refer to "Fixing the bugs," earlier in this chapter). If you fix several bugs and then run the regression test, it's hard to determine what caused the 17 new failures that appeared.

As the hare learned from the tortoise, slow and steady wins the race. Keep things as simple as possible. Fix one thing at a time and then retest everything.

Retesting everything one last time

Did I say retest everything? Yes. After you think that you've tested the application to death — after you're sure that you've squashed all the bugs that could possibly exist, it's time for one final test. This time, instead of running the test yourself, have someone else — someone who's totally unrelated to the development effort — conduct the entire test suite one more time. If you get a clean run this final time, you can truly say that you're finished. Break out the bubbly!

Chapter **6**

Understanding SQL's Procedural Capabilities

I n its original incarnation, SQL was conceived as a data sublanguage, the only purpose of which was to interact with relational databases. It was considered acceptable to embed SQL statements within procedural language code written in some full-featured language to create a fully functional database application. For a long time, however, users wanted SQL to have procedural capabilities so that there would be less need to switch back and forth between SQL and some other language in data-driven applications. To solve this problem, vendors started putting procedural capabilities in their implementations of SQL. These nonstandard extensions to the language ended up inhibiting cross-platform portability until several procedural capabilities were standardized with a new section of the ANSI/ISO standard in 1996. That new section is called Persistent Stored Modules (SQL/PSM), although it covers quite a few things in addition to stored modules.

WARNING

The SQL standard has made great progress in defining a standard way of handing procedural capabilities, but unfortunately, many database products still do their own thing when it comes to handling procedural code. This chapter follows the standard as defined in the SQL:2023 specifications, which may or may not work in your particular database package. Please consult the documentation for your specific database package for more detailed information.

Embedding SQL Statements in Your Code

In Book 5, Chapter 3, I discuss embedding SQL statements in applications written in one of several procedural languages. Even with the new procedural capabilities that were added to SQL with SQL/PSM, embedding is still necessary, but switches between languages are much less frequent. In its current version (SQL:2016), the ANSI/ISO SQL standard still describes a language that isn't computationally complete.

Introducing Compound Statements

SQL was originally conceived as a nonprocedural language that deals with data a set at a time rather than a record at a time. With the addition of the facilities covered in this chapter, however, this statement isn't as true as it used to be. SQL has become more procedural, although it still deals with data a set at a time. Because classic SQL (that defined by SQL-92) doesn't follow the procedural model — one instruction follows another in a sequence to produce a desired result — early SQL statements were stand-alone entities, perhaps embedded in a C++ or Visual Basic program. With these early versions of SQL, users typically didn't pose a query or perform some other operation by executing a series of SQL statements. If users did execute such a series of statements, they suffered a performance penalty. Every SQL statement executed requires a message to be sent from the client where the user is located to the server where the database is located; then a response must be sent in the reverse direction. This network traffic slows operations as the network becomes congested.

SQL:1999 and all following versions allow compound statements, made up of individual SQL statements that execute as a unit. This capability eases network congestion, because all the individual SQL statements in the compound statement are sent to the server as a unit and executed as a unit, and a single response is sent back to the client.

All the statements included in a compound statement are enclosed between a BEGIN keyword at the beginning of the statement and an END keyword at the end of the statement. To insert data into multiple related tables, for example, you use syntax similar to the following:

```
void main {
    EXEC SQL
        BEGIN
            INSERT INTO STUDENTS (StudentID, Fname, Lname)
                VALUES (:sid, :sfname, :slname) ;
            INSERT INTO ROSTER (ClassID, Class, StudentID)
                VALUES (:cid, :cname, :sid) ;
            INSERT INTO RECEIVABLE (StudentID, Class, Fee)
                VALUES (:sid, :cname, :cfee)
        END ;
/* Check SQLSTATE for errors */
}
```

This little fragment from a C program includes an embedded compound SQL statement. The comment about SQLSTATE deals with error handling. If the compound statement doesn't execute successfully, an error code is placed in the status parameter SQLSTATE. Placing a comment after the END keyword doesn't correct any errors, however. The comment is placed there simply to remind you that in a real program, error-handling code belongs in that spot. Error handling is described in detail in Book 4, Chapter 4.

Atomicity

Compound statements introduce a possibility for error that doesn't exist for simple SQL statements. A simple SQL statement either completes successfully or doesn't. If it doesn't complete successfully, the database is unchanged. This is not necessarily the case for a compound statement.

Consider the example in the preceding section. What if both the INSERT into the STUDENTS table and the INSERT into the ROSTER table took place, but because of interference from another user, the INSERT into the RECEIVABLE table failed? A student would be registered for a class but wouldn't be billed. This kind of error can be hard on a university's finances. The concept that's missing in this scenario is atomicity. An *atomic* statement is indivisible: It either executes completely or not at all. Simple SQL statements are atomic by nature, but compound SQL statements are not. You can make a compound SQL statement atomic, however, by specifying it as such. In the following example, the compound SQL statement is made safe by introducing atomicity:

```
void main {
    EXEC SQL
        BEGIN ATOMIC
            INSERT INTO STUDENTS (StudentID, Fname, Lname)
                VALUES (:sid, :sfname, :slname) ;
            INSERT INTO ROSTER (ClassID, Class, StudentID)
                VALUES (:cid, :cname, :sid) ;
            INSERT INTO RECEIVABLE (StudentID, Class, Fee)
                VALUES (:sid, :cname, :cfee)
        END ;
/* Check SQLSTATE for errors */
}
```

By adding the keyword ATOMIC after the keyword BEGIN, you can ensure that either the entire statement executes, or — if an error occurs — the entire statement rolls back, leaving the database in the state it was in before the statement began executing.

Variables

One feature that full computer languages such as C and BASIC offer that SQL didn't offer until SQL/PSM is variables. *Variables* are symbols that can take on a value of any given data type. Within a compound statement, you can declare a variable and assign it a value. Then you can use the variable in the compound statement. When you exit a compound statement, all the variables declared within it are destroyed. Thus, variables in SQL are local to the compound statement within which they are declared. Here's an example:

```
BEGIN
    DECLARE prezpay NUMERIC ;
    SELECT salary
    INTO prezpay
    FROM EMPLOYEE
    WHERE jobtitle = 'president' ;
END;
```

Cursors

You can declare a cursor within a compound statement. You use cursors to process a table's data one row at a time (see Book 3, Chapter 5 for details). Within a compound statement, you can declare a cursor, use it, and then forget it because the cursor is destroyed when you exit the compound statement. Here's an example:

```
BEGIN
    DECLARE ipocandidate CHAR(30) ;
    DECLARE cursor1 CURSOR FOR
            SELECT company
            FROM biotech ;
    OPEN CURSOR1 ;
    FETCH cursor1 INTO ipocandidate ;
    CLOSE cursor1 ;
END;
```

Assignment

With SQL/PSM, SQL finally gains a function that even the lowliest procedural languages have had since their inception: the ability to assign a value to a variable. Essentially, an assignment statement takes the following form:

```
SET target = source ;
```

In this usage, target is a variable name, and source is an expression. Several examples are

```
SET vfname = 'Brandon' ;
```

```
SET varea = 3.1416 * :radius * :radius ;
```

Following the Flow of Control Statements

Since its original formulation in the SQL-86 standard, one of the main drawbacks that prevented people from using SQL in a procedural manner has been its lack of flow of control statements. Until SQL/PSM was included in the SQL standard, you couldn't branch out of a strict sequential order of execution without reverting to a host language like C or BASIC. SQL/PSM introduces the traditional flow of control structures that other languages provide, thus allowing SQL programs to perform needed functions without switching back and forth between languages.

IF . . . THEN . . . ELSE . . . END IF

The most basic flow of control statement is the IF...THEN...ELSE...END IF statement. This statement means that if a condition is true, the statements following the THEN keyword should be executed. Otherwise, the statements following the ELSE keyword should be executed. Here's an example:

```
IF
    vfname = 'Brandon'
THEN
    UPDATE students
        SET Fname = 'Brandon'
        WHERE StudentID = 314159 ;
ELSE
    DELETE FROM students
        WHERE StudentID = 314159 ;
END IF
```

In this example, if the variable vfname contains the value Brandon, the record for student 314159 is updated with Brandon in the Fname field. If the variable vfname contains any value other than Brandon, the record for student 314159 is deleted from the students table.

The IF...THEN...ELSE...END IF statement is great if you want to take one of two actions, based on the value of a condition. Often, however, you want to make a selection among more than two choices. At such times, you probably should use a CASE statement.

CASE . . . END CASE

CASE statements come in two forms: the simple CASE statement and the searched CASE statement. Both kinds allow you to take different execution paths based on the values of conditions.

Simple CASE statement

A simple CASE statement evaluates a single condition. Based on the value of that condition, execution may take one of several branches, as in this example:

```
CASE vmanufacturer
    WHEN 'General Motors'
    THEN INSERT INTO DOMESTIC (VIN, Make, Model)
            VALUES (:vin, :make, :model) ;
    WHEN 'Ford'
```

```
THEN INSERT INTO DOMESTIC (VIN, Make, Model)
        VALUES (:vin, :make, :model) ;
WHEN 'Chrysler'
THEN INSERT INTO DOMESTIC (VIN, Make, Model)
        VALUES (:vin, :make, :model) ;
WHEN 'Studebaker'
THEN INSERT INTO DOMESTIC (VIN, Make, Model)
        VALUES (:vin, :make, :model) ;
ELSE INSERT INTO FOREIGN (VIN, Make, Model)
        VALUES (:vin, :make, :model) ;
END CASE
```

The ELSE clause handles everything that doesn't fall into the explicitly named categories in the THEN clauses.

WARNING

The ELSE clause is optional, but if it isn't included and the CASE statement's condition isn't handled by any of the THEN clauses, SQL returns an exception.

Searched CASE statement

A searched CASE statement is similar to a simple CASE statement, but it evaluates multiple conditions rather than just one. Here's an example:

```
CASE
    WHEN vmanufacturer  IN ('General Motors','Ford')
    THEN INSERT INTO DOMESTIC (VIN, Make, Model)
            VALUES (:vin, :make, :model) ;
    WHEN vmake IN ('Chrysler','Dodge','Plymouth')
       THEN INSERT INTO DOMESTIC (VIN, Make, Model)
            VALUES (:vin, :make, :model) ;
    WHEN vmodel IN ('Avanti','Lark')
       THEN INSERT INTO DOMESTIC (VIN, Make, Model)
            VALUES (:vin, :make, :model) ;
    ELSE INSERT INTO FOREIGN (VIN, Make, Model)
            VALUES (:vin, :make, :model) ;
END CASE
```

You prevent an exception by putting all cars that aren't domestic into the FOREIGN table. Because a car that doesn't meet any of the stated conditions may still be domestic, this practice may not be strictly accurate in all cases. If it isn't, you can always add another WHEN clause.

LOOP . . . END LOOP

The LOOP statement allows you to execute a sequence of SQL statements multiple times. After the last SQL statement enclosed within the LOOP . . . END LOOP statement executes, control loops back to the first such statement and makes another pass through the enclosed statements. The syntax is as follows:

```
SET vcount = 0 ;
LOOP
    SET vcount = vcount + 1 ;
    INSERT INTO asteroid (AsteroidID)
        VALUES (vcount) ;
END LOOP
```

This code fragment preloads your asteroid table with unique identifiers. You can fill in other details about the asteroids as you find them, based on what you see through your telescope when you discover them.

Notice the one little problem with the code fragment in the preceding example: It's an infinite loop. No provision is made for leaving the loop, so it will continue inserting rows into the asteroid table until the database management system (DBMS) fills all available storage with asteroid table records. If you're lucky, the DBMS raises an exception at that time. If you're unlucky, the system merely crashes.

For the LOOP statement to be useful, you need a way to exit loops before you raise an exception: the LEAVE statement.

LEAVE

The LEAVE statement works just like you might expect it to. When execution encounters a LEAVE statement embedded within a labeled statement, it proceeds to the next statement beyond the labeled statement, as in this example:

```
AsteroidPreload:
SET vcount = 0 ;
LOOP
    SET vcount = vcount + 1 ;
    IF vcount > 10000
        THEN
            LEAVE AsteroidPreload ;
    END IF ;
    INSERT INTO asteroid (AsteroidID)
```

```
        VALUES (vcount) ;
END LOOP AsteroidPreload
```

The preceding code inserts 10,000 sequentially numbered records into the asteroids table and then passes out of the loop.

WHILE . . . DO . . . END WHILE

The WHILE statement provides another method for executing a series of SQL
statements multiple times. While a designated condition is true, the WHILE loop
continues to execute. When the condition becomes false, looping stops, as in this
example:

```
AsteroidPreload2:
SET vcount = 0 ;
WHILE
    vcount < 10000 DO
        SET vcount = vcount + 1 ;
        INSERT INTO asteroid (AsteroidID)
            VALUES (vcount) ;
END WHILE AsteroidPreload2
```

This code does exactly the same thing that AsteroidPreload does in the preceding section. This is just another example of the oft-cited fact that with SQL,
you usually have multiple ways to accomplish any given task. Use whichever
method you feel most comfortable with, assuming that your implementation
allows it.

REPEAT . . . UNTIL . . . END REPEAT

The REPEAT loop is very much like the WHILE loop except that the condition is
checked after the embedded statements execute rather than before. Here's an
example:

```
AsteroidPreload3:
SET vcount = 0 ;
REPEAT
    SET vcount = vcount + 1 ;
    INSERT INTO asteroid (AsteroidID)
        VALUES (vcount) ;
    UNTIL X = 10000
END REPEAT AsteroidPreload3
```

TIP

Although I perform the same operation three ways in the preceding examples (with LOOP, WHILE, and REPEAT), you will encounter some instances in which one of these structures is clearly better than the other two. It's good to have all three methods in your bag of tricks so that when a situation like this arises, you can decide which tool is the best one available for the situation.

FOR ... DO ... END FOR

The SQL FOR loop declares and opens a cursor, fetches the rows of the cursor, executes the body of the FOR statement once for each row, and then closes the cursor. This loop makes processing possible entirely within SQL instead of switching out to a host language. If your implementation supports SQL FOR loops, you can use them as simple alternatives to the cursor processing described in Book 3, Chapter 5. Here's an example:

```
FOR vcount AS Curs1 CURSOR FOR
    SELECT AsteroidID FROM asteroid
DO
    UPDATE asteroid SET Description = 'stony iron'
        WHERE CURRENT OF Curs1 ;
END FOR
```

In this example, you update every row in the asteroid table by putting 'stony iron' in the Description field. This method is a fast way to identify the compositions of asteroids, but the table may suffer some in the accuracy department. Some asteroids are carbonaceous chondrites, and others are nickel–iron. Perhaps you'd be better off checking the spectral signatures of the asteroids and then entering their types individually.

ITERATE

The ITERATE statement provides a way to change the flow of execution within an iterated SQL statement. (The iterated SQL statements are LOOP, WHILE, REPEAT, and FOR.) If the iteration condition of the iterated SQL statement is true or not specified, the next iteration of the loop commences immediately after the ITERATE statement executes. If the iteration condition of the iterated SQL statement is false or unknown, iteration ceases after the ITERATE statement executes. Here's an example:

```
AsteroidPreload4:
SET vcount = 0 ;
WHILE vcount < 10000 DO
    SET vcount = vcount + 1 ;
```

```
   INSERT INTO asteroid (AsteroidID) VALUES (vcount) ;
   ITERATE AsteroidPreload4 ;
   SET vpreload = 'DONE' ;
END WHILE AsteroidPreload4
```

Execution loops back to the top of the WHILE statement immediately after the ITERATE statement each time through the loop until vcount equals 9999. On that iteration, vcount increments to 10000; the INSERT performs; the ITERATE statement ceases iteration; vpreload is set to DONE; and execution proceeds to the next statement after the loop.

Using Stored Procedures

Stored procedures reside in the database on the server rather than execute on the client — where all procedures were located before SQL/PSM. After you define a stored procedure, you can invoke it with a CALL statement. Keeping the procedure located on the server rather than the client reduces network traffic, thus speeding performance. The only traffic that needs to pass from the client to the server is the CALL statement. You can create this procedure in the following manner:

```
EXEC SQL
   CREATE PROCEDURE ForeignOrDomestic
      ( IN  manufacturer CHAR (20),
        OUT origin        CHAR (8) )
   BEGIN ATOMIC
      CASE manufacturer
         WHEN 'General Motors' THEN
            SET origin = 'domestic' ;
         WHEN 'Ford' THEN
            SET origin = 'domestic' ;
         WHEN 'Chrysler' THEN
            SET origin = 'domestic' ;
         WHEN 'Studebaker' THEN
            SET origin = 'domestic' ;
         ELSE
            SET origin = 'foreign' ;
      END CASE
   END ;
```

After you have created a stored procedure like the one in this example, you can invoke it with a CALL statement similar to the following statement:

```
CALL ForeignOrDomestic ('Toyota', origin) ;
```

The first argument is the input parameter fed to the ForeignOrDomestic procedure. The second argument is the output parameter that the procedure uses to return its result to the calling routine. In this case, it returns foreign.

Working with Triggers

Triggers are useful tools that you can use to execute SQL statements whenever certain changes are made in a database table. They're analogous to actions that occur in event-driven programming in modern procedural languages. If a predefined change is made in a database table, that event causes an associated trigger to fire, which in turn causes an SQL statement or block of SQL statements to execute. The triggered statement could cause another trigger to fire, as well as performing its stated action. There's no limit to the number of levels of nesting you can use for triggers.

One reason you may want to use a trigger is to create an audit trail. If a particular change is made in a table, you may want to record that fact in a log file somewhere. A trigger could cause an SQL statement to make a log entry. Another application of a trigger might be to maintain consistency among tables in a database. A particular change in one table might fire a trigger that causes corresponding changes to be made in other tables. You can even use a trigger to affect something outside the database. If a new row is inserted into an ORDERS table, for example, you could fire a trigger that wakes up and sets into motion a robot that starts to build the ordered product.

Here's the Backus-Naur Form (BNF) syntax for the statement that creates a trigger:

```
<trigger definition> ::=
  CREATE TRIGGER <trigger name>
    <trigger action time> <trigger event>
    ON <table name>[REFERENCING old or new values alias list]
    <triggered action>

<trigger action time> ::=
    BEFORE
  | AFTER
```

```
<trigger event> ::=
    INSERT
  | DELETE
  | UPDATE [ OF <trigger column list> ]

<trigger column list> ::= <column name list>

<triggered action> ::=
  [ FOR EACH { ROW | STATEMENT } ]
    [ WHEN <left paren> <search condition> <right paren> ]
    <triggered SQL statement>

<triggered SQL statement> ::=
    <SQL procedure statement>
  | BEGIN ATOMIC
      { <SQL procedure statement> <semicolon> }...
    END

<old or new values alias list> ::=
    OLD [ ROW ][ AS ] <old values correlation name>
  | NEW [ ROW ][ AS ] <new values correlation name>
  | OLD TABLE [ AS ] <old values table alias>
  | NEW TABLE [ AS ] <new values table alias>

<old values correlation name> ::= <correlation name>

<new values correlation name> ::= <correlation name>

<old values table alias> ::= <identifier>

<new values table alias> ::= <identifier>
```

Trigger events

Three different SQL statements — INSERT, DELETE, and UPDATE — can cause a
trigger to fire. A referential action can also cause a trigger to fire. If a referential-
integrity constraint is violated, for example, a trigger could fire, which would then
cause some appropriate action to take place. The optional REFERENCING clause
enables you to refer to table values before the trigger action takes place when
the OLD keyword is used, as well as to refer to table values after the trigger action
takes place when the NEW keyword is used.

In the CREATE TRIGGER statement, a table name is specified. If the trigger event is an INSERT, only an insert operation on the specified table causes the trigger to fire. Similarly, if the trigger event is a DELETE, only a delete operation on the specified table causes the trigger to fire. If the trigger event is an UPDATE on one or more columns in a table, only an UPDATE on those columns of the specified table causes the trigger to fire.

Trigger action time

A trigger can fire either immediately before the trigger event or immediately after it, as specified by the BEFORE or AFTER keyword.

It may seem odd that a trigger could fire *before* the event that causes it has even occurred. That's the magic of working in the computer world rather than the real world. The trigger is set up well in advance. It is only waiting for the triggering event to occur, but what is the triggering event? It is the execution of an SQL statement. Before a statement can be executed, it must be fetched and interpreted. Once it is interpreted, the DBMS knows whether it will cause a trigger to fire. If the trigger has been set up with the BEFORE keyword, it can be made to fire before the SQL statement that constitutes the triggering event is executed.

Triggered actions

There are two kinds of triggers:

>> **Row-level:** A *row-level* trigger is one whose triggered SQL statement is executed for every row modified by the triggering statement.

>> **Statement-level:** A *statement-level* trigger is one whose triggered SQL statement is executed only once, each time the triggering statement is executed.

The default triggered action is FOR EACH STATEMENT, if neither FOR EACH ROW nor FOR EACH STATEMENT is specified. The WHEN clause in a triggered action enables you to specify a condition. The trigger fires only if the condition evaluates to TRUE.

Triggered SQL statement

The triggered SQL statement can either be a single SQL statement or a BEGIN ATOMIC...END block containing multiple SQL statements. Here's an example:

```
CREATE TRIGGER notify
```

```
    AFTER INSERT ON MEMBERS
    FOR EACH STATEMENT
      BEGIN ATOMIC
        CALL send_email ('President', 'New member') ;
        INSERT INTO CHANGE_LOG
          VALUES ('MEMBERS', :vfirstname, :vlastname) ;
      END ;
```

Whenever a new row is inserted into the MEMBERS table, an email message is sent to the organization's president, informing her of the new member. At the same time, a new row is inserted into the CHANGE_LOG table, which records all insertions, deletions, and updates to any table in the database.

Using Stored Functions

A stored function is similar in many ways to a stored procedure. Collectively, the two are referred to as *stored routines.* They're different in several ways, including the ways in which they're invoked. A stored procedure is invoked with a CALL statement, and a stored function is invoked with a function call, which can replace an argument of an SQL statement.

Here's an example of a function definition, followed by an example of a call to that function:

```
CREATE FUNCTION Engine (test_engine_ID Integer)
    RETURNS NUMERIC (5,2)

    BEGIN ATOMIC
        DECLARE vdisplacement NUMERIC (5,2)
            DEFAULT '' ;
        SET vdisplacement = (SELECT Displacement FROM FORD
                          WHERE EngineID = test_engine_ID);
    RETURN vdisplacement;
    END ;
```

This function definition returns the displacement of the Ford engine whose engineID is supplied as input. The following SET statement contains a function call to Engine that retrieves the displacement of the engine identified by EngineID = 4004:

```
SET displace = Engine (EngineID)
    WHERE EngineID = 4004 ;
```

Passing Out Privileges

The various privileges that you can grant users are discussed in Book 1, Chapter 4. In most database packages, the database owner can grant the following privileges to other users:

>> The right to DELETE rows from a table

>> The right to INSERT rows into a table

>> The right to UPDATE rows in a table

>> The right to create a table that REFERENCES another table

>> The right of USAGE on a domain

SQL/PSM adds one more privilege that can be granted to a user: EXECUTE. Here are two examples:

```
GRANT EXECUTE on ForeignOrDomestic to SalesManager ;
GRANT EXECUTE on Engine to Mechanic ;
```

These statements allow the sales manager of the used-car dealership to execute the ForeignOrDomestic procedure and any mechanic in the shop to execute the Engine function. People who lack the EXECUTE privilege for a routine aren't able to use the routine.

Using Stored Modules

A *stored module* can contain multiple routines (procedures or functions) that can be invoked by SQL. Anyone who has the EXECUTE privilege for a module has access to all the routines in the module. Privileges on routines within a module can't be granted individually. Following is an example of a stored module:

```
CREATE MODULE mod1
   CREATE PROCEDURE ForeignOrDomestic
      ( IN manufacturer CHAR (20),
        OUT origin CHAR (8) )
   BEGIN ATOMIC
      CASE manufacturer
         WHEN 'General Motors' THEN
            SET origin = 'domestic' ;
         WHEN 'Ford' THEN
```

```
            SET origin = 'domestic' ;
        WHEN 'Chrysler' THEN
            SET origin = 'domestic' ;
        WHEN 'Studebaker' THEN
            SET origin = 'domestic' ;
        ELSE
            SET origin = 'foreign' ;
    END CASE
  END ;
```

```
  CREATE FUNCTION Engine (test_engine_ID Integer)
  RETURNS NUMERIC (5,2)

  BEGIN ATOMIC
     DECLARE vdisplacement NUMERIC (5,2)
         DEFAULT '' ;
     SET vdisplacement = (SELECT Displacement FROM FORD
                        WHERE EngineID = test_engine_ID);
  RETURN vdisplacement;
  END ;
END MODULE ;
```

The two routines in this module (ForeignOrDomestic and Engine) don't have much in common, but they don't have to. You can gather related routines into a single module, or you can stick all the routines that you're likely to use in a single module, regardless of whether they have anything in common.

Chapter **7**

Connecting SQL to a Remote Database

With a stand-alone desktop database system, communication is never an issue. The data-driven application you write has only one place to go for data: the database on your hard disk. Your desktop database management system (DBMS) provides the interface between your application code and the database. This simple situation, once very common, has largely been replaced by client/server database systems that reside on a local area network (LAN) or wide area network (WAN), or by Cloud-based systems such as Microsoft's OneDrive, Amazon's AWS, or Google Drive. In these more complicated configurations, you must communicate with different database back ends in different ways.

In this chapter, I discuss client/server systems. A simple client/server system has one server machine that hosts the database. Multiple client computers are connected to the server over a LAN. Users sit at the client machines, which execute your database application program. Larger systems can have multiple servers, each holding different databases. The part of your program written in a host language such as C++, C#, or Java is executed on the client machine, but the SQL is sent over the network to a server. Before it's sent to the server, the SQL must be translated into something the database understands. Several methods of doing this exist.

Native Drivers

The simplest form of communication between an application and a database is through a *native driver*. Figure 7-1 shows how a native driver specific to Oracle 23c connects your application to an Oracle 23c database.

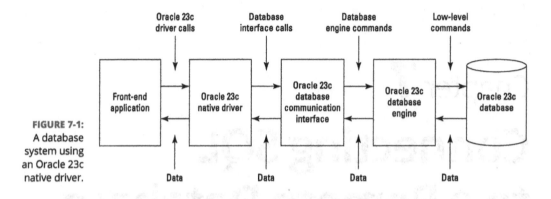

FIGURE 7-1:
A database
system using
an Oracle 23c
native driver.

This arrangement is not much different from that of a stand-alone desktop database system. The Oracle 23c native driver is specifically designed to take SQL from the application and translate it into Oracle 23c database commands. When the database returns a result set, the native driver translates it into a standard SQL result set and passes it back to the application.

Because native drivers are specifically designed to work with a particular database, they can be highly optimized for that specific situation and, thus, have very good performance. That specificity, which makes possible the native driver's greatest strength, is also its biggest weakness. When you build a database system that uses a native driver to connect to one type of database — say, Oracle 23c — the connection doesn't work with any other type of database, such as SQL Server.

When you write a database application, the part of the application that communicates with the database is called the application programming interface (API). When you're communicating to databases through native drivers, every native driver is different from all the others, so the API is different for each one, too. This situation complicates the design and development of applications that must deal with multiple data sources.

Native drivers are great if you know that the application you're writing will have to interface with only one specific data source, both now and in the future. You can't beat the performance of a well-designed native driver. If, however, your application may need to pull data from more than one source, you may want to consider one of the interface options that aren't product-specific. One of these options is ODBC, which is covered in the next section.

ODBC and Its Major Components

An application may need to access data in multiple databases of incompatible types. Incorporating multiple APIs into your code isn't a desirable solution.

Fortunately, you have a better way. Open Database Connectivity (ODBC) is a widely accepted standard method of communicating with most popular database formats. It accomplishes this task by adding an extra layer between the application and the database. Figure 7-2 shows this arrangement. It's unlikely that you'd want to connect any realistic application to five data sources, as shown in Figure 7-2, but with ODBC, you could.

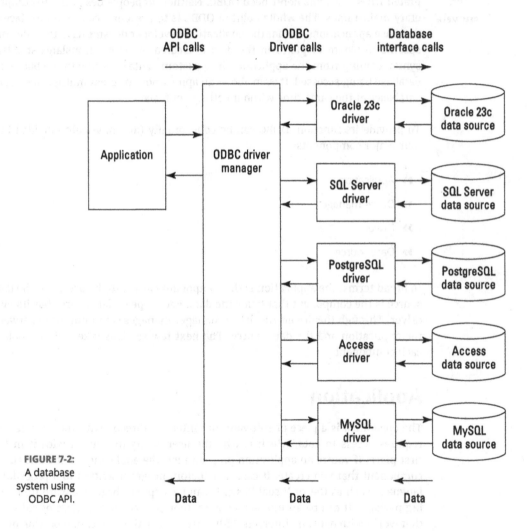

FIGURE 7-2:
A database system using ODBC API.

The application communicates directly with the driver manager. The front end of the driver manager always presents the same API to the application. The back end of the driver manager connects to a driver that's specific to the database on the back end. The driver in turn connects to the database. This arrangement means that you, as the application programmer, never have to worry about the details of how to connect to the database on the back end. All you have to do to be successful is make your program compatible with the ODBC API. The driver manager makes sure that the correct driver is in place to communicate with the database.

REMEMBER

ODBC is a direct response to the needs of developers who design applications to run on client/server systems. People designing for stand-alone PCs running integrated DBMS systems don't need ODBC. Neither do people designing for proprietary mainframes. The whole point of ODBC is to present a common interface to database applications so that the application developer doesn't have to write code specific to whatever platform the data is located on. ODBC translates standard syntax coming from the application into custom syntax specific to the back-end database being accessed. It even allows an application to access multiple back-end databases at the same time without getting confused.

To provide its function, ODBC can be conceptually (and physically) divided into four major components:

>> Application

>> Driver manager

>> Driver

>> Data source

In broad terms, the application is the component closest to the user, and the data source is the component that holds the data. Each type of data source has its own driver. Through the driver, the driver manager manages communication between the application and the data source. The next few sections take a closer look at each component.

Application

The *application* is a piece of software that interacts directly with the user. It also requires access to data, which is why the user wants to interact with it in the first place. If you're an application programmer, the application is the one ODBC component that you create. It can be a custom program written in a procedural language such as C++ or Visual Basic. It can be a spreadsheet or a word processing package. It can be an interactive query tool. Just about any piece of software that works with data and interacts with a user can be the application portion of an

ODBC system. The data accessed by the application can be from a relational database, from an Indexed Sequential Access Method (ISAM) file, or from a straight ASCII text file. ODBC provides a lot of flexibility in what kinds of applications can use it and in what kinds of data those applications can access.

Driver manager

The *driver manager* is a library (in Windows, a Dynamic-Link Library [DLL]) that provides a common interface to applications, regardless of what data source is being accessed. It performs such functions as the following:

» Determining which driver to load, based on the data source name supplied by the application

» Loading and unloading drivers

» Calling driver functions

» Implementing some functions itself

» Performing error checking

REMEMBER

A DLL is a library of routines linked to an application at runtime. In the case of a driver manager, the routines perform the various functions in the preceding list.

The value of the driver manager is that the application can make function calls to it without regard for which driver or data source is currently in use. After the application identifies the needed driver and data source by sending the driver manager a connection handle, the driver manager loads the driver and builds a table of pointers to the functions in that driver. The application programmer doesn't need to worry about maintaining a table of pointers to functions in the driver; the driver manager does that job under the covers.

Aside from the vendors of databases themselves, such as Microsoft and Oracle, driver managers are written and distributed by companies that specialize in database interfacing. Simba Technologies, Progress Software, Easysoft Limited, and OpenLink Software are examples of companies that provide the driver-manager and driver components of ODBC systems.

Drivers

Drivers are libraries that implement the functions of the ODBC API. Each driver has a common interface to the driver manager, but its interface to its data source is customized to that particular data source.

Companies that specialize in driver development, such as those listed in the preceding section, have developed and made available drivers for most of the popular data sources in use today. As a result, most people never need to write their own drivers. Only people who work with unusual data sources or require functions that aren't supported by standard drivers need to write their own drivers, using a procedural language such as C or Java.

DBMS-based drivers operate on multiuser systems operating in client/server mode. This mode of operation features a balance between the client and server machines, both of which do significant processing. The application, driver manager, and driver all reside on the client machine. Together, they comprise the client part of the client/server system.

The data source is composed of the DBMS, such as SQL Server, Oracle, or DB2, and the database itself. These components are located on the server machine. When the server hosts the DBMS as well as the database, it is called a two-tiered configuration. Figure 7-3 shows the two-tier configuration.

CAN ODBC DRIVERS PERFORM AS WELL AS NATIVE DRIVERS?

You may have heard that ODBC is good because it frees the application developer from having to customize applications for each potential target data source. You may also have heard that ODBC is bad because database access through an ODBC interface is slower than access through a database's native drivers. This criticism makes sense because it seems that going through an extra layer of processing cannot help but slow operation. In fact, database access with the first release of ODBC (ODBC 1.0) *was* significantly slower than the same access through a native driver. Going through an extra layer of processing does slow things. Using present-day ODBC, however, doesn't require you to go through that extra layer.

One big reason why ODBC 1.0 access was slow was because the early drivers that implemented it merely accepted SQL from the application and converted it to the DBMS's native API calls. This system has to be slower than a system that generates the native API calls in the first place. Performance of ODBC 2.0 and later drivers has been much better, largely due to the fact that these more recent drivers have been written to use the DBMS's underlying data stream protocol rather than the native API. Instead of making an ODBC call to make a native API call that then uses the data stream protocol, current ODBC drivers use the data stream protocol directly. With this architectural change, ODBC driver performance has become competitive with native driver performance, even exceeding it on some benchmarks.

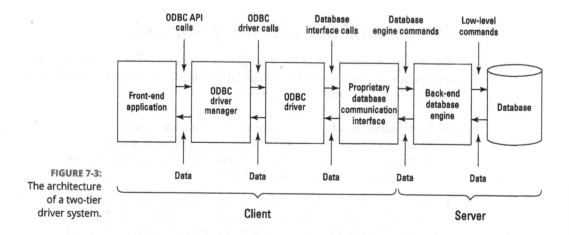

FIGURE 7-3:
The architecture
of a two-tier
driver system.

Labels in figure:
ODBC API calls · ODBC driver calls · Database interface calls · Database engine commands · Low-level commands

Front-end application · ODBC driver manager · ODBC driver · Proprietary database communication interface · Back-end database engine · Database

Data · Data · Data · Data · Data

Client · Server

Data sources

The data source, as the name implies, is the source of the data that's accessed by the application. It can be a spreadsheet file, an ASCII file, or a database under the control of a DBMS. The user needn't know the technical details of the data source, such as file type, DBMS, operating system, or hardware. The name of the data source is all he needs to know.

What Happens When the Application Makes a Request

Application development consists of writing, compiling, linking, executing, and debugging. When you get an application to function the way you want it to, you can release it to users. Applications that use ODBC are linked to the driver manager's import library at link time. The import library contains those parts of ODBC that deal with importing instructions from the application. In Windows, the import library is named ODBC32.LIB. In addition to ODBC32.LIB, a running application uses ODBC32.DLL and a driver that's compatible with the data source. ODBC32. DLL remains loaded in memory as long as any running application requires it. When the last ODBC-enabled application terminates, ODBC32.DLL is unloaded from memory.

Using handles to identify objects

ODBC makes extensive use of the concept of handles. A *handle* is an integer value that identifies an object used by an application. ODBC uses three types of handles that are related in a hierarchical fashion:

- » **Environment handle:** The *environment handle* is ODBC's global context handle. Every application that uses ODBC must allocate an environment handle and, when it finishes, free that handle. Every executing application has one (and only one) environment handle.

- » **Connection handle:** An application connects to one or more data sources. Each such connection is managed by a *connection handle,* which identifies the driver used in the connection for the routing of the ODBC function calls. The driver manager keeps a list of all connection handles associated with an environment handle. The application uses the connection handle to establish — and also to break — the connection to a data source. The connection handle also passes error codes for connection errors back to the application and sets connection options.

- » **Statement handle:** The third kind of handle used by ODBC is the *statement handle,* which processes SQL statements and catalog functions. When the application sends a function call that contains a statement handle to the driver manager, the driver manager extracts the connection handle from it to route the function call to the correct driver.

An application can have one (and only one) environment handle. Conversely, each environment handle can be assigned to one (and only one) application. A single environment handle can own multiple connections, each represented by a single connection handle. Each connection can own multiple statements, each represented by a single statement handle.

Figure 7-4 shows how to use environment handles, connection handles, and statement handles to establish a connection to a data source, execute some SQL statements, and then break the connection.

Following the six stages of an ODBC operation

An ODBC operation takes place in distinct stages. Each stage builds on the one that precedes it. Handles provide the mechanism for the exchange of commands and information. First, an environment is established. Next, a connection between application and data source is built. Then an SQL statement is sent to the data source for processing. Results are returned from the data source to the application. Finally, the connection is terminated.

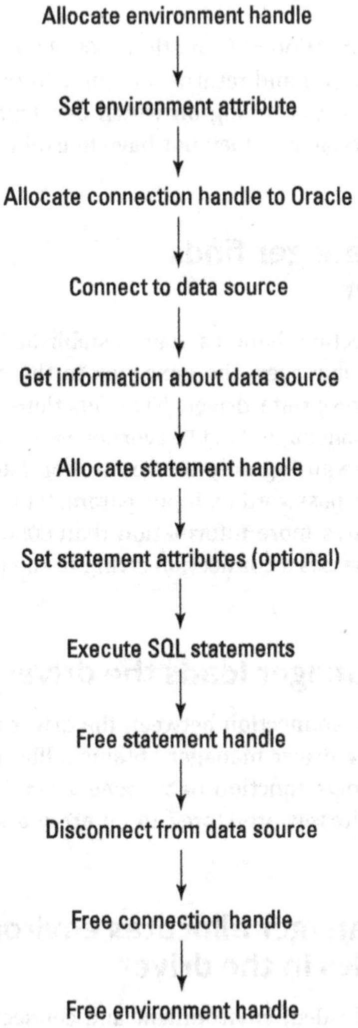

Allocate environment handle

↓

Set environment attribute

↓

Allocate connection handle to Oracle

↓

Connect to data source

↓

Get information about data source

↓

Allocate statement handle

↓

Set statement attributes (optional)

↓

Execute SQL statements

↓

Free statement handle

↓

Disconnect from data source

↓

Free connection handle

↓

Free environment handle

FIGURE 7-4:
Handles establish
the connection
between an
application and a
data source.

Stage 1: The application allocates environment and connection handles in the driver manager

ODBC-enabled applications communicate with the rest of the ODBC system by making function calls. The first step in the process is allocating an environment handle and a connection handle. Two invocations of the function call SQLAllocHandle do the job. The driver manager allocates space in memory for the requested handles and returns the handles to the application. The first invocation of SQLAllocHandle initializes the ODBC interface, in addition to allocating memory for global information. If the first SQLAllocHandle function executes successfully, execution can proceed to the second SQLAllocHandle function. This particular invocation of SQLAllocHandle allocates memory for a connection handle and its associated connection information. SQLAllocHandle takes the active environment handle as input and returns a pointer to the newly allocated connection handle as an output. Depending on which development tool they're using, application programmers may or may not have to explicitly allocate environment and connection handles.

Stage 2: The driver manager finds the appropriate driver

After environment and connection handles have established a link between the application and the driver manager, the next step in the process is linking the driver manager to the appropriate driver. Two functions are available for accomplishing this task: SQLConnect and SQLDriverConnect. SQLConnect is the simpler of the two functions, requiring only the connection handle, data source name, user identifier, and user password as input parameters. When the establishment of a connection requires more information than SQLConnect provides, SQLDriverConnect is used. It passes a connection string to the driver attached to the data source.

Stage 3: The driver manager loads the driver

In a Windows system, after the connection between the driver manager and the driver has been established, the driver manager obtains a library handle for the driver; then it calls the Windows function GetProcAddress for each function in the driver. The function addresses are stored in an array associated with the connection handle.

Stage 4: The driver manager allocates environment and connection handles in the driver

Now that the driver has been loaded, environment and connection handles can be called in it. The function SQLAllocHandle can be used for this purpose, as it was used to call the environment and connection handles in the driver manager. If the application uses the function SQLSetConnectOption to set options for the connection, the driver manager calls the driver's SQLSetConnectOption function to enable those options to be set.

Stage 5: The driver manager connects to the data source through the driver

At last, the driver manager completes the connection to the data source by calling SQLConnect or SQLDriverConnect. If the driver is a one-tier driver, there's no network connection to make, so this stage is trivial. If the driver is multitier, it calls the network interface software in the client machine, which connects to the server machine that holds the data source. To make this connection, the driver uses information that was stored in the ODBC.INI file when the data source name was created.

After the connection is established in a client/server system, the driver usually sends the username and password to the server for validation. If the username and password are valid, the driver returns a standard SQL_SUCCESS code to the driver manager. If they're not valid, the server returns an error code to the driver. Then the driver translates this error code to the standard ODBC error code and returns it to the driver manager as SQLSTATE, and the driver manager returns SQLSTATE to the application.

Stage 6: The data source (finally) executes an SQL statement

With the connection at last established, an SQL statement can be executed. Even this process, however, requires multiple stages. First, a statement handle must be allocated. The application does this by issuing an SQLAllocHandle call. When the driver manager receives this call, it allocates a statement handle and then sends an SQLAllocHandle call to the driver. Then the driver allocates its own statement handle before returning control to the driver manager, which returns control to the application.

After the statement handle has been allocated, an SQL statement can be executed. There is more than one way to do this, but the simplest is the SQLExecDirect function. SQLExecDirect takes a character string as input and sends it to the server. The character string should be a valid SQL statement. If necessary, the driver translates the statement from ODBC-standard SQL to commands understood by the data source on the server. When the data source receives the request for action, it processes the command and then returns any results to the application via the driver and driver manager. The exact details of this processing and how the results are returned to the client application may differ from one data source to another. These differences are masked by the driver so that the application always sees standard ODBC responses, regardless of what data source it is communicating with.

Following is a fragment of C code showing the allocation of environment, connection, and statement handles and connection to a data source:

```
SQLRETURN cliRC = SQL_SUCCESS;
int rc = 0;
SQLHANDLE henv; /* environment handle */
SQLHANDLE hdbc; /* connection handle */
SQLHANDLE hstmt; /* statement handle */
```

```
char dbAlias[SQL_MAX_DSN_LENGTH + 1];
char user[MAX_UID_LENGTH + 1];
char pswd[MAX_PWD_LENGTH + 1];

/* check the command line arguments */
rc = CmdLineArgsCheck1(argc, argv, dbAlias, user, pswd);
if (rc != 0)
{
  return 1;
}


/* allocate an environment handle */
cliRC = SQLAllocHandle(SQL_HANDLE_ENV, SQL_NULL_HANDLE, &henv);
if (cliRC != SQL_SUCCESS)
{
  printf("\n--ERROR while allocating the environment handle.\n");
  printf("  cliRC = %d\n", cliRC);
  printf("  line  = %d\n", __LINE__);
  printf("  file  = %s\n", __FILE__);
  return 1;
}

/* set attribute to enable application to run as ODBC 3.0 application */
cliRC = SQLSetEnvAttr(henv,
                 SQL_ATTR_ODBC_VERSION,
                 (void *)SQL_OV_ODBC3,
                 0);
ENV_HANDLE_CHECK(henv, cliRC);

/* allocate a database connection handle */
cliRC = SQLAllocHandle(SQL_HANDLE_DBC, henv, &hdbc);
ENV_HANDLE_CHECK(henv, cliRC);

/* connect to the database */
cliRC = SQLConnect(hdbc,
                 (SQLCHAR *)dbAlias, SQL_NTS,
                 (SQLCHAR *)user, SQL_NTS,
                 (SQLCHAR *)pswd, SQL_NTS);
DBC_HANDLE_CHECK(hdbc, cliRC);

/* allocate one or more statement handles */
cliRC = SQLAllocHandle(SQL_HANDLE_STMT, hdbc, &hstmt);
DBC_HANDLE_CHECK(hdbc, cliRC);
```

OLE DB

OLE DB is an interfacing technology developed by Microsoft as a replacement for ODBC. Whereas ODBC has enjoyed widespread acceptance outside of the Microsoft world, OLE DB has remained Microsoft-specific. OLE DB builds on ODBC but has additional functionality for interfacing with non-SQL data sources. Despite Microsoft's original intent for OLE DB, ODBC remains the dominant means for connecting applications to databases. The major strength of OLE DB is that you can use it to connect to just about any data source containing any type of data.

6
Working with Advanced Data Types in SQL: XML, JSON, and PGQ

Contents at a Glance

Chapter **1**

Using XML with SQL

XML stands for *Extensible Markup Language,* a general-purpose markup language that, like HTML, is a subset of SGML (Standard Generalized Markup Language). XML's primary purpose is to serve as a means of sharing information between information systems that could have very different architectures. SQL provides the worldwide standard method for storing data in a highly structured fashion, which enables users to maintain data stores of a wide range of sizes and efficiently extract from those data stores the information they want. XML has risen from a de facto standard to an official standard vehicle for transporting data between incompatible systems, particularly over the Internet. Bringing these two powerful methods together greatly increases the value of both. Now SQL can handle data that doesn't fit nicely into the strict relational paradigm that was originally defined by Dr. E.F. Codd. (Dr. Codd's role in the development of SQL is spelled out in Book 1, Chapter 1.) Likewise, XML can efficiently take data from SQL databases or send data to them. The result is information that's more readily available and easier to share.

REMEMBER

XML has come to be a popular means of sharing data over the Internet, particularly over the World Wide Web. Several derivatives of XML designed to carry specific kinds of data are in use. A few examples are RSS, XHTML, MathML, Scalable Vector Graphics, and MusicML. Most business-oriented databases never have to worry about handling XML data, but if you have an application that communicates with other applications across a network, using the XML SQL features can be a lifesaver.

Introducing XML

The XML language marks up text documents with start and end tags. The tags are in some way descriptive of the meaning of the text that they enclose. Key features are the character data itself, containers called elements, and the attributes of those elements. The data is structured as a tree, with a root element playing host to branch elements, which can in turn give rise to additional branches.

The fundamental unit of XML is a Unicode character. The ability to use both 8-bit and 16-bit versions of Unicode is required by the international XML specification. When characters are combined, they form an XML document. The document consists of one or more entities, each of which holds a portion of the document's characters.

The XML specification doesn't specify the names of the elements, the allowable hierarchy, or the meanings of the elements and attributes, as languages like HTML do. XML is much more flexible, leaving the specification of those items to a customizable schema. The XML specification concentrates on specifying what syntax is legal; it's the schema that supplements the syntax rules with a set of constraints. Such a constraint can restrict element and attribute names, as well as the structure of the containment hierarchy. An element named book, for example, could be restricted to contain no more than ten elements named chapter. A different schema could allow up to 20 chapters in a book.

Following are some of XML's salient characteristics:

- >> It's readable by both humans and machines.
- >> It supports Unicode, so even ideographic languages such as Chinese can be represented.
- >> It can represent a variety of common data structures, including records, lists, and trees.
- >> It's self-documenting, meaning that you can tell what it is doing just by looking at it.
- >> Its elements have a simple structure and, thus, are easily parsed.
- >> It adheres to an international standard.
- >> It's platform-independent.

Knowing the Parts of an XML Document

An XML document contains several parts. I describe them briefly in a moment, but first, check out a value assignment prototype:

```
<name attribute="value">content</name>
```

Here's how you'd use that prototype in describing the components of a popular game, expressed in XML:

```
<?xml version="1.0" encoding="UTF-8"?>
<game name="chess">
  <title>Chess game</title>
  <gameboard quantity="1">board</gameboard>
  <whitepiece quantity="1">king</whitepiece>
  <whitepiece quantity="1">queen</whitepiece>
  <whitepiece quantity="2">rook</whitepiece>
  <whitepiece quantity="2">bishop</whitepiece>
  <whitepiece quantity="2">knight</whitepiece>
  <whitepiece quantity="8">pawn</whitepiece>
  <blackpiece quantity="1">king</blackpiece>
  <blackpiece quantity="1">queen</blackpiece>
  <blackpiece quantity="2">rook</blackpiece>
  <blackpiece quantity="2">bishop</blackpiece>
  <blackpiece quantity="2">knight</blackpiece>
  <blackpiece quantity="8">pawn</blackpiece>
  <instructions>
    <action>Place pieces on their start squares.</action>
    <action>Play chess, white moving first.</action>
    <action>Play until someone wins or a draw is declared.</action>
    <action>Shake hands.</action>
  </instructions>
</game>
```

XML declaration

The first line of an XML document usually is its declaration. The declaration is optional but informative: It states the version of XML that's being used and may also contain information about character encoding and external objects that the document depends on. An XML declaration looks something like this:

```
<?xml version "1.0" encoding="UTF-8"?>
```

UTF indicates that a version of Unicode is being used that employs 1 to 4 bytes to hold a character. For alphabetic languages such as English, 1 byte (UTF-8) is fine. Chinese, for example, would use UTF-16, which uses a minimum of 2 bytes per character.

Elements

After the XML declaration, the rest of an XML document consists of elements. *Elements* may contain attributes and content, and they may be nested. An element starts with a start tag consisting of a name enclosed in angle brackets and ends with an end tag consisting of the same name preceded by a slash, also enclosed in angle brackets. The element's content is anything that appears between the tags. Here's an example of an element:

```
<action>Place pieces on their start squares.</action>
```

Nested elements

Elements can be nested inside other elements, as in this example:

```
<instructions>
    <action>Place pieces on their start squares.</action>
    <action>Play chess, white moving first.</action>
    <action>Play until someone wins or a draw is declared.</
  action>
    <action>Shake hands.</action>
</instructions>
```

The `instructions` element contains the four `action` elements.

The document element

Every XML document must have one (and only one) top-level element serving as the root of the tree structure. This element is called the *document* element. The XML description of a chess game given in the section titled "Knowing the Parts of an XML Document" is an example of an XML document element.

Empty elements

An element may exist but have no content. In such a case, it consists of nothing but its start and end tags. A couple of alternative syntax possibilities for an empty element are available. Here are the three possible syntaxes, all of which are equivalent:

```
<nothing></nothing>
<nothing/>
<nothing/>
```

You are probably saying to yourself, "That seems pretty worthless! Why would anybody want to do that?" Being able to set up empty elements is actually a very useful feature. Granted, you probably wouldn't write an XML element that looked like this:

```
<nothing></nothing>
```

But you might write one that looks like this:

```
<book name = "GAN"
  <title> = Great American Novel</title>
  <chapter></chapter>
  <chapter></chapter>
  <chapter></chapter>
  <chapter></chapter>
  <chapter></chapter>
  <chapter></chapter>
</book>
```

You are at the beginning of writing your first book. You don't have any content yet, but you know you want it to have six chapters. You can start out with the chapter elements empty and fill them one by one as you write. It's often a good idea to plan the skeleton of a project before starting right away with the detailed content.

Attributes

An element may or may not have attributes. *Attributes* are pairs of names and values included in the start tag — after the element name — which give you some information about the element. Attribute values must be enclosed in quotes, either single or double, and each attribute name should appear only once in an element.

```
<blackpiece quantity="2">rook</blackpiece>
```

In this example, the blackpiece element has one attribute: quantity, which has a value of 2. The quotes show that 2 is a character that represents the number 2 rather than being the number itself.

Entity references

As I discuss later in this chapter, in the section titled "Mapping identifiers to XML," XML is considerably more restrictive than SQL in terms of the characters it recognizes. Whereas SQL recognizes a large number of special characters, XML pretty much recognizes only the uppercase and lowercase letters, the integers, and a few punctuation marks. To include special characters in an XML document, you can use entity references. An *entity reference* is a placeholder that represents an entity — typically, an unusual character. An entity reference consists of an ampersand (&), the reference, and an ending semicolon (;). XML has five predeclared entity references:

» & (&)

» < (<)

» > (>)

» ' (')

» " (")

Here's an example of a predeclared XML entity that uses the entity reference for the ampersand:

```
<company>Smith &amp; Sons, Plumbing, Inc.</company>
```

When viewed in a web browser, this code displays the following:

Smith & Sons, Plumbing, Inc.

In addition to the five predeclared entity references, you can create additional ones by using the document's Document Type Definition (DTD) or XML schema. Here's an example of the declaration of an entity that hasn't been predeclared:

```
<?xml version="1.0" encoding=UTF-8"?>
<!DOCTYPE rtm [
  <!ENTITY reg "&#xAE;">
  <!ENTITY registered-TM "ACME&reg; Fireworks, Inc.">
]>
<rtm>
  &registered-TM;
</rtm>
```

AE is the hexadecimal code for the registered trademark symbol. When displayed in a browser, the `rtm` document appears as follows:

```
<rtm> ACME® Fireworks, Inc. </rtm>
```

Numeric character references

Another way of representing a nonstandard character is with a numeric character reference. This method just uses the decimal or hexadecimal code for a character. For decimal, the code is preceded by a # sign. For hexadecimal, for example, the code is preceded by #x. Here's a decimal example:

```
<trademark>ACME&#174; Fireworks, Inc.</trademark>
```

Here's a hexadecimal example:

```
<trademark>ACME&#xAE; Fireworks, Inc.</trademark>
```

Using XML Schema

XML Schema is one of several XML schema languages that are more powerful and flexible than the DTD used in "Entity references," earlier in this chapter. A *schema* is a set of rules that a valid XML document must conform to. XML Schema sets up such a set of rules but goes beyond that basic task to the extent of validating information that adheres to specific data types. It's particularly well suited to validating document processing software.

An XML schema definition (XSD) is an instance of XML Schema and usually has a file extension of `.xsd`. Here's an example of a simple XSD describing a member of the Oregon Lunar Society:

```
<xs:schema
 xmlns:xs=http://www.w3.org/2001/XMLSchema>
 <xs:element name="members" type="Members"/>
 <xs:complexType name="Members">
  <xs:sequence>
   <xs:element name="firstname" type="xs:string"/>
   <xs:element name="lastname" type="xs:string"/>
   <xs:element name="officeheld" type="xs:string"/>
  </xs:sequence>
 </ComplexType>
</xs:schema>
```

An XML document that conforms to this schema might look like the following:

```
<members
 xmlns:xsi=http://www.w3.org/2001/XMLSchema-instance
 xsi:noNameSpaceSchemaLocation="members.xsd">
  <firstname>Bryce</firstname>
  <lastname>Thoreau</lastname>
  <officeheld>Archivist</officeheld>
</members>
```

An XSD is written in XML Schema and applies constraints on the elements and attributes that may appear in the XML documents to which it applies. It also defines the relationships among the elements and attributes, as well as the types of data that they may contain. XSDs are used to validate XML documents. With constraints, if data appears in an XML document that the XSD considers to be invalid, an error flag is raised.

Relating SQL to XML

XML, like HTML, is a markup language, which means that it's not a full-function language such as C++ or Java. It's not even a data sublanguage such as SQL. Unlike those languages, however, it's cognizant of the content of the data it transports. Whereas HTML deals only with formatting the text and graphics in a document, XML gives structure to the document's content. XML itself doesn't deal with formatting. To do that, you have to augment XML with a style sheet. As it does with HTML, a style sheet applies formatting to an XML document.

SQL and XML provide two ways of structuring data so that you can save it and retrieve selected information from it:

>> SQL is an excellent tool for dealing with numeric and text data that can be categorized by data type and that has a well-defined size. SQL was created as a standard way to maintain and operate on data kept in relational databases.

>> XML is better at dealing with free-form data that can't be easily categorized. The driving motivations for the creation of XML were to provide a universal standard for transferring data between dissimilar computers and for displaying it on the World Wide Web.

The strengths and goals of SQL and XML are complementary. Each reigns supreme in its own domain and forms alliances with the other to give users the information they want, when they want it, and where they want it.

Using the XML Data Type

SQL:2003 introduced a new data type to SQL: the XML type. This means that conforming implementations can store and operate on XML-formatted data directly without first converting it to XML from one of the other SQL data types.

Although it's intrinsic to any implementation that supports it, the XML data type (including its subtypes) acts like a user-defined type (UDT). The XML type brings SQL and XML into close contact because it enables applications to perform SQL operations on XML content and XML operations on SQL content. You can include a column of the XML type with columns of any of the other predefined types covered in Book 1, Chapter 6 in a join operation in the WHERE clause of a query. In true relational database fashion, your database management system (DBMS) determines the optimal way to execute the query and then goes out and does it.

When to use the XML type

Whether you should store data in XML format depends on what you plan to do with that data. Here are some instances in which it makes sense to store data in XML format:

>> When you want to store an entire block of data and retrieve the whole block later.

>> When you want to be able to query the whole XML document. Some implementations have expanded the scope of the EXTRACT operator to enable extracting desired content from an XML document.

>> When you need strong typing of data inside SQL statements — meaning you want to severely restrict operations that mix data of different types. Using the XML type guarantees that data values are valid XML values and not just arbitrary text strings.

>> When you want to ensure compatibility with future, as-yet unspecified, storage systems that may not support existing types such as CLOB. (See Book 1, Chapter 6 for more information on CLOB.)

>> To take advantage of future optimizations that support only the XML type.

Here's an example of how you might use the XML type:

```
CREATE TABLE CLIENT (
    ClientName      CHAR (30)      NOT NULL,
    Address1        CHAR (30),
    Address2        CHAR (30),
```

```
        City              CHAR (25),
        State             CHAR (2),
        PostalCode        CHAR (10),
        Phone             CHAR (13),
        Fax               CHAR (13),
        ContactPerson     CHAR (30),
        Comments          XML(SEQUENCE) ) ;
```

This syntax stores an XML document in the Comments column of the CLIENT table, although not all implementations may support it yet. The document might look something like the following:

```
<Comments>
  <Comment>
    <CommentNo>1</CommentNo>
    <MessageText>Is VetLab equipped to analyze penguin blood?</MessageText>
    <ResponseRequested>Yes</ResponseRequested>
  </Comment>
  <Comment>
    <CommentNo>2</CommentNo>
    <MessageText>Thanks for the fast turnaround on the leopard seal sputum
sample.</MessageText>
    <ResponseRequested>No</ResponseRequested>
  </Comment>
</Comments>
```

When not to use the XML type

On many occasions, it doesn't make sense to use the XML type. Most data in relational databases today is better off in its current format than it is in XML format. Here are a couple of examples of when not to use the XML type:

>> When the data breaks down naturally into a relational structure with tables, rows, and columns.

>> When you need to do a comparison or sort on a data element, use the data element as a parameter to any scalar, built-in function other than ISNULL and COALESCE.

Mapping SQL to XML

Before you can exchange data between SQL databases and XML documents, the various elements of an SQL database must be translatable (mapped) into equivalent elements of an XML document, and vice versa. This translation needs to happen for several kinds of elements, as described in the following sections.

Mapping character sets to XML

In SQL, the character sets supported are implementation-dependent. This means that IBM's DB2 may support character sets that aren't supported by Microsoft's SQL Server, and SQL Server may support character sets that aren't supported by Oracle. Although the most common character sets are almost universally supported, using a less-common character set may make it difficult to migrate your database and application from one relational database management system (RDBMS) platform to another.

XML has no compatibility issue with character sets. It supports only one: Unicode. This is a good thing from the point of view of exchanging data between any given SQL implementation and XML. All the RDBMS vendors have to define a mapping between strings of each of their character sets and Unicode, as well as a reverse mapping from Unicode to each of their character sets. Luckily, XML doesn't also support multiple character sets. If it did, vendors would have a many-to-many problem, requiring many more mappings and reverse mappings.

Mapping identifiers to XML

What XML calls an identifier corresponds to what SQL calls a primary key. XML is much stricter than SQL in the characters it allows in identifiers. Characters that are legal in SQL but illegal in XML must be mapped to something legal before they can become part of an XML document. SQL supports delimited identifiers, which means that all sorts of odd characters (such as %, $, and &) are legal as long as they're enclosed within double quotes. Such characters aren't legal in XML, however. Furthermore, XML names that begin with the characters XML in any combination of cases are reserved and, thus, can't be used with impunity. SQL identifiers that begin with those letters have to be changed.

An agreed-on mapping bridges the identifier gap between SQL and XML. In moving from SQL to XML, all SQL identifiers are converted to Unicode. From there, any SQL identifiers that are also legal XML names are left unchanged. SQL identifier characters that aren't legal XML names are replaced by a hexadecimal code that takes the form _xNNNN_ or _xNNNNNNNN_, where N represents an uppercase hexadecimal digit. The underscore _ is represented by _x005F_, for example, and the colon is represented by _x003A_. These representations are the codes for the Unicode characters for the underscore and colon. The case in which an SQL identifier starts with the characters x, m, and l is handled by prefixing all such instances with a code in the form _xFFFF_.

Conversion from XML to SQL is much easier. All you need to do is scan the characters of an XML name for a sequence of _xNNNN_ or _xNNNNNNNN_. Whenever you find such a sequence, replace it with the character that the Unicode corresponds to. When you come across _x003A_, for example, replace it with :. If an XML name begins with the characters _xFFFF_, ignore them.

By following these simple rules, you can map an SQL identifier to an XML name and then back to an SQL identifier again. This happy situation, however, doesn't hold for a mapping from XML name to SQL identifier and back to XML name.

Mapping data types to XML

The SQL standard specifies that an SQL data type be mapped to the closest possible XML schema data type. The designation *closest possible* means that all values allowed by the SQL type are allowed by the XML schema type, and the fewest possible values not allowed by the SQL type are allowed by the XML schema type. XML facets, such as maxInclusive and minInclusive, can restrict the values allowed by the XML schema type to the values allowed by the corresponding SQL type. (A *facet* is a single defining aspect of a value space.) If the SQL data type restricts values of the INTEGER type to the range –2157483648<value<2157483647, in XML the maxInclusive value can be set to 2157483647, and the minInclusive value can be set to –2157483648. Here's an example of such a mapping:

```
<xsd:simpleType>
    <xsd:restriction base="xsd:integer">
        <xsd:maxInclusive value="2157483647"/>
        <xsd:minInclusive value="-2157483648"/>
        <xsd:annotation>
            <sqlxml:sqltype name="INTEGER"/>
        </xsd:annotation>
    </xsd:restriction>
</xsd:simpleType>
```

The annotation section retains information from the SQL type definition that isn't used by XML but may be of value later if this document is mapped back to SQL.

Mapping nonpredefined data types to XML

In the SQL standard, the nonpredefined data types include DOMAIN, DISTINCT UDT, ROW, ARRAY, and MULTISET. You can map each of these data types to XML-formatted data by using appropriate XML code. The next few sections show examples of how to map these types.

DOMAIN

To map an SQL domain to XML, first you must have a domain. For this example, create one by using a CREATE DOMAIN statement, as follows:

```
CREATE DOMAIN WestCoast AS CHAR (2)
    CHECK (State IN ('CA', 'OR', 'WA', 'AK')) ;
```

Now create a table that uses that domain, as follows:

```
CREATE TABLE WestRegion (
    ClientName          CHAR (20)          NOT NULL,
    State               WestCoast          NOT NULL
    ) ;
```

Here's the XML schema to map the domain to XML:

```
<xsd:simpleType>
    Name="DOMAIN.Sales.WestCoast">

    <xsd:annotation>
        <xsd:appinfo>
            <sqlxml:sqltype kind="DOMAIN"
                schemaName="Sales"
                typeName="WestCoast"
                mappedType="CHAR_2"
                final="true"/>
        </xsd:appinfo>
    </xsd:annotation>

    <xsd:restriction base="CHAR_2"/>

</xsd:simpleType>
```

From the appinfo element we see that a domain of type WestCoast exists in the Sales schema, and that the data in the domain is of the CHAR type with a maximum length of 2 characters.

When this mapping is applied, it results in an XML document that contains something like the following:

```
<WestRegion>
   <row>
   <ClientName>Nootka Enterprises</ClientName>
   <State>AK</State>
   </row>
   <row>
   <ClientName>Surfin' USA</ClientName>
   <State>CA</State>
   </row>
   <row>
   <ClientName>Cornelius Semiconductor</ClientName>
   <State>OR</State>
   </row>
   <row>
   <ClientName>Orca Inc.</ClientName>
   <State>WA</State>
   </row>
</WestRegion>
```

DISTINCT UDT

With a distinct UDT, you can do much the same things that you can do with a domain, but with stronger typing. Start by creating a distinct UDT with the help of a CREATE TYPE statement, like this one:

```
CREATE TYPE WestCoast AS CHAR (2) FINAL ;
```

The XML Schema to map this type to XML is as follows:

```
<xsd:simpleType>
   Name="UDT.Sales.WestCoast">

   <xsd:annotation>
      <xsd:appinfo>
         <sqlxml:sqltype kind="DISTINCT"
            schemaName="Sales"
            typeName="WestCoast"
            mappedType="CHAR_2"
            final="true"/>
      <xsd:appinfo>
   </xsd:annotation>
```

```
<xsd:restriction base="CHAR_2"/>

</xsd:simpleType>
```

This code creates an element that's the same as the one created for the preceding domain.

ROW

The ROW type enables you to cram a whole row's worth of information into a single field of a table row. You can create a ROW type in SQL as part of the table definition in the following manner:

```
CREATE TABLE CONTACTINFO (
    Name        CHAR (30)
    Phone       ROW (Home CHAR (13), Work CHAR (13))
) ;
```

Now you can map this type to XML with the following schema:

```
<xsd:complexType Name="ROW.1">

    <xsd:annotation>
        <xsd:appinfo>
            <sqlxml:sqltype kind="ROW">
                <sqlxml:field name="Home"
                    mappedType="CHAR_13"/>
                <sqlxml:field name="Work"
                    mappedType="CHAR_13"/>
            </sqlxml:sqltype>
        <xsd:appinfo>
    </xsd:annotation>

    <xsd:sequence>
        <xsd:element Name="Home" nillable="true"
            Type="CHAR_13"/>
        <xsd:element Name="Work" nillable="true"
            Type="CHAR_13"/>
    </xsd:sequence>

</xsd:complexType>
```

This mapping could generate the following XML for a column:

```
<Phone>
    <Home>(888)555-1111</Home>
    <Work>(888)555-1212</Work>
</Phone>
```

ARRAY

You can put more than one element in a single field by using an ARRAY type rather than the ROW type. In the CONTACTINFO table, for example, declare Phone as an array and then generate the XML Schema that maps the array to XML, as follows:

```
CREATE TABLE CONTACTINFO (
    Name        CHAR (30),
    Phone       CHAR (13) ARRAY [4]
) ;
```

Now you can map this type to XML with the following schema:

```
<xsd:complexType Name="ARRAY_4.CHAR_13">

    <xsd:annotation>
      <xsd:appinfo>
        <sqlxml:sqltype kind="ARRAY"
                        maxElements="4"
                        mappedElementType="CHAR_13"/>
      </xsd:appinfo>
    </xsd:annotation>

    <xsd:sequence>
      <xsd:element Name="element"
      minOccurs="0" maxOccurs="4"
      nillable="true" type="CHAR_13"/>
    </xsd:sequence>

</xsd:complexType>
```

This code would generate something like this:

```
<Phone>
    <element>(888)555-1111</element>
    <element>xsi:nil="true"/>
```

```
      <element>(888)555-3434</element>
   </Phone>
```

The element in the array containing xsi:nil="true" reflects the fact that the second phone number in the source table contains a null value.

MULTISET

The phone numbers in the preceding example could just as well be stored in a multiset as in an array. To map a multiset, use something akin to the following:

```
CREATE TABLE CONTACTINFO (
   Name          CHAR (30),
   Phone         CHAR (13) MULTISET
) ;
```

Now you can map this MULTISET type to XML with the following schema:

```
<xsd:complexType Name="MULTISET.CHAR_13">

   <xsd:annotation>
      <xsd:appinfo>
         <sqlxml:sqltype kind="MULTISET"
                         mappedElementType="CHAR_13"/>
      </xsd:appinfo>
   </xsd:annotation>

   <xsd:sequence>
      <xsd:element Name="element"
      minOccurs="0" maxOccurs="unbounded"
      nillable="true" type="CHAR_13"/>
   </xsd:sequence>

</xsd:complexType>
```

This code would generate something like the following:

```
<Phone>
   <element>(888)555-1111</element>
   <element>xsi:nil="true"/>
   <element>(888)555-3434</element>
</Phone>
```

Mapping tables to XML

You can map a table to an XML document. Similarly, you can map all the tables in a schema or all the tables in a catalog. Privileges are maintained by the mapping. A person who has the SELECT privilege on only some table columns is allowed to map only those columns to the XML document. The mapping actually produces two documents: one containing the data in the table and the other containing the XML schema that describes the first document. Here's an example of the mapping of an SQL table to an XML data-containing document:

```
<CUSTOMER>
    <row>
        <FirstName>Abe</FirstName>
        <LastName>Abelson</LastName>
        <City>Springfield</City>
        <AreaCode>714</AreaCode>
        <Telephone>555-1111</Telephone>
    </row>
    <row>
        <FirstName>Bill</FirstName>
        <LastName>Bailey</LastName>
        <City>Decatur</City>
        <AreaCode>714</AreaCode>
        <Telephone>555-2222</Telephone>
    </row>
      .
      .
      .
</CUSTOMER>
```

The root element of the XML document has been given the name of the table. Each table row is contained within a <row> element, and each <row> element contains a sequence of column elements, each named after the corresponding column in the source table. Each column element contains a data value.

Handling null values

Because SQL data may include null values, you must decide how to represent them in an XML document. You can represent a null value as nil or absent. If you choose the nil option, the attribute xsi:nil="true" marks the column elements that represent null values. Null values might be represented in the following way:

```
<row>
        <FirstName>Bill</FirstName>
```

```
        <LastName>Bailey</LastName>
        <City xsi:nil="true"/>
        <AreaCode>714</AreaCode>
        <Telephone>555-2222</Telephone>
</row>
```

If you choose the absent option, you could implement it as follows:

```
<row>
        <FirstName>Bill</FirstName>
        <LastName>Bailey</LastName>
        <AreaCode>714</AreaCode>
        <Telephone>555-2222</Telephone>
</row>
```

In this case, the row containing the null value is simply absent. No reference to it appears.

Creating an XML schema for an SQL table

You may remember from the section titled "Mapping tables to XML" that when mapping from SQL to XML, the first document generated is the one that contains the data, and the second document contains the schema information. As an example, consider the schema for the CUSTOMER document shown in that section.

```
<xsd:schema>
    <xsd:simpleType name="CHAR_15">
        <xsd:restriction base="xsd:string">
            <xsd:length value = "15"/>
        </xsd:restriction>
    </xsd:simpleType>

    <xsd:simpleType name="CHAR_25">
        <xsd:restriction base="xsd:string">
            <xsd:length value = "25"/>
        </xsd:restriction>
    </xsd:simpleType>

    <xsd:simpleType name="CHAR_3">
        <xsd:restriction base="xsd:string">
            <xsd:length value = "3"/>
        </xsd:restriction>
    </xsd:simpleType>
```

```
<xsd:simpleType name="CHAR_8">
  <xsd:restriction base="xsd:string">
    <xsd:length value = "8"/>
  </xsd:restriction>
</xsd:simpleType>

<xsd:sequence>
  <xsd:element name="FirstName" type="CHAR_15"/>
  <xsd:element name="LastName" type="CHAR_25"/>
  <xsd:element
    name="City" type="CHAR_25" nillable="true"/>
  <xsd:element
    name="AreaCode" type="CHAR_3" nillable="true"/>
  <xsd:element
    name="Telephone" type="CHAR_8" nillable="true"/>
</xsd:sequence>

</xsd:schema>
```

This schema is appropriate if the `nil` approach to handling nulls is used. The absent approach requires a slightly different element definition, as in this example:

```
<xsd:element
    name="City" type="CHAR_25" minOccurs="0"/>
```

This element specifies that the minimum number of occurrences of City is 0. In other words, the City field need not hold a value.

Operating on XML Data with SQL Functions

The SQL standard defines several operators, functions, and pseudofunctions that, when applied to an SQL database, produce an XML result or that, when applied to XML data, produce a result in standard SQL form. The functions include XMLELEMENT, XMLFOREST, XMLCONCAT, and XMLAGG. In the following sections, I provide brief descriptions of these functions, as well as several others that are frequently used when publishing to the web. Some of the functions rely heavily on XQuery, a new standard query language designed specifically for querying XML data. I say more about XQuery in Book 6, Chapter 3.

XMLELEMENT

The XMLELEMENT operator translates a relational value into an XML element. You can use the operator in a SELECT statement to pull data in XML format from an SQL database and publish it on the web. Here's an example:

```
SELECT c.LastName
    XMLELEMENT ( NAME "City", c.City ) AS "Result"
FROM CUSTOMER c
WHERE LastName="Abelson" ;
```

Here's the result returned:

LastName	Result
Abelson	`<City>Springfield</City>`

XMLFOREST

The XMLFOREST operator produces a list, or *forest*, of XML elements from a list of relational values. Each of the operator's arguments produces a new element. Here's an example of this operator:

```
SELECT c.LastName
    XMLFOREST (c.City,
               c.AreaCode,
               c.Telephone ) AS "Result"
FROM CUSTOMER c
WHERE LastName="Abelson" OR LastName="Bailey" ;
```

This code produces the following output:

LastName	Result
Abelson	`<City>Springfield</City>`
	`<AreaCode>714</AreaCode>`
	`<Telephone>555-1111</Telephone>`
Bailey	`<City>Decatur</City>`
	`<AreaCode>714</AreaCode>`
	`<Telephone>555-2222</Telephone>`

XMLCONCAT

XMLCONCAT provides an alternative way to produce a forest of elements. It does so by concatenating its XML arguments, as in this example:

```
SELECT c.LastName,
    XMLCONCAT(
        XMLELEMENT ( NAME "first", c.FirstName,
        XMLELEMENT ( NAME "last", c.LastName)
        ) AS "Result"
FROM CUSTOMER c ;
```

This code produces the following result:

LastName	Result
Abelson	\<first>Abe\</first>
	\<last>Abelson\</last>
Bailey	\<first>Bill\</first>
	\<last>Bailey\</last>

XMLAGG

XMLAGG, the aggregate function, takes XML documents or fragments of XML documents as input and produces a single XML document as output in GROUP BY queries. The aggregation contains a forest of elements. To illustrate the concept, take a look at the following query:

```
SELECT XMLELEMENT
    ( NAME "City",
        XMLATTRIBUTES ( c.City AS "name" ) ,
        XMLAGG (XMLELEMENT ( NAME "last" c.LastName )
                )
    ) AS "CityList"
FROM CUSTOMER c
GROUP BY City ;
```

When run against the CUSTOMER table, this query produces the following:

CityList

```
<City name="Decatur">
   <last>Bailey</last>
</City>
<City name="Philo">
   <last>Stetson</last>
   <last>Stetson</last>
   <last>Wood</last>
</City>
<City name="Springfield">
   <last>Abelson</last>
</City>
```

XMLCOMMENT

The XMLCOMMENT function enables an application to create an XML comment. Its syntax is as follows:

```
XMLCOMMENT ( 'comment content'
     [RETURNING
          { CONTENT | SEQUENCE } ] )
```

The example

```
XMLCOMMENT ('Back up database at 2 am every night.')
```

would create an XML comment that looks like this:

```
<!--Back up database at 2 am every night. -->
```

XMLPARSE

The XMLPARSE function performs a nonvalidating parse of a string to produce an XML value. You might use it like this:

```
XMLPARSE (DOCUMENT '   GREAT JOB!   '
    PRESERVE WHITESPACE )
```

The preceding code would produce an XML value that is either XML(UNTYPED DOCUMENT) or XML(ANY DOCUMENT). Which of the two subtypes would be chosen is implementation-defined.

XMLPI

The XMLPI function allows applications to create XML processing instructions. The syntax for this function is as follows:

```
XMLPI NAME target
    [ , string-expression ]
    [RETURNING
         { CONTENT | SEQUENCE } ] )
```

target identifies the target of the processing instruction (PI). string-expression is the content of the PI. This function creates an XML comment of the following form:

```
<? target string-expression ?>
```

XMLQUERY

The XMLQUERY function evaluates an XQuery expression (for more about XQuery, see Book 6, Chapter 3) and returns the result to the SQL application. The syntax of XMLQUERY is

```
XMLQUERY ( XQuery-expression
    [ PASSING { By REF | BY VALUE }
      argument-list ]
    RETURNING { CONTENT | SEQUENCE }
    { BY REF | BY VALUE } )
```

Here's an example of the use of XMLQUERY:

```
SELECT max_average,
    XMLQUERY (
          'for $batting_average in
                /player/batting_average
          where /player/lastname = $var1
          return $batting_average'
          PASSING BY VALUE
                'Mantle' AS var1,
          RETURNING SEQUENCE BY VALUE )
FROM offensive_stats
```

This statement returns the batting average for New York Yankees star Mickey Mantle stored in the `offensive_stats` XML document.

XMLCAST

The XMLCAST function is similar to an ordinary SQL CAST function but has some additional restrictions. XMLCAST enables an application to cast a value from an XML type to another XML type or to an SQL type. Similarly, you can use it to cast a value from an SQL type to an XML type. The restrictions are as follows:

>> At least one of the types involved — either the source type or the destination type — must be an XML type.

>> Neither of the types involved may be an SQL collection type, row type, structured type, or reference type.

>> Only the values of one of the XML types or the SQL null type may be cast to XML(UNTYPED DOCUMENT) or to XML(ANY DOCUMENT).

Here's an example:

```
XMLCAST ( CLIENT.ClientName AS XML(UNTYPED CONTENT)
```

The XMLCAST function is transformed into an ordinary SQL CAST. The only reason to use a separate keyword is to enforce the preceding restrictions.

Working with XML Predicates

Predicates return a value of TRUE or FALSE. Some new predicates have been added that specifically relate to XML.

DOCUMENT

The purpose of the DOCUMENT predicate is to determine whether an XML value is an XML document. It tests whether an XML value is an instance of either XML(ANY DOCUMENT) or XML(UNTYPED DOCUMENT). The syntax is as follows:

```
XML-value IS [NOT]
   [ANY | UNTYPED] DOCUMENT
```

If the expression evaluates to true, the predicate returns a TRUE value; otherwise, it returns a FALSE value unless the XML value is a null value, in which case it returns an UNKNOWN value. If you don't specify either ANY or UNTYPED, the default assumption is ANY.

CONTENT

You would use the CONTENT predicate to determine whether an XML value is an instance of XML(ANY CONTENT) or XML(UNTYPED CONTENT). The syntax is

```
XML-value IS [NOT]
    [ANY | UNTYPED] CONTENT
```

As is the case with the DOCUMENT predicate, if you don't specify either ANY or UNTYPED, ANY is the default.

XMLEXISTS

As the name implies, you can use this predicate to determine whether a value exists. Here's the syntax:

```
XMLEXISTS ( XQuery-expression
    [ argument-list ])
```

The XQuery expression is evaluated, using the values provided in the argument list. If the value queried by the XQuery expression is the SQL NULL value, the predicate's result is UNKNOWN. If the evaluation returns an empty XQuery sequence, the predicate's result is FALSE; otherwise, the result is TRUE. You can use this predicate to determine whether an XML document contains some particular content before using a portion of that content in an expression.

VALID

The VALID predicate is used to evaluate an XML value to see whether it's valid in the context of a registered XML schema. The syntax of the VALID predicate is more complex than is the case for most predicates, as you see in this example:

```
xml-value IS [NOT] VALID
[XML valid identity constraint option]
[XML valid according-to clause]
```

This predicate checks whether the XML value is one of the five XML types: XML(SEQUENCE), XML(ANY CONTENT), XML(UNTYPED CONTENT), XML(ANY DOCUMENT), or XML(UNTYPED DOCUMENT). Additionally, it may check whether the validity of the XML value depends on identity constraints and whether the value is valid with respect to a particular XML schema (the validity target).

There are four possibilities for the identify-constraint-option component of the syntax:

>> WITHOUT IDENTITY CONSTRAINTS

>> WITH IDENTITY CONSTRAINTS GLOBAL

>> WITH IDENTITY CONSTRAINTS LOCAL

>> DOCUMENT

If the identify-constraint-option syntax component isn't specified, WITHOUT IDENTITY CONSTRAINTS is assumed. If DOCUMENT is specified, it acts like a combination of the DOCUMENT predicate and the VALID predicate WITH IDENTITY CONSTRAINTS GLOBAL.

WITH IDENTITY CONSTRAINTS GLOBAL means that the value is checked not only against the XML schema, but also against the XML rules for ID/IDREF relationships. ID and IDREF are XML attribute types that identify elements of a document.

WITH IDENTITY CONSTRAINTS LOCAL means that the value is checked against the XML schema but not against the XML rules for ID/IDREF or the XML schema rules for identify constraints.

The XML valid according-to clause identifies the schema that the value will be validated against.

Chapter **2**

Storing XML Data in SQL Tables

The latest version of the ISO/IEC SQL specification (SQL:2016) details how to store XML data in an SQL-compliant database and operate on it with SQL. In this chapter, I cover SQL's basic data manipulation operations as applied to XML data. Because the primary focus of this book is SQL, I assume that you're already up to speed on XML.

Inserting XML Data into an SQL Pseudotable

Until recently, with regard to the relationship between SQL and XML, the emphasis has been on converting SQL table data to XML to make it accessible on the Internet. A more recent addition to the SQL standard addresses the complementary problem of converting XML data to SQL tables so that it can be easily queried using standard SQL statements. The XMLTABLE pseudofunction performs this operation. The syntax for XMLTABLE is

```
XMLTABLE ( [namespace-declaration,]
XQuery-expression
[PASSING argument-list]
COLUMNS XMLtbl-column-definitions
```

where argument-list is

```
value-expression AS identifier
```

and XMLtbl-column-definitions is a comma-separated list of column definitions, which may contain

```
column-name FOR ORDINALITY
```

or

```
column-name data-type
[BY REF | BY VALUE]
[default-clause]
[PATH XQuery-expression]
```

Here's an example of how you might use XMLTABLE to extract data from an XML document into an SQL pseudotable. A pseudotable isn't persistent — meaning that it isn't permanently stored — but in every other respect behaves like a normal SQL table, as in this example:

```
SELECT clientphone.*
FROM
   clients_xml ,
   XMLTABLE(
      'for $m in
         $col/client
      return
         $m'
   PASSING clients_xml.client AS "col"
   COLUMNS
      "ClientName" CHAR (30) PATH 'clientname' ,
      "Phone" CHAR (13) PATH 'phone'
   ) AS clientphone
```

This query retrieves the contents of the clientname and phone fields from the XML document named clients_xml, and places the result set into the ClientName and Phone columns of the SQL pseudotable named clientphone.

When run, the preceding code gives the following result:

```
ClientName                        Phone
-------------------------------   -------------
Abe Abelson                       (714)555-1111
Bill Bailey                       (714)555-2222
Chuck Wood                        (714)555-3333

(3 rows in clientphone)
```

If you want to make it persistent, you can create a table with a CREATE TABLE statement as follows:

```
CREATE TABLE clientphone AS
clients_xml ,
    XMLTABLE(
        'for $m in
            $col/client
        return
            $m'
    PASSING clients_xml.client AS "col"
    COLUMNS
        "ClientName" CHARACTER (30) PATH 'clientName' ,
        "Phone" CHARACTER (13) PATH 'phone'
    )
```

Creating a Table to Hold XML Data

Although you can create a table to hold XML data by using the CREATE TABLE statement wrapped around an XMLTABLE function, as shown in the preceding section, you can also create a table the old-fashioned way, specifying one or more columns as having the XML data type and inserting XML data into the table later. The process is just as simple as this:

```
CREATE TABLE CLIENT (
    ClientName      CHAR (30)       NOT NULL,
    Address1        CHAR (30),
    Address2        CHAR (30),
    City            CHAR (25),
    State           CHAR (2),
    PostalCode      CHAR (10),
```

```
Phone            CHAR (13),
Fax              CHAR (13),
ContactPerson    CHAR (30),
Comments         XML(SEQUENCE) ) ;
```

Tables can hold a mix of data of the XML data type and classic SQL data types, as shown in this example, or you could create a table in which all columns contain XML data.

Updating XML Documents

Currently, there's no standard way to update XML documents stored in persistent storage, such as an SQL database. Also, there's no standard way to modify transient XML documents, such as stock tickers. Furthermore, there's no standard way to add new data to an existing XML document. Methods for performing these operations haven't been added to the XQuery 1.0 standard because update operations carry some messy baggage, causing side effects that complicate operations.

Regardless of whether a standard method exists, you need to be able to modify XML documents. Following are some of the required tasks that you should be able to perform:

>> Insert new nodes into an instance of a data model at specified positions.

>> Change the value of a node in an instance of a data model.

>> Replace nodes in an instance of a data model.

>> Modify the properties of nodes in an instance of a data model.

>> Delete a node in an instance of a data model.

Because you clearly need to be able to update XML documents that reside in SQL databases, and because no universally recognized standard way of doing so exists, vendors of database management systems (DBMS) have developed proprietary solutions to the problem. In the next few sections, I briefly describe the Oracle and Microsoft solutions.

Discovering Oracle's Tools for Updating XML Data in a Table

Oracle provides three distinct methods of updating XML data in an Oracle database:

» **Document Object Model (DOM):** DOM was developed by the World Wide Web Consortium (www.w3.org). It provides methods for traversing the DOM representation of an XML document, retrieving values from individual nodes, inserting nodes, deleting nodes, and modifying the values of nodes.

» **Java application programming interface (API):** Another method uses a Java API that defines a class to represent the XML type, along with methods such as insertXML( ), updateXML( ), and deleteXML( ).

» **Update functions:** The third method is more closely related to SQL/XML. In SQL/XML, applications use ordinary SQL statements to access XML data stored as values of the XML type in tables. The SQL function XMLQUERY (discussed in Book 6, Chapter 1) evaluates an XQuery expression and returns the result of that evaluation to an SQL application.

   Oracle extends SQL/XML with several update functions:

   • APPENDCHILDXML, INSERTCHILDXML, and INSERTXMLBEFORE for inserting new data

   • DELETEXML for deleting data

   • UPDATEXML for updating existing data

In the next few sections, I look a bit more closely at the update functions.

WARNING

Oracle is trying to steer developers toward the XQuery tool (which I discuss in Book 6, Chapter 3). In Oracle 23c, the SQL/XML update functions are still available, but they're marked as deprecated. This means that Oracle plans on removing them in some future release.

APPENDCHILDXML

Unlike the row-and-column structure of an SQL database table, XML documents have a treelike structure. The tree has nodes and branches, with parent nodes branching out to child nodes. The ultimate parent node, called the *root* node, resides at the base of the tree. The APPENDCHILDXML function adds a child node to an existing node. The node it adds is the very last sibling of the existing node's current children.

Here's an example, using the CLIENT table from "Creating a Table to Hold XML Data," earlier in this chapter:

```
UPDATE CLIENT SET Comments =
  APPENDCHILDXML(Comments, 'Comments/Comment',
  XMLTYPE('<IssueClosed>Yes</IssueClosed>'))
  WHERE EXTRACTVALUE(Comments,
    '/Comments/Comment/ResponseRequested') = 'No';
```

The second argument of APPENDCHILDXML, 'Comments/Comment', is the XPath expression, which specifies a location within the document. The preceding code makes the following change in the XML document shown in Book 6, Chapter 1 (Xpath is a query language for selecting nodes from an XML document):

```
<Comments>
  <Comment>
    <CommentNo>1</CommentNo>
    <MessageText>Is VetLab equipped to analyze penguin blood?</MessageText>
    <ResponseRequested>Yes</ResponseRequested>
  </Comment>
  <Comment>
    <CommentNo>2</CommentNo>
    <MessageText>Thanks for the fast turnaround on the leopard seal sputum
    sample.</MessageText>
    <ResponseRequested>No</ResponseRequested>
    <IssueClosed>Yes</IssueClosed>
  </Comment>
</Comments>
```

The IssueClosed node has been added as the last child of the Comment node, where ResponseRequested has a value of No.

INSERTCHILDXML

Whereas APPENDCHILDXML adds a new node to the XML document tree, INSERTCHILDXML inserts a new value into the document at the node specified by the XPath expression. Following is an example:

```
UPDATE CLIENT SET Comments =
  INSERTCHILDXML(Comments, 'Comments/Comment', 'MessageText',
  XMLTYPE('<MessageText>I am only interested in gentoo penguins.
  </MessageText>'))
  WHERE EXTRACTVALUE(Comments,
    '/Comments/Comment/CommentNo') = 1;
```

This code adds another instance of `MessageText` to comment 1, with the following result:

```
<Comments>
  <Comment>
    <CommentNo>1</CommentNo>
    <MessageText>Is VetLab equipped to analyze penguin blood?</MessageText>
      <MessageText>I am only interested in gentoo penguins.</MessageText>
      <ResponseRequested>Yes</ResponseRequested>
  </Comment>
  <Comment>
    <CommentNo>2</CommentNo>
    <MessageText>Thanks for the fast turnaround on the leopard seal sputum
    sample.</MessageText>
    <ResponseRequested>No</ResponseRequested>
    <IssueClosed>Yes</IssueClosed>
  </Comment>
</Comments>
```

INSERTXMLBEFORE

The `INSERTXMLBEFORE` function inserts a new value *before* the node specified by the XPath expression. The following example shows the difference between `INSERTXMLBEFORE` and `INSERTCHILDXML`:

```
UPDATE CLIENT SET Comments =
  INSERTXMLBEFORE(Comments,'Comments/Comment/MessageText[1]',
  XMLTYPE('<MessageText>I am only interested in gentoo penguins.</
  MessageText>'))
WHERE EXTRACTVALUE(Comments,
    '/Comments/Comment/CommentNo') = 1;
```

This code adds another instance of `MessageText` to comment 1, before the existing instance. The result follows:

```
<Comments>
  <Comment>
    <CommentNo>1</CommentNo>
    <MessageText>I am only interested in gentoo penguins.</MessageText>
    <MessageText>Is VetLab equipped to analyze penguin blood?</MessageText>
      <ResponseRequested>Yes</ResponseRequested>
  </Comment>
  <Comment>
    <CommentNo>2</CommentNo>
    <MessageText>Thanks for the fast turnaround on the leopard seal sputum
    sample.</MessageText>
```

```
    <ResponseRequested>No</ResponseRequested>
    <IssueClosed>Yes</IssueClosed>
  </Comment>
</Comments>
```

The new addition to Comment 1 has been placed ahead of the original message.

DELETEXML

The DELETEXML function deletes the node matched by the XPath expression in the target XML document. In the example in this section, I remove the IssueClosed node from the Comments document. Here's the document before the deletion:

```
<Comments>
  <Comment>
    <CommentNo>1</CommentNo>
    <MessageText>Is VetLab equipped to analyze penguin blood?</MessageText>
    <ResponseRequested>Yes</ResponseRequested>
  </Comment>
  <Comment>
    <CommentNo>2</CommentNo>
    <MessageText>Thanks for the fast turnaround on the leopard seal sputum
    sample.</MessageText>
    <ResponseRequested>No</ResponseRequested>
    <IssueClosed>Yes</IssueClosed>
  </Comment>
</Comments>
```

Here's the deletion operation:

```
UPDATE CLIENT SET Comments =
  DELETEXML(Comments, 'Comments/Comment/IssueClosed')
  WHERE EXTRACTVALUE(Comments,
    '/Comments/Comment/ResponseRequested') = 'No';
```

The result is

```
<Comments>
  <Comment>
    <CommentNo>1</CommentNo>
    <MessageText>Is VetLab equipped to analyze penguin blood?</MessageText>
    <ResponseRequested>Yes</ResponseRequested>
  </Comment>
  <Comment>
    <CommentNo>2</CommentNo>
```

```
<MessageText>Thanks for the fast turnaround on the leopard seal sputum
sample.</MessageText>
<ResponseRequested>No</ResponseRequested>
</Comment>
</Comments>
```

UPDATEXML

The UPDATEXML function updates an existing value in an XML document. To see this function in operation, go ahead and change the ResponseRequested element of the Comments document. First, here's the document before the update:

```
<Comments>
  <Comment>
  <CommentNo>1</CommentNo>
  <MessageText>Is VetLab equipped to analyze penguin blood?</MessageText>
    <ResponseRequested>Yes</ResponseRequested>
  </Comment>
  <Comment>
  <CommentNo>2</CommentNo>
  <MessageText>Thanks for the fast turnaround on the leopard seal sputum
sample.</MessageText>
  <ResponseRequested>No</ResponseRequested>
  </Comment>
</Comments>
```

Here's the update operation itself:

```
UPDATE CLIENT SET Comments =
  UPDATEXML(Comments, 'Comments/Comment/ResponseRequested/text()', Maybe)
  WHERE EXTRACTVALUE(Comments,
    '/Comments/Comment/ResponseRequested') = 'Yes';
```

This operation produces the following result:

```
<Comments>
  <Comment>
    <CommentNo>1</CommentNo>
    <MessageText>Is VetLab equipped to analyze penguin blood?</MessageText>
    <ResponseRequested>Maybe</ResponseRequested>
  </Comment>
  <Comment>
  <CommentNo>2</CommentNo>
  <MessageText>Thanks for the fast turnaround on the leopard seal sputum
sample.</MessageText>
```

```
    <ResponseRequested>No</ResponseRequested>
  </Comment>
</Comments>
```

Oracle's extension functions UPDATEXML, INSERTCHILDXML, INSERTXMLBEFORE, DELETEXML, and UPDATEXML are transformation functions rather than true update functions. They don't update an XML value "in place," but return an updated copy of the value they've changed. When the functions are used with an SQL UPDATE statement, as shown here, this difference becomes moot.

Introducing Microsoft's Tools for Updating XML Data in a Table

Like Oracle, Microsoft provides more than one way to update XML data in its SQL Server 2022 DBMS:

>> **Using the modify( ) method as part of the SET clause of an SQL UPDATE statement:** A parameter determines whether the operation is an INSERT, UPDATE, or DELETE operation.

>> **Using a set of .NET classes:** Some of these classes provide methods for setting the values of nodes, inserting nodes into specified locations, deleting nodes, and replacing nodes.

>> **Using the OPENXML function:** This function is part of SQL Server's Transact-SQL implementation of the SQL language. This approach inserts data into a table that pulls its data from an XML document that's part of SQL Server's Transact-SQL implementation of the SQL language.

>> **Using updategrams:** An *updategram* is a template that contains <sync>, <before>, and <after> blocks. With an updategram, you can insert, delete, or update XML data in a database table.

.NET classes is a major topic in its own right, which I will not elaborate on here.

Inserting data into a table using OPENXML

OPENXML is a rowset provider that provides a rowset view over an XML document. To illustrate the use of OPENXML, the following example — using Microsoft's Transact-SQL — creates an internal example of an XML image, using sp_xml:preparedocument. Next, a SELECT statement uses an OPENXML rowset provider to operate on the internal representation of the XML document.

```
DECLARE @idoc int
DECLARE @doc varchar(1000)
SET @doc ='
<ROOT>
    <MEMBERS MemberID="9"
            FirstName="Sam"
            LastName="Shovel"
            OfficeHeld="Investigator"/>
</ROOT>
--Create an internal representation of the XML document.
EXEC sp_xml:preparedocument @idoc OUTPUT, @doc
-- Execute a SELECT statement that uses the OPENXML rowset provider.
SELECT    MemberID, FirstName, LastName, OfficeHeld
FROM      OPENXML (@idoc, '/ROOT/MEMBERS',1)
            WITH (MemberID    CHAR(15),
                  FirstName   CHAR(20),
                  LastName    CHAR(20),
                  OfficeHeld  CHAR(20) )
```

The query produces the following result:

MemberID	FirstName	LastName	OfficeHeld
9	Sam	Shovel	Investigator

The desired information was pulled from an XML document by an SQL SELECT statement, rather than from an SQL table.

Using updategrams to map data into database tables

An updategram works against the XML views provided by an annotated XSD or XDR schema. (XSD is an XML Schema Definition language used to define an XML schema, whereas XDR — XML-Data Reduced — is an older XML schema definition language.) One example of such a schema is the mapping schema, which has the information needed to map XML elements and attributes to the corresponding database tables and columns. The updategram uses this mapping information to update the database tables and columns.

Using an updategram namespace and keywords

All three of an updategram's keywords — <sync>, <before>, and <after> — exist in the namespace urn:schemas-microsoft-com:xml-updategram. You can use any namespace prefix that you want. In the examples in this section, I use updg as a namespace prefix to denote the updategram namespace.

Here's an example of the template:

```
<ROOT xmlns:updg="urn:schemas-microsoft-com:xml-updategram">
  <updg:sync [mapping-schema= "AnnotatedSchemaFile.xml"] >
    <updg:before>
      . . .
    </updg:before>
    <updg:after>
      . . .
    </updg:after>
  </updg:sync>
</ROOT>
```

The code references a mapping-schema named AnnotatedSchemaFile.xml. I discuss mapping schemas in the following section.

The three keywords are defined as follows:

» **<before>:** The state of a record instance before the update.

» **<after>:** The state the record instance is to have after the update.

» **<sync>:** A block that contains the <before> and <after> blocks. A <sync> block may contain more than one set of <before> and <after> blocks, which are always specified in pairs. A sync block is an atomic item; either all of it is processed or none of it is. In that sense, it's similar to a transaction in SQL. If you specify multiple <sync> blocks in an updategram and one of them fails, the other <sync> blocks proceed normally, unaffected by the failure. Thus, an updategram itself is *not* atomic.

You can insert, update, or delete data with an updategram. Which operation is performed depends on the contents of the <before> and <after> blocks:

» If the <before> block is empty but the <after> block contains a record instance, an insert operation is being performed.

» If the <before> block contains a record instance but the <after> block is empty, a delete operation is being performed.

» If both the <before> block and the <after> block contain a record instance, the record instance in the <before> block is being updated to the record instance in the <after> block.

Specifying a mapping schema

Because the tree structure of an XML document is fundamentally different from the row-and-column structure of an SQL table, there must be a translation from one structure to another for XML data to be placed in an SQL table, and vice versa. This translation is called a *mapping schema*. In the simplest case, each element in a ‹before› block or ‹after› block maps to a table, and each element's child element or attribute maps to a column in its corresponding table. This situation is called *implicit* or *default* mapping. If such simple correspondence between the XML document and the SQL table doesn't exist, you must explicitly specify a mapping schema in which the elements and attributes of the updategram match the elements and attributes of the mapping schema.

Implicit mapping

In many cases, an updategram can perform an update without an explicit mapping schema, relying on the default mapping schema instead.

INSERTING AN ELEMENT OF AN XML DOCUMENT INTO A RECORD IN AN SQL DATABASE

Look at this example of an insert operation that uses implicit mapping:

```
<ROOT xmlns:updg="urn:schemas-microsoft-com:xml-updategram">
  <updg:sync >
    <updg:before>
    </updg:before>
    <updg:after>
      <OLS.MEMBERS MemberID="9"
                   FirstName="Sam"
                   LastName="Shovel"
                   OfficeHeld="Investigator"
                   Email="hammett@book.com"
                   Phone="(503)555-8004"
                   Street="154 Polk St."
                   City="Carver"
                   State="OR"
                   Zip="97003"/>
    </updg:after>
  </updg:sync>
</ROOT>
```

This code inserts a new record into the MEMBERS table of the Oregon Lunar Society (OLS). For this code to work without an explicit mapping schema, the

MEMBERS element must map to the MEMBERS table in the OLS database, and the attributes specified in the ‹after› block must map to the columns of the MEMBERS table. In an insert operation, the empty ‹before› block is optional. You can leave it out if you want to.

UPDATING A RECORD IN AN SQL DATABASE FROM AN ELEMENT OF AN XML DOCUMENT

Here's an example of using an updategram to modify the information in an existing SQL table:

```
<ROOT xmlns:updg="urn:schemas-microsoft-com:xml-updategram">
  <updg:sync >
    <updg:before>
      <OLS.MEMBERS MemberID="9"/>
    </updg:before>
    <updg:after>
      <OLS.MEMBERS Phone="(503)555-5643"/>
    </updg:after>
  </updg:sync>
</ROOT>
```

This code updates the phone number for the person with MemberID 9. The updategram uses the columns in the ‹before› block to find the desired record. Because MemberID is the primary key of the MEMBERS table, by itself, it's sufficient to identify the desired row.

DELETING A RECORD IN AN SQL DATABASE WITH AN UPDATEGRAM

You can also delete one or more records from an SQL table by using an updategram. Here's an example that deletes two records from the MEMBERS table:

```
<ROOT xmlns:updg="urn:schemas-microsoft-com:xml-updategram">
  <updg:sync >
    <updg:before>
      <OLS.MEMBERS MemberID="8"/>
      <OLS.MEMBERS MemberID="9"/>
    </updg:before>
    <updg:after>
    </updg:after>
  </updg:sync>
</ROOT>
```

The fact that this updategram has content in its ⟨before⟩ block but an empty ⟨after⟩ block tells you that it's a delete operation.

Explicit mapping

If you're using an updategram to make a simple insertion, update, or deletion, implicit mapping using the default schema works well. If, however, you want to perform a complex update, such as inserting records into multiple tables that have a parent–child relationship, you need to specify a mapping schema to make sure that things end up where you want them. The mapping schema should be in the same directory as your updategram; otherwise, you need to specify the path to it.

Two kinds of mapping schema are in use, either of which will work.

CREATING AN UPDATEGRAM WITH AN XSD SCHEMA

XSD stands for *XML Schema Definition* and is the preferred method of specifying a mapping schema. Following is a mapping schema that maps the ⟨MEMBERS⟩ element to the OLS.MEMBERS table:

```
<xsd:schema xmlns:xsd="http://www.w3.org/2001/XMLSchema"
     xmlns:sql="urn:schemas-microsoft-com:mapping-schema">
  <xsd:element name="MEMBERS" sql:relation="OLS.MEMBERS" >
   <xsd:complexType>
       <xsd:attribute name="MemberID"
                      sql:field="MemberID"
                      type="xsd:integer"/>
       <xsd:attribute name="FirstName"
                      sql:field="FirstName"
                      type="xsd:string"/>
       <xsd:attribute name="LastName"
                      sql:field="LastName"
                      type="xsd:string"/>
       <xsd:attribute name="OfficeHeld"
                      sql:field="OfficeHeld"
                      type="xsd:string"/>
       <xsd:attribute name="Email"
                      sql:field="Email"
                      type="xsd:string"/>
       <xsd:attribute name="Phone"
                      sql:field="Phone"
                      type="xsd:string"/>
       <xsd:attribute name="Street"
```

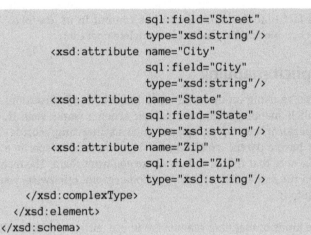

```
                    sql:field="Street"
                    type="xsd:string"/>
      <xsd:attribute name="City"
                    sql:field="City"
                    type="xsd:string"/>
      <xsd:attribute name="State"
                    sql:field="State"
                    type="xsd:string"/>
      <xsd:attribute name="Zip"
                    sql:field="Zip"
                    type="xsd:string"/>
    </xsd:complexType>
  </xsd:element>
</xsd:schema>
```

You'd want to save this mapping schema in an appropriately named file — say, MembersUpdateSchema.xml. Next, you'd want to save the following updategram in a file named Member9Updategram.xml in the same directory, as follows:

```
<ROOT xmlns:updg="urn:schemas-microsoft-com:xml-updategram">
  <updg:sync mapping-schema="MembersUpdateSchema.xml">
    <updg:before>
    </updg:before>
    <updg:after>
      <OLS.MEMBERS MemberID="9"
                   FirstName="Sam"
                   LastName="Shovel"
                   OfficeHeld="Investigator"
                   Email="hammett@book.com"
                   Phone="(503)555-8004"
                   Street="154 Polk St."
                   City="Carver"
                   State="OR"
                   Zip="97003"/>
    </updg:after>
  </updg:sync>
</ROOT>
```

That's it. You've specified your mapping schema by using XSD.

CREATING AN UPDATEGRAM WITH AN XDR SCHEMA

XDR, which is short for *XML Data Reduced*, is an older method of specifying a mapping schema that's gradually being replaced by XSD (covered in the preceding section). Here's an XDR schema that's equivalent to the XSD schema in the preceding section:

```
<?xml version="1.0" ?>
    <Schema xmlns="urn:schemas-microsoft-com:xml-data"
        xmlns:dt="urn:schemas-microsoft-com:datatypes"
        xmlns:sql="urn:schemas-microsoft-com:xml-sql">
    <ElementType name="MEMBERS" sql:relation="OLS.MEMBERS" >
        <AttributeType name="MemberID"/>
        <AttributeType name="FirstName"/>
        <AttributeType name="LastName"/>
        <AttributeType name="OfficeHeld"/>
        <AttributeType name="Email"/>
        <AttributeType name="Phone"/>
        <AttributeType name="Street"/>
        <AttributeType name="City"/>
        <AttributeType name="State"/>
        <AttributeType name="Zip"/>

        <attribute type="MemberID" sql:field="MemberID"/>
        <attribute type="FirstName" sql:field="FirstName"/>
        <attribute type="LastName" sql:field="LastName"/>
        <attribute type="OfficeHeld" sql:field="OfficeHeld"/>
        <attribute type="Email" sql:field="Email"/>
        <attribute type="Phone" sql:field="Phone"/>
        <attribute type="Street" sql:field="Street"/>
        <attribute type="City" sql:field="City"/>
        <attribute type="State" sql:field="State"/>
        <attribute type="Zip" sql:field="Zip"/>
    </ElementType>
    </Schema>
```

The older XDR schema definition language was created by Microsoft and is largely restricted to use with Microsoft products. The XSD schema definition language was created by the W3C international standards body and enjoys widespread use. It is more powerful, but also more complex than XDR.

REMEMBER

In these examples, I've made the attribute names in the schema the same as the corresponding attribute names in the SQL table. This practice isn't necessary, however. As long as it's clear which attributes correspond to which, the attributes can have different names. The same updategram that was created to work with the XSD schema will work with this one, too.

CREATING A MAPPING SCHEMA FOR TABLES WITH A PARENT–CHILD RELATIONSHIP

In "Implicit mapping," earlier in this chapter, I mention that you don't really need an explicit mapping schema for a simple update such as the one shown in that section. Providing such a schema does no harm, however. An explicit mapping schema is *required*, however, for a more complex update, such as insertions into two tables that have a parent–child relationship. Here's an example of an XSD schema that performs such an update:

```
<xsd:schema xmlns:xsd="http://www.w3.org/2001/XMLSchema"
    xmlns:sql="urn:schemas-microsoft-com:mapping-schema">
<xsd:annotation>
  <xsd:appinfo>
    <sql:relationship name="InvoiceToLine"
        parent="Sales.Invoice"
        parent-key="InvoiceNo"
        child="Sales.InvoiceLine"
        child-key="InvoiceNo"/>
  </xsd:appinfo>
</xsd:annotation>

<xsd:element name="Invoice" sql:relation="Sales.Invoice" >
  <xsd:complexType>
    <xsd:sequence>
      <xsd:element name="Line"
          sql:relation="Sales.InvoiceLine"
          sql:relationship="InvoiceToLine" >
        <xsd:complexType>
          <xsd:attribute name="InvoiceNo"
type="xsd:integer"/>
          <xsd:attribute name="ProductID"
type="xsd:integer"/>
          <xsd:attribute name="UnitPrice"
type="xsd:decimal"/>
          <xsd:attribute name="Quantity"
type="xsd:integer"/>

        </xsd:complexType>
      </xsd:element>
    </xsd:sequence>
      <xsd:attribute name="CustomerID" type="xsd:string"/>
      <xsd:attribute name="InvoiceNo"  type="xsd:integer"/>
      <xsd:attribute name="InvoiceDate"  type="xsd:date"/>
  </xsd:complexType>
```

```
   </xsd:element>
 </xsd:schema>
```

After you save this schema as InvoiceUpdateSchema.xml, you can reference it with an updategram. The following updategram uses this mapping schema to add a new invoice line record for Invoice 1010:

```
<ROOT xmlns:updg="urn:schemas-microsoft-com:xml-updategram">
  <updg:sync mapping-schema="InvoiceUpdateSchema.xml" >
    <updg:before>
      <Invoice InvoiceNo="1010"/>
    </updg:before>
    <updg:after>
      <Invoice InvoiceNo="1010" >
          <Line ProductID="17" UnitPrice="$5.95"
              Quantity="2"/>
      </Invoice>
    </updg:after>
  </updg:sync>
</ROOT>
```

An equivalent XDR schema could look like the following:

```
<?xml version="1.0" ?>
<Schema xmlns="urn:schemas-microsoft-com:xml-data"
        xmlns:dt="urn:schemas-microsoft-com:datatypes"
        xmlns:sql="urn:schemas-microsoft-com:xml-sql">

<ElementType name="Line" sql:relation="Sales.InvoiceLine" >
    <AttributeType name="InvoiceNo"/>
    <AttributeType name="ProductID"/>
    <AttributeType name="UnitPrice"  dt:type="fixed.14.4"/>
    <AttributeType name="Quantity"/>

    <attribute type="InvoiceNo"/>
    <attribute type="ProductID"/>
    <attribute type="UnitPrice"/>
    <attribute type="Quantity"/>
</ElementType>

<ElementType name="Invoice" sql:relation="Sales.Invoice" >
    <AttributeType name="CustomerID"/>
    <AttributeType name="InvoiceNo"/>
    <AttributeType name="InvoiceDate"/>
```

```
        <attribute type="CustomerID"/>
        <attribute type="InvoiceNo"/>
        <attribute type="InvoiceDate"/>
        <element type="Line" >
                <sql:relationship
                        key-relation="Sales.Invoice"
                        key="InvoiceNo"
                        foreign-key="InvoiceNo"
                        foreign-relation="Sales.InvoiceLine"/>
        </element>
    </ElementType>
</Schema>
```

Elementcentric mapping

Elementcentric updategrams, as the name implies, code items as elements. Elements contain child elements, which are the properties of the parent element. The parent element maps to a table, and the child elements map to columns in that table. Here's an example from the OLS database:

```
<ROOT xmlns:updg="urn:schemas-microsoft-com:xml-updategram">
<updg:sync >
  <updg:after>
    <OLS.MEMBERS>
        <MemberID>5</MemberID>
        <FirstName>Gus</FirstName>
        <LastName>Roderick</LastName>
        <OfficeHeld>Webmaster</OfficeHeld>
        <Email>hotrod@davenport.net</Email>
        <Phone>(503)555-9976</Phone>
        <Street>43 Ash St.</Street>
        <City>Silverton</City>
        <State>OR</State>
        <Zip>97078</Zip>
    </OLS.MEMBERS>
  </updg:after>
</updg:sync>
</ROOT>
```

Because no mapping schema was specified, this updategram uses implicit mapping.

Attributecentric mapping

In *attributecentric* mapping, the elements have attributes rather than child elements. The following updategram, which also uses implicit mapping, is an example of attributecentric mapping:

```
<ROOT xmlns:updg="urn:schemas-microsoft-com:xml-updategram">
<updg:sync >
  <updg:before>
  <updg:/before>
  <updg:after>
    <OLS.MEMBERS
        MemberID="5"
        FirstName="Gus"
        LastName="Roderick"
        OfficeHeld="Webmaster"
        Email="hotrod@davenport.net"
        Phone="(503)555-9976"
        Street="43 Ash St."
        City="Silverton"
        State="OR"
        Zip="97078"/>
    </OLS.MEMBERS>
  </updg:after>
</updg:sync>
</ROOT>
```

Mixed elementcentric and attributecentric mapping

It's possible to mix elementcentric and attributecentric mapping in the same updategram, although why you would want to do so is beyond me. The difference between the two approaches can lead to confusion. Anyway, here's an example:

```
<ROOT xmlns:updg="urn:schemas-microsoft-com:xml-updategram">
<updg:sync >
  <updg:before>
  <updg:/before>
  <updg:after>
    <OLS.MEMBERS
        MemberID="5"
        FirstName="Gus"
```

```
        LastName="Roderick"
        OfficeHeld="Webmaster"
        Email="hotrod@davenport.net"
        Phone="(503)555-9976">
        <Street>43 Ash St.</Street>
        <City>Silverton</City>
        <State>OR</State>
        <Zip>97078</Zip>
    </OLS.MEMBERS>
  </updg:after>
</updg:sync>
</ROOT>
```

Once again, this code uses implicit mapping.

Schemas that allow null values

Sometimes, the updategram you're using to insert values into an SQL table may not have a value for each of the table's columns. In such a case, you want to put a null value in the columns for which no value is specified. This issue arises because XML, like most computer languages other than SQL, doesn't support null values. You can handle this problem by assigning the xsi:nil attribute to any element in the updategram that may contain a null value. In the corresponding XSD schema, you must specify the XSD nillable attribute. Here's an example of such a schema:

```
<xsd:schema xmlns:xsd="http://www.w3.org/2001/XMLSchema"
      xmlns:sql="urn:schemas-microsoft-com:mapping-schema">
  <xsd:element name="MEMBERS" sql:relation="OLS.MEMBERS" >
   <xsd:complexType>
        <xsd:attribute name="MemberID"
                       sql:field="MemberID"
                       type="xsd:integer"/>
        <xsd:attribute name="FirstName"
                       sql:field="FirstName"
                       type="xsd:string"/>
        <xsd:attribute name="LastName"
                       sql:field="LastName"
                       type="xsd:string"/>
        <xsd:all>
          <xsd:element name="OfficeHeld"
                       sql:field="OfficeHeld"
                       type="xsd:string"
                       nillable="true"/>
```

```
        </xsd:all>
        <xsd:attribute name="Email"
                       sql:field="Email"
                       type="xsd:string"/>
        <xsd:attribute name="Phone"
                       sql:field="Phone"
                       type="xsd:string"/>
        <xsd:attribute name="Street"
                       sql:field="Street"
                       type="xsd:string"/>
        <xsd:attribute name="City"
                       sql:field="City"
                       type="xsd:string"/>
        <xsd:attribute name="State"
                       sql:field="State"
                       type="xsd:string"/>
        <xsd:attribute name="Zip"
                       sql:field="Zip"
                       type="xsd:string"/>
      </xsd:complexType>
    </xsd:element>
</xsd:schema>
```

A member of the OLS may not hold any office, so the OfficeHeld element is designated as nillable. Here's an example of an updategram that uses this schema:

```
<ROOT xmlns:updg="urn:schemas-microsoft-com:xml-updategram">
  <updg:sync mapping-schema="MembersUpdateSchema.xml">
    <updg:before>
    </updg:before>
    <updg:after>
      <OLS.MEMBERS MemberID="3"
                   FirstName="Tom"
                   LastName="Charges"
                   Email="waldo@magic.com"
                   Phone="(503)555-3211"
                   Street="132 22nd St."
                   City="Portland"
                   State="OR"
                   Zip="97245">
        <OfficeHeld xsi:nil="true">
        </OfficeHeld>
      </OLS.MEMBERS>
```

```
      </updg:after>
    </updg:sync>
  </ROOT>
```

With the schema used here, records can be inserted into the MEMBERS table from an updategram if the OfficeHeld attribute is absent, but that's not true for any of the other attributes. All the other attributes must contain definite values.

Chapter **3**

Retrieving Data from XML Documents

E arly in the development of XML, one of the primary concerns was the conversion of data stored in SQL databases to XML so that it could be transmitted to other, incompatible data stores or so that it could be displayed on the web. In Book 6, Chapter 1, I describe several SQL functions whose purposes are to perform such conversions. Converting XML to SQL is also an important endeavor because SQL has traditionally been the premier tool for extracting the information you want from a collection of data. This conversion usually takes the form of *shredding*, in which an XML document is torn apart and pieces of it flow into the columns of tables in an SQL database. Then queries can be made by using normal SQL SELECT statements.

Querying XML documents directly, without shredding them into an SQL database, is much more complicated; thus, that capability took a while longer to implement in standard form. In addition, many common examples of XML documents aren't readily shredded. The tree structure of an XML document can be difficult to translate into the row-and-column structure of a relational database. Consequently, several years of development of XML query facilities have been required to produce the XQuery standard, currently at version 3.1, which defines how to query an XML document directly and retrieve the information you want.

XQuery, like XML itself, is a vast topic, which I don't cover in detail here. I describe it briefly, however, and give some examples of its use. These examples are in no way comprehensive but should give you an idea of what you can do with XQuery. For an in-depth treatment, I recommend *Querying XML*, by Jim Melton and Stephen Buxton (published by Morgan Kaufmann Publishers).

XQuery

XQuery is a nonprocedural language specifically designed to retrieve desired information from XML documents, just as SQL is a nonprocedural language specifically designed to retrieve desired information from relational databases. Whereas relational databases are highly structured, XML documents can be characterized as semistructured. What an XML document looks like varies a lot more than what a relational database looks like.

REMEMBER

When I say that SQL or XQuery is a *nonprocedural* language, I mean that a query — whether expressed in SQL or XQuery — describes *what* to do but not *how* to do it. The how is left up to the engines that process the SQL or XQuery code.

Where XQuery came from

XQuery is the result of combining the best parts of several predecessor languages. For a long time, it's been clear that being able to query XML documents directly has great value. Several groups worked on the problem and came up with a variety of query languages. One of those languages is XQL, written in 1998 by Jonathan Robie, who worked for Software AG at the time. An unrelated language, also named XQL, was created at Fujitsu Labs at the same time, but never developed beyond the prototype stage.

At about the same time, a language named XML-QL emerged from a collaboration of several researchers. Stanford University joined the game with a project named Lore and a language named Lorel, which had object-oriented characteristics. At Institut National de Recherche en Informatique et en Automatique (INRIA), the French National Institute for Research in Computer Science and Control, a research language named YATL was developed. Rounding out the predecessors, a language named Quilt was developed by Don Chamberlin (one of the authors of SQL), Jonathan Robie, and Daniela Florescu, all of IBM.

Although XQuery probably owes more to Quilt than to any of the other predecessor languages, it takes ideas from all the others and benefits from all that has gone before.

What XQuery requires

The XQuery 3.1 language specification defines what must be true of a language for it to qualify as an XQuery implementation. Actually, it defines three levels. Some things *must* be true, others *should* be true, and some other things *may* be true. XQuery is evolving, and it's not yet clear what will be mandatory in the future.

Among the things that the XQuery 3.1 language specification defines are the following requirements:

» XQuery is a declarative language, and as such, it *must not* mandate an evaluation strategy. It describes what the processor should do, not how it should do it.

» XQuery *may* have more than one syntax binding, but it *must* have one syntax that's convenient for humans to read and one syntax expressed in XML that reflects the underlying structure of the query.

» XQuery *must* define standard error conditions that can occur during execution of a query.

XQuery 1.0 doesn't have any update capability, but an extension named XQuery Update 1.0 does. However, at the time of this writing, not all vendors support XQuery Update 1.0. Oracle and Microsoft, among others, offer proprietary update solutions (discussed in Book 6, Chapter 2).

XQuery functionality

The XQuery requirements document specifies several things that an XQuery implementation *must* do, as well as things that it *should* do and things that it *may* do. Here are some of those functionality requirements:

» XQuery *must* support operations on all data types in the XQuery data model.

» Queries *must* be able to express simple conditions on text, including on text that spans element boundaries. Element boundaries are specified by tags such as `<element></element>`. Text may go beyond such a boundary. If it does, queries must be able to express simple conditions on that text.

» Operations on collections *must* include support for universal and existential quantifiers. "All" is an example of a universal quantifier and "some" is an example of an existential quantifier. When Aristotle said, "All men are mortal," he was making a statement about all men, a universal statement. When he said, "Some men are Greeks," he was making an existential statement. A least one man is a Greek, but one cannot conclude from the statement that all men are Greeks.

>> XQuery *must* be able to combine related information from different parts of a given document or from multiple documents.

>> XQuery *must* be able to compute summary information from a group of related document elements (aggregation).

>> XQuery *must* be able to sort query results.

>> XQuery *must* support NULL values.

>> Queries *should* be able to operate on literal data. Literal data is the data itself, rather than some representation of the data.

>> Queries *must* be able to perform simple operations on names, such as testing for equality in element names and attribute names, and processing instruction targets. Queries *may* perform more powerful operations on names.

>> XQuery *should* support the use of externally defined functions on all data types of the XQuery data model.

>> XQuery *must* be able to provide access to environmental information, such as current date, time, and time zone.

These requirements are a partial list. XQuery 3.1 meets all the requirements I have listed as *must* or *should*. Other requirements in the XQuery Requirements may or may not have been met by XQuery 3.1.

Usage scenarios

The World Wide Web Consortium (www.w3.org) has developed a set of 77 use cases that cover 9 categories of queries. In each case, a query is applied to the supplied input data, and the expected results are given. You can use these use cases as a starting point in testing an XQuery implementation to see whether it's more or less working. An exhaustive test suite, which tests every possibility, would take thousands of such cases, but these 77 are a good start. In this section, I show you just one such case.

Because this book just happens to be about SQL, one category of data that you may want to query using XQuery is data stored in a relational database. The W3 XML Query Use cases document, which is available at www.w3.org/TR/xquery-use-cases, describes just how do to that in Paragraph 1.4. Paragraph 1.4.1 describes the database layout used for the test case, which I reproduce in this section.

The case takes data from a simplified version of an online auction. Three tables are involved: USERS, ITEMS, and BIDS. The USERS table contains information on buyers and sellers. The ITEMS table lists items currently for sale or that have recently been for sale. The BIDS table contains all the bids on record.

Here are the tables and the columns that they contain:

```
USERS (USERID, NAME, RATING)
ITEMS (ITEMNO, DESCRIPTION, OFFERED_BY, START_DATE, END_DATE,
       RESERVE_PRICE)
BIDS (USERID, ITEMNO, BID, BID_DATE)
```

USERID is the primary key of the USERS table; ITEMNO is the primary key of the ITEMS table, and the combination of USERID and ITEMID is the composite primary key of the BIDS table.

The relational database tables correspond to input documents named users.xml, items.xml, and bids.xml. The correspondence between the tables and the XML documents is specified by the following Document Type Definition (DTD):

```
<!DOCTYPE users [
  <!ELEMENT users (user_tuple*)>
    <!ELEMENT user_tuple (userid, name, rating?)>
      <!ELEMENT userid (#PCDATA)>
      <!ELEMENT name (#PCDATA)>
      <!ELEMENT rating (#PCDATA)> ]>
<!DOCTYPE items [
  <!ELEMENT items (item_tuple*)>
    <!ELEMENT item_tuple (itemno, description, offered_by,
          start_date?, end_date?, reserve_price?)>
    <!ELEMENT itemno (#PCDATA)>
    <!ELEMENT description (#PCDATA)>
    <!ELEMENT offered_by (#PCDATA)>
    <!ELEMENT start_date (#PCDATA)>
    <!ELEMENT end_date (#PCDATA)>
    <!ELEMENT reserve_price (#PCDATA)> ]>
<!DOCTYPE bids [
  <!ELEMENT bids (bid_tuple*)>
    <!ELEMENT bid_tuple (userid, itemno, bid, bid_date)>
      <!ELEMENT userid (#PCDATA)>
      <!ELEMENT itemno (#PCDATA)>
      <!ELEMENT bid (#PCDATA)>
      <!ELEMENT bid_date (#PCDATA)> ]>
```

The input data is contained in Table 3-1, Table 3-2, and Table 3-3.

TABLE 3-1

USERS

USERID	Name	Rating
U01	Tom Jones	B
U02	Mary Doe	A
U03	Dee Linquent	D
U04	Roger Smith	C
U05	Jack Sprat	B
U06	Rip Van Winkle	B

TABLE 3-2

ITEMS

ITEMID	Description	Offered_By	Start_Date	End_Date	Reserve_Price
1001	Red Bicycle	U01	1999-01-05	1999-01-20	40
1002	Motorcycle	U02	1999-02-11	1999-03-15	500
1003	Old Bicycle	U02	1999-01-10	1999-02-20	25
1004	Tricycle	U01	1999-02-25	1999-03-08	15
1005	Tennis Racquet	U03	1999-03-19	1999-04-30	20
1006	Helicopter	U03	1999-05-05	1999-05-25	50000
1007	Racing Bicycle	U04	1999-01-20	1999-02-20	200
1008	Broken Bicycle	U01	1999-02-05	1999-03-06	25

TABLE 3-3

BIDS

USERID	ITEMNO	Bid	Bid_Date
U02	1001	35	1999-01-07
U04	1001	40	1999-01-08
U02	1001	45	1999-01-11
U04	1001	50	1999-01-13
U02	1001	55	1999-01-15
U01	1002	400	1999-02-14
U02	1002	600	1999-02-16

USERID	ITEMNO	Bid	Bid_Date
U03	1002	800	1999-02-17
U04	1002	1000	1999-02-25
U02	1002	1200	1999-03-02
U04	1003	15	1999-01-22
U05	1003	20	1999-02-03
U01	1004	40	1999-03-05
U03	1007	175	1999-01-25
U05	1007	200	1999-02-08
U04	1007	225	1999-02-12

The XML representation of this tabular data serves as the input to the query. Following is a truncated version of the XML (truncated because the full XML files are lengthy, with nothing new beyond the first element in each):

```
<items>
  <item_tuple>
    <itemno>1001</itemno>
    <description>Red Bicycle</description>
    <offered_by>U01</offered_by>
    <start_date>1999-01-05</start_date>
    <end_date>1999-01-20</end_date>
    <reserve_price>40</reserve_price>
  </item_tuple>
  <!-- !!! Snip !!! -->

<users>
  <user_tuple>
    <userid>U01</userid>
    <name>Tom Jones</name>
    <rating>B</rating>
  </user_tuple>
  <!-- !!! Snip !!! -->

<bids>
  <bid_tuple>
    <userid>U02</userid>
    <itemno>1001</itemno>
    <bid>35</bid>
```

```
    <bid_date>1999-01-07</bid_date>
    </bid_tuple>
  <bid_tuple>
  <!-- !!! Snip !!! -->
```

Here's one of the queries run against this data: *List the item numbers and descriptions of all bicycles that currently have an auction in progress, ordered by item number.* This query is expressed in XQuery as follows:

```
<result>
  {
    for $i in doc("items.xml")//item_tuple
    where $i/start_date <= current-date()
      and $i/end_date >= current-date()
      and contains($i/description, "Bicycle")
    order by $i/itemno
    return
        <item_tuple>
            { $i/itemno }
            { $i/description }
        </item_tuple>
  }
</result>
```

Assuming that the current date is 1999-01-31, the expected result of the query is

```
<result>
    <item_tuple>
        <itemno>1003</itemno>
        <description>Old Bicycle</description>
    </item_tuple>
    <item_tuple>
        <itemno>1007</itemno>
        <description>Racing Bicycle</description>
    </item_tuple>
</result>
```

The auctions for the old bicycle and the racing bicycle were active on the last day of January 1999.

FLWOR Expressions

FLWOR means *for, let, while, order by,* and *return.* FLWOR expressions are to XQuery what SELECT expressions are to SQL. They're the constructs you use to ask questions of an XML document. A FLWOR expression must contain either a for clause or a let clause as well as a return clause; optionally, it may also include while and order by clauses. Here's the syntax of a FLWOR expression:

```
FLWORExpr ::= (ForClause | LetClause)+ WhereClause? OrderByClause? "return"
    ExprSingle

ForClause ::= "for" "$" VarName TypeDeclaration? PositionalVar? "in" ExprSingle
    ("," "$" VarName TypeDeclaration? PositionalVar? "in" ExprSingle)*

PositionalVar ::= "at" "$" VarName

LetClause ::= "let" "$" VarName TypeDeclaration? ":=" ExprSingle ("," "$"
    VarName TypeDeclaration? ":=" ExprSingle)*

WhereClause ::= "where" ExprSingle

OrderByClause ::= ("order" "by" | "stable" "order" "by") OrderSpecList

OrderSpecList ::= OrderSpec ("," OrderSpec)*

OrderModifier ::= ("ascending" | "descending")? ("empty" "greatest" | "empty"
    "least")? ("collation" URILiteral)?
```

In the preceding code, the following conventions are used:

>> "A?" means that A is optional.

>> "A|B" means either A or B but not both.

>> "A+" means one or more occurrences of A.

>> "A*" means zero or more occurrences of A.

To see how to use a FLWOR expression on an example XML document that corresponds to an SQL table, consider this sample document:

```
<?xml version="1.0" encoding="UTF-8"?>
<customer xmlns:xsi="http://www.w3.org/2001/XMLSchema-instance">
    <row>
        <FirstName>Abe</FirstName>
        <LastName>Abelson</LastName>
        <City>Springfield</City>
```

```
        <AreaCode>714</AreaCode>
        <Telephone>555-1111</Telephone>
    </row>
    <row>
        <FirstName>Bill</FirstName>
        <LastName>Bailey</LastName>
        <City>Decatur</City>
        <AreaCode>714</AreaCode>
        <Telephone>555-2222</Telephone>
    </row>
    <row>
        <FirstName>Chuck</FirstName>
        <LastName>Wood</LastName>
        <City>Philo</City>
        <AreaCode>714</AreaCode>
        <Telephone>555-3333</Telephone>
    </row>
</customer>
```

Keep this example in mind as you make your way through the fors, lets, whiles, order bys, and returns in the following sections.

The for clause

A FLWOR expression must have at least a for clause (or a let clause) and a return clause. For purposes of illustrating the effect of the for clause, here are a for fragment and the result of that much of a FLWOR expression:

```
for $c in customer/row
```

This code selects the row element in the customer XML document. The result is

```
$c:     <row>
            <FirstName>Abe</FirstName>
            <LastName>Abelson</LastName>
            <City>Springfield</City>
            <AreaCode>714</AreaCode>
            <Telephone>555-1111</Telephone>
        </row>
$c:     <row>
            <FirstName>Bill</FirstName>
            <LastName>Bailey</LastName>
            <City>Decatur</City>
            <AreaCode>714</AreaCode>
            <Telephone>555-2222</Telephone>
```

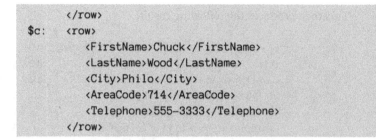

```
        </row>
$c:     <row>
            <FirstName>Chuck</FirstName>
            <LastName>Wood</LastName>
            <City>Philo</City>
            <AreaCode>714</AreaCode>
            <Telephone>555-3333</Telephone>
        </row>
```

The result includes three instances of the variable $c, each one being bound to a separate row element in the binding sequence from the original document. This result is called a *tuple stream*. The for clause iterates over the tuples in the binding sequence, binding the variable to each of the tuples in the sequence in turn.

The let clause

To show the effect of the let clause, I need a second document example to go along with the customer example. Here's that document:

```
<?xml version="1.0" encoding="UTF-8"?>
<product xmlns:xsi="http://www.w3.org/2001/XMLSchema-instance">
    <row rating="0">
        <ProdNo>101</ProdNo>
        <Name>Firecracker 1</Name>
        <Size>Big</Size>
    </row>
    <row rating="1">
        <ProdNo>102</ProdNo>
        <Name>Firecracker 2</Name>
        <Size>Huge</Size>
    </row>
    <row rating="3">
        <ProdNo>103</ProdNo>
        <Name>Firecracker 3</Name>
        <Size>Tremendous</Size>
    </row>
</product>
```

Whereas the for clause iterates over the items in the binding sequence, the let clause binds its variables with the entire sequence. A let clause that binds multiple variables generates a single tuple containing all the variable bindings. Here's an example:

```
let $c := /customer/row, $p := /product/row/ProdNo
```

This code produces the following result:

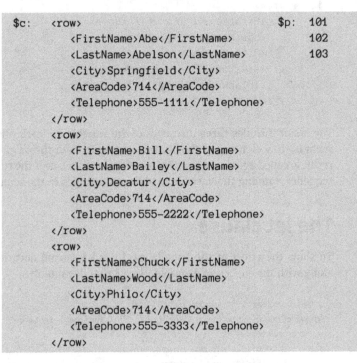

```
$c:    <row>                                          $p:   101
           <FirstName>Abe</FirstName>                       102
           <LastName>Abelson</LastName>                     103
           <City>Springfield</City>
           <AreaCode>714</AreaCode>
           <Telephone>555-1111</Telephone>
       </row>
       <row>
           <FirstName>Bill</FirstName>
           <LastName>Bailey</LastName>
           <City>Decatur</City>
           <AreaCode>714</AreaCode>
           <Telephone>555-2222</Telephone>
       </row>
       <row>
           <FirstName>Chuck</FirstName>
           <LastName>Wood</LastName>
           <City>Philo</City>
           <AreaCode>714</AreaCode>
           <Telephone>555-3333</Telephone>
       </row>
```

The where clause

The result of a for clause or a let clause contains some data that you want, but it likely also contains some irrelevant data that you don't want. You can filter out the data that you don't want with a where clause. Consider the following XQuery fragment:

```
for $p at $i in product/row
where $i = $p/@rating
```

This code produces the following result:

```
$p:    <row rating="3">                               $i 3
           <ProdNo>103</ProdNo>
           <Name>Firecracker 3</Name>
           <Size>Tremendous</Size>
       </row>
```

Only in the case of the last product does the element counter equal the value of the rating attribute.

The order by clause

The order by clause, as you would expect, specifies an order for the items in the result, according to the ordering specification (OrderSpec). The ordering specification contains a single expression (ExprSingle) and an optional ordering modifier (OrderModifier). You can add an order by clause to one of the query fragments in the preceding sections to see how it affects the result, as follows:

```
for $c in customer/row
order by $c/LastName descending
```

This code selects the row element in the customer XML document, listing the tuples in descending order by last name. The result is

```
$c:     <row>
            <FirstName>Chuck</FirstName>
            <LastName>Wood</LastName>
            <City>Philo</City>
            <AreaCode>714</AreaCode>
            <Telephone>555-3333</Telephone>
        </row>
$c:     <row>
            <FirstName>Bill</FirstName>
            <LastName>Bailey</LastName>
            <City>Decatur</City>
            <AreaCode>714</AreaCode>
            <Telephone>555-2222</Telephone>
        </row>
$c:     <row>
            <FirstName>Abe</FirstName>
            <LastName>Abelson</LastName>
            <City>Springfield</City>
            <AreaCode>714</AreaCode>
            <Telephone>555-1111</Telephone>
        </row>
```

Because you're ordering by last name in descending order, the record for Chuck Wood precedes that of Bill Bailey, which comes before the record for Abe Abelson.

The return clause

The return clause specifies what's returned by the FLWOR expression after all the other clauses have had a chance to have an effect. The ExprSingle in the return clause is evaluated once for each tuple produced by the combined activity of the other clauses. The result is a sequence of values. Adding a return clause to the query fragment in the preceding section to make a complete query results in the following:

```
<result>
    {
        for $c in doc("customer.xml")
        order by $c/row/LastName descending
        return
            <row>
                { $c/FirstName }
                { $c/LastName }
            </row>
    }
</result>
```

This code selects the row element in the customer XML document, listing the tuples in descending order by last name. Then it outputs the first and last names in the tuples. The result is

```
<result>
    <row>
        <FirstName>Chuck</FirstName>
        <LastName>Wood</LastName>
    </row>
    <row>
        <FirstName>Bill</FirstName>
        <LastName>Bailey</LastName>
    </row>
    <row>
        <FirstName>Abe</FirstName>
        <LastName>Abelson</LastName>
    </row>
</result>
```

XQuery versus SQL

The data in an XML document is in quite a different form from the data in an SQL table, but some similarities exist between the two worlds. XQuery's FLWOR expression corresponds to some extent with the SQL SELECT expression. Both expressions are used to retrieve the data you want from a collection of data, most of which you don't want at the moment.

Comparing XQuery's FLWOR expression with SQL's SELECT expression

Although XQuery's let clause has no analog in SQL, the XQuery for clause is related to the SQL FROM clause in that both specify the source of the data. XQuery's order by clause serves the same purpose that SQL's ORDER BY clause serves. In both XQuery and SQL, the where clause filters out data that you don't want to include in the result. SQL's GROUP BY and HAVING clauses have no analogs in XQuery.

Relating XQuery data types to SQL data types

Some of XQuery's data types correspond to SQL data types; others don't. XQuery has some data types that don't correspond to any SQL data types, and vice versa.

Table 3-4 lists the XQuery data types and, where applicable, the corresponding SQL types. Where no corresponding type exists, a dash serves as a placeholder.

TABLE 3-4 **XQuery 1.0 Data Types and Corresponding SQL Data Types**

XQuery 1.0 Data Types	SQL Data Types
xs:string	CHARACTER, CHARACTER VARYING, CHARACTER LARGE OBJECT, NATIONAL CHARACTER, NATIONAL CHARACTER VARYING, NATIONAL CHARACTER LARGE OBJECT
xs:normalizedString	—
xs:token	—
xs:language	—
xs:NMTOKEN	—
xs:NMTOKENS	—
xs:Name	—
xs:NCNAME	—
xs:ID	—
xs:IDREF	—
xs:IDREFS	—

(continued)

TABLE 3-4 *(continued)*

XQuery 1.0 Data Types	SQL Data Types
xs:ENTITY	—
xs:ENTITIES	—
xs:BOOLEAN	BOOLEAN
xs:decimal	NUMERIC, DECIMAL
xs:integer	INTEGER
xs:nonPositiveInteger	—
xs:negativeInteger	—
xs:long	BIGINT
xs:int	INTEGER
xs:short	SMALLINT
xs:byte	—
xs:nonNegativeInteger	—
xs:unsignedLong	—
xs:unsignedInt	—
xs:unsignedShort	—
xs:unsignedByte	—
xs:positiveInteger	—
xs:float	FLOAT, REAL
xs:double	FLOAT, DOUBLE
xs:error	—
xs:duration	—
xs:dateTime	TIMESTAMP WITH TIME ZONE, TIMESTAMP WITHOUT TIME ZONE
xs:date	DATE WITH TIME ZONE, DATE WITHOUT TIME ZONE
xs:time	TIME WITH TIME ZONE, TIME WITHOUT TIME ZONE
xs:gYearMonth	—
xs:gYear	—

XQuery 1.0 Data Types	SQL Data Types
`xs:gMonthDay`	—
`xs:gDay`	—
`xs:gMonth`	—
`xs:hexBinary`	`BINARY LARGE OBJECT`
`xs:base64Binary`	`BINARY LARGE OBJECT`
`xs:anyURI`	—
`xs:QName`	—
`xs:NOTATION`	—
`xdt:dayTimeDuration`	INTERVAL (day–time interval)
`xdt:yearMonthDuration`	INTERVAL (year–month interval)
`xs:anyType`	XML
`xs:anySimpleType`	—
`xdt:untyped`	—
Node types	Structured user-defined types (UDTs)
User-defined complex types	Structured UDTs
—	ROW
—	REF
List types and sequences	ARRAY
List types and sequences	`MULTISET`
—	`DATALINK`

Clearly, a lot more XQuery types are available than SQL types. In most cases, casting an SQL type to an XQuery type isn't a problem, but going the other way may be a challenge.

Chapter **4**

Using JSON with SQL

J ust as XML is a data interchange format for transmitting data from one platform to a different incompatible platform, JavaScript Object Notation (JSON) is another such format that performs that function. JSON is specifically designed to transfer unstructured or semi-structured data from one NoSQL database to a different, incompatible NoSQL database. As large and ever-increasing amounts of data are being stored in the semi-structured databases addressed by NoSQL technology, the need to share that data with databases adhering to the highly structured relational technology that is the domain of SQL has become clear. The SQL:2016 specification officially brought JSON into the SQL world, and the SQL:2023 specification provides enhancements to further help us work with JSON data objects. First, I explain the basics of SQL and JSON using the SQL:2016 specifications. Then I show how the SQL:2023 enhancements can help make working with JSON data much easier.

Using JSON with SQL

Organizations have been storing important data in relational databases for close to 40 years, in many cases representing the most critical assets those organizations have. Nowadays, huge amounts of unstructured and semi-structured data are being generated by sensors on the Internet of Things, as well as data coursing over the Internet from billions of users around the world. It is evident that there is value in being able to combine this data with the more structured data stored in relational databases. For this reason, SQL has been expanded to enable relational databases to ingest data in JSON format, and conversely to convert relational data into JSON format for consumption by non-relational data stores.

JSON supports several data types, as does SQL. However, the JSON types don't necessarily match up with the corresponding SQL types. As a result, SQL accepts only the two types that JSON and SQL have in common, character strings and binary strings. This means that any JSON data that you want to ingest into a relational database must first be converted into either character strings or binary strings.

In the reverse direction, data in relational tables can be transformed into JSON objects and arrays, using built-in functions.

To query JSON data stored in SQL tables, a new language named SQL/JSON path language is embedded in SQL operators. You can use these operators to query JSON data stored in relational database tables.

The SQL/JSON Data Model

The SQL/JSON data model is the solution to the problem that SQL and JSON store data in different ways. The SQL/JSON data model sits between the SQL world and the JSON world and can talk to each in its native language.

JSON data comes in a variety of forms, including JSON arrays, JSON objects, JSON members, JSON literal null values, JSON literal true values, JSON literal false values, JSON numbers, and JSON strings. SQL, on the other hand, has no counterpart for JSON arrays, JSON objects, or JSON members. Furthermore, JSON nulls, numbers, and strings are not exactly the same as SQL nulls, numbers, and strings. For its part, JSON has no counterpart for SQL datetime data. This "impedance mismatch" is addressed by a set of SQL/JSON items.

SQL/JSON items

JSON data, stored in the form of character or binary strings, can be parsed into SQL/JSON items. An SQL/JSON item can be an

>> SQL/JSON scalar

>> SQL/JSON null

>> SQL/JSON array

>> SQL/JSON object

SQL/JSON scalar

An SQL/JSON scalar is a non-null value of any of the following SQL types:

>> Character string, using Unicode characters

>> Numeric

>> Boolean

>> Datetime

SQL/JSON null

The SQL/JSON null differs from the SQL null in that it has a value distinct from any value of any SQL type, including the null type.

SQL/JSON array

An SQL/JSON array is an ordered list or zero or more SQL/JSON items. These items are called SQL/JSON elements of the SQL/JSON array. Array elements are separated by commas and enclosed in square brackets. For example:

```
[ 49.95, 67.60, "Swedish cabbage", false, "assertion"]
```

SQL/JSON object

A SQL/JSON object is an unordered collection of zero or more SQL/JSON members, where a member is a pair whose first value is a character string from the Unicode character set and whose second value is an SQL/JSON item. The first value of an SQL/JSON member is called the key, and the second value is called the bound value. Members are often called key/value pairs. They may also be called name/value pairs. SQL/JSON objects can be serialized by separating the members with commas and enclosing the entire object in curly braces. For example:

```
{ "name" : "Santa", "vehicle" : "sleigh", "home" : "North Pole" }
```

SQL/JSON sequences

An SQL/JSON sequence is an ordered list of zero or more SQL/JSON items. Such a sequence can be viewed as a *container* of zero or more SQL/JSON items.

Parsing JSON

The parsing operation is the importing of data in some external data format into the SQL/JSON data model. In most cases the import will be in the form of a Unicode character string, although other implementation-dependent formats are possible.

Serializing JSON

Serializing JSON is the opposite of parsing JSON. It is the exporting of values from the SQL/JSON data model back into the format of the external storage device. One restriction on this operation is that SQL/JSON datetimes cannot be serialized, and another is that SQL/JSON sequences of length greater than one also may not be serialized.

SQL/JSON Functions

Built-in functions perform the operations on JSON data. There are two types of SQL/JSON functions, query functions and constructor functions. Query functions evaluate SQL/JSON path language expressions against JSON values, producing corresponding values of SQL/JSON types, which are then converted to SQL types. I discuss SQL/JSON path language briefly later in this chapter.

Constructor functions use values of SQL types to produce JSON values, either JSON objects or JSON arrays. These JSON objects are represented as either SQL character strings or binary strings.

Query functions

There are several query functions, all of which share a common syntax. They all require a path expression, the JSON value to be input to that path expression for querying and processing, and possibly optional parameter values passed to the path expression.

The syntax is

```
<JSON API common syntax> ::=
    <JSON context item> <comma>
      <JSON path specification>
        [ AS <JSON table path name> ]
          [ <JSON passing clause> ]
<JSON context item> ::= <JSON value expression>
```

```
<JSON path specification> ::=
  <character string literal>
<JSON passing clause> ::=
  PASSING <JSON argument>
    [ { <comma> <JSON argument> } ] ]
<JSON argument> ::=
  <JSON value expression> AS <identifier>
```

The value expression contained in the preceding `<JSON context item>` is of the string type.

JSON value expression

As noted in the previous Backus-Naur Form (BNF) syntax definition, a JSON context item is just a JSON value expression. A JSON value expression is defined as

```
<JSON value expression> ::=
  <value expression> [ <JSON input clause> ]

<JSON input clause> ::= FORMAT <JSON representation>

<JSON representation> ::=
 JSON [ ENCODING { UTF8 | UTF16 | UTF32 } ]
 | Implementation-defined JSON representation option>
```

You see from this that a JSON value expression is a value expression with an optional input clause. The input clause specifies the format of the JSON representation, which specifies the encoding as either UTF8, UTF16, UTF32, or an implementation-defined representation.

Path expression

Following the JSON context item and a comma is the JSON path specification, which must be a character string literal. The table path name and passing clause are optional parts of the JSON path specification.

Passing clause

The passing clause, as the name implies, passes parameters to the SQL/JSON path expression.

JSON output clause

When JSON data returns to an application because of the operation of a function, the application author can specify the data type, format, and encoding of the JSON text created by the function. The syntax for the output clause is

```
<JSON output clause> ::=
  RETURNING ,data type>
  [ FORMAT <JSON representation> ]

<JSON representation> ::=
 JSON [ ENCODING { UTF8 | UTF16 | UTF32 } ]
 | Implementation-defined JSON representation option>

If FORMAT is not specified, then JSON format is assumed.
```

The SQL/JSON query functions are JSON_EXISTS, JSON_VALUE, JSON_QUERY, and JSON_TABLE. These functions evaluate path language expressions against JSON values. The results returned are values of SQL/JSON types, which are then converted to SQL types. Path language is described later in this chapter.

JSON_EXISTS

JSON_EXISTS determines whether a JSON value satisfies a search condition in the path specification. The syntax is

```
<JSON exists predicate> ::=
  JSON_EXISTS <left paren>
    <JSON API common syntax>
    [ <JSON exists error behavior> ON ERROR ]
  <right paren>
<JSON exists error behavior> ::=
  TRUE | FALSE | UNKNOWN | ERROR
```

If the optional ON ERROR clause is not included, the default assumption is FALSE ON ERROR. JSON_EXISTS evaluates the SQL/JSON path expression, returning a TRUE result if the path expression finds one or more SQL/JSON items.

Sample data that can be used to learn how to use the query functions, including JSON_EXISTS, can be found on pages 24 and 25 of Section 6 of the SQL Technical Report ISO/IEC TR 19075-6:2017(E), which can be downloaded from

```
https://standards.iso.org/ittf/PubliclyAvailableStandards/
c067367_ISO_IEC_TR_19075-6_2017.zip
```

The data consists of two columns, K and J of a table T. K is the primary key of the table, and J is the data. The table consists of key-value pairs or arrays of key-value pairs. JASON_EXISTS tests for the existence of a given character string literal in the JSON path expression. For example

```
SELECT T.K
FROM T
WHERE JSON_EXISTS (T.J, 'lax $.where') ;
```

The primary keys of the rows that contain the word 'where' are returned as the result set of the SELECT query. The keyword 'lax' refers to the error handling that is more forgiving than 'strict' error handling. It has no effect on the result of the query. $ is the accessor that accesses the word 'where' in the current JSON object.

JSON_VALUE

The JSON_VALUE function extracts a SQL scalar value from a JSON value. The syntax is

```
<JSON value function> ::=
  JSON VALUE <left paren>
    <JSON API common syntax>
    [ <JSON returning clause> ]
    [ <JSON value empty behavior> ON EMPTY ]
    [ <JSON value error behavior ON ERROR ]
  <right paren>
<JSON returning clause> ::= RETURNING <data type>
<JSON value empty behavior> ::=
    ERROR
  | NULL
  | DEFAULT <value expression>
<JSON value error behavior> ::=
    ERROR
  | NULL
  | DEFAULT <value expression>
```

As you can probably surmise, <JSON value empty behavior> tells what to return if the result of the SQL/JSON path expression is empty.

» NULL ON EMPTY means the result of JSON_VALUE is empty.

» ERROR ON EMPTY means an exception is raised.

» DEFAULT <value expression> ON EMPTY means that the value expression is evaluated and cast to the target type.

<JSON value error behavior> is similar. It specifies what to do if there is an unhandled error.

In the preceding JSON_EXISTS example, all the rows where the keyword 'where' was present in the J value column were returned. With JSON_VALUE, the value associated with a target keyword is returned. Using the same data set as the JSON_EXISTS example, where the keyword 'who' is paired with a person's name, the following SQL code will return the names of people from all the rows where the keyword 'who' is present.

```
SELECT T.K,
   JSON_VALUE (T.J, 'lax $.who') AS Who
FROM T ;
```

The result set will contain a column named K, containing the primary keys of the rows being returned, and a column named Who, containing the names that were paired with the 'who' keyword in the source data.

By default, JSON_VALUE returns an implementation-defined character string data type. The user can specify other types with a RETURNING clause.

JSON_QUERY

Although JSON_VALUE does a fine job of extracting a scalar from an SQL/JSON value, it is unable to extract an SQL/JSON array or an SQL/JSON object from an SQL/JSON value. JSON_QUERY performs those functions. The syntax for JSON_QUERY is

```
<JSON query> ::=
  JSON_QUERY <left paren>
    <JSON API common syntax>
    [ <JSON output clause> ]
    [ <JSON query wrapper behavior> ]
    [ <JSON query quotes behavior> QUOTES
       [ ON SCALAR STRING ] ]
    [ <JSON query empty behavior> ON EMPTY ]
    [ <JSON query error behavior> ON ERROR ]
  <right paren>
```

The ON EMPTY and ON ERROR clauses are similar to the ones in JSON_VALUE, and are handled the same way. The difference is that the user can specify behavior when either the empty case or the error case arises.

>> If <JSON output clause> is not specified, RETURNING JSON FORMAT is the default.

>> If ‹JSON query empty behavior› is not specified, then NULL ON EMPTY is the default.

>> If ‹JSON query error behavior› is not specified, then NULL ON ERROR is the default.

>> If ‹JSON query wrapper behavior› is not specified, then WITHOUT ARRAY is the default.

>> If ‹JSON query wrapper behavior› specifies WITH and if neither CONDITIONAL nor UNCONDITIONAL is specified, then UNCONDITIONAL is the default.

>> If the value of the ‹JSON context item› simply contained in the ‹JSON API common syntax› is the null value, then the result of ‹JSON query› is the null value.

Using the same sample data used for the JSON_EXISTS sample query and the JSON_VALUE sample query, you can add array data to the result set, along with the results obtained with the JSON_VALUE clauses.

```
SELECT T.K,
   JSON_VALUE (T.J, 'lax $.who') AS Who,
   JSON_VALUE (T.J, 'lax $.where' NULL ON EMPTY)
     AS Nali,
   JSON_QUERY (T.J, 'lax $.friends') AS Friends
FROM T
WHERE JSON_EXISTS (T.J, 'lax $.friends')
```

The WHERE JSON_EXISTS clause eliminates any rows that do not have a key-value pair for friends. If WITH ARRAY WRAPPER is specified, then array elements returned are enclosed in a pair of square brackets.

JSON_TABLE

The JSON_TABLE function is complicated, much more so than the other functions previously covered. It takes JSON data as an input and generates a relational output table from that data. The syntax definition for the simplest variant of the JSON_TABLE function takes up a full page. Nested paths and plan clauses add even more complexity to what is already pretty hard to comprehend. There is not enough room here to cover JSON_TABLE to the depth that it deserves. Instead, I refer you to page 35 and following of the SQL Technical Report ISO/IEC TR 19075-6 2017(E), which you can download from

```
https://standards.iso.org/ittf/PubliclyAvailableStandards/
c067367_ISO_IEC_TR_19075-6_2017.zip
```

Constructor functions

The SQL/JSON constructor functions construct JSON objects, arrays, and aggregates, based on information stored in relational tables. This is essentially the reverse of the operations performed by the SQL/JSON query functions.

JSON_OBJECT

The JSON_OBJECT function constructs JSON objects from explicit name/value pairs. The syntax is

```
<JSON object constructor> ::=
  JSON_OBJECT <left paren>
    [ <JSON name and value> [ { <comma>
         <JSON name and value> } ... ]
      [ <JSON constructor null clause> ]
      [ <JSON key uniqueness constraint> ] ]
    [ <JSON output clause> ]
  <right paren>
<JSON name and value> ::=
    [KEY] <JSON name> VALUE <JSON value expression>
  | <JSON name> <colon> <JSON value expression>
<JSON name> ::= <character value expression>
<JSON constructor null clause> ::=
    NULL ON NULL
  | ABSENT ON NULL
<JSON key uniqueness constraint> ::=
    WITH UNIQUE [ KEYS ]
  | WITHOUT UNIQUE [ KEYS ]
```

Some rules go along with this syntax:

» <JSON name> may not be NULL.

» <JSON value expression> may not be NULL.

» The <JSON constructor null clause>, if NULL ON NULL, produces a SQL/JSON null. If ABSENT ON NULL, it omits the key-value pair from the resulting SQL/JSON object.

» If no JSON constructor null clause is present, the default is NULL ON NULL.

JSON_OBJECTAGG

An application developer may want to construct a JSON object from an aggregation of the data in a relational table. If, for example, a table contains two columns, one with JSON names and the other with JSON values, the JSON_OBJECTAGG function can act on that data to create a JSON object. The syntax to perform this operation is

```
<JSON object aggregate constructor> ::=
  JSON_OBJECTAGG <left paren>
    <JSON name and value>
    [ <JSON constructor null clause> ]
    [ <JSON key uniqueness constraint> ]
    [ <JSON output clause> ]
  <right paren>
```

If `<json constructor null clause>` is absent, NULL ON NULL is the default.

JSON_ARRAY

To create a JSON array, based on a list of data items in a relational database table, use the JSON_ARRAY function. The syntax is

```
<JSON array constructor> ::=
    <JSON array constructor by enumeration>
  | <JSON array constructor by query>
<JSON array constructor by enumeration ::=
  JSON_ARRAY <left paren>
    [ <JSON value expression> [ { <comma>
        <JSON value expression> }... ]
      <JSON constructor null clause> ] ]
    <JSON output clause>
  <right paren>
<JSON array constructor by query> ::=
  JSON_ARRAY <left paren>
    <query expression>
    [ <JSON input clause> ]
    [ <JSON constructor null clause> ]
    [ <JSON output clause> ]
  <right paren>
```

JSON_ARRAY has two variants, one that produces its result from an input list of SQL values, and the other that produces its results from a query expression invoked from within the function. If the optional JSON constructor null clause is absent, the default is ABSENT ON NULL, which is the opposite of the default behavior for JSON_OBJECT.

JSON_ARRAYAGG

You see in the section on JSON_OBJECTAGG how you could construct a JSON object based on an aggregation of relational data. In the same way, you can construct a JSON array based on an aggregation of relational data. To do so, you use the JSON_ARRAYAGG constructor function. The syntax is

```
<JSON array aggregate constructor> ::=
  JSON_ARRAYAGG <left paren>
    <JSON value expression>
    [ <JSON array aggregate order by clause> ]
    [ <JSON constructor null clause> ]
    [ <JSON output clause> ]
  <right paren>
<JSON array aggregate order by clause> ::=
  ORDER BY <sort specification list>
```

If there is no JSON constructor null clause, the default is ABSENT ON NULL. The JSON array ORDER BY clause enables the developer to order output array elements according to one or more sort specifications, similar to the way an ORDER BY clause operates in an ordinary SQL statement.

IS JSON predicate

The IS JSON predicate tests whether a string purported to be JSON data is indeed valid JSON data. The syntax of the IS JSON predicate is

```
<JSON predicate> ::=
  <string value expression> [ <JSON input clause> ]
      IS [NOT] JSON
    [ <JSON predicate type constraint> ]
    [ <JSON key uniqueness constraint> ]
<JSON predicate type constraint> ::=
    VALUE
  | ARRAY
  | OBJECT
  | SCALAR
```

If the optional JSON input clause is not specified, then `FORMAT JSON` is the default. If the JSON key uniqueness constraint is not specified, then `WITHOUT UNIQUE KEYS` is the default.

JSON nulls and SQL nulls

JSON nulls are not the same as SQL nulls. In SQL, a zero-length string (`""`) is distinct from an SQL null value, which represents the absence of a definite value. In JSON, null is an actual value, and is represented by a JSON literal (`"null"`). JSON nulls must be distinguishable from SQL nulls. The developer must decide whether SQL null values are included in the JSON object or array being constructed, or whether they should be omitted from the object or array.

SQL/JSON Path Language

SQL/JSON path language is a query language used by the SQL/JSON query functions. It accepts a context item, a path specification, and a `PASSING` clause as inputs, potentially along with `ON ERROR` and other clauses, to execute the `JSON_EXISTS`, `JSON_VALUE`, `JSON_QUERY`, and `JSON_TABLE` functions. A path engine executes these functions and returns results to the function, which in turn passes the results on to the user.

In path language, the dollar sign ($) is the current context element, and the period (.) is an object member. Square brackets enclose array elements. From this you see that

» `$.name` denotes the value of the name attribute of the current JSON object.

» `$.phones[last]` denotes the last element of the array stored in the phones attribute of the current JSON object.

SQL:2023 JSON Enhancements

When the SQL:2016 specifications were defined, JSON was still a developing technology, so the specifications somewhat shoehorned support for JSON into the existing SQL standards. Now that the JSON standards are well defined, the new SQL:2023 standards have more fully incorporated support for JSON. This section describes the JSON features that have been added to the SQL:2023 specification.

The JSON data type

Perhaps the biggest addition to the SQL:2023 specification is the new `json` data type. The SQL:2016 specification stored JSON data as either character strings or binary strings in the table. Now, databases that support the SQL:2023 standard allow you to store JSON data in a `json` data type:

```
CREATE TABLE orders (
    orderid int not null primary key
    purchase json not null );
```

The product data field uses the new `json` data type, which allows you to store the data as JSON data objects, similar to the previous character method:

```
INSERT INTO orders (purchase)
VALUES ('{ "customer" : "Rich", "items" : {"product" : "Candy", "qty" : 5}}');
```

This may look exactly the same as when you use a character data type for the JSON data, but there is an advantage to using the `json` data type: You can add multiple data values in the same `INSERT` statement:

```
INSERT INTO orders (purchase)
VALUES ('{ "customer" : "Rich", "items" : {"product" : "Candy", "qty" : 5}}'),
VALUES ('{ "customer" : "Katie", "items" : {"product" : "Lentils", "qty" :
    2}}'),
VALUES ('{ "customer" : "Jessica", "items" : {"product" : "Soda", "qty" : 5}}');
```

A simple query of the table returns all the JSON data items:

```
SELECT purchase from orders;

{ "customer" : "Rich", "items" : {"product" : "Candy", "qty" : 5}}
{ "customer" : "Katie", "items" : {"product" : "Lentils", "qty" : 2}}
{ "customer" : "Jessica", "items" : {"product" : "Soda", "qty" : 5}}
```

The result set returns the data as JSON items. Now that the data is a JSON object, you can use JSON functions to handle the JSON data. For example. you can use the –> operator to return a specific JSON object field:

```
SELECT purchase -> 'customer' FROM orders;

"Rich"
"Katie"
"Jessica"
```

To retrieve the text value contained in a JSON object, use the --> operator:

```
SELECT purchase  -> 'items' --> 'product' FROM orders;

Candy
Lentils
Soda
```

The purchase -> 'items' bit returns the items as JSON objects; then -->
'product' returns the product as a text value.

Additional functions for the JSON data type

Because the SQL:2023 specification still supports the older string-based method
for storing JSON data, all the previous JSON functions defined in SQL:2016 still
apply (see the "SQL/JSON Functions" section), and you can now use these same
functions on json data type objects as well.

Besides the old JSON functions, the SQL:2023 specification defines several new
functions specifically for the json data type. Table 4-1 shows some of the more
common functions you may run into.

TABLE 4-1   **New JSON Functions**

Function	Description
array_to_json	Converts an SQL array to a JSON array.
json_array	Constructs a JSON array either from a series of values or from the results of a query.
json_build_array	Builds a JSON array from a text argument list.
json_build_object	Builds a JSON object from a text argument list.
json_each	Expands the specified JSON object into key/value pairs.
json_object	Creates a JSON object from a set of key/value pairs specified as text.
json_object_keys	Returns the keys specified in the JSON object.
json_typeof	Returns the JSON data type of the specified object.
row_to_json	Converts an SQL data row into a JSON object.
to_json	Converts any SQL value into a JSON object.

WARNING

Many SQL database products provided some type of JSON data support prior to the SQL:2023 specification. Consult the documentation for the database product you're using to see just what JSON features and functions it supports. Now that there is a formal specification for handling JSON data in an SQL database, most database products will eventually incorporate these standards in future releases.

Chapter **5**

Exploring Property Graph Queries

For most business operations, relational databases work perfectly fine for defining the entities contained in the business (such as employees, departments, customers, and orders) and their relationships (employees work in a department, and customers place orders). But not all data fits nicely in a relational database. One sticky point with the relational database model is how it handles many-to-many relationships between entities and how the different entities relate to each other outside the defined relationships (such as can an employee also be a customer?). The theory of property graph databases attempts to expand on these relationships, making it easier to perform complex SQL queries against complex data. The SQL:2023 specifications have added features to incorporate property graphs into the standard SQL language. This chapter explores just what property graph databases are and how to query them using SQL/PGQ.

What Are Property Graph Queries?

Property graph databases (also called *graph databases*) allow you to define objects as either *nodes* (also called *vertices* in some database packages) and *edges* (also called *relationships*). Nodes represent an entity in the database, such as an employee of a company or a customer of the company. Edges connect nodes using relationships — for example, an employee works for a company or a customer buys from a company. What makes property graph databases interesting are some of the unique relationships that nodes and edges can support:

>> Both nodes and edges can contain properties.

>> A node can be connected by multiple edges.

>> An edge can connect a node to itself.

>> Queries can follow the path between multiple nodes interconnected by multiple edges

Property Graph Query Language (PGQL) is a new language specifically for property graph databases. The SQL:2023 specifications expand the standard SQL language to incorporate the node and edge relationships created in property graph databases and call these new features SQL/PGQ. The SQL/PGQ standard incorporated into the SQL:2023 specification sets a standard that database companies can strive for to help standardize the use of property graph databases.

The next sections take a look at each of the interesting features provided by property graph databases.

Looking at node and edge properties

The relational database model allows you to define properties for each table, but property graph databases also allow you to define properties for the relationships between nodes. For example, an edge named worksfor can define the relationship between an employee node and a company node, and it can also contain a property, years, representing the number of years the employee has worked for that company.

This allows for greater flexibility when defining the database entities. You don't need to define properties only in node tables; you can also define properties in the relationships that they represent, making for a more logical distribution of the data.

Connecting nodes by multiple edges

To help simplify queries, you can define multiple edges connecting nodes. For example, you can have the worksfor edge defined between the employee and company nodes, but you can also have an employs edge that connects the company and employee nodes. Each edge can also contain different properties to help represent the different relationships, providing different information for queries based on what type of data you're looking for. This can help simplify what would be complex SQL JOIN queries that attempt to find specific types of data based on the node relationships.

Using edges to connect a node to itself

In relational databases you don't see a table that has a relationship to itself. However, with property graph databases this can be a common occurrence. For example, an employee node can have a bossof edge relationship to indicate which employees are the boss of other employees. This is yet another feature that can often help simplify otherwise complex queries.

Following paths with SQL queries

As nodes connect to other nodes using edges, paths can (and often do) develop. With relational databases, trying to query interrelated tables can be somewhat cumbersome, but with property graph queries you can easily specify a query path to retrieve data related in multiple edges.

Examining SQL/PGQ

The SQL:2023 specification adds support for property graph databases to the SQL standard using what's called *SQL/PGQ*. SQL/PGQ provides the additional SQL structures and query clauses required to work with property graph databases.

Figure 5-1 shows a diagram of a simple property graph database that relates employees, companies, and cities. The database contains three nodes:

» **Employee:** Defines the employee data for the company.

» **Company:** Defines the company data.

» **City:** Defines the city where employees live and where the companies are located.

The database also contains four edges:

» **worksfor:** Defines the company/employee relationship.

» **livesin:** Defines the employee/city relationship.

>> **bossof:** Defines an employer/employee relationship, indicating which employee works for whom.

>> **locatedin:** Defines the company/city relationship.

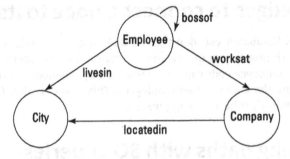

In the SQL/PGQ standard, both nodes and edges are defined as property graph tables. The SQL used to create them is very similar to what you'd use to create relational database tables, but just with an extra clause to define the table as either a node table or an edge table. For example:

```
CREATE TABLE Employee (
  EmpID Integer PRIMARY KEY,
  name VARCHAR(100)
) AS NODE;
```

This SQL creates the Employee table as a graph node. When you create a graph node, the database adds an extra data field named $node_id to the table. This value is used by the edge tables and SQL/PGQ queries to identify the different nodes.

You create edge graph tables similarly:

```
CREATE TABLE worksfor (
    startdate(DATE)
) AS EDGE;
```

As mentioned, edge relationships may main contain properties, such as the startdate property shown in this example. When you create an edge graph table, the database adds the startdate property data field to the table; it also adds three extra data fields to the table:

>> **$edge_id:** Uniquely defines the edge entity.

» $from_id: Identifies the parent node the edge connects to.

» $to_id: Identifies the child node the edge connects to.

You can then use the $node_id, $edge_id, $from_id, and $to_id data fields in your queries to determine the interrelationships between nodes and edges.

The SQL/PGQ standard defines the MATCH clause to help follow edge relationships between nodes in queries. A simple SQL/PGQ query would look like this:

```
SELECT Employee.name AS Employee, Company.name AS Company
FROM Employee, worksat, Company
WHERE MATCH (Employee-(worksat)->Company);
```

Notice that the FROM clause specifies both the node and edge tables involved in the query. Also, notice how the MATCH clause specifies the relationships between the Employee node, the worksat edge, and the Company node. This is the key to the simplicity of property graph queries. You can easily define a full path that includes multiple nodes and edges to determine the relationships between nodes that aren't directly connected.

The following section walks through an example that helps demonstrate the power of using property graph databases and SQL/PGQ.

Working with SQL/PGQ

Microsoft SQL Server supported property graph tables starting in version 2017 (but calls them *graph tables*). If you've downloaded and installed Microsoft SQL Server 2022 Express, you can experiment with property graph tables. The following sections walk through the process of creating node and edge tables.

Building the property graph tables

Follow these steps to create the property graph tables to represent the sample database shown in Figure 5-1.

1. **Open Microsoft SQL Server Management Studio and log into your Microsoft SQL 2022 database server.**

2. **Right-click the Databases folder, select New Database, type** MyGraph, **and click OK.**

   This creates the database MyGraph in the Databases folder.

3. **Click the MyGraph database and then click the New Query button at the top of the page.**

   This opens a new Query window.

4. **Create the Employee node table by entering the following text:**

```
CREATE TABLE Employee (
  EmpID Integer PRIMARY KEY,
  name VARCHAR(100)
) AS NODE;
```

5. **Click the Execute button to run the new query.**

   Figure 5-2 shows the results.

   If you click the Refresh icon for the Object Explorer window, you can see the new Employee table; however, it has been created in the Graph Tables folder, indicating that it's defined as a graph table.

6. **Follow the same process to create the City and Company node tables:**

```
CREATE TABLE City (
  CityID Integer PRIMARY KEY,
  name VARCHAR(100),
  state CHAR(2)
) AS NODE;

CREATE TABLE Company (
  CompID Integer PRIMARY KEY,
  name VARCHAR(100),
  city VARCHAR(100)
) AS NODE;
```

   Figure 5-3 shows how the tables should appear in the Object Explorer window. Notice that each of the node tables has a $node_id data field added to it.

7. **Follow the same process to create the worksfor, livesin, bossof, and locatedin edge tables in the Query window.**

   For this example, I don't define any properties for the edge tables:

```
CREATE TABLE worksat AS EDGE;
CREATE TABLE livesin AS EDGE;
CREATE TABLE bossof AS EDGE;
CREATE TABLE locatedin AS EDGE;
```

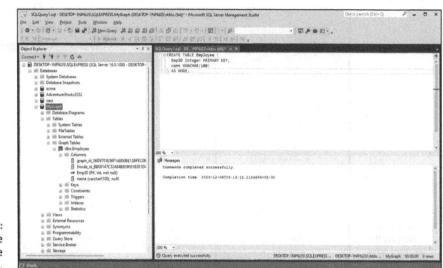

FIGURE 5-2:
Creating the
Employee
node table.

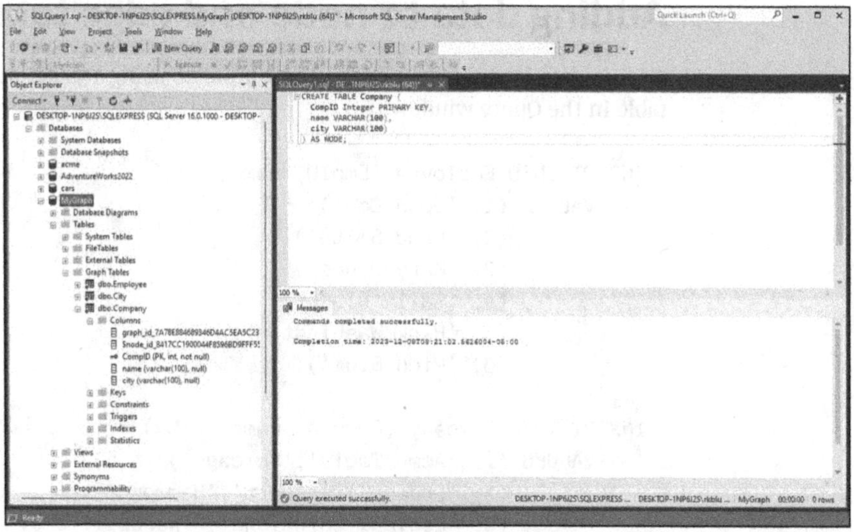

FIGURE 5-3:
The City and
Company node
tables added to
the database.

Figure 5-4 shows the data fields created in the worksat edge table. Notice that each of the edge tables contains the $edge_id, $from_id, and $to_id data fields by default.

Now that you've created the node and edge tables, you can add data to them as described in the next section.

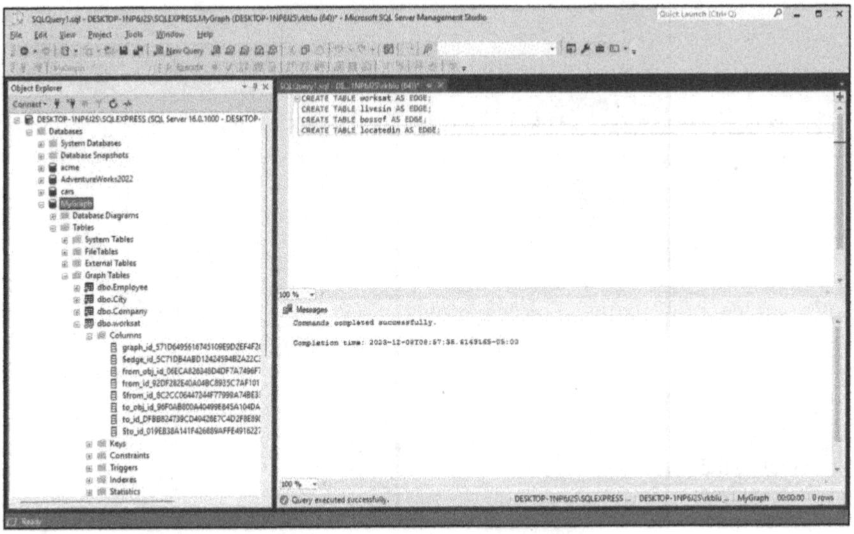

FIGURE 5-4:
Viewing the
worksat edge
table data fields.

Adding data to node and edge tables

Adding data to the node tables is as simple as using INSERT statements for each table in the Query window:

```
INSERT INTO Employee (EmpID, name)
    VALUES (1, 'John Doe')
         , (2, 'Fred Smith')
         , (3, 'Mary Jones')
         , (4, 'Sally Blank')
         , (5, 'Hank Washington')
         , (6, 'Rich Blum');

INSERT INTO Company (CompID, name, city)
    VALUES (1, 'Acme Tools','Chicago')
         , (2, 'Speedy Transport','Hammond')
         , (3, 'Logical Solutions', 'Naperville');

INSERT INTO City (CityID, name, state)
    VALUES (1,'Chicago','IL')
         , (2,'Hammond','IN')
         , (3,'Naperville','IL');
```

Nothing new here, just simple SQL for adding the data you need.

However, adding data to the edge tables is somewhat tricky. Each edge table data record must specify the $from_id and $to_id data fields for each node table that it connects, using the $node_id values from each node table. For example, if I wanted to add the livesin edge relationship relating John Doe (EmpID of 1) to the city Chicago (CityID of 1), I'd use the following INSERT statement:

```
INSERT INTO livesin
    VALUES ((SELECT $node_id FROM Employee WHERE EmpID = 1),
            (SELECT $node_id FROM City WHERE CityID = 1))
```

The first SELECT statement retrieves the $node_id value for John Doe from the Employees table, and the second SELECT statement retrieves the $node_id value for Chicago from the City table. To populate all the edge tables with some sample data, enter the following INSERT statements in the Query window and execute the query:

```
INSERT INTO worksat
    VALUES ((SELECT $node_id FROM Employee WHERE EmpID = 1),
            (SELECT $node_id FROM Company WHERE CompID = 1))
        , ((SELECT $node_id FROM Employee WHERE EmpID = 2),
            (SELECT $node_id FROM Company WHERE CompID = 2))
        , ((SELECT $node_id FROM Employee WHERE EmpID = 3),
            (SELECT $node_id FROM Company WHERE CompID = 3))
        , ((SELECT $node_id FROM Employee WHERE EmpID = 4),
            (SELECT $node_id FROM Company WHERE CompID = 1))
        , ((SELECT $node_id FROM Employee WHERE EmpID = 5),
            (SELECT $node_id FROM Company WHERE CompID = 2))
        , ((SELECT $node_id FROM Employee WHERE EmpID = 6),
            (SELECT $node_id FROM Company WHERE CompID = 3));

INSERT INTO livesin
    VALUES ((SELECT $node_id FROM Employee WHERE EmpID = 1),
            (SELECT $node_id FROM City WHERE CityID = 1))
        , ((SELECT $node_id FROM Employee WHERE EmpID = 2),
            (SELECT $node_id FROM City WHERE CityID = 2))
        , ((SELECT $node_id FROM Employee WHERE EmpID = 3),
            (SELECT $node_id FROM City WHERE CityID = 1))
        , ((SELECT $node_id FROM Employee WHERE EmpID = 4),
            (SELECT $node_id FROM City WHERE CityID = 1))
        , ((SELECT $node_id FROM Employee WHERE EmpID = 5),
            (SELECT $node_id FROM City WHERE CityID = 3))
        , ((SELECT $node_id FROM Employee WHERE EmpID = 6),
            (SELECT $node_id FROM City WHERE CityID = 3));

INSERT INTO locatedin
    VALUES ((SELECT $node_id FROM Company WHERE CompID = 1),
```

```
                     (SELECT $node_id FROM City WHERE CityID =1))
             , ((SELECT $node_id FROM Company WHERE CompID = 2),
                (SELECT $node_id FROM City WHERE CityID =2))
             , ((SELECT $node_id FROM Company WHERE CompID = 3),
                (SELECT $node_id FROM City WHERE CityID =3));

INSERT INTO bossof
    VALUES ((SELECT $node_id FROM Employee WHERE EmpID = 1),
            (SELECT $node_id FROM Employee WHERE EmpID = 4))
         , ((SELECT $node_id FROM Employee WHERE EmpID = 2),
            (SELECT $node_id FROM Employee WHERE EmpID = 5))
         , ((SELECT $node_id FROM Employee WHERE EmpID = 3),
            (SELECT $node_id FROM Employee WHERE EmpID = 6));
```

Now that all the node and edge tables have data, the next section walks through how to run some SQL/PGQ queries to retrieve data.

Querying data in graph tables

You use the MATCH clause to define the relationships between the nodes and edges that you want to query. For example, to find the company that each employee works at, you'd use the following query:

```
SELECT Employee.name as Employee, Company.name as Company
FROM Employee, worksat, Company
WHERE MATCH (Employee-(worksat)->Company);
```

The result of this query is shown in Figure 5-5.

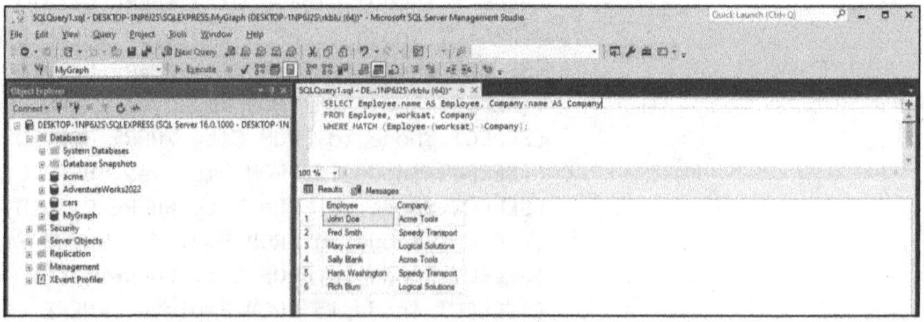

FIGURE 5-5:
The result of the worksat query.

For each employee in the Employee table, the query uses the worksat edge to find the related company in the Company table. To find the employees who work for John Doe, you'd use the bossof edge query:

```
SELECT employee2.name
FROM Employee employee1, bossof, Employee employee2
WHERE MATCH(employee1-(bossof)->employee2)
AND employee1.name='John Doe';
```

The result of this query is shown in Figure 5-6.

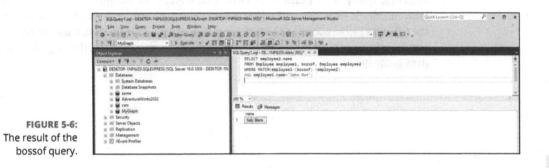

These queries may seem simple, but the real power in SQL/PGQ comes in trying to follow the path between multiple nodes and edges. For example, to query which employees work and live in the same city, you'd just need to use the following:

```
SELECT Employee.name AS Employee, City.name AS City
FROM Employee, worksat, Company, livesin, City, locatedin
WHERE MATCH (Employee-(worksat)->Company-(locatedin)->City
    AND Employee-(livesin)->City);
```

Notice the two paths used in the first part of the MATCH clause:

```
Employee-(worksat)->Company-(locatedin)->City
```

This query links all three node tables with the two edge tables to find which city the employee works in. Then you just use the AND Boolean operator to link the result of this query to the city the employee lives in. Figure 5-7 shows the results from this query.

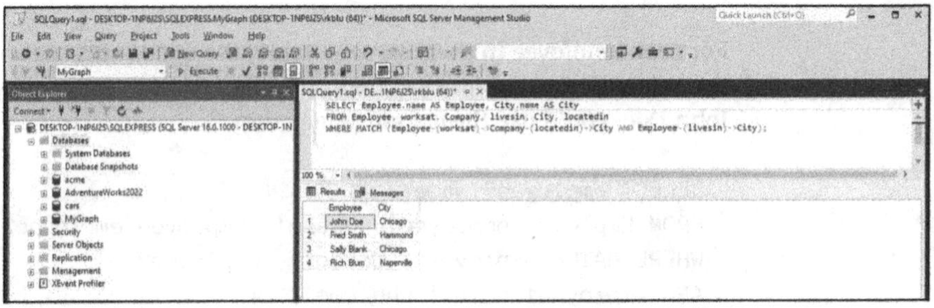

FIGURE 5-7:
The results from
finding which
employees work
and live in the
same city.

What would be a fairly complex SQL query turns into a somewhat routine SQL/PGQ query. This example is somewhat trivial, but imagine having a database with hundreds of nodes and edges. As you can see, property graph databases and the SQL/PGQ extensions to the SQL language can provide an easier way of retrieving data from complex data environments, which may very well be the future of data analysis.

7

Optimizing Your Database

Contents at a Glance

Chapter **1**

Tuning the Database

The word *tuning* is generally taken to mean optimizing an existing system that isn't operating at top capacity. Tuning doesn't do you much good, however, if your initial design isn't at least close to optimal in the first place. Tuning can take you only so far from your starting point. It's a lot easier to tune a slightly off-pitch B string on your guitar to a perfect B than it is to tune a G string up to a perfect B. (Also, you're a lot less likely to break the string.) Tuning for optimal performance should start in the initial design stage of a database, not at some later time when design decisions have been cast in concrete.

The performance of a database management system (DBMS) is generally judged by how fast it executes queries. Two types of operations are important: the retrieval of data from a database and the updating of records in a database. The speed at which records can be accessed is key to both types of operations, because you must locate a record before you can retrieve or update the data in it. The users' data model on which you'll base your database design is almost certainly structured in a way that isn't the best from a performance standpoint. The users are primarily concerned with functionality and may have little or no idea of how the design of a database affects how well it performs. You must transform the users' data into a conceptual schema that you actualize in the form of an Entity-Relationship (ER) model diagram. Recall that the Entity-Relationship data model and its associated diagrams are extensively covered in Book 1.

Analyzing the Workload

Optimal design of a database depends largely on how the database will be used. What kinds of queries will it be subjected to? How often will updates be made, compared with how often queries are posed? These kinds of questions try to get at what the workload will be. The answers to such questions have great bearing on how the database should be structured. In effect, the design of the database is tuned based on how it will typically be used.

To give you a sound foundation for designing your database to best handle the workload to which it will be subjected, draft a workload description. The workload description should include the following elements:

>> A list of all the queries you expect to be run against the database, along with an estimate of the expected frequency of each query compared with the frequencies of all the other queries and update operations

>> A list of all the update operations you expect to perform, along with an estimate of the expected frequency of each operation compared with the frequencies of all the other updates and queries

>> Your goal for the performance of each type of query and update

Queries can vary tremendously in complexity, so it's important to determine in advance how complex each query is and how that complexity will affect the overall workload. You can determine query complexity by answering a few questions:

>> How many relations (tables) are accessed by this query?

>> Which attributes (columns) are selected?

>> Which attributes appear in the WHERE clause, and how selective are the WHERE clause conditions likely to be?

Just as queries can vary a great deal, so can update operations. Questions regarding updates should include the following:

>> Which attributes appear in the WHERE clause, and how selective are the WHERE clause conditions likely to be?

>> What type of update is it: INSERT, DELETE, or UPDATE?

>> In UPDATE statements, which fields will be modified?

Considering the Physical Design

Among the factors that have a major impact on performance, few, if any, have a greater effect than indexes. On the plus side, indexes point directly to the desired record in a table, thereby bypassing the need to scan down through the table until you come upon the record you want. This feature can be a tremendous time-saver for a query. On the minus side, every time an insertion update or a deletion update is made to a table, the indexes on that table must be updated too, costing time.

When chosen properly, indexes can be a great help. When chosen poorly, indexes can waste resources and slow processing substantially.

Regarding indexes, you need to answer several questions:

>> Which tables should have indexes, and which should not?

>> For the tables that should have indexes, which columns should be indexed?

>> For each index, should it be clustered or unclustered? Recall that a table can have only one clustered index, and that it will give the greatest performance boost. The column used most often as a retrieval key should be the one with a clustered index. Other columns used as retrieval keys less frequently would get unclustered indexes.

I address all these questions in this chapter.

After you arrive at a conceptual schema and determine that you need to make changes to improve performance, what kinds of modifications can you make? For one thing, you could change the way you divide up your data among the tables in your design. For another, you could alter the level of normalization of your tables.

- » Often, you have more than one way to normalize a schema, and one such way may deliver better performance than others. You may want to change the way tables are defined to take advantage of a schema that gives you better performance than your current schema does.

- » Although this method may sound somewhat heretical, sometimes it pays to denormalize your schema and accept a risk of modification anomalies in exchange for a significant performance boost.

- » Contrary to the preceding point, sometimes it makes sense to take normalization a step further than you otherwise would — in effect, to overnormalize. This method can improve the performance of queries that involve only a few attributes. When you give those attributes a table of their own, sometimes you can speed retrievals. But be careful, because overnormalizing can have detrimental effects on performance as well, making for a fine balancing act.

You should carefully examine frequently run queries and updates to see whether rewriting them would enable them to execute faster. There's probably not much advantage to applying such scrutiny to queries that are rarely run, but after you have some history and notice the ones running continually, it may pay to give those queries an extra look to see whether they can be improved.

Choosing the Right Indexes

Indexes can improve the performance of database retrievals dramatically, for several reasons. One reason is that an index tends to be small compared with the table that it's indexing. This fact means that the index is likely to be in the cache, which is accessible at semiconductor-memory speed rather than on disk — a million-to-one performance advantage right there. Other reasons depend on the type of query being performed and on whether the index is clustered. I discuss clustering in the section "Clustering indexes."

Avoiding unnecessary indexes

Because maintaining indexes carries an overhead cost, you don't want to create any indexes that won't improve the performance of any of your retrieval or update queries. To decide which database tables shouldn't be indexed, consult the workload description you created as the first step in the design process (refer to "Analyzing the Workload," earlier in this chapter). This description contains a list of queries and their frequencies.

TIP

Here's a no-brainer: If a table has only a small number of rows, there's no point in indexing it. A sequential scan through relatively few rows executes quickly.

For larger tables, the best candidates for indexes are columns that appear in the query's WHERE clause. The WHERE clause determines which table rows are to be selected.

It's likely — particularly in a system in which a large number of different queries are run — that some queries are more important than others. Those queries are run more often, or they're run against more and larger tables, or getting results quickly is critical for some reason. Whatever the case, prioritize your queries, with the most important coming first. For the most important query, create indexes that give the best performance. Then move down the line, adding indexes that help the progressively less-important queries. Your DBMS's query optimizer chooses the best execution plan available to it based on the indexes that are present.

Different kinds of indexes exist, each with their own structure. One kind of index is better for some retrievals; another kind is better for others. The most common index types are B+ tree, hash, and ISAM (see "Choosing an index type," later in this chapter). Theoretically, for any given query, the query optimizer chooses the best index type available. Most of the time, practice follows theory.

Choosing a column to index

Any column that appears in a query's WHERE clause is a candidate for indexing. If the WHERE clause contains an exact-match selection, such as EMPLOYEE. DepartmentID = DEPARTMENT.DepartmentID, a hash index on EMPLOYEE. DepartmentID usually performs best. The number of rows in the EMPLOYEE table is sure to be larger than the number of rows in the DEPARTMENT table, so the index is of more use applied to EMPLOYEE than it is applied to DEPARTMENT.

REMEMBER

A hash index stores pairs of keys and values based on a pseudo-randomizing function called a hash function.

If the WHERE clause contains a range selection, such as EMPLOYEE.Age BETWEEN 55 AND 65, a B+ tree index on EMPLOYEE.Age will probably be the best performer. (A B+ tree is a balanced tree data structure whose leaves contain a sequence of key/pointer pairs.) If the table is rarely updated, an ISAM index may be competitive with the B+ tree index.

REMEMBER

ISAM indexes are small and can be searched quickly. However, if insertions or deletions are frequent, a table with ISAM indexing can quickly lose its efficiency advantage.

Tuning the Database

Using multicolumn indexes

If a `WHERE` clause imposes conditions on more than one attribute, such as `EMPLOYEE.Age BETWEEN 55 AND 65 AND EMPLOYEE.DeptName = 'Shipping'`, you should consider using a multicolumn index. If the index includes all the columns that the query retrieves (an index-only query), the query could be completed without touching the data table at all. This method could speed the query dramatically and may be sufficient motivation to include in the index a column that you otherwise wouldn't include.

Clustering indexes

Most database packages support the use of clustered indexes (although Oracle doesn't). A *clustered index* is one that determines the sort order of the table that it's indexing, as opposed to an *unclustered index, which* has no relationship to the sort order of the table.

Suppose that several queries of the EMPLOYEE table have a `WHERE` clause similar to `WHERE EMPLOYEE.LastName = 'Smith'`. In such a case, it would be beneficial to have a clustered index on EMPLOYEE.LastName. All the employees named Smith would be clustered in the index, and they'd be retrieved very quickly. Quick retrieval is possible because after you've found the index to the first Smith, you've found them all. Access to the desired records is almost instantaneous.

REMEMBER

Any given table can have only one clustered index. All other indexes on that table must be unclustered. Unclustered indexes can be helpful, but not as helpful as clustered indexes. For that reason, if you're going to choose one index to be the clustered index for a table, choose the one that will be used by the most important queries in the list of queries in the workload description (refer to "Analyzing the Workload," earlier in this chapter).

Consider the following example:

```
SELECT DeptNo
FROM EMPLOYEE
WHERE EMPLOYEE.Age > 29 ;
```

You can use a B+ tree index on Age to retrieve only the rows in which employee age is greater than 29. Whether this method is worthwhile depends on the age distribution of the employees. If most employees are 30 or older, the indexed retrieval won't do much better than a sequential scan.

Suppose that only 10 percent of the employees are more than 29 years old. If the index on Age is clustered, you gain a substantial improvement over a sequential scan. If the index is unclustered, however — as it's likely to be — it could require a buffer-page swap for every qualifying employee and will likely be more expensive than a sequential scan. I say that an index on Age is likely to be unclustered based on the assumption that at least one column in the EMPLOYEE table is more deserving of a clustered index than the Age column.

You can see from this example that choosing whether to create an index for a table column isn't a simple matter. Doing an effective job of choosing requires detailed knowledge of the data as well as of the queries run on it.

Figure 1-1 compares the costs of using a clustered index, an unclustered index, and a sequential scan to retrieve rows from a table.

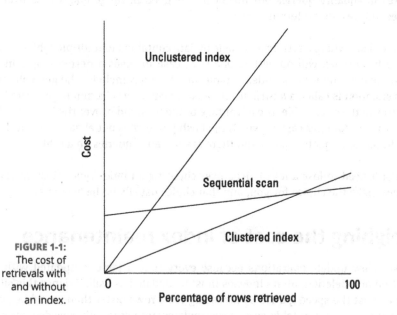

FIGURE 1-1:
The cost of retrievals with and without an index.

Figure 1-1 reveals a few things about the cost of indexes:

>> A clustered index always performs better than an unclustered index.

>> A clustered index performs better than a sequential scan unless practically all the rows are retrieved.

>> When one record is being retrieved, or a very few records are being retrieved, a clustered index performs much better than a sequential scan.

>> When one record is being retrieved, or a very few records are being retrieved, an unclustered index performs better than a sequential scan.

>> When more than about 10 percent of the records in a table are retrieved, a sequential scan performs better than an unclustered index.

That last point disproves the myth that indexing a table column that is used as a retrieval key always improves performance compared with the performance of a sequential scan.

Choosing an index type

In most cases, a B+ tree index is preferred because it does a good job on range queries as well as equality queries. Hash indexes are slightly better than B+ tree indexes in equality queries but not nearly as good in range queries, so overall, B+ tree indexes are preferred.

In some cases where a retrieval is made of data contained in multiple tables, however, a hash index will do better. One such case involves a nested loop join, in which the inner table is the indexed table and the index includes the join columns. (This situation is called a *hash join*.) Because an equality selection is generated for each row in the outer table, the advantage of the hash index over the B+ tree index is multiplied. Another case in which the hash join comes out ahead is when there is an important equality query and there are no range queries on a table.

TIP

You don't need to lose a lot of sleep over choosing an index type. Most database engines make the choice for you, and that choice usually is the best one.

Weighing the cost of index maintenance

Indexes slow update operations because every time a table is updated with an insertion or a deletion, all its indexes must be updated as well. Balance this situation against the speed gained by accessing table rows faster than would be possible with a sequential table scan. Even updates are potentially speeded because a row must be located before it can be updated. Nevertheless, you may find that the net benefit of some indexes doesn't justify their inclusion in the database, and you're better off dropping them. If you suspect that an index might be doing you more harm than good, run some test queries with the index both present and absent. Use the results to guide your decision.

Using composite indexes

Composite indexes are indexes on more than one column. They can give superior performance to queries that have more than one condition in the WHERE clause. Here's an example:

```
SELECT EmployeeID
FROM EMPLOYEES
WHERE Age BETWEEN 55 AND 65
    AND Salary BETWEEN 4000 and 7000 ;
```

Both conditions in the WHERE clause are range conditions. An index based on <Age, Salary> performs about as well as an index based on <Salary, Age>. Either one performs better than an index based only on <Age> or only on <Salary>.

Now consider the following example:

```
SELECT EmployeeID
FROM EMPLOYEES
WHERE Age = 57
    AND Salary BETWEEN 4000 and 7000 ;
```

In this case, an index based on <Age, Salary> performs better than an index based on <Salary, Age> because the equality condition on <Age> means that all the records that have Age = 57 are clustered by the time the salary evaluation is done.

Tuning Indexes

After the database you've designed has been in operation for a while, you should reevaluate the decisions you made about indexing. When you created the system, you chose indexes based on what you expected usage to be. Now, after several weeks or months of operation, you have actual usage statistics. Perhaps some of the queries that you thought would be important aren't run very often after all. Perhaps you made assumptions about what indexes would be used by the query optimizer, but now you find that limitations of the optimizer prevent it from using those indexes, to the detriment of performance.

Based on the actual performance data that you have now, you can tune your indexes. This tuning may entail dropping indexes that are doing you no good and merely consuming resources, or it may mean adding new indexes to speed queries that turned out to be more important than they first appeared.

For best results, tuning indexes must be an ongoing activity. As time goes on, the nature of the workload is bound to evolve. As it does, the best indexes to support the current workload need to evolve, too. The database administrator must keep track of performance and respond when it starts to trend downward.

Another problem, which appears after a database has been in operation for an extended period of time, might be called the tired index. A *tired index* is one that no longer delivers the performance advantage that it did when it was first applied to the database. When an index is fresh and new — whether it's a B+ tree index, an ISAM index, or some other kind — it has an optimal structure. As time goes on, insertions, deletions, and updates are made to the table that the index is associated with, and the index must adjust to these changes. In the process of making those adjustments, the structure of the index changes and moves away from optimality. Eventually, performance is affected enough to be noticeable. The best solution to this problem is to drop the index and then rebuild it. The rebuilt index once again has an optimal structure.

The only downside to this solution is that the database table must be out of service while its index is being rebuilt. The amount of time it takes to rebuild an index depends on several things, including the speed of the processor and the size of the table being indexed. For some databases, you may not even experience any downside. The database engine will rebuild indexes automatically as needed.

Tuning Queries

After your system has been running for a while, you may find that a query is running slower than you expect. Several possible causes exist, and you have several ways to fix the problem. Because you generally have several ways to code a query, all producing the same result, perhaps you could recode it, along with an appropriate change of indexes.

Sometimes, a query doesn't run as you expect because the query optimizer isn't executing the plan that you expect it to. You can check on this situation in most DBMSs by having the optimizer display the plan that it generated. It's quite possible that the optimizer isn't finding the best plan. Here are some possible causes:

>> Some query optimizers don't handle NULL values well. If the table you're querying contains NULL values in a field that appears in the WHERE clause, this situation could be the problem.

>> Some query optimizers don't handle arithmetic or string expressions well. If one of these expressions appears in the WHERE clause, the optimizer may not handle it correctly.

>> An OR connective in the WHERE clause could cause a problem.

>> If you expect the optimizer to select a fast but sophisticated plan, you could be disappointed. Sometimes, the best plan is beyond the capability of even high-end optimizers to find.

Some DBMSs give you some help in overcoming optimizer deficiencies. They enable you to force the optimizer to use an index that you know will be helpful or to join tables in the order that you know is best. For best results, a thorough knowledge of the capabilities and the deficiencies of your DBMS is essential, as is a good grasp of optimization principles.

Two possible culprits in performance problems are nested queries and correlated queries. Many optimizers don't handle these queries well. If a nested or correlated query isn't performing up to expectations, recoding it without nesting or correlation is a good thing to try.

Tuning Transactions

In an environment in which many users are using a database concurrently, contention for a popular resource can slow performance for everyone. The problem arises because a user locks a resource before using it and releases the lock when she is finished with it. As long as the resource is locked, no one else can access it.

Here are several things you can do to minimize the performance impact of locking:

>> **Minimize the amount of time that you hold a lock.** If you're performing a series of operations with a transaction, obtain your locks as late as possible and release them as soon as possible.

>> **Put indexes on a different disk from the one that holds the data files.** This practice prevents accesses to indexes from interfering with accesses to data.

>> **Switch to a hash index.** If a table is updated frequently, B+ tree indexes on its columns lose much of their advantage, because the root of the tree and the pages just below it must be traversed by every update. They become hot spots, meaning that they're locked frequently, becoming bottlenecks. Making the switch to a hash index may help.

Separating User Interactions from Transactions

Because computer instructions operate in the nanosecond realm and humans operate in the second or even minute realm, one thing that can really slow a database transaction is any interaction with a human. If that transaction happens to hold a lock on a critical resource, the application with which the user is interacting isn't the only one to suffer a delay. Every other application that needs that resource is brought to a screeching halt for an interval of time that could be billions of times longer than necessary.

The obvious solution is to separate user interactions from transactions. Never hold a lock on anything while waiting for a human to do something.

Minimizing Traffic between Application and Server

If you have a lot of applications running on a lot of client machines, all depending on data that resides on a server, overall performance is limited by the server's capacity to send and receive messages. The fewer messages that need to travel between client and server, the better. The smaller the messages that need to travel between client and server, the better.

One approach to this problem is to use *stored procedures* — precompiled application modules that run on the server rather than on the client. Their primary purpose is to filter result sets rather than send a big chunk of the database, so that only the needed data is transmitted to the client. This method can reduce traffic between the server and client machines dramatically.

Precompiling Frequently Used Queries

If you execute the same query repeatedly — say, daily or even hourly — you can save time by compiling it in advance. At runtime, executing the query is the only thing that needs to be done. The compilation is done only once and never needs to be repeated. The time savings due to this forethought adds up and becomes significant over the course of weeks and months.

Chapter 2

Tuning the Environment

omputer systems are subject to all kinds of failures: power failures, hardware failures, operating system failures, application program failures, and even database management system (DBMS) failures. These things happen; you can count on it. The important question you should ask yourself is "What happens when a failure occurs somewhere in my environment?" In critical applications, you don't want to lose any data, and you don't want to lose any more time than absolutely necessary.

Failures aside, you want your system to run as efficiently as possible. Inefficiencies can hamper productivity in many ways, sometimes slowing it to a crawl. In dealing with both failures and inefficiencies, the key to optimizing performance is tuning each part of your system. Your recovery system is designed to handle failures gracefully, but it must be tuned to operate at top efficiency. Your operating system and storage subsystem need to be tuned for the work that you're doing. Settings that would be appropriate for one job mix might be terrible for another. If you have multiple computers connected on a network, the way that they're connected can have a tremendous impact on performance. All these considerations are important, and they tend to interact, which makes optimizing them even more challenging.

In this chapter, I talk about some of the things you can do to ensure that you're getting the best performance out of your system that you can reasonably expect, given the budget and staff time that you can devote to maintaining an acceptable level of performance.

TIP

The tuning ideas suggested in this chapter assume you have access to the physical database server. These days, with the growing popularity of using the cloud to support applications, that may not be the case. If you're working in a cloud database environment, this chapter should at least give you some information to use when discussing performance issues with your cloud provider.

REMEMBER

The performance of a database system can vary dramatically — anywhere from lightning-fast to molasses-slow. Where your system sits on that spectrum is largely up to the decisions you make as a developer, the decisions the database administrator (DBA) makes, and the decisions the system administrator makes about how the operating system will run and what hardware it will run on. All these levels affect the ultimate performance of a database application.

Surviving Failures with Minimum Data Loss

Sooner or later, failures occur. That being the case, planning for those failures can make a big difference. Your plans should be aimed at minimizing the disruption that would be caused by downtime and loss of data. At any given time, the current copy of your database resides in two places: in stable storage in the form of hard disk drives and in a volatile solid-state memory called the *page buffer*. The page buffer contains the *working set* — the data currently being actively read and written by transactions that have been initiated by the executing program. The pages in the working set are destined to be written to disk, but that hasn't happened yet. If a failure occurs before a transaction commits or aborts, the recovery system must be able to return the database to a consistent state: either the state the database would have been in if the transaction had committed successfully or (in the case of an abort) the state the database was in before the transaction started.

What happens to transactions when no failure occurs?

In the absence of a failure, a transaction can end up in one of two ways: It will either commit or abort. When a transaction commits, it has completed successfully. This does *not* mean that the changes made by the transaction have been written to stable storage; it means that the changes are recoverable in the event of a failure, thanks to the logging feature (which I discuss later in this section). After the recovery operation is performed, the database is once again in a consistent state.

The other thing that a transaction can do is abort. A resource conflict, for example, may prevent a transaction from committing. This conflict isn't a failure, because nothing is broken; it's just a case of trying to do something at the wrong time. When a transaction aborts, a rollback is initiated. The database transaction log records every operation that takes place in the course of a transaction. The rollback operation consults the log and performs in reverse all the operations listed in it, restoring the database to the state it was in before the transaction started. This state is consistent. The transaction can be attempted again when conditions are more favorable. In many cases, conditions are favorable just as soon as the rollback completes. Whatever concurrent transaction caused the conflict has either committed or aborted, and now the contested resource is available.

What happens when a failure occurs and a transaction is still active?

If a failure occurs before a committed or aborted transaction has been written to disk, the database may be left in an inconsistent state. It's up to the recovery system to restore consistency. To do so, it makes use of the transaction log, which contains a record of what was done up to the point of the failure. This information can be used to restore consistency, either by reconstructing the committed transaction and writing it to disk or by erasing all record of the aborted transaction so that it has no effect on the database that exists on disk.

Tuning the Recovery System

Because it's a sure thing that failures will occur, it makes sense to plan ahead for them. A failure that you haven't planned for could result in a data loss severe enough to jeopardize the continued survival of your organization. Effective preparation requires that you understand what kinds of failures could happen, what the impact of such failures would be, and what you can do to mitigate that impact.

The most damaging failure is the one that causes irretrievable loss of data. Data can be irretrievably lost due to a variety of causes, based on the way that data is stored.

Volatile and nonvolatile memory

Two kinds of storage devices in common use today are subject to different failure modes:

>> **Volatile memory:** *Volatile memory* forgets everything if its power is interrupted, even for a fraction of a second. Thus, any kind of power failure can cause all data held in volatile memory to be lost.

>> **Nonvolatile memory:** Nonvolatile memory, as I'm sure you've guessed by now, doesn't lose its contents in the event of a power outage.

Another name for nonvolatile memory is *persistent* storage. The data persists even in the event of a three-day blackout after a major storm. When power is restored, the data is still there, just waiting for you.

You may wonder why computers have volatile memory at all. Because volatile memory forgets everything after a power interruption or processor reboot, why not use nonvolatile persistent storage for all the memory? The answer has to do with performance. Volatile main memory consists of semiconductor RAM chips, and nonvolatile persistent storage is implemented with hard disk drives. Semiconductor RAM can be as much as a million times faster than hard disks in terms of exchanging data with the processor. With a million-to-one speed advantage, volatile semiconductor RAM earns a place in every computer in which speed is a consideration.

A THIRD MEMORY CATEGORY

A third category of memory has come into use, which shares some of the characteristics of semiconductor RAM and some of hard disk drives. This is flash memory, as exemplified by memory sticks — also known as thumb drives or flash drives, and by "solid state disk" (SSD).

Flash drives and SSDs aren't really disk drives. They don't rotate like hard disk drives, which is good, because that fact makes them both faster and more reliable than hard disk drives. Like hard disk drives, they are non-volatile storage devices. However, they are typically more expensive per byte than a hard disk drive, and they are significantly slower than the RAM that makes up the main memory of a typical computer system. Because they are not as fast as semiconductor RAM and not as economical as a hard disk drive, SSD drives have found application at an intermediate level of cost performance between RAM and hard disk drives.

Now you may wonder why, if volatile RAM is a million times faster than nonvolatile hard disk storage and remedies have been developed for recovering from failures, you would ever want to use hard disk storage. The answer is cost. The cost of storing a bit on hard disk is much lower than the cost of storing the same bit in semiconductor RAM. A personal computer may have a 2TB hard disk but only 8GB of RAM. The difference in capacity reflects the difference in cost per bit.

Because both volatile and nonvolatile memory are subject to failure, you need strategies to cope with those failures. Because the failure modes are so different, the strategies you use also need to be different. How do you protect data against failures in a volatile memory system? For this discussion, I assume that the nonvolatile memory system is operating properly because it's unlikely that both the volatile and nonvolatile memory systems would fail at the same time. Such a failure is possible in the event of a building collapse or other major disaster, of course. There are ways of coping with even those eventualities, but those methods are beyond the scope of this book.

Memory system hierarchy

Modern memory systems are hierarchical in nature, with the fastest memory devices at the top of the memory hierarchy and the slowest at the bottom. The fastest devices are also the most expensive in terms of cost per bit stored. For this reason, it isn't feasible to populate a memory system completely with the fastest memory available.

Here's the hierarchy for a typical database server:

>> **CPU registers:** CPU registers are fastest because they're fabricated with the same process as the CPU itself, on the same chip. They're closest to the processing unit, so transit delays between the two are minimized.

>> **Level 1 cache:** Level 1 cache is a little slower than CPU registers.

>> **Level 2 cache:** Level 2 cache is slower yet.

>> **Level 3 cache (if present):** Level 3 cache may or may not be present. If it is, it's a little slower than Level 2 cache.

>> **Main memory:** Main memory is much slower than cache.

>> **Solid state disk (SSD):** Slower than main memory, but much faster than hard disk.

>> **Hard disk:** Hard disk is much, much, much slower than main memory.

>> **Magnetic tape:** Magnetic tape is so slow that it's used only for backup and archiving. You would never keep active data on magnetic tape.

CPU registers, cache, and main memory are all examples of volatile memory. When you lose power, you also lose all the data stored in those devices. Hard disks and magnetic tape are persistent storage devices. Data stored in such devices survives power outages. This isn't to say that persistent storage devices are invulnerable to failure; they just have different failure modes from those of volatile memory devices.

Hard disks and magnetic tape drives are machines that contain moving parts. Such devices fail catastrophically from time to time. If you use them long enough, they're sure to fail. When a hard disk fails, you lose all the data that was stored on it. A regular backup schedule, faithfully followed, can minimize your losses in such an event.

Putting logs and transactions on different disks

Volatile memory failures are inconvenient but not catastrophic if the information you need to recover to resume operation is stored on some nonvolatile medium, such as a hard disk. Clearly, you can't store the results of your computations directly on hard disk as you perform them; if you did, your processing would be reduced to hard disk speeds rather than the million-times-faster RAM speeds. You can do a few things, however, to minimize the amount of time that results spend in RAM before being written to disk. These methods involve transactions and logging. (I discuss transactions and logging in detail in Book 4, Chapter 2.)

The log is a record of every operation that alters the database in memory. It resides primarily on disk, but part of it — the page buffer — is in RAM. Writes of log entries to disk are made before the results of the corresponding transactions are written to disk. If a system failure or crash occurs, you can reconstruct any transactions that were in progress when the crash occurred. If a transaction had committed or aborted but had not yet been flushed to disk, the log on disk holds the information that enables the system to commit or roll back the transaction, as appropriate. By keeping the log on a disk separate from the disk that holds the database, performance during normal operation is maximized because writes to the log are sequential and no time is lost doing disk head seeks. This being the case, frequent writes to the log don't exact the same performance penalty that buffer flushes to the database do.

To understand why you should put a database's log on its own hard disk drive, you should understand how a hard disk drive is constructed and how it operates.

Hard disk drive construction

A hard disk drive contains a sealed enclosure that's protected from particulates in the air by a very effective air filter. Inside the enclosure, a spindle connected to a motor rotates at speeds on the order of 7,200 revolutions per minute (rpm). Attached to the spindle are several circular platters stacked one atop another within the enclosure. The platters are aluminum disks coated with a magnetic material. On each platter, a set of more than 1,000 concentric tracks are magnetically recorded. These tracks hold the data in the form of magnetic domains that are magnetized in one direction or the other. If a magnetic north pole is up, it represents a binary 1; if a south pole is up, it represents a 0.

An actuator moves an arm so that its tip, which holds a magnetic read/write head, can hover over any of the tracks. The read/write head, when reading, can sense whether it is flying over a north pole or a south pole and, thus, reads either 1 or 0. When writing, the head, which is an electromagnet, can flip the polarity of the domains it flies over, thus laying down a pattern of 1s and 0s. The top and bottom of every platter has an actuator arm and its associated read/write head. The set of corresponding tracks on all the platters — all the track 0s, for example, which are the outermost tracks — constitute a *cylinder*. All the heads in the stack are flying over the same cylinder at any given time.

Hard disk drive performance considerations

Because of the way that hard disk drives are constructed, and because mechanical movement is involved, there are limits to how fast a given byte or word can be read or written. The delay involved in a read or write has several components:

>> **Disk drive controller delay:** The time it takes the controller to determine whether it's being asked to do a read or a write and to determine the location that is to be read or written.

>> **Seek time:** The time it takes for the read/write head to move from whatever track it's currently on to the track that it needs to go to next.

>> **Settling time:** The time it takes for the jiggling to stop after the read/write head has arrived at the track it will operate on next.

>> **Rotational latency:** Even at 7,200 rpm, it takes a significant amount of time for a word of data to rotate all the way around the disk and come under the read/write head. If the desired word has just gone by when the head settles over a track, there will be a delay of up to 8 milliseconds before it comes around again.

>> **Read/write time:** The time it takes to do the read or write operation.

When you add up all the noted delays, it becomes clear why hard disk storage is so much slower than semiconductor RAM. The natural question that arises is "What can I do to minimize the delays inherent in the operation of hard disks?"

As it happens, a major part of the total delay involved in hard disk operation is due to the combination of seek time, settling time, and rotational latency. Minimizing these factors dramatically improves performance. The best way to minimize seek time and settling time is to do all your writes on the same cylinder so that you never have to do a seek. That's not possible, but what you *can* do is make all your writes to the same cylinder until it fills and then move to an adjacent cylinder. This practice minimizes both seek time and settling time. Furthermore, if you're writing sequentially along a track, rotational latency isn't an issue. You're always writing on the sector that immediately follows the one you've just written.

Because it's critical that log entries be written to disk sooner rather than later, dedicating an entire disk drive to the log is an obvious choice. Sequential writes to the log are as fast as possible because seek time, settling time, and rotational latency are all minimized.

TIP

For performance reasons, unless you're dealing with a read-only database, always locate a database's log on its own disk, not sharing the disk with any other function or any other database. This way, log writes are always to sequential sectors on the same disk cylinder, minimizing access time.

It's a given that any reasonable system employs transactions and logging. Transactions and logging are forms of insurance. They protect you from the worst effects of a failure, but you must pay a premium for that protection. Clearly, you want the protection, but you don't want to pay a higher premium for it than you have to. This is where tuning comes in. You make a trade-off between the time it takes to recover from a failure and performance during normal operation.

To minimize the time to recover from a failure, you should flush log entries from the page buffer located in RAM to hard disk frequently. The more often you make disk accesses, however, the greater the impact on performance. Somehow, you must find that sweet spot where time to recover from a failure is tolerable and normal operation performance is acceptable. Finding that sweet spot is the DBA's responsibility.

The DBA is the person with the power to determine how often the page buffer is flushed to disk. The specifics of how to do this vary from one DBMS to another. Consult the system administrator documentation for whichever product you are using for details on how to control the timing of buffer flushes.

Keep a detailed history of every time your system goes down for any reason, and use that knowledge to estimate the frequency of future failures. Combine that information with the results of the data you've recorded on the amount of time it takes to recover from a failure to decide how to set the buffer-flush timing parameters.

TIP

Tuning write operations

With a performance difference on the order of a million to one between semiconductor RAM and hard disk storage, the less frequently you write to disk, the better your performance is. Balancing that consideration is the fact that if you don't write to stable storage, you'll lose all your data in the event of a failure.

Before a transaction commits, it writes the "after" image of the change to the log disk. It may be quite a while after the change is made before the change is transferred from the buffer, which is in solid-state memory, to the stable storage of the data disk. The length of that interval affects performance.

If a failure occurs after the log has been updated with the result of a transaction but before the change has been made to the data disk, recovery isn't a problem. Thus, you can wait until a convenient time to store the changed data to disk. A convenient time would be when the disk read/write head happened to be located over the track you want to write to. In such a case, there would be no delay due to seek time and settling time.

Different DBMS products have different procedures for determining when it becomes advantageous to start looking for opportunities to make convenient writes. The buffer in solid-state memory is divided into pages. Whenever a change is made to a page, the page is marked as dirty. You never need to write a clean page out to disk, because its contents already match the contents of the corresponding disk location. Dirty pages, on the other hand, differ from their corresponding disk locations and eventually have to be written to disk, incurring the performance penalty that such an operation entails. Generally, when the percentage of dirty pages in the page buffer exceeds a certain threshold, the system starts looking for opportunities to make convenient writes.

You gain a considerable advantage in delaying writes to the data disk — an advantage that goes beyond the difference in speed between a write to buffer and a write to disk. If a memory location is *hot*, in the sense that it's being updated frequently, many of those updates may not need to be written to disk. Suppose that a memory location in the page buffer has a value of 4. In quick succession, it may be updated to 7, 17, 34, and 54. If the page that location is on isn't flushed to disk until the last of those writes takes place, the updates to 7, 17, and 34 are never written to disk, and the time that such writes would have taken is never consumed. This consideration strengthens the case for extending the amount of time before dirty pages are written to disk as long as possible without making recovery from failure unduly onerous.

Performing database dumps

In the preceding sections, I refer to hard disk storage as stable storage. This type of storage earns that description because it's nonvolatile. It doesn't lose its contents when the power goes out. Stable storage isn't immune to destruction, however. Hard disks *do* fail, and when they do, all the data on them is lost. To address this problem, system administrators perform periodic database dumps, in which the entire database is copied to offline media and stored in a safe place.

Database dumps are expensive because it takes a significant amount of time to copy a large database to an offline medium. In addition, the offline medium itself has a cost, as does the space taken up by it. For these reasons, you don't want to do dumps too often. On the other hand, you want to do them often enough. If a hard disk dies, all the changes that have been made since the last dump are gone. Can those lost transactions be reentered? If those transactions are important, you'd better find a way. How much of a hassle would it be to reenter the data? If it would be more than you're comfortable with, you may need to reevaluate your dump interval.

If you never dump your database, when your hard disk fails, you'll lose all your data — clearly, not an acceptable outcome. At the other extreme, if you perform dumps too frequently, you won't get any work done because your system is spending all its time doing database dumps. That's not acceptable either. Somewhere in the middle is an optimal dump interval.

No dump interval is best for everybody in every situation. Consider several points:

>> How hot is the database? How many changes are being made to it per second, per hour, per day, or per week?

>> How painful would it be to reenter updates that have been made since the last dump?

>> How long does a dump take, and how much does it affect productivity?

>> Am I using dumps for anything besides insurance against failure? Am I data mining dumps, for example? If so, how recent does the information need to be to be useful?

>> How much room for storing dumps do I have?

>> Can I recycle dump media from several generations back and use it again?

In many cases, doing a dump once per day is sufficient; you can schedule it at a time when activity is light. In other cases, doing a dump more or less frequently is appropriate. Taking all the preceding points into consideration, decide on the best dump interval for each of the databases for which you're responsible.

Setting checkpoints

Hard disk failures are almost always hard failures. In a *hard failure*, something physical is permanently and catastrophically damaged. In the case of a hard disk, this failure is the infamous disk crash. The term is descriptive, because when a disk crash occurs, you often hear a horrible scraping sound as one of the flying heads slams into its platter at speeds of up to 75 miles per hour.

Luckily, hard failures are relatively rare. Far more common are soft failures. In a *soft failure*, something unexpected has happened, and processing has stopped. Perhaps the dreaded Blue Screen of Death appears, featuring an indecipherable error message. Maybe the system just freezes and refuses to respond to anything you do. In cases such as these, rebooting the machine often clears the problem. Unfortunately, it also clears all your volatile, solid-state memory. Anything that hasn't already been flushed to disk is lost. Ideally, the log on disk has been updated recently, and you can reconstruct some of what was lost. The flushing of data from the page buffer to disk is called *checkpointing*.

You have two methods of writing data in the page buffer to hard disk stable storage:

>> **Write the buffer contents to disk one page at a time.** In this case, when it turns out that a page not currently in the buffer is needed and, as a consequence, is read from disk, it displaces a page that's already in the buffer. If that page is dirty, it must be written to disk before the new page can be read.

>> **Write the entire contents of the buffer to disk at the same time.** This operation is done at regular intervals called *checkpoints*. The more frequent your checkpoints are, the less data you lose in case of a soft failure or failure of any part of the system other than the hard disk subsystem. For this reason, setting frequent checkpoints is a good idea. Too-frequent checkpoints are bad, however, because a write to disk of the complete contents of the page buffer takes time that isn't being used productively. Here again, you have a trade-off between normal operating performance and the time and effort it would take to recover from a failure.

If you have good statistics on the frequency of failures that cause the loss of the contents of solid-state memory and the cost — both in lost productivity and extra expense — of recovery from those failures, you can make an informed decision about how frequently you should schedule checkpoints. Checkpoints have a cost in lost productivity, but not as great a cost as a dump. Checkpoints should be performed more frequently than dumps, but not so frequently that multiple checkpoints are likely to occur within the execution time of a typical transaction. Having multiple checkpoints while a transaction is active consumes time but doesn't deliver a corresponding reduction in recovery time.

Optimizing batch transactions

A transaction that causes multiple updates is called a *batch* transaction. Batch transactions can be problematic if they're long. If the page buffer fills while a batch transaction is in progress, it could initiate a rollback, and rolling back a lengthy transaction and then rerunning it can have a major impact on productivity. To address this concern, one option is to break the batch into smaller minibatches — but you must do this carefully. If a batch transaction is rolled back, it undoes every change that was made by the transaction up to the point of the rollback. If a batch is broken into, say, two minibatches, and a rollback occurs while the second minibatch is executing, the changes made by the first minibatch won't be rolled back, and the database is left in an inconsistent state.

One solution to this problem is to allow rollbacks only during the first minibatch of a series of minibatches. Doing so, however, severely limits what can be done in the subsequent minibatches. If the minibatches are truly independent, no problem exists, but such independence must be guaranteed to preserve the integrity of the database.

Tuning the Operating System

Because your operating system controls an application's access to input/output (I/O) devices and to hard disk memory, it can affect database application performance in many ways. You can do at least an equal number of things, however, to tune the operating system to improve performance. In the following sections, I touch on some of the major areas in which you can make a performance difference by acting on the operating system.

Scheduling threads

Practically all operating systems these days are multithreaded operating systems. Microsoft Windows is an example of one such operating system. Multithreading is what makes it possible for you to type text in a Microsoft Word document while your Microsoft Excel spreadsheet is recalculating values and your Microsoft Access database is performing a query. Meanwhile, your media player is piping your favorite song into your headphones. Each one of those tasks is performed by a thread of execution.

Multiple threads of execution don't operate simultaneously, although they seem to. Instead, they operate concurrently. First, a little bit of one task is executed; then a context switch suspends that thread of execution and activates another thread. This swapping goes on so rapidly that to a human observer, the threads appear to be executing at the same time. Operating systems have moved from single-threaded to multithreaded operation because of the great performance boost you get.

You may wonder why multithreading improves performance. After all, whether you interleave the execution of five tasks or have them run sequentially, you still have to execute all the instructions involved in those five tasks. In fact, it seems that multithreading should be slower than single threading because nonproductive overhead is involved with every task-switch operation.

Despite task switching overhead, multithreading substantially improves *throughput* — the total amount of work that gets done per unit time. Suppose that you have a typical organizational database system, with a database server holding the database and multiple client machines making queries or updates to that database. On the server, some of the database is in high-speed cache memory, some is in slower dynamic RAM, and some is stored on very-much-slower hard disk.

If the currently active thread needs to access a data item that is neither in cache nor RAM, a long delay occurs before it can proceed. There's no point in stalling everybody while that one thread waits for a response from the hard disk subsystem. As soon as the operating system is asked to go to hard disk for data, it can initiate that operation and then immediately suspend execution of the active thread and activate another thread that's ready to go. When the needed data becomes available from the hard disk subsystem, the original thread can be reactivated and run at full speed again.

Any application that's operating in a multithreaded environment with, say, four other applications isn't speeded by the multithreading process. All five applications, however, will finish sooner than they would have if they'd been run sequentially, because as one application is waiting for a slow operation to complete, the processor can productively be used by another application that's performing fast operations.

The scheduling of threads is a ripe area for tuning. One area in which tuning can make a big difference is context switching.

Context switching

At any given instant, the data that's being acted on in the processor is the *context* at that instant. All the data in all the processor's user-accessible registers make up the context. An instant later, a computation has been performed, and the context is different.

Before a context switch occurs, the context of an application must be saved so that when the application's thread is reactivated, the context can be restored and execution can proceed as though nothing had happened.

A context switch takes time. It takes time to save the context of the thread that's being replaced, and it takes time to restore the context of the thread that's replacing it. Some operating systems are more efficient at context switching than others. That efficiency rating could be a factor in choosing an operating system, depending on the mix of applications that will be running and on the number of applications that typically will be running concurrently.

Round-robin scheduling

Round-robin scheduling is the simplest algorithm for selecting which one of all the threads that are ready to run should run next. The operating system kernel maintains a queue of pointers to threads that are ready to run. It grabs the pointer to the next thread from the head of the queue and places the pointer to the currently executing thread at the tail of the queue. New threads are placed at the tail of the queue when they become ready to run.

Round-robin scheduling treats all threads as though they have equal importance. In a database environment, this assumption is likely to be valid, so round-robin scheduling is appropriate.

Priority-based scheduling

In *priority-based scheduling,* each thread is given a priority number, with higher-priority threads receiving higher numbers. Higher-priority threads are given preference by a part of the operating system called the scheduler. They run more often and for longer periods than other threads. The priority assigned to an application, as well as the level of service that a given priority level confers, are quantities subject to tuning.

Priority-based scheduling has a potential pitfall, called *priority inversion.*

Priority inversion

Suppose that you have three applications running on three different threads. One has high priority, one has medium priority, and one has low priority. Suppose further that the high-priority thread and the low-priority thread require the same resource. Here's what could happen:

1. The low-priority thread starts running and acquires an exclusive lock on the key resource.

2. The high-priority thread starts running and tries to acquire the key resource, but it fails because the resource is locked by the low-priority thread. This situation is a priority inversion, but it isn't too bad. It's called a *bounded priority inversion* because it lasts no longer than the critical section of the low-priority thread, after which the lock is released.

3. The medium-priority thread preempts the low-priority thread during the inversion. Now both the high-priority thread and the low-priority thread are idle. The medium-priority thread may even be preempted by another, higher-priority thread, which could delay the high-priority thread for an unacceptably long time, causing it to fail.

**TECHNICAL
STUFF**

This kind of unbounded priority inversion happened to the Mars Pathfinder spacecraft in 1997, halting the exploration of the red planet by the Sojourner rover until NASA engineers could figure out what had happened and upload a fix to the code.

Here are two possible solutions to the priority inversion:

» **Priority Inheritance Protocol (PIP):** One solution to the priority inversion problem is to institute the PIP. When a high-priority thread attempts to lock a resource that's already locked by a lower-priority thread, the priority of the lower-priority thread is automatically raised to match the priority of the high-priority thread. Thus, it can't be preempted by a medium-priority thread, and the priority inversion is only a bounded one.

» **Priority Ceiling Protocol (PCP):** Another solution is provided by the PCP. When a thread locks a resource, regardless of what its priority is, it's immediately promoted to the highest priority. It can't be preempted. Thus, when it exits its critical section and releases its lock on the resource, the ready thread with the highest priority can acquire that resource. This example is another case of a bounded priority inversion.

Clearly, if you use priority-based scheduling, you should also use some scheme such as PIP or PCP.

Deadlock

Deadlock is another problem related to resource acquisition. Suppose that two threads both need the same two resources, A and B:

1. Thread 1 acquires an exclusive lock on resource A.

2. Thread 2 acquires an exclusive lock on resource B.

3. Thread 1 attempts to acquire a lock on resource B but can't, so it waits, pending the availability of resource B.

4. Thread 2 attempts to acquire a lock on resource A but can't, so it waits, pending the availability of resource A.

5. Neither resource A nor resource B ever becomes available, and both applications 1 and 2 are deadlocked.

A common solution to this problem is for the operating system to notice that neither thread 1 nor thread 2 has made any progress after an interval during which progress should have been made. The operating system drops all locks held by both threads and delays them for different intervals before allowing them to run again. The delay intervals are tunable quantities. The best intervals are successful at breaking deadlocks practically all the time.

Determining database buffer size

Earlier in this chapter, I mention that the storage in a computer that runs database applications comes to two varieties: volatile and nonvolatile. Volatile memory is considered to be unstable storage because a power interruption or other failure that causes a machine reboot erases everything in it. Nonvolatile memory, by contrast, retains its information when such problems occur. The reason why nobody puts all his code and data in nonvolatile storage is that it's about a million times slower than the slowest form of volatile storage.

Clearly, the less often you have to go out to the nonvolatile storage on hard disk, the better. You enjoy a million-to-one performance advantage if you operate out of semiconductor RAM. For many applications, it's not feasible to retain your entire database in RAM, but you can afford to keep some of it in RAM (ideally, that portion of the database that you're most likely to need to access often). The portion of RAM that holds that heavily used portion of the database is called the *database page buffer*. Your DBA's tuning option is to decide on the size of the page buffer. If the page buffer is too small, you'll be going out to disk more often than you need to and will suffer serious performance degradation. If the page buffer is larger than it needs to be, you'll be paying for expensive RAM when you could be getting the same performance out of dirt-cheap disks. Somewhere in the middle is the optimum size.

If your hit rate on the page buffer is between 90 percent and 95 percent, you're probably doing about as well as you can expect. That result means that 9 times out of 10 or 19 times out of 20, when you need to access a data item, that item is in the buffer. If you're not getting a hit rate in that range, perhaps you could do better with a larger buffer — or perhaps not. Depending on your database, a 70 percent hit rate may be the best that you can do.

You can test the situation by gradually adding more RAM to the buffer until your hit rate plateaus. At that point, you know that adding any additional RAM to the buffer won't improve your performance and will only add to your cost.

Tuning the page usage factor

Another system parameter under the DBA's control is the amount of space on a page that's holding data. This parameter is called the page's *usage factor*. The higher the usage factor, the more data you can store in fast RAM compared with the amount that must remain on slow hard disk. This is a vote for high usage factors. If the usage factor is too high, however, a problem arises when you make several insertions or update records by replacing NULL values with data. Overflowing a page causes a major performance hit.

Tuning is important here. You need to be aware of the kinds of operations that are typically performed on the database. Are insertions common? If so, a lower usage factor is called for. If not, you'll get better performance by raising the usage factor.

Page usage factor is one of the many places where tuning means trying a setting, taking data, and then trying something else. After you have a good understanding of how your workload performs under the various usage factors, you can pick the one that will serve you the best most of the time.

Maximizing the Hardware You Have

In addition to the tweaks your DBA can make to the recovery system and the operating system, she can improve performance by making better use of the hardware. In this section, I look at just a few ways to maximize your hardware.

Optimizing the placement of code and data on hard disks

You already know from the discussion of hard disk drive construction earlier in this chapter that you can improve performance by locating data that will be read or written in sequential locations on the same track on your hard disk. Keeping the read/write head on the same track eliminates the delay due to seek time and settling time. For data transfers larger than a single track, staying on the same cylinder on the disk maintains the performance advantage.

When a hard disk is new or has recently been reformatted, you can enjoy good performance by carefully choosing the way in which you copy data to it. As time goes on and updates are made, that beautiful organization is gradually degraded, and your performance is degraded with it. One thing you can do to combat this degradation is defragment your disks regularly.

Another thing your DBA can do to improve performance is locate your most frequently used data on the cylinders in the middle of your hard disk. If your disk has cylinders numbered 0 through 1023, you should put the most heavily used data on cylinder 511, or at least near it. This practice is due to a statistical consideration. If the most heavily used data is clustered in the center of the disk, seeks tend to be short, decreasing the time it takes for the heads to settle over a track. Furthermore, on those occasions when the heads are over a high-numbered track or a low-numbered track, a high probability exists that they'll next need to go to one of the heavily used tracks, which is only half the radius of the disk away. Long seeks from, say, track 5 to track 1020 are rare.

Tuning the page replacement algorithm

The *page replacement algorithm* is the code that decides which page in the database page buffer to flush to disk when the buffer is full and a new page is needed. You want to flush out a page that is highly unlikely to be needed again soon. The best page to flush is predictable with a high degree of accuracy due to the fact that most applications have a key property called temporal locality. *Temporal locality* means that a page in the buffer that has been used recently is likely to be needed again soon. The flip side of this coin is that a page that hasn't been accessed in a long time probably won't be needed any time soon. Such a page is a prime candidate for flushing out to disk.

One page replacement algorithm that follows this line of reasoning is the least recently used (LRU) algorithm. Whenever a page must be replaced, the LRU algorithm flushes the page that has been in the buffer the longest time without being either read or written to. The LRU algorithm works very well in most cases.

Depending on what the application is doing, however, the LRU algorithm may be the worst possible option from a performance standpoint. If you monitor performance and notice excessive buffer page swapping, changing the page replacement algorithm may give you a substantial performance enhancement.

Tuning the disk controller cache

The disk controller cache is another area that the DBA can tune. Not only is a page replacement buffer located in the system's main memory, but also, a cache is located in the hard disk subsystem. How this cache is used can affect performance.

Cache usage is regulated by two distinct protocols. As it happens, the performance of read operations isn't affected by which of two protocols you use, but write performance definitely can be affected. The two protocols are

>> **Write-through:** When the write-through protocol is in effect, writes to disk are simultaneously written to both the cache and the disk. This means that every write operation is as slow as a disk write operation rather than as fast as a cache write operation. When you're operating under this protocol, the cache gives no advantage to write operations, but reads of data in the cache are fast.

>> **Write-back:** When the write-back protocol is in effect, writes to the disk subsystem go only to the cache, and a dirty bit is set to indicate that the contents of the cache differ from the contents of the corresponding locations on disk. Dirty pages are flushed to disk when convenient or when the page replacement algorithm replaces a dirty page with a new page loaded from disk.

For a lightly loaded system, the write-back protocol usually gives better performance because disk accesses are rare. For a heavily loaded system with frequent page swapping and more reading than writing, the write-through protocol may be better. Depending on your job mix, it may pay you to try both protocols, taking statistics for both. After you analyze your statistical data, choose the protocol that performs better.

Adding Hardware

If you didn't read the material in the preceding sections of this chapter, probably the first thought to come to mind when you determine that your system isn't performing the way it should is "I need new hardware." Perhaps that's true, but new hardware shouldn't be your first option. As demonstrated in the preceding sections, you can try a great many things besides adding new hardware.

When you've exhausted all the possibilities for improvement of the hardware you have, consider adding hardware. If you add hardware before performing the optimizations discussed in the preceding sections, you could easily be out the money without having addressed the real problem. Performance may not improve because your system's lagging performance wasn't due to a deficiency in the hardware after all. Nevertheless, if your system is optimized to the point at which it's doing the best that it can with the hardware it has, and you're still not getting the performance you need, perhaps upgrading your hardware will help.

Faster processor

One obvious choice is moving to a faster processor. This choice can be an expensive one, however, because you can't just plug a faster processor chip into your existing motherboard and expect a speedup. The support chips on the motherboard need to match the new processor, which means that you probably need to replace the motherboard and may have to move to faster RAM at the same time. You may as well buy a whole new box and give your existing box to your kid to play computer games on. (Wait — that won't work! Today's fast-action computer games with hyper-realistic graphics require the fastest processors on the planet. Your offspring will probably feel dissed if you try to palm off your obsolete processor on him.) At any rate, expensive or not, moving to a faster, more capable CPU may give you a significant performance boost.

More RAM

A less drastic upgrade than a computer switch-out, which may nonetheless make a big difference in performance, is adding RAM to your existing system. Adding RAM may enable you to support a bigger page buffer than you currently have, enabling you to keep more of your data in fast semiconductor memory. If this addition improves your page buffer hit rate, it could be a very economical way to improve performance.

Faster hard disks

Hard disk drives don't all have the same performance parameters. Seek time, settling time, rotational latency, controller cache size, and disk interface bandwidth are all things to look at (refer to "Hard disk drive performance considerations," earlier in this chapter). If the disks you currently have aren't up to the current state of the art, you might consider replacing them. Think carefully, however, before spending a lot of money on this idea. Although processor performance, RAM densities, and hard disk capacities have been improving at an exponential rate in accordance with Moore's Law, hard disk performance specifications haven't scaled nearly as rapidly. Although this year's hard disks have a lot more capacity than last year's, there may be little or no improvement in the speed at which you're able to read from and write to them.

More hard disks

Although trading up to faster hard disk drives may not give you the performance boost you're looking for, adding disk drives that are no faster than the ones you are using now may do the job. The advantage of having multiple disks is that while one disk is busy performing one operation, a second disk can be performing a second operation. Because the processor is operating so much faster than the disk drives, in an operation that entails a lot of disk accesses, multiple disks can operate at the same time. This parallelism could translate into a significant improvement in overall performance.

Solid State Disk (SSD)

For applications that demand the ultimate in performance, such as high-speed gaming, having one or two hundred gigabytes of SSD sitting between your RAM and disk storage can make a tremendous difference. It will also speed things up for business applications that have a large working set. If that working set is all on electronic media instead of having some of it on rotating media, you can expect a dramatic improvement in throughput.

RAID arrays

If you're going to spread your database across multiple disks anyway, you may as well configure those disks as a RAID array. RAID is an acronym for Redundant Array of Independent Disks, although it previously stood for Redundant Array of Inexpensive Disks. The disks in a RAID array are inexpensive because at any given time, the hard disk market has a sweet spot where you get the most bang for your buck, which in this case means the most megabytes per dollar. If the sweet spot happens to be 4TB, it's cheaper to buy five 4TB drives and configure them as a RAID array than it would be to buy a single 20TB drive (if you could even buy a 20TB drive at any price). The disks in the array are redundant in that your database information is recorded in more than one place. This safety feature is important for critical databases. If one of your disk drives were to fail and lose all its data, you could keep on operating by using the remaining disks. I give detailed coverage to RAID in Book 4, Chapter 1.

Working in Multiprocessor Environments

Until now, I've been talking primarily about a system that may have multiple client computers engaging in transactions with a database stored on a single database server. For large-enough databases in which performance is an important consideration, a distributed solution may be called for. This solution means not only multiple client computers, but multiple servers too.

Distributed databases are significantly more complex than single-server databases, and I don't go into that complexity much here. Instead, I briefly mention three main architectural choices for such systems.

The architecture chosen has a major effect on overall performance. For some types of applications, one architecture is clearly superior to the other two. For another architecture, the advantage goes to one of the other configurations. Your choices are

» **Tightly coupled architecture:** Several processors share the same main memory and disks. The processors operate in parallel on the same data, so this architecture is often best for large, highly integrated tasks.

» **Shared-disk architecture:** Each processor in the system has its own private main memory, but the hard disks are shared. This architecture is often best when a lot of computation must be done on related tasks that operate on the same data.

» **Shared-nothing architecture:** All the processors have their own private main memory and their own private hard disks. This architecture is appropriate when the application being run can be divided into independent subapplications.

Chapter **3**

Finding and Eliminating Performance Bottlenecks

D atabases generally start small and grow with time. Operations that could be performed in a reasonable amount of time with a small database gradually take longer as the database grows. This slowdown probably isn't due to any general inadequacy of the system, but to a specific link in the chain of operations that leads from a request to a result. That specific link is a *bottleneck*. Finding and eliminating bottlenecks is one of the main jobs of any person charged with maintaining a database. The ability to determine the cause of a performance shortfall, and to find a remedy, is valuable in any organization and can be highly rewarding, both intellectually and financially.

Pinpointing the Problem

Have you heard the old backwoods story about the frog in hot water? It goes like this:

> If you throw a frog into a pot of water that's practically boiling, it will jump out right away. If, however, you put a frog in a pot that's at a comfortable temperature and gradually turn up the heat, the frog won't notice that anything is amiss and will swim around contentedly until it's too late.

Sometimes, database users are like frogs. When they start using a new database application, they let you know right away if it's running slowly. If performance is good at first but then gradually degrades, however, they may not notice a difference until that difference is truly dramatic. Some problems manifest themselves right away, whereas others are slow to develop. As you might expect, the causes of the immediate problems tend to be different from the causes of the problems that develop slowly over time. In either case, a database specialist needs to know how to track down the source of the problem and then take appropriate action to fix it.

After the initial loading of data into a database, only two basic activities are performed on it: retrieving a selected portion of the data or updating the data. I count adding new data, deleting existing data, and changing existing data as being forms of updates. Some databases experience many more retrievals, called *queries*, than they do updates in a given interval. Other databases experience more updates, and some experience about an equal number of queries and updates.

Slow query

Users who are responsible for running queries, like the happily swimming frog, may not notice that their queries are running slower until someone comes by while one is running and remarks on how long it takes for a result to come back. At that point, the users call you. Now you get the chance to do a little detective work. Somewhere — whether it be in the application, the database management system (DBMS), the network link, the database server, or the storage subsystem — something has maxed out. Your job is to figure out what it is and restore performance to acceptable levels as soon as possible without replacing or upgrading the parts of the system that are *not* part of the problem. Your job is to find the bottleneck.

Slow update

Perhaps the problem is not with queries, but with updates. For a person making additions, changes, or deletions in a database, long waits between entering a change and having the system being ready to accept the next one can be frustrating at best and intolerable at worst. The causes for delays in updating tend to be different from the causes of slow responses to queries. Although the bottleneck may be different, your job is still the same: Find the source of the problem and then fix it. In the next section, I look at some of the likely causes of bottlenecks.

Determining the Possible Causes of Trouble

The main candidates for causing bottlenecks can be categorized in three areas: indexes, communication, and hardware. In this section, I explore these categories further.

Problems with indexes

Probably the number-one cause of less-than-optimal performance is improper indexing. Improper indexing may mean the lack of one or more indexes that should be present, but it could also mean the presence of indexes that should not be there.

B+ tree indexes

Several kinds of indexes exist, but the most common is the B+ tree index, (also called the B-tree index), in which B stands for *balanced*. A B+ tree has a treelike structure with a root node from which a row of branch nodes fan out. Another row of branch nodes may fan out from the first row, and so on for as many rows as the tree has. The nodes at the end of the chain of branch nodes are called *leaf nodes*. Leaf nodes have no children; instead, they hold the index values. The root node contains pointers to the first row of branch nodes. The first row of branch nodes contains pointers to the next row of branch nodes. The last row of branch nodes contains pointers to the leaf nodes. The leaf nodes contain pointers to rows in the table being indexed.

Index pluses and minuses

Indexes are valuable because they allow you to find a row in a data table after following a short chain of pointers, as opposed to scanning the table one row at a time until you reach the row you want. The advantage is even greater than it seems on the surface because indexes tend to be small compared with the data tables they're indexing. This means that the index is often entirely contained in cache memory, which in turn means that the target row in the data table is located at semiconductor RAM speeds rather than mechanical hard disk speeds, as would likely be the case for a full table scan.

The advantages aren't all on the side of indexing, however. Indexes tend to degrade in tables with frequent inserts and deletes. Deletes create empty leaf nodes, which fill space in cache without contributing and could cause the index to spill out of cache onto the hard disk, with the performance penalty that goes along with that. Eliminating the empty leaf cells requires a time-consuming index rebuild, during which no productive processing can take place.

Updates have an even greater impact on performance than delete operations do. An update that includes at least one indexed column consists of both a delete and an insert. Because an index is a table of pointers, updating an index changes the location of that pointer, requiring its deletion from one place and its insertion at another. Indexes on nonkey columns containing values that change frequently cause the worst performance hits. Updates of indexes on primary keys almost never happen, and updates of indexes on foreign keys are rare. Indexes that aren't highly selective (such as indexes on columns that contain many duplicates) often degrade overall performance rather than enhance it.

Index-only queries

Indexes have the capability to speed queries because they provide near-direct access to the rows in a data table from which you want to retrieve data. This arrangement is great, but suppose that the data you want to retrieve is entirely contained in the columns that comprise the index. In that case, you don't need to access the data table at all: Everything you need is contained in the index.

Index-only queries can be very fast indeed, which may make it worthwhile to include in an index a column that you otherwise wouldn't include, just because it's retrieved by a frequently run query. In such a case, the added maintenance cost for the index is overshadowed by the increased speed of retrievals for the frequently run query.

Full table scans versus indexed table access

How do you find the rows you want to retrieve from a database table? The simplest way, called a *full table scan*, is to look at every row in the table, up to the table's high-water mark, grabbing the rows that satisfy your selection condition as you go. The *high-water mark* of a table is the largest number of rows it has ever had. Currently, the table may have fewer rows because of deletions, but it still may have rows scattered anywhere up to and including the high-water mark. The main disadvantage of a full table scan is that it must examine every row in the table up to and including the high-water mark. A full table scan may or may not be the most efficient way to retrieve the data you want. The alternative is indexed table access.

As I discuss in the preceding section on the B+ tree index, when your retrieval is on an index, you reach the desired rows in the data table after a short walk through a small number of nodes on the tree. Because the index is likely to be cached, such retrievals are much faster than retrievals that must load sequential blocks from the data table into cache before scanning them.

For very small tables, which are as likely to be cached as an index is, a full table scan is about as fast as an indexed table access. Thus, indexing small tables is probably a bad idea. It won't gain you significant performance, and it adds complexity and size to your database.

Pitfalls in communication

One area where performance may be lost or gained is in the communication between a database server and the client computers running the database applications. If the communication channel is too narrow for the traffic, or if the channel is just not used efficiently, performance can suffer.

ODBC/JDBC versus native drivers

Most databases support more than one way of connecting to client computers running applications. Because these different ways of connecting employ different mechanisms, they have different performance characteristics. The database application, running on a client computer, must be able to send requests to and receive responses from the database, running on the database server. The conduit for this communication is a software driver that translates application requests into a form that the database can understand and database responses into a form that the application can understand.

You have two main ways of performing this function. One way is to use a native driver, which has been specifically written to interface an application written with a DBMS vendor's application development tools to that same vendor's DBMS back end. The advantage of this approach is that because the driver knows exactly what's required, it performs with minimum overhead. The disadvantage is that an application written with one DBMS back end in mind can't use a native driver to communicate with a database created with a different DBMS.

In practice, you frequently need to access a database from an application that didn't originally target that database. In such a case, you can use a generalized driver. The two main types are Open Database Connectivity (ODBC) and

Java-Based Database Connectivity (JDBC). ODBC was created by Microsoft but has been widely adopted by application developers writing in the Visual Basic, C, and C++ programming languages. JDBC is similar to ODBC but designed to be used with the Java programming language.

ODBC consists of a driver manager and the specific driver that's compatible with the target database. The driver performs the ODBC functions and communicates directly with the database server. One feature of the driver manager is its capability to log ODBC *calls*, which do the actual work of communicating between the application and the database. This feature can be very helpful in debugging a connection, but slows down communication, so it should be disabled in a production environment. ODBC drivers may provide slower performance than a native driver designed to join a specific client with a specific data source. An ODBC driver also may fail to provide all the functions for a specific data source that a native driver would. (I discuss drivers in more detail in Book 5, Chapter 7.)

Locking and client performance

Multiple users can perform read operations without interfering with one another, making use of a shared lock. When an update is involved, however, things are different. As long as an update transaction initiated by one client has a resource in the database locked with an exclusive lock, other clients can't access that resource. Furthermore, an update transaction can't place an exclusive lock on a resource that currently is held by a shared lock.

This situation is strong motivation for keeping transactions short. You should consider several factors when you find that a critical resource is being locked too long, slowing performance for everyone. One possibility is that a transaction's SQL code is written in an inefficient manner, perhaps due to improper use of indexes or poorly written SELECT statements. Hardware could also be the culprit. Most organizations put their limited IT budget dollars into keeping the servers upgraded because servers affect everyone, which is a good idea. You can't ignore the client computers in the process, however. It takes only one obsolete, slow client computer to slow processing for everyone by holding locks too long. If response in a multiuser environment seems to be slow even though you have a fast server, check the clients. For best performance, they should all be operating at comparable performance levels.

Application development tools making suboptimal decisions

Sometimes, an application development tool implements a query differently from what you'd get if you entered the same query directly from the SQL command prompt. If you suspect that lagging performance is due to your development tool, enter the SQL directly, and compare response times. If something that the tool is doing is indeed causing the problem, see whether you can turn off the feature that's causing extra communication between the client and the server to take place.

Determining whether hardware is robust enough and configured properly

Perhaps your queries are running slowly because your hardware isn't up to the challenge. It could be a matter of a slow processor, bus clock, or hard disk subsystem, or it could be insufficient memory. Alternatively, your hardware may be good enough but isn't configured correctly. Your database page buffer may not be big enough, or you may be running in a less-than-optimal mode, such as flushing the page buffer to disk more often than necessary. Perhaps the system is creating checkpoints or database dumps too frequently. All these configuration issues, if recognized and addressed, can improve performance dramatically without touching your equipment budget.

REMEMBER

You may well decide that you need to update some aspect of your hardware environment, but before you do, make sure that the hardware that you already have is configured in such a way that you have a proper balance of performance and reliability.

Implementing General Principles: A First Step Toward Improving Performance

In looking for ways to improve the performance of queries you're running, some general principles almost always apply. If a query violates any of these principles, you can probably make it run faster by eliminating the violation. Check out the suggestions in this section before expending a lot of effort on other interventions.

Avoid direct user interaction

Among all the components of a database system, the human being sitting at the keyboard is the slowest by far — almost a thousand times slower than a hard disk and more than a billion times slower than semiconductor RAM. Nothing brings a system to its knees as fast as putting a human in the loop. Transactions that lock database resources should never require any action by a human. If your application does require such action, changing your application to eliminate it will do more for overall system performance than anything else you can do.

Examine the application/database interaction

One important performance bottleneck is the communication channel between the server and a client machine. This channel has a design capacity that imposes a speed limit on the packets of information that travel back and forth. In addition to the data that gets transmitted, a significant amount of overhead is associated with each packet. Thus, one large packet is transmitted significantly faster than numerous small packets containing the same amount of information. In practice, this means that it's better to retrieve the entire set in one shot than to retrieve a set of rows one row at a time. Following that logic, it would be a mistake to put an SQL retrieval statement within a loop in your application program. If you do, you'll end up sending a request and receiving a response every time through the loop. Instead, grab an entire result set at the same time, and do your processing on the client machine.

Another thing you can do to reduce back-and-forth traffic is to use SQL's flow of control constructs to execute multiple SQL statements in a single transaction. In this case, the number-crunching takes place on the server rather than on the client. The result is, however, the same as in the preceding paragraph — fewer message packets traveling over the communication channel.

User-defined functions (UDFs) can also reduce client/server traffic. When you include a UDF in a SELECT statement's WHERE clause, processing is localized in the server, and less data needs to be transmitted to the client. You can create a UDF with a CREATE FUNCTION statement, and then use it as an extension to the SQL language.

Don't ask for columns that you don't need

It may seem like a no-brainer to not retrieve columns that you don't need. After all, doing so shuttles unneeded information across the communications channel, slowing operations. It's really easy, however, to type the following:

```
SELECT * FROM CUSTOMER ;
```

This query retrieves the data you want, along with a lot of unwanted baggage. So work a little harder and list the columns you want — *only* the columns you want. If it turns out that all the columns you want are indexed, you can save a lot of time, as the DBMS makes an index-only retrieval. Adding just one unindexed column forces the query to access the data table.

Don't use cursors unless you absolutely have to

Cursors are glacially slow in almost all implementations. If you have a slow-running query that uses cursors, try to find a way to get the same result without cursors. Whatever you come up with is likely to run significantly faster.

Precompiled queries

Compiling a query takes time — often, more than the time it takes to execute the query. Rather than suffer that extra time every time you execute a query, it's better to suffer it once and then reap the benefit every time you execute the query after the first time. You can do this by putting the query in a stored procedure, which is precompiled by definition.

Precompilation helps most of the time, but it also has pitfalls:

» If an index is added to a column that's important to a query, you should recompile the query so that it takes advantage of the new index.

» If a table grows from having relatively few rows to having many rows, you should recompile the query. When the query is compiled with few rows, the optimizer probably will choose a full table scan over using an index because for small tables, indexes offer no advantage. When a table grows large, however, an index greatly reduces the execution time of the query.

Tracking Down Bottlenecks

Tracking down bottlenecks is the fun part of database maintenance. You get the same charge that a detective gets from solving a mysterious crime. Breaking the bottleneck and watching productivity go through the roof can be exhilarating.

Your system is crawling when it should be sprinting. It's a complex construction with many elements, both hardware and software. What should you do first?

Isolating performance problems

As long as a wide variety of system elements could be involved in a problem, it's hard to make progress. The first step is narrowing down the possibilities. Do this by finding which parts of the system are performing as they should, thus eliminating them as potential sources of the problem. To paraphrase Sherlock Holmes, "When you eliminate all the explanations but one as being not possible, then whatever is left, however unlikely it may seem, must be true."

Performing a top-down analysis

A query is a multilevel operation, and whatever is slowing it could be at any one of those levels. At the highest level is the query code as implemented in SQL. If the query is written inefficiently, you probably need to look no further for the source of the problem. Rewrite the query more efficiently, and see whether that solves the problem. If it does, great! You don't have to look any further. If you don't find an inefficient query, however, or the rewrite doesn't seem to help, you must dig deeper.

DBMS operations

Below the level of the SQL code is a level where locking, logging, cache management, and query execution take place. All these operations are in the province of the DBMS and are called into action by the top-level SQL. Any inefficiencies here can certainly impact performance, as follows:

» Locking more resources than necessary or locking them for too long can slow operations for everybody.

» Logging is a vital component of the recovery system, and it helps you determine exactly how the system performs, but it also absorbs resources. Excessive logging beyond what's needed could be a source of slowdowns.

» Cache management is a major factor in overall performance. Are the right pages being cached, and are they remaining in the cache for the proper amount of time?

» Finally, at this level, are queries being executed in the most efficient way? Many queries could be executed a variety of ways and end up with the same result. The execution plans for these different ways can vary widely, however, in how long they take to execute and in what resources they consume while doing it. All these possibilities deserve scrutiny when performance is unacceptable and can't be attributed to poorly written queries.

Hardware

The lowest level that could contribute to poor performance is the hardware level. Look here after you confirm that everything at the higher levels is working as it should. This level includes the hard disk drives, the disk controller, the processor, and the network. Each of these elements could be a bottleneck if its performance doesn't match that of the other hardware elements.

HARD DISK DRIVES

The performance of hard disk drives tends to degrade over time, as insertions and deletions are made in databases and as files unrelated to database processing are added, changed, or deleted. The disk becomes increasingly fragmented. If you want to copy a large file to disk, but only small chunks of open space are scattered here and there across the disk's cylinders, pieces of the file are copied into those small chunks. To read the entire file, the drive's read/write head must move from track to track, slowing access dramatically. As time goes on, the drive gets increasingly fragmented, imperceptibly at first and then quite noticeably.

The solution to this problem is running a defragmentation utility. This solution can take a long time, and because of heavy disk accessing, it reduces the system's response time to close to zero. Defragmentation runs should be scheduled at regular intervals when normal traffic is light to maintain reasonable performance. Most modern operating systems include a defragmentation utility that analyzes your hard disk, tells you whether it would benefit from defragmenting, and then (with your consent) performs the defragmentation operation.

DISK CONTROLLER

The disk controller contains a cache of recently accessed pages. When a page that's already in disk controller cache is requested by the processor, it can be returned much faster than is possible for pages stored only on disk. All the considerations I mention in Book 7, Chapter 2 for optimizing the database page buffer in the processor apply to the disk controller cache as well. The choice of page replacement algorithm can have a major effect on performance, as can cache size.

PROCESSOR

The processor has a tremendous effect on overall system performance because it's the fastest component in the entire system. Processors just a few years old are significantly slower than those on the market today. Upgrading an older processor, along with all the ancillary circuitry that must be upgraded to support it, can make a significant difference in overall performance.

Many organizations have a regular program of replacing computers at regular intervals, such as every three years. The systems that get replaced are moved down to less-critical applications. This domino effect of hand-me-down computers ends with donation to charitable organizations. If your computer is more than about three years old, consider replacing it as a possible method of improving your performance, assuming that you've already investigated all the other sources of slowdown mentioned in this chapter.

NETWORK

The network is the final major subsystem that may be causing performance problems. If the performance of running queries from a client computer on a network is unacceptable, try running the same queries directly on the server. If the queries run significantly faster on the server, the server's processor may be more powerful, or the network connection between the server and the client may be a bottleneck. Tools for analyzing network traffic can give you some indication whether your network is slowing you.

As is the case with processors, network performance has been increasing steadily. If your network is starting to get a little old, you may be better served by one with state-of-the-art speed. It's worth looking into.

Partitioning

Suppose that you've done the top-down analysis advocated in the preceding section and have isolated your performance problem to one of the primary hardware subsystems: the hard disk drive, disk controller, processor, or network. Suppose further that you've done everything you can think of: defragmented your hard drives, optimized paging in your disk controller, optimized paging in your database page buffer, and analyzed the traffic on your network. Despite all these remedies, the problem persists. Partitioning offers another approach that may break the bottleneck.

Partitioning can be helpful if your performance problem is caused by exceeding the capacity of a critical system resource. Partitioning is essentially spreading out the work so that the overstretched resource doesn't get overloaded.

You can spread the work spatially, temporally, or both. *Spatial partitioning* means doing more things in parallel, which could entail moving to a multicore processor, adding hard disk drives to your RAID array, installing a bigger database page buffer, and so on. You get the idea. Wherever the bottleneck is, widen the neck to increase the flow rate through it.

The other thing to try is to increase temporal partitioning. In *temporal partitioning,* you don't make the neck of the bottle any wider; you just schedule workflow so that it's more evenly distributed in time. Don't run large update transactions at the same time that online query activity is high. Give users incentives to use the system across a broader range of times, rather than allow everybody to try to access the same resources at the same time.

Locating hotspots

Spreading the work away from an overloaded resource presupposes that you're able to determine which of the many components of your system is causing the bottleneck. Such overloaded resources are called *hotspots.* When a resource is hot, it's continually in use. If the resource is too hot, operations have to wait in line to use it. If the wait takes too long and results in aborts and rollbacks, performance is greatly affected. Fortunately, several tools are available, both at the operating-system level and at the database level, which you can use to monitor the performance of various aspects of your system and locate the hotspots. These performance monitoring tools, of course, vary from one operating system to another and from one DBMS to another. Check the documentation of your specific systems to determine what is available to you. After you locate a hotspot, you are well on your way to solving your performance problem. When you know what the overloaded system component is, you can apply the remedies discussed in this chapter to restore performance to an acceptable level. In the next section, I discuss several performance monitoring tools available on popular systems.

Analyzing Query Efficiency

Some kinds of problems slow everything that's running on a system. Other kinds of problems affect the performance of only one query or a few queries. For the class of problems that seem to affect only one or a few queries, the major DBMSs provide tools that you can use to track down the source of the problem. These tools come in three major categories: query analyzers, performance monitors, and event monitors. Each looks at a different aspect of the way a query is running. Based on what these tools tell you, you should be able to zero in on whatever is causing your system to perform less well than it should.

Using query analyzers

All the major DBMSs offer tools that give the database administrator (or other person responsible for the efficient operation of the database) a way of analyzing how well queries on the database are performing. In versions of Microsoft SQL Server before SQL Server 2005, the tool for this job was even named Query Analyzer. SQL Server 2005 represented a major break from the past in a number of ways. The functions that had been the province of Query Analyzer were incorporated into the new Microsoft SQL Server Management Studio, along with additional functionality useful for tuning query performance. This functionality is retained, along with a lot of other functionality in the version of SQL Server Management Studio included with SQL Server 2022.

Here's a brief introduction to SQL Server 2022's tuning tools (the Database Engine Tuning Advisor and the SQL Server Profiler) to give you an idea of what such tools look like and what they do. The operation of the tuning tools in SQL Server Management Studio differs in detail from the operation of similar tools for other DBMSs, but the overall functions are the same.

Figure 3-1 shows the main screen of Microsoft SQL Server Management Studio.

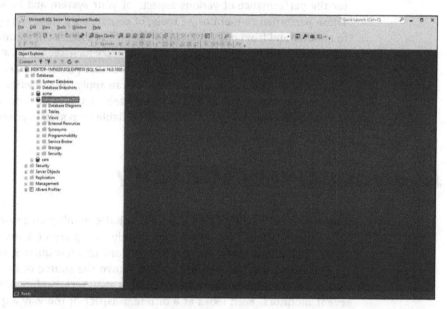

FIGURE 3-1:
Microsoft SQL
Server 2022
Management
Studio.

If you take a peek at the Object Explorer in the left pane of the Management Studio window (refer to Figure 3-1), you can see that I've connected to a database named AdventureWorks2022. This database is a sample SQL Server database provided by Microsoft. If you don't have it already, you can download it from www.msdn.microsoft.com. It contains sample data for a fictitious company.

Suppose that you're a manager at AdventureWorks, and you want to know what customers you have in the United States. You can find out with a simple SQL query. To draft a query in Management Studio, follow these steps:

1. **Click the New Query button at the left end of the Standard toolbar.**

   An SQL editor pane opens in the middle of the Management Studio window, as shown in Figure 3-2.

   TIP

   To remind yourself of the names of the tables in the AdventureWorks2022 database, you can expand the Databases node and then, from the items that appear below it, expand the Tables node in the tree in the Object Explorer in the left pane of the Management Studio window.

2. **Type your query in the editor pane, as shown in Figure 3-3.**

   The query

   ```
   SELECT FirstName, LastName FROM Person.Person
   WHERE LastName = 'Taylor' ;
   ```

   retrieves the names and phone numbers of everybody in the Contact table of the Person schema whose last name is Taylor.

3. **Execute the query by clicking the Execute button in the toolbar.**

   The result of the query shows up in the Results tab, as shown in Figure 3-4. The first several of the 83 people in the table whose last name is Taylor appear on the tab. You can see the rest by scrolling down.

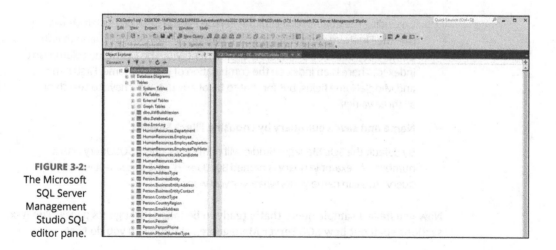

FIGURE 3-2:
The Microsoft
SQL Server
Management
Studio SQL
editor pane.

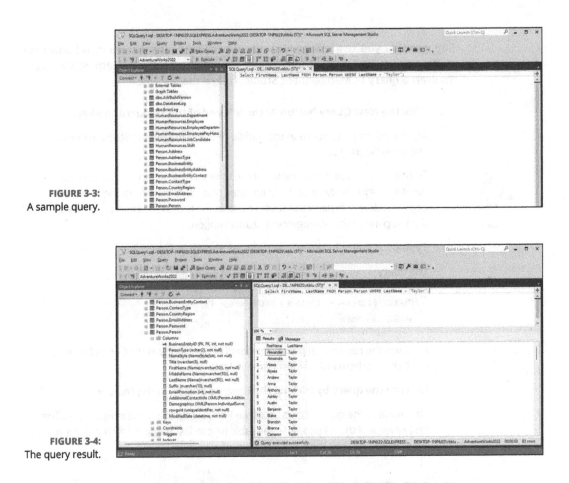

FIGURE 3-3:
A sample query.

FIGURE 3-4:
The query result.

Expanding the Column object of the Person.Person table on the left shows that the FirstName and LastName columns are a NVARCHAR field, and that the primary key of the Person table is BusinessEntityID. The LastName column isn't indexed. There is an index on the combination of the LastName, FirstName, and MiddleName fields, but for that to be of any use, we'd have to search on all three values.

4. Name and save your query by choosing File ⇨ Save As.

By default the SQL Manager Studio will name your query SQLQuery with a number. My example query is named SQLQuery1.sql because it was my first query. You can name yours whatever you want.

Now you have a sample query that's ready to be taken through its paces. The next sections spell out how SQL Server Management Studio lets you do that.

The Database Engine Tuning Advisor

The tool that SQL Server Management Studio provides for tuning queries is the Database Engine Tuning Advisor. To use this tool with the sample query created in the preceding section, follow these steps:

1. **In SQL Server Management Studio, choose Tools ⇨ Database Engine Tuning Advisor.**

   The Tuning Advisor window opens to the General tab, as shown in Figure 3-5.

   TIP

   SQL Server 2022 Express does not support the Database Engine Tuning Advisor. To follow the steps in this section, you must use one of the commercial SQL Server 2022 database products.

2. **When you're asked to connect to the server you're using, do so.**

3. **(Optional) The system has assigned a default session name, based on your login and the date and time; change this session name if you want to.**

4. **In the Workload section, choose the File radio button and then click the Browse for a Workload File button to the right of the long text box.**

5. **Find and select the query file that you just created.**

   For this example, I select SQLQuery1.sql.

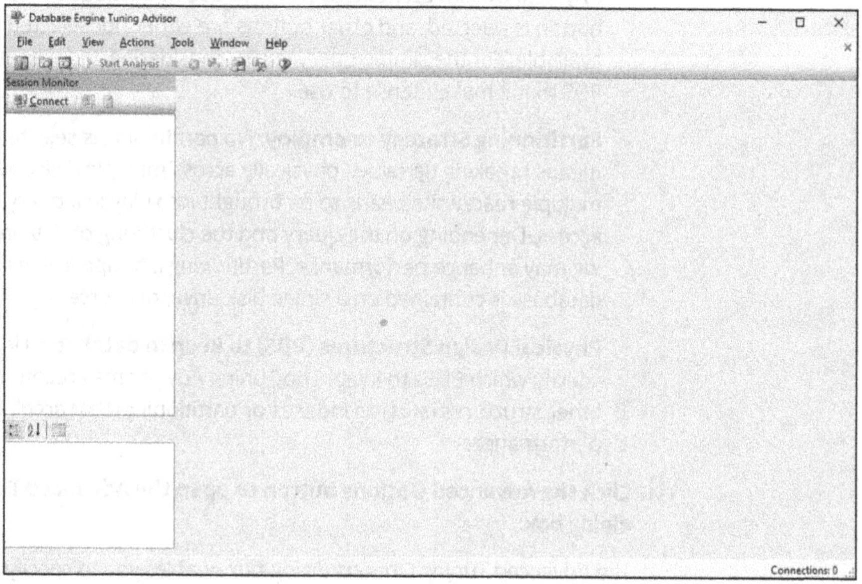

![Database Engine Tuning Advisor window screenshot]

FIGURE 3-5:
The Database Engine Tuning Advisor window.

Finding and Eliminating Performance Bottlenecks

6. Choose your database from the Database for workload analysis drop-down menu.

For this example, I choose AdventureWorks2022.

7. In the list of databases at the bottom of the Tuning Advisor window, select the check box next to the name of your database.

8. Make sure that the Save Tuning Log check box (at the bottom of the list of databases) is selected.

This option creates a permanent record of the tuning operation that's about to take place.

9. Click the Tuning Options tab to see what the default tuning options are — and to change them, if so desired.

TIP

The Limit Tuning Time check box in the top left corner is selected by default: Tuning can be so time-consuming that it severely affects normal production operation. To prevent this effect, you can set the maximum amount of time that a tuning session can take. When that maximum is reached, whatever tuning recommendations have been arrived at so far are shown as the result. If the tuning run had been allowed to run to completion, different recommendations might have been made. If your server is idle or lightly loaded, you may want to clear this check box to make sure that you get the best recommendation.

The three tuning options you can change are

- **Physical Design Structures (PDS) to use in database:** The Indexes radio button is selected, and other options are either not selected or not available. For the simple query you're considering, indexes are the only PDS that it makes sense to use.

- **Partitioning Strategy to employ:** No partitioning is selected. Partitioning means breaking up tables physically across multiple disk drives, which enables multiple read/write heads to be brought into play in a query, thereby speeding access. Depending on the query and the clustering of data in tables, partitioning may enhance performance. Partitioning isn't applicable if the entire database is contained on a single disk drive, of course.

- **Physical Design Structures (PDS) to keep in database:** Here, you can specify which PDSs to keep. The Tuning Advisor may recommend dropping other structures (such as indexes or partitioning) that aren't contributing to performance.

10. Click the Advanced Options button to open the Advanced Tuning Options dialog box.

The Advanced Tuning Options dialog box enables you to specify a maximum amount of memory use for the recommendations. In the process of coming up with a recommendation, the Tuning Advisor can consume considerable memory. If you want to set a limit on the amount it can commandeer, this dialog box is the place to do it. (The Online Index Recommendations check boxes allow you to specify where you want to see any recommendations for indexes that are generated.)

11. **Click OK to return to the General tab, confirm that your query file is specified in the Workload area, and then click the Start Analysis button to commence tuning.**

The Start Analysis button is in the icon bar, just below the Actions option on the main menu.

Depending on the sizes of the tables involved in the query, this process could take a significant amount of time. The Tuning Advisor keeps you apprised on progress as the session runs.

If the Tuning Advisor has concluded that tuning would not improve performance at all, the query is already as efficient as it can be.

When you complete the tuning run, you'll probably want to look at the Reports tab, which shows the details of the tuning run.

SQL Server Profiler

The Database Engine Tuning Advisor is just one tool that SQL Server Management Studio provides to help you optimize your queries. The SQL Server Profiler is another tool available under the Tools tab. Instead of operating on SQL scripts, it traces the internal operation of the database engine on a query, showing exactly what SQL statements are submitted to the server — which may differ from the statements written by the SQL programmer — and how the server accesses the database.

Choose Tools ⇨ SQL Server Profiler to start the SQL Server Profiler tool. After you log into your SQL server, the Trace Properties dialog box appears for the new trace. This traces all DBMS activity until you tell it to stop. Somewhere among all the things that are going on, actions relevant to your query are recorded. Figure 3-6 shows the General tab of the Trace Properties dialog box.

Figure 3-7 shows the Events Selection tab of the Trace Properties dialog box. In this example, the default selections are shown, selecting almost everything to be recorded. In many cases, this selection is overkill, so you should deselect the things that don't interest you. Click the Run button to start the trace, and then click the Execute button for your query in Management Studio to give the trace a query to operate upon.

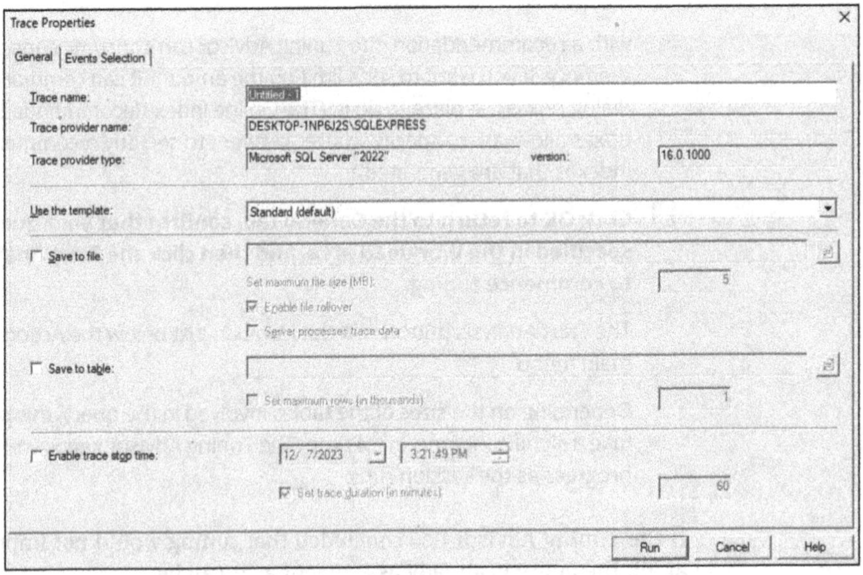

FIGURE 3-6:
The Trace
Properties
dialog box.

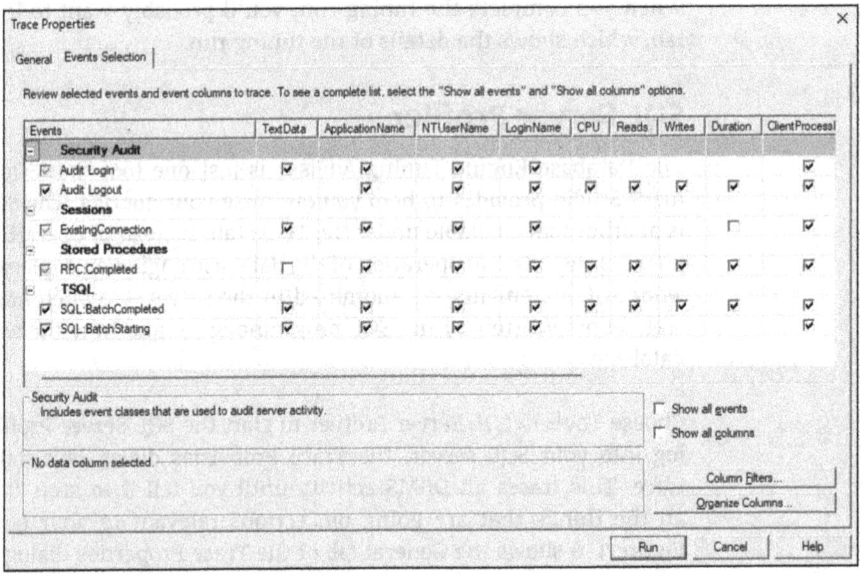

FIGURE 3-7:
The Events
Selection tab
of the Trace
Properties
dialog box.

A trace of SQLQuery1.sql dumps information about the EventClasses that you've specified for monitoring. Figure 3-8 is a view of the trace, showing the events that I selected. Data listed on the right side of the trace window include CPU usage, number of reads, number of writes, and time consumed by every event represented by a row in the trace file.

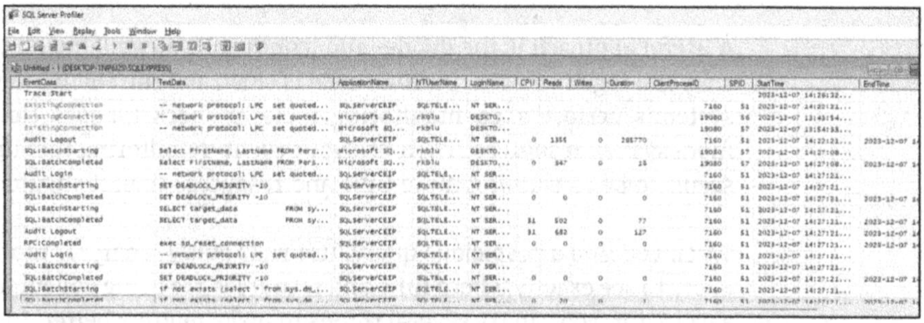

FIGURE 3-8:
Trace for a simple
query.

You can include many more event classes in a trace beyond the few that I display in this section. Check the Show All Events box in the Events Selection pane of the Trace Properties dialog box to display a host of them. You can break down a query to its constituent parts and see which parts are consuming the most time and resources. For the trace shown in Figure 3-8, I chose to monitor the acquisition and release of locks (and there were a lot of them). In cases in which you have little or no chance of deadlocks or lock contention, the trace will run faster if you choose not to monitor lock behavior.

REMEMBER

Queries aren't the only things that consume system resources. If you're experiencing performance problems, the source of the problem may be somewhere other than in a poorly performing query. Performance monitors are tools that give you a broader view of how a system is performing. Just remember that performance monitors aren't specifically related to database systems but are maintained by the operating system.

The Oracle Tuning Advisor

The Oracle Tuning Advisor analyzes a query presented to it and issues recommendations for rewriting it to improve performance. The learning curve for this tool is somewhat steeper than that for the SQL Server Database Engine Tuning Advisor, but after you master the syntax, it provides very helpful recommendations.

Finding problem queries

In a poorly performing multiuser, multitasking environment in which multiple queries are being run at any given moment, tracking the source of the problem may be difficult. Is the problem systemic? Are weaknesses in the server's processor, the server's memory, or the network slowing everything? Is one problem query gumming up the works for everyone? This last question is particularly important. If you can restore performance to a satisfactory level by tuning a query, doing so is a lot cheaper than making a major hardware upgrade that may not solve the problem.

A useful approach is the divide-and-conquer strategy. Find all the jobs that typically run together when performance is slow, and run them individually. Use your system's performance-monitoring tools to check for jobs that saturate one or more system resources. Then use your event-monitoring tool to find a query that seems to be consuming more time and resources than it should.

When you find a suspicious query, use your query-analyzer tool to look inside the query to see exactly where time and resources are being consumed. When you find a bad actor, you can try several things to make matters better. In the next sections, I discuss a few of those techniques.

Analyzing a query's access plan

A DBMS generates an access plan that describes how to execute a query. The details of the access plan depend on what the DBMS knows or can assume about what system resources are available and what the query needs. This knowledge is largely based on statistics that show how the system has been running lately on queries similar to the one for which the access plan is being developed.

CHECKING THE ACCESS PATH

After the query optimizer generates an access plan, check the plan to see how the query accesses table rows. Is it doing a full table scan? If a full table scan of a large table uploads a big chunk of the table into the database buffer, it could push data out of the buffer that other queries running concurrently will need soon. This situation won't show up as a performance bottleneck for the query you're looking at, but it affects the performance of the other queries running at the same time.

Interactions of this type are devilishly difficult to unravel and fix. Some DBMSs are smart enough to recognize this situation, and instead of following the normal practice of flushing the least recently used (LRU) pages from the buffer, they page out the big chunk because it's unlikely to be needed again soon after the scan.

In most situations, unless you're dealing with a very small table, indexed access is better than a full table scan. If your query's access plan specifies a full table scan, examine the plan carefully to see whether indexed access would be better. It may make sense to create a new index if the appropriate index doesn't exist.

Here are several reasons why indexed access tends to be better:

>> The target of an indexed access is almost always cached.
>> Table blocks reached by an index tend to be hotter than other blocks and consequently are more likely to be cached. These rows, after all, are the ones that you (and possibly other users) are hitting.

- Full table scans cache a multiblock group, whereas an indexed access retrieves a single block. The single blocks retrieved by indexed access are likelier to contain the rows that you and other users need than are blocks in a multiblock group that came along for the ride in a full table scan.

- Indexed accesses look only at the rows that you want in a retrieved block rather than every row in the block, thus saving time.

- Indexed accesses scale better than full table scans, which become worse as table size increases.

Full table scans make sense if you're retrieving 20 percent or more of the rows in a table. Indexed retrievals are clearly better if you're retrieving 0.5 percent or fewer of the rows in the table. Between those two extremes, the best choice depends on the specific situation.

FILTERING SELECTIVELY

Conditions such as those in an SQL WHERE clause act as filters. They exclude the table rows that you don't want and pass on for further processing the rows that you may want. If a condition specifies a range of index values for further processing, values outside that range need not be considered, and the data table itself need not be accessed as part of the filtering process. This filter is the most efficient kind because you need to look only at the index values that correspond to the rows in the data table that you want.

If the desired index range isn't determined by the condition, but rows to be retrieved are determinable from the index, performance can still be high because, although index values that are ultimately discarded must be accessed, the underlying data table needn't be touched.

Finally, if rows to be retrieved can't be determined from the index but require table access, no time is saved in the filtering process, but network bandwidth is saved because only the filtered rows need to be sent to the requesting client.

CHOOSING THE BEST JOIN TYPE

In Book 3, Chapter 4, I discuss several join types. Although the SQL code may specify one of the join types discussed there, the join operation that's actually executed is probably one of three basic types: nested-loops, hash, or sort-merge. The Query optimizer chooses one of these join types for you. In most cases, it chooses the type that turns out to be the best. Still, you should understand the three types and what distinguishes them from one another, as follows:

- **Nested-loops join:** A *nested-loops join* is a robust method of joining tables that almost always produces results in close to the shortest possible time. It works by filtering unwanted rows from one table (the driving table) and then joining the result to a second table, filtering out unwanted rows of the result in the process, joining the result to the next table, and so on until all tables have been joined and the fully filtered result is produced.

>> **Hash join:** In some situations, a hash join may perform better than a nested-loops join. This situation occurs when the smaller of the two tables being joined is small enough to fit entirely into semiconductor memory. Unwanted rows are discarded from the smaller table, and the remaining rows are placed in buckets according to a hashing algorithm. At the same time, the larger driving table is filtered; the remaining rows are matched to the rows from the smaller table in the hash buckets; and unmatched rows are discarded. The matched rows form the result set.

>> **Sort-merge join:** A *sort-merge join* reads two tables independently, discarding unwanted rows. First, it presorts both tables on the join key and merges the sorted lists. The presort operation is expensive in terms of time, so unless you can guarantee that both tables will fit into semiconductor memory, this technique performs worse than a hash join of the same tables.

Examining a query's execution profile

Perhaps you've examined an expensive query's access plan and found it to be about as efficient as can be expected. The next step is looking at the query's execution profile — the accounting information generated by the profiler. Among the pieces of information available are the number of physical and logical reads and the number of physical and logical writes. *Logical operations* are those that read or write memory. *Physical operations* are logical operations that go out to disk.

Other information available in the profile includes facts about locking. Of interest are the number of locks held and the length of time they're held. Time spent waiting for locks, as well as deadlocks and timeouts, can tell you a lot about why execution is slow.

Sorts are also performance killers. If the profile shows a high number of sorts or large areas of memory used for sorting, this report is a clue that you should pursue.

Resource contention between concurrently running transactions can drag down the performance of all transactions, which provides excellent motivation to use resources wisely, as I discuss in the following section.

Managing Resources Wisely

The physical elements of a database system can play a major role in how efficiently the database functions. A poorly configured system performs well below the performance that's possible if it's configured correctly. In this section, I review the roles played by the various key subsystems.

The disk subsystem

The way that data is distributed across the disks in a disk subsystem affects performance. The ideal case is to store contiguous pages on a single cylinder of a disk to support sequential *prefetching* — grabbing pages from disk before you need them. Spreading subsequent pages to similarly configured disks enables related reads and writes to be made in parallel. A major cause of performance degradation is disk fragmentation caused by deletions opening free space in the middle of data files that are then filled with unrelated file segments. This situation causes excessive head seeks, which slow performance dramatically. Disk fragmentation can accumulate rapidly in transaction-oriented environments and can become an issue over time even in relatively static systems.

Tools for measuring fragmentation are available at both the operating-system and database levels. Operating-system defragmentation tools work on the entire disk, whereas database tools measure the fragmentation of individual tables. An example of an operating-system defragmentation tool is the tool for Microsoft Windows, Optimize Drives utility, which you can access from the Search field. Figure 3-9 shows the result of an analysis of the disks on my workstation. Notice in Figure 3-9 that for some removable drives, optimization is not available.

In addition to being badly fragmented, this drive has very little free space, and none of that space is in large blocks, which makes it almost impossible to store a new database in a fragment-free manner.

With Optimize Drives, you can not only analyze the fragmentation of a disk drive, but also defragment it. Alas, this defragmentation usually is incomplete. Files that Optimize Drives can't relocate continue to impair performance.

DBMSs also have fragmentation analysis tools, but they concentrate on the tables in a database rather than look at the entire hard disk. SQL Server, for example, offers the sys.dm_db_index_physical_stats command, which returns size and fragmentation data for the data and indexes of a specified table or view. It doesn't fix the fragmentation; it only tells you about it. If you decide that fragmentation is excessive and is impairing performance, you must use other tools — such as the operating-system defragmentation utility — to remedy the situation.

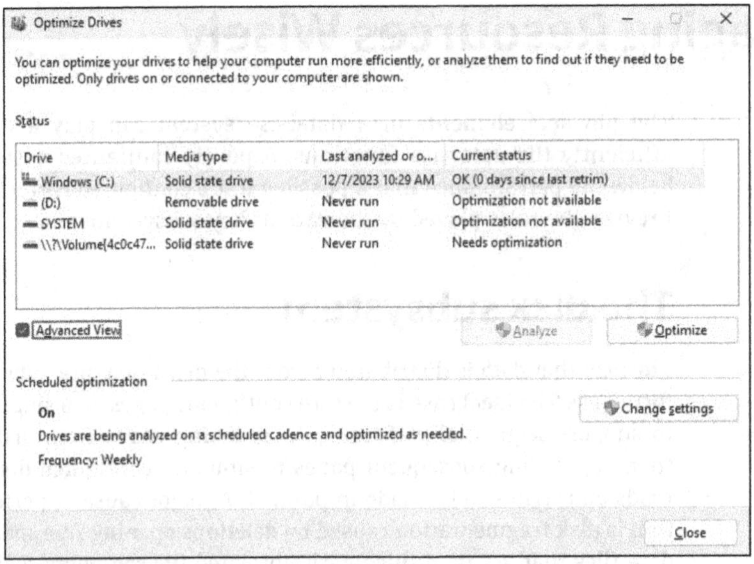

FIGURE 3-9:
An Optimize
Drives display
of a computer's
disk drives.

The database buffer manager

The job of the buffer manager is to minimize the number of disk accesses made by a query. It does this by keeping *hot pages* — pages which have been used recently and are likely to be used again soon — in the database buffer while maintaining a good supply of free pages in the buffer. The free pages provide a place for pages that come up from disk without the need to write a dirty page back to disk before the new page can be brought in.

You can see how good a job the buffer manager is doing by looking at the *cache–hit ratio* — the number of times a requested page is found in the buffer divided by the total number of page requests. A well-tuned system should have a cache–hit ratio of more than 90 percent.

In the specific case of Microsoft SQL Server running under Microsoft Windows, you can monitor the cache–hit ratio along with many other performance parameters from the Windows System Monitor. You can access the System Monitor from the Windows command prompt by typing **perfmon**. This launches the System Monitor in a window titled Reliability and Performance Monitor. From the menu tree on the left edge of the window, under Monitoring Tools, select Performance Monitor. This displays the Performance Monitor Properties dialog box. Open the Data tab and then click the Add button. This enables you to add counters that monitor many performance-related quantities, including cache–hit ratio.

TIP

Activating the System Monitor consumes resources, which affects performance. Use it when you are tracking down a bottleneck, but turn it off when you are finished before returning to normal operation.

Another useful metric is the number of free pages. If you check the cache–hit ratio and the number of free pages frequently under a variety of load conditions, you can keep an eye out for a trend that could lead to poor performance. Addressing such problems sooner rather than later is wise. With the knowledge you gain from regular monitoring of system health, you can act in a timely manner and maintain a satisfactory level of service.

The logging subsystem

Every transaction that makes an insertion, alteration, or deletion in the database is recorded in the log before the change is actually made in the database. This recovery feature permits reconstruction of what occurred before a transaction abort or system failure. Because the log must be written to before every action that's taken on the database, it's a potential source of slowdown if log writes can't keep up with the transaction traffic. Use the performance-monitoring tools available to you to confirm that there are no holdups due to delays in making log entries.

The locking subsystem

The locking subsystem can affect performance if multiple transactions are competing to acquire locks on the same object. If a transaction holds a lock too long, other transactions may time out, necessitating an expensive rollback.

You can track down the source of locking problems by checking statistics that are normally kept by the DBMS. Some helpful statistics are

>> Average lock wait time (the average amount of time a transaction must wait to obtain a lock)

>> Number of transactions waiting for locks

>> Number of timeouts

>> Number of deadlocks

Time spent waiting for locks should be low compared with total transaction time. The number of transactions waiting for locks should be low compared with the number of active transactions.

If the metrics cited here point to a problem with locks, you may be able to trace the source of the problem with a Microsoft Windows System Monitor or the equivalent event monitor in a different operating environment. Things such as timeouts and deadlocks appear in the event log and indicate what was happening when the event occurred.

8

Appendixes

Contents at a Glance

Appendix A

SQL:2023 Reserved Words

When you submit an SQL statement to a database engine for processing, the engine must parse your SQL statement to determine just what it is you want it to do. Because of that, there are many words that you can't use for database, table, or data field names; otherwise, the engine would get confused. These words are called *reserved words*.

Some database engines provide a way to use reserved words, such as enclosing them in quotes, but in general, it's never a good idea to use a reserved word in your database names. Here's a list of the reserved words to avoid when creating databases, tables, and data fields.

ABS	AS
ALL	ASENSITIVE
ALLOCATE	ASYMMETRIC
ALTER	AT
AND	ATOMIC
ANY	AUTHORIZATION
ANY_VALUE	AVG
ARE	BEGIN
ARRAY	BEGIN_FRAME
ARRAY_AGG	BEGIN_PARTITION
ARRAY_MAX_CARDINALITY	BETWEEN

BIGINT

BINARY

BLOB

BOOLEAN

BOTH

BTRIM

BY

CALL

CALLED

CARDINALITY

CASCADED

CASE

CAST

CEIL

CEILING

CHAR

CHAR_LENGTH

CHARACTER

CHARACTER_LENGTH

CHECK

CLASSIFIER

CLOB

CLOSE

COALESCE

COLLATE

COLLECT

COLUMN

COMMIT

CONDITION

CONNECT

CONSTRAINT

CONTAINS

CONVERT

CORR

CORRESPONDING

COUNT

COVAR_POP

COVAR_SAMP

CREATE

CROSS

CUBE

CUME_DIST

CURRENT

CURRENT_CATALOG

CURRENT_DATE

CURRENT_DEFAULT_TRANSFORM_
GROUP

CURRENT_PATH

CURRENT_ROLE

CURRENT_ROW

CURRENT_SCHEMA

CURRENT_TIME

CURRENT_TIMESTAMP

CURRENT_TRANSFORM_GROUP_
FOR_TYPE

CURRENT_USER

CURSOR

CYCLE

DATE

DAY

DEALLOCATE

DEC

DECFLOAT

DECIMAL

DECLARE

DEFAULT

DEFINE

DELETE

DENSE_RANK

DEREF

DESCRIBE

DETERMINISTIC

DISCONNECT

DISTINCT

DO

DOUBLE

DROP

DYNAMIC

EACH

ELEMENT

ELSE

ELSEIF

EMPTY

END

END-EXEC

END_FRAME

END_PARTITION

EQUALS

ESCAPE

EVERY	GET
EXCEPT	GLOBAL
EXEC	GRANT
EXECUTE	GREATEST
EXISTS	GROUP
EXP	GROUPING
EXTERNAL	GROUPS
EXTRACT	HANDLER
FALSE	HAVING
FETCH	HOLD
FILTER	HOUR
FIRST_VALUE	IDENTITY
FLOAT	IF
FLOOR	IN
FOR	INDICATOR
FOREIGN	INITIAL
FRAME_ROW	INNER
FREE	INOUT
FROM	INSENSITIVE
FULL	INSERT
FUNCTION	INT
FUSION	INTEGER

INTERSECT	LEADING
INTERSECTION	LEAST
INTERVAL	LEAVE
INTO	LEFT
IS	LIKE
ITERATE	LIKE_REGEX
JOIN	LN
JSON_ARRAY	LOCAL
JSON_ARRAYAGG	LOCALTIME
JSON_EXISTS	LOCALTIMESTAMP
JSON_OBJECT	LOWER
JSON_OBJECTAGG	LPAD
JSON_QUERY	LTRIM
JSON_TABLE	MATCH
JSON_TABLE_PRIMITIVE	MATCHES
JSON_VALUE	MATCH_NUMBER
LAG	MATCH_RECOGNIZE
LANGUAGE	MAX
LARGE	MEMBER
LAST_VALUE	MERGE
LATERAL	METHOD
LEAD	MIN

MINUTE

MOD

MODIFIES

MODULE

MONTH

MULTISET

NATIONAL

NATURAL

NCHAR

NCLOB

NEW

NO

NONE

NORMALIZE

NOT

NTH_VALUE

NTILE

NULL

NULLIF

NUMERIC

OCCURRENCES_REGEX

OCTET_LENGTH

OF

OFFSET

OLD

OMIT

ON

ONE

ONLY

OPEN

OR

ORDER

OUT

OUTER

OVER

OVERLAPS

OVERLAY

PARAMETER

PARTITION

PATTERN

PER

PERCENT

PERCENT_RANK

PERCENTILE_CONT

PERCENTILE_DISC	REGR_INTERCEPT
PERIOD	REGR_R2
PORTION	REGR_SLOPE
POSITION	REGR_SXX
POSITION_REGEX	REGR_SXY
POWER	REGR_SYY
PRECEDES	RELEASE
PRECISION	REPEAT
PREPARE	RESIGNAL
PRIMARY	RESULT
PROCEDURE	RETURN
RANGE	RETURNS
RANK	REVOKE
READS	RIGHT
REAL	ROLLBACK
RECURSIVE	ROLLUP
REF	ROW
REFERENCES	ROW_NUMBER
REFERENCING	ROWS
REGR_AVGX	RPAD
REGR_AVGY	RTRIM
REGR_COUNT	RUNNING

SAVEPOINT	SQRT
SCOPE	START
SCROLL	STATIC
SEARCH	STDDEV_POP
SECOND	STDDEV_SAMP
SEEK	SUBMULTISET
SELECT	SUBSET
SENSITIVE	SUBSTRING
SESSION_USER	SUBSTRING_REGEX
SET	SUCCEEDS
SHOW	SUM
SIGNAL	SYMMETRIC
SIMILAR	SYSTEM
SKIP	SYSTEM_TIME
SMALLINT	SYSTEM_USER
SOME	TABLE
SPECIFIC	TABLESAMPLE
SPECIFICTYPE	THEN
SQL	TIME
SQLEXCEPTION	TIMESTAMP
SQLSTATE	TIMEZONE_HOUR
SQLWARNING	TIMEZONE_MINUTE

TO	USING
TRAILING	VALUE
TRANSLATE	VALUES
TRANSLATE_REGEX	VALUE_OF
TRANSLATION	VAR_POP
TREAT	VAR_SAMP
TRIGGER	VARBINARY
TRIM	VARCHAR
TRIM_ARRAY	VARYING
TRUE	VERSIONING
TRUNCATE	WHEN
UESCAPE	WHENEVER
UNION	WHERE
UNIQUE	WHILE
UNKNOWN	WIDTH_BUCKET
UNNEST	WINDOW
UNTIL	WITH
UPDATE	WITHIN
UPPER	WITHOUT
USER	YEAR

Appendix B

Glossary

ActiveX control: A reusable software component that can be added to an application, reducing development time in the process. ActiveX is a Microsoft technology; ActiveX components can be used only by developers who work on Windows development systems.

aggregate function: A function that produces a single result based on the contents of an entire set of table rows; also called a *set function*.

alias: A short substitute or nickname for a table name.

API: *See* application programming interface (API).

applet: A small application written in the Java language, stored on a web server that's downloaded to and executed on a web client that connects to the server.

application programming interface (API): A standard means of communicating between an application and a database or other system resource.

assertion: A constraint specified by a CREATE ASSERTION statement (rather than by a clause of a CREATE TABLE statement). Assertions commonly apply to more than one table.

atomic: Incapable of being subdivided.

attribute: A component of a structured type or relation.

back end: That part of a database management system (DBMS) that interacts directly with the database. *See also* database management system (DBMS).

catalog: A named collection of schemas. *See also* schema.

client: An individual user workstation that represents the front end of a database management system (DBMS) — the part that displays information on a screen and responds to user input. *See also* front end *and* database management system (DBMS).

client/server system: A multiuser system in which a central processor (the server) is connected to multiple intelligent user workstations (the clients).

cluster: A named collection of catalogs. *See also* catalog.

CODASYL DBTG database model: The network database model. Note: This use of the term *network* refers to the structuring of the data (network as opposed to hierarchy) rather than to network communications.

collating sequence: The ordering of characters in a character set. All collating sequences for character sets that have the Latin characters (a, b, c) define the obvious ordering (a, b, c, . . .). They differ, however, in the ordering of special characters (+, -, <, ?, and so on) and in the relative ordering of the digits and the letters.

collection type: A data type that allows a field of a table row to contain multiple objects.

column: A table component that holds a single attribute of the table.

composite key: A key made up of two or more table columns.

conceptual view: The schema of a database. See also *schema.*

concurrent access: Two or more users operating on the same rows in a database table at the same time.

conditional value expression: A value expression that assigns different values to arguments, based on whether a condition is logically true. *See also* value expression.

constraint: A restriction you specify on the data in a database. *See also* deferred constraint.

cursor: An SQL feature that specifies a set of rows, an ordering of those rows, and a current row within that ordering.

Data Control Language (DCL): That part of SQL that protects the database from harm.

Data Definition Language (DDL): That part of SQL used to define, modify, and eradicate database structures.

Data Manipulation Language (DML): That part of SQL that operates on database data.

data redundancy: Having the same data stored in more than one place in a database.

data source: A source of data used by a database application. It may be a database, a spreadsheet, or a flat data file.

data sublanguage: A subset of a complete computer language that deals specifically with data handling. SQL is a data sublanguage of programming languages such as C++ and Java.

data type: A set of representable values.

database: A self-describing collection of integrated records. *See also* enterprise database, personal database, *and* workgroup database.

database administrator (DBA): The person ultimately responsible for the functionality, integrity, and safety of a database.

database engine: That part of a database management system (DBMS) that directly interacts with the database (serving as part of the back end). *See also* back end *and* database management system (DBMS).

database management system (DBMS): A set of computer programs that controls the creation, maintenance, and use of databases.

database publishing: The act of making database contents available on the Internet or over an intranet.

database server: The server component of a client/server system — the place where the database resides. *See also* client/server system.

datetime value expression: A value expression that deals with DATE, TIME, TIMESTAMP, or INTERVAL data. *See also* value expression.

DB2: A relational database management system (RDBMS) marketed by IBM Corp. *See also* relational database management system (RDBMS).

DBA: *See* database administrator (DBA).

DBMS: *See* database management system (DBMS).

DCL: *See* Data Control Language (DCL).

DDL: *See* Data Definition Language (DDL).

deferred constraint: A constraint that isn't applied until you change its status to immediate or until you COMMIT the encapsulating transaction.

deletion anomaly: An inconsistency in a multitable database that occurs when a row is deleted from one of its tables.

denial-of-service attack: An attack on a website mediated by a flood of messages coming in from large numbers of worm-infected computers that have been programmed to send a message to the target site at a specific time, overwhelming the site's ability to handle the traffic. *See also* worm.

descriptor: An area in memory used to pass information between an application's procedural code and its dynamic SQL code.

diagnostics area: A data structure, managed by the database management system (DBMS), that contains detailed information about the last SQL statement executed and any errors that occurred during its execution. *See also* database management system (DBMS).

distributed data processing: A system in which multiple servers handle data processing.

DML: See Data Manipulation Language (DML).

domain: The set of all values that a database item can assume.

domain integrity: A property of a database table column in which all data items in that column fall within the domain of the column.

driver: That part of a database management system (DBMS) that interfaces directly with a database. *See also* database management system (DBMS).

driver manager: A component of an ODBC-compliant database interface. On Windows machines, the driver manager is a dynamic link library (DLL) that coordinates the linking of data sources with appropriate drivers. *See also* Open Database Connectivity (ODBC).

dumb terminal: A combination keyboard/display device with no internal intelligence.

dynamic SQL: *See* dynamic Structured Query Language (SQL).

dynamic Structured Query Language (SQL): A means of building compiled applications that doesn't require all data items to be identifiable at compile time. *See also* Structured Query Language (SQL).

embedded SQL: *See* embedded Structured Query Language (SQL).

embedded Structured Query Language (SQL): An application structure in which SQL statements are embedded within programs written in a host language. *See also* Structured Query Language (SQL)

enterprise database: A database containing information used by an entire enterprise.

entity integrity: A property of a database table that is entirely consistent with the real-world object that it models.

exploit: An action that takes advantage of a security weakness of a software system to penetrate the system for a malicious purpose.

Extensible Markup Language (XML): A widely accepted markup language used as a means of exchanging data between dissimilar systems.

file server: The server component of a resource-sharing system. It doesn't contain any database management software.

firewall: A piece of software (or a combination of hardware and software) that isolates an intranet from the internet, allowing only trusted traffic to travel between them.

flat file: A collection of data records that contains only data — no metadata.

foreign key: A column or combination of columns in a database table that references the primary key of another table in the database.

forest: A collection of elements in an XML document. *See also* Extensible Markup Language (XML).

front end: That part of a database management system (DBMS), such as the client in a client/server system, that interacts directly with the user. *See also* database management system (DBMS).

functional dependency: A relationship between or among attributes of a relation.

graphical user interface (GUI): A digital interface where users interact with graphical objects such as icons, menus, and buttons.

GUI: *See* graphical user interface (GUI).

hierarchical database model: A tree-structured model of data.

host variable: A variable passed between an application written in a procedural host language and embedded SQL.

HTML: *See* Hypertext Markup Language (HTML).

Hypertext Markup Language (HTML): A standard formatting language for web documents.

implementation: A particular relational database management system (RDBMS) running on a specific hardware platform. *See also* relational database management system (RDBMS).

index: A table of pointers used to locate rows in a data table rapidly.

information schema: The system tables, which hold the database's metadata. *See also* metadata.

insertion anomaly: An inconsistency introduced into a multitable database when a new row is inserted into one of its tables.

interactive SQL: *See* interactive Structured Query Language (SQL).

interactive Structured Query Language (SQL): A real-time conversation with a database. *See also* Structured Query Language (SQL).

Internet: The worldwide network of computers.

Internetwork Packet Exchange/Sequenced Packet Exchange (IPX/SPX): A local area network (LAN) protocol. See also local area network (LAN).

intranet: A network that uses World Wide Web hardware and software but restricts access to users within a single organization.

IPX/SPX: *See* Internetwork Packet Exchange/Sequenced Packet Exchange (IPX/SPX).

Java: A platform-independent compiled language designed originally for web application development but now used in many contexts.

Java Database Connectivity (JDBC): A standard interface between a Java *applet* (or application) and a database. The JDBC standard is modeled after the ODBC standard. *See also* Open Database Connectivity (ODBC).

JavaScript: A script language that gives some measure of programmability to HTML-based web pages.

JavaScript Object Notation (JSON): An open standard file format used for asynchronous browser/server communication.

join: A relational operator that combines data from multiple tables in a single result table.

JSON: See JavaScript Object Notation (JSON).

local-area network (LAN): A collection of devices connected together in a physical location for the purpose of data transfer.

logical connectives: Used to connect or change the truth value of predicates to produce more-complex predicates.

malware: Software written to accomplish a malicious purpose.

mapping: The translation of data in one format to another format.

metadata: Data about the structure of the data in a database.

modification anomaly: A problem introduced into a database when a modification (insertion, deletion, or update) is made in one of the database tables.

module: A container for SQL statements.

module language: A form of SQL in which SQL statements are placed in modules, which are called by an application program written in a host language.

mutator function: A function associated with a user-defined type (UDT), having two parameters whose definition is implied by the definition of some attribute of the type. The first parameter (the result) is of the same type as the UDT. The second parameter has the same type as the defining attribute. *See also* user-defined type (UDT).

nested query: A statement that contains one or more subqueries.

NetBEUI: A LAN protocol. *See also* local area network (LAN).

network database model: A way of organizing a database to get minimum redundancy of data items by allowing any data item (node) to be directly connected to any other.

normal form: A technique of structuring a database to reduce data redundancy and improve data integrity. There are several levels of the normal form, such as first normal form, second normal form, and so on.

normalization: A technique that reduces or eliminates the possibility that a database will be subject to modification anomalies.

numeric value expression: A value expression that combines numeric values using the addition, subtraction, multiplication, or division operator. *See also* value expression.

ODBC: *See* Open Database Connectivity (ODBC).

object: Any uniquely identifiable thing.

Open Database Connectivity (ODBC): A standard interface between a database and an application that's trying to access the data in that database. ODBC is defined by the International Organization for Standardization (ISO) and the American National Standards Institute (ANSI).

Oracle: A relational database management system (RDBMS) marketed by Oracle Corp. *See also* relational database management system.

parameter: A variable within an application written in SQL module language.

personal database: A database designed for use by one person on a single computer.

PGQL: *See* Property Graph Query Language (PGQL).

phishing scam: A social-engineering ploy that induces victims to surrender confidential information by claiming to be a trusted source.

precision: The maximum number of digits allowed in a numeric data item.

predicate: A statement that may be either logically true or logically false.

primary key: A column or combination of columns in a database table that uniquely identifies each row in the table.

procedural language: A computer language that solves a problem by executing a procedure in the form of a sequence of steps.

property graph database: A way of organizing data that stores data in nodes and defines relationships between nodes as edges.

Property Graph Query Language (PGQL): A language for querying data stored in a property graph database.

query: A question you ask about the data in a database.

RAD tool: *See* rapid application development (RAD) tool.

rapid application development (RAD) tool: A proprietary, graphically oriented alternative or supplement to SQL. Several such tools are on the market.

RDBMS: See relational database management system (RDBMS).

record: A representation of some physical or conceptual object.

reference type: A data type whose values are all potential references to sites of one specified data type.

referential integrity: A state in which all the tables in a database are consistent with one another.

relation: A two-dimensional array of rows and columns containing single-valued entries and no duplicate rows.

relational database management system (RDBMS): A database server that stores data following the relational database method of using databases, tables, and data fields. *See also* database management system (DBMS).

reserved words: Words that have a special significance in SQL and can't be used as variable names or in any other way that differs from their intended use (refer to Appendix A).

row: A sequence of (`field name, value`) pairs.

row pattern recognition: A feature of the `FROM` clause that uses a `MATCH_RECOGNIZE` clause to retrieve rows that exhibit a pattern.

row value expression: A list of value expressions enclosed in parentheses and separated by commas.

scale: The number of digits in the fractional part of a numeric data item.

schema: The structure of an entire database. The information that describes the schema is the database's metadata. *See also* metadata.

schema owner: The person who was designated as the owner when the schema was created.

SEQUEL: A data sublanguage, created by IBM, that was a precursor of SQL.

set function: *See* aggregate function.

SQL/PGQ: An industry-standard data sublanguage designed to add property graph database queries to SQL.

SQL: *See* Structured Query Language (SQL).

SQL/DS: *See* Structured Query Language/Data System (SQL/DS).

string value expression: A value expression that combines character strings with the concatenation operator. *See also* value expression.

Structured Query Language (SQL): An industry-standard data sublanguage specifically designed to create, manipulate, and control relational databases. *See also* dynamic Structured Query Language (SQL), embedded Structured Query Language (SQL), and interactive Structured Query Language (SQL).

Structured Query Language/Data System (SQL/DS): A relational database management system (RDBMS) marketed by IBM Corp. *See also* relational database management system (RDBMS) *and* Structured Query Language (SQL).

Structured Query Language (SQL) injection attack: An attempt to penetrate the defenses of an SQL database application to gain control of the underlying database. *See also* Structured Query Language (SQL).

structured type: A user-defined type (UDT) expressed as a list of attribute definitions and methods instead of being based on a single predefined source type. *See also* user-defined type (UDT).

subquery: A query within a query.

subtype: A subtype of a second data type if every value of the first type is also a value of the second type.

supertype: A supertype of a second data type if every value of the second type is also a value of the first type.

table: A relation.

TCP/IP: *See* Transmission Control Protocol/Internet Protocol (TCP/IP).

teleprocessing system: A powerful central processor connected to multiple dumb terminals. *See also* dumb terminal.

transaction: A sequence of SQL statements whose effect isn't accessible to other transactions until all the statements are executed.

transitive dependency: A situation in which one attribute of a relation depends on a second attribute, which in turn depends on a third attribute.

translation table: A tool for converting character strings from one character set to another.

Transmission Control Protocol/Internet Protocol (TCP/IP): The network protocol used by the Internet and intranets.

trigger: A small piece of code that tells a database management system (DBMS) what other actions to perform after certain SQL statements have been executed. *See also* database management system (DBMS).

Trojan horse: A useful program that also has a secret payload. This payload, when activated inside a target computer, does what a malware writer wants rather than what the computer owner wants.

UDT: *See* user-defined type (UDT).

update anomaly: A problem introduced into a database when a table row is updated.

user-defined type (UDT): A type whose characteristics are defined by a type descriptor specified by the user.

value expression: An expression that combines two or more values. *See also* conditional value expression, datetime value expression, numeric value expression, *and* string value expression.

value function: A function that performs an operation on a single character string, number, or datetime.

view: A database component that behaves exactly like a table but has no independent existence of its own.

virtual table: A view.

virus: A self-replicating piece of software that spreads by attaching itself to other programs or to documents.

workgroup database: A database designed to be used by a department or workgroup within an organization.

World Wide Web: An aspect of the Internet that has a graphical user interface (GUI). The web is accessed by applications called *web browsers,* and information is provided to the web by installations called *web servers. See also* graphical user interface (GUI).

worm: A self-replicating form of malware that spreads via networks.

XML: *See* Extensible Markup Language (XML).

zombie spambot: One of a host of worm-infected computers spewing unsolicited advertising messages to lists of email addresses that the spammers have acquired. *See also* worm.

Index

Symbols and Numerics

A

partitioning, 692–693

performing top-down analysis, 690–692

precompiled queries and, 689

slow query, 682

slow update, 682–683

using query analyzers, 693–701

bottom up design, 501–510

Boyce-Codd Normal Form (BCNF), 161, 164–166

bugs, fixing, 511

business rules, 45, 486–487

Buxton, Stephen (author)

Querying XML, 116

C

C#, MySQL and, 458

CALL statement, 73, 523

candidate key, 207

cardinality

about, 233, 241

actual, 241

defined, 38

maximum, 39, 485

minimum, 39–41, 485–486

CARDINALITY function, 233–234, 241

Cartesian product/cross join, 330–332

CASCADE keyword, 429, 430

cascading delete, 311

CASE statement, 241, 243–244

CASE...END CASE statement, 518–519

CAST expression, converting data types with, 244–246

catalogs

defined, 721

in relational database model, 71, 72

CEIL/CEILING function, 235

CHARACTER LARGE OBJECT (CLOB) type, 111, 124, 221

character sets, mapping to XML, 557

character strings

about, 110

CHARACTER, 110–111, 124, 221

CHARACTER LARGE OBJECT (CLOB), 111, 124, 221

CHARACTER VARYING, 111

NATIONAL CHARACTER, 112, 221

NATIONAL CHARACTER LARGE OBJECT, 112

NATIONAL CHARACTER VARYING, 112, 221

CHARACTER type, 110–111, 124, 221

CHARACTER VARYING type, 111

CHARACTER_LENGTH function, 232

Cheat Sheet (website), 3

CHECK constraint, 127, 392

checking access path, 702–703

checkpoints

about, 404

setting, 669–670

CIL (Common Intermediate Language), 458

classic procedural languages, 462–463, 464–465

classifying users, 422

client, defined, 721

client/server system, defined, 721

CLOB (CHARACTER LARGE OBJECT) type, 111, 124, 221

CLOSE statement, 349–350

closing cursors, 356

cloud computing, 25

CLR (Common Language Runtime), 457

cluster, defined, 721

drivers

defined, 723

in ODBC, 535–537

DROP statement, 495

dumb terminal, defined, 724

Durability, in ACID test, 396–397

dynamic cache sizing, 62

Dynamic Link Library (DLL), 450

dynamic SQL, defined, 724

dynamic string building, 376–377

E

edge properties, 634

edges. *See* relationships

education, for protection, 389

elementcentric mapping, 594, 595–596

elements, in XML documents, 550–551

eliminating

anomalies, 161–164

many-to-many relationships, 487–490

unneeded locks, 412

Ellisonn, Larry, 54

ELSE clause, 242, 519

embedded Structured Query Language (SQL), 101–104, 724

embedding

SQL in applications

about, 466–467

Java applications, 470

Oracle Pro*C applications, 467–470

Perl applications, 470

PHP applications, 471

using SQL with other .NET languages, 472

using SQL with Visual Basic .NET applications, 471

SQL statements, 514

empty elements, 550–551

ensuring data validity, with domains, 210–211

entering

data with SQL, 505

values

about, 219–220

column values, 220

literal values, 220–221

row values, 220

special variables, 222–223

variables, 222

enterprise database, defined, 724

entities

determining, 484

in Entity-Relationship (ER) models, 33–34

ID-dependent, 43

relationships and, 484–487

strong, 41–43

subtype, 43–45

supertype, 43–45

weak, 41–43

entity class, 33

entity instance, 33

entity integrity, 182–183, 724

entity references, in XML documents, 552–553

Entity-Relationship (ER) model

about, 32–33

advanced concepts, 41–45

building, 483–487

complex relationships, 50–51

converting to relational models, 172

designing, 170–171

drawing diagrams, 38–41

examples, 45–50

normalizing, 490–491

MySQL
  about, 62–63, 454
  C and, 458
  C# and, 458
  C++.NET and, 458
  Java and, 459
  Perl and, 459
  PHP and, 459
  Python and, 459
  website, 63

N

NAMES ARE clause, 104
NASA, 13
NATIONAL CHARACTER LARGE OBJECT
    type, 112
NATIONAL CHARACTER type, 112, 221
NATIONAL CHARACTER VARYING type,
    112, 221
native drivers, 532
natural join, 334–335
nested elements, 550
nested queries
  defined, 296, 726
  tuning statements containing, 312–318
nested-loops join, 703–704
.NET languages
  SQL Server and, 457–458
  using SQL with other, 472
NetBEUI, defined, 726
network, 692
network database model, 19–20, 726
network-layer firewalls, 388
N:M (many-to-many) relationship, 17, 36,
    176, 487–490
node properties, 634

nonexistence, testing for, 305
nonhandled conditions, 437
nonpredefined data types, mapping to
    XML, 559–563
nonprocedural, SQL as, 101
nonprocedural languages, 463–464
nonrelational NoSQL model, 25
nonrepeatable read, 399–400
nonvolatile memory, 662–663
normal forms
  about, 161
  defined, 726
  higher, 164–166
normalization
  defined, 726
  Entity-Relationship (ER) model, 490–491
  relational models, 172–174
  simplifying relationships using, 51
NOT, 269–270
NOT EXISTS predicate, 304–305
NOT IN predicate, 255–256
NOT LIKE predicate, 257–258
NOT NULL constraint, 89, 126–127, 182,
    404–405
NULL value, 243, 258–259
null values
  about, 596–598
  handling, 564–565
  managing, 125
NULLIF expression, 243–244
numeric character references, in XML
    documents, 553
NUMERIC type, 108, 124, 221, 393
numeric value expressions, 237–238, 726
numeric value functions
  about, 227, 231

procedural languages
  combining SQL with
    about, 464
    classic procedural languages, 464–465
    object-oriented procedural languages, 465–466
  comparing SQL with
    about, 462
    classic procedural languages, 462–463
    nonprocedural languages, 463–464
    object-oriented procedural languages, 463
  defined, 727
  interfacing SQL with, 455–460
procedures (module), 474
processors
  about, 691–692
  speed of, 678
programming errors, 394
project scope
  about, 482–483
  determining, 143–144
property graph databases
  about, 633–634
  connecting nodes by multiple edges, 634–635
  connecting nodes to itself, 635
  defined, 727
  edge properties, 634
  following paths with SQL queries, 635
  node properties, 634
  SQL/PGQ
    about, 635–637
    adding data to node and edge tables, 640–642
    building property graph tables, 637–640
    querying data in graph tables, 642–644

Property Graph Query Language (PGQL), 634, 727. See also SQL/PGQ
proposals, 479–480
protected attribute, 120
pseudo-random hash function, 194
public, 422
Python, MySQL and, 459

Q

quantified comparison operator, 298
quantified subqueries, 301–304
queries
  about, 276–277
  ad hoc, 87
  analyzing efficiency of, 693–704
  data in graph tables, 642–644
  defined, 727
  finding problems, 701–704
  HAVING clause, 289–293
  OR logical connective, 293–294
  ORDER BY clause, 285–289
  precompiling frequently used, 658
  SELECT DISTINCT, 277–280
  temporary tables, 280–285
  tuning, 656–657
query analyzers, 693–701
query expression cursors, 347
query functions, 620–625
query optimizer, 190
query type, indexes and, 191–193
Querying XML (Melton and Buxton), 116

R

RAD (rapid application development) tool, defined, 727
RAID. See Redundant Array of Independent Disks (RAID)

V

VALID predicate, 572–573

value expression, defined, 729

value functions, 227, 729

values

  entering

    about, 219–220

    column values, 220

    literal values, 220–221

    row values, 220

    special variables, 222–223

    variables, 222

  subqueries

    returning multiple, 296–298

    returning single, 298–304

VARCHAR type, 111, 124, 221

variables

  about, 222

  compound statements and, 516

VBA (Visual Basic for Applications), 449–450, 456–457

views

  creating, 78–83

  data for access privileges, 423–424

  defined, 729

  multitable, 78, 80–83

  in relational database model, 69–70

  single-table, 78–79

  updating, 94–95

virtual table, defined, 729

viruses, 370–372, 729

Visual Basic for Applications (VBA), 449–450, 456–457

Visual Basic .NET applications, using SQL with, 471

volatile memory, 662–663

vulnerabilities, 383–387, 388–389

W

Warning icon, 3

weakening isolation levels, 413–414

Web Developer, 384–385

websites

  Cheat Sheet, 3

  HP Scrwalr, 385

  HP WebInspect, 385

  IBM Security AppScan, 385

  MariaDB, 63

  MySQL, 63

  Oracle, 62

  SQL Map, 385

  Web Developer, 384

  World Wide Web Consortium, 579, 602

WHENEVER clause, 437–438

where clause, 610

WHERE clause

  about, 251–253, 508

  ALL predicate, 259–262

  ANY predicate, 259–262

  comparison predicates, 253

  deleting data from tables using, 93–94

  DISTINCT predicate, 263

  EXISTS predicate, 262–263

  indexes and, 651–652

  LIKE predicate, 257–258

  logical connectives, 268–270

  MATCH predicate, 264–268

  NOT IN predicate, 255–256

  NOT LIKE predicate, 257–258

About the Authors

Allen G. Taylor: Allen is a 40-year veteran of the computer industry and the author of more than 40 books, including *SQL For Dummies, Crystal Reports 2008 For Dummies, Database Development For Dummies, Access 2003 Power Programming with VBA,* and *SQL Weekend Crash Course.* He lectures internationally on databases, networks, innovation, astronomy, and entrepreneurship as well as health and wellness. He also teaches database development through a leading online education provider. For the latest news on Allen's activities, check out his online courses (at `https://pioneer-academy1.teachable.com`) and his blog (at `www.allengtaylor.com`). You can contact Allen at `allen.taylor@ieee.org`.

Richard Blum: Rich has worked in the IT industry for more than 35 years as a network and systems administrator. During that time, he has had the opportunity to work with lots of different operating systems, including IBM mainframes and Windows, Netware, UNIX, and Linux servers, as well as many different database systems such as Oracle, Informix, Microsoft SQL, PostgreSQL, and MySQL. Over the years, he has also volunteered for several nonprofit organizations to help support small networks that had little financial support. Rich is the author of several Linux-based books for total Linux geeks and teaches online courses in programming. When he's not busy being a computer nerd, Rich enjoys playing organ, piano, and bass guitar, and spending time with his wife, Barbara, and their two daughters, Katie Jane and Jessica.

Dedication

This book is dedicated to the many teachers, authors, coworkers, friends, students, and online posters who have helped expand my computer knowledge over these many years.

"The way of a fool is right in his own eyes, but a wise man listens to advice." — Proverbs 12:15 (ESV)

—Richard Blum

Author's Acknowledgments

Allen G. Taylor: First and foremost, I would like to acknowledge the help of Jim Melton, editor of the ISO/ANSI specifi cation for SQL. Without his untiring efforts, this book — and indeed SQL itself as an international standard — would be of much less value. I would also like to thank my project manager, Maureen Tullis, my development and copy editor Scott Tullis, and executive editor, Katie Mohr, for their key contributions to the production of this book. Thanks also to my agent, Carole McClendon of Waterside Productions, for her support of my career.

From Richard Blum: First, all praise and glory go to God, who through His Son makes all things possible, and gives us the gift of eternal life.

A special thanks to Allen for his amazing and excellent work with the past editions of *SQL All-in-One For Dummies*. I jumped onto this project in the 4th Edition, and it has been my pleasure to update the text to the latest SQL standards.

Many thanks go to the great people at John Wiley & Sons for their help and guidance in writing this book. Thanks to Steve Hayes for offering me the opportunity to pick up this project. Also, many thanks to Elizabeth Kuball for helping keep the project focused and on track! Ken Hess has done an excellent job of finding my mistakes and making suggestions to help make this book better — thanks! Thanks also goes to Carole Jelen at Waterside Productions for arranging this gig and keeping my book-writing career on track.

Finally, I'd like to thank my parents, Mike and Joyce Blum, for constantly stressing education over goofing off, as well as my wife, Barbara, and two daughters, Katie Jane and Jessica, for their love and support, especially while I was working on this project.

Publisher's Acknowledgments

Executive Editor: Steven Hayes
Editor: Elizabeth Kuball
Technical Editor: Ken Hess

Production Editor: Pradesh Kumar
Cover Image: © Sashkin/Adobe Stock Photos